The Derbyshire Family Commentary

ISAIAH

Doug Derbyshire

Copyright © 2020 Douglas Derbyshire

All rights reserved. No part of this book may be reproduced
or used in any manner without the prior written permission of the copyright owner,
except for the use of brief quotations in a book review.

To request permissions, contact the publisher at admin@TellTheKids.com

Hardcover ISBN: 978-1-953935-03-8
Electronic Book ISBN: 978-1-953935-05-2

Library of Congress Control Number: 2020922709

First Revised hardback edition December 2020

Editor: Diane Hamilton
Cover Design: Nick Zink

Scripture taken from the New King James Version®. Copyright © 1982 by Thomas Nelson. Used by
permission. All rights reserved.

Scripture quotations marked ESV® are taken from The Holy Bible, English Standard Version®, copyright © 2001 by Crossway, a
publishing ministry of Good News Publishers. Used by permission. All rights reserved.

Scripture quotations marked HCSB and CSB are taken from the Holman Christian Standard Bible®, Used by Permission HCSB
©1999,2000,2002,2003,2009 Holman Bible Publishers. Holman Christian Standard Bible®, Holman CSB®, and HCSB® are federally
registered trademarks of Holman Bible Publishers.

Scriptures marked KJV are taken from the KING JAMES VERSION (KJV): KING JAMES VERSION, public domain.

Scriptures marked NIV are taken from the NEW INTERNATIONAL VERSION (NIV): Scripture taken from THE HOLY BIBLE,
NEW INTERNATIONAL VERSION ®. Copyright© 1973, 1978, 1984, 2011 by Biblica, Inc.™. Used by permission of Zondervan

Scripture quotations marked NLT are taken from the Holy Bible, New Living Translation, copyright ©1996, 2004, 2015 by Tyndale
House Foundation. Used by permission of Tyndale House Publishers, a Division of Tyndale House Ministries, Carol Stream, Illinois
60188. All rights reserved.

Scripture quotations marked YLT are taken from the 1898 YOUNG'S LITERAL TRANSLATION OF THE HOLY BIBLE by J.N.
Young, (Author of the Young's Analytical Concordance), public domain.

Printed by Ingram Spark in the USA

Tell The KIDS LLC
7700 Skylake Drive
Fort Worth TX 76179

TellTheKids.com

Preface

One evening as I knelt in the presence of the Lord, He moved me to pray once again for my children. Gary was maybe 6 or 7 years old at the time. I began, solemnly at first, but after some time, my composure left me and I began to cry out my prayer. Tears filled my eyes, my body shook, and I raised clenched fists in a battle of prayer, pleading with my Lord to fill the souls of my children with the fullness of His presence, and fill the hearts and minds of my children with a love for His Word. I don't remember how long I knelt in prayer, but I do remember when He graciously drew near. I heard in my mind God's words from Isaiah 59:21, "As for Me, this is the covenant that I will make with (you) says the Lord, My Spirit who is upon you, and My words which I have placed in your mouth, shall not depart from your mouth, nor from the mouth of your children, nor from the mouth of your children's children from this time on and forever more." I immediately rose from my place of prayer, confident that my Lord had heard my request. And for the past 20 years I have had no greater joy than seeing the Lord bring these words to pass for our family. While we were all together under the same roof in Bangkla we gathered together as a family to study God's Word at dinners each evening and early Sunday mornings before church each week. I kept those notes from our times together in God's Word and have written them down for us here. I have added some thoughts here and there, but the heart of these notes came from our studies together as we sought to fill our family and our minds with God's Word that He might make better use of us for His purposes. Our times together have given me notes on nearly all the Bible. I will continue to put them together into a more useful form, and pass them on to you as each section is completed.

…………to my mom, whose love for God's Word overflowed into my life so that I became filled with a love for God's Word at an early age.

…………to my dad, whose study on the book of Job ignited a fire in my blood to study God's Word book by book and verse by verse.

…………to my four children, whose obedience to God's Word and heart to take it to the next generation has filled your mom and I with joy.

…………and to Cheryl, whose love for me and tireless provision for our family, has enabled me to endure. For years you woke the children and had them ready for breakfast and family Bible study at 6 a.m. every morning. May the Lord bless you for what you have done for me, for our children, and for the cause of Christ in the lives of so many others. You are the most wonderful individual I have ever met. For over 37 years you have been a continual, precious, loving, untiring blessing to me personally and to the cause of Christ. I am so deeply grateful to you, so happily in love with you, and so overwhelmingly thankful to our Lord who has given you to me. You are such a dear, gifted, and enthusiastically hard-working partner, as we minister together in the care of God's people and bring the lost to the Savior.

Foreword to Volume 3

My thoughts on Isaiah comprise the third volume of our family commentary. To me, this remains a "family commentary," because many of my notes on these passages came from our family devotions when the six of us sat around the living room and discussed together the great things of God. I am still so grateful for those days when I could sit and listen to your understanding of God's Word. It is also a "family commentary" because Mom and the four of you were continually in my mind as I wrote down these thoughts.

How can I not think of you when I read:

54:11-13
O you afflicted one, tossed with tempest, and not comforted, behold, I will lay your stones with colorful gems, and lay your foundations with sapphires. I will make your pinnacles of rubies, your gates of crystal, and all your walls of precious stones. <u>**All your children shall be taught by the LORD, and great shall be the peace of your children.**</u>

Reading these words, while seeing God's kindness extended toward our family, moved me to write:

Isaiah writes of a future day when the house of Israel had collapsed. Their homes, homeland, hopes, and family lines lay in ruins. But here, our Lord promises to make them beautiful once again. He would beautify their homes, houses of worship, and future with the precious stones of His favor. As Solomon decorated the temple with "precious stones" to reflect the beauty of the Lord (II Chronicles 3:6), the Lord promises here to adorn His people with precious stones of beauty once more. Verse 13 describes the motherlode of precious stones, the vein of precious metals, which is the source of the spiritual sapphires which beautify God's people. "All your children shall be taught by the LORD." Oh, the joy of seeing the eternal God teach your children! Nothing glorifies, beautifies, enriches a family as when the Spirit of God is seated at the family dining table and teaches your children as you eat. Nothing compares to the precious work of the Savior as He calls your children to sit with Him in daily devotions while He teaches His great truths to their spiritual ears. Oh, how beautiful is the family that sees the Savior teach their children how to follow Him, serve Him, and devote themselves to His will and ways. Solomon set precious stones in the wall of the temple "for beauty," and our Lord teaches our children the great things of God so that our families might be filled with the beauty of the Father. From my seat on the hill of fatherhood, I have seen nothing more beautiful than this sight of my Father teaching my children. The encouragement is more excellent still because He is careful to say: "All your children" shall be taught by the Lord. One black sheep, one wayward son, a single daughter who does not care for the Lord, can bring great grief to godly parents. But the Lord has granted me this blessing that He speaks of here. My Lord has granted me the unsurpassed blessing of teaching <u>all</u> my children. Gary, Jonathan, Becky, and Sandi have all been called to my Savior's table of instruction and have heard and have obeyed His voice instructing them on the way that they should go. I am deeply, deeply grateful. When the Lord is the great Teacher of our children, He makes them to prosper and He fills them with peace. "And great shall be the peace of your children." The law of the Lord brings beauty to families, and His instructions fill children with peace. "Those who love your teachings will find true peace, and nothing will defeat them" (Psalms 119:165 NCV)." Prosperity and peace. Beauty and abundance. These are the blessings that our Lord brings when He comes to teach our children. Let us crave nothing but God and let us dread nothing but sin – not only for ourselves, but also for our children. Let us leave off praying for shallow blessings for our children. Let us plead with the Lord that He will sit with them each day and teach them His ways. For true prosperity and true peace will belong to our children and to their children when they listen to and obey the magnificent tutoring of our Lord.

I was moved to think of our family again when I read:

38:18-19
For Sheol cannot thank You, death cannot praise You; those who go down to the pit cannot hope for Your truth. The living, the living man, he shall praise You, as I do this day; <u>the father shall make known Your truth to the children.</u>

Reading Hezekiah's thoughts on making God's truth known to his children re-filled me with concern for our coming generations:
... If man's great work is to see God praised, His next great effort is to "make known Your truth to the children." Hezekiah will fail here. His son, Manasseh, will rebel against the Lord. Let us not fail. Let us pray for the next generation! We must make God's truths known to our children. Let us teach them God's ways, let us praise the Lord openly so our children can see the proper response to God's goodness. We must praise God and

teach our children to praise God. The benefit for doing so can hardly be overstated! Jonadab made a vow to serve the Lord over 200 years before Jeremiah was born. He commanded his children to follow in his footsteps – to serve the Lord and abstain from alcohol (Jeremiah 35:6) -- and almost 300 years later we find his descendants still committed to following his example! Generations upon generations committed to God and blessed by God (Jeremiah 35:19) because their father was faithful to God and made known God's truths to his children. Praise the Lord for His goodness; make His truths known to the next generation. This was Hezekiah's desire. May it be ours as well.

So many times, as I read Isaiah's words, I thought of our family. I was deeply convicted over the parents' responsibility and opportunity to bless their descendants as I read:

37:33-35
Therefore thus says the LORD concerning the king of Assyria: "He shall not come into this city, nor shoot an arrow there, nor come before it with shield, nor build a siege mound against it. By the way that he came, by the same shall he return; and he shall not come into this city," says the LORD. For I will defend this city, to save it for My own sake <u>and for My servant David's sake.</u>

Just look at what these words say about the lasting effect of a family's devotion to the Lord! My comments on these verses included:

Remarkably, God says that His second reason for defending Jerusalem is "for My servant David's sake." Amazing. David lived and died nearly 300 years before Isaiah and Hezekiah faced the Assyrian invasion. 300 years! And yet, God says that the reason He will deliver His people from Assyria is for the sake of His servant David. How long will our legacy last? How long will God continue to bless our children and their children for the sake of our service and devotion to Him? Not only is it reasonable to hope for this, it is proper for us to expect this! Deuteronomy 7:9 says, "Therefore know that the LORD your God, He is God, the faithful God who keeps covenant and mercy for a thousand generations with those who love Him and keep His commandments." What a precious thought. Through the mercies of my precious Savior, my devotion to His commands may bless my descendants for untold generations! Let us be faithful to God! Let us serve Him, honor Him, and obey Him! So much good can rise from one man's devotion to the Creator! David served the Lord in his generation (Acts 13:36), but the reward for his service was passed on to his descendants for generations on end. Let us be rightly inspired by these words to invest heavily in godly service today. The long-term dividends arising from our present godly devotion are incalculable.

And in chapter 22, Isaiah's words regarding Hilkiah, made me think of the "glorious throne" that all godly children become for their parents:

22:23-25
I will fasten him as a peg in a secure place, and he will become a glorious throne to his father's house. **They will hang on him all the glory of his father's house, the offspring and the posterity, all vessels of small quantity, from the cups to all the pitchers. "In that day," says the LORD of hosts, "the peg that is fastened in the secure place will be removed and be cut down and fall, and the burden that was on it will be cut off; for the LORD has spoken."**

Shebna was unreliable. He was looking out for his own interests and failed to carry out the purposes of God and failed to care for the people of God. As a result, he "will be removed and be cut down and fall." In contrast, God will "fasten" Hilkiah like "a peg in a secure place." Hilkiah would be solid and dependable, like a nail driven deep into the frame of a hardwood house. A thick nail driven deep in a hardwood wall can hold up virtually anything you hang on it. And so Hilkiah will represent the coming Son of God upon whom we can hang all our hopes and needs. He will become "a glorious throne to his father's house." What a joy to a family when sons and daughters rise up to glorify God and bring honor to their family name; when their faith and service shine like a "glorious throne." Proverbs 23:24 says, "The father of the righteous will greatly rejoice, and he who begets a wise child will delight in him." So will Hilkiah be for his father. And so, my four children have been for me. Like a glorious throne they have blessed my house with their service to the Lord and efforts to remain holy. May the Lord bless my children with this same joy that I have been allowed to know.

And, of course, Isaiah 59:21 forever will be a blessing to me as I think of that blessed pre-dawn morning in His presence praying for my children. The Lord's words, through Isaiah in that verse, provided not just great inspiration for this volume of the family commentary, but for all the volumes, and for all our precious times together studying His Word and serving Him together as a family of faith. Our Lord has called all of us to diligently study His Word and to devotedly take care of His people as we pass on to others what His Word has been teaching us. I am so deeply grateful that studying God's Word and serving Him has become a family effort. The gratitude that swept over me as I prayed for my children so long ago, has been matched and more by the past 25 years of watching my Lord call my children to Himself. I am so eternally grateful. John wrote, "I have no greater joy than to hear that my children walk in the truth" (III John 1:4). I am so grateful that my Lord has condescended to grant me this highest of joys. God has called my children to Himself. We find in Isaiah 59:21 that it is the heart of the Lord to do that very thing – and His hand on our children has proven to be a joy of the highest possible magnitude. Neither John nor I can find its equal.

I wrote my first commentary on the Bible when I was 12, entitling it simply, <u>Notes on The Bible, by Doug Derbyshire, 6th grade</u>. And for the past 46 years, the highlight of my days has continued to be sitting with the Lord in prayer and praise, and then holding His Word in my hands and memorizing, studying, and meditating on every word. It is a joy to give you this collection of my thoughts on Isaiah, knowing that all of you share my deep love for God's Word and remain faithful to join me each day in reading, obeying, and trembling at His Word (Isaiah 66:2). May the Lord grant that this effort might be some blessing to you Cheryl, and to you Gary, Jonathan, Becky, and Sandi. You all are such a dear blessing to me.

-Doug Derbyshire
September 22, 2020

Isaiah 1

1:1-3
The vision of Isaiah the son of Amoz, which he saw concerning Judah and Jerusalem in the days of Uzziah, Jotham, Ahaz, and Hezekiah, kings of Judah. Hear, O heavens, and give ear, O earth! For the LORD has spoken: "I have nourished and brought up children, and they have rebelled against Me; the ox knows its owner and the donkey its master's crib; but Israel does not know, My people do not consider."

Isaiah's 66-chapter vision from the Lord is recorded for our continual benefit. The vision is said to concern only Judah and Jerusalem, but Isaiah's vision clearly has profound implications and applications for us today. He immediately calls on all of heaven and earth to "give ear" to what he has to say. God's word is applicable, yes, it is essential for every man and every woman in every town, from every walk of life, in every nation on earth. The vision is "concerning Judah and Jerusalem." But the heavens and the earth are called upon to pay careful attention to what the vision details, so we are right to concentrate on what Isaiah says, and to make all effort to declare to all nations all that God says in His Word. Everything God says to Jerusalem applies to us today. What He expects from His people in Judah, He expects from us. That which incurred God's wrath then, still incurs His wrath today. Those things that grieved the Lord when Jerusalem did them, will grieve the Lord today if we also do them.

God calls Isaiah's listeners His "children." He has "nourished" them. God has "brought up" the nation of Judah as a mother and father raise up a family. As the nation's loving Lord and Father, God "brought up" His people out of the land of Egypt (Exodus 29:46, I Samuel 10:18).   Even after His children were no longer a fledgling nation -- no longer "children," as it were, God continued to bring them up – to tend to them and care for them like a father cares for his own. Psalms 30:3 says, "O Lord, You brought my soul up from the grave; You have kept me alive, that I should not go down to the pit." Psalms 40:2 says, "He also brought me up out of a horrible pit, out of the miry clay, and set my feet upon a rock, and established my steps." And yet, after all God has done to "bring up" His children – establishing their nation, protecting them from death and danger, and setting their feet on solid ground, after lavishing them with all His provisions, "Israel does not know" how to respond rightly to God's relentless Fatherly love, and "My people do not consider" how they should express appropriate gratitude for all that God has done for them.

People are smart. It is remarkable how brilliant mankind has proven itself to be. We can make airplanes. We can fly to the moon. We can split atoms in two. We make computers, duct tape, and suitcases with wheels on the bottom. People are smart – made so by our Creator. Mankind, therefore, is completely without excuse when his actions prove him to be even more stupid than a donkey or an ox. A donkey can figure out where he comes from, and an ox recognizes his owner. Brute beasts like oxen and donkeys "know their owner and appreciate his care" (NLT). There is, therefore, no excuse for anyone to fail to recognize God and to fail to offer Him His rightful appreciation and devotion. Only a fool says there is no God (Psalms 14:1). Even an ox knows that, and even a donkey knows enough to stay close to his provider. God's point is plain. The people of Judah have turned their backs on their Creator and Provider, the One who had brought them up when they had been very low. Isaiah's vision begins with a scathing critique: the people of Judah have abandoned their devotion to God. And unfaithfulness to God proves people to be more brutish than donkeys and less intelligent than an ox.

1:4
Alas, sinful nation, a people laden with iniquity, a brood of evildoers, children who are corrupters! They have forsaken the LORD, they have provoked to anger the Holy One of Israel, they have turned away backward.

God's people have "forsaken the LORD." It is hard to imagine a more shameful descriptor. To know God and then forsake God is inexcusable. God is perfect. His work is perfect (Deuteronomy 32:4). His way is perfect (II Samuel 22:31). His knowledge is perfect (Job 37:16). His law is perfect (Psalms 19:7). His will for us is perfect (Romans 12:2). God is perfect in every way. And He has revealed Himself to us perfectly and extended to us a perfect invitation to draw near to Him and enjoy His perfect pleasures forever. To be granted a taste of God's perfections and then forsake Him, is betrayal and treason and infidelity at the highest level. It cannot be surprising that when men and women forsake the Lord that it "provoke(s) to anger the Holy One of Israel." Mankind cannot reject God with impunity. Forsaking Him angers Him.

We see here two certain results of rejecting God – God is incited to anger, and men decline into sin. Those who have forsaken God are called "a sinful nation," "a people laden with iniquity," "a brood of evildoers," and "children who are corrupters." This is the certain outcome of forsaking God. Those who would think to create a moral state apart from God face inevitable failure. Men without God are "sinful." Women without God are "laden with iniquity," and children not taught God's ways will corrupt the morals taught them by their conscience. This is the state of the people to whom Isaiah writes, people who have forsaken God and permitted themselves to sin. Their sin and unfaithfulness have provoked God to anger. Isaiah writes to turn his readers from their sin so that they might avoid God's wrath.

1:5-6
Why should you be stricken again? You will revolt more and more. The whole head is sick, and the whole heart faints. From the sole of the foot even to the head, there is no soundness in it, but wounds and bruises and putrefying sores; they have not been closed or bound up, or soothed with ointment.

With a heart for reconciliation, our Lord strikes those He loves. He says in Revelation 3:19 "Those whom I love, I reprove and discipline, so be zealous and repent." God uses discipline and misery to call people to their senses and turn their hearts back to Him. But when God's loving discipline fails to dislodge us from our deliberate intent to rebel, what is the use of further discipline? God asks rhetorically, why should I grant you further discipline when it will only see you "revolt more and more"? God calls attention to the horrible result of His people's rebellion. Their "whole head is sick." Their "whole heart faints." From head to toe they are covered in "wounds and bruises and putrefying sores." Let this picture sink in – in God's eyes, sinners appear "putrefying." Sin wounds our conscience, bruises our integrity, and putrefies our soul. Sinners must seek treatment before their malignant sinfulness infects them through and through. Who in their right mind would sit in pain and disease when the remedy lies so easily available right before their eyes? Our loving Lord stands ever ready to bind our wounds of guilt with forgiveness, and to heal our sores of regret with kindness, but rebellion refuses us access to the Great Physician. Jeremiah 8:22 says: "Is there no balm in Gilead, Is there no physician there? Why then is there no recovery for the health of the daughter of my people?" There is balm in Gilead. The Great Physician is on call ready to heal the wounds of sin, but sin will not be soothed if there is no repentance. Hosea 6:1 tells the response God desires from those He chastens, "Come, and let us return to the LORD; for He has torn, but He will heal us; He has stricken, but He will bind us up." Repentance and returning to the Lord will grant us healing. Persistent rebellion, as shown here, however, will be like a festering sore in our soul, sickening our spiritual vitality, and depriving us of the treatment plan of the Great Physician, who alone can heal the wounds of guilt and shame.

1:7-8

Your country is desolate, your cities are burned with fire; strangers devour your land in your presence; and it is desolate, as overthrown by strangers. So the daughter of Zion is left as a booth in a vineyard, as a hut in a garden of cucumbers, as a besieged city.

In verses 5 and 6 God likened the effects of Judah's sin to a disease that had ravaged their body. Now He moves to a new picture to illustrate the effects of their nation-wide rebellion. Twice, God says that sin has caused their nation to be "desolate." They are "burned with fire." Their nation is devoured, "overthrown," "besieged." Jerusalem, "the daughter of Zion," was once "the joy of the whole earth," "the city of the great King" (Psalms 48:2). But sin has diminished this city so badly that it is now no more glorious than a lean-to in a cucumber patch. When the people lived in righteousness, God lived with them in Zion (Psalms 74:2). But sin has made the Lord unwelcome there, and His departure has made the city unlivable – "it is desolate." Such is the certain outcome of sin – sin leaves us desolate, diminished, and ultimately, "burned with fire." May sin's nightmarish endpoints give us the good sense to refuse to entertain any notion of enjoying any of sin's fleeting short-term pleasures.

1:9
Unless the LORD of hosts had left to us a very small remnant, we would have become like Sodom, we would have been made like Gomorrah.

Judah had sinned just as Sodom had, and the utter destruction that God meted out on Sodom is well recorded in Genesis 19. Judah's sin and deserved destruction, was following the same course as that of Gomorrah, with total annihilation the projected final result. But in mercy, and in keeping with His covenant with Abraham, God withholds a remnant, "a very small remnant" from the total ruin their sins deserved. We are left breathless by the emotion of Isaiah's words. Judah's sins had brought them to the brink of extinction – but the Lord of hosts has chosen to leave them with a very small remnant – a memorial to both God's mercy and to the rebellion that so nearly destroyed an entire people group. "Through the LORD's mercies we are not consumed" (Lamentations 3:22). "The wages of sin is death" (Romans 3:23), and apart from our Lord's mercies we would all "become like Sodom," shamed and shattered, just like Gomorrah. We read Isaiah's words and shudder to think how close we are to destruction. Without the protection of the Lord of hosts, we would all perish like Sodom. Sin is our enemy -- evil desires war against our soul (I Peter 2:11). Satan is our enemy -- he is constantly looking to devour us (I Peter 5:8). And the world assaults us with more enemies still. With such a cloud of enemies in us and around us, what hope could we have of surviving if the Lord of hosts was not on our side? Blessedly, He is on our side, preserving His elect, and safeguarding His "remnant." God is on our side! And "if it had not been the LORD who was on our side, let Israel now say – if it had not been the LORD who was on our side, when men rose up against us, then they would have swallowed us alive, when their wrath was kindled against us; then the waters would have overwhelmed us, the stream would have gone over our soul; then the swollen waters would have gone over our soul. Blessed be the LORD, who has not given us as prey to their teeth. Our soul has escaped as a bird from the snare of the fowlers; the snare is broken, and we have escaped. Our help is in the name of the LORD, who made heaven and earth" (Psalms 124:1-8).

1:10-11
Hear the word of the LORD, you rulers of Sodom; give ear to the law of our God, you people of Gomorrah: "To what purpose is the multitude of your sacrifices to Me?" Says the LORD. "I have had enough of burnt offerings of rams and the fat of fed cattle. I do not delight in the blood of bulls, or of lambs or goats."

Judah's sin has made them look so much like the evil people of these two infamous cities that God calls them Sodom and Gomorrah. God's question in verse 11 provides us with invaluable instruction: religious acts by unrighteous people are pointless, they serve absolutely no spiritual "purpose." The people are called "corrupters" in verse 4, and here we see that their moral bankruptcy has corrupted even their most sacred efforts. The sacrificial system that God Himself gave to them has been ruined by their unrighteousness. No religious effort is of any spiritually cleansing worth when offered by sinful hearts. No religious acts can cleanse a sinful soul, and here we see that this is true, even for God-authored religious efforts. Repentance and obedience to God's decrees sanctify our spiritual efforts and make our religious offerings "a sweet-smelling aroma, an acceptable sacrifice, well pleasing to God" (Philippians 4:18). But we are here solemnly reminded that "To obey is better than sacrifice" (I Samuel 15:22). Disobedience contaminates our good deeds and desecrates our religious acts. We must obey God's word in every arena of life, or all our religious acts are futile.

1:12-13
"When you come to appear before Me, who has required this from your hand, to trample My courts? Bring no more futile sacrifices; incense is an abomination to Me. The New Moons, the Sabbaths, and the calling of assemblies – I cannot endure iniquity and the sacred meeting."

God continues to decry religious effort delivered by sinful hearts. God's view of corrupt people carrying out religious acts is brought into striking contrast with how man views his spiritual endeavors. What unrepentant sinners call "attending church" God calls "trampling My courts!" Offerings made by sinners intending to foster good will with God, the Lord calls "futile sacrifices." Incense intended to please God becomes offensive to Him when offered by people living in sin. God cannot stand sacred meetings when the assemblers are filled with sin. We are granted the remarkable opportunity and privilege of gathering together and entering the presence of God (Matthew 18:20), where we may offer Him our expressions of devotion and gratitude. But we are not permitted to enter the presence of God and drag our sin in with us. When we try it – when we go to church, when we offer sacrifices to God with sinful and unrepentant hearts, we trample His courts and desecrate our place of worship. God cannot stand it, and we must not allow it.

1:14-15
Your New Moons and your appointed feasts My soul hates; they are a trouble to Me, I am weary of bearing them. When you spread out your hands, I will hide My eyes from you; even though you make many prayers, I will not hear. Your hands are full of blood.

God ordained the sacrifices of the New Moons (Numbers 28:11-15), and when those offerings were given by worshippers they were "a sweet aroma" before the Lord (Numbers 28:13). God appointed feasts for His people to observe (Exodus 23:14-16), and they were considered "holy" and "sacred" when celebrated by His obedient children. These same feasts and these same sacrifices however, when observed by disobedient children, were "a trouble" to God. Sinfulness in worshippers made these religious efforts a weariness to the God who cannot tire. With frightening clarity, God says, "My soul hates" these religious rites when carried out by sinful people. The new moon sacrifices and the appointed feast days were ordained by God to draw mankind to communion with Him and be a joy to both creature and Creator. But like maggots in our favorite food, so is sin in our acts of worship. Sin spoils our offering and turns God-ordained, God-pleasing actions into abhorrent acts that He detests. They sicken Him and make Him tired of watching our worship. Sin ruins our public worship and destroys our private prayers as well. A prayer of repentance God will always hear – but we are reminded here that the unrepentant sinner has no assurance that God will listen to any prayer other than repentance. God repeats this warning in Isaiah 59:1-2, "Behold the LORD's hand is not shortened, that it cannot save; nor His ear heavy, that it cannot hear. But your iniquities have separated you from your God; and your sins have hidden His face from you, so that He will not hear." He says it again in Micah 3:4 "Then they will cry to the LORD, but He will not hear them; He will even hide His face from them at that time, because they have been evil in their deeds." Sin makes worship futile and prayers left unheard. Oh let us examine ourselves! Let us cry out like David in Psalm 139 "Search me, O God, and know my heart… and see if there is any wicked way in me." May God reveal our sin to us quickly that we might repent quickly and thus restore holiness to our worship and make our prayers hearable.

1:16-17
Wash yourselves, make yourselves clean; put away the evil of your doings from before My eyes. Cease to do evil, learn to do good; seek justice, rebuke the oppressor; defend the fatherless, plead for the widow.

Our Lord has invited us to come (Isaiah 55:1, Revelation 22:17). We are invited to enter His presence, to rejoice in His favor, and to enjoy His blessings forever. The invitation comes with requirements, however. In Matthew 22, the invitation went out from the king bidding everyone to come to his son's wedding celebration. The people come, but one man arrives without proper attire, and he is thrown out. Here, Isaiah describes for us the proper attire that is the required dress code for all who would seek to worship God and enjoy His presence. First, we must "wash" ourselves and make ourselves "clean." We are permitted, yes, we are invited to come into the presence of God. But we are not permitted to draw near to God and drag our sin in with us. The invitation to draw near to God is inextricably bound with the command to be holy. "Draw near to God and He will draw near to you. Cleanse your hands, you sinners; and purify your hearts, you double-minded" (James 4:8).

We must "put away" all evil and "learn to do good." No one has to teach us to do evil. We are sadly skilled at sinning even before we can read. A toddler can sin without any training at all, and unskilled, uneducated adults are just as adept at sinning. Educated, highly skilled, busy professionals are also sadly superb at sinning. We can sin even when we are hard pressed to find time to do anything else. No one needs training or instruction to sin. In contrast, we must "learn to do good." We must study God's word, seek to know His will and ways, and then intentionally put His instructions into practice. Psalms 119:33 says, "Teach me, O LORD, the way of Your statutes, and I shall keep it to the end." Psalms 143:10 says, "Teach me to do Your will, for You are my God; Your Spirit is good. Lead me in the land of uprightness." And Psalms 25:4-5 says the same thing - "Show me Your ways, O LORD; teach me Your paths. Lead me in Your truth and teach me, for You are the God of my salvation; on You I wait all the day."

Then, in addition to cleansing ourselves from evil and learning to do good, we are commanded to "seek justice, rebuke the oppressor; defend the fatherless, plead for the widow." <u>It is essential for us to see that holy living is not simply living without breaking any rules.</u> If our life is to be pleasing and honoring to our Lord we must also fight for justice in our cities, defend the weak from oppressors, provide safe haven for orphans and others who are desperate, and take care of widows and all who have needs that they cannot meet themselves. Holy living will move us to take up swords and fight as Saul did for the sake of Jabesh Gilead in I Samuel 11. Godly hearts will be moved to take care of orphans as David does for Mephibosheth in II Samuel 9. Those moved to rid themselves of evil will also be moved to take care of widows as the early church did in Acts 6. Purity in our souls will move us to "rebuke the oppressor" as Elijah rebukes Ahab in I Kings 21 and Nathan rebukes David in II Samuel 12. Let us cleanse our hands and purify our hearts as required of all who would walk rightly with our Lord. But let us also fight to defend the oppressed and strain to provide for the needy as Isaiah reminds us to do here.

1:18
"Come now, and let us reason together," says the LORD. "Though your sins are like scarlet, they shall be as white as snow; though they are red like crimson, they shall be as wool."

With a plea to the intelligence and working conscience of His people, the Lord invites us to "reason together," to discuss this matter reasonably so that a mutually pleasing, logical conclusion might be reached. The people have sinned. They have turned their backs on God, devoted themselves to other gods and made the conscious decision to rebel against the laws of God that He has written in His Word and chiseled in their conscience. This sin has led to terrible repercussions: God is angered. They have forfeited access to His blessings. Their nation is weak and oppressed by powerful enemies. And their eternal souls, like their kingdom in Judah, are destined for destruction. "Come now"! Our Lord cries out, let's be reasonable about this! Your present woeful condition and your future mournful condemnation are rooted in your sin – but I am offering to take away your sin! If you will but repent of your sins, I will turn your scarlet sins into snow white redemption. If you will repent, I will forgive. God's constant call for repentance will ring out continually through the pages of Isaiah. Our Lord's relentless demand for righteousness will persist through Isaiah's prophecy. God's condemnation for evil, immoral, sacrilegious living will echo unchanging from Isaiah's day to ours. But so will this Divine offer found nestled here in Isaiah 1:18. God's people often memorize this verse, and rightly so. The outcome of sin is horrible, but the gift of God that washes away the stain and guilt of sin is made readily available. All reasonable people must surely see that it is in our own best interest to "come now" and reconcile with the Lord so that the stain of our sin might be removed.

1:19-20
If you are willing and obedient, you shall eat the good of the land; but if you refuse and rebel, you shall be devoured by the sword; for the mouth of the LORD has spoken.

If we are "willing" to submit to God, if we are willing to be obedient to His commands, we will "eat the good of the land." God is good, and He is good to those who are His. But if we "refuse and rebel" our destruction is assured – "for the mouth of the LORD has spoken." God reigns supreme over the universe. God is love – but He is no one to be trifled with. God is Spirit – we cannot see Him -- but He does not live in dark shadowed corners of the galaxy where no one can find Him. He "has spoken" to us. He has made plain His will and ways. He has spoken through our conscience, He has spoken through His creation, He has spoken through His written Word. In fact, Hebrews 1:1 says that He has spoken in "many ways" (ESV). It is inexcusable and it is condemning for any creature to hear God speak and then not rush to obey. God has spoken to the world, and if we are "willing and obedient" we will be eternally blessed. But disobedience and rebellion will never be excused. "The mouth of the LORD has spoken." There are only two possible outcomes: obedience and blessings, or disobedience and doom.

1:21-23
How the faithful city has become a harlot! It was full of justice; righteousness lodged in it, but now murderers. Your silver has become dross, your wine mixed with water. Your princes are rebellious, and companions of thieves; everyone loves bribes, and follows after rewards. They do not defend the fatherless, nor does the cause of the widow come before them.

The woefully sad commentary on the spiritual state of Jerusalem is given here. The city which was once called the "city of the great King" (Psalms 48:2), loyal to God, "the faithful city" is now compared to a harlot. Faith and fidelity have left the city. David cried over this very thing, when "the faithful disappear from among the sons of men" (Psalms 12:1). When they were faithful to God, the city was full of justice and righteous people lived in every neighborhood. Now the city is full of murderers. Those who have put to death their devotion to God are much inclined to put to death their fellow man. "The city has become dross." Everything of spiritual value has died away. Faith in God is precious (I Peter 1:7), and when a city loses its faith in God and faithfulness to God, not only is this precious commodity lost, but everything else of value is lost as well! Your silver has become dross! If you take the dross out of the silver, precious jewelry can be created (Proverbs 25:4). But if you choose the dross and throw out the silver, you leave yourself with nothing of value. You are like "wine mixed with water," and leave a foul taste in the mouth of the Creator.

It is common to find scoundrels and impish boys who have never been taught good morals in the company of criminals, but the spiritual state of Jerusalem has rotted so badly that now even the city's princes have joined the ranks of rebellious delinquents and have become "companions of thieves." Leaders are shameful and so are the rank and file. "Everyone loves bribes." Rather than finding joy in doing their duty, the people are only looking out for personal gain. Rather than use their position to provide for others, they seek opportunity to put bribe money in their pockets. Good men find reward enough in a job well done. Evil men are only motivated by personal gain and are ever looking for "rewards." Faithfulness to God will move His people to "look out not only for his own interests, but also for the interests of others" (Philippians 2:4). But when faith in God leaves the city, so does integrity – people will look for bribes rather than seek justice. And when faith in God leaves, so does concern for the needy and oppressed. The cause of the fatherless and the widow is forgotten in the stampede to look out for one's own personal interests

1:24-26
Therefore the Lord says, the LORD of hosts, the Mighty One of Israel, "Ah, I will rid Myself of My adversaries, and take vengeance on My enemies. I will turn My hand against you, and thoroughly purge away your dross, and take away all your alloy. I will restore your judges as at the first, and your counselors as at the beginning. Afterward you shall be called the city righteousness, the faithful city."

Jerusalem has abandoned God, and no one who rejects God can reasonably expect to do so without severe repercussions. Even in our dealings with common man, such actions as snubbing a person of power, will put you at risk. How much more is the obvious danger for those who would think to reject "the LORD of hosts, the Mighty One of Israel?" Not surprisingly, God will eventually get rid of His adversaries and "take vengeance" on those who set themselves against Him. What is surprising – marvelously surprising -- is God's intention behind His removal of His enemies. "I will restore." God does not take vengeance on His enemies to cast men from His sights forever. No, He punishes to restore our right standing with Him. He will restore righteous judges who will lead the people with justice rather than seek bribes and personal gain. He will restore counselors to the people who will be able to teach them the words and ways of God. He will restore for them their reputation so that they will once again be called "the city of righteousness, the faithful city." What a blessed reminder that God judges, God punishes, but God restores. His heart to punish us is not that we might be destroyed, but that He might purge away our dross, and take away all the impurities that shame us and make us unfit for His service.

1:27
Zion shall be redeemed with justice, and her penitents with righteousness.

We are redeemed, bought back to sonship with our Maker "with justice." God's redeeming love is conveyed to us on the wings of mercy, but His mercy is carried by the winds of justice. Mercy without justice soon erodes to coddling, evil and empowering sinners to remain addicted to their sin. Holy God does not coddle sinners, nor permit them to persist in disobedience, nor allow sin to go unpunished. If we are to be saved, we must be rescued by God's mercy. But for God's perfect holiness to be satisfied, justice must be upheld. Apart from the death of Christ, satisfying the laws of God demanding that the wages of sin be death, no one could be saved, for "without the shedding of blood, there is no remission of sin" (Hebrews 9:22). Let us ponder again, that we are "redeemed with justice." This redemption with justice required the death and suffering of our Lord Jesus Christ. We were bought (in mercy and justice) "at a price" (I Corinthians 6:20a). Remembering how great that price was, let us then "glorify God with our body and our spirit, which are God's" (I Corinthians 6:20b).

Our Lord redeems us with His justice and His mercy, and we lift up our hands and receive His gift of redemption with faith and with "righteousness." The people that God has redeemed from their sin are here called "penitents." They are "repentant people" (NLT). Just as it was not naked mercy, but mercy clothed with justice that God demonstrated in redeeming His people. So it is not naked faith, but faith clothed in righteousness that is the response that our Lord requires of us. We often delight in discussing the mercy of God and the faith of man when we discuss God's plan of salvation, and well we should. But this verse provides a reminder of the justice of God and the righteousness of man that are woven together with mercy and faith as essential fibers in the fabric of our salvation.

1:28
The destruction of transgressors and of sinners shall be together, and those who forsake the LORD shall be consumed.

    No distinction is made between "sinners" and "those who forsake the LORD." It is equally evil, it is equally condemnable to be a sinner and to be a God-rejecter. The conscience of man that teaches him to reject sin also teaches him to seek God – so sin and unbelief are equally united in evil, and will receive equal punishment from their Maker.

1:29-30
For they shall be ashamed of the terebinth trees which you have desired; and you shall be embarrassed because of the gardens which you have chosen. For you shall be as terebinth whose leaf fades, and as a garden that has no water.

    Terebinth trees were sites of pagan worship. "The gardens" were similar places where spirits and foreign gods were venerated. When God comes to destroy sinners and unbelievers (verse 28), those who worship in these places "shall be ashamed." To be caught red-handed in improper conduct is embarrassing. To be caught red-handed by someone in authority is horrifying. And to be caught red-handed by the One who "has power to cast into hell" (Luke 12:5) is mortifying. After spending years praying to and placating gods and spirits that cannot save, they will face the eternal God who judges mankind, and see in an instant that their garden has no water – the object of their worship has no substance, no power, no ability to save. On judgment day all religious and irreligious men and women will discover (too late) that which Nebuchadnezzar discovered long ago – that "there is no other God who can deliver" when our life is on the line (Daniel 3:29).

1:31
The strong shall be as tinder, and the work of it as a spark; both will burn together, and no one shall quench them.

    Personal strength, personal power and influence will be of no value to us on judgment day. On the contrary, the works and evil deeds of successful sinners will simply add fuel to their self-destructive flames. "The strong shall be as tinder." As dry tinder burns promptly and easily, so will be the fate of evil men and unbelievers on judgment day. And the "spark" which sets them on fire is their own works. Their very works, the very ill-gotten gains that evil men and women often work so hard to procure, will, on judgment day, be both the fuel and the spark that ignites the fire of their destruction. Perhaps on earth, evil men and unbelievers are blinded to the fact that their life work condemns them. But on Judgment Day, "each one's work will become clear; for the Day will declare it" (I Corinthians 3:13). On judgment day, those found in the gardens of false religion (verse 29) and those whose life work fails to give honor to God "will burn." While there is still time, let us expend all possible energy to see all men reconciled with God and work for His glory. For on Judgment Day, it will be too late for further warnings. Those who do not obey the Lord and do not work for Him will be burned, "and no one shall quench them."

Isaiah 2

2:1-2
The word that Isaiah the son of Amoz saw concerning Judah and Jerusalem. Now it shall come to pass in the latter days that the mountain of the LORD's house shall be established on the top of the mountains, and shall be exalted above the hills; and all nations shall flow to it.

Chapter 2 begins exactly as chapter 1 announcing that Isaiah's vision is "concerning Judah and Jerusalem." And just as in chapter 1, we are again shown that although the vision is specifically directed toward Judah, it clearly relates to the entire world, for the vision declares that one day "all nations" will flow to "the mountain of the LORD's house" that is established in Jerusalem. Isaiah's vision is not that one day there will be a mass migration of people to Israel, but that "in the latter days," perhaps in our day, there will be world-wide revival when the Lord our God "shall be exalted above the hills," when the people of the earth will come to God, not by ones and twos, but by the millions. They will stream to Him, they will "flow" to Him. The world has been granted glimpses of this already. Great revivals have shaken England and America and other nations as well. These city-wide and nation-wide revivals grant us a taste of the spiritual wonders to come. They stir excitement in our souls as we look ahead to the day when God's invitation to man is no longer ignored, when the mercy and justice of God are matched by the faith and heart for holiness in man. Is this vision just describing the New Jerusalem in Heaven, or might we see this here on earth? Jesus taught us to pray that we might not need to wait for heaven to see the dawn of this day of revival. We are to pray that God's kingdom would come and His will be done right now on earth just as it is in heaven. Revival! What a joyous thing to contemplate. When our whole family is completely devoted to God, our city streams to God, and then one nation after another flows to God in gratitude and praise. Let us pray that God will hasten the day when "All the ends of the world shall remember and turn to the Lord, and all the families of the nations shall worship before You" (Psalms 22:27). Let us long for this day when "All nations whom You have made shall come and worship before You, O Lord, and shall glorify Your name" (Psalms 86:9). This day is coming! May our soul take proper delight in this wonderful expectation.

2:3
Many people shall come and say, "Come, and let us go up to the mountain of the LORD, to the house of the God of Jacob; He will teach us His ways, and we shall walk in His paths." For out of Zion shall go forth the law, and the word of the LORD from Jerusalem.

What a beautiful picture is painted for us here! "Many people" encouraging one another to go and worship the Lord. "He will teach us His ways, and we shall walk in His paths." It is to man's eternal good that God is willing to teach us His ways, and it is pleasing to our Lord when man chooses to walk in His paths. God teaches us because He is good. "Good and upright is the LORD; therefore He teaches sinners in the way" (Psalms 25:8). And good men hang on His every word, longing for God to teach them more and more. Psalms 25:4 says "Show me Your ways, O LORD; teach me Your paths." Psalms 119:35 says, "Make me walk in the path of Your commandments, for I delight in it." It is evidence that our soul has been cleansed by God's forgiveness and His Spirit reigns inside us when we "delight" in hearing God teach and delight just as much in walking in His ways. The child of God loves to hear God's voice, to read His words in the scriptures, and then he delights in waking up each morning, intent on walking in the paths God has set before Him. Evil men, unregenerate men find God's word uninspiring and hard to understand. They complain that sermons are boring, and then they chaff under the requirements for holiness that the Lord teaches. But God's people love His Word! They love His teachings! And they love to walk in the paths of God's instruction.

It is not difficult to know God's will – "He will teach us His ways." And it is not difficult to spot a godly man in the crowd – he is the one who delights in walking in God's path. What a wonderful picture: "(God) will teach us His ways, and we shall walk in His paths." May this beautiful arrangement be continually demonstrated in us.

2:4
He shall judge between the nations, and rebuke many people; they shall beat their swords into plowshares, and their spears into pruning hooks; nation shall not lift up sword against nation, neither shall they learn war anymore.

War is the natural outflow of men living together in sinful disobedience to God on earth. As long as men rebel against God, they will readily find cause to war against one another. There are righteous wars when men must rise up to fight against tyranny and injustice. God "teaches my hands to make war" (Psalms 18:34), so that we can carry out His just causes in wars of that sort. And there are unrighteous wars when men simply want to take what other people have (James 4:1). But when people set their heart on worshipping God on His holy mountain (verse 2) and walking in His paths (verse 3) they will find no further need for war. The weapons that were once used to destroy people will be refashioned into instruments to provide for the needs of people. When all nations flow to worship as in verse 2, all nations will cease to fight each other as in verse 4. God will "judge between the nations." God will "rebuke many people." And His judgments and His rebuke prove to be the antidote that cures the world of war. When God rises in judgment, He "delivers all the oppressed of the earth" (Psalms 76:9). And when He rebukes the nations, the chariot and the warhorse are put to rest (Psalms 76:6). When God thunders out His judgments, the oppressed need no one else to defend them and the wicked are ashamed to arm themselves with unholy intentions. Our future as children of God is very bright. God "will teach us His ways" (verse 3), and in His holy schoolhouse, His people will have no need to "learn war anymore."

2:5
O house of Jacob, come and let us walk in the light of the LORD.

The world can be a dark place. Bad things happen to good people. Difficulties arise for which no cure appears possible. Poverty, illness, friendships lost, and a variety of sorrows can cast very dark shadows on our world. Blessedly, children of God of the house of Jacob are granted ready access to the light. We "are all sons of the light and sons of the day. We are not of the night nor of darkness" (I Thessalonians 5:5). Psalms 119:105 says, "Your word is a lamp to my feet and a light to my path." No matter how dark circumstance appears, light shines when we open God's word. Isaiah's hearers were living through dark days. But he invites them here to look to the light of God's word for hope and instruction and vision. His words offer the same inspiration for us today. What a joy it is in trials to know that "The LORD my God will enlighten my darkness" (Psalms 18:28). When enemies darken our doorstep, the light of God's word reassures us with Psalms 27:1 – "The LORD is my light and my salvation; whom shall I fear?" When darkness seems to hide the future and we cannot tell which way to go, our Lord, Himself will be the light that shows the way. Psalms 89:15 says, "Blessed are the people who know the joyful sound! They walk, O LORD, in the light of Your countenance." Isaiah's grand invitation beckons us today! The world can be a dark place. But we do not need to sit dazed in the dark, doze off in the dark, become muddled or confused or depressed in the dark. Jesus said, "I am the light of the world. He who follows Me shall not walk in darkness, but have the light of life" (John 8:12). Our Lord has called us "out of darkness into His marvelous light" (I Peter 2:9). It is "marvelous" to walk in the light of our Lord! So, then, with such a delightful invitation and opportunity to walk in the light of God's glory, let us do so, enjoying the glow of the presence of God and reflecting it for the benefit of others, so that we, too, may "shine like lights in the world" (Philippians 2:15).

2:6-9

For You have forsaken Your people, the house of Jacob, because they are filled with eastern ways; they are soothsayers like the Philistines, and they are pleased with the children of foreigners. Their land is also full of silver and gold, and there is no end to their treasures; their land is also full of horses, and there is no end to their chariots. Their land is also full of idols; they worship the work of their own hands, that which their own fingers have made. People bow down, and each man humbles himself; therefore do not forgive them.

God has "forsaken" his people because they are full. Just as we cannot pour more water into a glass already full of something else, so God cannot fill His people with His blessings when they have filled themselves with other things. Judah is filled with 8 unholy and unhelpful things that have ruined their opportunity for God to pour into them the riches of His kindness. Verse 6 begins the list: "they are filled with eastern ways." They are filled with "soothsayers like the Philistines." And they are filled with "the children of foreigners." The people of Judah have filled their ears with the advice of soothsayers and the religions of "eastern ways." Their nurseries are filled with the cries of children birthed from unholy unions. And if we choose to fill our ears with noises such as these, God will not blend His voice with the brash sounds of rebellion. He will "forsake" His people, He will leave them to their own devices rather than mix His voice with such unholy background noise.

Verse 7 continues the list. God has rejected His people because their land is full of "silver and gold." Their land is full of "treasures." And the land is full of "horses" and "chariots." It is our Lord's heart to fill us with His blessings. "I give wealth to those who love me, filling their houses with treasures" (Proverbs 8:21, NCV). But if we find our own way to fill our lives with our own riches, we leave Him no room to fill us up with His. I Peter 1:18 warns that silver and gold are "corruptible" and cannot save us. James 5:3 warns us that heaping up ill-gotten treasure will testify to our poverty with God and only serve to "eat our flesh like fire" in the last days. And Deuteronomy 17:16 warned the people not to multiply horses because that was an attribute of pagan nations and God would protect them from any action that would tempt them to "return" to the lifestyle of godless people. Idol worshippers trust in horses, godless people trust in chariots, but God's desire for His people is that we might trust in the name of the Lord our God (Psalms 20:7).

Verse 8 completes the list of things Judah has filled themselves with, saying that the land is full of "idols" and "the work of their own hands." It is God's good pleasure to save us by His mercy. But Jonah recognized that those who fill their hand with worthless idols will forfeit their own mercy (Jonah 2:8). God's anger toward idol worshippers can hardly be overstated. In Leviticus 26:30 God says, "My soul shall abhor" those who worship idols. Judah has filled themselves with everything from horses to idols, leaving no room for God's blessings. They have forsaken God for the sake of lesser things, and the height of the tragedy is realized when God is said to forsake His people in verse 6. Isaiah then affirms the appropriateness of God's actions in verse 9. Isaiah writes, "The people bow down" before idols – it is humiliating to watch. Their conscience has taught them that idols cannot save them from sin. Their brain tells them plainly that lifeless idols have no power to save them from anything at all. And yet they insist on rejecting

God and filling themselves with idol nonsense. "Each man humbles himself," each man humiliates himself with his idolatry. It is shameful for grown men to worship idols. It is unforgiveable. David said, "I hate those who worship worthless idols" (Psalms 31:6 NLT). Isaiah's sentiment is hardly any softer, praying for God to withhold His forgiveness from those who offend Him by their idol worship.

2:10-11
Enter into the rock, and hide in the dust, from the terror of the LORD and the glory of His majesty. The lofty looks of man shall be humbled, the haughtiness of men shall be bowed down, and the LORD alone shall be exalted in that day.

The sheer glory of God's majesty is enough to send men to their knees. The prospect of God's holy gaze piercing into our sinful soul brings "terror" to our hearts. It is frightful for thinking men to contemplate the day when our open failures and secret wicked thoughts will be evaluated and judged by such a mighty and witheringly holy God. With no way to hide our sinfulness, and no way to stand up against God's holy gaze, man will, ostrich-like, bury his face in the ground and try to hide under a rock. God is great. We are not. The closer we are to God, the more strikingly clear this becomes. Let us bow before the Lord in humility and submission today so that we will be found already in the proper posture when Christ returns to judge us all in "that day" to come. Godly men and women delight to exalt our Lord today and call out to others to do the same. Psalms 34:3 says, "Oh, magnify the LORD with me, and let us exalt His name together." But the ungodly and unbelieving will be forced against their will to exalt Him in "that day" to come. One way or another, "the LORD alone shall be exalted." If we will humble ourselves and submit to His Lordship today, we will be exalted with Him in "that day" (I Peter 5:6). If, however, we exalt ourselves with "lofty looks" and "haughtiness," we will look frighteningly foolish when we stand and then fall before the glory of God's holy majesty on "that day."

2:12-17
For the day of the LORD of hosts shall come upon everything proud and lofty, upon everything lifted up – and it shall be brought low – upon all the cedars of Lebanon that are high and lifted up, and upon all the oaks of Bashan; upon all the high mountains, and upon all the hills that are lifted up; upon every high tower, and upon every fortified wall; upon all the ships of Tarshish, and upon all the beautiful sloops. The loftiness of man

ISAIAH 2

shall be bowed down, and the haughtiness of men shall be brought low; the LORD alone will be exalted in that day,

The sin of pride is pictured plainly for us here. Isaiah's listeners are not here condemned for immorality or injustice. They are condemned for their pride. "The day of the LORD," the wrath of God will come upon "everything proud and lofty." Nowhere in this discourse will these objects of God's wrath be called "evil." In fact, they are described in considerably complimentary fashion. They are called tall trees, high mountains, strong towers, fortified walls, and beautiful boats. The people are doing nothing that would put them in jail. They are breaking no laws, they are not cheating on tests, and they are not guilty of violent crimes. But they have become "proud and lofty." And this sin is disgusting to God. Proverbs 6:16 says that there are six things that the Lord hates – there are seven things "that are an abomination to Him." And number one on that list is "a proud look" (Proverbs 6:17). God is great. We are not. The Lord alone is to be exalted. It is the height of man's glory to exalt God's majesty, and it is the height of man's folly when he exalts his own. Proverbs 29:23 says, "A man's pride will bring him low," and that is the message here as God pronounces imminent judgment on the proud, when "the loftiness of man shall be bowed down, and the haughtiness of men shall be brought low." On "that day," on judgment day, "the LORD alone will be exalted." There will be no temptation to exalt oneself on the day when the Lord God at last reveals Himself in glory. But today, it is sadly easy to fail here. It is remarkable how little we need to accomplish before we fill ourselves with pride. We pass a single challenge, overcome a single foe, build a single "beautiful sloop" and suddenly we think that we deserve praise. Let us cling to the attitude of John the Baptist who understood that "He must increase but I must decrease" (John 3:30). It needn't be a painful process to teach ourselves humility. The humble spirit that God desires is not instilled in us by self-deprecation, but by gazing continually on the wonderful face of our Lord. In His presence, entranced by His glory, our own humility is best enjoyed.

2:18
But the idols He shall utterly abolish.

Of all the sins of man, idolatry is one of the most curious. The intelligence of man would seem to make idolatry a sin only for children. As soon as boys and girls grew up, they would realize that "idols are silver and gold, the work of men's hands. They have mouths, but they do not speak; eyes they have, but they do not hear; noses they have, but they do not smell;

they have hands, but they do not handle; feet they have, but they do not walk; nor do they mutter through their throat" (Psalms 115:4-7). There should be no way that a rational human being could ever believe that a hand-carved idol has supernatural power. And yet, intelligent men and women from Isaiah's day to ours, continue to clutch the idols around their neck and bow before the idols in their temples. Their conscience demands the belief in God, but their flesh rebels against the constraints of holiness – and so idolatry persists. But it will not persist forever. One day, God will "utterly abolish" the idols that men cling to in self-deception. Sadly, those who worship these idols will share their idol's fate as the following verses describe.

2:19-22
They shall go into the holes of the rocks, and into the caves of the earth, from the terror of the LORD and the glory of His majesty, when He arises to shake the earth mightily. In that day a man will cast away his idols of silver and his idols of gold, which they made, each for himself to worship, to the moles and bats, to go into the clefts of the rocks, and into the crags of the rugged rocks, from the terror of the LORD and the glory of His majesty, when He arises to shake the earth mightily. Sever yourselves from such a man, whose breath is in his nostrils; for of what account is he?

On Judgment Day, when God openly reveals His glory and pronounces His verdict on sinners and rebels, unbelievers will want to hide. "The terror of the LORD and the glory of His majesty, when He arises to shake the earth mightily," will come as a stunning contrast to the mute, lifeless, powerless idol they wear around their neck. They will be suddenly, horribly embarrassed by the object of their worship. They will snap the string that holds their god and fling it into holes in the ground and caves of the hills where the moles and bats will be appropriately uninterested. God, the One true God, is Creator of the universe and is able "to shake the earth mightily." All other gods are mute and impotent, and a horrifying embarrassment to those who hold them when God shakes the skies and judges the earth. Isaiah tells his readers to "sever yourselves from such a man." Stay as far from idol worshippers as possible. As the Lord warned Moses to get away from the tents of Korah, Dathan, and Abiram in Numbers 16, so we are warned here to separate ourselves from these who will incur God's wrath by their offensive devotion to gods they made up themselves.

Isaiah 3

3:1-3
For behold, the Lord, the LORD of hosts, takes away from Jerusalem and from Judah the stock and the store, the whole supply of bread and the whole supply of water; the mighty man and the man of war, the judge and the prophet, and the diviner and the elder; the captain of fifty and the honorable man, the counselor and the skillful artisan, and the expert enchanter.

God delights in giving good things to His people. Psalms 84:11 says, "No good thing will He withhold from those who walk uprightly." This wonderful provision, however, in no way applies to those who refuse to "walk uprightly." Righteousness is the vessel that is specially designed to receive heaven's blessings. Without holy service to God, we are left without a proper receptacle for God to pour His blessings into, and without God's blessings, our situation, as we see here, becomes desperate. Mankind is incapable of feeding himself. If he rebels against God's lordship, he forsakes God's provision and famine will result. "The stock and the store," our bread and our water are provided by God in mercy, and here these things are withheld by God in judgment. Famines of bread and a thirst for water are devastating, but spiritual famines, where God no longer speaks to His people (because no one is listening), are even worse. Amos 8:11 says, "'Behold, the days are coming,' says the Lord GOD, 'That I will send a famine on the land, not a famine of bread, nor a thirst for water, but of hearing the words of the LORD.'" God's judgment brings both a famine of food and a dearth of leadership. It is God who provides the world with leaders who protect people from evil men and provide for those who are needy. Romans 13:1 says, "...there is no authority except from God, and the authorities that exist are appointed by God." But if men reject God's plan, they deny themselves God's provision, and anarchy joins famine as outcomes of their ungodliness. Judges 21:25 provides a clear example of this relationship – the people rebelled against God, God's judgment fell, His provisions were lost, and then "everyone did what was right in his own eyes." Self-centered anarchy reigns when God does not. When individuals turn away from God, the effects on society are catastrophic. In judgment on their rebellion, God removes the nation's pillars. The soldiers who protect their borders are gone. The judges who right wrongs and the prophets who teach wrong from right are also gone. Civic leaders, religious leaders, military leaders, and on down to counselors, artists, and experts in every arena imaginable are all removed from their society because they have removed God from their priorities. The fall of nations begins with unbelief and ungodliness in the hearts of the people. May the somber message of these verses have its proper effect on us.

3:4-5
I will give children to be their princes, and babes shall rule over them. The people will be oppressed, every one by another and every one by his neighbor; the child will be insolent toward the elder, and the base toward the honorable.

Insolent children and disrespectful adults are the so-called gifts that God "will give" to those who do not honor Him. When our children obey us and church members honor their leaders, we can happily lift up our gratitude to our Lord, for apart from His blessings, we would not be able to enjoy such things. When God-inspired wisdom reigns in the hearts of His people, princes and noble men rule the land (Proverbs 8:16). But without God's guidance "babes shall rule." These baby rulers will have neither the strength to fight against evil nor the discernment to choose right paths for themselves, and so "the people will be oppressed, every one by another and every one by his neighbor." Without a heart to serve the Lord, the leaders here lose their heart to serve their people. And similarly, without a heart to honor the Lord, the people lose their desire to honor their leaders. Oppression from poor quality leaders and insolence and disrespect from base people – these things haunt godless societies in our day just as they did in the day when Isaiah wrote these words.

3:6-7
When a man takes hold of his brother in the house of his father, saying, "You have clothing; you be our ruler, and let these ruins be under your power," in that day he will protest, saying, "I cannot cure your ills, for in my house is neither food nor clothing; do not make me a ruler of the people."

It is amazing how far people are willing to degrade themselves in order to avoid submitting to God. If they will submit to God as Sovereign Lord, He will delight their souls with displays of His glory, "for God is the King of all the earth" (Psalms 47:7). "He is clothed with power" (Psalms 65:6), and He is clothed with majesty" (Psalms 93:1). But if people are uninspired by the holiness of God, they will likely be unimpressed by the majesty of God, and would rather bow before a low-life lackey who owns his own shirt, than bow before a Holy God clothed in righteousness. With imposed insight, however, the would-be leader in Isaiah's prophecy refuses to lead the rag-bound rabble of unrepentant paupers saying, "I cannot cure your ills." That much is certain. God alone can cure us of our hell-bent destiny, and repentance alone will grant us an appointment with the Great Physician.

3:8
For Jerusalem stumbled, and Judah is fallen, because their tongue and their doings are against the LORD, to provoke the eyes of His glory.

The people of Judah stumbled and fell, their families broke apart and their nation was destroyed "because their tongue and their doings are against the LORD." In Matthew 12:36 Jesus warned that "for every idle word men may speak, they will give account of it in the day of judgment." We are frighteningly capable of offending our Creator by the things that we say. We must guard our words! James 1:26 says it plainly, "If anyone among you thinks he is religious, and does not bridle his tongue but deceives his own heart, this one's religion is useless." In fact, we see here that his religion is "useless" to protect him from the wrath of God that has been "provoke(d)" by his irreligious, vulgar speech. Then, in addition to Jerusalem's offensive words, his actions, his "deeds" (ESV) have provoked God to wrath as well. Every soul of man is under the vigilant watch care of the Lord. No one is too insignificant to avoid God's scrutiny, and no one is too prominent to be above His examination. We must be ever mindful of how God views the works of our hands, for it is altogether possible for us to "provoke" Him to wrath if we soil our hands with dirty deeds. Proverbs 24:12 probes us with the question, "He who keeps your soul, does He not know (what you do)? And will He not render to each man according to his deeds?" We have been given proper notice. The words of our tongue and the "doings" of our hands are judged by God. When heaven's cross examination assesses our words and our deeds, may we be found pleasing rather than provoking.

3:9
The look on their countenance witnesses against them, and they declare their sin as Sodom; they do not hide it. Woe to their soul! For they have brought evil upon themselves.

Woe to the soul that does not hide his sin. David was called a man after God's own heart (Acts 13:22), not because he never sinned, but because his response to sin was so pleasing in God's eyes. David mourned over his sin, repented and regretted his sin. He did not defend it, and he certainly did not flaunt it. Godly men are not perfect beings that never sin. But godly men cry over their sins, repent of those sins, and strive to protect themselves from ever failing like that again. Here, we see that Jerusalem has fallen so far from God that they no longer mourn their sin. Adam hid from God after he sinned. But the men here do not hide, "they declare" it openly. Shame is a proper response to sin. When people no longer feel ashamed of their sin -- "woe to their soul." Flaunting sin like Sodom, will incur God's wrath and lead to our destruction, just as it did to Sodom.

3:10-11
Say to the righteous that it shall be well with them, for they shall eat the fruit of their doings. Woe to the wicked! It shall be ill with him, for the reward of his hands shall be given him.

II Peter 3:15 says that the patience of the Lord gives people time to be saved. Sadly, people often misuse the time allotted to them and deceive themselves into thinking that God's patience in dealing out judgment is evidence that he will never give out judgment. But Galatians 6:7 warns us not to be duped into thinking that we can sin without consequence: "Do not be deceived, God is not mocked; for whatever a man sows, that he will also reap." We will reap what we sow. "It shall be well" with the righteous, because their obedience will be rewarded by the Lord. "Surely there is a reward for the righteous" (Psalms 58:11). In contrast, "Woe to the wicked" – for exactly the same reason. Their wickedness will glean for them "the reward" that their evil acts deserve. "For He repays man according to his work, and makes man to find a reward according to his way" (Job 34:11).

3:12
As for My people, children are their oppressors, and women rule over them. O My people! Those who lead you cause you to err, and destroy the way of your paths.

When God was their ruler, He promised to strengthen and protect His people so mightily that "Five of you shall chase a hundred, and a hundred of you shall put ten thousand to flight; your enemies shall fall by the sword before you" (Leviticus 26:8). But when His people rejected Him as Lord, they rejected their own Protector, and now, left defenseless, even "children" are able to oppress them. Their king is gone, their mighty men are gone, their leaders are all dead, or captive, or maimed, or hiding. Only the women are left to take care of the shambles of society that remains. The sight of such a proud nation reduced to such a humiliating state causes God to cry out, "O My people!" You have rejected My love and My protection – and to what end? You have chosen false gods and frail and fallible men to lead you in my stead, and those you have chosen to follow "cause you to err." We must be careful who we follow! God will lead us to peace beside still waters (Psalms 23:2). God leads us in the truth (Psalms 25:5). God leads us to everlasting life (Psalms 139:24). But the seductive words of evil leaders "leads down to death" (Proverbs 2:18). God leads us in the paths of righteousness (Psalms 23:3). But wicked leaders "destroy" that path and lead to final disgrace. Oh, let us choose our leaders well! And let us faithfully follow along the path of our great Shepherd, adopting David's prayer as our own: "My soul follows close behind You; Your right hand upholds me" (Psalms 63:8).

3:13-15
The LORD stands up to plead, and stands to judge the people. The LORD will enter into judgment with the elders of His people and His princes: "For you have eaten up the vineyard; the plunder of the poor is in your houses. What do you mean by crushing My people and grinding the faces of the poor?" Says the Lord God of hosts.

As both Prosecutor and Judge, the Lord stands to make His case against His own people – for He is their Defender as well! The evidence in the case is overwhelming. Stolen merchandise is found in their homes! "The plunder of the poor is in your houses." Rather than care for the poor, the people have oppressed and taken advantage of those in need. The imagery is striking. Those that have turned their backs on God are "crushing" God's people, they are "grinding the faces of the poor" into the ground. They are accused of a criminal lack of compassion. They have trampled and ruined "the vineyard" – God's chosen people (Isaiah 5:7). We are commanded to take care of our brothers in Christ and provide for the poor in our nation. Deuteronomy 15:11 says, "I command you, saying, "You shall open your hand wide to your brother, to your poor and your needy, in your land.'" In Heaven's eyes, failure to show compassion on the needy and care for fellow believers is a criminal offense and warrants the Lord standing up in the court of our conscience and casting judgment on those who are negligent of their Christian duty.

3:16-17
Moreover the LORD says: "Because the daughters of Zion are haughty, and walk with outstretched necks and wanton eyes, walking and mincing as they go, making a jingling with their feet, therefore the Lord will strike with a scab the crown of the head of the daughters of Zion, and the LORD will uncover their secret parts."

David's favorite thing in life to do was to "behold the beauty of the Lord" (Psalms 27:4). When we become more enamored with our own beauty than we are with the "beauty of the Lord," we place ourselves in danger of receiving God's rebuke, and Psalms 39:11 says, "When with rebukes You correct man for iniquity, You make his beauty melt away like a moth." As a sad example of this, we see the beauty of the daughters of Zion melting away in an instant as judgment on their evil heart that chose to exalt their own beauty rather than God's.

3:18-23
In that day the Lord will take away the finery: the jingling anklets, the scarves, and the crescents; the pendants, the bracelets, and the veils; the headdresses, the leg ornaments, and the headbands; the perfume boxes, the charms, and the rings; the nose jewels, the festal apparel, and the mantles; the outer garments, the purses, and the mirrors; the fine linen, the turbans, and the robes.

ISAIAH 3

The quality that God finds most beautiful in His people is holiness. Psalms 29:2 urges us to "Give unto the LORD the glory due to His name; worship the LORD in the beauty of holiness." "The beauty of holiness." What a precious picture. Righteous acts, caring for the church, holy living, these are the "finery" that God wishes to see His people adorned with. Psalms 33:1 adds another "charm" that the Lord finds pleasing to look at -- "praise from the upright is beautiful." I Peter 3:4 also adds to the list of things that God finds beautiful, saying that "the incorruptible beauty of a gentle and quiet spirit" is an ornament which is "very precious in the sight of God." It is possible to please God with our beauty – but the things which make us beautiful in His eyes are not always the "festal apparel" that men and women find pretty. But if we will not make ourselves beautiful in God's sight, concentrating only on what others say is attractive, we will face "that day" when our Lord "will take away the finery." He will "take away" the things that give us useless beauty. The women of Judah in Isaiah's day had a long list of beauty products: crescents, mantles, and turbans joined the more familiar bracelets, rings, and jewels. But all these things will be stripped from their wearers and tossed aside like so much excess baggage. On "that day," only holiness, praise, and godly acts of service will be allowed to adorn our faith as we approach the judgment seat of our Lord. May we be found not lacking in these things which God finds beautiful.

3:24-26
And so it shall be: instead of a sweet smell there will be a stench; instead of a sash, a rope; instead of well-set hair, baldness; instead of a rich robe, a girding of sackcloth; and branding instead of beauty. Your men shall fall by the sword, and your mighty in the war. Her gates shall lament and mourn, and she being desolate shall sit on the ground.

If we will simply respond to God's love for us and love Him in return, if we will cleanse our lives in response to His holy presence, if we will obey Him as is fitting for the creature to obey his Creator -- then He will make our lives a thing of beauty (Isaiah 61:3) and He will not only make us strong, but He will allow our descendants to become mighty as well -- "Blessed is the man who fears the LORD, who delights greatly in His commandments. His descendants will be mighty on earth" (Psalms 112:1-2). But if we reject the Lord, these precious promises of beauty and strength are lost! Oh, the tragedy that rebellion and unbelief bring us! Verse 24 says that the women of the world will lose their beauty and verse 25 says that the men of the world will lose their strength, and verse 26 pictures the sorrow that will ensue when the lost people of the world will "lament and mourn" their lost potential and "sit on the ground" wondering why they let such promises of beauty and might slip through their fingers for the sake of the fleeting satisfaction of sin. When we serve God and take care of His people, we become a "sweet-smelling aroma" that is "well pleasing to God" (Philippians 4:18). When we turn our back on God, however, we become a "stench" wafting up as evidence of the rottenness in our souls. In obedience, our hope is that "the beauty of the LORD our God (will) be upon us" (Psalms 90:17). But in disobedience, "baldness" and "branding" – humiliation and scarring replace the beautiful hope that abides in the hearts of God's children. Psalms 96:6 says, "Strength and beauty are in His sanctuary." Sadly, all those who refuse to serve the Lord in His sanctuary will be found weak and repulsive in God's eyes. Let us run to church. Let us run to worship the Lord, for it is His good will to make all His children beautiful (Ecclesiastes 3:11). But if we forsake Him, we forsake the beautiful life and spiritual strength that He lavishes on those that are His.

Isaiah 4

4:1
And in that day seven women shall take hold of one man, saying, "We will eat our own food and wear our own apparel; only let us be called by your name, to take away our reproach."

    The judgment of God on the sins of Jerusalem and Judah will leave the nation shattered. Oh, if we could only see in advance the degradation and humiliation that will always, eventually arise as a result of sin. In verses 2 and 3 of chapter 3, God said that He would punish the nation by taking away their mighty men and their warriors, as well as their judges, prophets, diviners, elders, captains, counselors, and the nation's experts in various fields. Verse 6 of chapter 3 says that the nation will deteriorate so badly that anyone with clothes on his back will be deemed worthy of being king. And here, we see that the women will be so desperate to find a decent man, that their qualifications for a husband will be even less than that! War and famine and personal wickedness will make husbands so hard to find that 7 women will grab the arm of any man they can find so that they can at least avoid the disgrace of being childless. Wretched women married to wretched men are a blight on society. But decent women married to wretched men because they can find no one better is a sign of a sick society reeling from the stench of their sin that has brought on them the judgments of God.

4:2
In that day the Branch of the LORD shall be beautiful and glorious; and the fruit of the earth shall be excellent and appealing for those of Israel who have escaped.

The "Branch of the LORD" is Jesus the Messiah. Jeremiah 23:5, Jeremiah 33:15, Zechariah 3:8, and Zechariah 6:12 also refer to the Messiah as the Branch. We are prone to believe that the glory of the Lord is somehow dependent on our well-being. It is not. The sin and sad state of Judah was vividly described in chapter one and in the first verse of chapter two. Despite the sorry state of God's people, however, "the Branch of the LORD" is unalterably "beautiful and glorious." We can reflect His beauty and glory by obedience, or we can provide contrast to His glory and beauty through rebellion. Either way, the Branch of the Lord is glorious and provides "excellent and appealing" fruit to those who escape His judgment and are blessed with the joys of His favor.

There is a radical shift in focus from verse one to verse two. Both verses begin the same way, "in that day," but the focal point in verse one is the degradation of man that is the result of sin. The focus of verse two, however, is the glory of God manifested in the Branch of the Lord. Sin brings injury and shame, abasement and desperation. Jesus, the Branch of the Lord, brings us beauty and glory, excellence and things that are "appealing" to the eye and to the soul. All "who have escaped" the grip of sin and the judgments of God will be able to enjoy all the comforts and splendors of walking in union with the Savior.

4:3-4
And it shall come to pass that he who is left in Zion and remains in Jerusalem will be called holy – everyone who is recorded among the living in Jerusalem. When the Lord has washed away the filth of the daughters of Zion, and purged the blood of Jerusalem from her midst, by the spirit of judgment and by the spirit of burning.

At the end of time, books will be opened that have recorded the deeds and misdeeds of all the world's peoples since Adam and Eve (Revelation 20:12). On that Day of Judgment, the Book of Life will be opened and anyone whose name is not recorded in that book will be "cast into the lake of fire" (Revelation 20:15). Those who are "recorded" in that book, however, are said here to "be called holy" and admitted as residents in the New Jerusalem. We will be called holy, "not by works of righteousness which we have done" (Titus 3:5), but because the Lord has washed away our filth through His death on the cross and purged our blood with His blood that was shed as the awful price required to make us clean. We are "washed," we are "purged," and our names are recorded among the inhabitants of the heavenly Jerusalem through the "spirit of judgment" and the "spirit of burning." "Our God is a consuming fire" (Hebrews 12:29). The fire of His judgment consumes the carnal acts of his saints (I Corinthians 3:13-15) and consumes all the life's efforts of those who persisted with evil hearts of unbelief. All who come to Jesus will be baptized, will be purified with the Holy Spirit and with fire (Matthew 3:11). The end result of the fiery judgments of our Lord is wonderful – we "will be called holy." What a precious thought. The great enemy which forbids us from entering the presence of our Lord is sin. And on this great day of judgment, we will be purged from that sin, our filth will be washed away, we will be dressed in white (Revelation 7:9), and we will enjoy unadulterated fellowship with our Savior forever.

4:5-6
Then the LORD will create above every dwelling place of Mount Zion, and above her assemblies, a cloud and smoke by day and the shining of a flaming fire by night. For over all the glory there will be a covering. And there will be a tabernacle for shade in the daytime from the heat, for a place of refuge, and for a shelter from storm and rain.

When the Lord calls His people to Himself at the end of time, it will again be as when He first called His people out of Egypt (Exodus 13:21). There will be no mistaking His direction -- a cloud of smoke will guide us by day and a pillar of flaming fire will guide us by night. Neither will we need to fear enemies or the elements because He will be a shade from the heat and a shelter from storm. Direction and protection. These two great provisions from our Lord began in Eden, were highlighted in Exodus 13, will be brought to full completion when our Lord comes to dwell with us in this New Jerusalem (Revelation 21), and are, even now, the blessed expectation of His people. Psalms 43:3 says, "Oh, send out Your light and Your truth! Let the lead me; let them bring me to Your holy hill and to Your tabernacle." And Psalms 5:11 says, "let all those rejoice who put their trust in You; let them ever shout for joy, because You defend them."

Isaiah 5

5:1-2
Now let me sing to my Well-beloved a song of my Beloved regarding His vineyard: my Well-beloved has a vineyard on a very fruitful hill. He dug it up and cleared out its stones, and planted it with the choicest vine. He built a tower in its midst, and also made a winepress in it; so He expected it to bring forth good grapes, but it brought forth wild grapes.

Chapter 5 is a song. It is sung by Isaiah to his beloved Lord, his "Well-beloved" Lord. God loves me. And I love Him in return. This precious love-relationship provides the answers to the deepest mysteries of life, provides hope in the deepest trials of life, and provides joy that surpasses all understanding day after day throughout all the years of our life. "I am my beloved's and my beloved is mine" (Song of Solomon 6:3). This is the relationship that inspires Isaiah's song. May our love for our Lord, springing in response to His love for us, be the inspiration for everything we do.

Isaiah's Beloved, the God who created all things, has planted a vineyard. All creation is His, but this vineyard is particularly special. He has planted it and nurtured it and protected it with extraordinary care – and with high expectations. "He expected it to bring forth good grapes." God established the nation of Israel with a unique calling, remarkable provisions, and miraculous interventions. But "for everyone to whom much is given, from him much will be required" (Luke 12:48). All those who have tasted the good things of God, who have been instructed with the deep truths of His word, and have been blessed by the joys of forgiveness and reconciliation are commanded to "bear fruits worthy of repentance" (Matthew 3:8). John 15:16 says, "You did not choose Me, but I chose you and appointed you so that you might go and bear fruit – fruit that will last." We are not called and chosen and rescued by our Lord to sit on our laurels. It is "expected" that all who have been touched by the love of God will bear fruit that is pleasing in His sight. God expected His vineyard Israel to bring forth good fruit – and it did not. Isaiah finds this inexcusable. So must we. Let us be diligent to "walk worthy of the Lord, fully pleasing Him, being fruitful in every good work and increasing in the knowledge of God" (Colossians 1:10).

5:3-4
And now, O inhabitants of Jerusalem and men of Judah, judge, please, between Me and My vineyard. What more could have been done to My vineyard that I have not done in it? Why then, when I expected it to bring forth good grapes, did it bring forth wild grapes?

God asks Isaiah's listeners to "judge, please, between Me and My vineyard." Who is to blame here? Why have My people failed to "bring forth" "fruits worthy of repentance" (Matthew 3:8)? God asks, "What more could I have done?" "Did I do something wrong?" We cringe before such an obvious question -- the perfections of our Lord provide the easy, yet uneasy answer, that all of the fault lies with God's people. God has provided everything we need to spiritually thrive. II Peter 1:3 says that the power of our Lord "gives us everything we need for living a godly life" (NLT). Verses 1-2 detailed all the wonderful things that God had done for His vineyard, just as the Scriptures detail the myriad of things that God has done for His people. God has given us counsel (Psalms 16:7). He has given us His shield of salvation (Psalms 18:35). He has given us food (Psalms 111:5), light (Psalms 118:27), and life itself (Psalms 119:50). What more could God do for us that He has not already done? Let us be diligent to "bring forth good grapes," to make sure that our life yields fruit that is pleasing to our Savior. God "expects" His kindnesses to yield fruitfulness in our lives. As a son delights in making his father proud, let us take proper delight in meeting our Lord's expectations.

5:5-7
And now, please let Me tell you what I will do to My vineyard: I will take away its hedge, and it shall be burned; and break down its wall, and it shall be trampled down. I will lay it waste; it shall not be pruned or dug, but there shall come up briers and thorns. I will also command the clouds that they rain no rain on it. For the vineyard of the LORD of hosts is the house of Israel, and the men of Judah are His pleasant plant. He looked for justice, but behold, oppression; for righteousness, but behold, a cry for help.

Verse 7 tells us two specific fruits that the Lord was expecting from His people, His "vineyard." He looked for "justice" and He looked for the fruit of "righteousness" -- but he found none. In the place of justice, the people oppressed their fellow man, and instead of the song of righteous living, only "a cry for help" from those who suffered at their wicked hands was heard. God has done His part. He has planted a vineyard with tender care. He has nurtured it, protected it, and provided all the things needful for growth and fruitfulness. But His people have defied their nature and dishonored their Creator by failing to bear the fruit that should have flowed naturally from their vines. Jesus allowed us to see the extent of God's dissatisfaction with lives that bear no spiritual fruit in Matthew 21. Matthew 21:19 records the encounter: "And seeing a fig tree by the road, He came to it and found nothing on it but leaves, and said to it, "Let no fruit grow on you ever again." Immediately the fig tree withered away." Let there be no mistake. God is love, but that in no way means that He tolerates laziness, lack of compassion, or wickedness in His people. If we will not bear fruit for our Creator, His displeasure will mean the loss of our protection and our lives will be "trampled down." If we will bear fruit for His kingdom He will prune us so that we will bear more fruit (John 15:2), but if we make no effort to bear the fruit that He desires, John 15, Matthew 21:19, and our verses here all remind us that our Lord will not allow us to bear fruit for anyone else either.

5:8-10
Woe to those who join house to house; they add field to field, till there is no place where they may dwell alone in the midst of the land! In my hearing the LORD of hosts said, "Truly, many houses shall be desolate, great and beautiful ones, without inhabitant. For ten acres of vineyard shall yield one bath, and a homer of seed shall yield one ephah."

ISAIAH 5

In an effort to advance their own fame and their own fortune, the well-to-do of Isaiah's day had added property after property to their vast possessions. Isaiah is not impressed. He solemnly warns those who would increase their own kingdom without effort to advance God's kingdom – "Woe to those who join house to house…" They have abandoned the great work of serving God's people and advancing God's kingdom – and the result will be devastating. Their houses "shall be desolate." And their lands and investments will fail to yield the anticipated fruit. Re-emphasizing His point from verses 1-7, God again expresses for Isaiah's readers this essential truth – if we refuse to bear fruit that is pleasing to God, He will not allow us to amass "fruit that will last" (John 15:16) for ourselves either. It is offensive to our Creator for us to approach His throne now with our requests or approach His throne later on judgment day – and come to Him empty-handed. God says in Exodus 34:20, "None shall appear before Me empty-handed." Deuteronomy 16:16 says the same thing, "They shall not appear before the LORD empty-handed." God has given this life to us on earth *on lease* (Luke 20:9). If we fail to offer to Him the fruits from the land and lives that He has leased to us, He will be justifiably angered and will make our unfruitful lives "desolate."

5:11-13
Woe to those who rise early in the morning, that they may follow intoxicating drink; who continue until night, till wine inflames them! The harp and the strings, the tambourine and flute, and wine are in their feasts; but they do not regard the work of the LORD, nor consider the operation of His hands. Therefore my people have gone into captivity, because they have no knowledge; their honorable men are famished, and their multitude dried up with thirst.

What a striking picture of how differently God views partying and leisure than man views these things. Isaiah's cry goes out – woe to those who party from morning to night! Severe judgment is coming to those who drink and lounge and enjoy life but "do not regard the work of the LORD." The sin that is condemned here is not immorality, dishonesty, or violent crimes. God is pronouncing woe and judgment on those who live for pleasure and leisure rather than live to diligently carry out "the work of the LORD." Look at the picture God gives us. The people are continually feasting – but God says they are "famished." If we feed only our mouths, our souls will starve, and God has no use for the spiritually scrawny. The people are drinking continually all day long, yet God says they are "dried up with thirst." In

Isaiah 55:2 God asks the same people, "Why do you spend money for what is not bread, and your wages for what does not satisfy?" If they will devote themselves to doing "the work of the LORD" rather than feeding their belly's appetite, their soul will "delight itself" in abundance. Working for the Lord is very satisfying for both body and soul. In John 4:34 Jesus told His disciples, "My food is to do the will of Him who sent Me, and to finish His work." If we will devote ourselves to our Father's work, we will love our work, our soul will find delight in our days, and we will feel richly satisfied. Isaiah's hearers however, refused to put their hand to their Father's plow. They ate and drank and partied. And their life of leisure made them spiritual weaklings, their souls were "famished" and "dried up." Isaiah laments that the result of their life of leisure was that "my people have gone into captivity." Their captivation with leisure led to captivity among their enemies. May the point not be lost on us. Eventually, the outcome will always be regret and shame and captivity if we choose a life of leisure rather than a life devoted to the work of the Lord.

5:14-15
Therefore Sheol has enlarged itself and opened its mouth beyond measure; their glory and their multitude and their pomp, and he who is jubilant, shall descend into it. People shall be brought down, each man shall be humbled, and the eyes of the lofty shall be humbled.

Verse 12 depicted God's people as revelers who abandoned the work of the Lord for the sake of partying and leisure. And here, Isaiah says that the grave (Sheol) will feast on those who give themselves to feasting. The world can be very deceptive. When multiple successes provide us with personal fame and fortune, our personal "glory" may dupe us into thinking that our life and afterlife are secure. But fame and glory are fleeting. These things will also be cast into Sheol. When we are surrounded by a "multitude" of people who all seem to testify that leisure is god and God is a myth, the sheer number of people all saying the same (God-deprecating) things can deceive us into thinking that they are correct. But popular thinking is often not right thinking, and in the end, "the multitude" along with their pomp and popularity will be cast into Sheol as well. Living for oneself can be so full of personal incentives and lead to so many happy moments that we can be deceived into thinking that being happy now is more significant than serving God now. But "he who is jubilant," he who lives for his personal well-being and happiness will be cast into Sheol just the same. The grave has a very wide mouth. It swallows whole even those who are puffed up and big-headed. No matter how big we are, at the mouth of the grave "people shall be brought down." Everyone, no matter how rich or strong or popular or happy – everyone "shall be humbled" before the face of death, whose mouth easily swallows the greatest of men. But even before the gaping jaws of death, we have a great hope! Death awaits all those who "do not regard the work of the Lord" (verse 12), but I Corinthians 15:58 says, "Be steadfast, immovable, always abounding in the work of the Lord, knowing that your labor is not in vain in the Lord." Look what happens when we will turn our backs on personal glory and popular thinking and live, instead, to serve the Lord our God – I Corinthians 15:54 says, "Death is swallowed up in victory"! Death will swallow all those who live for themselves. But those who love and live for the Savior will live to see the day when death itself is swallowed whole.

5:16-17
But the LORD of hosts shall be exalted in judgment, hallowed in righteousness. Then the lambs shall feed in their pasture, and in the waste places of the fat ones strangers shall eat.

Sadly, on earth, God is often denied the praise He deserves. But this is only a temporary situation. "In judgment" -- on judgment day, "The LORD of hosts shall be exalted." He is patient with men now, and men often mistake His patience for an opportunity to disregard Him. But on that Day of Judgment He will be exalted. He will be exalted in praise by those who love Him, and He will be exalted in exacting justice on those who do not. God "shows himself holy" (ESV) in righteousness. God seems to tolerate wickedness today, but on judgment day He will show for all to see His holy intolerance of sin. And at last, all those who are His, all His "lambs" will "feed in their pasture." They will receive all the full measure of God's provision in paradise. On earth, the righteous may become weakened by fasting (Psalms 109:24) while the wicked grow fat (Deuteronomy 32:15), but in righteousness and judgment, God will see to it that "the fat ones," the ones who grew fat by unholy means, will have the fruit of their labors taken away and given to "strangers" that were more righteous than they. These two verses remind us of three eternal truths: God will be exalted; His people will enjoy eternity in paradise; and the wicked may thrive for a time and grow fat, but they will lose all they have amassed. May these truths grant us great comfort for ourselves, and great pity and compassion for the lost, knowing that unless they repent, their demise is at hand.

5:18-19
Woe to those who draw iniquity with cords of vanity, and sin as if with a cart rope; that say, "Let Him make speed and hasten His work, that we may see it; and let the counsel of the Holy One of Israel draw near and come, that we may know it."

If a runner in the Olympics stepped up to the starting blocks dragging a heavy cart behind him, it would be obvious to all that he was about to lose. Spiritually speaking it is much the same. Hebrews 12:1 says, "let us lay aside every weight, and the sin which so easily ensnares us, and let us run with endurance the race that is set before us." Life is like a race, and if we run it dragging along a cart full of sins and distractions, it will be obvious to all that we are doomed. Sin and unholy cares destroy our opportunity to be victorious in life and in the afterlife. This is obvious! The trouble is that the people of Israel dragged their cart of sin with "cords of vanity." The ESV and other translations say, "cords of falsehood," and the NIV renders it "cords of deceit." Those who rebel against God drag their sins around, deceiving themselves into thinking that the weight of sin doesn't matter, or at least that the weight of small sins doesn't matter, or that the weight of their own personal pet sins is excused by their special circumstances. But the weight of sin – all sin -- not only matters, it is deadly. The weight of sin will cause sinners to be disqualified from the race of life and disqualified from passing through the finish line of heaven's gates. We must unencumber ourselves from all sins and unholy distractions, for the Lord, our righteous Judge, is watching how we race.

In verse 19 Isaiah quotes his detractors as they heckle him – Where is God? We don't see Him! Let Him hurry up and judge us if He is real. Let Him "draw near and come, so that we can know (whether or not we need to obey Him)." Peter faced the same argument from the unbelieving crowd. In II Peter 3:4 he wrote: this will be the argument of those who would rather sin than obey God -- "Jesus promised to come back, did he? Then where is he? Why, as far back as anyone can remember, everything has remained exactly the same since the world was first created" (NLT). Jesus faced the same sarcastic unbelief even as He hung on the cross to redeem mankind. Much like the people scoffed at Isaiah and sneered at Peter, the unbelieving crowd mocked Jesus in Matthew 27:42 saying, "He saved others; Himself He cannot save. If He is the King of Israel, let Him now come down from the cross, and we will believe Him." But those of us with eyes to see are not easily cowed by the criticisms of those who run the race of life dragging their sins and unbelief in a wheel-less cart behind them. Isaiah was not intimidated by the critics, he pronounced woe upon them. Let us follow his example.

5:20
Woe to those who call evil good, and good evil; who put darkness for light, and light for darkness; who put bitter for sweet, and sweet for bitter!

God has given the people of the world great guides to show us how to live. The human conscience is remarkable. Transcending nationality and culture, man's conscience teaches him right from wrong. Man is capable of "searing" his conscience (I Timothy 4:2), however, and so God gives us His written word which surpasses our conscience as an even better guide to what is good and what isn't. "Woe to those" who turn their backs on these great guides and decide that they have the right to determine for themselves what is good and what is evil. It is one thing to make a fleeting error in judgment and then quickly repent – but it is completely inexcusable for anyone to stare evil in the face and declare it "good." This is a sign that people have seared their own conscience with a hot iron, they have sunk to the depths of depravity and sought to redefine "good" as that which is pleasing to themselves, and that which is "evil" as that which hinders their personal enjoyments. Everyone would doubt the sense of someone who put a sugar cube on their tongue and called it bitter – so, too, we have cause to doubt the sense of those who call something good, even though God's word calls it evil. Surely, they must realize that God will have the last word. And when he does, "Woe to those who call evil good."

5:21
Woe to those who are wise in their own eyes, and prudent in their own sight!

Isaiah continues to pronounce woe on those whose actions set them up for incurring God's judgment. Those who believe that they are "wise" enough to need no input from God, those who value their opinions more highly than God's revealed truths are headed for eternal disaster. Proverbs 26:12 says, "Do you see a man wise in his own eyes? There is more hope for a fool than for him." Our only hope for entering heaven is for us to live lives that please the One that made both earth and heaven. If we trust that our wisdom is superior to the written truths of God, we have no hope for pleasing Him, and so no hope at all of entering heaven. A fool has more hope for getting into heaven than a smart guy who trusts in his own theories about how people can take care of their eternity. Proverbs 3:7 says,

"Do not be wise in your own eyes; fear the LORD and depart from evil." We don't have to be smart to get into heaven. We need to be obedient, exhibiting a holy fear of the One who reigns over death and the Day of Judgment. Those wise in their own estimation lose their fear of God's wrath, and so do not feel the necessity to "depart from evil," having determined that their sins are not eternally significant. We are allowed to ask for wisdom from God (James 1:5). But Isaiah's early readers had placed themselves in a very dangerous place because they had determined that they needed no wisdom from God, feeling that they were already wise enough to take care of their eternal destiny all on their own. This thinking is doomed thinking. Woe to those who think that they are so smart that they do not need God's mercy.

5:22-23
Woe to men mighty at drinking wine, woe to men valiant for mixing intoxicating drink, who justify the wicked for a bribe, and take away justice from the righteous man!

Isaiah pronounces another in his series of woes on those who stand far off from God. Woe to those who think that holding their liquor is an admirable quality. Perhaps there is little condemnation given for those who are poor drinkers, but woe to those who are skilled at it. Ephesians 5:18 says, "Don't be drunk with wine, because that will ruin your life. Instead, let the Holy Spirit fill and control you." We must not allow ourselves to be under the sway of anything that is "intoxicating." The voice of intoxicating drink can drown out the voice of the Spirit and may well lead, not just to embarrassing moments of drunkenness, but lifelong shameful flaws of character that are likely to "ruin" our life. Isaiah sees a direct correlation between a love for drinking and corruption (taking bribes) and injustice. Being filled with the Spirit will move us to self-denial and a passion for things that are holy. Being filled with wine leads to further cravings for personal pleasures and further unholy passions. "Woe to those who are mighty at drinking wine." The love of wine leads to so many evils. May our family respond rightly to Isaiah's warning.

5:24-25
Therefore, as the fire devours the stubble, and the flame consumes the chaff, so their root will be as rottenness, and their blossom will ascend like dust; because they have rejected the law of the LORD of hosts, and despised the word of the Holy One of Israel. Therefore the anger of the LORD is aroused against His people; He has stretched out His hand

against them and stricken them, and the hills trembled. Their carcasses were as refuse in the midst of the streets. For all this His anger is not turned away, but His hand is stretched out still.

God is love (I John 4:8). But God is also "a consuming fire" (Hebrews 12:29). We are reminded again how much our sin angers God. "As the fire devours the stubble" so God's anger will devour sinners. As "the flame consumes the chaff" so the wrath of God will burn hot before the face of those who sin against Him. We must understand (and help others understand) that those who reject the law of the Lord and those who despise the word of the Holy One cannot expect to do so with impunity. God has taught us His laws that we might live according to His ways. But if we reject His laws He will be angered. God has spoken to us through His word that we might hear His voice – but if we despise His message of love and holiness, He will consume us with the fire of His wrath and justice. The outcome of the unleashed wrath of God is frightful: the carcasses of the disobedient will fill the streets. The value of human life is inestimably high – but creation's obligation to glorify the name of the Lord of hosts is even higher. Failure to honor God demands a death sentence. And though the Lord is remarkably patient, there will come a point in the life of every rejecter when God will say, "Enough." I have shown you kindness and mercy without end, and you have "rejected" Me; you have "despised" Me. Those who reject and despise God will not survive. How could they expect anything else but execution if they would brazenly spurn the love of omnipotent, holy God? Hebrews 2:3 asks, "How shall we escape if we neglect so great a salvation?" Sin angers God. These verses make it impossible to ignore this fact. Let us respond rightly with holy fear and loving obedience. Let us delight in the law of the Lord of hosts, and let us cherish and obey the word of the Holy One of Israel. The reward for doing so is beyond reckoning, and failure to do so is condemning.

5:26-30
He will lift up a banner to the nations from afar, and will whistle to them from the end of the earth; surely they shall come with speed, swiftly. No one will be weary or stumble among them, no one will slumber or sleep; nor will the belt on their loins be loosed, nor the strap of their sandals be broken; whose arrows are sharp, and all their bows bent; their horses' hooves will seem like flint, and their wheels like a whirlwind. Their roaring will be like a lion, they will roar like young lions; yes, they will roar and lay hold of the prey; they will carry it away safely, and no one will

deliver. In that day they will roar against them like the roaring of the sea. And if one looks to the land, behold, darkness and sorrow; and the light is darkened by the clouds.

"If God is for us, who can be against us?" (Romans 8:31) But if God is against us, what hope do we have? Here we see that as a result of Israel's rebellion against God, He has called out Israel's enemies against them. And He has decreed that Israel's enemies will deal a devastating blow to His people. God will "whistle to them from the end of the earth." All nations, good and bad, are at our Lord's beck and call. Before the King of creation, all nations are like the family dog on the farm. Wherever the dog is, whether on the front porch or on the back forty, he will "come with speed, swiftly" when the master whistles for him. When Israel travelled from Egypt to the Promised Land, the Lord decreed that He would take care of every detail of their provision. In Deuteronomy 29:5 He said, "I have led you forty years in the wilderness. Your clothes have not worn out on you, and your sandals have not worn out on your feet." Now, however, because of Israel's rebellion, this promise is made to their enemies. God will make sure that Israel's enemies come quickly. They will not feel tired, their equipment will not break down, their weapons will be frightfully efficient, and they will come brimming with confidence, roaring like a lion. It is a sad day when God summons pagans to afflict His people because His people have turned their backs on Him. It is a day of "darkness and sorrow." Psalms 27:1 says, "The LORD is my light and my salvation; whom shall I fear? The LORD is the strength of my life; of whom shall I be afraid?" With God as our light and our Savior, we need fear no one. But those who turn a blind eye to His light and reject His offer of salvation have real cause to fear many things, and condemn themselves to "darkness and sorrow," unable to see God's provisions, and unable to know the joy of His protection.

Isaiah 6

6:1
In the year that King Uzziah died, I saw the Lord sitting on a throne, high and lifted up, and the train of His robe filled the temple.

On the heels of mourning the death of his king, Isaiah has a remarkable encounter with God. In Revelation 4, John is granted a vision of heaven, and the first thing John sees is this same throne with the Lord God, Creator of all things seated there in glory. God reigns supreme in heaven. His glory dominates the view of everyone there. He is high and lifted up, and His majesty commands the attention and the submission of everyone in heaven's domain. On earth "we do not yet see all things put under Him" (Hebrews 2:8), but in heaven, God will no longer shroud His glory. There are times when God may grant us glimpses of His majesty, but even then, He still chooses to veil His full power on earth (Habakkuk 3:4 ESV). But in heaven, His power and authority, His grandeur and holiness, His superiority over all creation is fully revealed. People may fool themselves into thinking that their eternity is secure even if they do not allow Him to reign over their hearts. But on judgment day, when the glory of God is revealed as it was revealed to Isaiah here, His children will be so glad that He is their God and

Savior. Sadly, the unbelievers and disobedient will be horror-stricken by this sight, seeing that the God they rejected, reigns as their Judge. Isaiah saw God's glory clearly. Blessed are those who have not seen and yet believe.

6:2-3
Above it stood seraphim; each one had six wings: with two he covered his face, with two he covered his feet, and with two he flew. And one cried to another and said: "Holy, holy, holy is the LORD of hosts; the whole earth is full of His glory!"

Reinforcing the uniqueness of Isaiah's encounter with God in heaven, he describes the seraphim that fly in continual praise around God's throne. No one else in all of scripture describes these beings. They are "the burning ones," that is how the Hebrew translates. As far as we can tell, they are employed in constant praise to the Lord of hosts who sits on the throne of heaven. Their praise centers on God's holiness. "Holy, holy, holy is the LORD of hosts." God is holy. He never sins, He is never prone to sinning. He is distinct, He is set apart from everything else that exists. Everything about His thoughts and acts and plans are perfect. If events befall us that tempt us to question God's intentions for us, may the words of the seraphim remind us that whatever may befall us on earth, God's perfect holiness transcends description, establishing our firm foundation for worshipping Him and submitting to His will. The seraphim declare that "the whole earth is full of His glory!" It is fascinating to see that from heaven's vantage point our earth is full of God's glory. From our lowly view, we may, and often do miss this. We see pain and rebellion. We see pride and oppression. But heaven sees that "the whole earth is full" of God's glory. Saints are rewarded, sin is punished. God is glorified in the praises of His people. God is glorified in the destruction of sinners. God is glorified as He cares for His children, God is glorified as He shows patience with prodigals, God is glorified as He shows mercy on the repentant, and God is glorified when He punishes those who refuse to do His will. The whole earth is full of the glory of God! As an ant cannot see the majesty of the forest because his vantage point is so small, so man has difficulty appreciating the glory of God manifested on earth because his vision is restricted by his physical and spiritual limitations. But heaven's host sees it plainly! The earth is full of the glory of God! The world is bursting with praise! Jesus felt it in Luke 19:40 when He told the doubters that the stones that lay beside Him on the roadside were bursting with the desire to glorify the Lord of hosts with their praise. May the Lord help us see what the seraphim see. God is holy. And the whole earth is full of His glory. Oh, how He deserves our praise!

ISAIAH 6

6:4-5
And the posts of the door were shaken by the voice of him who cried out, and the house was filled with smoke. So I said: "Woe is me, for I am undone! Because I am a man of unclean lips, and I dwell in the midst of a people of unclean lips; for my eyes have seen the King, the LORD of hosts."

The door to heaven's temple was shaken when the seraphim declared the holiness of the Lord. Psalms 18:7 says that God's anger shakes the earth. Psalms 29:8 says, "The voice of the LORD shakes the wilderness." And Ezekiel 38:20 says that all creation will one day shake when we are brought into the presence of God. Here, the mere mention of God's holiness shakes the foundations of the temple in heaven. The temple shakes and Isaiah is unraveled by what he sees and hears. God is holy. And the declaration of His holiness in the presence of His glorious splendor moves Isaiah to fear for his life. It is interesting that fear is the emotion that God's holiness evokes. Revelation 15:4 makes note of this fact as well, "Who shall not fear You, O Lord, and glorify Your name? For You alone are holy." We can ponder the various reasons that cause God's holiness to incite fear in man, and we can see it plainly exemplified here. In the presence of Holy God, Isaiah feels "undone." He is deserving of judgment because "I am a man of unclean lips, and I dwell in the midst of a people of unclean lips." The closer we are to God, the more broken we will be about our sinfulness. For godly men, their greatest pain, their greatest inner distress will always be their own sin, and their second greatest pain will be the sin of others ("I dwell in the midst of a people of unclean lips.") Isaiah sees God! He is high and lifted up! His holiness is exalted! And in the presence of Holy God, Isaiah falls in broken remorse over his sin. Brokenness over sin is the hallmark of a godly man serving in the presence of His Lord. As much as we crave it, the absence of sin is not within our grasp (I John 1:8) – but brokenness over sin and sorrowful repentance, as exemplified by Isaiah, is not only possible, but has been given to us as the instinctive reaction that spontaneously washes over us when we enter our Father's presence. God has made known to mankind His commandments. He has communicated His word so that we will not sin (I John 2:1). But when sin undoes us, as it did Isaiah, let us fall to our knees in broken, repentant sorrow, which is not to be regretted (II Corinthians 7:10), and let us look upward, expectantly, assured that His hand of mercy will "cleanse us from all unrighteousness" (I John 1:9).

6:6-7
Then one of the seraphim flew to me, having in his hand a live coal which he had taken with the tongs from the altar. And he touched my mouth with it, and said: "Behold, this has touched your lips; your iniquity is taken away, and your sin purged."

In verse 5 Isaiah crumbles beneath the weight of his sin in the face of Holy God. He cries out his confession in verse 5 and his cleansing flies to him in verse 6. If we confess our sins our Lord is faithful to immediately, suddenly forgive us of those sins, and to cleanse us of all our unrighteousness (I John 1:9). Before the face of Holy God, righteous men are horror-stricken and completely undone by the shame of their sin. We are children of God! We should not sin! We have no excuse for sinning. We have been taught God's Word, we have been filled by His Spirit, and we have been inspired by holy examples. And yet, despite all these blessed advantages, we still bring sorrow to our Lord and shame on our own head by disobeying God's commands. Children and rascals may feel a small sting of shame when caught in wrongdoing – but that is nothing compared to the shame felt by godly men when they are confronted with their wrongs before the face of their beloved and holy God. "Woe is me, for I am undone" is the rational, soul-wrenching cry that erupts from the lips of godly men mourning their sin at the feet of their beloved Lord. In the face of such sorrow over sin, what overwhelming joy is granted God's children as we read Isaiah's account of his moments in heaven, for it is not just to Isaiah that God grants cleansing for sin, no, He offers this same cleansing to all of us. "For You, Lord, are good, and ready to forgive, and abundant in mercy to all those who call upon You" (Psalms 86:5). Isaiah confesses his specific sin, and his sin is specifically healed in exact precision. And the healing seraphim, sent to him by the Great Physician, declares him completely cured of the malignancy of sin. "Your iniquity is taken away and your sin is purged." What a blessed hope is ours that our sin can be purged just as Isaiah's was. What a blessing. "Blessed is he whose transgression is forgiven, whose sin is covered" (Psalms 32:1).

6:8
Also I heard the voice of the Lord, saying: "Whom shall I send, and who will go for Us?" Then I said, "Here am I! Send me."

Verse 8 continues the blessed sequence of holy initiatives by God and the godly responses by Isaiah. Isaiah's record of the event provides us with something of a blueprint for God's continued works among us, His people, and the responses that He desires of us. God invites His creation to encounter the glory of His presence (verse 1). Our sin in the face of His holiness grieves us and we cry out in repentance (verse 5). In mercy, He rushes in to forgive us (verse 6). And in response, we rush out to serve Him (verse 8). David summarized Isaiah's same responses in Psalm 51 when he wrote, "Hide Your face from my sins, and blot out all my iniquities.... Then I will teach transgressors Your ways, and sinners shall be converted to You" (Psalms 51:9,13). A heart to serve the Lord in all areas of life, and particularly in the arena of sharing God's message with the lost, is the proper, intended outcome of God's merciful forgiveness that cleanses us from all sin. Isaiah reminds us that God's forgiveness not only saves us from our hell-bound destiny, it springboards us into His life-long service. Receiving our Savior's forgiveness, and then displaying no heart to serve Him immediately and wholeheartedly is to hold His forgiveness in contempt. Let us gratefully accept our Lord's invitation to draw near to Him as Isaiah did (James 4:8). His holiness will reveal our embarrassing flaws. Let us be quick to repent, and then, as we bask in the flood of His forgiveness, let us run to serve Him, serve His purposes, and serve His church. It is our only proper response.

6:9-10
And He said, "Go, and tell this people: 'Keep on hearing, but do not understand; keep on seeing, but do not perceive.' Make the heart of this people dull, and their ears heavy, and shut their eyes; lest they see with their eyes, and hear with their ears, and understand with their heart, and return and be healed."

God's words here are troubling. Isaiah's response in verse 11 shows that he was troubled by the weight of God's message, so we are right to feel weighted by the words as well. God sends Isaiah as His messenger to Judah. But Isaiah is not sent to soften the hearts of God's people, but to harden them. The result of Isaiah's preaching will be that his hearers will "keep on hearing" but they will never understand. They will "keep on seeing" Isaiah's godly example before them, but they will be so spiritually "dull" that no amount of good preaching or godly examples will save them.

In Matthew 23:37 we see our Savior's heart as He sends out His invitation to those who are apart from Him – "How often I wanted to gather your children together, as a hen gathers her chicks under her wings." Our Lord holds His hands aloft and invites everyone He finds to come to Himself (Matthew 22:9). But rejecting the invitation of the Most High God is a spiritual crime of the highest possible magnitude, and is punishable by the most awful retribution imaginable. God punishes unbelief with further unbelief. He punishes evil intentions with "dull" hearts that do not feel the sting of guilt. He punishes failure to comply with failure to "understand." He punishes nauseating rebellion with cancerous unbelief that cannot be healed. God calls us to Himself, but if we reject His call, there is no guarantee that He will call again. In righteous indignation, we see Him promise that He will not call these people again. He will not allow them to come to their senses. He will not open their eyes to the truth and will deny them His healing forgiveness.

Jesus quotes these verses in Matthew 13 and says that this passage is the very reason that He teaches in parables. He taught in parables "because" they did not believe in Him. Then John 12 quotes this passage to explain why people failed to believe even after seeing Jesus do astounding miracles. They did not believe "because" God "blinded their eyes and hardened their hearts." Later, Paul quotes this same passage in Acts 28, saying that his unbelieving hearers were exemplifying the words of Isaiah when they heard the riches of the truths of Christ and remained unmoved. Paul <u>again</u> quotes this passage in Romans 11, using Isaiah's words here to explain why some heard the gospel to the saving of their souls, and some heard the same gospel and remained unrepentant. Clearly, these two verses are deeply important to understand! Four times in the New Testament, twice by Jesus, and twice by Paul, Isaiah's words here are reiterated to teach us that it is the will of God to blind the eyes and block the understanding of some. He does so in response to unbelief, and He does so to incite unbelief in the hearts of those bent on sin. When we feel a twinge of conscience, when we feel remorse over sin, when we read God's word and are overwhelmed with the wonder of its truths, when we feel unquenchably confident in God's yet-unseen provisions, when all our labors are motivated by an unflinching, unbridled faith in the Creator God, let us bow humbly and thank our Savior for these blessings. These things are not granted to all men. God punishes unbelief with further unbelief, and God incites unbelief in those intent on sinning. Knowing that apart from His elective grace we would be among that crowd, let us be unceasing in our gratitude, and just as unceasing in our intercession, pleading with our Savior as Moses did in Exodus 32 that He might yet lift the veil from the eyes of those who are perishing.

6:11-13

Then I said, "Lord, how long?" And He answered: "Until the cities are laid waste and without inhabitant, the houses are without a man, the land is utterly desolate, the LORD has removed men far away, and the forsaken places are many in the midst of the land. But yet a tenth will be in it, and

will return and be for consuming, as a terebinth tree or as an oak, whose stump remains when it is cut down. So the holy seed shall be its stump."

    Isaiah is brokenhearted over God's declaration that He is going to harden His people's hearts rather than heal their afflictions. Isaiah can't imagine that God will discard His people forever and he cries out, "Lord, how long?" In the middle of his trial, David asked the same question that Isaiah now asks at the onset of his. In Psalms 13:1 David writes, "How long, O LORD? Will You forget me forever? How long will You hide Your face from me?" David cannot foresee the outcome of his trial, but in faith he writes in Psalms 13:5, "I have trusted in Your mercy; my heart shall rejoice in Your salvation." In David's case, he could not know how long the trial would last, but he trusted in God's mercy to carry him through. It may seem that if we could know from the beginning how long our illness, poverty, broken relationships, and various trials will last, that it would help us remain hopeful and faithful in the storm. In Isaiah's case here, however, knowing the length of the trial is hardly of any comfort. God's punishment will last a very long time. It will continue until "the land is utterly desolate." His hand of justice will bring terror on Isaiah's people "until the cities are laid waist and without inhabitant." He will allow "a tenth" of the people to survive, but even they will "be for consuming" or as the NASV says, even the remnant will be "subject to burning." But even here, even in the announcement of God's severest judgment on His people, His mercy glimmers still. The great oak tree of Israel will become a stump. And that stump will be charred and burned away, but from that stump will grow "the holy seed." The holy seed growing up from the blackened stump will produce the Branch described in Isaiah 11:1. That seed will produce the "true vine" from John 15. And by faith today, we can be grafted (Romans 11) into the holy tree that has risen from that holy seed. God's people have sinned, and sinned repeatedly, and their sins have angered their holy God. His patience is supernatural – He continued to safeguard His people even after hundreds of years of rebellion. But at last His anger toward sin will have its day – and it will be a very long day. Let us read and be moved again by God's unshakeable love for His creation that moves Him to spare a remnant even among peoples that have been intent on sinning for generations. And let us again, renew our fear of sin, being reminded here that "The Lord is longsuffering and abundant in mercy, forgiving iniquity and transgression; but He by no means clears the guilty, visiting the iniquity of the fathers on the children to the third and fourth generation" (Numbers 14:18).

Isaiah 7

7:1-2
Now it came to pass in the days of Ahaz the son of Jotham, the son of Uzziah, king of Judah, that Rezin king of Syria and Pekah the son of Remaliah, king of Israel, went up to Jerusalem to make war against it, but could not prevail against it. And it was told to the house of David, saying, "Syria's forces are deployed in Ephraim." So his heart and the heart of his people were moved as the trees of the woods are moved with the wind.

    Ahaz and his people fall under the attack of a powerful enemy. Syria and Israel have united forces and deployed their armies in Ephraim in preparation for invading the land of Judah. The story is such an encouragement to God's people that the writer cannot wait to tell us what happened. He begins his narrative by telling us how the story ends before telling us how desperate the situation was. Two powerful armies attacked Judah, "but could not prevail against it." So much worry can be avoided if we already know the outcome before we begin a battle. Who worries about a final exam when an "A" is already guaranteed? Who worries about an expensive purchase when the money is already in their pocket? Isaiah's rendition of

ISAIAH 7

the story of the Syrian/Israeli invasion begins with the outcome in view. Judah's enemies "could not prevail." May we stand equally reassured, knowing that the Writer of our history has also told us the end of our story. "The gates of hell shall not prevail" (Matthew 16:18 ESV). The invasion of Rezin and Pekah moved the hearts of Ahaz and his people to tremble in fear. But God's hand of protection is on them, so they did not need to be afraid. We need not be like "the trees of the woods" that are "moved with the wind." Like Isaiah's rendition of the story here, the end of our troubles is already likewise assured. "The angel of the Lord encamps all around those who fear Him, and delivers them" (Psalms 34:7). "The righteous cry out, and the LORD hears, and delivers them out of all their troubles" (Psalms 34:17). "Many are the afflictions of the righteous, but the LORD delivers him out of them all" (Psalms 34:19). God has already assured us that the various trials that fall on us will "work together for good" (Romans 8:28). Let us not be over-moved by troubles when the final victory is already in our view.

7:3-4
Then the LORD said to Isaiah, "Go out now to meet Ahaz, you and Shear-Jashub your son, at the end of the aqueduct from the upper pool, on the highway to the Fuller's Field, and say to him: 'Take heed, and be quiet; do not fear or be fainthearted for these two stubs of smoking firebrands, for the fierce anger of Rezin and Syria, and the son of Remaliah."

The Lord tells Isaiah to take his son and deliver a message to the king. (What a blessing when our sons and daughters join us in the ministry.) God's message to Ahaz and His people is to "keep calm" (NIV), "stop worrying" (NLT), and both the ESV and the NKJV here say, "be quiet." Stress often makes us say things that should not be said. We are prone to take out our stress on our loved ones, sometimes causing more injury with our words than the actual problem causes. We are prone to vent frustrations with those nearby, sometimes articulating lack of faith or God-directed anger in the process. The Scriptures commend Job for his handling of the terrible tragedies that befell him at Satan's hand. After losing his children, his wealth, and his health Job 2:10 says, "in all this Job did not sin with his lips." He then sat silent with his friends for 7 days. But then Job 3:1 opens with, "After this Job opened his mouth and cursed the day of his birth." Then for the next 30 some chapters Job and his friends say one non-God-exalting thing after another. Job was better off when he was quiet. After God draws near and challenges Job's understanding, Job says, "Behold, I am vile; what shall I answer You? I lay my hand over my mouth. Once I have spoken, but I will not answer; yes, twice, but I will proceed no further." Our Lord would spare Ahaz (and us) the pain of saying stupid stuff while in the throes of stressful times. "Be quiet." Rather than vent our frustrations, let us quietly wait for the Lord's provisions. Psalms 131:2 provides us with a good example when David writes, "Surely I have calmed and quieted my soul, like a weaned child with his mother; like a weaned child is my soul within me." As a child takes comfort in his mother's ability to provide for all his needs, so we can take even greater assurance knowing that our Lord certainly can provide all our needs. God calls the king of Syria and the king of Israel "two stubs of smoking firebrands." To Ahaz, these kings and their armies threaten to destroy his entire nation. To God, these same two men look like smoldering cigarette butts. When trials and tensions mount, let us be quiet and wait for the Lord to rescue in His time. When pain and tension mount, Micah 7:5 advises us to "guard the doors of your mouth." Then, in Micah 7:7 he lays out his plan for what he will do when pressure and stress threaten to drown him: "I will look to the LORD; I will wait for the God of my salvation; my God will hear me."

7:5-9
Because Syria, Ephraim, and the son of Remaliah have plotted evil against you, saying, "Let us go up against Judah and trouble it, and let us make a gap in its wall for ourselves, and set a king over them, the son of Tabel" – thus says the Lord GOD: "It shall not stand, nor shall it come to pass. For the head of Syria is Damascus, and the head of Damascus is Rezin. Within sixty-five years Ephraim will be broken, so that it will not be a people. The head of Ephraim is Samaria, and the head of Samaria is Remaliah's son. If you will not believe, surely you shall not be established."

The king of Syria and the king of Israel have secretly "plotted evil" against God's people in Judah. Their plotting was in secret, but God knows all the details of their under-handed schemes, and He declares to Ahaz and His people, "it shall not stand, nor shall it come to pass." Their evil plans will be overturned by God's protective hand. Moreover, Israel has thought to destroy the people of Judah, but their evil intentions will backfire, causing their own nation to "be broken, so that it will not be a people." What they intended to inflict on others, God will return on their own head. This is a common theme of God's judgments. Obadiah 1:15 says, "For the day of the

LORD upon all the nations is near; as you have done, it shall be done to you; your reprisal shall return upon your own head."

After promising protection, God tells His people what they must do: "If you will not believe, surely you shall not be established." Our faith must hold strong in times of trial if God's promises to us are to yield their greatest effect. We must have faith that God's commands should be obeyed even when our flesh tells us otherwise. We must have faith that God's love for us is true, even when harsh circumstance suggests otherwise. And we must be faithful to God and faithful to His purposes even when our strength begins to wane. For if we will remain faithful to Him, our eternity is secure and His provision and protection are assured. But "if you do not believe, surely you shall not be established." What a shame when God's promises are not brought to fruition in the lives of His people because they are "not being mixed with faith in those who heard (them)" (Hebrews 4:2). God promises to safe-guard His children, and we believe His word. This simple arrangement is to our eternal benefit. Let us then "believe to the saving of the soul" (Hebrews 10:39).

7:10-13
Moreover the LORD spoke again to Ahaz, saying, "Ask a sign for yourself from the LORD your God; ask it either in the depth or in the height above." But Ahaz said, "I will not ask, nor will I test the LORD!" Then he said, "Hear now, O house of David! Is it a small thing for you to weary men, but will you weary my God also?"

To overcome the combined forces of Israel and Syria, Judah will need a miracle. God, in His kindness to His people has promised to provide that miracle, but delivering His people is not God's ultimate goal. It is God's desire to increase the faith of His people so that they will give Him glory. God does not want anyone to doubt where the upcoming miracle is coming from, so He will give His people a sign, providing proof of His omnipotence and proof of His promised protection. Ahaz, however, has no desire to see God glorified and so refuses to ask for any sign that will give credence to what God says. Isaiah is disgusted by the king's refusal to ask for a sign so that God's hand will be seen. Ahaz was a wicked king and his evil reign was a weariness to men. Bringing grief to men was certainly bad enough, but Isaiah shouts out, "will you weary my God also?" It is frightening to think that we are able to make God tired of us! Failure to demonstrate faith in God is a weariness to the One who cannot tire. Unhappy with His disciples' weak faith, Jesus says in Mark 9:19, "O faithless generation, how long shall I be with you? How long shall I bear with you?" God created the universe in 6 days. There is nothing that He cannot do. In response to this great truth, man's necessary response is simple. Trust God. Obey God. Give Him glory. Any lesser response is a weariness to our Creator.

7:14
Therefore the Lord Himself will give you a sign: behold, the virgin shall conceive and bear a Son, and shall call His name Immanuel.

God offers Ahaz a sign that will bless his faith and grant him courage to persevere. Ahaz refuses God's offer, so instead, God gives him a sign that will bless the faith and provide courage to persevere to the believers of future generations. The sign may have meant little to Ahaz, but for us today, God's promise in Isaiah 7:14 (and recalled in Matthew 1:23) remains wonderfully precious. Through a miraculous, immaculate conception, a Son will be born who will be called "Immanuel." "God with us." From the very beginning, God revealed His heart to walk in close communion with the people He has made -- in Genesis 3:8 we see our Lord coming to walk with Adam and Eve in the cool of the day. Adam's sin marred that relationship, but did not destroy it forever, and here God provides us with the dear promise that He will walk in close communion with men and women once again. On this side of Calvary, we are able to find so much more joy in this promise than Ahaz could see. Ahaz' lack of faith caused him to miss out on being granted a sign that would be a blessing to him and his people – but his loss meant a great blessing to us, for this "sign" foretelling the coming of Jesus to earth remains an encouragement to us today, and continues to be a focal point of songs and sermons especially at Christmas time when we again concentrate our attentions on the remarkable fact that Jesus, the Son of God came to live with us here on earth. Immanuel, God with us. We do not serve a God who is aloof from us. We can know Him, relate to Him, understand Him, and serve Him in tangible ways. The sign given to Ahaz is a blessing given to us, reminding us of God's glorious and gracious intentions to dwell in close communion with His people.

7:15
Curds and honey He shall eat, that He may know to refuse the evil and choose the good.

Immanuel, God with us, will come to eat and sleep and serve with man. He will not come to live in palaces and feast with kings. He will eat curds and honey – simple foods that the common man eats. He will not use His divine power for selfish or unholy purposes, He will "refuse the evil and choose the good." Jesus, Immanuel, did not come to enjoy the pleasures of life, and He certainly did not come to partake in the sensual sins of life. He came to champion a life that was not subservient to the desires of the flesh. He came to exemplify a life that would lead to abundant fulfillment on earth and eternal paradise in heaven. Yes, but not only that, He came to provide an abundant life of fulfillment on earth and eternal paradise in heaven. This life of abundance on earth and eternal paradise in heaven only comes through reconciliation with our Maker, and that reconciliation only comes through Immanuel, God with us, who came to eat, and sleep, and serve with common man, and who refused the evil and chose the good.

7:16-17
For before the Child shall know to refuse the evil and choose the good, the land you dread will be forsaken by both her kings. The LORD will bring the king of Assyria upon you and your people and your father's house – days that have not come since the day that Ephraim departed from Judah.

Many believe Isaiah's prophecy regarding Immanuel has a double fulfillment. The greater, broader fulfillment was with the coming of Jesus, the Messiah, "God with us." But many believe that the son that was prophesied of in verse 14 also referred to the younger son of Isaiah (Maher-Shalal-Hash-Baz) that is spoken of in chapter 8. If so, this would explain the meaning of verse 16 which implies that in a very short time, before the child grows up, the great danger imposed by the armies of Syria and Israel that seems so threatening now, will completely melt away. "The land you dread," the nations of Syria and Israel, appear terrorizing. But soon their ominous threat will simply vanish away. Let us "dread" nothing but sin. None of the troubles of this world can separate us from the love of our Lord. And the loving, omnipotent hand of our Lord can sweep away all our troubles in the blink of an eye. But sin stands distinct from all of the world's sorrows and dangers, for unlike pain, unlike danger, unlike any terror the world can throw at us, sin separates us from God, and ruins our right to ask for rescue (Isaiah 59:2). The present danger that faces Ahaz and his people is a small matter. What he should be worried about is the coming judgment of God when He will "bring the king of Assyria upon you and your people" and execute judgment on the nation of Judah for their rebellion against their Creator. Let us keep our focus properly riveted. Let us not be over-moved by the trials and perils that threaten us today. It is important, however, to keep our watch out for judgment day that will come "upon you and your people and your father's house." Some people live in safety now, and some people live in the line of fire now, but one day, all our loved ones and all our family line will inevitably face the judgment that "the LORD will bring." Let us not be distracted by lesser dangers.

7:18-19
And it shall come to pass in that day that the LORD will whistle for the fly that is in the farthest part of the rivers of Egypt, and for the bee that is in the land of Assyria. They will come, and all of them will rest in the desolate valleys and in the clefts of the rocks, and on all thorns and in all pastures.

Judah has refused to honor God, and in response, the Lord will bring judgment on them. He will call judgment on His people with a whistle – just as He said in Isaiah 5:26. All too often, people fool themselves into thinking that somehow they will be able to avoid God's holy judgment. Perhaps they feel too insignificant for God to care about their sin, or they feel so important that they are above judgment, or perhaps they feel that some good deed of theirs will make them immune to God's judgment. But God would warn people here not to be deceived by this way of thinking. Judgment for their sin is coming – and no one will avoid it. The armies that bring God's judgment will be like bees and flies that fill even the most out-of-the-way valleys and crawl into the most secretive clefts of the rocks. Good pastures will fall under the judgment, as well as overlooked thorny places. No one will be strong enough to overcome God's judgment and no one will be so insignificant that he will avoid God's judgment. Judgment Day, like the coming of the armies of Egypt and Assyria in Isaiah's day will come on everyone. We had best prepare ourselves well.

7:20
In the same day the Lord will shave with a hired razor, with those from beyond the River, with the king of Assyria, the head and the hair of the legs, and will also remove the beard.

In II Kings 16, Ahaz strips out all of the silver and gold that was found in the house of the Lord and sends it as a present to Tiglath-Pileser, the king of Assyria, saying, "I am your servant and your son. Come up and save me from the hand of the king of Syria and from the hand of the king of Israel, who rise up against me." Rather than reach out to his loving Lord who had already promised to deliver him, Ahaz spends all he has to bribe a pagan king to do what God had already ordained would be done. Bad things happen when we misplace our confidence. Psalms 118:8-9 says simply, "It is better to trust in the LORD than to put confidence in man. It is better to trust in the LORD than to put confidence in princes." Sadly, Ahaz will trust in that which David says is better not to trust, and the results will be abject humiliation. He will hire a pagan to do God's work. He has misplaced his confidence, and the tragic result is that Assyria will become little more than "a hired razor" that will shave Judah bald. The shame and humiliation that was felt by men in Isaiah's day when they lost their beard is compared to the shame and humiliation that inevitably befalls men and women when they trust in anything other than God to save them.

7:21-22
It shall be in that day that a man will keep alive a young cow and two sheep; so it shall be, from the abundance of milk they give, that he will eat curds; for curds and honey everyone will eat who is left in the land.

Opinions vary regarding Isaiah's intended point here, but it seems that he is communicating that the outcome of God's judgment by the hand of Assyria will leave the land so desolate that where great herds once grazed, only a cow and a couple sheep will remain. Even so, God will provide for the remnant that survives. They will not have much, but they will have enough to live on. Even when God chastises and disciplines His people, He provides.

7:23-25
It shall happen in that day, that wherever there could be a thousand vines worth a thousand shekels of silver, it will be for briers and thorns. With arrows and bows men will come there, because all the land will become briers and thorns. And to any hill which could be dug with the hoe, you will not go there for fear of briers and thorns; but it will become a range for oxen and a place for sheep to roam.

It is so sad to see how useless and valueless men and lands become when God is not exalted. When God was praised as Lord over Judah, the land was full of vineyards that were worth a thousand shekels each. But when God was ignored, both men and land lost their value. Farmland became wilderness, and those who once prospered in peace by the fat of the land, now had to arm themselves just to scrounge for the scraps that were left. It is deceptive nonsense to believe that we could be better off trusting in anything other than God Himself. Ahaz felt that trusting in Assyria was a better bet than trusting in God, and this is the result of his poor choice. So, will it likely befall us if we ever deceive ourselves into thinking that we would be better off playing, working, or resting on the Lord's day rather than give Him His due honor. So, too, will it likely be our lot if we ever think that trusting in our own abilities or trusting in a benefactor's resources are more likely to grant us success than trusting in our Lord. Let us make our life's great priorities continually center on God's name, God's Word, and God's people. If we will keep His kingdom at the forefront of our priorities, we will find that His purposes lead to our well-being. Proverbs 28:25 says, "The one who trusts in the Lord will be enriched" (ESV). Abandoning God, however, means forfeiting His blessings, with briers and thorns in lands and lives the unhappy result.

Isaiah 8

8:1-2
Moreover the LORD said to me, "Take a large scroll, and write on it with a man's pen concerning Maher-Shalal-Hash-Baz. And I will take for Myself faithful witnesses to record, Uriah the priest and Zechariah the son of Jeberechiah."

God's message in chapter 8 is terribly important. He insists that Isaiah "take a large scroll" and write down everything he hears God say. When God first gave Moses the Ten Commandments, Exodus 31:18 tells us "when He had made an end of speaking with him on Mount Sinai, He gave Moses two tablets of the Testimony, tablets of stone, written with the finger of God." This time, however, despite the import of the message, God instructs Isaiah to use "a man's pen" to record the message that will be important to him personally, to his nation in the days to come, and to us in our day as well. Isaiah will have a son, and just as the angel told Zacharias the name of his son before even his wife conceived (Luke 1:13), so now, God tells Isaiah that he will have a son, and will call his name Maher-Shalal-Hash-Baz – a unique name for a sadly commonplace situation. God's people have rebelled, and a foreign army has been summoned (God has whistled for them – Isaiah 7:18) to punish them for their sins. Their loss will be the gain of foreign pagans as Isaiah's son's name prophesies, for his name means "speeding to the plunder, hurrying to the spoil," signifying the rush that will ensue to procure the valuables left by the victims of Assyria's onslaught. Assyria will first defeat Judah's enemies – Syria and Israel, but quickly they will turn their destructive power on Judah as well. God tells Isaiah he will have a son, He foretells the demise of the Jewish nation, and His words urge all of us in the present day to apply these words personally and "wait on the LORD" and to "hope in Him" (verse 17). With such important matters contained within the message's content, carrying such significant implications to so many people on so many levels, no wonder God took such care to make sure His words were penned accurately. He hand-picked the faithful Uriah and Zechariah as His recorders. When God moves to speak to His people today, may He find our family similarly faithful to His purposes and thus useful in conveying His words to saints and sinners alike.

8:3-4
Then I went to the prophetess, and she conceived and bore a son. Then the LORD said to me, "Call his name Maher-Shalal-Hash-Baz; for before the child shall have knowledge to cry 'My father' and 'My mother,' the riches of Damascus and the spoil of Samaria will be taken away before the king of Assyria."

The people of Judah are terrified of the impending attack on them by the combined armies of Syria and Israel. They see no hope for rescue, and they certainly do not look to God for help. But Isaiah's son will be a sign to them. Though it appears that the armies massed against them are unstoppable, God says that before the child is old enough to cry out "mommy, daddy!" God will make their seemingly inescapable threat completely melt away. Let us not fear the dangers of the world. "God is our refuge and strength, a very present help in trouble" (Psalms 46:1), and He can deliver us from or through any trial. As He delivered Judah from their enemies, so He is faithful today to deliver us. Disbelieving this, Judah looked to Assyria to save them rather than to their God who summoned Assyria – a mindset that would lead to terrible repercussions. They should have followed David's example in Psalms 108:12 when he prayed to the Lord, "Give us help from trouble, for the help of man is useless."

8:5-8

The LORD also spoke to me again, saying: "Inasmuch as these people refused the waters of Shiloah that flow softly, and rejoice in Rezin and in Remaliah's son; now therefore, behold, the Lord brings up over them the waters of the River, strong and mighty – the king of Assyria and all his glory; he will go up over all his channels and go over all his banks. He will pass through Judah, he will overflow and pass over, he will reach up to the neck; and the stretching out of his wings will fill the breadth of Your land, O Immanuel."

The Lord leads His people to enjoy "still waters," that He here calls "the waters of Shiloah." "The river of God is full of water" (Psalms 65:9). It always provides all the needs of those who come to quench their thirst there. God's waters are "still waters." They never overflow their banks, and never flood or cause harm to those who drink from them. Unlike God's "softly" flowing waters of refreshment, "the waters of the River," the king of Assyria, will initially appear to be a flood of relief, but will soon overflow his usefulness and make life miserable for Judah. God "turns a wilderness into pools of water" (Psalms 107:35), that bless His people and establish their cities. The waters from the river of Assyria, however, "will reach up to the neck" and threaten to drown all those who trusted in them. Sadly, the people had ready access to God's river of life, but they "refused the waters" that God provided, preferring instead, the raging river of Assyria that would soon wreak havoc on their nation like a natural disaster. Were it not for the rescuing wings of Immanuel, God with us, their trust in Assyria would have caused them total ruin.

8:9-10

Be shattered, O you peoples, and be broken in pieces! Give ear, all you from far countries. Gird yourselves, but be broken in pieces; gird yourselves, but be broken in pieces. Take counsel together, but it will come to nothing; speak the word, but it will not stand, for God is with us.

Assyria will gird themselves for war against Judah, but they will be "broken in pieces." Three times, God repeats the message. Assyria will be "broken in pieces." No one can logically expect to survive if they stand in defiant opposition to God, and their expectation can hardly differ if they gird themselves to fight against His children. In fulfillment of these words, as the armies of Assyria surrounded Jerusalem, God declared in II Kings 19:34 -- "I will defend this city, to save it For My own sake and for My servant David's sake." And because God does not change, we have good cause to anticipate that He will protect us in today's day just as He protected His people in Isaiah's day. David wrote, "Let all those rejoice who put their trust in You; let them ever shout for joy, because You defend them; let those also who love Your name be joyful in You. For You, O Lord, will bless the righteous; with favor You will surround him as with a shield" (Psalms 5:11-12). The wicked can "take counsel together," they can put their heads together and plan out schemes to oppress God's people, "but it will come to nothing." They can "speak the word" – breathe out threats and curses and hurl out insults on our faith in our Creator as the Assyrians do before the wall in II Kings 18. But their threats and curses and insults "will not stand" because "God is with us," as His name "Immanuel" implies, and greater is He who is in us than he who is in the world (I John 4:4).

8:11
For the LORD spoke thus to me with a strong hand, and instructed me that I should not walk in the way of this people, saying:

God is the Lord. He reigns in heaven and holds sway over the universe. He sustains life on earth by the word of His power. He is not simply one voice among many offering religious opinions. He speaks to us (what an overwhelming privilege is ours to be allowed to hear the words of God!), but He does not speak with suggestions or timid requests. God's words are commands. Here He speaks to Isaiah "with a strong hand." The NLT says, "The Lord has said to me in the strongest terms…" We must listen when God speaks. We must obey when God commands. And this is His command: we must not "walk in the way" of the worldly people around us. The Lord's scathing rebuke of His people in Hosea 7:8 was that "Ephraim has mixed himself among the peoples." We are commanded to "come out from among (the people of the world) and be separate, says the Lord. Do not touch what is unclean, and I will receive you" (II Corinthians 6:17). God says the same thing in Leviticus 20:26 – "And you shall be holy to Me, for I the LORD am holy, and have separated you from the peoples, that you should be Mine." We are to live in the world, but we must keep ourselves "unspotted from the world" (James 1:27). Psalms 1:1 maintains that we are blessed when we do not walk with ungodly people, we do not stand in the company of unrepentant sinners, and we do not sit with those who scorn those who are more righteous than they. "Come out from among them, and be ye separate, saith the Lord" (II Corinthians 6:17 KJV). God's words to Isaiah stand as a message to us. We must not live like the people around us live. Let us not mimic them or envy them. James uses strong language when he says: "Friendship with the world" is to become the enemy of God (James 4:4). And God uses "a strong hand" when He says the same thing to Isaiah. Our lifestyle should be obviously distinguishable from the "the way of this (ungodly) people."

8:12-13
"Do not say, 'A conspiracy' concerning all that this people call a conspiracy, nor be afraid of their threats, nor be troubled. The LORD of hosts, Him you shall hallow; let Him be your fear, and let Him be your dread."

We are not to fear, regardless of how many people gather together to conspire against us. God has promised that He will never leave us (Hebrews 13:5), so we can say with confidence: "The Lord is my helper; I will not fear. What can man do to me?" (Hebrews 13:6). People can, indeed, cause us considerable discomfort. But God's control over our eternal destiny is so vastly more significant that man's ability to hurt us should seem paltry by comparison. God is the Holy One "who is ready to judge the living and the dead" (I Peter 4:5). Since our eternal destiny and our present state of mind rest in His providence, let us fear His judgments rather than the threats of men, and let us dread the thought of not pleasing Him, rather than dread the backlash of not conforming to the expectations of ungodly people in power. If ever we stand at a crossroads, unsure of which path to take, let us tremble in fear before the presence of the Lord at our side; let us dread the thought of displeasing Him – this is the key to wisdom, and the key to direction when we are unsure how to move forward. "Who are those who fear the LORD? He will show them the path they should choose" (Psalms 25:12). For "the fear of the LORD is the beginning of wisdom" (Psalms 111:10).

8:14-15
He will be as a sanctuary, but a stone of stumbling and a rock of offense to both the houses of Israel, as a trap and a snare to the inhabitants of Jerusalem. And many among them shall stumble; they shall fall and be broken, be snared and taken.

To godly men and women in trouble, God is a sanctuary, a safe haven, where we can find rest and safety for our bodies, peace for our mind, and eternal happiness for our soul. Isaiah 26:3 says, "You will keep him in perfect peace, whose mind is stayed on You." But to the belligerent and disobedient, the same Sanctuary that protects and provides for us turns out to be "a stone of stumbling," a "rock of offense," "a trap and a snare" for them. God's reign is a comfort to His children, but a "stone of stumbling" to others. They will chaff under His rule, resist His authority, and stumble over His requirements for holiness. God will be a "rock of offense" to unbelievers. They will be offended by the exclusivity of His gospel and they will be offended by His claim that their chosen lifestyle transgresses His laws of holiness. God, "as a sanctuary," will be a refuge to His children, but will be like a "trap and a snare" to those who reject Him. Those who choose to stand in defiant disobedience to the Lord will prefer to be anywhere other than in His holy presence, but they will find that they are "snared in the work of (their) own hands" (Psalms 9:16), unable to flee from the presence of the holy Lord that they have offended with their impure thoughts and actions. The sanctuary of the Lord will be for them a trap that will not let them escape from the punishment of their sins. Like running into the house to get out of the storm, God's children can find shelter from the storms of life and find warmth and security in the inviting comforts of the Sanctuary. In contrast, unbelievers and disobeyers, coming to this same Sanctuary, will "fall and be broken" on its stone steps outside. Jesus said, "Whoever falls on that stone will be broken; but on whomever it falls, it will grind him to powder" (Luke 20:18).

8:16
Bind up the testimony, seal the law among my disciples.

The NLT fleshes out Isaiah's statement beautifully, "I will write down all these things as a testimony of what the LORD will do. I will entrust it to my disciples, who will pass it down to future generations." Let us "bind up" in our heart all that we read of God's attributes and actions. When Mary heard the testimony of the shepherds, she "treasured up all these things and pondered them in her heart" (Luke 2:19 NIV). Let us do the same with the treasured testimonies of the inspired writers of God's word here in our hands. Let us treasure the words of God and then teach them, "entrust" them to the next generation of believers. Let us delight in the law of the Lord and in the inspired testimonies of His people in His word. Proverbs 6:21-23 calls us to "bind them continually upon your heart; tie them around your neck. When you roam, they will lead you; when you sleep, they will keep you; and when you awake, they will speak with you. For the commandment is a lamp, and the law a light..." Proverbs 7:1-3 gives the same instruction, "My son, keep my words, and treasure my commands within you. Keep my commands and live, and my law as the apple of your eye. Bind them on your fingers; write them on the tablet of your heart." Let us bind up God's word in our heart, treasure it, contemplate on it, roll it over our minds over and over again. And then, let us pass it on to others who will seal this treasure in their hearts as well. What a precious thought.

8:17
And I will wait on the LORD, who hides His face from the house of Jacob; and I will hope in Him.

Isaiah's response to the national crisis around him is inspired and inspiring. It calls us to imitate him today. Enemy armies threaten his nation, and closer enemies trouble him with personal threats (verse 12). Yet in the face of these external dangers and uncertainties, Isaiah does not falter. "I will wait on the LORD." "I will hope in Him." God has hidden His face from the house of Judah, but with extreme faith, Isaiah knows He is there just the same, and like David, he stands undeterred in his confidence in his Creator. Isaiah shares David's sentiments when he wrote, "I lift my eyes to the hills. From where does my help come? My help comes from the LORD who made heaven and earth" (Psalms 121:1-2 ESV). "I wait for the LORD, my soul waits, and in His word I do hope. My soul waits for the Lord more than those who watch for the morning -- Yes, more than those who watch for the morning" (Psalms 130:5-6). Likewise, Micah, too, retained unwavering faith in God in the face of life's insecurities. Life is full of dangers, and Micah noted that neither friends nor family could be counted on to provide the deliverance we desperately seek – "Therefore," Micah says, "I will look to the LORD; I will wait for the God of my salvation; my God will hear me" (Micah 7:7). God has clearly warned that He will hide His face from "children in whom is no faith" (Deuteronomy 32:20). But those who seek Him will find Him (Jeremiah 29:13), and those who wait on Him will be renewed with strength (Isaiah 40:31). Let us join Isaiah, and those like him, who do not panic when crisis comes. Let us be calm and resolute, "wait on the Lord" and "hope in Him." Those who do so are never disappointed.

8:18
Here am I and the children whom the LORD has given me! We are for signs and wonders in Israel from the LORD of hosts, who dwells in Mount Zion.

As a family united together in service to our Lord, may the riches of this verse bring us deep and abiding joy. Isaiah lifts up his eyes and sets his pen on his scroll to write of the emotion filling his heart as he writes of his united family standing before the Lord and before the nation, openly declaring their devotion to the purposes of God. "Here am I and the children whom the LORD has given me!" Isaiah's son Shear-Jashub went with him, at God's command, to meet with the king with a message from the Lord. Shear-Jashub was both the messenger and the message, for his name means "a remnant shall return." Isaiah's son Maher-Shalal-Hash-Baz was given to Isaiah as a son and to the nation as a sign signifying the imminent destruction of their enemies (verse 3). And, certainly most famously, Isaiah's middle son was named Immanuel, "God with us" as a sign of the coming Messiah. Isaiah's wife, too, was a godly woman, a "prophetess" (verse 3), and together they stand as a family in devotion to their Lord. "Here am I and the children whom the LORD has given me!" It is an unmatchable joy to stand before the Lord, hand in hand with one's family in His service (III John 4). God has done "wonders" in and through Isaiah's family, and his children are used as "signs" to show God's future and present plans for His people. All families that are allowed to serve the Father with complete unity and unbridled devotion are rightfully carried to incomparable heights of joy – for we see that our Savior delights to see this just the same. In a wholly remarkable passage, Hebrews 2:11-13 says that Jesus is not ashamed to call us His "brethren." Hebrews quotes Isaiah's words here, showing that Jesus shares Isaiah's sentiments and rejoices to stand hand in hand with His saints before the throne and say, "Here am I and the children whom the LORD has given me!" This wonderful picture of Isaiah's family is inspiring, but it is also a prophecy of Jesus' family. Isaiah's words foretell Jesus saying the same thing about His children of faith as He stands before His Father in heaven. Our Lord and Savior is not ashamed to be related to us! (Hebrews 2:11) What a precious thought. He gathers us around His throne in heaven and announces His joy over His family, just as Isaiah rejoiced over his sons -- "Here am I and the children whom the LORD has given Me!" Our Savior rejoices over His children. Isaiah rejoiced over his sons. And it is my unending joy to rejoice over the family that my Lord has given me. It is my constant plea with my Lord that He might continue to call all of us to His presence and to His service that we might be a blessing to His people and a joy to our Savior in keeping with the wonderful example provided here of Isaiah and his family.

8:19
And when they say to you, "Seek those who are mediums and wizards, who whisper and mutter," should not a people seek their God? Should they seek the dead on behalf of the living?"

Apparently, it was an all-too-common practice for God's people to consult witches and wizards who would conjure up spirits of the dead for advice. We see King Saul do this in I Samuel 28. Isaiah gives two quick reasons to dissuade his hearers from this detestable practice. Sadly, he did not use scripture as the foundation for his argument. He could have easily referred to Leviticus 19:31 - "Give no regard to mediums and familiar spirits; do not seek after them, to be defiled by them: I am the LORD your God." He could have quoted Leviticus 20:6 - "And the person who turns to mediums and familiar spirits, to prostitute himself with them, I will set My face against that person and cut him off from his people." Or he could have reiterated the psalmist's warning when he said that those who "ate sacrifices made to the dead... provoked (God) to anger with their deeds, and the plague broke out among them" (Psalms 106:28-29). But his people had grown so cold to the word of God that Isaiah knew this tact would do him no good. Blessedly, God's ways are logical and straightforward. Thinking men with a working conscience will love God's ways when they are taught them, even if they did not have the advantages of solid Bible teaching in the past. Isaiah's argument for calling his people to reject the consultations of mediums and wizards rests on two questions. The first was, "Should not a people seek their God?" Even pagan nations with wooden gods on a string will clutch their muted idols and seek their help in time of need. If heathen nations with no loyalties other than to their own self interests are loyal enough to seek help from their own god before seeking counsel from others – how much more should Judah "seek their God" before thinking to enlist the aid of lesser foreign spiritualists? Secondly, almost humorously, Isaiah asks, "Should they seek the dead on behalf of the living?" How helpful can dead people be to living people? The dead have no power to bless or curse the lives of the living. Abel's godly example *in life* can inspire us to emulate him even today (Hebrews 11:4), but after men die, they are denied opportunity to influence the living (Luke 16:19-31). This should be intuitively obvious to all, and Isaiah urges his hearers to listen to reason, even if their rebellious heart has moved them to stop listening to God.

8:20
To the law and to the testimony! If they do not speak according to this word, it is because there is no light in them.

Crisis has come to Judah. Enemy armies are at the door. What should they do? Isaiah cries out his answer! "To the law!" "To the testimony!" When danger and uncertainties abound, we have a single acceptable response! Go to God's law and see what He says to do! Listen to the testimony of God's servants that is recorded in His word and go do likewise! When trials surround us, our response should be automatic – go to God's Word. When we face difficult decisions, our path is set in stone – go to God's Word. Isaiah's cry goes out – stop consulting mediums and wizards, stop asking dead people to help you. Stop listening to "the way of this people" (verse 11). Go to God's law for your answers! Go to the testimony of the saints in His word for your inspiration! There can be but one explanation for anyone who consults any spiritual or intellectual advisor before consulting God's Word – "there is no light in them." There can be only one explanation for any advisor who gives counsel that conflicts with God's Word – "there is no light in them." Both the advisee and the advisor have no light in them. They are blind guides who lead blind followers. They are intentionally in the dark, for they have doused God's guiding light. Jesus tells us to avoid those who reject God's Word for the sake of human counsel, and to reject counselors who ignore God's Word. In Matthew 15:14 He told the disciples, "Let them alone. They are blind leaders of the blind. And if the blind leads the blind, both will fall into a ditch." Jesus is the light of the world. In John 8:12 He said, "I am the light of the world. He who follows Me shall not walk in darkness, but have the light of life." As the light of the world, He has given us His word to guide our steps. Psalms 119:105 says, "Your word is a lamp to my feet and a light to my path." And Proverbs 6:23 says, "the commandment is a lamp, and the law a light." To reject this light is to doom oneself to being either a blind guide or a blind follower with the end result being the same for both. Some days are hard. There are dark days even for the godliest of men. But when our days are darkest, let us look "to the law and to the testimony." The Word of God casts light on every dilemma.

8:21-22
They will pass through it hard-pressed and hungry; and it shall happen, when they are hungry, that they will be enraged and curse their king and their God, and look upward. Then they will look to the earth, and see trouble and darkness, gloom of anguish; and they will be driven into darkness.

The unbelieving and sinful in Isaiah's day will "pass through" their imminent trial and they will be far worse off after their trial than at the beginning. In Psalms 119:71 David wrote, "It is good for me that I have been afflicted, that I may learn Your statutes." Sadly, Judah's afflictions will yield no good outcome in them. They will grow "hard-pressed and hungry" in their difficult days, and rather than look to the Lord for provision, they will "look upward" in seething rage and curse both their king and their God. Cursing God will cut them off from their only hope of deliverance. When they finish their rants against God, they will come back to earth and be forced to lie in the bed that they have made for themselves. They will be surrounded by "trouble and darkness, gloom of anguish." Psalms 119:143 says, "Trouble and anguish have overtaken me, yet Your commandments are my delights." But without God's word to delight us, trials simply add gloom to trouble and anguish to gloom. Trials and troubles move godly men to trust in God and they move corrupt men to curse God. Being hard-pressed and hungry moves God's saints to find delight in His words to them. But this same pressure and stress and hunger will drive base men and women "into darkness" where only trouble and gloom and anguish await.

Isaiah 9

9:1-2
Nevertheless the gloom will not be upon her who is distressed, as when at first He lightly esteemed the land of Zebulun and the land of Naphtali, and afterward more heavily oppressed her, by the way of the sea, beyond the Jordan, in Galilee of the Gentiles. The people who walked in darkness have seen a great light; those who dwelt in the land of the shadow of death, upon them a light has shined.

The Assyrian invasion is coming. The people in Isaiah's day with decent insights likely saw it coming already, and Isaiah's prophecy made it clear that judgment was on its way. God's people would be "distressed." Zebulun and Naphtali, along with the rest of Israel would be struck hard by this judgment of God that "oppressed her," but her "gloom" would not last forever. In the midst of this prophecy of God's judgment comes a prophecy of deliverance, not just for Israel, but for all the peoples of the world. In Galilee of the Gentiles, those who "walked in darkness have seen a great light." Those who once lived in the darkness of hardship as well as the darkness of spiritual ignorance are now granted the light. This promise of light dawning on distressed people is not just given to the household of Israel, it is given to all the people of the world who live in "the shadow of death." Adam's sin doomed man to die, and our own sin dooms us to death in hell, and this specter of death, this "shadow" of death hung over every man and woman from Adam onward – until a light shined. Isaiah writes in the past tense, as if Jesus had already come. "A light has shined." Jesus has come in the flesh, and He is "the light of the world" (John 8:12). He has come to deliver all the distressed peoples of the world that walk in darkness of understanding and under the curse of sin. Matthew 4:15-16 quotes these verses to show Jesus' fulfillment of this prophecy during His ministry in Galilee. Luke 1:78-79 speaks of Jesus, the "Dayspring" who will come to light the way for all the peoples of the world, "to give light to those who sit in darkness and the shadow of death, to guide our feet into the way of peace." Jesus is "the true Light which gives light to every man coming into the world" (John 1:9). Isaiah's prophecy brought the light of hope to people who lived in very dark times, and the light of His glory is hardly less joyous to us today. "Happy are those who hear the joyful call to worship, for they will walk in the light of your presence, LORD" (Psalms 89:15 NLT).

9:3-5
You have multiplied the nation and increased its joy; they rejoice before You according to the joy of harvest, as men rejoice when they divide the spoil. For You have broken the yoke of his burden and the staff of his shoulder, the rod of his oppressor, as in the day of Midian. For every warrior's sandal from the noisy battle, and garments rolled in blood, will be used for burning and fuel of fire.

Verse 2 says that "a light has shined." Verse 6 says "a Child is born." And verses 3-5 tell of the wonderful blessings that accompany the coming of Jesus, the Messiah, the Child who is the Light of the world. The nation will be "multiplied," and the people's joys will be "increased." The coming of Jesus and the preaching of His apostles led to a great many people added to the roll call of the faithful (Acts 6:7, Acts 9:31). It was the will of our Lord, however, not only to increase the number of His disciples, but to increase the joy of His followers as well. "These things I have spoken to you, that My joy may remain in you, and that your joy may be full" (John 15:11). Jesus brings His people joy. Like the satisfaction of the farmer in "the joy of the harvest," like the joy of the victorious soldier when he is rewarded with the spoils of war, so is the joy of those who trust in Him. We are filled with joy because our Lord has broken the "yoke" of the law (Acts 15:10) and freed us from "the rod of His wrath" (Lamentations 3:1). "As in the day of Midian" (Judges 7), in the battle against their enemies, so Jesus will deliver His children from their battle with sin.

9:6
For unto us a Child is born, unto us a Son is given; and the government will be upon His shoulder. And His name will be called Wonderful Counsellor, Mighty God, Everlasting Father, Prince of Peace.

The Messiah, God's Son, came to earth to redeem mankind from the penalty of their sins. But the majesty of the Messiah's redemptive work did not begin on the cross, it began when the "Child (was) born," from the moment that the "Son (was) given." Jesus is our Wonderful Counsellor, He is our Mighty God, He is our Everlasting Father, and He is our Prince of Peace, but His work began as a Child, as a Son who was given from His Heavenly Father to His earthly parents to grow up carrying the weight of the world on His young shoulders.

Jesus is our Wonderful Counsellor. The fads and trendy ideas of the world may seem like wisdom for a while, but "the counsel of the LORD stands forever, the plans of His heart to all generations" (Psalms 33:11). Long after the counsel of men has proved unreliable, it is "the LORD's counsel that will stand" (Proverbs 19:21). Psalms 16:7 says, "I will bless the LORD who has given me counsel," because our Lord is a Wonderful Counsellor.

Jesus is our Mighty God. During His time on earth He was "mighty in deed and word" (Luke 24:19), and we can entrust to Him our desperate needs because still today He is "mighty to save" (Isaiah 63:1). We can face trials and the threat of danger without fear because our Jesus is a Mighty God. Zephaniah 3:17 says, "The Lord your God is in your midst, a mighty one who will save; he will rejoice over you with gladness; he will quiet you by his love; he will exult over you with loud singing." What good news this is! God is not mighty to slay us, He is mighty to save us! In His might He calls us to Himself! "The Mighty One, God the LORD, has spoken and called the earth from the rising of the sun to its going down" (Psalms 50:1). Let us trust Him for our deliverance, let us run to Him when He calls to us to receive His salvation, for our Lord Jesus is our Mighty God!

Jesus is our Everlasting Father. He said it plainly in John 10:30 – "I and My Father are one." Proverbs 17:6 says, "The glory of children is their father," reminding us of the joy and glory that is ours to have Jesus as our Everlasting Father. And how can we respond to such a privilege of being called the sons of Jesus, our Everlasting Father? Hebrews 12:9 (NIV) says, "we have all had human fathers who disciplined us and we respected them for it. How much more should we submit to the Father of spirits and live!" Jesus is our Everlasting Father. He never dies, and neither does His Paternal love for us. Let us submit to Him and live!

Jesus is our Prince of Peace. Luke 1:79 says that Jesus, the "Dayspring from on high," came to "guide our feet into the way of peace." The world can be an unsettling place. There are matters that happen, conflicts on the outside and fears on the inside (II Corinthians 7:5), that can plague even the most faithful believer with temporary anxieties. But Jesus, the Prince of Peace, provides the cure for all these worries and uncertainties that come to disquiet our soul. In John 16:33 Jesus says, "These things I have spoken to you, that in Me you may have peace. In the world you will have tribulation; but be of good cheer, I have overcome the world."

Generations before Jesus' birth, Isaiah provides this four-fold descriptor of our Savior and Lord. What a soul-enriching enterprise it is to ponder, again, the attributes of our Savior that were known and spoken of long before He came to earth. Jesus is "Everlasting." He has been wonderful and mighty, and He has been our Counsellor and Father and Prince of Peace since before time began and will remain so for eternity. And blessedly, today, He is all this for us right now.

9:7
Of the increase of His government and peace there will be no end, upon the throne of David and over His kingdom, to order it and establish it with judgment and justice from that time forward, even forever. The zeal of the LORD of hosts will perform this.

Jesus came as a child, a Son who would redeem men from their sins, and then gather the redeemed together as a "holy nation," His own "special people" (I Peter 2:9). He would "govern" His people with "justice" and "righteousness" (ESV). This "kingdom" of the redeemed would begin very small – just a few shepherds and wise men, and a handful of others. From its humble roots in a stable, however, the kingdom which our Savior governs has continued to "increase" from that day to this -- and will never stop increasing. The "increase" of this kingdom will have "no end." Our Savior came to save! And He came to govern the saved in a holy kingdom that would never stop increasing and would last forever. Jesus will "establish" His kingdom! He will continually increase the number of His citizen-saints, and He will forever bless them with unending peace. From certain vantage points, in certain eras, and in certain places, it may appear that Christ's kingdom is losing ground. But we are assured here that this will never be the case. "Of the increase of His government and peace there will be no end." His kingdom will forever be increasing. Fanatics who would attempt to destroy Christ's people are doomed to fail, because "the zeal of the LORD of hosts" will overpower all attempts to block His kingdom's advances. What a blessed assurance we find here. With the same zeal that Christ exhibited for His Father's house (John 2:17), He will increase His kingdom of the saints. Just as He overturned tables in His zeal to uphold true worship, so He will overturn efforts to oppose His kingdom's expansion, and with that same zeal, He will turn away attacks that would tear at His people's peace.

9:8-12

The LORD sent a word against Jacob, and it has fallen on Israel. All the people will know – Ephraim and the inhabitant of Samaria – who say in pride and arrogance of heart: "The bricks have fallen down, but we will rebuild with hewn stones; the sycamores are cut down, but we will replace them with cedars." Therefore the LORD shall set up the adversaries of Rezin against him, and spur his enemies on, the Syrians before and the Philistines behind; and they shall devour Israel with an open mouth. For all this His anger is not turned away, but His hand is stretched out still.

God has "sent a word" against His people, and when God speaks, everyone "will know" what He says. He speaks through His written word, through His prophets, and through our conscience so that no one will miss His invitation of redemption and His warning of judgment for the unredeemed. Those who hear Him (which is "all the people" – everyone) and yet despise what He says, place themselves in grave danger. With remarkable mercy, He rebukes and disciplines His people so that they will repent of their foolish rebellion. But here, in "pride and arrogance of heart," God's people despise God's call for repentance and declare that they do not seek God's approval. What God has destroyed in judgment, they intend to rebuild – stronger than before. Rather than seek God's blessings, they will persist in their own pursuit of self-empowered self-advancement. This double rejection of God is condemning. He has called His people to Himself, and they have refused to come. So, He disciplined them to help them come to their senses. But His discipline only moved them to more pride and more rebellion. For those who reject both God's blessings and His rebukes, there is nothing left to give them except God's anger. He will first set enemy armies all around His people, spurring their enemies on, until they "devour

Israel with an open mouth." But even that will not be enough. "His anger is not turned away." God's wrath is forever "stretched out" against those who despise Him with this double rejection – rejecting both His blessings and His discipline. God speaks to us. What a blessed thought. But when "He sent a word" to His people in Isaiah's day they refused to obey His commands – and their refusal incurred His wrath and destroyed their nation. Let all thinking men respond fittingly to the obvious lesson.

9:13-17

For the people do not turn to Him who strikes them, nor do they seek the LORD of hosts. Therefore the LORD will cut off head and tail from Israel, palm branch and bulrush in one day. The elder and honorable, he is the head; the prophet who teaches lies, he is the tail. For the leaders of this people cause them to err, and those who are led by them are destroyed. Therefore the LORD will have no joy in their young men, nor have mercy on their fatherless and widows; for everyone is a hypocrite and an evildoer, and every mouth speaks folly. For all this His anger is not turned away, but His hand is stretched out still.

With an offer of forgiveness for the repentant, the Lord has disciplined His people, but they "do not turn to Him" for His help or for His forgiveness. They do not "seek the LORD of hosts." They do not seek to be reconciled with Him. They do not seek His blessings. They do not seek His approval. Those who reject God can certainly have no realistic hope other than incurring His wrath. Here, in response to His people's rejection, God promises to "cut off" the elders and the "honorable," the leaders of the people who taught their followers to reject God's authority. God will also "cut off" "the prophet who teaches lies." Religious leaders who deceive their followers with false messages will be destroyed along with those that they have misinformed. There is no excuse permissible for those who are taken in by false spiritual teaching, and there is certainly no leniency shown for those who lead others in believing spiritual lies. Usually, seeing young people grow up to take their place in the world fills older onlookers with joy. When young people reject God, however, He finds "no joy in their young men." God is not spontaneously pleased with the arrival of the younger generation. If young men reject Him, He finds no joy in them, and their sin will move God to withhold His mercy from the needy within their borders. If men sin as a group, God will judge them by the group – even orphans and widows will incur the same judgment as healthy young men when their rebellion is the same as that of the healthy young men. Their spiritual depravity will outweigh their physical neediness, and God will view them as a people to be punished rather than a people to be pitied.

Verse 17 provides valuable insight into how God views those who know Him but do not obey Him. "Everyone is a hypocrite and an evildoer, and every mouth speaks folly." From Heaven's perspective, those who reject God are hypocrites, evildoers, and fools. It is hypocrisy to condemn the wrongs of others, but not condemn oneself for personal wrongs (Luke 6:42). It is hypocrisy to know God, yet keep one's heart far from Him (Mark 7:6). It is hypocrisy to sense the need to be righteous, and yet be driven by self-indulgence (Matthew 23:25). God views "everyone" (everyone!) who rejects Him as a hypocrite. They know Him, but do not give Him glory. They are hypocrites. And God's anger toward them will not be "turned away."

God views all who reject Him as "an evildoer." The world is not divided into 3 types of people: God followers, sinners, and good people who don't believe in God. Heaven only sees two peoples: those made righteous by faith and "evildoers." It is impossible to please God without faith (Hebrews 11:6), because there are no righteous people without faith (Galatians 2:16). Without faith accessing God's grace to wash away our sins (Ephesians 2:8), we are all "evildoers" in His sight, and God's anger toward evildoers will not be "turned away."

"Every mouth" that communicates unrepentant disbelief in God "speaks folly." It is folly, it is the height of foolishness, to disobey or disbelieve God. Psalms 53:1 declares that only a fool would say that there is no God. And only a fool would recognize that God is real and then choose to disobey Him. All in heaven plainly see that all those who trust in God and obey Him are rewarded eternally, and all who reject Him are condemned. So from Heaven's perspective, it is folly to reject God. It is a sin against the intelligence of man to reject God, and God's anger toward those who are guilty of the evil of foolishness will not be "turned away."

9:18-21

For wickedness burns as the fire; it shall devour the brier and thorns, and kindle in the thickets of the forest; they shall mount up like rising smoke. Through the wrath of the LORD of hosts the land is burned up, and the people shall be as fuel for the fire; no man shall spare his brother. And he shall snatch on the right hand and be hungry; he shall devour on the left hand and not be satisfied; every man shall eat the flesh of his own arm. Manasseh shall devour Ephraim, and Ephraim Manasseh; together they shall be against Judah. For all this His anger is not turned away, but His hand is stretched out still.

ISAIAH 9

Chapter 9 concludes with even more fiery punishments that are meted out on those who choose "wickedness" over righteousness, preferring lesser gods that accept their sin, rather than the Almighty God who demands holiness. Isaiah rebukes those whose "wickedness burns as the fire." Sin is like a fire. It burns and destroys those who fuel its flames. The destructive outcome of sin burns like fire destroying marriages, families, careers, and their potential for accomplishing wonderful things in life. The people have sinned, and now they are forced to face the destruction that the fire of their sin has kindled. Frighteningly, that's not the end of it -- fast approaching from the other side is the fire of God's wrath that burns those who despise His grace. "Through the wrath of the LORD of hosts, the land is burned up." God fights fire with fire. People who prefer a life of sin rather than a life of holiness, and people who choose lesser gods (or no god) rather than a life of service to Almighty God, are caught between these two great wind-swept fires – the destructive power of their own sin, and the fire of God's judgment. Psalms 11:6 says, "Upon the wicked He will rain coals; fire and brimstone and a burning wind shall be the portion of their cup." Psalms 97:3 makes the same point, "A fire goes before Him, and burns up His enemies round about." Jude 1:23 calls on us to save people who have given themselves to sin, "pulling them out of the fire." The fire of sin ruins the lives of men and women. The fire of God's judgment burns for eternity. Let us devote ourselves to the work of spiritual firemen, rescuing sinners from the flames.

Unity and brotherly love overflow in the lives of those who set their hearts on loving God. In Acts 2:44 all the believers happily met together constantly and shared with one another all they had. Acts 4:32 says that all the believers were "of one heart and of one soul" (KJV). In contrast, those who reject God will scorch their conscience so completely that their hatred for their fellow man will steadily grow until, eventually, they will deteriorate into cannibalism. "Every man shall eat the flesh of his own arm." There may be a thin veneer of love that embroiders the cloak of sin, but let no one be fooled. When the fires of the consequences of sin and of judgment grow hot, everyone will turn on one another. "No man shall spare his brother." Let all those who are tempted to discard God's love for the sake of the love of someone else take heed. Those who reject God, will soon enough reject us as well. The only loyalties that are fire-proof are those that are bound by cords of God's love. All other bonds of love and loyalty will melt away into self-serving cannibalism as soon as things get hot.

Isaiah 10

10:1-2
"Woe to those who decree unrighteous decrees, who write misfortune, which they have prescribed to rob the needy of justice, and to take what is right from the poor of My people, that widows may be their prey, and that they may rob the fatherless."

    God pronounces woe on those who "rob" the needy of justice and take from the poor rather than provide for the poor. We are reminded that the life that our Lord requires of us is not simply a life that abides by commandments and avoids sins of dishonesty and immorality. God requires us to defend the weak and to assure justice to those who cannot protect themselves from predators. If our strength is insufficient to grant justice and defend the weak against their enemies, then we are at least required to take care of them in their need. It is no less our responsibility to provide for the poor than it is for us to obey the Ten Commandments and carry out the Great Commission. God's people are accused of failing in this matter, and even worse, rather than protect the innocent and take care of the needy, they have oppressed the innocent and taken advantage of the poor! "Woe to those" who do such things. God considers a lack of compassion to be comparable to stealing – they "rob" the fatherless rather than care for them. God also considers turning a blind eye to injustice to be comparable to stealing – they "rob the needy of justice." By all means, let us strive to be righteous. But by all means, let us be reminded that righteousness in the sight of God includes protecting and providing for the weak and needy. "Woe to those" who forget the heart of God and put selfish desires above the basic needs of others.

10:3-4
"What will you do in the day of punishment, and in the desolation which will come from afar? To whom will you flee for help? And where will you leave your glory? Without Me they shall bow down among the prisoners, and they shall fall among the slain." For all this His anger is not turned away, but His hand is stretched out still.

God asks the question of His people by the pen of Isaiah, but His question rings out demanding an answer from all people in every age. "What will you do in the day of punishment?" "To whom will you flee for help?" What will become of your earthly glory when judgment day arrives? God promptly gives the only answer that will save us – "Without Me" you will be imprisoned, and you will die. When God asks, "What will you do on judgment day?" "Who will you look to for help?" "What will become of your personal glory amassed by your deeds on earth?" There is only one set of answers to God's questions that will save us: 'I will look to my Savior for mercy. I will flee to my Father's arms for grace. At the end of my days my glory will be caught up in the glory of who God is and what He has done, not at all in who I am and what I have done.' Judgment day is coming for all humanity, and we must prepare ourselves with the right attitude and the right answer when that day comes. What will you do in the day of punishment? Blessedly, we can say that we will be safe in the arms of our Savior's forgiveness. We have set our eyes on the hills, and see our Savior coming, and it is He who comes to bring us our "help." And the only glory we seek is the glory we give to our Father as we glorify Him with our faith, with our obedience and with our praise.

10:5-6
Woe to Assyria, the rod of My anger and the staff in whose hand is My indignation. I will send him against an ungodly nation, and against the people of My wrath I will give him charge, to seize the spoil, to take the prey, and to tread them down like the mire of the streets.

We are reminded here that everyone is subservient to God. Not all men are obedient to God, but everyone like it or not, intentionally or not, is subservient to God. Assyria, with its self-absorbed, polytheistic, God-despising worldview is nothing more than a "rod" in God's hand, a "staff" which God uses to accomplish His purposes. The people of Assyria would never think to intentionally carry out God's will – yet they will do exactly that. They will trample God's people who have become "an ungodly nation" just as God has decreed. We can choose to be obedient, or we can choose to be merely subservient. Either way, God's will is accomplished – we will either glorify Him by praising Him for saving us, or we will glorify Him by being punished for our rebellion. We can happily, intentionally rush to do our Father's will, and receive our reward, or we can be like the Assyrians and accomplish God's purposes unwittingly. "Woe to Assyria," woe to those who only inadvertently carry out God's will even though they were intent on serving themselves. In the New Testament, Judas acts like Assyria. He accomplishes God's will – it was God's will for His Son to redeem His people on the cross – but Matthew 26:24 says the same thing about him that Isaiah says about Assyria: "The Son of Man indeed goes just as it is written of Him, but *woe to that man* by whom the Son of Man is betrayed! It would have been good for that man if he had not been born."

10:7-11
Yet he does not mean so, nor does his heart think so; but it is in his heart to destroy, and cut off not a few nations. For he says, "Are not my princes altogether kings? Is not Calno like Carchemish? Is not Hamath like Arpad? Is not Samaria like Damascus? As my hand has found the kingdoms of the idols, whose carved images excelled those of Jerusalem and Samaria, as I have done to Samaria and her idols, shall I not do also to Jerusalem and her idols?"

Continuing His rebuke of Assyria, God highlights Assyria's many misunderstandings. God has whistled (Isaiah 7:18) for Assyria to come and punish Israel and Judah for His name's sake. But Assyria "does not mean" to do anything for God's sake. "His heart," Assyria's intentions, are completely self-centered. Assyria believes that they are conquering Israel and Judah for personal gain – that is incorrect. They are conquering Israel by God's power and for God's purposes – and failure to understand this will lead to their demise. Assyria's second misunderstanding is that he thinks far too highly of himself. "Are not my princes altogether kings?" Proverbs 16:18 warns us that "Pride goes before destruction, and a haughty spirit before a fall." This will prove all too true for Assyria – their destruction awaits, even as they plan the destruction of others. Assyria's third misconception is that they think all religions are the same. The NLT renders verse 10 as, "Yes, we have finished off many a kingdom whose gods were far greater than those in Jerusalem and Samaria." Assyria thought that the power of their army surpassed the power of all gods everywhere. But our God is the God of gods, our God is the Lord of kings (Daniel 2:47), He is not like the idols of foolish peoples. God is not mute, He is not immobile, He is not conquerable. "The LORD shall reign forever" (Psalms 146:10). Failure to understand this has eternal repercussions.

10:12-14
Therefore it shall come to pass, when the LORD has performed all His work on Mount Zion and on Jerusalem, that He will say, "I will punish the fruit of the arrogant heart of the king of Assyria, and the glory of his haughty looks." For he says: "By the strength of my hand I have done it, and by my wisdom, for I am prudent; also I have removed the boundaries of the people, and have robbed their treasuries; so I have put down the inhabitants like a valiant man. My hand has found like a nest the riches of the people, and as one gathers eggs that are left, I have gathered all the earth; and there was no one who moved his wing, nor opened his mouth with even a peep."

Assyria is a rod in the hand of God that He will use to punish Israel and Judah. Rather than fear God's judgments, however, Assyria brings down God's judgment on their head as well. For though they saw how God punished the proud and the self-centered, they insisted on following the same pattern of living as that which brought God's judgment on Judah. Assyria's victories made them "arrogant." Rather than give God thanks for their victories, they mistakenly claimed that "by the strength of my hand I have done it, and by my wisdom, for I am prudent." James 4:16 says that arrogant boasting is evil. Assyria's boastful attitude is evil, and they will soon find out for themselves that God punishes evil.

10:15
Shall the ax boast itself against him who chops with it? Or shall the saw exalt itself against him who saws with it? As if a rod could wield itself against those who lift it up, or as if a staff could lift up, as if it were not wood!

An ax is useless without an arm – and a strong arm at that. Likewise, a saw is useless without a skilled handler. As ridiculous as it would be for an ax to boast that he was stronger than the arm that wields it, as nonsensical as it would be for a saw or a rod or a staff to claim that they were greater than the one who put them to use, so is it ludicrous for a man or woman to boast that they could take care of themselves without God. Everything we have, we have from God – "Every good gift and every perfect gift is from above, and comes down from the Father of lights, with whom there is no variation or shadow of turning" (James 1:17). From heaven's viewpoint we look insanely evil when we boast of our possessions, when all of our possessions were handed to us from God. Everything we successfully accomplish, we accomplish through the strength of the Lord's arm that wields us. "Without Me you can do nothing" (John 15:5). From heaven's perspective, we look insanely evil when we boast of our own accomplishments, even though we are little more than a stick in God's hand. No wonder James calls boasting "evil." It is insanely evil. An ax can do absolutely nothing without an arm. We can do absolutely nothing without our Lord. Let us ask Him to use us. Let us give Him all the glory when He does.

10:16-17
Therefore the Lord, the Lord of hosts, will send leanness among his fat ones; and under his glory He will kindle a burning like the burning of a fire. So the Light of Israel will be for a fire, and his Holy One for a flame; it will burn and devour his thorns and his briers in one day.

Assyria is guilty of the sin of boasting, and in punishment, the Lord will "send leanness among his fat ones." If Assyria will not honor God in his prosperity, God will grant him poverty to help him see the need to clothe himself in humility, for "God resists the proud, but gives grace to the humble" (I Peter 5:5). Assyria's power appears unconquerable, his defenses impenetrable, his riches inexhaustible. Contrary to appearances, however, he is extremely vulnerable. "Under his glory," beneath the fabric and foundation of his stability, God will "kindle a burning." The Lord of hosts can burn away the glory of man in the blink of an eye. Let all thinking men and women take note! Let us avoid boasting and pride with all possible intensity! For all his greatness, Assyria was flammable. His possessions and conquests simply added more fuel to the fire of God's judgment. God is not only our Creator, He is our Sustainer! Psalms 54:4 says, "The Lord is the sustainer of my life" (CSB). The moment He stops sustaining us we burn out and our accomplishments burn up. God will light a fire under the glory of those who reject Him, and all that they have acquired will burn away. But fire not only burns – it brightens. At the same time that God's fire is burning away Assyria's pride, it is glowing as the "Light of Israel." His "Holy One" is shining brightly to provide hope and direction to the people that seek Him. Those who boast that they do not need God will be consumed in the fire of His judgment, but those who seek His direction and mercy will be granted the light of the Holy One. Our God is a "consuming fire" (Deuteronomy 4:24). Our Lord is the "light of the world" (John 8:12). We must follow the light of His path or we will be consumed in the fire of His judgment.

10:18-19
And it will consume the glory of his forest and of his fruitful field, both soul and body; and they will be as when a sick man wastes away. Then the rest of the trees of his forest will be so few in number that a child may write them.

The fire of God's judgment will "consume the glory" of "his forest," Assyria's massive army. II Kings 19:35 tells of the day when this prophecy was fulfilled, the day when Sennacherib awoke one morning and found that the angel of the Lord had executed 185,000 of his soldiers during the night. The survivors, "the trees of his forest," were so few in number that a child could count them. Apart from God's blessings, we are very vulnerable. Even if we have an army of friends, even if we are armed with powerful friends and powerful weapons, those who reject God will fall down like "a sick man" who "wastes away."

10:20
And it shall come to pass in that day that the remnant of Israel, and such as have escaped of the house of Jacob, will never again depend on him who defeated them, but will depend on the LORD, the Holy One of Israel, in truth.

God's intended outcome will come to pass. He has disciplined His people and He has punished His enemies so that His people will "depend on the LORD, the Holy One of Israel, in truth." God's desire for us is that we will face all challenges and every crisis with the prayer of Psalms 62:7 (CSB) "My salvation and glory depend on God; my strong rock, my refuge, is in God." Certainly, everyone must understand that it is in our best interest to depend on God for our needs rather than seek the aid of anyone else. Psalms 33:18 (CSB) says, "Now the eye of the Lord is on those who fear Him -- those who depend on His faithful love." When we despise God's "faithful love," when we ask for help from seemingly powerful people rather than look to God to supply our needs, we follow the example of Judah in our passage here, who looked to Assyria for his rescue rather than trusting in "the Holy One of Israel." God will not disappoint those who "depend" on Him. A husband would be rightly offended if his wife asked for money from another man when he had the money she needed in his pocket. So, too, God is offended when we turn our backs on His provision and indicate that we find others more trustworthy than He is. In Judah's case, God destroyed Assyria and stripped away everything else His people trusted in, so that they would lift up their eyes and be convinced once again of God's great power and God's great love for those who trust in Him.

10:21-23
The remnant will return, the remnant of Jacob, to the Mighty God. For though your people, O Israel, be as the sand of the sea, a remnant of them will return; the destruction decreed shall overflow with righteousness. For the Lord GOD of hosts will make a determined end in the midst of all the land.

Both the great mercy of God and the great judgment of God are highlighted here. Both the great hope of the faithful and the ominous future of the disobedient are brought to light. God's people have sinned, and "the destruction decreed" on those who sin will certainly come to pass. God's justice must be satisfied. Sin leads to death, and when great numbers of people sin, there will, of necessity, be the death of great numbers of people just as God has "decreed." Though Israel was once a populous and prosperous nation, with a populace "as the sand of the sea" in number, "the destruction decreed" will bring them very low. God "will make a determined end" of their rebellion. It is frightful to consider the dismal prospects of any person or people if God decides to "make a determined end" of them. Paul quotes these verses in Romans 9:27-28 to explain why the Jewish nation had been brought to such a catastrophic low point in their history. The doom that awaits sinners should make us all shudder with fear and leap away from sin as soon as temptation creeps up behind us. Sin brings "destruction" and a "determined end" to our personal hopes for lasting well-being. But even as the doom that awaits sinners is painted freshly before us, so too is the hope that is granted God's children: "The remnant will return." In Micah 4:7 God promises, "I will make the lame a remnant, and the outcast a strong nation; so the LORD will reign over them in Mount Zion from now on, even forever." And Micah responds to

God's rescue of the remnant with praise. "Who is a God like You, pardoning iniquity and passing over the transgression of the remnant of His heritage? He does not retain His anger forever, because He delights in mercy." God's justice will always prevail, which will spell judgment and doom for millions. But "He delights in mercy" which provides hope for all who call on His name for deliverance (Joel 2:32).

10:24-25
Therefore thus says the Lord GOD of hosts: "O My people, who dwell in Zion, do not be afraid of the Assyrian. He shall strike you with a rod and lift up his staff against you, in the manner of Egypt. For yet a very little while and the indignation will cease, as will My anger in their destruction."

When God draws near, often His first instruction to His listener is just as it is here, "do not be afraid." The massive Assyrian army's invasion is imminent. There appears to be good cause for alarm, if not outright panic. But the Lord calms the fears of His people: "do not be afraid of the Assyrian." Assyria will attack, he will "strike you with a rod" and threaten with "his staff" of cruel power, but he will face his demise sooner than Judah will face theirs. God's anger will abate, and He will require Assyria's "indignation" to "cease." God's anger toward Judah will be redirected by His mercy, and Assyria's "indignation," their cruel attack on Judah, will be redirected by the desire for self-preservation when God's anger toward them threatens their "destruction." God's assurances here remind us of David's assurance in Psalms 3:6 – "I will not be afraid of ten thousands of people who have set themselves against me all around." Today, when we sense fear creeping in, may we be reminded of how often God sends this message to His people: "Do not be afraid." And may Psalms 56:3 be our prayer, "Whenever I am afraid, I will trust in You."

10:26-27
And the LORD of hosts will stir up a scourge for him like the slaughter of Midian at the rock of Oreb; as His rod was on the sea, so will He lift it up in the manner of Egypt. It shall come to pass in that day that his burden will be taken away from your shoulder, and his yoke from your neck, and the yoke will be destroyed because of the anointing oil.

We are called upon to have faith in God. But it is not blind faith that is required. God tells Judah not to fear the Assyrian (verse 24), and despite the cruel nature of the Assyrians, despite their successful triumphs over numerous neighboring nations, despite the size and power of their army, the people of Judah have good cause to trust God's promise of deliverance. Gideon's challenge in facing the Midianite army with only 300 men was even more desperate than Judah's fight against the Assyrians. And yet God delivered the nation when His people executed Oreb, the Midianite prince, on the rock of Oreb after a miraculous God-wrought victory (Judges 7). Israel's desperation as they fled the Egyptian army in Exodus 14 was also greater than the current Assyrian threat, and yet God delivered His people as well, drowning Israel's enemies when Moses' "rod was on the sea." So then, far from being a far-fetched illogical hope, Judah has excellent cause to believe God's assurances that He will take the Assyrian "burden" off of His people's shoulder and take the "yoke" of fear and war from off their neck. God will anoint His people with the oil of His protection in the presence of their enemies (Psalms 23:5). And He has commanded the nations, "Saying, 'Do not touch My anointed ones, and do My prophets no harm'" (Psalms 105:15).

10:28-32

He has come to Aiath, he has passed Migron; at Michmash he has attended to his equipment. They have gone along the ridge, they have taken up lodging at Geba. Ramah is afraid, Gibeah of Saul has fled. Lift up your voice, O daughter of Gallim! Cause it to be heard as far as Laish – O poor Anathoth! Madmenah has fled, the inhabitants of Gebim seek refuge. As yet he will remain at Nob that day; he will shake his fist at the mount of the daughter of Zion, the hill of Jerusalem.

Isaiah foretells the coming march of the Assyrian army toward Jerusalem, listing the cities that will be overwhelmed by Sennacherib's forces. The invasion will devastate God's people. "Ramah is afraid." Gibeah of Saul and Madmenah flee from the atrocities that the Assyrian soldiers commit. The inhabitants of Gebim "seek refuge." And all Isaiah can say about Anathoth is "O poor Anathoth!" Assyria will "shake his fist" at God's people, defying their God and threatening their existence as a nation. And it is this defamation of God and venomous threat hurled at God's people that will lead to Assyria's undoing. II Kings 18 and 19 tell of Sennacherib's threats toward Israel and insults toward God. Verse 32 here says that the king of Assyria will "shake his fist" at God's people and II Kings 19:4 says that he came to "reproach the living God." And so it is not surprising that God would respond powerfully to Assyria's blasphemous curses, determined to defend His people and His name. In II Kings 19:22 God asks Sennacherib, king of Assyria, "Whom have you reproached and blasphemed? Against whom have you raised your voice, and lifted up your eyes on high?" Then God says, "But I know your dwelling place, your going out and your coming in, and your rage against Me. Because your rage against Me and your tumult have come up to My ears, therefore I will put My hook in your nose and My bridle in your lips, and I will turn you back by the way which you came." "For I will defend this city, to save it for My own sake and for My servant David's sake!" (II Kings 19:27-28,34). It is certainly a self-defeating act of defiance to "shake (a) fist" at the Almighty God or threaten His beloved children. God is determined to defend His people (Psalms 5:11), and He is determined that His name "is to be praised" (Psalms 113:3). All who will join Assyria in raising their fist in defiance, will also join Assyria when God lowers His hand in judgment.

10:33-34
Behold, the Lord, the LORD of hosts, will lop off the bough with terror; those of high stature will be hewn down, and the haughty will be humbled. He will cut down the thickets of the forest with iron, and Lebanon will fall by the Mighty One.

God is the Mighty One, and everyone else is like a twig. He will "lop off" the branches that oppose Him. He will "take away" (John 15:2) every branch that fails to carry out His will. Having a high self-esteem provides no protection whatsoever against God's judgments – "the haughty will be humbled." Those who are held in high esteem by society are similarly unprotected – "those of high stature will be hewn down." Often, "what is highly esteemed among men is an abomination in the sight of God" (Luke 16:15). The only thing that matters is how God esteems us. Let us then, devote ourselves to those things which grant us high esteem in the eyes of our Lord. Proverbs 3:3-4 says that if we will show mercy to the needy and proclaim God's truth that we will find "favor and high esteem in the sight of God and man." Let us diligently reflect God's mercy toward those in need and proclaim God's truths to the nations. For those who shake their fist (verse 32) in defiance against God rather than bear much fruit in devotion to God will be "cut down" and "fall" at the hand of "the Mighty One."

Isaiah 11

11:1-2
There shall come forth a Rod from the stem of Jesse, and a Branch shall grow out of his roots. The Spirit of the LORD shall rest upon Him, the Spirit of wisdom and understanding, the Spirit of counsel and might, the Spirit of knowledge and of the fear of the LORD.

Isaiah's prophecy has been given; it will surely come to pass. Both Assyria, Judah's oppressor, and Judah itself will be destroyed. The great difference, however, is that Judah will rise again. The flower of his glory will fade, the trunk of his power will be hewn down, but from his roots "a Branch shall grow." A "Rod" will rise from the "stem of Jesse." From David's line of kings will rise the King of kings. The Spirit of the Lord will "rest upon Him." This is how John the Baptist knew that Jesus was this Branch, this Messiah, because in John 1:32 he says, "I saw the Spirit descending from heaven like a dove, and He remained upon Him." John saw the Spirit of God "remained" on Jesus, He came to "rest upon Him" as evidence that Jesus, the Messiah, was the Branch that would rise from the stem of Jesse and establish God's kingdom.

In addition, the Spirit of "wisdom and understanding" would rest upon Jesus. Jesus' wisdom exceeded the wisdom of Solomon (Matthew 12:42). In Matthew 13:54 the crowds listening to Jesus were astonished by His teaching and wondered out loud, "Where did this Man get this wisdom?"

Added to that, Jesus the Branch, would be filled with the Spirit of "counsel and might." Some people can offer decent advice, but they possess no power or sway to provide the strength needed to carry out their instructions. Jesus, however, provides both the counsel that will show us how to win, as well as the power to overcome the struggle before us. He is both a "Wonderful Counsellor" and our "Mighty God" (Isaiah 9:6). His counsel is founded in omniscience and His might is founded in omnipotence so we can trust what He says and trust that He is able to accomplish His purpose in us when we obey Him.

In addition to all that, the Branch will also be filled with the Spirit of "knowledge and of the fear of the LORD." Some men are smart, some are impressively smart. But too often, they sadly replace fear of the Lord with pride in their intelligence. Jesus, however, for all His immeasurable knowledge and wisdom and might, exemplifies constant fear of the LORD and submission to His Father's will. Ah, can we take in all that this Branch is to us? He teaches us how to live, empowers us as we live, and exemplifies the life that He calls us to live. Judah will fall – his judgments failed him, his power failed in the face of his enemies, and he despised God rather than choose to serve Him with holy fear. But the Branch will rise and provide the solution to all those failures that led to Judah's demise. His insights will be fueled with wisdom and understanding, His mighty hand will overcome the power of any and all enemies that confront His kingdom, and He will show us that fear of the Lord and submission to His mastery will establish us forever so that we will never face the sting of sinful failure that doomed the nation of Judah.

11:3-5

His delight is in the fear of the LORD, and He shall not judge by the sight of His eyes, nor decide by the hearing of His ears; but with righteousness He shall judge the poor, and decide with equity for the meek of the earth; He shall strike the earth with the rod of His mouth, and with the breath of His lips He shall slay the wicked. Righteousness shall be the belt of His loins, and faithfulness the belt of His waist.

Jesus, the Branch, has His delight "in the fear of the LORD." Honoring the Father, serving Him, submitting to His will, is the Messiah's delight. He will judge the earth. John 5:22 says "For the Father judges no one, but has committed all judgment to the Son." But He does not judge by looking at the outward appearance. He does not rely on His eyes and ears to discern the truth. He judges with true righteousness, knowing the truth, able to distinguish between the guilty and the innocent by His omniscient understanding of everyone's heart. The poor will not be disadvantaged when they face His judgments, and the meek will find that He upholds their righteous cause. Verse 4 offers an interesting phrase: "He shall strike the earth with the rod of His mouth." God's Word is a rod. As a rod is used to beat the back of a fool (Proverbs 26:3), so God's Word strikes a blow to a wayward man's conscience. The rod of God's Word beats those who are "devoid of understanding" (Proverbs 10:13), but it also comforts the righteous (Psalms 23:4) and delivers the soul of His children from hell (Proverbs 23:14). There is no struggle for the Branch to overthrow the wicked. "The breath of His lips" is all that is needed to execute His judgment on them. The Lord, the Branch from the seed of David reigns! And He reigns with righteousness and faithfulness. All those who long for a world where oppression, crime and violence are removed and virtue is rewarded will love the coming of the Branch. Those who hunger and thirst for righteousness will be filled with joy, because the Branch will reign wearing righteousness as a belt around His waist. Acts 17:31 says that God "has appointed a day on which He will judge the world in righteousness by the Man whom He has ordained. He has given assurance of this to all by raising Him from the dead." Judah was facing dreadfully dark times as Isaiah wrote his prophecy. But what a wonderful promise of hope is offered here! Jesus, the righteous Branch, will come and reign over His people! May the promise of His second coming provide us in our day with the same joyous hope that it offered Isaiah's readers in his day.

11:6-9
The wolf also shall dwell with the lamb, the leopard shall lie down with the young goat, the calf and the young lion and the fatling together; and a little child shall lead them. The cow and the bear shall graze; their young ones shall lie down together; and the lion shall eat straw like the ox. The nursing child shall play by the cobra's hole, and the weaned child shall put his hand in the viper's den. They shall not hurt nor destroy in all My holy mountain, for the earth shall be full of the knowledge of the LORD as the waters cover the sea.

ISAIAH 11

The world is a dangerous place. There are wolves and cobras, wars and cancer. The world is full of vipers and bears, villains and bullies. But the world did not begin this way. In Eden, when Adam and Eve lived under the caring hand of their Creator, the world was a supremely safe place. Only when God does not reign does danger lurk. Isaiah foretells the day when the Branch, the righteous Savior, will come and restore God's reign and end the reign of terror that sin ushered in. One day soon, "the earth shall be full of the knowledge of the LORD as the waters cover the sea," and when knowledge of the Lord predominates, when submission to His will prevails, danger will disappear. "They shall not hurt nor destroy in My holy mountain." This is the happy outcome anticipated by the missionary. It is heart-wrenching to talk to people day after day who have never heard the gospel story, who have no "knowledge of the LORD" and so live in the shadow of death and with multiple fears in life. But it is our joy to spread the great news to the nations so that knowledge of the Holy One will at last fill the earth "as the waters cover the sea" just as Isaiah prophesies here.

11:10
And in that day there shall be a Root of Jesse, who shall stand as a banner to the people; for the Gentiles shall seek Him, and His resting place shall be glorious.

Jesus, the "Root of Jesse," stands before the whole earth "as a banner to the people." He beckons the nations to "come to Me all you who labor and are heavy laden, and I will give you rest" (Matthew 11:28). His banner waves in the wind and beckons all who thirst to "come to Me and drink" (John 7:37). His banner fills the sky calling sinners to come for forgiveness and the weak to come to Him for strength. He invites the embattled to join the ranks of His soldier-saints and overcome the world. His banner summons all the nations of the world to "seek Him" and when they find Him they will find His resting place "glorious." "Gentiles shall seek Him." All the nations will see their need for a Savior and they will come to Jesus. And He will not abandon those who seek Him to stumble around in the dark. He is on His holy hill waving aloft His banner inviting the world to join His family of faith. All those who seek Him will find Him (Jeremiah 29:13) because His banner is unfurled in plain view of every soul on earth. What a blessed picture. Our Captain mounted on His charger, our King seated on His throne, elevated high above the earth in full view of all the nations. He has unfurled His banner and He is inviting the peoples of the world to join His ranks both in His glorious war against unrighteousness and in the glorious peace of His "resting place." The Lord is my banner (Exodus 17:15). He waves to me, He summons me. He is in plain view and the sight of Him is inspiring.

11:11-12
It shall come to pass in that day that the LORD shall set His hand again the second time to recover the remnant of His people who are left, from Assyria and Egypt, from Pathros and Cush, from Elam and Shinar, from Hamath and the islands of the sea. He will set up a banner for the nations, and will assemble the outcasts of Israel, and gather together the dispersed of Judah from the four corners of the earth.

God's people in Judah will be defeated and they will be dispersed. Some will be taken captive into Assyria and Babylon. Others will flee captivity and be "outcasts" that disperse into "the four corners of the earth." But "the Lord knows those who are His" (II Timothy 2:19). He knows where His children are. He keeps careful track of His sheep even when no one else pays them any attention at all. And at the time of His choosing, "He will set up a banner for the nations" and "gather together" all that He has reserved for Himself from the nations of the world. He rescued His people from Egypt, and He will rescue them "again the second time" when He moves to "recover the remnant of His people" from the ravages of living as foreigners in an unbelieving world. We take encouragement from these verses that remind us that God does not change. Because He delivered His people from Egypt, it is not surprising that He promises to deliver them a "second time" when they are captives and outcasts in other nations, and it is altogether reasonable for us to anticipate that He will deliver us from our current crisis just the same.

11:13-14
Also the envy of Ephraim shall depart, and the adversaries of Judah shall be cut off; Ephraim shall not envy Judah, and Judah shall not harass Ephraim. But they shall fly down upon the shoulder of the Philistines toward the west; together they shall plunder the people of the East; they shall lay their hand on Edom and Moab; and the people of Amon shall obey them.

At the time Isaiah wrote, Judah and Israel (Ephraim) had been divided, warring nations for generations. But when the Lord moves to "recover the remnant of His people" (verse 11), they will return to the Promised Land as a unified people once more. They will be surrounded by enemies from the east and from the west, but as a people united, they will overcome their adversaries and accomplish God's purposes. Jeremiah 3:18 says, "In those days the house of Judah shall walk with the house of Israel, and they shall come together out of the land of the north to the land that I have given as an inheritance to your fathers." This prophecy is given in wonderful detail in Ezekiel 37:15-28. God will unify His people and "the nations also will know that I, the LORD, sanctify Israel, when My sanctuary is in their midst forevermore" (Ezekiel 37:28).

11:15-16
The LORD will utterly destroy the tongue of the Sea of Egypt; with His mighty wind He will shake His fist over the River, and strike it in the seven streams, and make men cross over dry-shod. There will be a highway for the remnant of His people who will be left from Assyria, as it was for Israel in the day that he came up from the land of Egypt.

The language here is wonderfully metaphorical, but we can see the meaning (at least a sparkling facet of its meaning) clear enough. As God opened a "highway" from captivity in Egypt to deliverance in the Promised Land, so will He do again, opening a new highway that will bring home the dispersed in Assyria. God once dried up seas and rivers to allow His people to overcome these obstacles "dry-shod," and He will do so again, delivering His people from the waters of oppression and floods of violence. The Lord will bring His people to the Promised Land, not on an overgrown forest trail or along an unmarked course in the desert, but He will bring His people home on a highway. Proverbs 15:19 says, "the way of the upright is a highway." God's road of rescue for His people held captive in Assyria was a superhighway. God's intended path for us, His road of deliverance for us, is similarly well-lit, well-marked, and well mapped out in the pages of His word.

Isaiah 12

12:1
And in that day you will say: "O LORD, I will praise You; though You were angry with me, Your anger is turned away, and You comfort me."

    We cannot disregard the fact that God is angered when we disobey Him. "God is angry with the wicked every day" (Psalms 7:11). It is right to fear sin out of fear of God's anger. Our blessings on earth are forfeited and our hope for eternity in heaven is dissolved if the Creator of earth and the Ruler of heaven is angry with us. When our conscience is in pain because of sin, it follows suit that we would cry out with the words of Psalms 85:5 -- Oh Lord! "Will You be angry with us forever? Will You prolong Your anger to all generations?" Blessedly, we are reminded here that God's anger toward His children is not forever. Even though we have sinned, yet we have been granted the hope of seeing our Lord's anger "turned away." Repentance on our part and the work of reconciliation on our Savior's part, turn away God's wrath. And once His wrath is turned away, His mercy and forgiveness pour out to "comfort" us. Oh, the comforting presence of our forgiving Lord! Psalms 94:19 voices the emotion well, "In the multitude of my anxieties within me, Your comforts delight my soul." Our sin angers God and threatens to be our soul's ruin, but God's forgiveness brings us incomparable comfort that is the delight of our now-forgiven soul. Our rightful response to God's comfort is praise. "O LORD, I will praise You." God has forgiven us. He has comforted us – He, Himself, has become our Comforter. II Corinthians 1:3 says that He is the "God of all comfort!" May all of us who have been comforted by our merciful Savior sing out our praise to Him as our verse says here. We sin, but our repentance and Christ's redemptive sacrifice on the cross turn away God's wrath and carry to us His comfort instead. And in response, we rise up to praise Him. The natural response of those who have tasted the comforts of our Lord is to sing out: "Praise the LORD! Praise the LORD, O my soul! While I live I will praise the LORD; I will sing praises to my God while I have my being" (Psalms 146:1-2).

12:2
"Behold, God is my salvation, I will trust and not be afraid; for YAH, the LORD, is my strength and song; He also has become my salvation."

Many of us need rescuing from a great many menaces, and all of us need rescue from the sin that threatens our eternal fate. But in the face of earthly dangers that loom over our safety, and in the face of our own sin which threatens our eternity, God's children are blessed with an unshakeable assurance, "God is my salvation." An embattled soldier's morale would not be lifted by news that a group of unarmed school children was arriving to reinforce his position. News of the imminent arrival of an entire division of his army's best troops, however, would cheer him considerably. Similarly, we are encouraged knowing that the One coming to save us is no ordinary man with dubious character and limited power. God is our salvation. Our Rescuer is omnipotent, omniscient, and He loves us. Who could ask for a better Savior? Our rescue is certain. Our salvation is assured, for God is our salvation and He cannot possibly fail to deliver us from even our most powerful enemy. We can "trust and not be afraid," because, by grace, through faith (Ephesians 2:8), God "has become (our) salvation." He is our salvation and He is our "strength and song." Psalms 118:14 says the same thing, "The Lord is my strength and song, and He has become my salvation." Psalms 28:7 says, "The LORD is my strength and my shield; my heart trusted in Him, and I am helped; therefore my heart greatly rejoices, and with my song I will praise Him." By His grace our God has saved us, with His strength He upholds us, and with our song we praise Him in return. By virtue of His saving grace, He has become the focus of our songs of joy, the very essence of the songs of praise we sing. "Oh sing to the LORD a new song! Sing to the LORD, all the earth. Sing to the LORD, bless His name; proclaim the good news of His salvation from day to day. Declare His glory among the nations, His wonders among all peoples. For the LORD is great and greatly to be praised; He is to be feared above all gods" (Psalms 96:1-4).

12:3
Therefore with joy you will draw water from the wells of salvation.

Our salvation from sin and death, our assurance that God has saved us and has reserved a place for us in heaven, is a well from which we can draw a constant supply of soul-refreshing waters that grant us vision for our future and strength for the trials of here and now. The waters from the wells of salvation allow us to endure hardship now, knowing that our reward is awaiting us in heaven. These waters allow us to endure the harsh criticisms of the world, knowing that our Savior is pleased to save us. Knowing that we are bound for heaven provides us with an eternal joy that is not driven away by temporary threats. The waters from "the wells of salvation" provide a deep, constant satisfaction for our soul. Access to these living waters (John 7:37-38), however, only comes through God's grace through our faith in His Son (Ephesians 2:8). Attempts to find satisfaction for our soul through any other means will not only disappoint us, they will make us culpable in the eyes of the Lord who offers us free access to His salvation. Jeremiah 2:13 says, "For My people have committed two evils: they have forsaken Me, the fountain of living waters, and hewn themselves cisterns--broken cisterns that can hold no water." The wells of salvation provide unending confidence and hope for those who draw their water there. All other efforts to find satisfaction and salvation for the soul will only lead to "broken cisterns that can hold no water."

12:4
And in that day you will say: "Praise the LORD, call upon His name; declare His deeds among the peoples, make mention that His name is exalted."

Salvation! "In that day" of our soul's salvation we will say, "Praise the LORD"! The spontaneous response to being saved is to praise the Rescuer. God's name is to be exalted for He has reached down and saved us out from among the unbelieving peoples of the world. Psalms 106:47 (ESV) says, "Save us, O Lord our God, and gather us from among the nations, that we may give thanks to your holy name and glory in your praise." God saves, and we "declare His deeds among the peoples" in response. Our personal salvation sparks the inner drive to world missions. God has saved me; I am bound for heaven. Therefore, I will declare His deeds among the peoples of the world so that they can be saved too. It is not just our personal salvation that drives us to world missions, however. The greatness of God, the wonder of "His deeds," the glory of His name all compel us to do the work of a missionary. Our soul is compelled to declare His deeds and His truths to the ends of the earth and to call on all men everywhere to join us in exalting His great name. We are again drawn to Psalms 96 just as we were in verse 2. Psalms 96:2-5 says, "Sing to the LORD, bless His name; proclaim the good news of His salvation from day to day. Declare His glory among the nations, His wonders among all peoples. For the LORD is great and greatly to be praised; He is to be feared above all gods. For all the gods of the peoples are idols, but the LORD made the heavens."

12:5
Sing to the LORD, for He has done excellent things; this is known in all the earth.

    The ESV highlights the imperative for missions in this song of praise, "Sing praises to the Lord, for he has done gloriously; let this be made known in all the earth." The greatness of God and His excellent works on behalf of mankind inspire us not only to praise Him, but to make Him known "in all the earth." Our Lord has done "excellent things." We are moved to awe over His creation of the galaxy. We read with amazement His many works on behalf of His people in the Old Testament. The acts of His Spirit in the New Testament amaze us further still. But perhaps most amazing of all is as Mary prayed in Luke 1:49, "He who is mighty has done great things for me." God has done excellent things, we marvel at them. But the praise from our lips is not simply to acknowledge His greatness, we sing with deep gratitude as well as great awe, for our Lord, our great God, has not just done excellent things, He has done these excellent things for us. And the kindness He has shown to us is available to all the peoples of all the nations the world over. We should "let this be made known in all the earth."

12:6
Cry out and shout, O inhabitant of Zion, for great is the Holy One of Israel in your midst!

    Our God is great! He is holy! And He lives in our midst. He is not a far-off god of myths or fairy tales. He is Immanuel, God with us (Isaiah

7:14). His nearness to us allows us to take comfort as Asaph did in Psalms 74:12 – "God is my King from of old, working salvation in the midst of the earth." Zephaniah 3:17 says, "The LORD your God in your midst, The Mighty One, will save; He will rejoice over you with gladness, He will quiet you with His love, He will rejoice over you with singing." Zechariah 2:10 blesses us with the same message, "Sing and rejoice, O daughter of Zion! For behold, I am coming and I will dwell in your midst," says the LORD." Our Lord walked with Adam and Eve in the midst of the garden (Genesis 3:8). He walked with the people of Israel in the midst of their camp (Deuteronomy 23:14). And today, He continues to assure us that "where two or three are gathered together in My name, I am there in the midst of them" (Matthew 18:20). Our God is very near. His nearness grants us ready access to His tender mercies which moves us to "cry out" our prayers to Him, knowing that He has drawn near to hear us and sit with us in our trials. And the glory of His presence moves us to "shout" out our praise and confident expectations of triumph for our omnipotent God is at our side. Our God is in our midst. Let us not ignore our Savior as He stands by our side. Let us "pray without ceasing" (I Thessalonians 5:17), seeing that His nearness invites constant conversation. Let us guard every word and every thought, knowing that He hears us speak and knows our thoughts. And let us rejoice and praise and even shout as our verse suggests here, filled with joy in knowing that our Almighty God, the Holy One of Israel, is able to conquer all our fears and overcome all our troubles. And He is in our midst.

Isaiah 13

13:1-3
The burden against Babylon which Isaiah the son of Amoz saw. "Lift up a banner on the high mountain, raise your voice to them; wave your hand, that they may enter the gates of the nobles. I have commanded My sanctified ones; I have also called My mighty ones for My anger – those who rejoice in My exaltation."

Isaiah's visions began with a pronouncement of judgment on the people of Judah (chapter 1). Judgment begins with the house of God (I Peter 4:17), but "if it begins with us first, what will be the end of those who do not obey the gospel of God?" After pronouncing judgment on Judah for their sins in chapter 1, God foretells the fall of Israel and Syria in chapter 7, the fall of Assyria in chapter 10, and now the vision of judgment on the unbelieving and disobedient moves to Babylon here in chapter 13. Isaiah is commanded to "lift up a banner on the high mountain," and to "raise your voice to them." It is God's intention to make His will known to the peoples of the earth. If our actions please Him, His Spirit and His word will tell us so. And if our actions move Him to anger, His Spirit and His word will communicate that as well. There is no reason for anyone to arrive at judgment day and be surprised at the Lord's handling of their eternity. He has lifted up a banner on a high hill, he has raised a loud voice communicating His message to our conscience. God has told us what His will is, and He has called out His people to accomplish it. God has called out His "sanctified ones," He has equipped His "mighty ones," He has chosen to accomplish His purposes through those "who rejoice in My exaltation." He has chosen a people to accomplish His mission – and in this case, the mission is the destruction of Babylon.

13:4-5
"The noise of a multitude in the mountains, like that of many people! A tumultuous noise of the kingdoms of nations gathered together! The LORD of hosts musters the army for battle. They come from a far country, from the end of heaven – the LORD and His weapons of indignation, to destroy the whole land."

God will gather together "kingdoms of nations" to overthrow Babylon. Though Babylon's empire was vast, and his armies great, his power was inconsequential compared to God's unlimited resources. He is seen here mustering an army to do battle with Babylon – a battle Babylon cannot win. It is God's intention to "destroy the whole land." God is able to appoint any ruler or topple any ruler at His discretion. God "removes kings and raises up kings" (Daniel 2:21). God raised up Assyria to punish wicked Israel and Syria. He raised up Babylon to punish wicked Assyria, and He will raise up the Medes and Persians to punish the wickedness of Babylon. The reign of wicked men does not last very long. Isaiah's prophecy was given some 150 years or so before Babylon was overthrown. But God desired that His people would know in foresight, and He desires us to know in hindsight, that wickedness will not go unpunished. Let us walk holy with the Lord today, for the lessons of yesterday remind us that those who oppose Him will be overthrown.

13:6-8
Wail, for the day of the LORD is at hand! It will come as destruction from the Almighty. Therefore all hands will be limp, every man's heart will melt, and they will be afraid. Pangs and sorrows will take hold of them; they will be in pain as a woman in childbirth; they will be amazed at one another; their faces will be like flames.

It is remarkable how quickly our self-confidence can melt away. When God's judgment comes, when the Day of the Lord is at hand, "all hands will be limp, every man's heart will melt, and they will be afraid." There are some today who still shake their fist at God and claim that if given the opportunity they would give God an earful of their complaints against Him. But that is plainly not the case. When judgment day comes, those who oppose God "will be in pain as a woman in childbirth." The pain of a guilty conscience becomes unbearable when God draws near. In Job 31:37, Job cries out his innocence and declares that if provided opportunity, he would defend his actions before the Lord. Job is so confident that he says if God would invite him to come, "like a prince I would approach Him." But when God does come near, Job says, "Behold, I am vile; what shall I answer You? I lay my hand over my mouth. Once I have spoken, but I will not answer; yes, twice, but I will proceed no further." Then, after God speaks the second time, Job has the same response, "I have heard of You by the hearing of the ear, but now my eye sees You. Therefore I abhor myself, and repent in dust and ashes." If this is the reaction to the presence of God from the lips of righteous Job, what is the hope of anyone less righteous than he when at last they are allowed admittance into the Master's presence on judgment day? It is important for all men everywhere to realize that "the Day of the Lord is at hand." Our judgment day and the Day of the Lord's return are imminent. It is in our best interest to reconcile with our God before that day arrives.

13:9-11
Behold, the day of the LORD comes, cruel, with both wrath and fierce anger, to lay the land desolate; and He will destroy its sinners from it. For the stars of heaven and their constellations will not give their light; the sun will be darkened in its going forth, and the moon will not cause its light to shine. I will punish the world for its evil, and the wicked for their iniquity; I will halt the arrogance of the proud, and will lay low the haughtiness of the terrible.

Though Isaiah's vision is said to be foretelling the destruction of Babylon (verse 1), his prophecy clearly has wider applications. When God's fierce anger toward sinners is unleashed, the light of the sun and moon and stars are put out. The prophecy names Babylon specifically, but verse 11 says that God "will punish the world for its evil," not just Babylon. Revelation 14:16 and 18 all refer to the judgment of God that will destroy Babylon. In John's prophecy it seems that "Babylon" refers to a city without borders that is comprised of all the wicked and rebellious God-despisers on the earth. Isaiah seems to do the same here, his prophecy including both the destruction of the nation of Babylon 150 years later, as well as the destruction of all "the world" that rejects His lordship and rebels against Him. Perhaps it seems like it for a time, but no one gets away with murder. No one gets away with any evil. God "will punish the world for its evil. The "wicked" will be destroyed because of their "iniquity." God will "halt the arrogance of the proud," and He will "lay low the haughtiness of the terrible." Jesus is the light of the world (John 8:12), and those who reject Him face very dark days ahead.

13:12-16
I will make a mortal more rare than fine gold, a man more than the golden wedge of Ophir. Therefore I will shake the heavens, and the earth will move out of her place, in the wrath of the LORD of hosts and in the day of His fierce anger. It shall be as the hunted gazelle, and as a sheep that no man takes up; every man will turn to his own people, and everyone will flee to his own land. Everyone who is found will be thrust through, and everyone who is captured will fall by the sword. Their children also will be dashed to pieces before their eyes; their houses will be plundered and their wives ravished.

Isaiah foretells the answer to the prayer in Psalms 137:8-9 -- "O daughter of Babylon, who are to be destroyed, happy the one who repays you as you have served us! Happy the one who takes and dashes your little ones against the rock!" Babylon will conquer many nations with barbarity and cruelty, and the time is coming when they will be repaid in kind. Though they will become a prosperous, wealthy nation, God's judgment will lay them so low that it will be harder to find a man than it is to find a wedge of fine gold on the ground. God will "shake the heavens" to rain down His anger on Babylon. "The earth will move out of her place." Nothing is stable, nothing can support us, not even the earth can hold up beneath our feet when God moves to punish rather than protect. Babylon once hunted down their enemies like a lion, but they will become like a "hunted gazelle" or a lost sheep. One after another their citizens will suffer the brutal death of being thrust through with a sword. Babylon has treated their victims cruelly, and when God at last vents the anger of His retribution, the result is terrifying. Children are dashed to pieces before the eyes of their parents – the scene is too disturbing to contemplate. Obadiah 1:15 says, "as you have done, it shall be done to you; your reprisal shall return upon your own head." This is horrifyingly pictured here in the prophecy of the demise of the kingdom of Babylon.

ISAIAH 13

13:17-19
Behold, I will stir up the Medes against them, who will not regard silver; and as for gold, they will not delight in it. Also their bows will dash the young men to pieces, and they will have no pity on the fruit of the womb; their eye will not spare children. And Babylon, the glory of kingdoms, the beauty of the Chaldeans' pride, will be as when God overthrew Sodom and Gomorrah.

Some 150 years before the fall of Babylon, God reveals to Isaiah the means by which He will destroy them. The Lord will call out the Medes, and together with the Persians, they will conquer "the beauty of the Chaldean's pride." A century and a half later, on October 12, 539 BC, God will give another advanced announcement of His judgment on Babylon. In Daniel 5, the very night that the Medes and Persians attack and overthrow Babylon, God will place His handwriting on the wall confirming what Isaiah says here. Babylon will become immensely powerful, and yet, for all their power, they are helpless to defend themselves before the Lord Almighty. Though they are "the glory of kingdoms," they will be as easily and completely destroyed as Sodom and Gomorrah. Those who are completely given to sin will be completely destroyed by our righteous God.

13:20-22
It will never be inhabited, nor will it be settled from generation to generation; nor will the Arabian pitch tents there, nor will the shepherds make their sheepfolds there. But wild beasts of the desert will lie there, and their houses will be full of owls; ostriches will dwell there, and wild goats will caper there. The hyenas will howl in their citadels, and jackals in their pleasant palaces. Her time is near to come, and her days will not be prolonged.

God commonly decrees justice and judgment on those who refuse to do His will. Less commonly, however, does He completely destroy a people for their sins as He did with Sodom and Gomorrah. But this is what He promises to do with the sinful Babylonians (verse 22). Babylon will be destroyed – and "it will never be inhabited" again. In 539 BC, Darius the Mede conquered the city, but it continued to thrive for a time. Alexander the Great wanted to make it his capital in 323 BC but he died in Babylon, and the city steadily declined until it finally disappeared in fulfillment of Isaiah's prophecy here. Andrew Davis' commentary tells us that when the Roman emperor Trajan went to visit Babylon in AD 116, he found only rubble. The city was abandoned. And still today only archeological ruins remain. "It is a fearful thing to fall into the hands of the living God" (Hebrews 10:31).

Isaiah 14

14:1-2
For the LORD will have mercy on Jacob, and will still choose Israel, and settle them in their own land. The strangers will be joined with them, and they will cling to the house of Jacob. Then people will take them and bring them to their place and the house of Israel will possess them for servants and maids in the land of the LORD; they will take them captive whose captives they were, and rule over their oppressors.

"The LORD will have mercy on Jacob." We may be called upon to endure painful trials and testings. Our obedience may lead to cruel treatment from the world, or our sin may require painful discipline from the Lord as in Israel's case here. But our comfort today is the same comfort that Isaiah offers to Israel: The Lord will have mercy on His people. Judgment is required to maintain holiness in the body of Christ. But mercy triumphs over judgment (James 2:13), it outlasts it, carries on long after the gavel of judgment falls, for it is not judgment, but mercy which endures forever (Psalms 107:1). Mercy sets the righteous back on their feet after they have fallen, mercy restores communion with the Father when prodigals return home. Mercy cleanses us from the sins of our youth (Psalms 25:7). God's mercy is the source of our joy in times of trouble (Psalms 31:7). When our "foot slips" it is God's mercy which holds us up (Psalms 94:18). When circumstance or sin bring us low, let us not take comfort in the strength of our hand, but in the mercy of our Master, for "The LORD takes pleasure in those who fear Him, in those who hope in His mercy" (Psalms 147:11).

Here, God's mercy will not only bring Israel home from their captivity in Babylon, His mercy toward Israel will spill over to the peoples nearby, so that "strangers will be joined with them." Those who had once been ignorant of God's mercy, will now be recipients of His grace when He calls His people home. We are right to expend all possible energy and resources to see that strangers and foreigners are brought into the kingdom of God, seeing that it is God's heart to call them to Himself.

14:3-8
It shall come to pass in the day the LORD gives you rest from your sorrow, and from your fear and the hard bondage in which you were made to serve, that you will take up this proverb against the king of Babylon, and say: "How the oppressor has ceased, the golden city ceased! The LORD has broken the staff of the wicked, the scepter of the rulers; he who struck the people in wrath with a continual stroke, he who ruled the nations in anger, is persecuted and no one hinders. The whole earth is at rest and quiet; they break forth into singing. Indeed the cypress trees rejoice over you, and the cedars of Lebanon, saying, 'Since you were cut down, no woodsman has come up against us.'"

Wicked Babylon will be dethroned and the world will rejoice. Proverbs 28:12 says, "when the wicked arise, men hide themselves." The people of the earth hid themselves from the oppression and violence of Babylon as long as she ruled, but when her evil reign "ceased," the people could come out of hiding and "break forth into singing," because no longer did the vassals of the Babylonian tyrant "come up against us." Similarly, Proverbs 29:2 says, "When the righteous are in authority, the people rejoice; but when a wicked man rules, the people groan." As long as Babylon reigned, all the people who suffered under their cruelty groaned. But Isaiah promises that the day is coming that the Lord will "give rest from your sorrow, and from your fear and the hard bondage in which you were made to serve." Babylon's rule will end, his staff will be broken, his scepter of power removed, and God's people will rejoice. In the verses soon to come, Isaiah's prophecy against Babylon will prove to extend to the entirety of the evil kingdom of Lucifer, and here we are given a glimpse of the global nature of Isaiah's words when he says "the whole earth is at rest and quiet" when Babylon is deposed. Wicked kingdoms may last for a day, but soon enough they will all be thrown down. Satan may oppress the world of men for a time, but he, too, will be "broken," his reign of terror will cease. The whole earth will rest in peace and quiet and break forth into singing when the day comes that God reigns and the enemies of sin and Satan, oppression and death no longer "come up against us."

14:9-11
"Hell from beneath is excited about you, to meet you at your coming; it stirs up the dead for you, all the chief ones of the earth; it has raised up from their thrones all the kings of the nations. They all shall speak and say to you: 'Have you also become as weak as we? Have you become like us? Your pomp is brought down to Sheol, and the sound of your stringed instruments; the maggot is spread under you, and worms cover you.'"

Misery loves company, and at least poetically speaking, this is true in hell as well. When Babylon is at last put down and her chiefs are cast into hell, the denizens of hell are "excited" to see that Babylon was no exception – all evil men and all evil empires are cast down – their "pomp is brought down to Sheol." No matter how much gold and prosperity covered them in life, only maggots and worms "cover" them in death. Neither the splendor of riches, nor the magnificence of power will protect a man from judgment and death. Tyrants and thieves, those who abuse their power and enrich themselves by ill-gotten gains will all "lie down alike in the dust, and worms cover them" (Job 21:26). And if we are not careful to give God His due honor, Herod's fall from eminence in Acts 12:23 reminds us that the worms may not wait until the grave to consume us.

14:12-15
"How you are fallen from heaven, O Lucifer, son of the morning! How you are cut down to the ground, you who weakened the nations! For you have said in your heart: 'I will ascend into heaven, I will exalt my throne above the stars of God; I will also sit on the mount of the congregation on the farthest sides of the north; I will ascend above the heights of the clouds, I will be like the Most High.' Yet you shall be brought down to Sheol, to the lowest depths of the Pit."

Isaiah's prophecy concerning the fall of Babylon moves seamlessly into a picture of the fall of Satan, here called "Lucifer, son of the morning." It was in Satan's heart to "ascend into heaven," to ascend to the throne of heaven and exalt himself "above the stars of God." The foolishness of his ambition, the sinfulness of his conceit is highlighted when he says, "I will be like the Most High." God has uttered His voice and made the truth known, "I am God, and there is no other; I am God, and there is none like Me" (Isaiah 46:9). Satan may have had brilliant moments – he is called "son of the morning." But the conceit of men and devils that moves them to think that they need not submit to God, or that they themselves are God, exposes the darkness within them. Lucifer thought to exalt himself above his Maker, and thus doomed himself "to the lowest depths of the Pit." Revelation 20:1-3 says, "then I saw an angel coming down from heaven, having the key to the bottomless pit and a great chain in his hand. He laid hold of the dragon, that serpent of old, who is the Devil and Satan, and bound him for a thousand years; and he cast him into the bottomless pit, and shut him up and set a seal on him, so that he should deceive the nations no more till the thousand years were finished."

14:16-17
Those who see you will gaze at you, and consider you, saying: "is this the man who made the earth tremble, who shook kingdoms, who made the world as a wilderness and destroyed its cities, who did not open the house of his prisoners?"

In II Samuel 1:27, David mourned the loss of his dear friend Jonathan with the famous words, "How the mighty have fallen." David used those words to mourn the loss of his godly friend. Here, we see the world expressing that sentiment in happiness over the destruction of evil Babylon. Babylon had once "made the earth tremble" with his power. He "destroyed cities," turning prosperous towns into an empty "wilderness." With his irresistible power, Babylon used their prisons to exact revenge on their enemies rather than maintain justice in the land, imprisoning enemies and never freeing them regardless of the pettiness of their wrongs. But now, the world stares at the rubble that was once an empire and marvels that such complete devastation could come to such a powerful kingdom. Psalms 37:38 says, "...transgressors shall be destroyed together; the future of the wicked shall be cut off." It makes no difference to God if the evil is perpetrated by a 90-pound weakling or a world empire, all transgressors of His laws "shall be destroyed together." No evil one is too insignificant to avoid His judgments, and no one is too powerful to overcome His judgments. David offers this warning to those who would think to trust in their own power rather than trust in their obedience to God's laws: "Why do you boast in evil, O mighty man? The goodness of God endures continually. Your tongue devises destruction, like a sharp razor, working deceitfully. You love evil more than good, lying rather than speaking righteousness. Selah. You love all devouring words, you deceitful tongue. God shall likewise destroy you forever; He shall take you away and pluck you out of your dwelling place, and uproot you from the land of the living" (Psalms 52:1-5).

14:18-21
"All the kings of the nations, all of them, sleep in glory, everyone in his own house; but you are cast out of your grave like an abominable branch, like the garment of those who are slain, thrust through with a sword, who go down to the stones of the pit, like a corpse trodden underfoot. You will not be joined with them in burial, because you have destroyed your land and slain your people. The brood of evildoers shall never be named. Prepare slaughter for his children because of the iniquity of their fathers, lest they rise up and possess the land, and fill the face of the world with cities."

When kings die, they are laid to rest "in glory." They are entombed in a place of honor as a continual memorial of their reign. In contrast, the evil acts of Babylon's kings will assure that no one will want to memorialize the time of their rule. Rather than be entombed in glory, their corpses will simply be "trodden underfoot." Rather than be enshrined in honor, they will be tossed on a bonfire "like an abominable branch." They will be thrown in the trash heap like a bloodied, torn garment. "The brood of evildoers shall never be named." Good men do not make memorials to wretched men, even if those wretches were kings. Their evil sons are put away and their evil reign is brought to an end, lest their evil deeds be perpetuated and "fill the face of the world with cities" of evil-intentioned people. Babylon had conquered kingdom after kingdom until it amassed a great empire that stretched across much of the known world. But their evil acts made it so that no memorial would be built in Babylon's honor. Psalms 9:5-6 (ESV) reminds us that this is no exception, this is God's general rule: "You have rebuked the nations; you have made the wicked perish; you have blotted out their name forever and ever. The enemy came to an end in everlasting ruins; their cities you rooted out; the very memory of them has perished." Proverbs 10:7 says it simply: "The memory of the righteous is blessed, but the name of the wicked will rot."

14:22-23

"For I will rise up against them," says the LORD of hosts, "And cut off from Babylon the name and remnant, and offspring and posterity," says the LORD. "I will also make it a possession for the porcupine, and marshes of muddy water; I will sweep it with the broom of destruction," says the LORD of hosts.

One of the Lord's most precious promises to His people is that He will always preserve for them a remnant. Though Israel rebels against Him, He will preserve a remnant that holds true to their devotion to Him. Though the nation is destroyed by enemies and taken away captive to foreign lands, yet God will preserve a remnant that will survive these disasters so that the people of Israel will never die out. This promise is denied the evil kingdom of Babylon. God will cut off from Babylon both their "name and remnant." Today, there are no Babylonians. God has swept that nation away "with the broom of destruction" and it no longer exists. Comparatively, Israel was a small nation, and from their captivity in Babylon to the Holocaust, they seemed at the brink of extinction numerous times. But God's promise to leave them a remnant has proven true. Babylon, on the other hand, was a great, expansive dominion, seemingly unconquerable, and certainly much more likely than Israel to last forever. But their inheritance was passed down to porcupines and their dominion was reduced to muddy water. Let us not be over-awed by the temporary achievements and momentary glory of the wicked. Psalms 37:27 encourages us to "depart from evil, and do good; and dwell forevermore." Then Psalms 37:28-29 continue the thought that is exemplified here by the disappearance of Babylon and the persistence of Israel, "For the LORD loves justice, and does not forsake His saints; they are preserved forever, but the descendants of the wicked shall be cut off. The righteous shall inherit the land, and dwell in it forever."

14:24-27

The LORD of hosts has sworn, saying, "Surely, as I have thought, so it shall come to pass, and as I have purposed, so it shall stand: that I will break the Assyrian in My land, and on My mountains tread him underfoot. Then his yoke shall be removed from them, and his burden removed from their shoulders. This is the purpose that is purposed against the whole earth, and this is the hand that is stretched out over all the nations. For the LORD of hosts has purposed, and who will annul it? His hand is stretched out, and who will turn it back?"

Finishing His discourse pronouncing doom on Babylon, the Lord now turns the discussion to Assyria's imminent demise. Once again, we see that although the prophecy is said to be aimed at Assyria specifically, the warning carries world-wide, timeless implications, for he says, "This is the purpose that is purposed against the whole earth." Assyria is condemned for their evil, but it is God's intention, it is His purpose to rid the world of all nations and individuals who share in their sin. Isaiah 23:9 speaks to that purpose: "The LORD of hosts has purposed it, to bring to dishonor the pride of all glory, to bring into contempt all the honorable of the earth." "God resists the proud" (I Peter 5:5). In fact, "Everyone proud in heart is an abomination to the Lord; though they join forces, none will go unpunished" (Proverbs 16:5). God rebukes the proud, the accursed, those who stray from His commandments (Psalms 119:21). It is His intention to do so, He has purposed to do so, and as He purposes, "so it shall come to pass." God "will break the Assyrian" for his crimes of pride and vainglory, and it is His intention to continue to do the same to those who imitate the sin of the Assyrians in our day. Let all thinking men take note.

14:28-32

This is the burden which came in the year that King Ahaz died. "Do not rejoice, all you of Philistia, because the rod that struck you is broken; for out of the serpent's roots will come forth a viper, and its offspring will be a fiery flying serpent. The firstborn of the poor will feed, and the needy will lie down in safety; I will kill your roots with famine, and it will slay your remnant. Wail, O gate! Cry, O city! All you of Philistia are dissolved; for smoke will come from the north, and no one will be alone in his appointed times." What will they answer the messengers of the nation? That the LORD has founded Zion, and the poor of His people shall take refuge in it.

The Lord has already issued a proclamation announcing doom on Babylon and Assyria, and now He turns to Philistia. The Philistines are warned not to be encouraged by the temporary silence of their enemies. Although "the rod that struck (them) is broken" – the enemy nations around them are currently subdued – these enemies will return as "a fiery flying serpent" that will leave Philistia with no survivors. Today, there are no Philistines. Their "roots" were killed with famine. No one escaped. Isaiah's prophecy announces that the "fiery flying serpent" of God's judgment will slay their remnant. Throughout Israel's history, God's people have endured His judgments and discipline over and over again. But the promise of a

ISAIAH 14

"remnant," the promise that God would preserve a portion of His people that would remain true to Him and receive His blessings remained a sustaining hope throughout those trials. This hope is not extended to the evil Philistines. They will be "dissolved." In contrast, the poor and weak of Israel will be far better off. The poor and needy among God's people will be fed by God's own hand, they will "lie down in safety." God will dismantle Philistia, and they will disappear forever. But He "has founded Zion" and it will endure forever. "For God will save Zion and build the cities of Judah" (Psalms 69:35). For the LORD has chosen Zion; He has desired it for His dwelling place: 'This is My resting place forever; here I will dwell, for I have desired it. I will abundantly bless her provision; I will satisfy her poor with bread. I will also clothe her priests with salvation, and her saints shall shout aloud for joy'" (Psalms 132:13-16). May Isaiah's prophecy that Philistia would be "dissolved" because of their evil acts have its proper effect on us, seeing that it is not simply Philistia, but the whole world that is under this prophecy. II Peter 3:11-12 tells us what this should mean to us: "Therefore, since all these things will be dissolved, what manner of persons ought you to be in holy conduct and godliness, looking for and hastening the coming of the day of God, because of which the heavens will be dissolved, being on fire, and the elements will melt with fervent heat?" One day, the sky and the elements of the earth will dissolve just like Philistia as a result of the sins of man. Since this will certainly be the case, let us exercise all possible diligence in living our lives "in holy conduct and godliness, looking for and hastening the coming of the day of God." Philistia has already dissolved, and one day the whole earth will suffer the same fate. But "the LORD has founded Zion" and all His people "shall take refuge in it." Let us walk humbly and holy with the Lord, so that when the wicked are dissolved around us we can rejoice that "the righteous has a refuge" (Proverbs 14:32) that will keep us safe when the world melts away.

Isaiah 15

15:1-4
The burden against Moab. Because in the night Ar of Moab is laid waste and destroyed, because in the night Kir of Moab is laid waste and destroyed, he has gone up to the temple and Dibon, to the high places to weep. Moab will wail over Nebo and over Medeba; on all their heads will be baldness, and every beard cut off. In their streets they will clothe themselves with sackcloth; on the tops of their houses and in their streets everyone will wail, weeping bitterly. Heshbon and Elealeh will cry out, their voice shall be heard as far a Jahaz; therefore the armed soldiers of Moab will cry out; his life will be burdensome to him.

    Chapter 14 describes the fall of Babylon and Assyria, and now Isaiah's string of prophecies against Judah's God-less neighbors turns to Moab. Long ago, Moab enjoyed God's blessings and protection. The nation was founded by the descendants of Lot, and in Deuteronomy 2:9 God says to Moses, "Do not harass Moab, nor contend with them in battle, for I will not give you any of their land as a possession, because I have given Ar to the descendants of Lot as a possession." To whom much is given, however, much will be required (Luke 12:48), and if we mishandle the blessings provided us, those blessings will be "taken away" (Matthew 25:29) and given to others. Such is the case for Moab. As a people, they have rejected the God of their father, Lot, and so, as a people, they will be destroyed. Their trouble moves them to go "up to the temple" and weep before their man-made gods, but they will find no solace there. "Everyone will wail, weeping bitterly" at the destruction of their nation. Their "armed soldiers" have been entrusted with the protection of their nation, but their strength will fall far short of that which is needed to save their people and they will join with the people of Moab's cities and "cry out" their mourning over the death of their nation.

15:5-6
My heart will cry out for Moab; his fugitives shall flee to Zoar, like a three-year-old heifer. For by the Ascent of Luhith they will go up with weeping; for in the way of Horonaim they will raise up a cry of destruction, for the waters of Nimrim will be desolate, for the green grass has withered away; the grass fails, there is nothing green.

Though Moab and Judah have been enemies for generations, Isaiah is moved to tears by the announcement of Moab's doom. "My heart will cry out for Moab." Zoar was in Judah, and when Moab is invaded, its people will flee to Zoar in Judah for refuge, because their own land has been delivered up to "destruction" and "there is nothing green" remaining in their land. Isaiah is moved to compassion by the thought of Moab's people stricken with terror and fleeing their homeland to come take refuge within Judah's borders. God takes no pleasure in the death of the wicked (Ezekiel 33:11), and so neither does Isaiah. Proverbs 24:17 says, "Do not rejoice when your enemy falls, and do not let your heart be glad when he stumbles." The old adage, "I wouldn't wish that on my worst enemy," certainly applies here, as Isaiah cries out in pity when his enemy, Moab, falls under the judgments of God. As children of God, it is our work to rescue people from judgment and mourn over the lost, not gloat over their destruction.

15:7-9
Therefore the abundance they have gained, and what they have laid up, they will carry away to the Brook of the Willows. For the cry has gone all around the borders of Moab, its wailing to Eglaim and its wailing to Beer Elim. For the waters of Dimon will be full of blood; because I will bring

more upon Dimon, lions upon him who escapes from Moab, and on the remnant of the land.

Moab will be destroyed. Their sin and rejection of God will be their undoing. And of all their earthly possessions that they have amassed, they can only take what they can carry to their new home in exile. Earthly treasures are very little comfort to those who have lost their family and are running for their lives. Unlike Babylon, a remnant of Moab will be preserved, likely for the sake of their father, Lot. But those who escape the fall of Moab will have witnessed the death of many of their loved ones – "the waters of Dimon will be full of blood," and their own danger will not have passed even after they successfully pass into neighboring countries. Lions will prey upon the escapees, danger upon danger will fall on the people of Moab until the dead fill the waters of Dimon with their blood and the living are filled with terrors that never seem to end. Such is the end of the nation of Moab. It began in a cave when Lot's oldest daughter slept with her drunken father, and it will end with the nation's terrorized survivors returning to the caves to hide from the judgments of the Lord that will come upon them at the appointed time.

Isaiah 16

16:1-2
Send the lamb to the ruler of the land, from Sela to the wilderness, to the mount of the daughter of Zion. For it shall be as a wandering bird thrown out of the nest; so shall be the daughters of Moab at the fords of the Arnon.

Many, perhaps even the vast majority of experts say that "send the lamb to the ruler of the land" refers to a call upon the refugees from Moab to send tribute to the King of Judah. The writers of the NLT version are so sure that this is true that they have made it not only their interpretation of the verse, but their translation of the verse! The NLT rendering of Isaiah's words are: "Moab's refugees at Sela send lambs to Jerusalem as a token of alliance with the king of Judah." I am not alone, however, in feeling that there is more to Isaiah's words than that. Since the institution of the Passover in Exodus 12, God's people have been taught that the sacrifice of the lamb was required if God's judgment was to be averted. Here, God's judgment on Moab is foretold. Their nation will be destroyed, and the survivors will flee "to the wilderness" like a "wandering bird thrown out of the nest." A bird too young to fly, thrown from its nest will not survive long. It will wander for a moment, but unless there is intervention, it will not survive. So is the fate of Moab. The remnant will survive, but only a very little while. They will wander here and there until other dangers put an end to their wandering. In Exodus 12, Egypt and Israel had but a single hope to save their firstborn – the blood of the lamb. In Revelation 12, the saints in heaven overcame Satan by the same means – the blood of the Lamb (Revelation 12:11). And in every age between the Passover to the final Day of Judgment, all peoples from Moab to America continue to have but a single hope to rescue them from the judgment of God. We depend on the Lamb to make us right with the Ruler of the land. Unless Moab abandoned their heathen gods and offered a sacrifice for their sins before the Ruler of the land, their remnant would survive only temporarily. Like a baby bird thrown out of its nest, Moab will not live long without the help of the Ruler of the land, and Isaiah invites them to seek His aid – send Him a lamb – offer your sacrifices to Almighty God. He is our only hope for salvation.

16:3-4
"Take counsel, execute judgment; make your shadow like the night in the middle of the day; hide the outcasts, do not betray him who escapes. Let My outcasts dwell with you, O Moab; be a shelter to them from the face of the spoiler. For the extortioner is at an end, devastation ceases, the oppressors are consumed out of the land.

Isaiah has been prophesying the doom and downfall of Moab since the beginning of chapter 15. But as God so often does, He provides a way to be saved from the coming judgment to those who would listen. In Daniel chapter 4, God provides King Nebuchadnezzar with a prophecy of his future – he will be driven from men and eat grass like an ox, because his ways displeased the Most High God. But even as He delivers the pronouncement of coming judgment, God provides a way out. In Daniel 4:27, Daniel urges the king with this advice, "break off your sins by being righteous, and your iniquities by showing mercy to the poor. Perhaps there may be a lengthening of your prosperity." Similarly, even as Moab's doom is foretold, his means of gaining God's blessings are provided. Moab's future is in peril, but Judah's peril is upon them already. The Assyrian army is upon them, and although the Assyrian "extortioner" is soon to come to "an end," and although his "devastation" will soon cease, for the moment, Judah is sorely oppressed. God calls on Moab to shelter His people in their time of need. Moab's time of need is quickly coming – God has already warned them of this certainty.

ISAIAH 16

But if Moab will care for the Lord's fugitives today, they will help secure a warm welcome for their nation in the future, when the day comes that they must flee as fugitives to Judah.

16:5
In mercy the throne will be established; and One will sit on it in truth, in the tabernacle of David, judging and seeking justice and hastening righteousness."

Unlike the kingdoms of this world which are established on power and military genius, God's throne will be established in mercy. God does not sit on His throne wielding power over enslaved subjects that He has conquered with cruelty. No, God sits on His throne offering freedom from the guilt and penalty of sin that He provides His people in mercy. "Our God is merciful" (Psalms 116:5), and this is blessed news to the fleeing Moabites, and blessed news in our ears today.

The Lord our God is the One who reigns on His throne "in truth." Man-made religions and non-religions offer people lies of comfort. It is comforting to think that the idol around your neck can protect you from danger. It is comforting to believe that you are god and are accountable to no one but yourself. The Moabites found comfort in their god Chemosh, enjoying the thought that they had a god that existed for their own personal well-being. But Jeremiah 48:13 says, "Moab shall be ashamed of Chemosh," because, in truth, Chemosh was a human invention and not God at all. In truth, man-made idols cannot help anyone with anything. In truth, men are not God and are accountable to His judgments. It is only a temporary comfort that is provided by belief in false gods. But the Creator, the Almighty One reigns in truth. His comforts last an eternity because He reigns in truth. It is God's lovingkindness and truth that "continually preserve "us (Psalms 40:11). God's truths preserve the safety of both our body and soul. Psalms 91:4 says, "He shall cover you with His feathers, and under His wings you shall take refuge; His truth shall be your shield and buckler."

The throne that Isaiah is discussing here, in the middle of his prophecy against Moab, arises from "the tabernacle of David." Many feel this is a reference to the righteous reign of Hezekiah, but we can hardly miss the allusion to the Messiah, who sprang from the tabernacle, the household, of David. Jesus came judging – John 5:22 says that the Father has "committed all judgment to the Son." Jesus came "seeking justice." Matthew 12:18 says that Jesus, "will declare justice to the Gentiles," and Matthew 12:20 says that He "sends forth justice to victory."

The verse ends with an interesting phrase, the King will come "hastening righteousness." The ESV says that He is "swift to do righteousness." Men may hesitate to do the right thing because it is personally dangerous, or because it causes them to oppose powerful people, but the Messiah has no such hesitations. He makes righteousness an urgent matter. As a man suffering a heart attack requires emergency medical care, so our soul requires emergent righteousness. We cannot be lax, we cannot be slow to act, and we cannot be apathetic about our righteousness. We must imitate the One on the throne who reigns in truth and mercy and who is "swift to do righteousness." The wicked are "swift in running to evil" (Proverbs 6:18), and we must be even more instant in our pursuit of holiness.

16:6-7
We have heard of the pride of Moab – he is very proud – of his haughtiness and his pride and his wrath; but his lies shall not be so. Therefore Moab shall wail for Moab; everyone shall wail. For the foundations of Kir Hareseth you shall mourn; surely they are stricken.

The pride of Moab lives to see the fall of Moab just as Proverbs 16:18 predicts – "Pride goes before destruction, and a haughty spirit before a fall." And Moab will wail over his personal hardships. Pride and self-pity are among the most common attributes of those who are far from God. Being successful in life, but far from God in spirit, moves men to dwell on their personal glory. Nebuchadnezzar exemplifies this all too well. In Daniel 4:30 we find him praising himself on a rooftop saying, "Is not this great Babylon, that I have built for a royal dwelling by my mighty power and for the honor of my majesty?" On the other hand, facing tragedy in life while far from God in spirit moves men to grovel in self-pity. Here we find Moab exemplifying both of these God-forsaking attributes. "Moab shall wail for Moab." Godless, hopeless, purposeless wailing is heartbreaking. Godly, hopeful, purposeful sorrow is quite a different matter. II Corinthians 7:10 says, "For godly sorrow produces repentance leading to salvation, not to be regretted; but the sorrow of the world produces death." Sadly, Moab's sorrow was of the second sort. They were not lamenting their sin, they were not repenting of unbelief, they were simply crying over adversity. And their sorrow would foreshadow their death.

16:8-9
For the fields of Heshbon languish, and the vine of Sibmah; the lords of the nations have broken down its choice plants, which have reached to

Jazer and wandered through the wilderness. Her branches are stretched out, they are gone over the sea. Therefore I will bewail the vine of Sibmah, with the weeping of Jazer; I will drench you with my tears, O Heshbon and Elealeh; for battle cries have fallen over your summer fruits and your harvest.

Moab was not a friend to Judah. It is quite likely that Isaiah did not have a single Moabite friend. Yet in the face of the pronouncement of certain doom on Moab's people, Isaiah cries out in pity just as he did in 15:5. As we boldly call people to repent, as we sternly call on the people around us to turn from sin and live holy lives, it is good for us to pity those who are apart from God and grieve when judgment and other sorrows befall them. Isaiah grieves over the destruction of the fields and vines and choice plants of Moab. Moab had such great potential! The land was so capable of blessing man and glorifying God. But now that potential was lost in a landslide of judgment that was precipitated by a torrent of sin. God pities the lost (Jonah 4:11). Jesus reveals that the heart of God grieves over man's unbelief (Luke 18:24). Let us never be soft on sin, but let us be gentle with sinners, pitying those who do not know God, and grieving over those who deny themselves God's salvation.

16:10-11
Gladness is taken away, and joy from the plentiful field; in the vineyards there will be no singing, nor will there be shouting; no treaders will tread out wine in the presses; I have made their shouting cease. Therefore my heart shall resound like a harp for Moab, and my inner being for Kir Heres.

When God is our portion in life, when He is all we desire and all our delight is in Him, our joy is secure even when our fields of service are not "plentiful" and even when the "vineyards" fail. "Though the fig tree may not blossom, nor fruit be on the vines; though the labor of the olive may fail, and the fields yield no food; though the flock may be cut off from the fold, and there be no herd in the stalls -- yet I will rejoice in the LORD, I will joy in the God of my salvation" (Habakkuk 3:17-18). When God is not our focus, however, "gladness is taken away" as soon as hardship falls. When people reject God as their Savior, they find that they have also rejected the Sustainer of their joy in trial. "Gladness is taken away" from Moab because the fields which sustained their livelihood were taken away. But when the Lord is the One that sustains us, we can join David in saying, "You have put gladness in my heart, more than in the season that their grain and wine increased" (Psalms 4:7). Proverbs 10:28 says, "The hope of the righteous will be gladness, but the expectation of the wicked will perish." The gladness of the righteous is sustained in trial and the gladness of the unbeliever is "taken away" in trial, and the level of the trial has very little to do with it. Moab mourns, and Isaiah mourns with them, hearing, as it were, a harp sounding out a funeral dirge for an entire nation. They mourn because their land has been destroyed. In the presence of God there is fullness of joy (Psalms 21:6). But Moab has rejected the presence of God, so their "gladness is taken away."

16:12
And it shall come to pass, when it is seen that Moab is weary on the high place, that he will come to his sanctuary to pray; but he will not prevail.

When Moab's defenses fail, when his crops fail, when inescapable suffering appears imminent, Moab turns to his god – "he will come to his sanctuary to pray." It is hardly surprising. When men and women come to the realization that they are hopelessly incapable of rescuing themselves from their plight, even irreligious people tend to pray. Sadly, but again, not surprisingly, "he will not prevail." His prayers will not help him. Man-made gods can do nothing that their makers and followers cannot do. If Moab is helpless to overcome the judgment against him, his god cannot help him either. There is only one God that can do more than His believers can do. Nebuchadnezzar had this realization made plain when he watched three boys walk around uninjured in a burning fiery furnace. Seeing that their God could do things that the boys could not, Nebuchadnezzar said, "There is no other God who can deliver like this" (Daniel 3:29). The God who made heaven and earth can deliver us from anything. Other gods may appear helpful for a time -- as long as troubles are not extraordinary. But when all hope is lost, when personal power is no longer enough, no other God "can deliver." On judgment day, (and here we see that Moab's day of judgment will be no exception), no god can deliver except the One who created the world and died on the cross and came back to life again. Moab prays, "but he will not prevail." His prayers fail because he prays to the wrong god. He prays to a god that is not God. In contrast, those who pray to their Creator have this promise, "If My people who are called by My name will humble themselves, and pray and seek My face, and turn from their wicked ways, then I will hear from heaven, and will forgive their sin and heal their land" (II Chronicles 7:14).

16:13-14

This is the word which the LORD has spoken concerning Moab since that time. But now the LORD has spoken, saying, "Within three years, as the years of a hired man, the glory of Moab will be despised with all that great multitude, and the remnant will be very small and feeble."

God pronounces judgment on Moab, but once again, as He does so often, He gives them time (three years) before the judgment will fall. He gives even the most hardened rebel time to repent. The patience of the Lord "gives people time to be saved" (II Peter 3:15 NLT). Unlike Babylon, a remnant of Moab will survive, at least for a time, but "the remnant will be very small and feeble." The "glory" of their nation will "be despised" and the "great multitude" of their populous nation will disappear. The glory of man is a fleeting thing. I Peter 1:24 reminds us that "All flesh is as grass, and all the glory of man as the flower of the grass. The grass withers, and its flower falls away." Seeing that the state of our well-being on earth is completely in the hands of the eternal God, let us hold loosely the present comforts and successes that we are allowed to enjoy, knowing that it is God's grace and not our innate talents that has allowed us these enjoyments. If we fail to give Him glory, He can remove our glory at any moment, just as He does here with unrighteous Moab. "Thus says the LORD: 'Let not the wise man glory in his wisdom, let not the mighty man glory in his might, nor let the rich man glory in his riches; but let him who glories glory in this, that he understands and knows Me, that I am the LORD, exercising lovingkindness, judgment, and righteousness in the earth. For in these I delight,' says the LORD" (Jeremiah 9:23-24).

Isaiah 17

17:1-3
The burden against Damascus. "Behold Damascus will cease from being a city, and it will be a ruinous heap. The cities of Aroer are forsaken; they will be for flocks which lie down, and no one will make them afraid. The fortress also will cease from Ephraim, the kingdom from Damascus, and the remnant of Syria; they will be as the glory of the children of Israel," says the LORD of hosts.

In quick succession, the Lord has pronounced judgment on Babylon (chapter 13), Assyria, Philistia (chapter 14), and Moab (chapter 15 and 16). Now, He declares His judgment on wicked Damascus and the nation of Syria, here called "the cities of Aroer." We are not surprised by the judgment against them. Damascus was a city famous for its idolatry and they had recently invaded Judah with the intent of destroying the kingdom of God's people there. What is striking, however, is the inclusion of Israel in the judgment on Syria. Israel had joined Syria in an unholy union (II Kings 16:5) and helped Syria attack their brothers in Judah. Here, we see that those who partner with evil men in their business will also join with them in their

ISAIAH 17

judgment. "The fortress also will cease from Ephraim." At one time, God was the fortress of Israel. Psalms 31:3 says, "For You are my rock and my fortress; therefore, for Your name's sake, lead me and guide me." Israel abandoned God as their fortress, however, and in doing so they found themselves without protection when judgment drew near. The warning is loud and clear. Israel became allies with an unholy partner, and the result was an unenviable inclusion in their judgment. "Do not be deceived: 'Bad company ruins good morals'" (1 Corinthians 15:33 ESV). Choosing our friends poorly, partnering with evil people, ruins morals, ruins reputations, and ruins nations as Israel sadly demonstrates here.

17:4-6
"In that day it shall come to pass that the glory of Jacob will wane, and the fatness of his flesh grow lean. Yet gleaning grapes will be left in it, like the shaking of an olive tree, two or three olives at the top of the uppermost bough, four or five in its most fruitful branches," says the LORD God of Israel.

It is a joy to good parents to leave a legacy behind for their children. The thought of leaving an inheritance that will bless our descendants brings joy to our soul. We are comforted by the thought that our children will be better off than we were. These comforts, however, are denied the people of Israel. "The glory of Jacob will wane," the successes and victories of the parents will not be passed on to their children. "The fatness of his flesh grow lean," their children will be worse off than their parents. Their glory as a nation will fade and their numbers will dwindle -- an entire harvest from the family tree will be reduced to a handful of olives. Such is the pitiful outcome of a generation that turns its back on God. Proverbs 13:22 says, "A good man leaves an inheritance to his children's children, but the wealth of the sinner is stored up for the righteous." Here, we see that when Israel no longer had godly men to pass on a heritage of faithfulness to their children, their children suffered the consequences just as Proverbs 3:35 foresees: "the wise shall inherit glory, but shame shall be the legacy of fools." Foolishly, Israel has rejected the Lord and so denied themselves the blessings that God prepares for those who obey Him. "The righteous shall inherit the land, and dwell in it forever" (Psalms 37:29), but "evildoers shall be cut off" (Psalms 37:9) – as Israel sadly demonstrates here.

17:7-8
In that day a man will look to his Maker, and his eyes will have respect for the Holy One of Israel. He will not look to the altars, the work of his hands; he will not respect what his fingers have made, nor the wooden images nor the incense altars.

The outlook for a people who have rejected God is very bleak. The previous 4 chapters all demonstrate this with disquieting clarity. The farther we are from God, the darker our future becomes. But no matter how bleak that future appears, all a man must do to change his destiny is to turn his back on sin and other gods and "look to his Maker." Here, that blessed change of heart that transforms eternal destinies is anticipated: one day "a man will look to his Maker." One day, men from every nation will look to their Maker and seek His favor and submit to His Lordship. They will revere "the Holy One of Israel," and they will despise wooden idols and acts of worship that elevate created things over the Creator. One day, "at the name of Jesus every knee will bow, in heaven and on earth and under the earth" (Philippians 2:10 NLT). One day, all men will come to their senses and acknowledge that God reigns, that He is holy, and that all other gods are unworthy of respect. Sadly, for many people, this day of realization will come with agonizing remorse on judgment day. But not everyone will wait until it is too late to declare their love and allegiance for the Lord. God's call continues to ring out across the nations summoning the world's people to Himself. He speaks through missionaries and preachers, through His written word and through the spoken testimonies of His saints, He speaks through dreams and visions, and through our God-directed conscience all for the purpose of compelling mankind to "look to his Maker." And, blessedly, many do just that. In Isaiah 45:22, God sends out the invitation: "Look to Me, and be saved, all you ends of the earth! For I am God, and there is no other." And it remains man's greatest moment of insight when he responds by saying, "Therefore I will look to the LORD; I will wait for the God of my salvation; my God will hear me" (Micah 7:7).

17:9-11
In that day his strong cities will be as a forsaken bough and an uppermost branch, which they left because of the children of Israel; and there will be desolation. Because you have forgotten the God of your salvation, and have not been mindful of the Rock of your stronghold, therefore you will plant pleasant plants and set out foreign seedlings; in the day you will make your plant to grow, and in the morning you will make your seed

to flourish; but the harvest will be a heap of ruins in the day of grief and desperate sorrow.

Forgetting God will make the fruit of all our labors come to nothing. Our life's work will be reduced to "a heap of ruins in the day of grief and desperate sorrow." We must see that this prophecy toward the children of Israel is applicable to everyone – everyone! Let no one be deceived by temporary successes – no matter how grand those successes may be. Building a financial empire, reigning over a multinational empire, or holding popular sway over crowds does not, in any way, protect anyone from all of their labors turning into "a heap of ruins" and a day of "grief and desperate sorrow" if they leave God out of their purposes. Psalms 68:19 says, "Blessed be the Lord, Who daily loads us with benefits, the God of our salvation!" How can we forget the God of our salvation? If there were several options available that were capable of providing salvation from sin and hell, perhaps God's salvation plan could be overlooked. But in Isaiah 43:11 God gives us this reminder: "I, even I, am the LORD, and besides Me there is no savior." Since God alone provides salvation, forgetting Him as Israel does here, will certainly be catastrophic. Psalms 9:17 says, "The wicked shall be turned into hell, and all the nations that forget God." Psalms 50:22 highlights the matter further: "Now consider this, you who forget God, lest I tear you in pieces, and there be none to deliver." May our Lord be our constant focus, may our family conversations constantly be centered on His purposes and His many kindnesses to us, so that there is no way that our family could forget our God even for a moment. May this complaint against Israel, that they have forgotten their Rock, the God of their salvation, never be possible for us. Instead, let us join the cry of Psalms 95:1 "Oh come, let us sing to the LORD! Let us shout joyfully to the Rock of our salvation." Let us sing to our Lord. Let us praise Him in public and in private and in our family devotions. We must not forget all that He has done for us! Furthermore, let us not be anxious when trials come, because "He only is my rock and my salvation; He is my defense; I shall not be greatly moved" (Psalms 62:2). Let us ever remind ourselves and remind one another that our God is a Rock, our God is the God of our salvation. We can trust Him to deliver us from our current trouble. Let us keep our Lord, our Rock of salvation foremost in our thoughts, foremost in our conversations, foremost in our plans and intentions, for He is worthy of our devotion and because forgetting Him dooms the fruit of our life's work to nothing more that "a heap of ruins," and cause us to suffer the "grief and desperate sorrow" of those who must mourn over a life poorly spent.

17:12-14
Woe to the multitude of many people who make a noise like the roar of the seas, and to the rushing of nations that make a rushing like the rushing of mighty waters! The nations will rush like the rushing of many waters; but God will rebuke them and they will flee far away and be chased like the chaff of the mountains before the wind, like a rolling thing before the whirlwind. Then behold, at eventide, trouble! And before the morning, he is no more. This is the portion of those who plunder us, and the lot of those who rob us.

Like an angry mob rushes through the streets of the city pillaging and destroying, so the nations of the world rush around the earth, making noise, shouting protests, and defying God's authority. The mob is large, "the multitude of many people" join together in their loud demonstration against their Creator. God will put up with their defiance for a time, but Psalms 65:7 says that soon enough He will "still the noise of the seas, the noise of their waves, and the tumult of the peoples." "As the horse rushes into the battle" (Jeremiah 8:6), so the unbelievers of the world will rush to overthrow God's sovereignty and plunder His people. But the world's rebellion will be quelled without effort. "God will rebuke them," and the thunder of His rebuke will be all that is required to make sinners "flee far away" as if they were "chaff of the mountains before the wind." Like a whirlwind blows paper away, so will the breath of God's rebuke drive away His enemies and the enemies of His people. God will quiet the world's boisterous rebellion simply and suddenly. Psalms 46:6 says, "The nations raged, the kingdoms were moved; He uttered His voice, the earth melted." With such certain doom spelled out against those who imagine to rebel against God, who in their right mind would refuse to submit to Him? Psalms 2:1 asks, "Why do the nations rage, and the people plot a vain thing?" It is vanity to rebel against God's lordship. All who attempt it will suffer the same fate as those who rush to fight against the will of God in our verses here. In Revelation 19, armies of sinners join Satan in a war against God and lose. In Revelation 20, an army of sinners joins Satan in a war against God and lose again. And these in Isaiah 17 that fight against God and His people will naturally suffer the same fate. There is no hope for those who would fight against Omnipotence.

Isaiah 18

18:1-3
Woe to the land shadowed with buzzing wings, which is beyond the rivers of Ethiopia, which sends ambassadors by sea, even in vessels of reed on the waters, saying, "Go, swift messengers, to a nation tall and smooth of skin, to a people terrible from their beginning onward, a nation powerful and treading down, whose land the rivers divide." All inhabitants of the world and dwellers on the earth: when he lifts up a banner on the mountains, you see it; and when he blows a trumpet, you hear it.

After reading multiple authors from multiple eras, it remains difficult to interpret with certainty the meaning behind this chapter. Even the first word is controversial, many saying that the "woe" that is used in the NKJV here should be "Ah," or "Ho!" because it is more of a call to listen than it is a call for condemnation. Indeed, the nation does not seem to be condemned here, merely discussed. Adding to the mystery, the nation being addressed is not certain. I am prone to agree with those who say that Isaiah's words are aimed at Ethiopia, although the description clearly says it is "beyond the rivers of Ethiopia," making even that claim uncertain. Perhaps the passage is an allusion to the events surrounding II Kings 19 when the king of Ethiopia came up to fight against the Assyrian army that was besieging Jerusalem, providing a temporary reprieve from the Assyrian attack. Isaiah's listeners may have had an easier time understanding him because "all inhabitants of the world and dwellers on the earth" could "see it" and "hear it" – whatever Isaiah was talking about.

18:4-6
For so the LORD said to me, "I will take My rest, and I will look from My dwelling place like clear heat in sunshine, like a cloud of dew in the heat of harvest." For before the harvest, when the bud is perfect and the sour grape is ripening in the flower, He will both cut off the sprigs with pruning hooks and take away and cut down the branches. They will be left together for the mountain birds of prey and for the beasts of the earth; the birds of prey will summer on them, and all the beasts of the earth will winter on them.

Some of this chapter may be mysterious, but verse 4 gives us a very pleasant picture of our Lord. Though the peoples of the world are in a riotous tumult against Him and against His people (17:12), yet the Lord is at perfect peace as the world rages below Him. He takes His "rest" in His "dwelling place," untroubled by the matters that trouble others. As if sitting on His porch on a cool sunny day, so the Lord finds enjoyment in His dwelling place. Like the pleasant feeling of sunshine on your face on a bright cool day, like the refreshing sprinkle of dew-like raindrops on a warm afternoon, so God dwells among His people, comfortable and at peace. And when the Lord enjoys the peace of His dwelling place, there is great joy for His people. "For the LORD has chosen Zion; He has desired it for His dwelling place: 'This is My resting place forever; here I will dwell, for I have desired it. I will abundantly bless her provision; I will satisfy her poor with bread. I will also clothe her priests with salvation, and her saints shall shout aloud for joy'" (Psalms 132:13-16). God's enemies rage, His people appear to be in danger, but God will take care of His people and rid them of their enemies without even needing to break a sweat. He will "cut down the branches" of those who rail against Him. With His pruning hooks He will cut off the buds and blossoms of His enemies – cut them off in their prime – and their destruction will provide a feast for the birds and beasts of the earth. This 3-verse stanza almost certainly foretells the destruction of Assyria, but God's people find good cause to take joy in these words in any age. The mayhem of the world does not cause God unrest. He enjoys His rest in His dwelling place, and blessedly, that resting place is with us. And when God is at rest in us, we too can be at rest.

18:7
In that time a present will be brought to the Lord of hosts from a people tall and smooth of skin, and from a people terrible from their beginning onward, a nation powerful and treading down, whose land the rivers divide -- to the place of the name of the Lord of hosts, to Mount Zion.

People are drawn to bring presents to the Lord of hosts. The soul of man is created with spiritual insight teaching us that it is proper to give honor to whom honor is due (Romans 13:7). The closer we are to God -- the more powerfully His Spirit works and speaks within us -- the greater this inner urging calls out to us to bring presents to our Creator. Psalms 76:11 says, "Let all who are around Him bring presents to Him who ought to be feared." But this cry in our soul to bring gifts to God is not just ringing out in so-called Christian nations, it is heard by everyone in every nation, even among those who would call themselves unbelievers. Psalms 68:18 says that God has "received gifts among men, even from the rebellious." Everywhere, the great and small on earth are drawn to bring gifts to God. Psalms 68:29 says, "Because of Your temple at Jerusalem, kings will bring presents to You." Psalms 72:10 says, "The kings of Tarshish and of the isles will bring presents; the kings of Sheba and Seba will offer gifts." Here, we see that "a people tall and smooth of skin," a people "terrible from their beginning onward," a nation that is "powerful and treading down" will bring a present to the Lord of hosts.

This heart of man to bring presents to God will often move us to give presents to both our Lord and to those who serve Him. I suspect that this verse is specifically talking about Ethiopia bringing gifts to God and to Hezekiah, His servant, after God's death angel executed 185,000 Assyrian soldiers and miraculously delivered Judah from Sennacherib's army. II Chronicles 32:22-23 says, "Thus the LORD saved Hezekiah and the inhabitants of Jerusalem from the hand of Sennacherib the king of Assyria, and from the hand of all others, and guided them on every side. And many brought gifts to the LORD at Jerusalem, and presents to Hezekiah king of Judah, so that he was exalted in the sight of all nations thereafter." Multiple scriptures repeatedly demonstrate this Spirit-directed heart of men to give presents, not only to God, but to those who are close to Him. The Egyptians are moved to give presents to the Israelites as they leave Egypt (Exodus

12:35-36). The Queen of Sheba brings Solomon gifts in I Kings 10:10. And the woman of Shunem gives gifts to Elisha in II Kings 4.

As our family serves the Lord faithfully as missionaries, pastors, and servants of His church, let us acknowledge this tendency of God's people to generously pour out kindness on God's servants. Let us always understand that these gifts given to us arise from the hearts of godly people to give honor to God. The gifts are to God, and it is only because we faithfully serve our Lord, that these gifts pass through our hands on their way to Him. Let us hold these gifts loosely in our hands, humbly acknowledging that they honor our Lord, not us. Let us always be ready to decline these gifts as Abram does with Sodom's gifts in Genesis 14:22-23, as Elisha does with Naaman's gifts in II Kings 5:16, and as Daniel does with Belshazzar's gifts in Daniel 5:17. Let us take great care that gifts to us do not become a hindrance to the gospel as the gifts to Gideon in Judges 8:22-27. Let us not think highly of ourselves when God's people give to us because they see God in us. Let us rather humbly treasure the fact that God is with us and that we are blessed to be His servants as Mary does with the gifts from the wise men and the affirmations of the shepherds (Luke 2:19). We must not seek gifts (Philippians 4:17), but when God's people entrust their gifts to us, we must strive to see that those gifts bring glory to their Lord and our Lord – the love of their life, and the love of ours. God's people are generous people; and they are compelled by their love for God to follow His example and give to His children. Jesus said, "it is more blessed to give than to receive" (Acts 20:35). If, then, we are called upon to receive from the generosity of God's people, let us be on our guard. Let us be humble, grateful, and diligent to see to it that all good things that befall us lead to the encouragement of God's people and the furtherance of God's kingdom.

Isaiah 19

19:1
The burden against Egypt. Behold, the LORD rides on a swift cloud, and will come into Egypt; the idols of Egypt will totter at His presence, and the heart of Egypt will melt in its midst.

Unlike idols which must be carried everywhere they go, the Lord our God "rides on a swift cloud." He goes wherever He wishes, and He arrives suddenly, often when He is not expected. His arrival brings joy to His children and praises to their lips. Psalms 68:4 (NLT) calls on us to "Sing praises to God and to his name! Sing loud praises to him who rides the clouds. His name is the LORD – rejoice in his presence!" Those who worship Him will rejoice when our Lord flies to us on the clouds. There are many, however, who are not moved to joy when the Lord appears. "The idols of Egypt will totter at His presence, and the heart of Egypt will melt in its midst." When God draws near, idols totter. "When the Philistines took the ark of God, they brought it into the temple of Dagon and set it by Dagon. And when the people of Ashdod arose early in the morning, there was Dagon, fallen on its face to the earth before the ark of the LORD. So they took Dagon and set it in its place again. And when they arose early the next morning, there was Dagon, fallen on its face to the ground before the ark of the Lord. The head of Dagon and both the palms of its hands were broken off on the threshold; only Dagon's torso was left of it" (I Samuel 5:2-4). Like Dagon, Egypt's idols will totter and fall before the unmatchable glory and power of the Lord of hosts. And following the example of their idols, the heart of Egypt's people will melt. "Their soul melts because of trouble" (Psalms 107:26). When God draws near the hearts and souls of men melt, and their nation melts with them. "The mountains melt like wax at the presence of the LORD, at the presence of the Lord of the whole earth" (Psalms 97:5). It is God's good pleasure to grant a multitude of blessings even on those who rebel against Him. He provides sunshine and rain for both the evil and the good (Matthew 5:45). In years of plenty, when troubles are few and blessings abound, unbelievers are happy to credit their idols with their good fortune and pat themselves on the back for their successes. Ultimately, however, there will come a day when God will draw near. And on that day, idols totter, men melt, false gods are exposed as imposters, and the successes of men prove hollow. Such is the prophesied fate of Egypt here.

19:2-4

"I will set Egyptians against Egyptians; everyone will fight against his brother, and everyone against his neighbor, city against city, kingdom against kingdom. The spirit of Egypt will fail in its midst; I will destroy their counsel, and they will consult the idols and the charmers, the mediums and the sorcerers. And the Egyptians I will give into the hand of a cruel master, and a fierce king will rule over them," says the Lord, the LORD of hosts.

Through the pen of Isaiah, the Lord foretells the fall of Egypt that would soon come as a result of civil wars that God would incite within their borders. It will not be foreign invasion, but brothers fighting against brothers that will cause "the spirit of Egypt" to "fail in its midst." Brotherly love is a fruit of the Spirit. When God draws near to His people in love, His people are spontaneously infused with unity and a deep love for one another. I John 4:12 says that "if we love one another, God abides in us." And when God abides in us, we will be moved to love one another, for we are "taught by God to love one another" (I Thessalonians 4:9). But when God leaves us, when sin and unbelief have separated us from the Lord our God, the call for unity that resonates from His Spirit is replaced by a call to war against our fellow man. Personal lusts lead to interpersonal war (James 4:1), and without the Spirit of God within us quelling those evil passions "everyone will fight against his brother." In addition to civil war, Egypt will be destroyed from within when the Lord moves to "destroy their counsel." "Where there is no counsel, the people fall" (Proverbs 11:14), and so Egypt will fall when God removes their wise counsellors and the people consult idols and witches and sorcerers instead. "Blessed is the man who walks not in the counsel of the ungodly" (Psalms 1:1), and cursed is the man who seeks ungodly counsel as Egypt does here. They will "fall by their own counsels" (Psalms 5:10), their choice of wicked counsel will be their undoing.

May this judgment on Egypt cause us all to be on our guard. We must study God's Word and rush to obey Him. The home of evil counsellors is right next door to the house of simple disobedience. If our neighbors see that we have "despised the counsel of the Most High (Psalms 107:11), they will rush to take His place. And the result of heeding the advice of evil counsellors is devastating. God will give the people of Egypt "into the hand of a cruel master, and a fierce king will rule over them." Failure to submit to God will never lead to freedom. It will always lead to the pain of subservience to a "cruel master."

19:5-7

The waters will fail from the sea, and the river will be wasted and dried up. The rivers will turn foul; the brooks of defense will be emptied and dried up; the reeds and rushes will wither. The papyrus reeds by the River, by the mouth of the River, and everything sown by the River, will wither, be driven away, and be no more.

When we are walking with our Lord, He uses our weaknesses for His great purposes. His immeasurable strengths are made perfect in our weakness (II Corinthians 12:9). But apart from Him, if we deny Him the throne of our lives, the best things we have in life become useless, our finest qualities become tainted and trivial, and our personal strengths are all "emptied and dried up" when measured by heaven's standards. Here, we see that the power of Egypt, the center of its strength and resource, the Nile River, "will turn foul" when God's hand of blessing is removed from their nation. "Everything sown by the River," everything that the nation gained by the Nile, every blessing provided by the Nile will be "driven away, and be no more." So will all natural gifts and abilities that are not used for our Savior's purposes. Great gifts are reduced to dross when they are not used for God's glory, and they will soon be taken away from us and given to others as illustrated by the story of the lazy servant in Matthew 25 if we refuse to use all our gifts and resources for God's glory. Those who will not use their resources to do God's will are doomed to see their strength dried up, their glory stripped away, and the fruit of their life's work wither away. In contrast, those who delight in the law of the Lord, those who meditate on His words day and night and devote themselves to obeying what that word says will "be like a tree planted by the rivers of water, that brings forth its fruit in its season, whose leaf also shall not wither; and whatever he does shall prosper" (Psalms 1:3).

19:8-10
The fishermen also will mourn; all those will lament who cast hooks into the River, and they will languish who spread nets on the waters. Moreover those who work in fine flax and those who weave fine fabric will be ashamed; and its foundations will be broken. All who make wages will be troubled of soul.

With the loss of the Nile, the nation's fishermen "will mourn." Their livelihood has dried up and no matter how industrious they are, they catch nothing and "lament" the loss of their profession and productivity. Their hopelessness will spread to the entire nation's labor force, "all who make wages will be troubled of soul." The backbone of a nation's strength is their working class, and when the people lose their vision to work, the nation's "foundations will be broken" and their hope for a prosperous future is lost. Haggai 2:4 says, "'be strong, Zerubbabel,' says the LORD; 'and be strong, Joshua, son of Jehozadak, the high priest; and be strong, all you people of the land,' says the LORD, 'and work; for I am with you,' says the LORD of hosts." When God is with us, He inspires us to work. His work inspires us to work. The promises of His blessings inspire us to work. The opportunity to serve His people and His purposes inspires us to work. Basking in the presence of God, all work becomes incredibly significant, and God's people are inspired to expend all possible energy and effort to accomplish every task, big and small in a manner that will glorify our Maker. "Whatever your hand finds to do, do it with your might" (Ecclesiastes 9:10). In the absence of God's presence, in the absence of hope that He will bless the outcome of our efforts, however, men lose their drive to work. Such is the case for Egypt as foretold here. God will revoke His blessings on their land, their idolatry will distance themselves from their Maker, and the result will be "all who make wages will be troubled of soul."

19:11-15
Surely the princes of Zoan are fools; Pharaoh's wise counselors give foolish counsel. How do you say to Pharaoh, "I am the son of the wise,

the son of ancient kings?" Where are they? Where are your wise men? Let them tell you now, and let them know what the LORD of hosts has purposed against Egypt. The princes of Zoan have become fools; the princes of Noph are deceived; they have also deluded Egypt, those who are the mainstay of its tribes. The LORD has mingled a perverse spirit in her midst; and they have caused Egypt to err in all her work, as a drunken man staggers in his vomit. Neither will there be any work for Egypt, which the head or tail, palm branch or bulrush, may do.

The judgments of the Lord on Egypt continue to devastate every facet of life there. Their religion will fail them (verse 1). Civil war will shatter their security (verse 2). The Nile River will dry up (verse 5), and their economy will collapse (verse 10). And now, while seemingly at their lowest, Pharaoh's counselors will fail him as well. They are unable to assess God's purposes for Egypt and cannot prescribe a solution for the total ruin that the nation faces. We have a perfect prescription provided to us in scripture when we lack the wisdom needed to overcome powerful enemies and overwhelming challenges. James 1:5 says, "If any of you lacks wisdom, let him ask of God, who gives to all liberally and without reproach, and it will be given to him." Without a relationship with God, however, this simple means of gaining wisdom is denied Pharaoh's counselors and they are left without understanding. Sadly, as is too often the case, however, the counselors simply replace wisdom with deceit. Bereft of wisdom, they turn to deception to maintain their place of honor in the eyes of their nation. Rather than seek God's direction, they have "deluded Egypt." They have duped the people into thinking that recovery is possible without repentance. Success is possible without sinlessness. And good outcomes are possible without God. This is a lie. A common lie, a (nearly) timeless lie, but it is a lie that will destroy Egypt and destroy all in our day who will be "deluded" by it.

19:16-17
In that day Egypt will be like women, and will be afraid and fear because of the waving of the hand of the LORD of hosts, which He waves over it. And the land of Judah will be a terror to Egypt; everyone who makes mention of it will be afraid in himself, because of the counsel of the LORD of hosts which He has determined against it.

In Isaiah's day, women were defenseless. They were not taught to use weapons, they were not given opportunities in education or business. Their possessions were in the name of their husbands or fathers. Without a male protector, they were extremely vulnerable. In this prophecy against Egypt,

Isaiah says that the entire nation will become defenseless, vulnerable, and afraid, like a woman with no one to protect her. Interestingly, the Lord's judgments on Egypt will move them to fear His people. Egypt's population, military, and economy dwarfed Judah's. And yet, when the Lord waved His hand of judgment on them, "the land of Judah will be a terror to Egypt." In Joshua 2:9 Rahab tells the Lord's spies, "the terror of you has fallen on us...all the inhabitants of the land are fainthearted because of you." Now, just as God's hand on Israel caused Jericho to fear His people, so here, the absence of God's blessings on Egypt will cause them to fear His people just the same. God often causes the people of the world to fear His people, not just to protect us, but to draw to Himself those who are far off. Esther 8:17 says, "in every province and city, wherever the king's command and decree came, the Jews had joy and gladness, a feast and a holiday. Then many of the people of the land became Jews, because fear of the Jews fell upon them." May our family be so inextricably bound to God's purposes, may our devotion to our Lord be so obvious, that those who love God will love us, and that even when we are weaker than anyone we know, the hands of God are so visibly cupped around us that those who fear our Father will be moved to fear His presence in us as well.

19:18
In that day five cities in the land of Egypt will speak the language of Canaan and swear by the LORD of hosts; one will be called the City of Destruction.

Opinions vary on the location of the "City of Destruction," but the picture is clearer when Isaiah speaks of five cities in the land of Egypt speaking the language of Canaan and swearing loyalty to the Lord of hosts. The movement within Egypt to seek God's blessings will be so widespread that the majority of 5 entire cities will proclaim their allegiance to God. Their focus on the God of Israel will move them to learn the language of the people of Israel. After 17 verses describing God's judgments against Egypt, we rejoice to see that some of Egypt's people will respond as God intends. In Revelation 3:19 the Lord says, "As many as I love, I rebuke and chasten. Therefore be zealous and repent." God punishes, but He binds up and heals those who seek His forgiveness. "Come, and let us return to the LORD; for He has torn, but He will heal us; He has stricken, but He will bind us up" (Hosea 6:1). Here, we see Egypt respond well to God's chastening. The men of Revelation 16:9 blasphemed God more and more when He punished their sins. Egypt, however, will respond much better. Rather than curse God they will swear to serve Him, rather than speak evil of Him, they will learn to speak the language of His word.

19:19-20
In that day there will be an altar to the LORD in the midst of the land of Egypt, and a pillar to the LORD at its border. And it will be for a sign and for a witness to the LORD of hosts in the land of Egypt; for they will cry to the LORD because of the oppressors, and He will send them a Savior and a Mighty One, and He will deliver them.

In rapid succession, God has pronounced judgment on Babylon (chapter 13), Assyria and Philistia (chapter 14), Moab (chapter 15 and 16), Syria and Israel (chapter 17), and mentions Ethiopia in chapter 18. All peoples are under God's authority and subject to God's judgment. Their (temporary) devotion to other gods provides them with absolutely no protection from God's ultimate punishment for sin. But here, after describing God's judgment on Egypt, we are reminded that although all nations of the world are subject to God's punishment, they are also *all* blessed with the opportunity to repent and be reconciled with their Maker! Peter declares in Acts 10:35, "in every nation whoever fears Him and works righteousness is accepted by Him." And here we see that one day, Egypt will fear the Lord and work righteousness, and their repentance will make them accepted by the Lord and He will deliver them. Egypt, the land full of idolatry and pagan ways, will one day "build an altar to the LORD in the midst of Egypt, and a pillar to the LORD at its border." They will trust in God and cry out to Him to deliver them, and He will hear their cry. Egypt will be granted "a Savior." The Mighty One will "deliver them." Perhaps this prophecy was partially fulfilled when Egypt was delivered from various assailants over time, but we cannot fail to acknowledge that Jesus is the Savior and Mighty One who will rescue Egypt. One day, many in Egypt will turn to the Lord. They will build an altar and worship Him. They will set up a pillar and exalt Him, they will see their need and cry out to Him. And the Lord will see their hearts from heaven, and He will send them Jesus, their Savior and our Savior. Just as Paul said in Romans 9:25, "Those who were not my people I will call 'my people,' and her who was not beloved I will call 'beloved.'" Though Egypt had long been idol worshippers and enemies of God's people, yet, when they repent, God forgives and rescues and lives among them, so that what was once promised to Israel is extended to all people who trust in Him: "The Lord your God is in your midst, a mighty one who will save; he will rejoice over you with gladness; he will quiet you by his love; he will exult over you with loud singing" (Zephaniah 3:17 ESV).

19:21
Then the LORD will be known to Egypt, and the Egyptians will know the LORD in that day, and will make sacrifice and offering; yes, they will make a vow to the LORD and perform it.

What a remarkable prophecy is presented here! One day Egypt will turn to God. They will know God, vow to serve Him, and present their offerings before Him. "Blessed is the nation whose God is the LORD" (Psalms 33:12), and one day, Egypt will be a very blessed nation. Psalms 46:10 says, "Be still, and know that I am God. I will be exalted among the nations, I will be exalted in the earth!" One day, Egypt will know God, and God will be exalted among this nation that had rejected Him for thousands of years. Eternal life is granted those who know God (John 17:3), and this gift of gifts will be granted Egypt when they repent and turn to the Lord. Paul says that there is nothing better than knowing God (Philippians 3:8) -- knowing our Maker inspires us to freely give all we have for His purposes, and to sacrifice all we have for His glory. The Egyptian believers will feel Paul's same emotion as they come to know the Lord. They will rush to make sacrifices and offerings, they will "make vows to the Lord and fulfill them" (HCS). Remarkable. Egypt will know God and serve Him. If Egypt can be saved, we are encouraged with the suddenly brighter prospects of all the other nations of the earth, remembering that it is the Lord's intention that "the earth will be filled with the knowledge of the glory of the LORD, as the waters cover the sea" (Habakkuk 2:14).

19:22
And the LORD will strike Egypt, He will strike and heal it; they will return to the LORD, and He will be entreated by them and heal them.

God strikes, and God heals. Psalms 141:5 says, "Let the righteous strike me; it shall be a kindness." When God strikes, it is indeed, a great kindness, causing the unrepentant to serve as deterrents to those who would think to follow their evil example, and allowing the righteous to come to their senses and return to their loving Lord. God strikes sinners, but He heals the wounded when they repent and regret their former ways. Our Lord "heals the brokenhearted and binds up their wounds" (Psalms 147:3). Our Lord forgives all our iniquities and heals all our diseases (Psalms 103:3). One day, Egypt will pray the sinner's prayer of Psalms 41:4 and say, "LORD, be merciful to me; heal my soul, for I have sinned against You." And when they do, mercy and healing will be granted Egypt, just as is granted all who come to God in reverence and repentance.

ISAIAH 19

19:23-25
In that day there will be a highway from Egypt to Assyria, and the Assyrian will come into Egypt and the Egyptian into Assyria, and the Egyptians will serve with the Assyrians. In that day Israel will be one of three with Egypt and Assyria – a blessing in the midst of the land, whom the LORD of hosts shall bless, saying, "Blessed is Egypt My people, and Assyria the work of My hands, and Israel My inheritance."

We have here yet another remarkable passage. Egypt, Assyria, and Israel will all be united, knit together in close union by their mutual submission and service to their Creator. "The Egyptians will serve with the Assyrians." And Israel will be the "blessing" in their midst, for it was through Israel that the word of God came to man, and it was through Israel that Christ the Redeemer came to bless the world with the means for salvation. Egypt and Assyria had been bitter enemies. But their warring will cease when they are united in Christian love. Those who find peace with God will find instant cause to find peace with their fellow man. Those who love God will be innately moved to love others who love Him too. Egypt once enslaved Israel, Assyria invaded Israel, but these past offenses will be forgotten and forgiven as these three nations, once so, so different, become united by their common love for their Savior and Creator. Egypt, Assyria, and Israel allied in godly service. After reading the previous 22 books of the Bible, who could have imagined such a possibility? The evil acts and blasphemous taunts of the Egyptians and Assyrians are well documented repeatedly in scripture. We are reminded here, however, that it is not God's good pleasure to destroy the people He has made. "God did not send His Son into the world to condemn the world, but that the world through Him might be saved" (John 3:17). Assyria, Egypt, and Israel will be allied, unified, and sanctified in serving the Lord together. They will serve the Lord together, and they will be blessed by the Lord together. We are right to be re-inspired to preach to and pray for even the most incorrigible people we know. Look at the possibilities that are exemplified before us – warring, hateful, pagan, murderous blasphemers are transformed by the blessings of God's grace into a unified people who serve Him and honor Him. We have no cause to doubt that God can transform men and nations in the same way today.

Isaiah 20

20:1-4
In the year that Tartan came to Ashdod, when Sargon the king of Assyria sent him, and he fought against Ashdod and took it, at the same time the LORD spoke by Isaiah the son of Amoz, saying, "Go, and remove the sackcloth from your body, and take your sandals off your feet." And he did so, walking naked and barefoot. Then the LORD said, "Just as My servant Isaiah has walked naked and barefoot three years for a sign and a wonder against Egypt and Ethiopia, so shall the king of Assyria lead away the Egyptians as prisoners and the Ethiopians as captives, young and old, naked and barefoot, with their buttocks uncovered, to the shame of Egypt."

    In 711 BC, Sargon's armies took Ashdod, one of the five chief cities of the Philistines. Fearing that the Assyrians would soon come after them, many in Judah set their hope on Egypt and Ethiopia to defeat the terribly cruel and powerful forces of Assyria. God would not have His people trust in feeble powers that could not save, so He foretells for His people the imminent destruction of Egypt and Ethiopia to deter them from unwisely depending

ISAIAH 20

on a doomed ally. To highlight the prophecy, as a constant picture of the future, God commands Isaiah to walk "naked and barefoot" for three years. It is less probable that Isaiah was totally nude, but rather for three years he walked about fulfilling his prophet's duties dressed only in the barest of modest attire, shedding the usual outer garments customary for honored men of his high station. God's people were wise to heed His warning through Isaiah. Assyria went on to destroy the armies of Egypt and Ethiopia. Coffman's commentary says that Egyptian records picture the captives "with their buttocks uncovered" being led away to captivity in Assyria. The glory of Egypt will be shamed by their humiliating defeat at the hands of Assyria. God's people are warned not to put their trust in people and nations that are helpless to provide any lasting benefit.

20:5-6
"Then they shall be afraid and ashamed of Ethiopia their expectation and Egypt their glory. And the inhabitant of this territory will say in that day, 'Surely such is our expectation, wherever we flee for help to be delivered from the king of Assyria; and how shall we escape?'"

The Egyptian-Ethiopian dynasty was the most powerful force the people of Judah knew. When that great army fell to Assyria, God's people asked, where can we go now? Where can we flee for safety now? What hope is there that we can "be delivered from the king of Assyria; and how shall we escape?" It is interesting that Sennacherib saw the same thing that God saw and unwittingly agrees with God when he says to Jerusalem's defenders in II Kings 18:21 -- "Now look! You are trusting in the staff of this broken reed, Egypt, on which if a man leans, it will go into his hand and pierce it. So is Pharaoh king of Egypt to all who trust in him." It is good for us to come to the end of our rope and find that God is our only hope. The result of this warning from Isaiah is a happy one. King Hezekiah finds no hope in trusting in Egypt, and goes directly to God for protection from the invading Assyrian army. In II Kings 19:15 he goes to the Lord and prays, "O LORD God of Israel, the One who dwells between the cherubim. You are God, You alone, of all the kingdoms of the earth. You have made heaven and earth." Then in verse 19 his prayer ends with, "Now therefore, O LORD our God, I pray, save us from his (Assyria's) hand, that all the kingdoms of the earth may know that You are the LORD God, You alone." Psalms 20:7 says that some people trust in horses, and some people trust in chariots (from Egypt perhaps), "but we trust in name of the Lord our God." And our "hope does not disappoint" (Romans 5:5).

Isaiah 21

21:1-2
The burden against the Wilderness of the Sea. As whirlwinds in the South pass through, so it comes from the desert, from a terrible land. A distressing vision is declared to me; the treacherous dealer deals treacherously, and the plunderer plunders. Go up, O Elam! Besiege, O Media! All its sighing I have made to cease.

Verse 9 tells us that this is a vision against Babylon. The vision is "distressing." It is distressing to see even the ungodly destroyed. Godly men mourn the loss of the world's people that are judged and destroyed because they refused to give God glory. God commands Media and Elam to besiege and plunder Babylon. The nation that had betrayed and plundered others will be betrayed and plundered by the Medes and the Persians in Daniel 5. In II Kings 20, the king of Babylon sends emissaries and presents to Hezekiah. It may have seemed that Babylon had kind intentions toward God's people. But this prophecy was to serve as a warning not to trust this nation that "deals treacherously." Judah must not trust Babylon in their fight against Assyria, just as they were warned not to trust Egypt in chapters

19 and 20. Babylon was a treacherous nation and was doomed to fall at the hands of Elam and Media. They could not be trusted. They could not be depended upon. And Hezekiah's warm welcome and friendship with them will prove very costly (II Kings 20:17-18). We must choose our friends carefully. Befriending the treacherous and becoming partners with those doomed to receive God's punishments is certain to cause us grief as well. "A companion of gluttons shames his father" (Proverbs 28:7). "A companion of harlots wastes his wealth" (Proverbs 29:3). "The companion of fools will be destroyed" (Proverbs 13:20). And the warning here is that the companions of Babylon will be destined for similar misfortunes. Let us, instead join David and become the companion of all those who keep God's precepts (Psalms 119:63). Let us walk with God and befriend those who also walk with Him. The "whirlwinds" of judgment blow hard against the ungodly. Let us not be found near them when these winds gust up to blow them away.

21:3-4
Therefore my loins are filled with pain; pangs have taken hold of me, like the pangs of a woman in labor. I was distressed when I heard it; I was dismayed when I saw it. My heart wavered, fearfulness frightened me; the night for which I longed He turned into fear for me.

The sight of the coming judgment on Babylon greatly "distressed" Isaiah. "(He) was dismayed when (he) saw it." Judgment falling on wicked men fills righteous Isaiah with pain and fear. The sight of God breaking the back of kingdoms and empires as easily as a child breaks a stick is frightening. The terrible power of the Lord, combined with His utter intolerance for sin, fills thinking men with dread when they consider that apart from His great grace, this great wrath and power could be unleashed on them just the same. "It is a fearful thing to fall into the hands of the living God" (Hebrews 10:31), and it is a fearful thing to see others fall into His hands of judgment as well. Isaiah exemplifies the godly response to judgments being meted out on the unrighteous. Sorrow and sympathy for others, fear and self-examination for oneself. When we see judgment fall on the disobedient, Paul tells us, "Do not be haughty, but fear" (Romans 11:20). Punishment and judgment are not just intended to penalize the guilty, but to provide further incentive for the righteous to continue to keep themselves pure. Judgments and punishments on the ungodly are prophesied by God and publicized by His servants so "that the rest also may fear" (I Timothy 5:20).

21:5-10
Prepare the table, set a watchman in the tower, eat and drink. Arise, you princes, anoint the shield! For thus has the LORD said to me: "Go, set a watchman, let him declare what he sees." And he saw a chariot with a pair of horsemen, a chariot of donkeys, and a chariot of camels, and he listened earnestly with great care. Then he cried, "A lion, my Lord! I stand continually on the watchtower in the daytime; I have sat at my post every night. And look, here comes a chariot of men with a pair of horsemen!" Then he answered and said, "Babylon is fallen, is fallen! And all the carved images of her gods He has broken to the ground." Oh, my threshing and the grain of my floor! That which I have heard from the LORD of hosts, the God of Israel, I have declared to you.

God declares the coming destruction of Babylon. It is good to see again that when God speaks, He expects, yes, He demands that we pay careful attention to what He says and set ourselves to earnestly look for those things which He tells us are coming. Many feel that verse 5 is a picture of Belshazzar's feast in Daniel 5. It was during that very feast that Babylon fell. God tells Isaiah to "set a watchman" and carefully scan the horizon for the day that Babylon is destroyed. The vigilance to which God calls Isaiah is fascinating since Babylon will not be completely destroyed until long after Isaiah passes away. But even if Isaiah's eyes do not see Babylon's final day, His spiritual vision of the event is clear enough. He sees the Medes and Persians, he sees their kings and horsemen riding up to conquer Babylon. God has called Isaiah to be a watchman, to stand his post and be attentive to the task of watching out for the fulfillment of God's words. And Isaiah fulfills his duty before the Lord admirably. "I stand continually on the watchtower in the daytime; I have sat at my post every night." Let us be equal to the example Isaiah sets before us. Let us be vigilant in our responsibilities as watchmen and proclaimers of His truths. Isaiah is faithful to these things. He watches for the works of the Lord day and night and then declares to others what He sees God do and what he hears God say. "That which I have heard from the LORD of hosts, the God of Israel, I have declared to you." God has spoken! He has revealed to us "the things which are, and the things which will take place after this" (Revelation 1:19). Let us be vigilant! Let us stand like watchmen as Isaiah did and scan life around us for the works of God that we might bear testimony to His doings. And let us carefully search out His written word that we might join Isaiah in declaring to others what we "have heard from the LORD of hosts."

"Babylon is fallen, is fallen!" Isaiah's words are repeated by the angel in Revelation 14:8 and again in Revelation 18:2. Babylon worshipped gods that they made themselves. Isaiah's warning here joins the angel's warning in Revelation that we must separate ourselves from people like this. "Come out of her, my people, lest you share in her sins, and lest you receive of her plagues" (Revelation 18:4).

21:11-12
The burden against Dumah. He calls to me out of Seir, "Watchman, what of the night? Watchman, what of the night?" The watchman said, "The morning comes, and also the night. If you will inquire, inquire; Return! Come back!"

We have a short and cryptic prophecy against "Dumah" which many think refers to Edom. Great empires are judged – Egypt and Assyria and Babylon. And tiny nations are judged – Edom and Moab. No one is ever too powerful to overcome God's judgment, and no one is so insignificant that he can avoid God's judgment. God will judge the nations. We must prepare ourselves and act as a watchman to warn and inspire all peoples to prepare themselves as well. We may warn many who do not care about our message. They may sarcastically call out, "what of the night?" Where is this judgment, this night of terror that you talk about? II Peter 3:3-4 says, "scoffers will come in the last days, walking according to their own lusts, and saying, 'where is the promise of His coming? For since the fathers fell asleep, all things continue as they were from the beginning of creation.'" Some may scoff at our message, others may respond immediately in repentance and submission. Still others may "inquire." They may not be fully convinced on their first hearing, they may even debate us as we speak. But they are moved by the truth and seek to carefully examine what we say. And when they "inquire," let us be ready with good answers. Let us stand at our post as a watchman for the world. Let us clearly and boldly tell others what we hear God say and what we see Him do. And if they want to know more details, let us be ready. Let us give Isaiah's invitation: "if you will inquire, inquire"! If anyone has questions for us, let them ask away! And we will be ready with the answers – "Return" to God; "come back" to Him so that He might cleanse your sins and guide your path. "Thus says the LORD of hosts: 'Return to Me,' says the LORD of hosts, 'and I will return to you,' says the LORD of hosts" (Zechariah 1:3).

21:13-17
The burden against Arabia. In the forest in Arabia you will lodge, O you traveling companies of Dedanites. O inhabitants of the land of Tema, bring water to him who is thirsty; with their bread they met him who fled. For they fled from the swords, from the drawn sword, from the bent bow, and from the distress of war. For thus the LORD has said to me: "Within a year, according to the year of a hired man, all the glory of Kedar will fail; and the remainder of the number of archers, the mighty men of the people of Kedar, will be diminished; for the LORD God of Israel has spoken it."

God's word of judgment against the disobedient and unbelieving peoples of the world continues, this time foretelling the fall of Arabia. The enemy would come (probably Assyria), and Arabia's various people groups would flee from "the distress of war." But war would overtake them and leave them greatly "diminished." No one can successfully flee from God's judgments on us. No matter how much the nomadic people of Arabia try to distance themselves from God's punishments, "within a year" they will fall. "Where can I go from Your Spirit? Or where can I flee from Your presence?" (Psalms 139:7). The longing to draw near to God will always succeed (James 4:8); and the desire to flee from Him will always fail. Let us choose our desired destination wisely.

Isaiah 22

22:1-4
The burden against the Valley of Vision. What ails you now, that you have all gone up to the housetops, you who are full of noise, a tumultuous city, a joyous city? Your slain men are not slain with the sword, nor dead in battle. All your rulers have fled together; they are captured by the archers. All who are found in you are bound together; they have fled from afar. Therefore I said, "Look away from me, I will weep bitterly; do not labor to comfort me because of the plundering of the daughter of my people."

Isaiah is granted a revelation of the future of his people and it moves him to "weep bitterly." God had revealed His ways and will to His people. Their home was "the Valley of Vision." To them had been granted visions of God's love, and visions of His blessings on the faithful, and visions of His punishments on the ungodly. But the people of Jerusalem had closed their eyes to these visions from the Lord, and the result was devastating. The people are slain. Sadder still, they died, not honorably in defense of their homes, but as they "fled together" with their backs to the battle. Those who were not slain were "captured by the archers." Archers did not usually capture anyone. They shot their volleys from afar, depending on the heavily armed swordsmen and spearmen to do the hand-to-hand fighting. But Jerusalem had lost their will to fight. They were vision-less, dispirited, and weak. They had no fight in them, so that even lightly armed troops could capture them with ease. Isaiah is mortified by the picture. The people who were supposed to reflect the glory of God were destroyed in humiliating fashion. They were bereft of holiness, so God left them bereft of power. Isaiah warns people not to try to comfort him. The death of his people left him beyond consolation. May the sight of sinners doomed to destruction fill us with Isaiah's godly sorrow. May sorrow for sin move us to intercede for sinners, for our intercession serves the same purpose as God's words of prophetic warning here – that men doomed by their sin might yet change their ways and reconcile with God while there is still time.

22:5-7
For it is a day of trouble and treading down and perplexity by the Lord GOD of hosts in the Valley of Vision – breaking down the walls and of crying to the mountain. Elam bore the quiver with chariots of men and horsemen, and Kir uncovered the shield. It shall come to pass that your choicest valley shall be full of chariots, and the horsemen shall set themselves in array at the gate.

This Day of Judgment on Jerusalem at the hands of their enemies will be a day of "tumult, trampling, and bewilderment" (HCS). Isaiah's people were religious, but they were ungodly. And "perplexity," "bewilderment," and "confusion" (ESV and NLT) will be the common reaction of ungodly, but religious people when the judgment of God overtakes them. We see this bewilderment exhibited by those judged in Matthew 7:22 – "Many will say to Me in that day, 'Lord, Lord, have we not prophesied in Your name, cast out demons in Your name, and done many wonders in Your name?'" This same confusion is voiced by the ungodly religious people suffering judgment in Matthew 25:44 – "Lord, when did we see You hungry or thirsty or a stranger or naked or sick or in prison, and did not minister to You?" Neither fake loyalty to the true God nor true loyalty to false gods are protective! Impure devotion to the true God is useless to the soul. Avid devotion to false gods is also condemning rather than saving. But this insight is denied those who have sold themselves to sin (Romans 7:14), and so when judgment day befalls them, they are shocked, though they should not be, and they are bewildered, though their conscience had warned them long before.

22:8-11
He removed the protection of Judah. You looked in that day to the armor of the House of the Forest; you also saw the damage to the city of David, that it was great; and you gathered together the waters of the lower pool. You numbered the houses of Jerusalem, and the houses you broke down to fortify the wall. You also made a reservoir between the two walls for the water of the old pool. But you did not look to its Maker, nor did you have respect for Him who fashioned it long ago.

The people of Jerusalem had done so many things to protect themselves. They had put on their armor, they had diverted the waters around Jerusalem as both a defense and a provision during siege (II Kings 20:20). They had gathered and numbered their soldiers from the houses of Jerusalem, and they had fortified their wall of defense. They had done everything humanly possible to protect themselves. But that was their undoing. They had done everything humanly possible to protect themselves, but they had offended their Creator who alone was capable of truly defending them. They did not "respect" Him, they did not "look to" their Maker for their protection and direction. It is the epitome of self-destructive behavior to disrespect God and look away from Him when trouble draws near. In Zephaniah 1:6 God says, "I will destroy those who used to worship me but now no longer do. They no longer ask for the LORD's guidance or seek my blessings" (NLT). Jerusalem's refusal to "look to its Maker" was condemning. In contrast, those who look to the Lord will never be disappointed. Psalms 123:2 says, "Behold, as the eyes of servants look to the hand of their masters, as the eyes of a maid to the hand of her mistress, so our eyes look to the LORD our God, until He has mercy on us." And Micah 7:7 calls out with that same assurance, "I will look to the LORD; I will wait for the God of my salvation; my God will hear me." Let us be grateful and good stewards of the resources and strengths that our Lord gives us. But let us not be pridefully dependent on these things. Only the Lord can protect us from the significant enemies of life, and only our Lord can overcome the obstacles that hinder our progress in efforts that truly matter. Let us look to our Maker. Those who do so will not be disappointed and those who fail to do so are doomed.

22:12-14
And in that day the Lord GOD of hosts called for weeping and for mourning, for baldness and for girding with sackcloth. But instead, joy and gladness, slaying oxen and killing sheep, eating meat and drinking wine: "Let us eat and drink, for tomorrow we die!" Then it was revealed in my hearing by the LORD of hosts, "Surely for this iniquity there will be no atonement for you, even to your death," says the Lord GOD of hosts.

God calls us all to a life of holiness, a life that honors Him. Humanity fails readily in this God-given quest to be holy, but in mercy, His Spirit moves us to weep and mourn for our sins and troubles and to turn to Him in repentance and remorse. Here, however, rather than repenting and mourning over their sin and sin-caused sorrows, the people party! They intentionally live for sensual pleasures in the here-and-now rather than preserve their soul with holiness for the sake of eternal joys. God responds with a resounding, frightening judgment: "Surely for this iniquity there will be no atonement." Those who repent and mourn over sin will find the Lord "faithful and just to forgive all our sins and to cleanse us from all unrighteousness" (I John 1:9). But if you revel in sin rather than mourn over sin "there is no atonement for you." "Godly sorrow produces repentance leading to salvation" (II Corinthians 7:10). Here, the people's lack of godly sorrow caused them to remain unrepentant and ultimately denied them salvation. In wonder and awe, Jacob lifted his eyes to the Lord and marveled that he was so unworthy to be the recipient of "all the truth which You have shown Your servant" (Genesis 32:10). It is man's greatest privilege to understand and know God (Jeremiah 9:24). But when God reveals His will and ways to us through His Word spoken to our conscience or through His Word written in the pages of His scriptures, we must respond rightly! If He is angry, we must fear. If He rejoices, we must rejoice. If He rebukes, we must repent, if He beckons, we must draw near. If He commands, we must obey! Here, God rebuked His people, He called them to repent and mourn over their sins – and they did not. They sneered at His revelation to them, they seared their conscience with disobedience, and they cheered and reveled over their sin rather than repent and bask in the joys of forgiveness. God finds this unforgiveable. To hear our Creator speak in our spiritual ear and ignore what He says is unforgiveable. "Surely for this iniquity there will be no atonement for you." It is a frightful pronouncement on an inexcusable act. May all in our day take full warning.

22:15-18

Thus says the Lord GOD of hosts: "Go, proceed to this steward, to Shebna, who is over the house, and say: 'What have you here, and whom have you here, that you have hewn a sepulcher here, as he who hews himself a sepulcher on high, who carves a tomb for himself in a rock? Indeed, the LORD will throw you away violently, O mighty man, and will surely seize you. He will surely turn violently and toss you like a ball into a large country; there you shall die, and there your glorious chariots shall be the shame of your master's house.'"

God turns, for a moment, from His judgments on countries and kingdoms to bring judgment on Shebna, who was over the royal house in Jerusalem. He held a privileged position and had lofty aspirations. He had carved out an impressive sepulcher for himself on the high ground overlooking Jerusalem, apparently with the expectation of being held in honor by future generations. Shebna thought that his footing in society was rock solid, his security and success were seemingly assured. But his solid footing with men gave him absolutely no credibility with God, and the day was fast approaching that his hopes would be dashed on those rocks that he thought to honor himself with. He would not die and be buried with honor in his gilded tomb as he supposed. God would "toss (him) like a ball" into a faraway nation where he would die and be buried in shame. The glorious chariots that once carried him in honor, vaunting his high status among men, will now showcase his shame. Other versions render Isaiah's meaning as Shebna, himself, "shall be the shame of your master's house." He used his position for personal gain rather than the purposes of God, and this will turn out to be his eternal shame.

22:19-21

So I will drive you out of your office, and from your position he will pull you down. Then it shall be in that day, that I will call My servant Eliakim the son of Hilkiah; I will clothe him with your robe and strengthen him with your belt; I will commit your responsibility into his hand. He shall be a father to the inhabitants of Jerusalem and to the house of Judah.

Our soul should take proper delight in the thought that God has chosen us to carry out His purposes on earth. He has given us talents (Matthew 25:15), He has given us work to do (Acts 13:2), He has equipped us (II Timothy 3:17) to carry out the calling (II Timothy 1:9) which He has called us to carry out. God has appointed us to serve Him (John 15:16). He has appointed us to carry out a specific task given specifically to us to carry out

(Acts 22:10). Recognizing that the great purpose of our life as well as the daily duties entrusted to us are assigned to us by our Creator, will rightly fill us with godly pride in our life's work and with humble determination to carry out the tasks He has assigned to us. Life is short, but it is terribly important. God has given each of us a great commission that we must spend all our resources and energies to carry out. Nothing that God has called us to do is viewed as a mundane task in heaven. That which God has called us to do must be carried out to the letter. If we fail to carry out our part of the work that God has appointed us to do, He will give our work to someone else. "I will commit your responsibility into (someone else's) hand." Shebna was assigned the great work of watching over the king's house. But he failed in his responsibility, looking out for himself, rather than caring for the people in his charge, and seeking to make a name for himself rather than exalting the name of God. For his failure, God removes him from his office and gives his work to Eliakim the son of Hilkiah, who will be endowed with honor and strength from God so that he can accomplish the purposes of God. God's purposes must be carried out to the letter, and He is certain to make sure that they are. He assigns His great purposes to His people (what a privilege!), and if we fail in our responsibilities, He will give our work to someone else. When Saul failed, God gave his office and responsibilities to David (I Samuel 15:28). When Judas failed, the Lord gave his office and responsibilities to Matthias (Acts 1:26). And Eleazar and Ithamar were appointed as priests when their brothers Nadab and Abihu failed (Numbers 3:4). God's purposes must be carried out. He entrusts these purposes to us, His people, and we must expend all possible devotion to carrying out His decrees to the letter. If we turn from His work to indulge in our play, if we turn from His work to pursue our own purposes, if we disqualify ourselves from His work with our own sin, we risk the same judgment that fell on Shebna here, "I will drive you out of your office, and from your position he will pull you down."

22:22
The key of the house of David I will lay on his shoulder; so he shall open, and no one shall shut; and he shall shut, and no one shall open.

Suddenly, Isaiah's prophecy concerning Shebna and Eliakim swells to a majestic, even divine magnitude. Shebna failed, so Eliakim will rise to take his place, and no one will be able to resist him: "he shall open, and no one shall shut; and he shall shut, and no one shall open." This same descriptor is used for our risen Lord in Revelation 3:7 -- "And to the angel of the church in Philadelphia write, 'These things says He who is holy, He who is true, He who has the key of David, He who opens and no one shuts, and shuts and no one opens.'" Like Shebna, the priests of Israel will fail, and like Hilkiah, Jesus will rise to accomplish the purposes of God in their stead. And He will not fail. No one will resist Him. When He opens opportunities, no one can obstruct Him. When He shuts the mouths of lions and devils, no one can open them. He is irresistible, immovable, and unstoppable. Ultimately, no one can impede His progress, obstruct His determinations, or hinder His intentions. Shebna failed. But God will not fail. He will raise up Hilkiah, and He will raise up His Son to carry out His great intentions for man. Let us rise up to join our Lord in service to our Father! The keys of the house of David, the keys to life that were once given to Hilkiah are now in the hands of our Savior, and since He is for us, who now can be against us?

22:23-25

I will fasten him as a peg in a secure place, and he will become a glorious throne to his father's house. They will hang on him all the glory of his father's house, the offspring and the posterity, all vessels of small quantity, from the cups to all the pitchers. "In that day," says the LORD of hosts, "the peg that is fastened in the secure place will be removed and be cut down and fall, and the burden that was on it will be cut off; for the LORD has spoken."

Shebna was undependable. He was looking out for his own interests and failed to carry out the purposes of God and failed to care for the people of God. As a result, he "will be removed and be cut down and fall." In contrast, God will "fasten" Hilkiah like "a peg in a secure place." Hilkiah would be solid and dependable, like a nail driven deep into the frame of a hardwood house. A thick nail driven deep in a hardwood wall can hold up virtually anything you hang on it. And so Hilkiah will represent the coming Son of God upon whom we can hang all our hopes and needs. He will become "a glorious throne to his father's house." What a joy to a family when sons and daughters rise up to glorify God and bring honor to their family name, when their faith and service shine like a "glorious throne." Proverbs 23:24 says, "The father of the righteous will greatly rejoice, and he who begets a wise child will delight in him." So will Hilkiah be for his father. And so, my four children have been for me. Like a glorious throne they have blessed my house with their service to the Lord and efforts to remain holy. May the Lord bless my children with this same joy that I have been allowed to know.

Isaiah 23

23:1-5
The burden against Tyre. Wail, you ships of Tarshish! For it is laid waste, so that there is no house, no harbor; from the land of Cyprus it is revealed to them. Be still, you inhabitants of the coastland, you merchants of Sidon, whom those who cross the sea have filled. And on great waters the grain of Shihor, the harvest of the River, is her revenue; and she is a marketplace for the nations. Be ashamed, O Sidon; for the sea has spoken, the strength of the sea, saying, "I do not labor, nor bring forth children; neither do I rear young men, nor bring up virgins." When the report reaches Egypt, they also will be in agony at the report of Tyre.

We must choose our friends carefully. It is man's natural tendency to befriend the powerful and enjoy the company of the rich, sensing that their power and rich possessions may rub off on us. Often, that is indeed the case. The friends of the rich often get richer. Friends of the powerful grow in power. Tarshish weeps at the fall of Tyre, Egypt is in agony when Tyre is destroyed, because the riches of Tyre put money in their pocket as well. But those who share in the profits of the wicked will also risk sharing in the demise of the wicked when the judgments of God finally fall. Tyre was "a marketplace for the nations." Tyre helped everyone get richer. So everyone liked her. Tyre's prosperity made them popular with everyone – except God. And in the end, the only thing that matters is our standing with our Creator. Popularity proved to provide absolutely no protection against God's judgments. Riches and power were similarly unable to protect Tyre from God's punishment for sin. Proverbs 11:4 warns us that: "Riches do not profit in the day of wrath, but righteousness delivers from death." Let us seek righteous friends, not rich friends. Let us long for holiness, not pine for possessions, knowing that "He who trusts in his riches will fall, but the righteous will flourish like foliage" (Proverbs 11:28).

23:6-9
Cross over to Tarshish; wail, you inhabitants of the coastland! Is this your joyous city, whose antiquity is from ancient days, whose feet carried her far off to dwell? Who has taken this counsel against Tyre, the crowning city, whose merchants are princes, whose traders are the honorable of the earth? The LORD of hosts has purposed it, to bring to dishonor the pride of all glory, to bring into contempt all the honorable of the earth.

Money is power, so they say. And so Tyre's "merchants are princes." Their money acts like an army giving them sway over men and power to execute their wishes. Riches and honor often go together. Rich men are honored by most every society. And so Tyre's traders had become "the honorable of the earth." But I Chronicles 29:12 tells us that "both riches and honor come from (God)" and He can remove these things just as easily as He can provide them. If we fail to credit Him with our successes and make sure that our good name glorifies His great name, He declares here that it is His intention to "destroy your pride and show his contempt for all human greatness" (NLT). Proverbs 29:23 says, "A man's pride will bring him low, but the humble in spirit will retain honor." Proverbs 15:25 promises that "The LORD will destroy the house of the proud." Here that promise is kept as Isaiah's prophecy declares that The LORD of hosts has "purposed" to bring an end to the boasting of the rich and powerful merchants of Tyre. Let us hold our money and possessions loosely in our hands, seeking to use these things for God's glory and not our own. Let us not be overly moved by the praises of men, seeing that man's praise is fleeting, and is hardly an indicator of how God feels about us. Tyre had riches and honor aplenty, and it did them no eternal good. Their pride in these things brought them only "dishonor" and "contempt" in heaven's eyes, and sends a warning to us not to follow in the footsteps of the self-confident.

23:10-12
Overflow through your land like the River, O daughter of Tarshish; there is no more strength. He stretched out His hand over the sea, He shook the kingdoms; the LORD has given a commandment against Canaan to destroy its strongholds. And He said, "You will rejoice no more, O you oppressed virgin daughter of Sidon. Arise, cross over to Cyprus; there also you will have no rest."

God has given the awful command to destroy the strongholds of Tyre (here called Canaan). They have enjoyed prosperity and success for a long time, but their sin and pride meant that it was just a matter of time before God's judgment fell, and that time has finally come. They "will rejoice no more." As long as God withholds His judgments, evil men find many reasons to rejoice and celebrate. But when judgment day arrives, nothing that once brought joy will be able to cheer the hearts of the rebellious. They will try to flee the presence of God as Jonah did in Jonah 1, but they will fail in their attempt just as he did. They will "cross over to Cyprus," but life in Cyprus will provide them with "no rest." The reward for righteous work on earth is rest in heaven. "And I heard a voice from heaven saying, 'Write this down: Blessed are those who die in the Lord from now on. Yes, says the Spirit, they are blessed indeed, for they will rest from all their toils and trials; for their good deeds follow them!'" (Revelation 14:13 NLT). In contrast, as verse 12 illustrates, the punishment for unrighteous work on earth is "no rest" forever. "The smoke of their torment ascends forever and ever; and they have no rest day or night, who worship the beast and his image, and whoever receives the mark of his name" (Revelation 14:11). This is the plain forewarning of our righteous God toward those who are bent on sin and unbelief: "I swore in My wrath, they shall not enter My rest" (Hebrews 4:3). God denies rest from the sinful nation of Tyre here, and He will deny it again on judgment day to any and all who choose to rebel against Him. Since, then, God has promised heaven's rest to His people (Hebrews 4:1), but this holy rest is denied the rebellious both now and forever, "Let us therefore be diligent to enter that rest, lest anyone fall according to the same example of disobedience" (Hebrews 4:11).

ISAIAH 23

23:13-14
Behold, the land of the Chaldeans, this people which was not; Assyria founded it for wild beasts of the desert. They set up its towers, they raised up its palaces, and brought it to ruin. Wail, you ships of Tarshish! For your strength is laid waste.

Babylon, "the land of the Chaldeans" will rise up and destroy Tyre. To punish Tyre, God will make something out of nothing. He will make "this people which was not" into an army that cannot be stopped. Assyria subdued the Chaldeans with ease, finding it little more than a place where "wild beasts of the desert" roamed. This place that had once been brought to ruin will rise up and ruin Tyre. Isaiah calls on Tarshish to wail and cry over the impending doom of Tyre, for everyone who profited from Tyre's prosperity will be ruined when Tyre's "strength is laid waste."

Let us not bemoan our lowly estate. God can raise us up to accomplish His great purposes as easily as He raised up Babylon to carry out His work long ago. And let us not allow our well-being to be connected in any way to the well-being of wicked partners. Tarshish depended on Tyre for their prosperity, and when God's judgments fell on Tyre, Tarshish suffered in the fall-out. Let us not be unequally yoked with those who indifferently disobey God without concern. Let us separate ourselves from the misdeeds of unbelievers so that we will be found far from them when judgment falls.

23:15-18
Now it shall come to pass in that day that Tyre will be forgotten seventy years, according to the days of one king. At the end of seventy years it will happen to Tyre as in the song of the harlot: "Take a harp, go about the city, you forgotten harlot; make sweet melody, sing many songs, that you may be remembered." And it shall be, at the end of seventy years, that the LORD will deal with Tyre. She will return to her hire, and commit fornication with all the kingdoms of the world on the face of the earth. Her gain and her pay will be set apart for the LORD; it will not be treasured nor laid up, for her gain will be for those who dwell before the LORD, to eat sufficiently, and for fine clothing.

Everyone works for God. Wittingly or unwittingly, intentionally or against our will, the fruit of everyone's labor eventually "will be set apart for the LORD." All that we do for our personal pleasure "will not be treasured nor laid up." In Matthew 25:28 the Lord says, "take the talent from him, and give it to him who has ten talents." And again, in Luke 19:24, Christ, the nobleman says, "Take the mina from him, and give it to him who has ten minas." Similarly, here, God takes Tyre's treasures and gives them to those "who dwell before the LORD." God considers devotion to any religious precept other than Creator-directed worship to be "fornication," it is spiritual impurity. Tyre's lack of God-directed commitment makes her a "harlot" in the eyes of heaven. Let those who believe in the notion that all religions are good take proper warning. God finds false religion offensive. And He decides what false religion includes. Failure to worship God is spiritual adultery. Belief that all religions are good is spiritual polygamy. God consistently compares man's unfaithfulness to his Creator with sexual impurity and marital infidelity. Ezekiel 23:37 says that those who fell away from God "committed adultery with their idols." We must keep our religious efforts and spiritual beliefs pure before our Creator. And we must call on the peoples of the world to do the same. We must warn the religious harlots and spiritual polygamists of the world, for if they spurn their Creator's love, He will "deal with" them just as He declares here that He will "deal with Tyre."

Isaiah 24

24:1-3
Behold, the LORD makes the earth empty and makes it waste, distorts its surface and scatters abroad its inhabitants. And it shall be: as with the people, so with the priest; as with the servant, so with his master; as with the maid, so with her mistress; as with the buyer, so with the seller; as with the lender, so with the borrower; as with the creditor, so with the debtor. The land shall be entirely emptied and utterly plundered, for the LORD has spoken this word.

From chapter 13 to chapter 23 Isaiah declared God's judgments on one country after another. Now, chapter 24 will serve as a sort of climax to this theme, calling the reader ("Behold!") to see that the day is coming when God will bring total destruction to all the world's peoples because of their sin. The earth is populated by 8 billion people. But when God gives vent to His anger, He will "empty" the earth and lay it waste. When people sin as a group, God judges as a group – all sinners will share together in paying the penalty for sins. It will make no difference if we are religious (priests) or powerful (masters), all will suffer the same judgment that is meted out by a just God on unjust sinners. Buyers and sellers will receive the same judgment. Debtors and bankers will likewise receive the same punishment. No matter how different people may appear on the outside, their inner sinfulness will be the common denominator that will cause them to suffer the same consequences. Sin always results in judgment. "The LORD has spoken this word": all unrepentant sinners are destined to incur the same punishment from the judge of all humanity, "For God shows no partiality" (Romans 2:11). I Peter 1:17 tells us how we should respond to Isaiah's words here: "remember that the heavenly Father to whom you pray has no favorites when he judges. He will judge or reward you according to what you do. So you must live in reverent fear of him during your time as foreigners here on earth" (NLT).

24:4-6
The earth mourns and fades away, the world languishes and fades away; the haughty people of the earth languish. The earth is also defiled under its inhabitants, because they have transgressed the laws, changed the ordinance, broken the everlasting covenant. Therefore the curse has devoured the earth, and those who dwell in it are desolate. Therefore the inhabitants of the earth are burned, and few men are left.

The final days before the earth is destroyed are described here by Isaiah. "The earth mourns." "The world wastes away and withers" (HCS). And the best and brightest among the world's peoples fade into oblivion in the days leading up to the time when "the curse has devoured the earth." This lamentable future is on the horizon because: "the earth is defiled under its inhabitants." Sin not only defiles the sinner, but everything the sinner touches. Mothers scold their children when their muddy feet leave dirty tracks throughout the house, and here God announces His judgment on those whose sinful feet have trampled the earth, leaving it grossly marred with their defiled imprints. One day the world will come to an end, it will be devoured, it will fade away, having been defiled by "its inhabitants" who are charged with a 3-fold offence. The world's peoples are first accused of having "transgressed the laws." At Sinai, God gave Israel the Ten Commandments and a long list of other laws that would guide them in the ways of holy living. But the world is not condemned here for disobeying the Mosaic Law, they are condemned for transgressing the laws written by their Creator in the hearts and conscience of every man and woman on earth. The law of God is written in our heart (Psalms 37:31). Hebrews 8:10 says, "For this is the covenant that I will make with the house of Israel after those days, says the LORD: I will put My laws in their mind and write them on their hearts; and I will be their God, and they shall be My people." But Romans 2:15 tells us that this beautiful promise is not just given to the nation of Israel, but to the world at large as well. When men and women the world over obey their conscience, they clearly show that "the work of the law (is) written in their hearts, their conscience also bearing witness." Our Creator has written His laws in the hearts of His creation, and the earth is condemned when mankind rebels against those laws.

Secondly, judgment is pronounced on the earth because its inhabitants have "changed the ordinance." Leviticus 18:4 gives the command: "You shall observe My judgments and keep My ordinances, to walk in them: I am the LORD your God." But the peoples of the world try to change God's ordinances. Rather than following God's ordinances for righteous living, they follow self-made ordinances for leisure living. The ordinances of God are designed to keep our attentions focused on holy matters, to remind us of our sins and the price that it cost to forgive us our sins. The ordinances of God provide rules to live by and means by which we can be spiritually healthy. But the unbelievers of the world find little use for spiritual holiness and a right standing with God, and so they change these ordinances into a means for personal gain and a means by which they can feel good about themselves regardless of how God feels about them.

And thirdly, judgment falls on the earth because its inhabitants have "broken the everlasting covenant." In Genesis 9:16 the Lord says, "The rainbow shall be in the cloud, and I will look on it to remember the everlasting covenant between God and every living creature of all flesh that is on the earth." The everlasting covenant between God and man means that God will safeguard the earth. He created all things at the dawn of time, and today, in keeping with His "everlasting covenant," He "holds all creation together" (Colossians 1:17 ESV) so that tsunamis, meteors, earthquakes, and the like do not tear the earth apart. In Jeremiah 11:10, God says that His people have "broken My covenant." They had given themselves to sin and they had worshipped other gods. These two acts of treason broke the covenant that bound them with their Creator. As a result, Jeremiah 11:11 pronounces that "calamity" will befall God's people. Here, we see that the peoples of the world will similarly unite in rebellion against God – they will sin against their Spirit-infused conscience and they will worship false gods. When they refuse to uphold their part of the covenant, at long last when the time for mercy has passed, God will no longer uphold His part of the covenant. He will no longer hold the earth together; He will bring calamity on creation, and the world "fades away."

24:7-9
The new wine fails, the vine languishes, all the merry-hearted sigh. The mirth of the tambourine ceases, the noise of the jubilant ends, the joy of the harp ceases. They shall not drink wine with a song; strong drink is bitter to those who drink it.

Wine, fun-loving ("merry-hearted") friends, and music are all gifts to the world to cheer the troubled and heighten the happiness of those who are already having a good time. But none of these things can compensate for the soul-jarring sorrow that ensues when sinners are forced to face the fact that their sin and unbelief has brought them to utter ruin. Despite deceptive indications to the contrary, sin always results in sorrow. "The joy of our heart has ceased; our dance has turned into mourning. The crown has fallen from our head. Woe to us, for we have sinned!" (Lamentations 5:15-16). The great news is that sin can be forgiven. Joy can return to those who repent. Our passage here cries out to warn us that although sin can be forgiven, the sorrow that stems from unrepented sin never goes away. Jeremiah 30:15 warns: "Why do you cry about your affliction? Your sorrow is incurable. Because of the multitude of your iniquities, because your sins have increased, I have done these things to you." Unrepented sin leads to "incurable" sorrow. What a frightening thought.

24:10-13
The city of confusion is broken down; every house is shut up, so that none may go in. There is a cry for wine in the streets, all joy is darkened, the mirth of the land is gone. In the city desolation is left, and the gate is stricken with destruction. When it shall be thus in the midst of the land among the people, it shall be like the shaking of an olive tree, like the gleaning of grapes when the vintage is done.

When God's judgment falls, when men are forced to receive the wages of their sins, "confusion" reigns. Everything seems so perfect to the sinner while under the delusion that he can sin without consequence. But then the judgment of God falls on him and he is bewildered. Insight left him long ago, so only confusion remains as his companion when he is left alone with his guilt. Those who once felt so confident in their rebellion against God will suddenly become confused when judgment falls. Like the prodigal they will ask, where did my friends go? Where did all my money go? Why is the wine gone, the joy gone, and why have the parties ended? He will seek the help of righteous friends, but as God closed the door of the ark in Genesis 7:16, so sinners will find "every house is shut up," all opportunity for escape from God's wrath in the solace of godly company has passed. One day the Lord will shake the earth like a man shakes the branches of an olive tree, and the wicked will fall like fat olives. Sadly, when the Lord shakes the earth in judgment, "few men are left" (verse 6). Let us not join the "confusion" of those who believe they can sin without consequence. Those who cry for wine and wicked pleasures will also be the ones who cry over the loss of their joy when their sin brings them face to face with "desolation" and "destruction." "Joy is darkened" and "the mirth of the land is gone" when men abandon the pursuit of God for any lesser goal. Let us take proper warning. The joys and mirth of sin and sinners are soon "darkened." Let us intentionally seek our joy in the Lord, rather than in the passing pleasures of sin. Let us say with the psalmist, "my soul shall be joyful in the LORD; it shall rejoice in His salvation" (Psalms 35:9). For although the joys of sin darken quickly, the joy of sitting in the presence of our God never ends. "You will show me the path of life; in Your presence is fullness of joy; at Your right hand are pleasures forevermore" (Psalms 16:11).

24:14-16

They shall lift up their voice, they shall sing; for the majesty of the LORD they shall cry aloud from the sea. Therefore glorify the LORD in the dawning light, the name of the LORD God of Israel in the coastlands of the sea. From the ends of the earth we have heard songs: "Glory to the righteous!" But I said, "I am ruined, ruined! Woe to me! The treacherous dealers have dealt treacherously, indeed, the treacherous dealers have dealt very treacherously."

The transitions may not be easy to follow, and not everyone agrees on Isaiah's intended meaning, but we appear to be granted here a glimpse of two godly responses to the coming of God's judgment. The preceding verses pictured God emptying the earth and removing all joy from the world as punishment for the sins of the people. Here, the righteous, God-fearing people of the world lift up a song of praise to the "majesty of the LORD." The "ends of the earth" praise the God of Israel because He has punished sinners and executed justice on the guilty. The righteous of the world rejoice to see God uphold justice and defend His holy name. Psalm 149 pictures this so wonderfully as the psalmist's call for praise weaves seamlessly with his joy in being able to partake in the Lord's execution of justice on sinful peoples. "Praise the Lord! Sing to the Lord! Sing to the Lord a new song, and His praise in the assembly of saints. Let Israel rejoice in their Maker; let the children of Zion be joyful in their King. Let them praise His name with the dance; let them sing praises to Him with the timbrel and harp. For the LORD takes pleasure in His people; He will beautify the humble with salvation. Let the saints be joyful in glory; let them sing aloud on their beds. Let the high praises of God be in their mouth, and a two-edged sword in their hand, to execute vengeance on the nations, and punishments on the peoples; to bind their kings with chains, and their nobles with fetters of iron; to execute on them the written judgment – this honor have all His saints. Praise the LORD!"

Then, after showing how the righteous people of the world responded to the news of God's judgments on the wicked, Isaiah appears to share his reaction to the news of judgment falling on the wicked world: "I am ruined, ruined! Woe to me!" The "treacherous" people of the world have "dealt very treacherously" with their Creator and are deservedly doomed to die. But Isaiah cannot join in the songs of those who praise the Lord in righteous celebration. Instead of righteous joy, Isaiah is filled with righteous sorrow. For although the two described reactions seem so dissimilar, they both reflect the righteous heart of God. Even while some are rightly rejoicing and praising God for His righteous right hand, Isaiah mourns the destruction of so many of those that turned their backs on God, knowing that God takes "no pleasure in the death of the wicked" (Ezekiel 33:11).

24:17-18
Fear and the pit and the snare are upon you, O inhabitant of the earth. And it shall be that he who flees from the noise of the fear shall fall into the pit, and he who comes up from the midst of the pit shall be caught in the snare; for the windows from on high are open, and the foundations of the earth are shaken.

No one can hide from God's judgments. Those who run from their fear of death will fall in the "pit of destruction" (Psalms 55:23), and those who try to avoid the pit are trapped again by the "snares of death" (Psalms 18:5). Amos 5:19 says the same thing, those who will try to avoid God's punishments will simply go from one punishing situation to another: "it will be as though a man fled from a lion, and a bear met him! Or as though he went into the house, leaned his hand on the wall, and a serpent bit him!" "The windows from on high are open." The eyes of heaven can see every evil act of every evil man, and can see precisely where every evil man hides. In Genesis 7:11 "the windows of heaven were opened" and the floodwaters brought judgment and death to everyone who refused to honor God. There was nowhere to hide to avoid the judgment brought about by the open windows of judgment in Noah's day, nor will there be any escape when God's judgments are poured out of these open windows in any other era. Those who dishonor God are on very shaky ground. "The foundations of the earth are shaken" when God judges the disobedient. By contrast, those who serve the Lord faithfully "are receiving a kingdom which cannot be shaken." So then, since the world falls apart for those who refuse to serve God, and "a kingdom which cannot be shaken" is promised to those who do, let us determine to "serve God acceptably with reverence and godly fear" (Hebrews 12:28).

24:19-20
The earth is violently broken, the earth is split open, the earth is shaken exceedingly. The earth shall reel to and fro like a drunkard, and shall totter like a hut; its transgression shall be heavy upon it, and it will fall, and not rise again.

"Its transgression shall be heavy upon it." We are reminded again of the immensity of the weight of sin. Who can ever hope to get away with even the least of sins? "The earth is violently broken" when the weight of sin crashes into it like a meteor. "The earth is split open" when the weight of sin slams into it like an axe splits kindling for the fire. If a planet cannot hold up under the weight of the sin heaped upon it by its people, it can hardly be surprising that individuals who sin are even more helpless in their effort to bear the weight of their guilt. Apart from God's hand of mercy lifting the burden of our sin from our shoulders, we would all be crushed beneath the weight of our sin. Those made righteous by the forgiveness of their Savior can rise again when their Lord lifts the weight of sin and guilt from their soul, but those not made righteous by forgiveness will be forced to bear the weight of sin forever without hope of relief. "A righteous man may fall seven times and rise again, but the wicked shall fall by calamity" (Proverbs 24:16). The weight of sin is simply overwhelming. No one can rise to look in the face of his Maker while the crushing weight of sin presses his soul hell-ward. But look! Even now there is hope for those who groan under the weight of sin! Ezekiel 33:10 (NLT) says, "Son of man, give the people of Israel this message: You are saying, 'Our sins are heavy upon us; we are wasting away! How can we survive?'" Then verse 11 gives God's famous answer! He takes no delight in watching the wicked be crushed to death by the weight of sin. Even now the call rings out to all men and women everywhere: Repent! Follow the sound of the Savior's voice! In mercy, He will take the weight of sin and the crushing weight of guilt from your soul. Let all thinking men everywhere come to their senses and admit that they cannot bear the weight of their sin alone. David provides a godly example. In Psalms 38:4 he prays, "my iniquities have gone over my head; like a heavy burden they are too heavy for me." The weight of sin moves him to continue in Psalms 38:17-18 -- "I am ready to fall, and my sorrow is continually before me. For I will declare my iniquity; I will be in anguish over my sin." Sin is heavy. But God's arms of mercy are very strong. The weight of sin drives us to our knees, but blessedly, "The LORD lifts up the humble" (Psalms 147:6). Apart from Christ, the wicked will fall "and not rise again." Blessedly, that is not our lot. "Your brother will rise again" is the promise our Lord gave to Martha in John 11:23, and is the promise yet given to the repentant and trusting in our day.

24:21-23
It shall come to pass in that day that the LORD will punish on high the host of exalted ones, and on the earth the kings of the earth. They will be gathered together, as prisoners are gathered in the pit, and will be shut up in the prison; after many days they will be punished. Then the moon will be disgraced and the sun ashamed; for the LORD of hosts will reign on Mount Zion and in Jerusalem and before His elders, gloriously.

"it shall come to pass in that day..." at the end of time the Lord will bring His final judgments on the people of the earth. The pride and power of kings and all who "exalted" themselves over their Maker will at last be stripped away. They will be defeated without a fight. They will be gathered together in the pit that serves as a prison for the disobedient. In the pit of judgment no distinction is made between leaders and followers, sinners of high rank and sinners of the rank and file. "They will be gathered together." Their souls were knit together in life in a common disdain for their Maker, and they will be joined together in the second death, incurring the common judgment meted out against all who traded away an eternity in the company of their Father in heaven for the sake of temporary pleasures and pretended autonomy on earth. It is not surprising that the glory of kings is forgotten on judgment day – even the sun and the moon are "disgraced" because their light pales compared to the light of the "LORD of hosts." Revelation 21:23 says, "The city (of heaven) had no need of the sun or of the moon to shine in it, for the glory of God illuminated it. The Lamb is its light." Those who trust in the Lamb will rejoice in the delight of basking in the glory of the light of the Lamb. But those who refused to honor God in life will join with the sun and moon and be "disgraced" and "ashamed" at the judgment. The brilliance of the unveiled glory of the Son will not comfort those who refused to honor their Creator in life. It will simply more fully display the foolishness of their unbelief and the evil of their secret sins. Happily, this is not our lot. All of us who love the Lord and have basked in His forgiveness on earth, will bask in His glory in heaven. And unlike the shame and disgrace that is felt by unbelievers, we will join our family of faith as in Psalms 34:5 that declares, "They looked to Him and were radiant, and their faces were not ashamed."

Isaiah 25

25:1
O LORD, You are my God. I will exalt You, I will praise Your name, for You have done wonderful things; Your counsels of old are faithfulness and truth.

It is good to remember again, to repeat the refrain once more: "O LORD, You are my God." As children are moved to tell their beloved parents "I love you" again and again, as husbands and wives are moved to tell each other over and over "I love you," so God's people are moved over and over again to join Isaiah and lift our eyes toward heaven and say once more, "O LORD, You are my God." Children see their parents tirelessly provide for them, and so are provided with a continuous stream of reasons to love them. Wives see their husbands provide so tirelessly for the family, husbands see their wives so tirelessly fill the home with love and acts of kindness, and so, daily, they are granted reasons to repeat their love for one another. Similarly, as Isaiah contemplates the goodness of God, he affirms once more, "O LORD, You are my God." "For You have done wonderful things." The kindnesses of our Lord are "new every morning" (Lamentations 3:23), the "wonderful things" that He does for us are repeated and multiplied day after day. And since our Lord does not tire in doing wonderful things for us, let us not tire in affirming our love and allegiance to Him. "O LORD, You are my God." There are many gods out there. There are many religions to choose from, but what compares to the "wonderful things" that our God has done for us? Mary expressed these same feelings Isaiah displays here. She exalts our Lord, she praises His name because "He who is mighty has done great things for me, and holy is His name" (Luke 1:49). Let us remember the wonderful things that God has done for us and exalt Him, praise Him, and affirm once more that He is our God.

His "counsels of old are faithfulness and truth." We acknowledge that there are many gods and many religions to choose from, but we agree with Peter in John 6:68, "Lord, to whom shall we go? You have the words of eternal life." Let us bless the Lord who has given us His infallible counsel (Psalms 16:7). "The counsel of the LORD stands forever, the plans of His heart to all generations" (Psalms 33:11), so we are right to exalt Him. God's counsels are faithful and true. God has done wonderful things for us. So we exalt Him. We praise His name. And we happily, gratefully sing again, "O LORD, You are my God."

25:2-3
For you have made a city a ruin, a fortified city a ruin, a palace of foreigners to be a city no more; it will never be rebuilt. Therefore the strong people will glorify You; the city of the terrible nations will fear You.

There is no state of man, there is no modern, advanced, enlightened state that man can attain that will set him above his Maker. Great cities that rebel against God will be brought to "ruin." No one by strength of arm or strength of argument can defy God. He turns the "fortified" places of men into a "ruin." Those who live in a palace and enjoy the luxury of worldly riches but are spiritually bankrupt will be similarly brought to ruin and disappear. This is the solemn warning of verse 2. Verse 3, however, suddenly cheers us with the blessed result of the demonstration of the power and punishments of God. God's judgments on rebellious people, who once trusted in their own strength, will move thinking men everywhere to give Him His due honor. "Strong people will glorify You"! Those who once trusted in their "fortified cities," their strong back and brilliant mind, will despise their own strength and praise God for His. "Terrible nations will fear You." Those who once used their power to make others live in fear, will repent and kneel in godly fear of the Lord of hosts. We tend to think of countries as "Christian nations" or "non-Christian nations," but it is clearly God's intent to draw all peoples to Himself and receive glory from all the nations of the world. David saw this in Psalms 102:15, saying, "the nations shall fear the name of the LORD, and all the kings of the earth Your glory."

25:4-5
For You have been a strength to the poor, a strength to the needy in his distress, a refuge from the storm, a shade from the heat; for the blast of the terrible ones is as a storm against the wall. You will reduce the noise of aliens, as heat in a dry place; as heat in the shadow of a cloud, the song of the terrible ones will be diminished.

Verse 2 said that God brings ruin to the rich, but here we find Him granting "strength to the poor." In verse 2 He toppled cities, here He upholds "the needy in his distress." God destroys great men in the pinnacle of their power, so that men will not trust in themselves, but in the One who truly wields power. And God gently cares for the troubled people of the world so that men can lift their eyes off their hurts and trust in the One who provides everlasting healing. Our Lord provides "a refuge from the storm." Psalms 107:29 says, "He calms the storm, so that its waves are still." Pressures at work, sickness at home, worries in our head and heart can all beat on us like a storm. But here we have a precious reminder. We have a refuge from the storm. We can kneel before our Lord, and there under His wings, the noise of life's storms is quieted. In the shelter of our Savior's approval, we are not drenched by the rains of sorrow, we are not blown away by the shock of sudden loss. "The blast" of the winds of trouble beat against us "as a storm against the wall." The bitter cold of life's storms are real, but the wall of God's comforts holds strong, so that: "We are hard-pressed on every side, yet not crushed; we are perplexed, but not in despair; persecuted, but not forsaken; struck down, but not destroyed – always carrying about in the body the dying of the Lord Jesus, that the life of Jesus also may be manifested in our body" (II Corinthians 4:8-10). Our Lord's comforts quiet "the noise" of the scorn of unbelievers. His comforts are like the shade of a cloud that protects from the hot, glaring attacks of our critics. The world is full of "terrible" people, but God will quiet them too. Our Lord grants His people both strength to endure our trials and comforts to ease our trials. What a precious thought.

ISAIAH 25

25:6
And in this mountain the LORD of hosts will make for all people a feast of choice pieces, a feast of wines on the lees, of fat things full of marrow, of well-refined wines on the lees.

Isaiah continues to praise the Lord for His many blessings. He judges the unrighteous (v2), and He strengthens the needy (v4). Here, we see that the Lord's provisions for His people are compared to a party, a day of feasting and celebration that will be "for all people." Our Lord invites the entire world to come to celebrate forever the joys of walking rightly with the Creator of the universe. "Blessed are those," Revelation 19:9 says, who are "invited to the marriage feast of the Lamb" (HCS). As our body delights in good food, so our soul finds delight in the fellowship of our Creator. Psalms 63:5 describes this feeling, "My soul shall be satisfied as with marrow and fatness, and my mouth shall praise You with joyful lips." Our Lord has invited us to feast with Him, to enjoy His presence and His good blessings forever. Our responsibility is to accept His offer and to align our intentions, actions, and priorities with His good will so that He will not find us unworthy of His invitation. Matthew 22:8 gives the warning in a parable, "Then he said to his servants, "The wedding is ready, but those who were invited were not worthy." Then Matthew 22:11 describes the master's displeasure when he sees a man at the wedding feast who was not clothed in proper attire. Let us strive to be found worthy of our Master's invitation to feast with Him. Let us "walk worthy of the calling with which (we) were called" (Ephesians 4:1). Let us clothe ourselves in righteousness (Revelation 19:8) so that we will conform to the dress code of this celebration of celebrations, this party of parties – the marriage feast of the Lord of hosts.

25:7-8
And on this mountain He will swallow up the covering which is over all peoples, even the veil which is stretched over all nations. He will swallow up death for all time, and the Lord GOD will wipe tears away from all faces, and He will remove the reproach of His people from all the earth; For the LORD has spoken.

Isaiah's readers in his day could take comfort from his words promising that they would be delivered from the oppression of their enemies. But we can hardly miss that Isaiah's promise extends far beyond Judah's rescue from their invaders. Paul refers to Isaiah's words here in I Corinthians 15:54 when he writes, "Then, when our dying bodies have been transformed into bodies that will never die, this Scripture will be fulfilled: 'Death is swallowed up in victory'" (NLT). Our Lord invites us to come live life as if feasting on the finest foods of the soul continually (verse 6). And here, we see this invitation extends beyond death, beyond our time here on earth. Our sorrows on earth will end, "The Lord GOD will wipe tears away from all faces." But our joy in being seated at a spiritual feast in the presence our Lord and Savior will never end! Death will be swallowed up and disappear. "And God will wipe away every tear from their eyes; there shall be no more death, nor sorrow, nor crying. There shall be no more pain, for the former things have passed away" (Revelation 21:4). Our God will one day remove all our sorrows. He will remove death. And He will "remove the reproach of His people from all the earth." Psalms 22:6 says, "I am a worm, and no man; a reproach of men, and despised by the people." On earth, our detractors find reason to despise us. We trust in a God they cannot see. We sacrifice pleasures for a cause that fails to inspire them. We defer our hope to heaven while they indulge in self-gratification in the here and now. And we prepare ourselves with holiness for a judgment they cannot see coming. But the day is imminent when the ridicule and reproach of our fault-finders is "removed." The psalmist laments in Psalms 42:10, "As with a breaking of my bones, my enemies reproach me, while they say to me all day long, "Where is your God?" Our Lord sees that for His sake we have "borne reproach" (Psalms 69:7). He sees when "zeal for Your house has eaten me up, and the reproaches of those who reproach You have fallen on me" (Psalms 69:9). God sees it, and it is His good will to "remove the reproach from His people." The time is soon coming when our Lord will descend from heaven with a shout (I Thessalonians 4:16) and call all His people to Himself. And as we kneel before His throne, our reproach will melt away. Everyone will know that we chose very wisely. We were oh so right to follow our Lord! Death is gone. Sorrow is gone. Our reproach from the lips of our critics is gone. All these things will soon enough be "swallowed up in victory."

25:9
And it will be said in that day: "Behold, this is our God; we have waited for Him, and He will save us. This is the LORD; we have waited for Him; we will be glad and rejoice in His salvation."

Such a great day is described here! The day when we can join the joyous privilege of Moses and see God! When we will lift our eyes and "see Him as He is" (I John 3:2). "Behold, this is our God!" This hope before us of the day when we will see God inspires us to "wait." While others indulge in immediate physical pleasures, we wait for heaven's bliss. While others store up treasures they can only enjoy on earth, we wait for the return on our investments in heaven. While others seek the praise of men, we wait for God's approval. Those who trust in God wait for God. And the blessings that come to those who wait for God are many.   Isaiah 40:31 says that those "who wait on the LORD shall renew their strength; they shall mount up with wings like eagles, they shall run and not be weary, they shall walk and not faint." Psalms 37:9 says that those who wait on the Lord will "inherit the earth." And here, two more blessed results of waiting on God are listed. Those who wait on the Lord now, rest in the promise that "He will save us." Proverbs 20:22 says simply, "Wait for the LORD, and He will save you." We are especially thankful for this saving outcome of our waiting on God, seeing that there are no other options for the salvation of our soul -- "there is no other God who can deliver like this" (Daniel 3:29). Seeing that God saves those who wait for Him, and there is no salvation awaiting those who trust in anything else, we are rightly "glad and rejoice in His salvation." Our joy in the provision of God's salvation does not begin in heaven, we are "glad and rejoice in His salvation" right now! Hannah's delight in God's rescue did not wait for heaven to begin. I Samuel 2:1 says, "And Hannah prayed and said: 'My heart rejoices in the Lord; my horn is exalted in the Lord. I smile at my enemies, because I rejoice in Your salvation.'" The joy that fills the soul of those who know that God has saved them knows no bounds. It buoys our spirit even when floods of sorrows would otherwise overwhelm us. David longed for everyone to know this joy that emanates from the assurance of God's salvation. In Psalms 70:4 he wrote, "Let all those who seek You rejoice and be glad in You; and let those who love Your salvation say continually, 'Let God be magnified!'" One day we will see God. And we will love what we see. Today, we wait for Him. But the sight of His glory will be worth the wait. One day we will enter the presence of our God in heaven. We will be saved forever from the guilt and stain and repercussions of sin. We wait for that day. And as we wait, "we will be glad and rejoice in His salvation."

25:10-12
For on this mountain the hand of the LORD will rest, and Moab shall be trampled down under Him, as straw is trampled down for the refuse heap. And He will spread out His hands in their midst as a swimmer reaches out to swim, and He will bring down their pride together with the trickery of their hands. The fortress of the high fort of your walls He will bring down, lay low, and bring to the ground, down to the dust.

The previous verses highlighted the joy of those who wait on God's salvation. That is contrasted here with the horror that awaits all those who choose not to cling to God for that salvation. Those who disbelieve God declare themselves to be the enemies of God, represented here by the nation of Moab. God's people will be lifted up (Psalms 30:1), but God's enemies will be "trampled down." Just as at Jericho, God will bring down and lay low the walls that people build to defend themselves against God's commands and God's judgments. No wall of argument or personal preference grants us impunity from God's laws. Some build walls of self-declared autonomy, foolishly feeling that this pretend independence protects them from God's authority. It does not. God will bring this wall "down to the dust." Some build walls of God-less religion, foolishly feeling that any spiritual effort is as good as another and provides equal protection for the soul. That is not true. God will "bring down" those walls to the dust as well, and all who trusted in them will be bitterly, eternally disappointed.

Isaiah 26

26:1-2
In that day this song will be sung in the land of Judah: "We have a strong city; God will appoint salvation for walls and bulwarks. Open the gates, that the righteous nation which keeps the truth may enter in."

"In that day," on judgment day, God's people will sing. While others cry out songs of disappointment and remorse, lamenting their unbelief, we will sing and rejoice in our salvation. We sing because our soul holds citizenship in a "strong city." Our detractors, our pains, our frailties cannot touch us there. The very walls around our city are made of our salvation. While others regret their sin and mourn their unbelief that denied them the right to enter this city of heaven, God's people will stride to the city gates and hear the great command sound out from the watchtower of heaven saying, "open the gates, that the righteous nation which keeps the truth may enter in." Those who enter the city gates are "righteous," they are imputed righteousness (Romans 4:6) through the blood of their Savior. Those who have not been made righteous by the cleansing power of Jesus' blood cannot "enter in." Only the "righteous" are admitted through the gates, only the one who "keeps the truth" is let inside. They believe the truth and they obey the truth, and this response to the truth grants them citizenship in heaven. Some 600 years later, Jesus revealed in John 14:6 that He is the truth, re-emphasizing Isaiah's words here that it is (only) those who believe the Truth and obey the Truth that "may enter in" when judgment day arrives.

26:3
You will keep him in perfect peace, whose mind is stayed on You, because he trusts in You.

This verse was written on the little chalkboard beside our family dining table for a long time. The blessed result of a wonderful enterprise is succinctly stated. Those whose hearts and minds are "fixed" (NLT) on God are blessed with "perfect peace." Ah, let us fix our minds on our Lord. Let us constantly think of His greatness and His many perfect attributes. Let us constantly recall to mind how kind He has been to our family. Let us think on His love for us and how basking in His presence exceeds all other joys of this world. Let us consider the great task He has commissioned us to carry out. Let us meditate on His word to us, let us ponder the deep truths He has revealed to us, let us roll over and over in our minds all that He has done in the past and all that He promises to do in the days to come. Let us meditate on His precepts and contemplate His ways (Psalms 119:15), for when we do, He has promised to keep us "in perfect peace." The world can be a very unsettling place. Anxiety, even among believers, has reached epidemic proportions in our day. Our Lord here offers the cure to the fears and worries that would cripple our godly service – the mind that is "stayed on" Jesus is kept in perfect peace. In John 14:27 Jesus repeated Isaiah's promise, "Peace I leave with you, My peace I give to you; not as the world gives do I give to you. Let not your heart be troubled, neither let it be afraid." "God has called us to peace" (I Corinthians 7:15), and if we will set our minds to continually contemplate His goodness, if we will take our eyes off the waves of our troubles and gaze instead on the wonderful eyes of our Savior, "the peace of God, which surpasses all understanding, will guard your hearts and minds through Christ Jesus" (Philippians 4:7). When our heart is fixed on the truths of God, the peace of God will rule in our heart (Colossians 3:15). Thinking about God heightens our trust in God. So let us think about Him continually, for the trust that flows from godly contemplation leads to "perfect peace."

26:4
Trust in the LORD forever, for in YAH, the LORD, is everlasting strength.

Young's Literal Translation renders the last phrase as: "Jehovah is a rock of ages." The literal rendition inspired the words of the old hymn, "Rock of Ages, cleft for me, let me hide myself in Thee." We can trust in God forever because He is an everlasting strength, an everlasting rock, a rock of strength and immutability that provides our soul with a bedrock of power that never ends, never changes, and vanquishes every opponent. If we will "go in the strength of the Lord GOD" (Psalms 71:16), our strength will never not be enough, because His strength is "everlasting strength." If God is the strength of my heart and my portion forever" (Psalms 73:26) no burden can overwhelm me because His strength is "everlasting strength." Oh "blessed is the man whose strength is in You" (Psalms 84:5) because the strength of our mind and strength of our back and the strength of our friends will always fade with time, but God's strength is "everlasting strength." Blessed are those who trust in the strength of the Lord, and not in their own abilities. What a blessed state of godly confidence is ours when our thoughts are those of Psalms 18:2 – "The LORD is my rock and my fortress and my deliverer; my God, my strength, in whom I will trust; my shield and the horn of my salvation, my stronghold."

26:5-6
For He brings down those who dwell on high, the lofty city; He lays it low, He lays it low to the ground, He brings it down to the dust. The foot shall tread it down – the feet of the poor and the steps of the needy.

See the contrast between those that are elevated to lofty perches of power on earth, and those who trust in the Lord's "everlasting strength" (verse 4). There are people who are godless, but not powerless. They oppress families and cities and empires with their self-serving powers. But those whose power emanates from military, financial, political, or intellectual capabilities will all be brought down to the dust. They may "dwell on high" for a while. They may enjoy influence in their "lofty city" for a time. But see their final, humiliating destiny! They will be so thoroughly abased that even the poorest and neediest of God's people will stand like giants before them, walking right over them as they enter the gates of heaven. Blessed are the poor in spirit (Matthew 5:3), for they will inherit the kingdom of heaven, while the rich and powerful, but godless people of the world, are doomed to be crushed "down to the dust" outside heaven's walls. Our Lord "raises the poor out of the dust, and lifts the needy out of the ash heap" (Psalms 113:7), and He condemns lofty unbelievers to take their place. Let us not envy the short-lived acclaim of unrighteous people. Asaph wrote in Psalm 73, "My steps had nearly slipped. For I was envious of the boastful, when I saw the prosperity of the wicked...pride serves as their necklace; violence covers them like a garment. Their eyes bulge with abundance; they have more than heart could wish. They scoff and speak wickedly concerning oppression; they speak loftily." But Asaph forgets his envy of the lofty speech of the wicked when he remembers in verses 18-19 the punishment that God has decreed for them, "You cast them down to destruction. Oh, how they are brought to desolation, as in a moment! They are utterly consumed with terrors." "The lofty city" is a dangerous place to live. Let us prefer to bow before the feet of our Lord and serve alongside the poor and needy in His family of faith. James 4:10 says, "Humble yourselves in the sight of the Lord, and He will lift you up." But if we exalt ourselves before the Lord, desiring to "dwell on high," He will cast us down.

26:7
The way of the just is uprightness; O Most Upright, You weigh the path of the just.

The ESV translates Isaiah's words as: "The path of the righteous is level; you make level the way of the righteous." This rendering echoes David's sentiments when he wrote in Psalms 26:12, "My foot stands in an even place." Our God, the One who is "Most Upright," will guide His people in the way that is certain to lead to eternal success. God makes the path before His children level, He makes it even so that His people can walk unhindered along the path that leads to His approval and His rewards. He clears the path of obstacles so that "nothing causes them to stumble" (Psalms 119:165). Our Lord calls us to Himself, and He lights the path and makes it plain for all to see. He levels it and clears it of obstacles so that no one can complain that their way to God was blocked by outside forces. This great promise, however, is given only to "the just," it only applies to "the righteous." When sin enters the heart of a man, it affects his spiritual eyesight so that he sees all manner of detours and alternate paths that reroute him around righteousness and onto paths that do not lead to God's approval and His rewards. Sin creates massive upheavals in the course of life that disrupt the level path that God sets before the righteous, creating jagged crags and deep rifts that prevent us from enjoying the level path and even ground that God sets before the feet of those who obey Him. "The path of the righteous is level." "But the way of the ungodly shall perish" (Psalms 1:6). Let thinking men choose their way of life wisely.

26:8
Yes, in the way of Your judgments, O LORD, we have waited for You; the desire of our soul is for Your name and for the remembrance of You.

"The desire of our soul is for Your name." What a blessed state of mind is ours when all we desire is to glorify God's name, when zeal for His house eats us up, when holy jealousy for His honor fuels our actions, when devotion to His cause drives our priorities, and when personal desires are forgotten, completely overwhelmed by the hunger to bring honor to the name of our Lord and Savior. Let us agree with Psalms 8:9 and cry out "O LORD, our Lord, how excellent is Your name in all the earth!" Let us praise His name forever (Psalms 44:8). Let us commit to seeing that His name is "remembered in all generations" (Psalms 45:17). May the desire of our soul be so caught up in honoring the name of the Lord that we join Psalms 86:12 and sing "I will praise You, O Lord my God, with all my heart, and I will glorify Your name forevermore." "The desire of our soul is for Your name." May our family echo this sentiment. We desire no name for ourselves, only that God's name would be glorified in our family. "Not unto us, O LORD, not unto us, but to Your name give glory, because of Your mercy, because of Your truth" (Psalms 115:1). In John 12:28, Jesus revealed that this was the desire of His eternal soul when He prayed, "Father, glorify Your name." "Then a voice came from heaven, saying, 'I have both glorified it and will glorify it again.'" It is the Son's desire to glorify the name of the Father. It is the Father's will that His name be glorified among men. And so, we must be right when our heart leaps within us in agreement with Isaiah's words here. "The desire of our soul is for Your name."

26:9
With my soul I have desired You in the night, yes, by my spirit within me I will seek You early; for when Your judgments are in the earth, the inhabitants of the world will learn righteousness.

Before going to bed at night, Isaiah's last thoughts returned to the Lord. He desired to sit with the Lord once more, to think about Him, to bask in His glory and in His many kindnesses. He "desired" the Lord's presence, he desired his Lord's approval. He desired to know Him more, please Him more, and set his focused attention on the Lord his God one more time before going to sleep. Then, in the morning, his mind raced instantly back to the

Lord once more: "by my spirit within me I will seek You early." We cannot help seeing how David expressed these same sentiments, "O God, You are my God; early will I seek You; my soul thirsts for You; my flesh longs for You in a dry and thirsty land where there is no water" (Psalms 63:1). And then in Psalms 63:6, David continues to express the same feelings that Isaiah describes here, "I remember You on my bed, I meditate on You in the night watches." Our heart leaps inside us as we read Isaiah and David describe their souls' craving for the presence of the living God. Our soul craves the presence of our Lord just the same! We rise early to meet with Him! We lie down at night thinking about Him! When we are alone we meditate on all His works, and when we are with others we talk of His amazing deeds (Psalms 77:12). "As the deer longs for streams of water, so I long for you, O God" (Psalms 42:1). Let us crave nothing but God, and let us readily, continually indulge in this holiest of cravings! Before we sleep, let us fill our minds with the joys of knowing Him, and when we rise in the morning, let us fill our minds with plans for serving Him. Psalms 16:11 says, "In Your presence is fullness of joy," so we find good cause to crave His presence from dawn to dark and in every minute in between, just as Isaiah and David once wrote, and our own soul now confirms.

26:10-11
Let grace be shown to the wicked, yet he will not learn righteousness; in the land of uprightness he will deal unjustly, and will not behold the majesty of the LORD. LORD, when Your hand is lifted up, they will not see. But they will see and be ashamed for their envy of people; yes, the fire of Your enemies shall devour them.

We have been created to be holy, like our Creator (Leviticus 11:44). The allurements of earth and the cravings of our flesh deter us from this pursuit of holiness, so our Lord grants us 2 great gifts to help us remain determined in the quest to be pure. The first was mentioned in verse 9 – seeing the judgments of God, realizing that God punishes the impure compels the thinking "inhabitants of the world" to "learn righteousness." It takes no great intelligence, simply the slightest spiritual perceptiveness to see that if the omnipotent God has promised to severely punish sinners, then it is in our best interest to "learn righteousness" and keep ourselves from sin. Then, secondly, God's great grace moves us to be righteous. Seeing such an outpouring of kindnesses from such a holy God moves the inhabitants of the world with even the slightest spiritual perceptiveness to "seek righteousness" (Zephaniah 2:3) as a proper show of gratitude for the grace that

God has shown. Sadly, even these 2 great gifts from our Lord do not sway a great many men. They defy God's judgments and demean God's grace by enjoying His good gifts but refusing to "learn righteousness" in return.

Here, verse 10 discusses a tragic, but all-too-common scenario. God shows grace to men, but men refuse to "learn righteousness." They "deal unjustly" with God, and this condemns them to an eternity apart from Him, never being able to "behold the majesty of the LORD." The Lord's "hand is lifted up" to do His wonderful works before them, but they refuse to acknowledge His authority; "they will not see" the truth of His love and majesty even when it is presented right in front of their eyes. Jesus spoke to this very matter in Matthew 13:13 when He said, "Therefore I speak to them in parables, because seeing they do not see, and hearing they do not hear, nor do they understand." God speaks, but the wicked refuse to understand. God gives grace, but the rebellious refuse to turn to Him in thanks. God works wonders for all to see, but the wicked refuse to see that His works on their behalf compel them to honor Him with works of their own. But people cannot remain blind forever. At the appointed time "they will see and be ashamed." God will finally reveal His glory and authority unmistakably and unavoidably. And at last, the wicked and rebellious who had refused to "learn righteousness," who had dealt "unjustly" with their Maker, and who had refused to see the truth, they will together "be ashamed" for their unrighteousness and unbelief.

26:12
LORD, You will establish peace for us, for You have also done all our works in us.

The ESV renders the last phrase as "you have done for us all our works." We would have good cause to feel anxious if our salvation depended on our own works. We would be right to worry if our entrance into heaven depended on how many good works we did on earth. Blessedly, on Calvary, our Lord established "peace for us." We are at peace because we know with certainty that our Savior has done the work required to cleanse us from sin and grant us admittance into His good graces in heaven. We have been granted peace with God through our Lord Jesus Christ (Romans 5:1) because He has "made peace through the blood of His cross" (Colossians 1:20). Everything required to cleanse our sin, reconcile us to our Maker, and grant us eternity in heaven has already been done by the saving, loving, and substitutionary works of Jesus. So then, since He has established peace for us, and has done all our works for us, what remains for us to do? Matthew

5:16 tells us that we are to "Let your light so shine before men, that they may see your good works and glorify your Father in heaven." I find it fascinating that because our Lord has done all our works for us – we are compelled to work. That even though all the works necessary for our salvation have already been accomplished by our Savior, we are able to shine before men on earth and glorify our God in heaven by demonstrating good works. Our Lord has already done all our work for our sake. So now, let us strive to do all His work for His name's sake.

26:13-14
O LORD our God, masters besides You have had dominion over us; but by You only we make mention of Your name. They are dead, they will not live; they are deceased, they will not rise. Therefore You have punished and destroyed them, and made all their memory to perish.

God's people in the Old Testament, New Testament, and in our day have had masters and leaders that have been oppressive. Like Nebuchadnezzar in Daniel 3, the Philippian magistrates in Acts 16, and like communist and radical Muslims in our day, they threaten violence against those who worship God. Or, like Nabal in I Samuel 25, like Festus in Acts 26, and like many anti-Christian groups in our day, they make a mockery of God's people. Across the ages there have been those that "have had dominion over us" for a time. The extent of their authority and the tenure of their influence has been severely limited, however. They may inflict injury on our body and mind, but they cannot touch our soul. Their influence may bring hardship all the days of our life, but they cannot touch us once we reach our heavenly destination. Isaiah admits that there are many people and nations more powerful than those in God's army, but he does not revere them. "we worship You alone" (NLT). "We remember Your name alone" (HCS). God will make even the memory of oppression and oppressors "to perish." Isaiah is so certain that God will destroy evil leaders who wreak havoc on His people, he writes in the past tense. "They are dead." "They are deceased." "You have punished and destroyed them, and made all their memory to perish." Let us not be shocked when evil men and women hold power and sway over homes and communities and nations. It has been that way for a very long time. But let us take comfort knowing that their influence is short lived. We are not to fear them. Matthew 10:28 says, "do not fear those who kill the body but cannot kill the soul. But rather fear Him who is able to destroy both soul and body in hell." We are to focus, instead, on the kingdom and dominion of the Lord our God. The seemingly impressive works of wicked kings and kingdoms will be forgotten, and "all their memory" will vanish away. But in striking contrast, the smallest, quietest efforts carried out by the meekest servants in God's kingdom will be remembered and rewarded forever (Matthew 10:42, Mark 14:9).

26:15
You have increased the nation, O LORD, You have increased the nation; You are glorified; You have expanded all the borders of the land.

"You are glorified." Isaiah rejoices because God is "honored" (HCS), He is "glorified" in the eyes of those who have watched Him expand the borders and increase the prosperity of His people. May all God's blessings toward us turn out to glorify His name just the same. May our walk with God be so obvious and so well-known that any honor shown to us will honor Him. Anything that blesses God's kingdom will bless us. And any blessing to us will glorify our Lord. When God increases David's greatness in Psalms 71:21, David praises Him in Psalms 71:22. God blesses His people in Psalms 115:14-15, and the people bless Him in verse 18. Such is as it should be -- God's blessings on us result in His name being glorified. God has blessed our family. He has so richly blessed our family. I am grateful. May we return all our Lord's blessings in praise. May our prayer always be: Father, You have "increased" our blessings, You have "expanded" the borders of our influence. May You be "glorified" in all You have done for us. God's blessings on Judah glorified His name. May His blessings on us have the same result.

26:16
LORD, in trouble they have visited You, they poured out a prayer when Your chastening was upon them.

The steadfast, unwavering, patient love of God is without equal. When people are "in trouble," they "visit" their Creator and He grants them entrance to His throne. When people finally return to the Lord after suffering under His "chastening," He hears their prayer. This single verse seems to summarize the entire book of Judges. In that book, God's people live out a seemingly endless cycle of extended rebellion and temporary repentance – returning to God only after their sin and God's chastening have made them too miserable to remain apart from Him. Jonah personally exhibits this trait that his entire nation had demonstrated over and over again. In Jonah 2:2, he prays from the belly of the fish, "I cried out to the LORD because of my affliction, and He answered me." The only reason Jonah prays, is that he is miserable! He appears to have little love for God, no heart to serve Him, and no obvious intent to glorify Him. And yet, with personal pain as Jonah's singular motivation for praying, God still answers him in kindness! Better yet, Hosea 5:15 tells us that the Lord's kindness to Jonah was no exception, it is, in fact, His general rule. In that verse, the Lord says, "I will return again to My place till they acknowledge their offense. Then they will seek My face; in their affliction they will earnestly seek Me." In the very next verse (Hosea 6:1), Hosea urges his people to respond to this great invitation from the Lord, "Come, and let us return to the LORD; for He has torn, but He will heal us; He has stricken, but He will bind us up." Let us pour our prayers heavenward when "trouble" and "chastening" have brought us low. The Lord "is a refuge in times of trouble" (Psalms 9:9) – even when our "trouble" is all our own fault. It is not our Lord's pleasure to watch us struggle for air in the waters of failure and distress. Remarkably, wonderfully, God says in Psalms 50:15 that it is His good pleasure for us to: "Call upon Me in the day of trouble; I will deliver you, and you shall glorify Me."

26:17-18

As a woman with child is in pain and cries out in her pangs, when she draws near the time of her delivery, so have we been in Your sight, O LORD. We have been with child, we have been in pain; we have, as it were, brought forth wind; we have not accomplished any deliverance in the earth, nor have the inhabitants of the world fallen.

God's people have been "in pain." The severity of their agony is compared to a woman giving birth. Just as a woman "cries out in her pangs," so God's people have cried out, perhaps screamed out in pain. But unlike a woman in labor who soon forgets all her pain when she sees the face of her newborn baby (John 16:21), Israel has only "brought forth wind." All their labor and pain and distress have failed to deliver a blessing to anyone. Their labor pains were severe but led to no deliverance. We are reminded that our Lord can redeem our pains to accomplish His wonderful purposes. But apart from Him, pain on its own does not secure rescue for anyone. When our heart is in our Savior's hands, painful chastening and bitter life lessons can yield "the peaceable fruit of righteousness to those who have been trained by it" (Hebrews 12:11). But apart from the "training" and sustaining hands of our Lord, when these same "labor pains" of chastening and hardship fall on unbelievers, I Thessalonians 5:3 says that "they shall not escape." The lesson is easy to apply. Let us press ever closer to the training, sustaining hands of our Lord, so that hardship will yield the peaceable fruit of righteousness rather than simply add pain to imperfection and add further suffering to the sting of guilt.

26:19
Your dead shall live; together with my dead body they shall arise. Awake and sing, you who dwell in dust; for your dew is like the dew of herbs, and the earth shall cast out the dead.

    Isaiah calls on his readers to consider and rejoice in the prospects of our resurrection. "Your dead shall live"! Together with my dead body they shall arise"! Let us "Awake and sing"! Today we "dwell in dust." In some wonderful ways we are only a little lower than the angels (Psalms 8:5), but in many ways we are not much higher than a worm. Psalms 22:6 says, "I am a worm, and no man; a reproach of men, and despised by the people." We live in the dust and are trampled on by any number of oppressors. But Isaiah encourages us not to sleep away this time in the dust. "Awake!" "Sing!" For our resurrection is coming! The dead shall live again! Those who live in the dust with Christ will rise again to be with Christ in heaven forever (I Thessalonians 4:16). What a blessed thought. Heaven awaits us just on the other side of death. The thought compels us to wake up and sing out praises to the One who will convey our mortal body into the eternal joys of life in heaven. Psalms 57:8 (NLT) says, "Wake up, my soul! Wake up, O harp and lyre! I will waken the dawn with my song." Let us not sleep away our time on earth! We have much praise to give and little time to give it! Ah, in heaven we will have the blessed opportunity to praise God forever, but right now, here on earth, we have the unique once-in-an-eternity opportunity to sing God's praises from the dust, to lift up our song of praise in the joy of the *anticipation* of our resurrection. Isaiah grants a dear encouragement to those who are grieving the loss of their loved ones. "Your dead shall live." Jesus said, "I am the resurrection and the life. Whoever believes in me, though he die, yet shall he live" (John 11:25, ESV). May this assurance move us to do as Isaiah calls us to do, "Awake and sing."

26:20-21
Come, my people, enter your chambers, and shut your doors behind you; hide yourself, as it were, for a little moment, until the indignation is past. For behold, the LORD comes out of His place to punish the inhabitants of the earth for their iniquity; the earth will also disclose her blood, and will no more cover her slain.

Today, it is good for us to kneel before our Lord and plead with Him to show mercy on the unbelieving. It is right for us to shake the gates of heaven with our intercessory prayers, echoing God's heart by vehemently pleading with Him to save the lost, desiring "all men to be saved and to come to the knowledge of the truth" (I Timothy 2:4). Today, it is right for us to "make a wall, and stand in the gap before (God) on behalf of the land, that (He) should not destroy it (Ezekiel 22:30). Today it is right for us to "Go into all the world and preach the gospel to every creature" (Mark 16:15), hungering to rescue every possible soul from the effects of sin and unbelief. Today, it is right for us to pray for and preach to the lost. But the day is coming when the opportunity to rescue sinners will be past. On that day, Isaiah says, we will, "as it were," quietly kneel in the safety of our house of worship, in our private room of prayer and shut the door behind us. When God, at last, unleashes His righteous anger on those who persist in their "evil heart of unbelief" (Hebrews 3:12), it will be best for us to "hide... for a little moment, until the indignation is past." Today, men find excuses for their sins and arguments supporting their unbelief. They think themselves worthy of special permission to sin and special exemptions from punishment. But on the day when God rises to punish sin and unbelief, no sin will be excused and no sinner will be exempt. The earth will "disclose" all her dark secrets and private sins, and no one will be able to cover their guilt or hide from their due punishment. Today, we must work to save men's souls, for the time is coming when "no one can work" (John 9:4). We will simply hide in a chamber of prayer, as it were, in the blessed safety of our Father's mercy, quietly grateful that our precious Jesus has saved us from this "wrath to come" (Matthew 3:7).

Isaiah 27

27:1
In that day the LORD with His severe sword, great and strong, will punish Leviathan the fleeing serpent, Leviathan that twisted serpent; and He will slay the reptile that is in the sea.

Chapter 26 ended with a fear-invoking forewarning that the Lord will "punish the inhabitants of the earth for their iniquity." Chapter 27 begins by extending God's promised punishments on the wicked to include Satan, who is the tempter (Matthew 4:3) and accuser (Revelation 12:10) of those that face that judgment. Here, Satan is called "Leviathan," the serpent, just as he was called in Genesis 3. Two more descriptors are added, however. He is the "fleeing" serpent and he is that "twisted" serpent. In Luke 3:7, John the Baptist asks the scathing question, "Brood of vipers! Who warned you to flee from the wrath to come?" John then tells the crowd the only alternative to fleeing God's wrath that is available to us: "Bear fruits worthy of repentance." Apparently, both men and devils have the same 2 alternatives. We can repent and bear fruits worthy of that repentance, or we can set out on a life-long, hopeless effort to "flee the wrath to come." Satan tempts and accuses and troubles and devours people, but his evil efforts are the last-gasp efforts of a retreating, yes, fleeing foe.

Secondly, Satan is "that twisted serpent." God gives good gifts to men (Ephesians 4:8). Everything God makes is good (Genesis 1:10, etc.). But Satan, along with "unstable men" take the good things of God and "twist" them "to their own destruction" (II Peter 3:16). At the appointed time, the Lord will "slay" that reptilian devil that has harassed men since his failed rebellion eons ago. Satan is a "fleeing serpent." But in the end, he will have no place to hide. His final demise is already described in Revelation 20:10, "The devil, who deceived them, was cast into the lake of fire and brimstone where the beast and the false prophet are. And they will be tormented day and night forever and ever."

27:2-3
In that day sing to her, "A vineyard of red wine! I, the LORD, keep it, I water it every moment; lest any hurt it, I keep it night and day."

Like a gardener lovingly weeds and waters the plants that he has tended since he first placed their seeds in the ground, so the Lord says He cares for His people. He keeps his garden well-watered, He makes sure no trespassers trample through and cause "hurt," and as a concerned gardener covers his favored plants when there is danger of a nighttime frost, so the Lord safeguards His people "night and day." In Psalm 80, Asaph compares God's people to a vineyard, just as the Lord does here. In verse 8 he writes, "You have brought a vine out of Egypt; You have cast out the nations, and planted it. You prepared room for it, and caused it to take deep root, and it filled the land." But Israel's sins caused them to lose God's favor and lose His blessings on them. So, in verses 14-15 Asaph prays, "Return, we beseech You, O God of hosts; look down from heaven and see, and visit this vine and the vineyard which Your right hand has planted, and the branch that You made strong for Yourself." Here, God seems to answer that prayer. In chapter 5, Isaiah sang a song comparing Israel to a disappointing, unfruitful vineyard that had ruined God's wonderful efforts on their behalf. But here, our loving Lord, in forgiveness and mercy, declares that He will return to His beloved vineyard, and tend it with love and skill and watch care once more. "I keep it night and day." What a precious thought. "Behold, He who keeps Israel shall neither slumber nor sleep. The LORD is your keeper; the LORD is your shade at your right hand. The sun shall not strike you by day, nor the moon by night. The LORD shall preserve you from all evil; He shall preserve your soul. The LORD shall preserve your going out and your coming in from this time forth, and even forevermore" (Psalms 121:4-8).

27:4-5
"Fury is not in Me. Who would set briers and thorns against Me in battle? I would go through them, I would burn them together. Or let him take hold of My strength, that he may make peace with Me; and he shall make peace with Me."

We continue to see the contrast between God's intention to punish His vineyard, Israel, in chapter 5, and His intention to protect and make peace with His "vineyard" in our verses here. God is holy, and He requires that His people follow Him in holiness. When we fail in personal holiness, He will chasten us in love. But once chastened and brought back to our senses, our Lord runs to us with forgiveness as the father does the prodigal in Luke 15. Hosea 6:1 says, "Come, and let us return to the LORD; for He has torn, but He will heal us; He has stricken, but He will bind us up." In Isaiah 5:6 the Lord allows "briers and thorns" to rise up in His vineyard as a punishment for their sin. But the time for punishment is now past, and those who would act like "briers and thorns" and trouble God's people for reasons of their own will find that they are fighting against God Himself. Briers and thorns may be a severe nuisance for a garden, but they are no trouble to God at all. "Who would set briers and thorns against Me in battle?" Like a thorn bush trying to hold back a tank in battle, so will God's enemies melt away when He comes to "burn them together" as He works to protect His people. It is God's desire to "make peace" with His people. Jesus came and "preached peace to you who were afar off and to those who were near." What a blessed thought to know that we are at peace with God, that we have "peace with God through our Lord Jesus Christ" (Romans 5:1). Psalms 29:11 says, "The LORD will give strength to His people; the LORD will bless His people with peace." The ESV turns the Lord's words into an invitation, "Let them make peace with me, let them make peace with me." "There is no peace," says the LORD, "for the wicked" (Isaiah 48:22). But for those who will repent and strive to bear works worthy of that repentance, we have been promised the never-ending reward of eternal peace with God.

27:6
Those who come He shall cause to take root in Jacob; Israel shall blossom and bud, and fill the face of the world with fruit.

God chose Israel as His own special people. "For the LORD has chosen Jacob for Himself, Israel for His special treasure" (Psalms 135:4). In Jeremiah 30:22 God says to Israel, "You shall be My people, and I will be your God." God never intended, however, for His blessings toward and calling to Israel to be limited only to that (tiny) nation. God's intentions for Israel were that His people would "fill the face of the world with fruit." The truth that God taught to Israel would be passed on to the peoples of the world, and the blessings that God showered on Israel would overflow to every nation the world over. "The root of the righteous yields fruit" (Proverbs 12:12), fruit that will bless the whole world and fruit that will last forever. "You didn't choose me. I chose you. I appointed you to go and produce fruit that will last" (John 15:16 NLT). As God's children today, let us strive to "fill the face of the world with fruit." Let us keep a global perspective even as we faithfully carry out our local mission. God called Jeremiah to be a "prophet to the nations" (Jeremiah 1:5), even though he never (willingly) travelled out of his home country. Similarly, it is God's will that all His children (all His children!), strive to fill the face of the world with the fruit of their labors for His kingdom. Jacob's root will anchor deep in the blessings of God. Israel's buds will blossom beautifully as a reflection of the glory of her Creator – and all so that the world will be filled with the fruit of faith and devotion of God's servants. "God, our own God, shall bless us. God shall bless us, and all the ends of the earth shall fear Him" (Psalms 67:6b-7).

27:7-9
Has He struck Israel as He struck those who struck him? Or has He been slain according to the slaughter of those who were slain by Him? In measure, by sending it away, you contended with it. He removes it by His rough wind in the day of the east wind. Therefore by this the iniquity of Jacob will be covered; and this is all the fruit of taking away his sin: when he makes all the stones of the altar like chalkstones that are beaten to dust, wooden images and incense altars shall not stand.

Judgment on unbelievers and punishment for sinners is a certainty. Equally certain is that on judgment day, "wooden images and incense altars shall not stand." Those who cling to the mercies of God and place their faith in the cleansing blood of the Son will find that when judgment day arrives "the iniquity of (those who trust in God) will be covered." All who entrust their eternity to an idol, however, will find that "wooden images and incense altars shall not stand." Incense cannot wash away sins. Wooden images cannot convey their believers into heaven. Jeremiah 10:8 gives clear warning, "A wooden idol is a worthless doctrine." No amount of sincerity on the part of the worshiper can infuse a wooden statue with the power to cleanse souls and carry those souls into heaven. Wooden images "shall not stand" when men and women kneel before their Maker on judgment day. They will fall like Dagon before the Lord (I Samuel 5) and be the source of catastrophic disappointment for their followers. Those who foolishly claim that all religions lead to heaven or that all religions lead to God should take careful note of Leviticus 26:30. In that verse, God warns His people that if they leave Him to follow other gods and other religions that He will "destroy your high places, cut down your incense altars, and cast your carcasses on the lifeless forms of your idols; and My soul shall abhor you." God abhors idol religion. Neither the images, nor those who believe in them will stand on judgment day. On that day, every knee shall bow, and every tongue confess that Jesus Christ, and He alone, is Lord (Philippians 2:10).

27:10-11
Yet the fortified city will be desolate, the habitation forsaken and left like a wilderness; there the calf will feed, and there it will lie down and consume its branches. When its boughs are withered, they will be broken off; the women come and set them on fire. For it is a people of no understanding; therefore He who made them will not have mercy on them, and He who formed them will show them no favor.

Having "no understanding" has horrible consequences. God "will not have mercy on them." God will "show them no favor," when people fail to develop understanding. Psalms 32:9 sends out the warning, "Do not be like the horse or like the mule, which have no understanding, which must be harnessed with bit and bridle, else they will not come near you." We were made to understand that God is great and we can "come near" Him. We have been created to understand that God blesses those who are near Him, God forgives those who are near Him, and that the purpose and highest joy of existence is in drawing near to Him. If we fail to develop and act upon this fundamental "understanding" we bring judgment on ourselves. Proverbs 2:2 urges us to "apply your heart to understanding." And Proverbs 2:3 urges us still further to "lift up your voice for understanding." "Understanding will keep you safe" (Proverbs 2:11 NLT), while our verses here tell us that a lack of understanding will disqualify us from God's mercy. "Good understanding gains favor," but our verses here remind us that failure to develop understanding excludes us from gaining God's favor. The invisible attributes of God are clearly seen in His creation (Romans 1:20). Failure to understand the origins of the universe and failure to understand what pleases the Originator of the universe is inexcusable and condemning.

27:12-13
And it shall come to pass in that day that the LORD will thresh, from the channel of the River to the Brook of Egypt; and you will be gathered one by one, O you children of Israel. So it shall be in that day; the great trumpet will be blown; they will come, who are about to perish in the land of Assyria, and they who are outcasts in the land of Egypt, and shall worship the LORD in the holy mount at Jerusalem.

What a wonderful double prophecy Isaiah provides us here! The sins of Israel will cause them to flee to Egypt and to be taken captive to Assyria and Babylon. But "in that day" the Lord will gather His children back to Himself, "one by one" they will be restored, no one will be overlooked. None of God's people will be forgotten. He will not be content with the 99 (Matthew 18:12), but will make sure that every one of His chosen lambs is accounted for. In the same way, "in that day," at the end of time, "the LORD will thresh" the peoples of the world and call His own chosen ones to Himself. And just as He summoned His dispersed children back to Himself in the Old Testament, so He will do at the end of time – "the great trumpet will be blown" and His people will be gathered together one by one to meet their Lord. "The trumpet of God" (I Thessalonians 4:16) will be blown and the living saints will join with the resurrected saints to "meet the Lord in the air." And from that time on, God's people will never again be dispersed by captivity or death. They "shall worship the LORD in the holy mount at Jerusalem" – the "New Jerusalem" (Revelation 21:2) that will be the home and house of worship for all God's people forever.

Isaiah 28

28:1
Woe to the crown of pride, to the drunkards of Ephraim, whose glorious beauty is a fading flower which is at the head of the verdant valleys, to those who are overcome with wine!

    The prideful men and women of Ephraim are compared to drunkards. They wear a "crown of pride." In contrast to the godly people in verse 5 whose trust in God is like a "crown of glory." The people of Ephraim crown themselves with delight in their own accomplishments, their own abilities, and their own positions of privilege. Taking pride in oneself is much like being intoxicated with alcohol. Drunks think they look clever, while those sober around them look on them with scorn. Their drunkenness often places them at risk of great danger, yet they are tranquilized, unaware of the peril they are in. Those who wear the crown of pride are much the same. God looks on them with scorn, even while they think they look so good. Their pride places them at the brink of destruction (Proverbs 16:18), but they are tranquilized and unaware of the danger they are in. The strength and beauty that the ungodly take pride in "is a fading flower." The source of their pride will not last forever. Their crown will corrode and fade away, just like the fleeting successes they once took pride in. Woe to those who choose to wear the crown of pride. "A man's pride will bring him low" (Proverbs 29:23). "When pride comes, then comes shame" (Proverbs 11:2). It is inevitable. Pride in oneself will always lead to shame. As soon as we are brought into the presence of the Lord, our glories will instantly pale in the face of His, and the very things that we once took pride in will immediately bring us shame instead. Unless, that is, our pride is in our Lord. If our crown is our trust in our Creator, then our crown will shine all the brighter when we are ushered into His presence. Woe to those who take pride in anything other than their Savior's glories. All other sources of pride will bring us low and cause us shame.

28:2-4
Behold, the Lord has a mighty and strong one, like a tempest of hail and a destroying storm, like a flood of mighty waters overflowing, who will bring them down to the earth with His hand. The crown of pride, the drunkards of Ephraim, will be trampled underfoot; and the glorious beauty is a fading flower which is at the head of the verdant valley, like the first fruit before the summer, which an observer sees; he eats it up while it is still in his hand.

God is "mighty and strong," and prideful men are not. At best, man's glory is "a fading flower." But even if they were like a towering oak tree, they would still be "trampled underfoot" by God's omnipotence. God brings tempests and storms and floods that will sweep the pride of men downstream as easily as a child picks an apple and "eats it up" in a moment's time. Again, Isaiah's prophecy contains a double meaning. The Assyrians are mighty and strong in the hands of the Lord, and they will destroy Ephraim with ease. And for those who fail to learn the lesson provided through Assyria's destruction of Ephraim, the same ending is assured – those who ignore the glory of God and take delight in their own personal glory will be destroyed by God's judgments just as Ephraim was destroyed by Assyria long ago.

28:5-6
In that day the LORD of hosts will be for a crown of glory and a diadem of beauty to the remnant of His people, for a spirit of justice to him who sits in judgment, and for strength to those who turn back the battle at the gate.

ISAIAH 28

In contrast to the woes meted out on those who take pride in themselves, look here at the list of blessings adorning those who trust in the Lord of hosts! To the believer, the Lord of hosts will, Himself, be "a crown of glory." The glory of men will always, inevitably fade away. No matter how pretty a girl is, no matter how strong a man is, no matter how rich or smart or powerful we become, all of these "crowns" will fade away. But if Jesus is our pride and joy, the source of our pride will never lose its luster. I Peter 5:4 affirms for us that "when the Chief Shepherd appears, you will receive the crown of glory that does not fade away."

Secondly, when our confidence and pride is in "the LORD of hosts," we will receive a "diadem of beauty." The beauty of the LORD our God will be upon us (Psalms 90:17). And unlike our outward beauty which melts away like a moth (Psalms 39:11), the presence of our Lord within us fills our souls with an "unfading beauty" (I Peter 3:4 NLT) "which is so precious to God."

Thirdly, those that trust in the Lord of hosts, and not in their own power, will receive "a spirit of justice." It is a great blessing to God's people when their leaders at every level seek justice, not personal advancement. God fills His followers with a heart to humbly give up their own rights and privileges, while at the same time strive diligently to assure justice and safety to the oppressed and needy around them.

Then, fourthly, God grants "strength to those who turn back the battle at the gate." Once again, we are reminded that life is a battle. It is a "good fight" (II Timothy 4:7). But here we are promised that all those who trust in God will be empowered for the fight before them. When the enemy marches to "the gate" of our souls, when we battle conflicts on the outside and fears on the inside (II Corinthians 7:5), God will give us "strength." It is good for us to put our confidence in the Lord, for "the LORD will give strength to His people" (Psalms 29:11). Life is a fight. Life is a battle. Blessedly, "You have armed me with strength for the battle; You have subdued under me those who rose up against me" (Psalms 18:39).

Those who take pride in their personal beauty and their personal strength "have their reward" (Matthew 6:2). But we are unenvious of their pleasures, for the rewards offered those whose pride and joy is in Christ far exceed the benefits of those who take pride in themselves. Unlike their temporary, fading enjoyments, the Lord of hosts has promised us "a crown of glory," "a diadem of beauty," "a spirit of justice," and "strength to those who turn back the battle at the gate." We find that these rewards far exceed those enjoyed by others.

28:7-8

But they also have erred through wine, and through intoxicating drink are out of the way; the priest and the prophet have erred through intoxicating drink, they are swallowed up by wine, they are out of the way through intoxicating drink; they err in vision, they stumble in judgment. For all tables are full of vomit and filth; no place is clean.

Condemnation is brought on God's people because they have "erred through wine." Perhaps there is a way for Spirit-filled men and women to drink alcohol and not "err," (I have some doubt), but it is clear in this passage that the people of God have marred their precious relationship with their Creator for the sake of the joys of drinking. "Intoxicating drink" has put them "out of the way," the effects of alcohol have deterred them from God's ways and moved them to step into harm's way instead. Their vision is diminished, their insights are damaged. Their judgment is impaired, and their discernment is crippled. And all for the sake of drinking. Psalms 18:24 says, "the LORD has recompensed me according to my righteousness, according to the cleanness of my hands in His sight." But here, the people have disqualified themselves from God's full rewards because "no place is clean" when they foul their lives with alcohol. The picture could hardly be clearer or more disgusting. The "tables" of their service "are full of vomit and filth." There are some who say that they can consume "intoxicating drink" and it does not affect their intimacy with the Lord nor impair their service to Him. This is clearly not the message delivered here. The kingdom of heaven is compared to a wedding feast (Revelation 19:9), and while blessed with the company of the Son our Savior, there is no need to fast, and the enjoyments of intoxicating drink are holy (Luke 5:34). But we live in the day when our Lord is yet "taken away" (Luke 5:35) from us, and so, it is right for us to fast, to abstain from alcohol, to discipline our body (I Corinthians 9:27) and to keep our wits about us so that we are not "disqualified" from godly service.

28:9-10

"Whom will he teach knowledge? And whom will he make to understand the message? Those just weaned from milk? Those just drawn from the breasts? For precept must be upon precept, precept upon precept, line upon line, line upon line, here a little, there a little."

How do you teach toddlers who know almost nothing? How do you teach people who can't tell their right hand from their left (Jonah 4:11)? Here, God gives His spiritual education system. He teaches "precept upon precept," He teaches "line upon line," and grants His people gradually increasing spiritual insights, "here a little, there a little." God starts with very basic concepts with us -- Exodus 20 starts with 10 core precepts: don't kill people, don't worship any other god except your Creator, etc. In Isaiah's day and ours, God teaches us with incremental revelations of His will and ways. It is not expected that brand new believers can articulate the doctrine of the trinity or explain the ministry of Melchizedek hours after coming to faith. It is expected, however, that when God teaches us layer by layer, line by line, concept building on concept, that, once taught, we will not require remedial lessons. We will accept God's word as fact, we will remember what He has taught, and we will rightly apply what He teaches to our daily lives. The writer of Hebrews expressed his dissatisfaction with his readers because "you need someone to teach you again the first principles of the oracles of God" (Hebrews 5:12). His desire was to leave the "discussion of the elementary principles of Christ," and move on to deeper spiritual truths – but he could not delve into some depths of spiritual understanding because his readers had become "dull of hearing" (Hebrews 5:11). God is patient with us. He teaches spiritual truths just as moms and dads teach their toddlers, one concept at a time. In grateful response to His patient instruction, let us hungrily hang on every word He teaches. Let us join with David and say, "Teach me, O LORD, the way of Your statutes, and I shall keep it to the end" (Psalms 119:33). Let us not be like the Hebrews who had to be retaught lessons they should never have forgotten. Instead, may our response to the privilege of hearing the instructions of our Lord forever be: "I will never forget Your precepts, for by them You have given me life" (Psalms 119:93).

28:11-13
For with stammering lips and another tongue He will speak to this people, to whom He said, "This is the rest with which you may cause the weary to rest," and, "This is the refreshing"; yet they would not hear. But the word of the LORD was to them, "Precept upon precept, precept upon precept, line upon line, line upon line, here a little, there a little," that they might go and fall backward, and be broken and snared and caught.

God's spiritual education system is without flaw. He teaches us "precept upon precept," incrementally adding "line upon line" of lessons and spiritual reasoning that will allow His people to grow in spiritual maturity. Sadly, His people in Isaiah's day failed to learn this way. God teaches them little by little as they are able to absorb His truths – but despite His perfect means of teaching, and the perfect content of His teaching, His people will refuse to understand. Their failure will require them to endure a different means of education – they will be taught "with stammering lips and another tongue." The Assyrians will come with foreign speech and foreign weapons and will conquer Israel, sending their children into captivity into a foreign land where their lessons will be delivered in a foreign tongue. There are grave consequences for failing in God's school of spiritual understanding. When God teaches, let us learn! And then, once taught, let us pass on to others what our Lord has told to us. Hebrews 5:12 says, "by this time you ought to be teachers." It is God's intention to teach us His ways. He will teach us little by little, precept upon precept. And then, once taught, it is His intention for us to go and teach others what we have learned from our Lord.

28:14-15
Therefore hear the word of the LORD, you scornful men, who rule this people who are in Jerusalem, because you have said, "We have made a covenant with death, and with Sheol we are in agreement. When the overflowing scourge passes through, it will not come to us, for we have made lies our refuge, and under falsehood we have hidden ourselves."

Death and judgment are inevitable. Every man and every woman will face death. Every man and every woman will face judgment. The blessed news is that we do not have to face death alone, nor do we need to fear the horrible outcome of judgment. All of us who trust and obey our Creator have this wonderful promise, "The eternal God is your refuge, and underneath are the everlasting arms" (Deuteronomy 33:27). Scornfully rejecting God as their refuge, however, the rulers of Jerusalem have made "lies" their refuge and hidden themselves "under falsehood." Death and judgment are coming for everyone. But all too common, people join the rulers of Jerusalem and hide themselves under lies. They believe the lie that there is no God. Or they believe the lie that God does not mind their personal sins. Or they believe the lie that it is better to take care of their here and now rather than their hereafter. Here, the rulers believed that they had made "a covenant with death." If it were not so tragic, their foolishness would be laughable. Death makes no treaties. We cannot bargain with death (as we will see in verse 18). We can, however, take refuge in the eternal God, and rest safely in His everlasting arms. "The righteous has a refuge in his death" (Proverbs 14:32). But for those who make lies their refuge, death will expose that their soul is utterly, eternally without defense.

28:16
Therefore thus says the Lord GOD: "Behold, I lay in Zion a stone for a foundation, a tried stone, a precious cornerstone, a sure foundation; whoever believes will not act hastily."

    Behold! Our Lord lays a solid, sure foundation for us to stand on, a rock-solid foundation we can bank our life on. Our Lord lays for us a precious stone for this foundation. We do not fear that it will let us down, for it is a "tried" stone. Untold millions have entrusted their eternities to this saving stone and have found it to hold true. We find in I Peter 2:6 that Jesus is this "precious cornerstone," and like a stone-sure foundation He proves dependable when we base our whole life on Him, commit our life's priorities to Him, and establish our house and home upon Him. Those who trust in this sure foundation, this rock of defense, find it completely dependable. They will stand on this rock with confidence, unmoved by the disappointments and storms of life. Others are quick to forget their faith in God. A loved one dies, and with grieving rage they hastily turn their back on their Maker. Some offer up a prayer, and if it is not answered, they hastily turn from God with deeply-set disappointment. But "whoever believes" will not act so "hastily" when sorrow or disappointment beat against them. They stand ever more securely on the solid rock that is the sure foundation of their soul's eternal well-being.

28:17
Also I will make justice the measuring line, and righteousness the plummet; the hail will sweep away the refuge of lies, and the waters will overflow the hiding place.

    Men who reject God tend to mystify or rather "mistify" Judgment Day with a complicated, self-serving set of principles. Their opening line describing their understanding of judgment may begin with something like: "Good people go to heaven and bad people go to hell." But what differentiates a bad person from a good person is a trickier matter to define, and most include exoneration for wrongs done personally. This difficulty for people to actually define who is good and who is bad moves them to believe the lie that they themselves can decide who is good and who is bad, and that they can decide for themselves if they have done enough to qualify themselves as "good." It is a lie (and really should make no sense to a rational person) to think that individuals can choose for themselves what the qualifications are for reaching heaven. Those who reject God take comfort in lies of this sort; in fact, they take shelter in a "refuge of lies." It is comforting for sinners to believe the lie that God is not real. It is further comforting for them to believe the lie that He overlooks their own personal sins. And they prefer to believe that enjoying the pleasures of sin in the here and now is more satisfying than assuring the security of their soul in the hereafter. But God's method of judgment will "sweep away" all the mist and false security of these lies. The hail and flood waters of God's pure judgment will sweep away everything that men try to build in an attempt to excuse away their sins. The judgments of God are not shrouded in mystery, they have no double standard, and they are always followed to the letter. God makes "justice" the "measuring line." God will show absolute justice in His judgment. There will be no leniency for those who meant well. There will be no wiggle room allowed for those who only sinned a little bit. Rich people are judged with the same justice as the poor. Education, good looks, deep pockets, and friendly smiles do not sway God at all. None of these things affect our eternal destiny. God's judgment uses "justice" as "the measuring line." God also uses "righteousness" as His "plumb line" (ESV). Do we pass, or do we fail? God's judgment is based on "righteousness." Once again, we see that pretty looks, kind words, family connections, and strength in mind or body do us no good on Judgment Day. The only thing that matters is, does our righteousness stand perfectly straight when compared with God's righteous plumb line? Without a perfectly righteous soul, no man can enter heaven. There are no exceptions. Righteousness is the plumb line God uses to prove who meets the qualifications for heaven and who does not. Man-made schemes for reaching heaven will be swept away. Personally-devised evaluations for deciding ones' fitness for heaven will be drowned out in a deluge of God's judgments, because righteousness is the only thing that is weighed in the balance; righteousness is the only thing that is held up to God's plumb line when He judges us. Those with "imputed righteousness" (Romans 4:6) granted by Jesus their Savior find this verse comforting. For all others, however, for anyone who thinks that they can reach heaven by any other means other than a lifetime of absolute, unblemished, pure righteousness – this verse stands as a solemn warning.

28:18-19

Your covenant with death will be annulled, and your agreement with Sheol will not stand; when the overflowing scourge passes through, then you will be trampled down by it. As often as it goes out it will take you; for morning by morning it will pass over, and by day and by night; it will be a terror just to understand the report.

In verse 15 we find the "scornful men" of Jerusalem had thought to make "a covenant with death." Here, God says that this covenant will be "annulled." Jesus alone holds the keys to Hades and death (Revelation 1:18). Hezekiah pleaded with the Lord that death's grip on him might be released for a time, and God granted his request (II Kings 20). But it is sheer folly to think that anyone can sign a unilateral treaty that death will find binding. Isaiah makes plain that their "agreement with Sheol will not stand." Those who scorned God's authority and thought that they could control their destiny with death will find that death tramples them down as it trampled the king's officer in II Kings 7:17. They had thought that they could spurn God and avoid death, but they will find that there is nowhere they can go to flee from God's presence and there is nowhere they can go to avoid death. Death will haunt them "morning by morning." It will haunt them "by day and by night." The "terror" of death will never leave them. Such is the fate of those who try to circumvent God's authority and fool themselves into thinking that the power of life and death is in their hands.

28:20-22
For the bed is too short to stretch out on, and the covering so narrow that one cannot wrap himself in it. For the LORD will rise up as at Mount Perazim, He will be angry as in the Valley of Gibeon – that He may do His work, His awesome work, and bring to pass His act, His unusual act. Now therefore, do not be mockers, lest your bonds be made strong; for I have heard from the Lord GOD of hosts, a destruction determined even upon the whole earth.

The people of Israel have scorned God and thought that they could make a "covenant with death," and an "agreement" with Sheol (verse 15) that would protect them from danger and judgment. But with a vivid, visual image, God reveals how their "agreement" appears from heaven's perspective. Their bargain with death is like a tall man lying on a short bed. His feet hang over the edge awkwardly, even comically. He can't rest and looks ridiculous when he tries. His blanket is so short it doesn't reach his knees, failing to protect him from the cold and exposing his nakedness. So are those who wrap themselves in the lie that they are safe from God's judgments because they have made a private agreement with death and heaven that will allow them to live and die on their own terms without consequence. Our Creator is infuriated by this unreasonable trust in self-made, nonbinding deals-that-dictate-one's-destiny-apart-from-God. "He will be angry" with those who think they can leave Him out of their plans for life, death, and eternity. He will destroy them like He did His enemies in Joshua 10 as He "cast down large hailstones from heaven on them" when He "killed them with a great slaughter at Gibeon." The Lord will "rise up" and bring judgment on unbelievers like He did at Mount Perazim when He broke through His enemies "like a breakthrough of water" (II Samuel 5:20).

Isaiah reaches out to his readers with a heartfelt warning. Do not mock God's warnings! Do not leave Him out of your plans for eternity! "I have heard from the Lord GOD of hosts, a destruction (is) determined even upon the whole earth." It is God's intention to destroy those who do not worship Him, fail to honor Him, and do not seek Him. "I will destroy those who used to worship me but now no longer do. They no longer ask for the LORD's guidance or seek my blessings" (Zephaniah 1:6 NLT). The horror and tragedy of the Creator destroying so much of humanity is difficult to contemplate. It is His "strange work," it is His "disturbing task" (HCS). It is hard to imagine so much destruction – but it is reality. Men who trust in self-made protection plans for their eternal well-being and ignore God's stated requirements for us are like a grown man trying to cover himself with a baby blanket. Death and judgment are coming for every person on earth. Those who are covered by the forgiveness of the Father (Psalms 85:2) will find nothing to fear in death or in judgment. But those who face judgment covered only with their home-made false-security blanket face a determined destruction.

28:23-26

Give ear and hear my voice, listen and hear my speech. Does the plowman keep plowing all day to sow? Does he keep turning his soil and breaking the clods? When he has leveled its surface, does he not sow the black cumin and scatter the cumin, plant the wheat in rows, the barley in the appointed place, and the spelt in its place? For He instructs him in right judgment, His God teaches him.

Admittedly, my understanding of this parable differs somewhat from many who are much smarter than I. The parable is given in 2 couplets – verses 23-26 and verses 27-29. Both couplets end very similarly, and my thoughts on these wonderful verses center on this repeated summary. Verse 22 ended with the horrifying announcement that God has determined to destroy the entirety of the human race that does not trust Him and obey Him. This news rightly causes us deep, solemn concern for humanity – the dozens that we know and love that we know are doomed apart from God – and the billions, yes, billions of people that we do not know personally, but who are also eternally doomed by their estrangement from their Creator. But here we are given good reason to hope! The penalty for disregarding God in life is terrible. Choosing unwisely in this matter leads to the most horrifying outcome imaginable. Blessedly, perhaps surprisingly, Isaiah's follow up parable to this news is that mankind has been provided with the wonderful capacity to choose wisely in this matter! God has made man smart. He is smart enough to know how to plow a field and smart enough to know what kind of seed thrives in what kind of soil. Man is able to demonstrate agricultural know-how as well as spiritual insights because God "instructs him in right judgment." "God teaches him" how to feed himself, and "God teaches him" how to get to heaven. In light of the horrors that await those who respond poorly to God's revelation, we are right to give all glory to God and all thanks to Him for His kindness in instructing us "in right judgment." Jacob basked in this joy and it brought him deep humble gratitude as He lifted His prayer to God in Genesis 32:10 saying, "I am not worthy of the least of all the mercies and of all the truth which You have shown Your servant." God has taught us His wonderful truths! Man didn't learn how to farm because he was lucky – God taught him how to farm. And He taught us how to get to heaven and avoid destruction. Because it is God's desire not just to feed man, but to protect him, provide for him, bless him, nurture him, and dwell with him forever in heaven. And He has not kept the way to right standing with Him secret! He has taught us "right judgment"! What a blessed thought. God has taught us what we need to know – about how to thrive on earth and how to be conveyed one day to heaven.

28:27-29
For the black cummin is not threshed with a threshing sledge, nor is a cartwheel rolled over the cummin; but the black cummin is beaten out with a stick, and the cummin with a rod. Bread flour must be ground; therefore he does not thresh it forever, break it with his cartwheel, or crush it with his horsemen. This also comes from the LORD of hosts, who is wonderful in counsel and excellent in guidance.

The parable begun in verse 23 continues. God has taught men how to farm. Man has learned the different means required to extract different grains by various means, because God taught him how to do that. It is God's benevolent will to make men smart. God is "wonderful in counsel and excellent in guidance." Who could ask for a better Counsellor than we have? How could we ever hope for more excellent guidance than what our

Creator promises to provide? Man is in desperate need of spiritual insight. His eternity hinges on making the right decision regarding the means required to save his soul from sin. Blessedly, remarkably, awe-inspiringly, God Himself provides us with wonderful counsel and excellent guidance. Let us echo David's thoughts in Psalms 16:7 – "I will bless the LORD who has given me counsel; my heart also instructs me in the night seasons." Let us gratefully take joy in knowing that "The counsel of the LORD stands forever, the plans of His heart to all generations" (Psalms 33:11). And let us rightly rejoice, knowing that "You will guide me with Your counsel, and afterward receive me to glory" (Psalms 73:24). No one goes to hell out of ignorance. God has made known to us the path of life (Psalms 16:11). People do not go to hell because they don't know any better. People are smart – made so by their Creator. Judgment comes on unbelievers, not because they were denied good counsel, but "Because they rebelled against the words of God, and despised the counsel of the Most High" (Psalms 107:11). I find the words in this parable deeply uplifting. My God is my guide in life. He teaches me in the "way everlasting" (Psalms 139:24). "This is God, our God forever and ever; He will be our guide even to death" (Psalms 48:14). What a precious thought.

Isaiah 29

29:1-4
Woe to Ariel, to Ariel, the city where David dwelt! Add year to year; let feasts come around. Yet I will distress Ariel; there shall be heaviness and sorrow, and it shall be to Me as Ariel. I will encamp against you all around, I will lay siege against you with a mound, and I will raise siege-works against you. You shall be brought down, you shall speak out of the ground; your speech shall be low, out of the dust; your voice shall be like a medium's, out of the ground; and your speech shall whisper out of the dust.

Judgment "begins with us" (I Peter 4:17). Judgment and punishment for sin are coming for everyone, and God's judgment on the sins of unbelievers will pick up quickly in verse 5, but it is God's stated priority to discipline and correct His people before moving on to respond with judgment in the lives of unbelievers. Sadly, Jerusalem, here called "Ariel," seems oblivious to God's impending judgment. They continue year after year in their God-dishonoring lifestyle, enjoying feast after feast, while their soul becomes more and more spiritually famished. Here, God declares war on His people's rebellion. He will "distress" His people. He will bring "heaviness and sorrow" on His people. We must not forget that it is God's intention to make sure that we are holy, not make sure we are happy. If we refuse to repent of our sin, He will see to it that we encounter "distress" because of our sin and that sin fills us with "sorrow." Psalms 147:6 says, "The LORD lifts up the humble; He casts the wicked down to the ground," and here we see Him casting His rebellious people into "the dust." Their speech will be reduced to groans as if their ribs were bruised by the trampling of the Lord's discipline. In Psalms 44:25, the writer pleads for the Lord's intervention, crying out, "our soul is bowed down to the dust; our body clings to the ground." This is the response the Lord desires here -- many times people have better spiritual insights after being trampled in the dust than they do while on top of the world.

29:5-8
Moreover the multitude of your foes shall be like fine dust, and the multitude of the terrible ones like chaff that passes away; yes, it shall be in an instant, suddenly. You will be punished by the LORD of hosts with thunder and earthquake and great noise, with storm and tempest and the flame of devouring fire. The multitude of all the nations who fight against Ariel, even all who fight against her and her fortress, and distress her, shall be as a dream of a night vision. It shall even be as when a hungry man dreams, and look – he eats; but he awakes, and his soul is still empty; or as when a thirsty man dreams, and look – he drinks; but he awakes, and indeed he is faint, and his soul still craves: so the multitude of all the nations shall be, who fight against Mount Zion.

The soul of man has cravings. Our soul craves holiness. Our soul craves companionship with our Creator. It craves the approval of our Creator. These holy cravings, however, can be replaced. We can feed our soul with other things that can appease its spiritual hunger pangs – at least for a while. We can replace the craving for our Creator's approval with a craving for the approval of society or the approval of a lover. We can replace the hunger to be holy with physical cravings. But the pursuit of all these things, even gorging ourselves on these things will ultimately leave our soul "empty." The Assyrians attacked Israel with the intent of conquest. But verse 8 tells us that when they had conquered their enemies and taken their spoil and basked in their victory that each man would find, in the end, that "his soul is still empty." If we will feed our soul with the things it craves, our soul will overflow with satisfaction. Our soul craves to be holy, and

ISAIAH 29

Matthew 5:6 assures us that, "Blessed are those who hunger and thirst for righteousness, for they shall be filled." Our soul craves for the presence of our Creator. And when we yield to our soul's craving and throw ourselves into the pursuit of God, our soul will delight in our fellowship with Him. In Psalms 63:1 David prays, "O GOD, You are my God; early will I seek You; my soul thirsts for You; my flesh longs for You in a dry and thirsty land where there is no water." And when David feeds this craving of his soul, he writes in Psalms 63:5 – "My soul shall be satisfied as with marrow and fatness, and my mouth shall praise You with joyful lips."

Let us seek to be holy. Let us seek the presence of God and His approval. Our soul craves these things and delights in them when they are found. Every other pursuit will leave the soul of man empty. After conquering the world, after conquering the heart of a lover, after succeeding in a life-long dream, even after a man or woman gains all these things, even then, "his soul is still empty" if his success is unaccompanied by the presence and approval of his Creator.

29:9-10
Pause and wonder! Blind yourselves and be blind! They are drunk, but not with wine; they stagger, but not with intoxicating drink. For the LORD has poured out on you the spirit of deep sleep, and has closed your eyes, namely, the prophets; and He has covered your heads, namely, the seers.

With a vivid description of Israel's tragic state, God says that His people are "blind" and "drunk." Though their eyes can see just fine, they have become spiritually blind. Though they may have abstained from wine, their souls drunkenly "stagger" from lack of spiritual insight. Though their eyes are wide open, their spirits have fallen into a "deep sleep." The picture could hardly be bleaker. The blind, the drunken, and the sleeping are all alike in their inability to see the dangers around them. They do not recognize danger and cannot formulate a plan to be rescued when it approaches. God's displeasure and His judgment rapidly approach, but Isaiah sadly shows that God's people are unaware. They are blind; they are drunk; they are asleep, and so, have no hope for rescue.

God says that those who have rejected Him are "blind." "The LORD opens the eyes of the blind" (Psalms 146:8), but if we reject Him, we condemn ourselves to spiritual blindness.

The Lord says that those who reject Him are "drunk." In Deuteronomy 29:6 the Lord takes note of His people's heart to know Him – "You have not drunk wine or similar drink, that you may know that I am the Lord your God." Those who seek to know God and strive to please Him are prone to spurn intoxicants, considering them unhelpful distractions from their holy pursuit. And verse 10 here indicates that the inverse is also true – those who spurn the Lord are enamored with wine and similar drink as a welcome distraction from the call of their conscience to reconcile with their Creator. And even those who do not drink, act as if they did – their souls stagger and reel from being "drunk" on the delusion that life has meaning apart from harmony with our Creator.

Thirdly, the people are in a "deep sleep." Jonah ran from God and is soon found sleeping in the depths of his escape boat (Jonah 1:5). Those who do not seek God are asleep. They have closed their eyes to the things that matter eternally and need to wake up before the day of judgment overtakes them. Those whose hearts yearn for the presence and approval of God stir their souls awake. The psalmist is so intent on seeing God worshiped that he sings out in Psalms 132:4 – "I will not give sleep to my eyes or slumber to my eyelids, until I find a place for the LORD, a dwelling place for the Mighty One of Jacob." And David sings out in Psalms 57:8 – "Wake up, my soul! Wake up, O harp and lyre! I will waken the dawn with my song" (NLT). Those whose hearts love the presence of God stir their souls awake to sing His praise and carry out His purposes. Those who do not love the Lord are content to sleep their lives away. They are alert to nothing spiritually significant; they are awake only to carry out tasks of temporary import. They are in desperate need of someone to wake them – but here we see that their wakers are asleep as well! The Lord has given His people prophets to be their eyes and seers to be their watchmen – but the prophets have their eyes closed and the seers have their heads covered. Our verses here depict a people that are spiritually asleep, and whose spiritual guides have fallen asleep as well. The people in Jesus' day were much the same. The Jews could not see that Jesus was the Way and the spiritual blindness of their Pharisee leaders made them "blind guides" (Matthew 23:16) – blind leaders of the blind, prompting Jesus to say in Matthew 15:14 -- "Let them alone. They are blind leaders of the blind. And if the blind leads the blind, both will fall into a ditch." Let us intently, intensely keep our eyes fixed on Jesus, the author and finisher of our faith (Hebrews 12:2). This is our best protection from the blindness, drunkenness, and sleepiness that causes Israel to be condemned here. Riveting our attention on Jesus will keep our eyes awake through the night watches so that we can meditate on His words (Psalms 119:148). It will keep us sober (Titus 2:12), and it will open our eyes, that we may see wondrous things from His law, and not be blind

(Psalms 119:18). What a horrifying thing to consider – that we could be created for the glory and pleasure of God, and yet live our whole life asleep, drunken, and blind to that purpose for living. May the Lord anoint our eyes with eye salve that we may see (Revelation 3:18) the glorious purpose to which our Lord has called us and avoid the drunkenness and blindness that imperil those who take their eyes off their Creator.

29:11-12

The whole vision has become to you like the words of a book that is sealed, which men deliver to one who is literate, saying, "Read this, please." And he says, "I cannot, for it is sealed." Then the book is delivered to one who is illiterate, saying, "Read this, please." And he says, "I am not literate."

God speaks to mankind. The thought is wholly remarkable to consider. The wonder of God's willingness to speak to man is met here, however, with the horror of rebellious man's inability to decipher what God is saying. God has revealed His truths to the world "like the words of a book." But man is sadly capable of blinding himself to the understanding of those words. Some men are "literate," they are spiritually attuned people that are cognizant of the fact that we must give attention to spiritual matters. They should be able to understand God's communications to us – but here we see that their rebellion against God has caused the book of God's revelation to be "sealed." Others are "not literate." I Corinthians 2:14 describes them: "the natural man does not receive the things of the Spirit of God, for they are foolishness to him; nor can he know them, because they are spiritually discerned." God reveals the truth of the origins and purposes of the universe to man. It is man's highest privilege to be granted access to the revelation of the heart of God. And it is mankind's highest offense when men and women desecrate this sacred privilege – when their sin seals up God's words so that they cannot see His truths and when their rebellion against the authority of God makes their souls illiterate to spiritual things. God has spoken, He has revealed "the whole vision" to His people. But in Isaiah's day, many could not see what He was saying, and others could not discern what He meant. May we take better care of this sacred privilege of knowing the heart of God.

29:13-14

Therefore the LORD said: "Inasmuch as these people draw near with their mouths and honor Me with their lips, but have removed their hearts far from Me, and their fear toward Me is taught by the commandment

of men, therefore, behold, I will again do a marvelous work among this people, a marvelous work and a wonder; for the wisdom of their wise men shall perish, and the understanding of their prudent men shall be hidden."

Jesus quotes Isaiah's words here in Matthew 15:8-9 and applies the meaning for our understanding. The Pharisees knew God's laws well. They proclaimed themselves to be ardent God-followers. They were very careful to "honor (God) with their lips." But their hearts were far from God – and since God "looks at the heart" (I Samuel 16:7) and God weighs the heart (Proverbs 21:2), we see that a proud, unloving, disobedient heart cannot be atoned for by a religious tongue in Isaiah's day, in Jesus' day, or in our day either. In Matthew 15, Jesus taught specifically that sermons and spiritual discussions are reduced to condemnable religious rhetoric if they are not accompanied by loving care for the needy – especially loving care for one's needy parents. And loyal devotion to man-made religion is viewed by Jesus as hypocrisy and a betrayal of one's conscience when it is unaccompanied by a devotion and love for the Creator, Sustainer, and Savior of the world. The Jews talked religion well. But their actions spoke louder than their words, revealing that a cold heart of unbelief was thinly veiled by their words of feigned devotion. In response to this state of His people, God promises that He, too, will make sure that His actions speak louder than His words. He will "do a marvelous work," He will do "a marvelous work and a wonder" that will put to shame the "wisdom" and clever words of those who express love for Him in word but not in deed, and who communicate religiosity with their tongue, but communicate spiritual inconsistency with their heart.

When we consider God's words here, we find the implication of this text overwhelming. God is troubled because the hearts of His people are far from Him. For all God's limitless power, for all His boundless authority and endless existence – He is amazingly, remarkably, intensely personal. His desire is to relate heart-to-heart with the people that He has created. His desire is for us to draw near to Him (James 4:8); His desire is for us to take shelter beneath His wings (Matthew 23:37); His desire is for our hearts to be truly His (II Chronicles 16:9). And when men remove their hearts far from Him, He is moved to rise from His throne and call us back to Himself. God is eternal, limitless, omniscient, and omnipresent. Yet He is warmly, invitingly personal. He invites us to draw near and is troubled when we do not. Let us guard our hearts so that we do not let them slip absent-mindedly from constant God-directed adoration. God is troubled when our hearts are far from His – the thought should add even greater drive to draw ever and always nearer to Him.

29:15-16
Woe to those who seek deep to hide their counsel far from the Lord, and their works are in the dark; they say, "Who sees us?" and, "Who knows us?" Surely you have things turned around! Shall the potter be esteemed as the clay; for shall the thing made say of him who made it, "He did not make me"? Or shall the thing formed say of him who formed it, "He has no understanding"?

We cannot hide from the Lord and we cannot tell the Lord what to do. The truth seems obvious, and yet it is remarkable how often men and women act as if this were not the case. We tend to think that if no one else sees our sin – God doesn't see it either. If our secret thoughts are hidden from those around us, we tend to suspect that God doesn't know of our wicked plans either. "Woe to those" who think they can "hide their counsel" – who think they can hide their unholy plans and sinful contemplations from the all-seeing eyes of God. And woe to those who think they can tell God what to do. The obvious folly of this effort is clear to everyone – except the billions of people who "have things turned around" and foolishly maintain that their personal moral code and personal religious views take precedence over God's revelation regarding these matters. From Isaiah's day to ours people want the right to decide for themselves what sin is, what the punishment for sin is, when mercy should be shown, and when justice should be carried out. And when God's ways conflict with their personal penchant, they have the condemnable audacity to say "(God) has no understanding." It takes little religious understanding – just simple child-like logic to understand that "the thing formed" cannot deny the preeminence of "him who formed it." Sadly, spiritual rebellion against the Creator's calling causes so many people to embrace what no rational creature should ever be tempted to believe – that the commands of God are subservient to personal preference. "Woe" to those who think like that. Woe to the many, many people who think like that.

29:17-21
Is it not yet a very little while till Lebanon shall be turned into a fruitful field, and the fruitful field be esteemed as a forest? In that day the deaf shall hear the words of the book, and the eyes of the blind shall see out of obscurity and out of darkness. The humble also shall increase their

joy in the LORD, and the poor among men shall rejoice in the Holy One of Israel. For the terrible one is brought to nothing, the scornful one is consumed, and all who watch for iniquity are cut off – who make a man an offender by a word, and lay a snare for him who reproves in the gate, and turn aside the just by empty words.

The spiritual insights of God's people have failed them. The previous two verses showed how they had foolishly thought to either hide from God or pompously think to tell Him what to do. But in mercy, the Lord decrees here that He will remedy this problem. He will take their barren land and turn it into a "fruitful field." He will allow the deaf to hear Him speak. He will allow the blind to see His truths. The proud and scornful will be removed, but those who humbly seek His blessings will find that He shall "increase their joy in the LORD." Adding blessing upon blessing, those who have no worldly riches will find their heavenly reward more than ample compensation -- "the poor among men shall rejoice in the Holy One of Israel."

God revealed His power and taught His commands at mount Sinai – and His people rebelled against Him and staggered into spiritual blindness and drunkenness and sleep (verse 9). And what will be God's response? When rebellion caused men to become blind and deaf and unfruitful – the blessed message from Isaiah here is that God promises to give sight to the blind, allow the deaf to hear, and turn their vain efforts into fruitful endeavors. Such is the all-surpassing marvel of the mercies of God. When the eyes of men cannot see God, when their ears become deaf to His calling, and when their heart falls far from Him, He heals their eyes and ears and hearts. What a blessed thought. Matthew 11:5 says that Jesus worked so that "The blind see and the lame walk; the lepers are cleansed and the deaf hear; the dead are raised up and the poor have the gospel preached to them." But here we see that God's heart to carry out this healing work in the eyes and ears and hearts of sinful man began long before the Son was sent from Heaven. God opens eyes and ears to the truth. I am so grateful that this is true! The mercies of God grant no solace for those who reject Him – "the scornful one is consumed" and "all who watch for iniquity are cut off." But mankind has been created with the God-given instinct to reach out in the darkness and silence to seek a Savior (Acts 17:27). And blessedly, the people here are promised eyes and ears to guide them as God directs their search.

29:22-24

Therefore thus says the LORD, who redeemed Abraham, concerning the house of Jacob: "Jacob shall not now be ashamed, nor shall his face

now grow pale; but when he sees his children, the work of My hands, in his midst, they will hallow My name, and hallow the Holy One of Jacob, and fear the God of Israel. These also who erred in spirit will come to understanding, and those who complained will learn doctrine."

Israel will be sorely threatened by their enemies. The Assyrian menace will loom so frightfully that it will appear that the future of the entire nation of Israel is doomed. But God promises that the future of His people is not bleak, and the face of His nation will not "grow pale." And the blessed sign of God's intention to bless the nation's prosperity is seen in their children. God calls the children of Israel "the work of My hands." It is a supreme comfort to godly parents to see that their children are not only in God's hands, they were formed by God's hands. There are no joys greater than the privilege of seeing the evidence of God's work in our children. Seeing my Lord form my children, grow my children, and grant them physical and spiritual gifts for His purposes is a dear gift to me – and this gift is here promised to the entire nation of Israel. The blessed outcome of God's blessed gift is penned as well: "they will hallow My name, and hallow the Holy One of Jacob, and fear the God of Israel." Seeing holiness, spiritual-giftedness, and God's protection on the next generation moves everyone to "honor" God's name and "stand in awe" (HCS) of the God of Israel. What a blessing when the younger generation rises up to call their fathers back to the Lord! The faithfulness of the young will compel those "who erred in spirit" to come back to their senses and "come to understanding." And those who "complained" how God ran the world will stop their senseless complaints when younger, wiser men teach them sound "doctrine." The ESV and other translators render the final phrase as: those who complained will "accept instruction." It is no shame for older men and women to be taught by younger people when the young are the work of God's hands. When the young rise up to know God, obey God, and proclaim God's truths; when the young rise up gifted by God, anointed by God, and filled with the Spirit of God – the other generations will "come to understanding," they will stop complaining about things that do not matter, and they will find themselves inspired to rise up and emulate the "children" that God has used to turn their hearts back to their Creator.

Isaiah 30

30:1-2
"Woe to the rebellious children," says the LORD, "Who take counsel, but not of Me, and who devise plans, but not of My Spirit, that they may add sin to sin; who walk to go down to Egypt, and have not asked My advice, to strengthen themselves in the strength of Pharaoh, and to trust in the shadow of Egypt!"

Sin prevents us from being right with God. But sin is not simply violent crimes and open dishonesty. Here, the Lord talks about a transgression that is perhaps less considered, but that prevents us from being right with God just the same. God's "rebellious children" have offended Him because they "take counsel, but not of Me." God promises to give counsel to those who seek His direction. In Psalms 32:8 He says, "I will instruct you and teach you in the way you should go; I will guide you with My eye." But if we are not looking at His face, we will not be able to discern what His eyes are telling us. The Lord is standing at the door of our hearts (Revelation 3:20), ready to come in and give us counsel – but if we refuse to welcome Him in, we deprive ourselves of His guidance. In Daniel 4, Nebuchadnezzar has a second dream. He cannot discern its meaning, but he foolishly takes his problem to the magicians and soothsayers for counsel – even though Spirit-filled Daniel is right there. This is the sin that Israel is condemned for here. They have serious problems facing them. The Assyrian army is poised to destroy their nation. In desperation they "take counsel" – an intelligent course of action – "but not of Me" – a sinful, offensive course of action that breaks their relationship with God. Their advisers recommend that they flee to Egypt, or that they ally with Egypt in their war against Assyria. They are encouraged to "strengthen themselves in the strength of Pharaoh." Seeking help in trouble, ports in storms, and allies in lonely fights would certainly seem reasonable. But God says that Egypt's strength is a "shadow." It cannot provide the rescue that Israel really needs. Such is often the case when we take counsel from any source but the Lord. Their advice is carnal and earthly, designed to provide only financial success, physical fitness, warm human relations, and creature comforts. But we see here that God finds it sinfully offensive, He says that it adds sin upon sin, when we make plans and seek the advice of people without carefully, prayerfully consulting Him.

God promises to guide us with His eye! So let us keep our eyes on His face. God alone is omniscient, so His counsel far surpasses all other advice in wisdom. God is the only One we desire to please, so His counsel is the only advice we should follow. There is a direct correlation with how much we love our Lord and how quick we are to run to His presence and seek His counsel. As soon as trouble begins, those who love the Lord run to Him, bow before Him, cling to His feet, and then look to His eyes and ask for counsel and provision. Those who do not love the Lord either ask for no counsel and rely on their own abilities, or look for advice from non-Divine sources. "Rebellious children" do not ask their parents for advice, and people who do not love God seek counsel from smart people before they seek counsel from Him. Is God our all in all? If so, let us be wary of the popular books and counsels of smart people, and let us agree with Asaph's psalm: "You will guide me with Your counsel, and afterward receive me to glory. Whom have I in heaven but You? And there is none upon earth that I desire besides You. My flesh and my heart fail; but God is the strength of my heart and my portion forever" (Psalms 73:24-26).

30:3-5
Therefore the strength of Pharaoh shall be your shame, and trust in the shadow of Egypt shall be your humiliation. For his princes were at Zoan, and his ambassadors came to Hanes. They were all ashamed of a people

who could not benefit them, or be help or benefit, but a shame and also a reproach.

Rather than "take counsel" (verse 1) with the Lord, His people followed conventional logic that supported an alliance with Egypt in their war with Assyria. They had made an "alliance" (HCS) to help fight their enemies, but the alliance was "against My will" (verse 1 HCS), and here we see the repercussions of making a pact with people that God does not approve of. "The strength of Pharaoh shall be your shame." Egypt will prove to be powerless to stop the Assyrian war machine, and all who trusted in them for help will be ashamed. Emissaries from Zoan and Israel's ambassadors "came to Hanes" to strike a deal and seal an alliance against a common enemy. But the pact would provide neither "help or benefit" to either party. Egypt's power was a "shadow." There was no substance to it. It could not deliver Israel in their crisis. So will be the end of all who put their trust in anyone or anything other than our Creator. Those who trust in money will be ashamed when their money corrodes and proves unable to purchase for us a place in heaven (James 5:3). Jesus' parable in Luke 18:9-14 shows how those who "trusted in themselves" will be ashamed on judgment day. Those who trust in money, those who trust in themselves, and those who trust in friendships with the world will all be disappointed. In contrast, Romans 10:11 says, "Whoever believes on Him will not be put to shame." Let us be sure to entrust our future, as well as our current endeavors to the care and counsel of our true Savior, and not foolishly entrust important matters to the protection of alliances and advisors which cannot save.

30:6-7
The burden against the beast of the South. Through a land of trouble and anguish, from which came the lioness and lion, the viper and fiery flying serpent, they will carry their riches on the backs of young donkeys, and their treasures on the humps of camels, to a people who shall not profit; for the Egyptians shall help in vain and to no purpose. Therefore I have called her Rahab-Hem-Shebeth.

The Lord describes the trek of Israel's ambassadors through the hostile land "of the South." To reach Egypt, they had to pass through a dangerous wilderness, full of hostile creatures, all so that they could give away their "treasures" and "riches" in a fool's errand. They would give away all their earthly goods "in vain and to no purpose." What a tragedy when men foolishly spend themselves on things that do them no good. Isaiah 55:2 will ask this poignantly, "Why do you spend money for what is not bread, and your wages for what does not satisfy?" Israel rejects God's deliverance and seeks, instead, to save themselves by the military might of Egypt. But Egypt cannot help them. God gives Egypt a new name: Rahab-Hem-Shebeth – "Rahab stands idle." Rahab was a mythical dragon – a powerful figure. But "idle" powers are just as helpless to save us as idol powers. Let us take care where we spend and where we store our treasures (Luke 12:34), so that we do not waste our livelihood on things that cannot save us.

30:8-9
Now go, write it before them on a tablet, and note it on a scroll, that it may be for time to come, forever and ever; that this is a rebellious people, lying children, children who will not hear the law of the LORD;

The Lord decrees that a written record be made that will forever bear witness that the people in Isaiah's day were "rebellious," "lying," and refused to listen to God's law. We are told that books of this sort are being written constantly by the scribes of heaven and will be opened and read on judgment day. In Revelation 20:12 John writes, "I saw the dead, small and great, standing before God, and books were opened. And another book was opened, which is the Book of Life. And the dead were judged according to their works, by the things which were written in the books." Like it or not, our biography is written in heaven. It is not an autobiography. We do not get to choose the stories that are included and the ones that are left out. Our deeds and words and attitudes are recorded as a perpetual witness for us or against us. Having been adequately forewarned then, let us take great care to guard our deeds and words and attitudes so that the record of our lives will not be an embarrassment as Israel's is here, but will be a blessing to the readers "forever and ever."

30:10-11
Who say to the seers, "Do not see," and to the prophets, "Do not prophesy to us right things; speak to us smooth things, prophesy deceits. Get out of the way, turn aside from the path, cause the Holy One of Israel to cease from before us."

Verse 9 said that the people of Isaiah's day were "children who will not hear the law of the LORD." They refused to listen to God, and in place of His decrees they wanted "smooth things" and "deceits." God's call to man tends to rock our boat (Jonah 1:4), upset our business plans (John 2:15), and turn our world upside down (Acts 17:6). These things can make life rough for a while – and Godless men like things "smooth." Sadly, the Israel of

Isaiah's day was not unique. So many, many people from so many places in our day and in every age have faced and continue to face this same challenge. When God's word creates conflict in my daily life, what will I choose? So many would rather have a smooth life based on "deceit" than a turbulent life founded on the truth. They do not care about "right things" – those things that make us right with God. They only care about "smooth things" – things that will make them comfortable. This insistence on having an easy life rather than a holy life leads men to a state of mind that is tantamount to spiritual insanity. They cry out to their spiritual leaders with the demand that they "rid us of the Holy One of Israel" (HCS). Of all God's precious gifts to us, surely, His greatest is that He condescends to live among us, to draw near to us, to speak to us, to enter our heart's door and commune with us. He is Immanuel, God with us (Isaiah 7:14). But in the utter insanity of self-declared autonomy, in the madness of man's rebellion, he tells God to go away. As the Gadarenes pleaded with Jesus to leave their region (Mark 5:17), so the people of Israel ask their (false) prophets to rid them of the troubling, conscience-stinging presence of their Creator. The decision to choose the "passing pleasures of sin" over the never-ending joy of the glory and presence of our loving, all-powerful Creator and Sustainer of the universe is mystifying. Who in their right mind would tell God to go away? Such is the blinding power of sin. Oh, let us flee sin! Small sins, hidden sins, sins that seem common to man – let us flee them in horror! See the insanity sin causes in seemingly intelligent creatures! It will lead us to reject an audience with the King of Creation who sits supremely on His throne eternally -- for the sake of a sin that provides only seconds of enjoyment.

30:12-14
Therefore thus says the Holy One of Israel: "Because you despise this word, and trust in oppression and perversity, and rely on them, therefore this iniquity shall be to you like a breach ready to fall, a bulge in a high wall, whose breaking comes suddenly, in an instant. And He shall break it like the breaking of the potter's vessel, which is broken in pieces; He shall not spare. So there shall not be found among its fragments a shard to take fire from the hearth, or to take water from the cistern."

The tragic outcome of sin and unbelief are here described. Israel has collectively opted to "despise this word." They have despised the words of God. They have despised the opportunity to pray and seek God's blessings and have chosen instead, to use "oppression and perversity" to get their way. In Isaiah 26:1, the people rejoice because they are "surrounded by the walls of God's salvation" (NLT). But here we have a picture of what happens when people reject God's plan to save us. Our sin becomes a "breach" in the wall of God's protection. Like a small crack expanding in a great dam, sin places a crack, then a breach in the wall that the Holy One of Israel has raised up around us to protect our soul. The result is the sudden collapse of walls and lives that were built apart from God. The destruction is so complete that there are not enough fragments of the wall remaining to hold coals from a fire or carry water from a well. Such is the total destruction destined for those who "despise this word." Let us not despise "this word" that our Lord has communicated to us. Let us cling to it, study it, meditate on it, and rush to obey it. The result of failing to do so is completely devastating.

30:15-16
For thus says the Lord GOD, the Holy One of Israel: "In returning and rest you shall be saved; in quietness and confidence shall be your strength." But you would not, and you said, "No, for we will flee on horses" – therefore you shall flee! And, "We will ride on swift horses" – therefore those who pursue you shall be swift!

The Lord invites His people to trust Him for their salvation, and His plan for salvation requires no special powers on their part. All they have to do is "(return) and rest." If we would save our soul and save ourselves from a multitude of hardships, we are not required to creatively discover an innovative soul-saving remedy – we simply need to return to the Lord. "Return to Me, and I will return to you, says the LORD of hosts" (Malachi 3:7). Furthermore, we are not required to fight and scratch and crawl our way through temptation and various trials to reach heaven's gates and God's earthly provisions. All we need to do is "rest" in Him. Psalms 37:7 encourages us to "Rest in the LORD, and wait patiently for Him." If we will simply rest in the arms of our Lord, we will find that our soul is in a very safe place. Deuteronomy 33:27 assures us that "The eternal God is (our) refuge, and underneath are (His) everlasting arms." If we will rest in His arms, He will grant us His "everlasting" protection plan. "Returning" to God, and finding "rest" in His arms, this is God's plan for us to preserve our own well-being. Psalms 116:7 gives the same two-fold recommendation: "Return to your rest, O my soul, for the LORD has dealt bountifully with you."

Despite God's clear recommendation, and Psalm 116's reminder that we have good cause to return to God and rest in His promises, the people of Israel do not listen to Isaiah's urging. Rather than rest in their Lord, they choose to "flee on horses." And when warned that this plan seems unlikely to succeed, they argue that "we will ride on swift horses." But no one is fast enough to elude all life's woes. Judgment will catch up to us soon enough. We cannot reasonably hope to avoid all trouble. We can, however, take God up on His offer and return to Him and rest in the joy of His presence and in the hope of His promises. There is a rest that awaits the people of God (Hebrews 4:9). "Therefore, since a promise remains of entering His rest, let us fear lest any of you seem to have come short of it" (Hebrews 4:1).

30:17
One thousand shall flee at the threat of one, at the threat of five you shall flee, till you are left as a pole on top of a mountain and as a banner on a hill.

What a turn of events and disruption of destiny is the inevitable outcome of rebellion against God. In Leviticus 26:8 God promises that if His people will obey Him that "Five of you shall chase a hundred, and a hundred of you shall put ten thousand to flight; your enemies shall fall by the sword before you." Now, in the face of their disobedience, the exact opposite outcome is determined: a thousand of them will flee "at the threat of one," and if any five enemies appear, the whole nation of Israel will flee in fear. Valor and victory are the predetermined rewards bestowed on those who remain loyal to God, and fear and failure are the predictable finishes for those who reject Him. May Israel's failure provide adequate incentive for us to "deny ungodliness and worldly lusts and live soberly, righteously, and godly in this present world" (Titus 2:12 KJV), so that we can lay claim to the promise of Leviticus 26:8, rather than fall under the condemnation of Isaiah 30:17.

30:18
Therefore the LORD will wait, that He may be gracious to you; and therefore He will be exalted, that He may have mercy on you. For the LORD is a God of justice; blessed are all those who wait for Him.

The godly activity of waiting is pictured for us here. We tend to have a natural proclivity for impatience. "I hate waiting" is a line that is commonly spoken, whereas, "I love long lines" may never have been said by anyone anywhere. But here, we see God offer to wait. What a fascinating thought. "The LORD will wait." His desire is to be "gracious" to us. And to prove Himself most gracious, it is sometimes necessary for Him to wait. He must wait for us to recognize our need, lest His kindnesses be missed. He must wait for us to look to Him for our provision, lest His rescue be misconstrued as the result of our own personal prowess. God's desire is that "He will be exalted" and that we will have mercy shown. And often, to accomplish the greatest good -- to exalt His own name, to show mercy on His people, and to be most "gracious" to us, He must wait. We tend to want Him to be quicker in executing revenge on our enemies and punishing the wicked people of the world, but, once again, we need not be impatient. We are assured here that "the LORD is a God of justice." He will certainly exact justice on those who are oppressive and cruel. But He has purpose behind His waiting before administering justice. As II Peter 3:9 affirms, "The Lord is not slow to fulfill His promise as some count slowness, but is patient toward you, not wishing that any should perish, but that all should reach repentance." God waits for us, so that He can be gracious to us. And in response, we "wait for Him" and are "blessed." We have great needs – and we expectantly await our Lord's blessed provision. Earth is not our home, and we wait expectantly for the blessings of heaven. We wait patiently for the Lord and are blessed because He hears our prayers (Psalms 40:1). We wait for our Lord and are blessed because we wait in the wonderful company of His saints as they wait on His name along with us (Psalms 52:9). Blessed are all those who wait for the Lord. We are happy and blessed to wait for our Lord, inspired all the more to do so, seeing that He has been willing to wait for us.

30:19-20
For the people shall dwell in Zion at Jerusalem; you shall weep no more. He will be very gracious to you at the sound of your cry; when He hears it, He will answer you. And though the Lord gives you the bread of adversity and the water of affliction, yet your teachers will not be moved into a corner anymore, but your eyes shall see your teachers.

Life can be filled with tears. Godliness is no protector against sorrow, seeing that even sinless Jesus was "a Man of sorrows and acquainted with grief" (Isaiah 53:3). But we are comforted here, seeing that our Lord is "gracious" to those who cry. "He hears" the sound of our sorrow and He answers the prayers of His troubled people. God is a "very present help in trouble" (Psalms 46:1) and when He draws near with His "very present help" we are comforted by His kindness and so "weep no more." "And though the Lord give you the bread of adversity and the water of affliction, yet your Teacher will not hide himself anymore, but your eyes shall see your Teacher" (ESV). Our Lord is both our Comforter and our Teacher. He cheers us in the midst of trials and guides us on how to get through the trials. The driving rain of troubles can severely diminish our vision. We often cannot see how we should respond, how to overcome, or why the trial came our way. But we can see our Teacher. No matter how adversely tears and driving rains affect our vision, we can always see our Lord. We may not be able to see answers to all life's hardships, we may not be able to see good defeat evil in every skirmish. "But we see Jesus" (Hebrews 2:9). Our Lord is not hidden in a "corner." Our Teacher, our Guide, our Comforter is with us in trials. He hears the sound of our cries and He answers. He sees our need, and blessedly, He allows us to see His face.

30:21
Your ears shall hear a word behind you, saying, "This is the way, walk in it," whenever you turn to the right hand or whenever you turn to the left.

As Philip heard the word of the Lord behind Him saying, "Go near and overtake this chariot" (Acts 8:29), as the Spirit told Peter to travel with the three men to Caesarea, so God's people are here heartened by the expectation that our Lord will guide us in our lifelong pursuits and our day to day decisions. We do not need to climb a mountain and hear advice from a faraway guru. Our God is walking with us, speaking "a word behind you" so that we can know His will and have access to His guiding voice in every endeavor in every moment of life. James 1:5 says, "If any of you lacks wisdom, let him ask of God, who gives to all liberally and without reproach, and it will be given to him." And here we see that the Lord's wise counsel is so "liberally" given that it is freely available to us continuously day and night. His voice speaks to our spiritual ear and guides us to go left or right at each fork in life's road. Oh, how we need to hear His voice guiding thoughts and guiding our steps! And, oh, how immeasurably blessed we are to have our Lord provide for us just what we need. Eli instructed Samuel to listen carefully and say, "Speak, LORD, for your servant hears" (I Samuel 3:9) when the Lord called to him in the middle of the night. Now, we find an invitation to hear the words of the Lord spoken to us both day and night. Let us listen, and rush to obey, overwhelmed by the priceless privilege that is ours to hear our Creator speak.

30:22-26
You will also defile the covering of your images of silver, and the ornament of your molded images of gold. You will throw them away as an unclean thing; you will say to them, "Get away!" Then He will give the rain for your seed with which you sow the ground, and bread of the increase of the earth; it will be fat and plentiful. In that day your cattle

will feed in large pastures. Likewise the oxen and the young donkeys that work the ground will eat cured fodder, which has been winnowed with the shovel and fan. There will be on every high mountain and on every high hill rivers and streams of waters, in the day of the great slaughter, when the towers fall. Moreover the light of the moon will be as the light of the sun, and the light of the sun will be sevenfold, as the light of seven days, in the day that the LORD binds up the bruise of His people and heals the stroke of their wound.**

When God's people throw away all idols, the result is magnificent. God gives rain in its season, food is "plentiful," and even their cattle and other domesticated animals glean the benefits of idol-less lives devoted wholly to God. Rivers provide clean water, God destroys His people's enemies, and previous blessings will suddenly be multiplied seven-fold. All as a result of God's people discarding their false gods. Like a former smoker who is now disgusted by the same smoke that once addicted him, so God's people are here depicted as despising the idols and images they once worshipped. Only while one is living under the dark cloak of sin can idols appear worthy of worship. When sin is despised, idols will also be despised. When the glories of God are displayed before us, idols will appear dirty and vile, and the very things that were once idolized will be thrown away "as an unclean thing."

30:27-28
Behold, the name of the LORD comes from afar, burning with His anger, and His burden is heavy; His lips are full of indignation, and His tongue like a devouring fire. His breath is like an overflowing stream, which reaches up to the neck, to sift the nations with the sieve of futility; and there shall be a bridle in the jaws of the people, causing them to err.

God's burning anger is described here. He sends a "devouring fire" and "an overflowing stream" to destroy His enemies. Isaiah's prophecy was initially uttered against Assyria's cruel attack on Israel and blasphemous attack on God (Isaiah 36:20), but his words apply to God's response to all peoples of all nations that think to rebel against Him. It is God's intention to "sift the nations with the sieve of futility." The ESV renders it "the sieve of destruction." God does not randomly hand out judgments, nor does He grant random blessings. He "sifts" the nations and deals with them in keeping with the outcome of His sifting. In Amos 9:9 God says, "For surely I will command, and will sift the house of Israel among all nations, as grain is sifted in a sieve; yet not the smallest grain shall fall to the ground." God sifts the nations, separating the wheat from the chaff, the pure from the impure, and saving out saints from among sinners. His anger is hot, "His burden is heavy." But for all of that, He will not allow the fires of His judgment to scorch a single one of His beloved children. In war there is always collateral damage. Innocents suffer. But this is not the case with God's judgment. It is God's intention to "sift the nations" and Amos 9 says that as a result, "not the smallest grain shall fall to the ground." No sinner will escape God's sifting, and none of God's children, no matter how small and seemingly insignificant, will fall with those who have incurred God's wrath.

30:29-30
You shall have a song as in the night when a holy festival is kept, and gladness of heart as when one goes with a flute, to come into the mountain of the LORD, to the Mighty One of Israel. The LORD will cause His glorious voice to be heard, and show the descent of His arm, with the indignation of His anger and the flame of a devouring fire, with scattering, tempest, and hailstones.

It is a worshipful experience to see God execute judgment on those that oppress His people and reject Him as Lord. His followers are filled with "gladness of heart" and a song on their lips, as if they were going to a "holy festival," as if they were going to a praise gathering on the mountain of the Lord. There are times, perhaps, when the Lord seems silent. Evil people do terrible things, and it seems like God doesn't say anything about it. We suffer loss and groan under our trials, and it seems like God doesn't have anything to say on our behalf. But God will not stay silent for long. "His glorious voice" will be heard condemning the unjust and consoling His children. Those who are consumed with the distress of seeing evil triumph and saints in pain will not be disappointed when they pray, "To You I will cry, O LORD my Rock: do not be silent to me, lest, if You are silent to me, I become like those who go down to the pit" (Psalms 28:1). Psalms 39:12 is confident that "the Lord will not be silent at my tears." And Psalms 50:3 is confident that He will not be silent before the wicked. "Our God shall come, and shall not keep silent; a fire shall devour before Him, and it shall be very tempestuous all around Him." "The LORD will cause His glorious voice to be heard." What a blessed thought. David muses on the glory of the voice of the Lord in Psalms 29:3-9 -- "The voice of the LORD is over the waters; the God of glory thunders; the LORD is over many waters. The voice of the LORD is powerful; the voice of the LORD is full of majesty. The voice of the

LORD breaks the cedars, yes, the LORD splinters the cedars of Lebanon. He makes them also skip like a calf, Lebanon and Sirion like a young wild ox. The voice of the LORD divides the flames of fire. The voice of the LORD shakes the wilderness; the LORD shakes the Wilderness of Kadesh. The voice of the LORD makes the deer give birth, and strips the forests bare; and in His temple everyone says, "Glory!"

30:31-33
For through the voice of the LORD Assyria will be beaten down, as He strikes with the rod. And in every place where the staff of punishment passes, which the LORD lays on him, it will be with tambourines and harps; and in battles of brandishing He will fight with it. For Tophet was established of old, yes, for the king it is prepared. He has made it deep and large; its pyre is fire with much wood; the breath of the LORD, like a stream of brimstone, kindles it.

Verse 31 begins with a foretelling of the defeat of Assyria, when the voice of the Lord will beat them down. But many say that the chapter's end in verse 33 depicts, not just Assyria's doom, but the doom of all those that war against God. "Tophet was established of old." Tophet, also called Gehenna, is a valley near Jerusalem where the Canaanites, and some depraved Jews sacrificed their children in the fires that burned there. Gehenna is the term Jesus used as His term for Hell in Matthew 5:29, Matthew 10:28 and elsewhere. Many feel that Isaiah's allusion to Tophet here, described as a "fire with much wood" and "like a stream of brimstone" is describing not just the death of Assyria's 185,000 soldiers as they encamped around Jerusalem (II Kings 19:35), but foretells the fires of hell that await all who are not right with God. Hell is "deep and large." It is widened to make room for the untold millions who refuse to submit to God's authority. "Through the voice of the LORD Assyria will be beaten down." No one will survive rebellion against the voice of the Lord. Let us then devote our voice to warning and pleading with the people around us so that they will turn from their Godlessness and submit to His authority, and not follow in the path of the Assyrians that leads to Hell.

Isaiah 31

31:1
Woe to those who go down to Egypt for help, and rely on horses, who trust in chariots because they are many, and in horsemen because they are very strong, but who do not look to the Holy One of Israel, nor seek the LORD!

Psalms 20:7 says, "Some trust in chariots, and some in horses; but we will remember the name of the LORD our God." Those who trust in God will be glad they did, but those who trust in Egypt, horses, or chariots will be disappointed, just as Psalms 20:8 says: "They (those who trust in Egypt, horses and chariots) have bowed down and fallen; but we (who trust in the Lord) have risen and stand upright." The Assyrian army was riding down upon Israel. Israel had no chance to win the war on their own, so some went as ambassadors to Egypt to ask them to come help, and others fled to Egypt in an attempt to hide from danger there. God says that neither effort will succeed. "Woe" to them, doom awaits them, if they choose to seek help from lesser powers than the omnipotent Holy One of Israel. Let us not seek help from unholy powers. II Corinthians 6:14 warns, "Do not be unequally yoked together with unbelievers. For what fellowship has righteousness with lawlessness? And what communion has light with darkness?" And our verse here warns Israel in Isaiah's day, and us in our day, not to depend on unbelievers for our safety or provisions. Generations after Isaiah, Ezra faced this temptation as he prepared to travel the dangerous trek to Jerusalem. He could ask King Artaxerxes for soldiers to protect his people on the way, or he could trust in God. Ezra 8:22 describes his decision, "I was ashamed to request of the king an escort of soldiers and horsemen to help us against the enemy on the road, because we had spoken to the king, saying, 'The hand of our God is upon all those for good who seek Him, but His power and His wrath are against all those who forsake Him.'" Later, Ezra 8:23 tells the blessed result of Ezra's confidence and dependence on the Lord, "So we fasted and entreated our God for this, and He answered our prayer."

God is "very strong." And He is determined to show Himself faithful to those who "seek" Him. Let us "Seek the LORD and His strength; seek His face evermore!" (I Chronicles 16:11). Our Lord invites us to seek Him in times of trouble. In fact, He formed us from birth, inherently designed to seek Him. Acts 17:26-27 plainly says that men and women were created and their dwelling place predetermined "so that they should seek the Lord." We were created with the instinct embedded within us to seek the Lord. If bears do not obey their instinct and hibernate, they are in grave danger, if birds do not obey their instinct to fly south for the winter, their lives will likewise be in jeopardy. Similarly, men are in danger when they refuse to "seek the LORD" as their instincts demand. If anyone refuses to seek God in times of need he must go "out of the way" (Romans 3:12 KJV), he must alter the 'natural' inclination of his soul to do so. And the Lord will hold him accountable for this failure to obey his God-given instinct and refuse to seek His Creator's blessings in time of need. Failure to seek the Lord in times of crisis is a crime against the conscience of man, and this is the crime that Israel is accused of here. The Assyrian threat is staggering. They must have God's help to survive. Their conscience teaches it and their circumstances demand it – and yet they refuse and seek help from a lesser power. The lesson for us is plain. Doom awaits those who refuse to "seek the LORD."

31:2-3
Yet He also is wise and will bring disaster, and will not call back His words, but will arise against the house of evildoers, and against the help of those who work iniquity. Now the Egyptians are men, and not God; and their horses are flesh, and not spirit. When the LORD stretches out His hand, both he who helps will fall, and he who is helped will fall down; they all will perish together.

It is useless to look for allies in rebellion against God. Israel turned their back on God and looked for help from Egypt instead. But Egypt cannot replace God! "Egyptians are men, and not God!" They cannot help in the things that matter most. So will be the final realization of all who place their dreams in the hands of people. Turning our back on God and consuming ourselves, instead, with a lover, a business, a game, or anything else that is "not God" that is "not spirit" will unquestionably fail to see us through to judgment day. God's people provide wonderful blessings of encouragement and strength to one another in their pursuit of carrying out their Savior's work. Friends in the faith and godly leaders bless one another. Friends out-of-the-faith, unholy allies, and ungodly leaders, however, provide one another with nothing of lasting value. They both "will fall down." "They all will perish together." There is no alliance on earth that can stand against the Lord when He "stretches out His hand" to judge us. The terrible danger of alliances with ungodly people and "friendship with the world" (James 4:4) is that it tends to do exactly what it does here – deceives people into thinking they are safe and in good company, when they are not.

31:4-5
For thus the LORD has spoken to me: "As a lion roars, and a young lion over his prey (when a multitude of shepherds is summoned against him, he will not be afraid of their voice nor be disturbed by their noise), so the LORD of hosts will come down to fight for Mount Zion and for its hill. Like birds flying about, so will the LORD of hosts defend Jerusalem. Defending, He will also deliver it; passing over, He will preserve it."

In the preceding verses, God rebuked His people for their unholy, unwise alliance with Egypt, and here He tells them how unnecessary that alliance is. God is already determined to defend His people! Why do they feel the need to seek aid from others, when God stands to protect them, like a lion defending His prey? God is "defending" them, God will "deliver" them, God promises to "preserve" His people. What need do they have to turn to others for what God has already promised to provide? Psalms 91:2 says, "I will say of the LORD, 'He is my refuge and my fortress; my God, in Him I will trust.'" When we place our confidence in our Lord as in Psalms 91:2, a host of reassurances follow. "Surely He shall deliver you from the snare of the fowler and from the perilous pestilence" (Psalms 91:3). "Because you have made the LORD, who is my refuge, even the Most High, your dwelling place, no evil shall befall you, nor shall any plague come near your dwelling" (Psalms 91:9-10). And Psalms 91:14-15 reaffirms: "Because he has set his love upon Me, therefore I will deliver him; I will set him on high, because he has known My name. He shall call upon Me, and I will answer him; I will be with him in trouble; I will deliver him and honor him." Let us set our hope in the presence and promises of God. For in the shelter of His power and kindness, we will be protected from the temptation of seeking provision and protection from unholy allies.

31:6-7
Return to Him against whom the children of Israel have deeply revolted. For in that day every man shall throw away his idols of silver and his idols of gold – sin, which your own hands have made for yourselves.

"In that day," in the day that the Lord defends His people (verse 5), they will respond by throwing away their idols of silver and gold. "Sinful hands" (NLT) make idols, but here we see that grateful hearts seek to cleanse those hands and "return to Him" from whom they had once revolted. It is a wonderful day when a man chooses to "throw away his idols." Many men prefer idols because they can see idols, and they cannot see God. But blessed are those who do not see and yet believe (John 20:29). Men often prefer idols because God demands holiness and idols allow indiscretions. But blessed are those who seek to be holy because their Creator is holy. "The idols of the nations are silver and gold, the work of men's hands" (Psalms 135:15), but our God is not like theirs. We did not make our God. He made us. Isaiah accused his listeners of making gods "for yourselves." But those who throw those idols away delight in the understanding that rather than making a god for ourselves, we can take joy in our God who created us for Himself (Colossians 1:16). Seeing God rise up to rescue them from Assyria moved His people to throw away their idols of silver and gold. May the vision of our Lord rising up on the cross to rescue us from sin move us to discard any present-day idols that would divert our devotion from our Creator.

31:8-9
"Then Assyria shall fall by a sword not of man, and a sword not of mankind shall devour him. But he shall flee from the sword, and his young men shall become forced labor. He shall cross over to his stronghold for fear, and his princes shall be afraid of the banner," says the LORD, whose fire is in Zion and whose furnace is in Jerusalem.

Isaiah prophecies of the fall of the Assyrian army. II Kings 19:35 details the fall, when an angel of the Lord, not the sword of man, executes 185,000 Assyrian soldiers on "a certain night." God is determined to defend His people. He will wave His standard over His soldier-saints, and His enemies "shall be afraid of the banner." The people of God can happily say, "The Lord is my Banner" (Exodus 17:15) -- He inspires His people to war, and the sight of Him strikes fear in the hearts of the enemy. Our God stands with us in times of trouble, and His banner waves high over-head so that we can always lift our eyes and see that He is with us through the smoke and haze of life's battles. God's "fire" is with us. "Our God is a consuming fire" (Hebrews 12:29), and His ministers serve Him like "a flame of fire" (Psalms 104:4). Our God is Immanuel, God with us. He lives with us, walks with us, protects us and guides us. He is God, and He does not sit quietly in a corner of the universe and let the world carry on as it pleases. "Our God shall come, and shall not keep silent; a fire shall devour before Him, and it shall be very tempestuous all around Him" (Psalms 50:3). God's presence on Mount Sinai was "like the smoke of a furnace" (Exodus 19:18), and even now, His "furnace is in Jerusalem" refining and purifying His people, burning away our spiritual dross so that we can shine for His purposes. Assyria will rise up and attack God's people, but the banner of the Lord will make him fear, the fire and furnace of the Lord will burn away his plans, and the angel of the Lord will destroy him completely. Such is the doom prophesied for Assyria, and such is the encouragement given all of us who trust in the Lord. Life is a battle, it is waged on the battlefield, not viewed from a lounge chair. But the battle is the Lord's (I Samuel 14:47). And He will use His sword, His banner, His fire, and His furnace to protect us, inspire us, and to destroy our enemies.

Isaiah 32

32:1-2
Behold, a king will reign in righteousness, and princes will rule with justice. A man will be as a hiding place from the wind, and a cover from the tempest, as rivers of water in a dry place, as the shadow of a great rock in a weary land.

The power of kings and rulers on earth is often, sadly, unaccompanied by righteousness. Those who rule over homes, workplaces, and kingdoms are often self-serving tyrants who take advantage of the weak rather than rescue them. Often, their power deludes them into thinking that they are accountable to no one and this moves them to take no thought for personal holiness or give little care to providing justice for those who can do nothing for them in return. But Isaiah looks to the day when "a king will reign in righteousness." The Messiah will come, the King of kings (I Timothy 6:15) will come and He will reign in righteousness. "The gift of righteousness will reign in life through the One, Jesus Christ" (Romans 5:17). What a beautiful picture of our King Jesus is given in verse 2. He will be "a hiding place from the wind." When the storms and winds of life gust up against us, our Savior-King is a shelter from the howling tempests of failures and fears and tormenters and trials. At times our Lord lifts His hand and says, "Peace, be still!" and the winds and storm around us are calmed by His presence (Mark 4:39). At other times, the winds and storms around us never seem to stop, but we are protected from them because we are "founded on the rock" (Matthew 7:25) that is a "hiding place from the wind." On our knees, kneeling in the presence of our King, the wind cannot touch us, for He is "a cover from the tempest."

Our King is also like "rivers of water in a dry place." "The river of God is full of water" (Psalms 65:9). He quenches the spiritual thirst of all who trust in Him. When our "strength has dried up like sunbaked clay" (Psalms 22:15, NLT), our King leads us beside the still waters (Psalms 23:2). When our soul longs to be fulfilled, when our spirit thirsts for hope and peace and the presence of our Lord, He is like "rivers of water in a dry place." When our "soul thirsts for God, for the living God" (Psalms 42:2), we will find Him very near to quench our thirst. The world can be "a dry place." Its temporary nature and its frequent disappointments leave us thirsty for the eternal, for the soul-satisfying – and we find this fulfillment in our King who reigns in righteousness. When our thirsty soul cries out as David does in Psalms 63:1 -- "O God, You are my God; early will I seek You; my soul thirsts for You; my flesh longs for You In a dry and thirsty land where there is no water," we know that we will not be disappointed, for our King has sent out His promise: "If anyone thirsts, let him come to Me and drink" (John 7:37). Our King provides a pure river filled with the waters of life (Revelation 22:1). All who trust in Him will find their thirst for life satisfied.

Our King is also compared to "the shadow of a great rock in a weary land." As the Lord provided the gourd to provide shade for Jonah, so our King will be for us as a "great rock" that will provide constant shade from the heat and glare of life's hottest stressors. "The Lord stands beside you as your protective shade" (Psalms 121:5, NLT). The Lord is a "hiding place" when the storms of life beat down. He is living water when our soul is dry. And He is shade when life gets hot. What a beautiful picture of our King who will reign in righteousness.

And as we read these wonderful descriptors of our Lord, let us take appropriate inspiration from the line "and princes will rule with justice." The King is righteous and safeguards His people. He nurtures them and protects them. He is a haven. He is an ever-present help in time of need. And His "princes" act like He does. He reigns "in righteousness." His princes "rule with justice." And just as His princes work to emulate His righteousness, so they also seek to imitate His protective nurture of His people. The "princes" of the kingdom of God – the pastors, elders, leaders, and shepherds of God's people are called to lead just as our King leads. Because He is righteous, let us vehemently guard our righteousness. And as He protects and cares for His people, let us rise to do the same.

32:3-4
The eyes of those who see will not be dim, and the ears of those who hear will listen. Also the heart of the rash will understand knowledge, and the tongue of the stammerers will be ready to speak plainly.

Isaiah looks forward to the wonderful effect that the reign of our righteous King will have on His people. When Jesus, our King of kings reigns over us, He infuses vitality into our eyes and ears and heart and tongue. When our Lord reigns, our eyes "will not be dim." God's presence with us and His commandments for us are continually "enlightening the eyes" of His people (Psalms 19:8). As the Lord enlightened Elisha's eyes to His chariots of fire that others could not see (II Kings 6:17), as the Lord opened the eyes of Paul's hearers so that they might be turned from darkness to light and from the power of Satan to God (Acts 26:18), so our King will do for all His subjects. He will not let their eyes be "dim." He will grant us the remarkably blessed privilege of seeing the light (Psalms 36:9). He allows us to see His face in righteousness (Psalms 17:15). He grants us the wonderful joy of seeing "the works of God" (Psalms 66:5). And taking the dimness from our eyes, our Lord permits all His people to "see His glory" (Psalms 97:6). Oh, the wonderful effect that God has on our eyes! Once we were blind, but now we see, and oh how grand these sights have proven to be!

In addition to the healing work on our eyes, our Great Physician-King also restores our ears, giving us the insight that we must "listen" to everything His Spirit says to us. We must not take this for granted. Not everyone who hears God speak, listens to what He says. It is an inexcusable, yet all-too-common malady of man – hearing the words of God, but failing to listen and apply what He commands. Let us rejoice with proper gratitude each time we feel ourselves inspired to say, "speak, Lord, for Your servant is listening" (I Samuel 3:9, HCS), for we see here that our desire to listen to God is actually a gift that our King extends to His people. Without this gift, we are prone to fall under the condemnation of those described in II Chronicles 33:10 "And the LORD spoke to Manasseh and his people, but they would not listen."

Our heart also, is blessed by the righteous reign of our King. Some people are naturally smart. Some minds are impressively brilliant. But others are not that way by nature. They are "rash," they leap to conclusions, they are quickly stumped by life's puzzles. But when our righteous King comes to reign in power, even the "rash will understand knowledge." Our King will grant understanding to our heart so that we "have more understanding than all (our) teachers, for Your testimonies are (our) meditation" (Psalms 119:99).

And joining our eyes and ears and heart, our tongue also is granted a Royal endowment of power when our righteous King comes to reign. "The tongue of stammerers will be ready to speak plainly." When Moses feared the repercussions of his poor speaking ability, the Lord blessed him with this same promise given through Isaiah here: "Go, and I will be with your mouth and teach you what you shall say" (Exodus 4:12). Jesus spoke of this same gift in Luke 12:11-12 – "Now when they bring you to the synagogues and magistrates and authorities, do not worry about how or what you should answer, or what you should say. For the Holy Spirit will teach you in that very hour what you ought to say." When God reigns in lands and lives His sanctifying work changes our tongue just as it changes our hearts and minds. He teaches us what we should talk about, He teaches us how to articulate what we now want to discuss, He fills our words with passion, emotion, weight, and wisdom so that He will be magnified in our speech, and our hearers will be moved to align themselves rightly with the King of kings.

Our God is king. His kingdom is vast and extends across millennia and continents. But for all its vastness, His kingdom is intensely personal. He gives each of His people eyes so they can see the truth, ears so that we can best pay attention to His commands, a heart to understand His ways, and a tongue so that we can clearly articulate His ways to others. Our Lord's reign over the universe touches us and changes us personally. When we are reconciled with God, our eternal destiny is changed, this is true. But we are personally bettered, we are individually perfected even now as we live under the rule and reign of the King who reigns in righteousness. Our eyes and ears and heart and tongue – every part of us is made new "so that we can be mirrors that brightly reflect the glory of the Lord. And as the Spirit of the Lord works within us, we become more and more like him and reflect his glory even more" (II Corinthians 3:18).

32:5-8
The foolish person will no longer be called generous, nor the miser said to be bountiful; for the foolish person will speak foolishness, and his heart will work iniquity: to practice ungodliness, to utter error against the

ISAIAH 32

LORD, to keep the hungry unsatisfied, and he will cause the drink of the thirsty to fail. Also the schemes of the schemer are evil; he devises wicked plans to destroy the poor with lying words, even when the needy speaks justice. But a generous man devises generous things, and by generosity he shall stand.

Although the specific wording of this passage varies widely among the major translators, the underlying theme remains constant – when our King reigns in righteousness over His people (verse 1), fools and misers and evil schemers are seen for what they are and lose their place of influence in society. Wherever God does not reign, a trio of spiritual misfits rise to take His place. Fools, misers, and those with "wicked plans" are allowed to lead when the Creator's leadership is refused. Look at the degradation that tears at cities and peoples when they turn from the Lord. Fools who "utter error against the LORD" are placed in leadership. Fools, who cannot tell their right hand from their left (Jonah 4:11), are called upon to give counsel and direction. Misers and "scoundrels" (ESV) who "keep the hungry unsatisfied" as Nabal does in I Samuel 25 are left in charge when God is denied His rightful place on the throne. And evil schemers who "destroy the poor with lying words" as Ahab does to Naboth in I Kings 21, are likewise allowed to reign when God is rejected. But when the Lord comes to "reign in righteousness" as verse 1 describes, this trio of virtue-less sham leaders is cast out and God's righteous followers come to lead instead. Instead of leaders who devise "wicked plans," the people are granted godly leaders who devise "generous things" for their people. And where the wicked once propped up their power by taking advantage of the weak, God's leaders earn the respect and loyalty of their people when they stand "by generosity." Multiple adjectives are used to describe ungodly leaders. They are "foolish" and miserly, they "work iniquity" and "practice ungodliness." They speak false things of God, deny help to the needy, and devise wicked plans. Interestingly, only one adjective is used to describe the godly men who come to lead others under the blessed rule of their righteous King: they are "generous." "A generous man devises generous things, and by generosity he shall stand." As servants of God and leaders of His people, let us not lose sight of this trait that should be inherent in all those who would lead and feed our Lord's sheep. Godly leadership and generosity go hand in hand, as exemplified by Cornelius the centurion who was "a devout man and one who feared God with all his household, who gave alms generously to the people, and prayed to God always" (Acts 10:2). By all means, let us "stand by faith" (II Corinthians 1:24). Let us stand unwavering for truth and righteousness

(Ephesians 6:14). But with equal faithfulness, let us stand by generosity. Let us gladly, generously, freely give from the generous supply that God has given to us and promptly provide for the needs of His people.

32:9-11
Rise up, you women who are at ease, hear my voice; you complacent daughters, give ear to my speech. In a year and some days you will be troubled, you complacent women; for the vintage will fail, the gathering will not come. Tremble, you women who are at ease; be troubled, you complacent ones; strip yourselves, make yourselves bare, and gird sackcloth on your waists.

Those who "are at ease" are called upon to "tremble." Those who are "complacent" are condemned. In Zephaniah 1:12 the Lord says that He will "punish the men who are settled in complacency" and here we see that complacency in women is equally abhorrent in the eyes of the Lord. Godly men and women view life as a "good fight" (II Timothy 4:7). Godly men and women "have a mind to work" (Nehemiah 4:6, II Thessalonians 3:10). Rest for the godly is coming in heaven, but our days on earth are to be filled with striving and toil, wrestling, and labor. Colossians 1:29 says, "For this I toil, struggling with all his energy that he powerfully works within me" (ESV). Ephesians 6:12 says that we "wrestle" against the powers and rulers "of the darkness of this age." And II Thessalonians 3:8 says that Paul "worked with labor and toil night and day." Life is too important to live out from a lounge chair! God's works must be accomplished! His kingdom must be expanded! Men and women that He has created are facing severe troubles and we must take care of them. Many men "do not have faith" and we must inspire them to believe! Sinners must be turned from the error of their ways, new believers must be trained up in the faith, saints nearby must be encouraged, and the gospel must be taken to the lost in distant lands. Backsliders must be returned to the fold, children need to be nurtured, and sin in our own hearts must be crushed. We must spend day and night studying and meditating on God's word, and then spend day and night teaching others what God's word has taught to us. Oh, there is so much work to do in life! Complacency is a sinister evil! Feeling "at ease" is a silent cancer in the life of a believer. Jesus said, "I must work the works of Him who sent Me while it is day; the night is coming when no one can work" (John 9:4). When we abandon the work of our Lord and become complacent, we forsake our Lord's example and follow, instead, the hell-bound example of the rich man in Luke 12:19 who said, "Soul, you have many goods laid up for many years;

take your ease; eat, drink, and be merry." Our rest is coming soon enough. But it is not today! Today we work! Today we fight! Let us fear a life of ease and refuse to allow complacency to settle down within us. "My Father never stops working, so why should I?" (John 5:17 NLT).

32:12-15
People shall mourn upon their breasts for the pleasant fields, for the fruitful vine. On the land of my people will come up thorns and briers, yes, on all the happy homes in the joyous city; because the palaces will be forsaken, the bustling city will be deserted. The forts and towers will become lairs forever, a joy of wild donkeys, a pasture of flocks – until the Spirit is poured upon us from on high, and the wilderness becomes a fruitful field, and the fruitful field is counted as a forest.

The people of Isaiah's day had turned their backs on God, and they will come to "mourn" this decision. Life apart from their Lord will devastate their nation. Fruitful fields will become "thorns and briers." "The palaces will be forsaken" and "the bustling city will be deserted." They had depended on their "forts and towers" to protect them from enemies, but these things will be reduced to dens and lairs for wild donkeys. And the land is doomed to stay in this degraded, disgraced condition "until the Spirit is poured upon us from on high." But when the Spirit of the Lord returns in grace and forgiveness, He makes "all things new" (Revelation 21:5). The wilderness of sin becomes a "fruitful field" of righteous efforts which grows to become a forest of blessings in the land. Oh, the blessings that overflow in us when "the Spirit is poured upon us from on high." In Acts 2:17 Peter quotes the prophet Joel and rejoices that "it shall come to pass in the last days, says God, that I will pour out of My Spirit on all flesh; your sons and your daughters shall prophesy, your young men shall see visions, your old men shall dream dreams." Without the Spirit of the Lord in us, our lives become barren and abased, as the land of Israel faces here. But our Lord has promised to pour out His Spirit on His people so that we can continually bask in His presence and rejoice in the blessings that His Spirit provides. When "the Spirit is poured upon us from on high," our frailties are replaced with His power, our confusion is replaced with His omniscience, and our problems are overturned in the fountain of His blessings. Poor insight, physical infirmity, and harsh circumstances can all serve to make our lives look like Israel does here – full of thorns and briers, forsaken, and deserted; so this wonderful picture that illustrates God's promise from Joel 2:28 is deeply uplifting to us. The Spirit of God – our Comforter, Counselor, and

Helper (John 14:16 KJV, NLT, ESV) has been promised to us! And He teaches us "all things" (John 14:26) and He gifts us and empowers us (I Corinthians 12:11) to meet every challenge. What a blessed thought.

32:16-17
Then justice will dwell in the wilderness, and righteousness remain in the fruitful field. The work of righteousness will be peace, and the effect of righteousness, quietness and assurance forever.

See the blessed results of living holy lives before the Lord. The "work of righteousness" is peace, and the "effect of righteousness" is "quietness and assurance forever." If we are plagued by worry, if anxiety nags at us at night, let us take note of our Savior's offered cure: "righteousness." Let us fix our hearts on our own purity before the Lord, and His forgiveness and cleansing mercies will be extended to us, lifting our guilt and filling our hearts with peace. The peace that flows from a heart made clean can quiet *any* storm life can throw at us. The noise of a tumultuous world is replaced with "quietness." Uncertainties are replaced with "assurance." And anxiety is replaced with "peace." In a world where anxiety runs rampant, even in the church, this message seems especially important. When financial, family, and health crises emerge – let us guard our personal holiness as our primary means of safeguarding our peace of mind. Spiritual holiness leads to emotional peace – "Righteousness and peace have kissed" (Psalms 85:10). We need not flee suffering to enjoy peace, we need only to guard, at all costs, our personal holiness.

32:18-20
My people will dwell in a peaceful habitation, in secure dwellings, and in quiet resting places, though hail comes down on the forest, and the city is brought low in humiliation. Blessed are you who sow beside all waters, who send out freely the feet of the ox and the donkey.

When men and women seek comfort, seek easy living, and become "complacent" (verses 9-11), God is angered and warns them to be "troubled" (verse 11), mourning their lack of insight. But when men and women seek to walk with their Creator in righteousness (verse 17), the result is "a peaceful habitation," "secure dwellings," and "quiet resting places." It is fascinating to see how God rewards His righteous followers with the same gifts of peace and tranquility that were sought by those that He condemns in verses 9-11. We are taught here (in verses 9-20) the important truth that peace is a wonderful reward, but it makes an unholy objective. See how similar godly rewards and unholy pursuits can appear! Complacency is evil, but God gives "quiet resting places" to His saints. Seeking to live "at ease" is vile to God, but He gives His people "peaceful habitation." Verse 17 above reminds us that it is the "work" of righteousness that brings peace, not lounging and easy living. Romans 2:10 promises peace "to everyone who *works* what is good." God promises peace and safety to His saints who devote themselves to righteous efforts. But making peace and safety our central aim condemns us! Paul warns us in I Thessalonians 5:3 "For when they say, 'Peace and safety!' then sudden destruction comes upon them, as labor pains upon a pregnant woman. And they shall not escape." Complacency, with a focus on personal safety and easy living is condemning. Let us, instead, seek righteousness and guard our personal holiness at all costs – this is the key to lasting peace.

Isaiah 33

33:1
Woe to you who plunder, though you have not been plundered; and you who deal treacherously, though they have not dealt treacherously with you! When you cease plundering, you will be plundered; when you make an end of dealing treacherously, they will deal treacherously with you.

Hezekiah made a pact with Assyria and paid for them to leave his nation alone (II Kings 18:13-16). But the king of Assyria "dealt treacherously" with Judah and soon returned with an army to conquer God's people. In Psalms 119:158 David writes, "I see the treacherous, and am disgusted, because they do not keep Your word." He writes again in Psalms 25:3 – "let no one who waits on You be ashamed; let those be ashamed who deal treacherously without cause." Seeing people "plunder" and murder and treacherously cheat their fellow man moves godly men and women to feel "disgusted." We are assured, however, that no one gets away with murder – or any other sin. Obadiah 1:15 says, "For the day of the LORD upon all the nations is near; as you have done, it shall be done to you; your reprisal shall return upon your own head." Treacherous, murderous men will certainly face their "reprisal" from the Lord. Perhaps we would prefer the Lord to be more immediate in His response to treacherous, violent people, but His response is certain. He will answer David's prayer: those who deal murderously and treacherously with others will "be ashamed." Assyria will certainly be ashamed. 185,000 soldiers will die at the hands of God's death angel outside Jerusalem, and their king will be murdered treacherously by his own sons (II Kings 19:35-37). "As you have done, it shall be done to you."

33:2-4
O LORD, be gracious to us; we have waited for You. Be their arm every morning, our salvation also in the time of trouble. At the noise of the tumult the people shall flee; when You lift Yourself up, the nations shall be scattered; and Your plunder shall be gathered like the gathering of the caterpillar; as the running to and fro of locusts, He shall run upon them.

Isaiah prays in verse 2, and his knowledge of God grants him assurance of the Lord's sure response in verses 3 and 4. Isaiah asks the Lord to "be our strength every morning" (HCS). Isaiah is facing a "time of trouble." If God does not help them, Isaiah and his people will not survive. But while some despair, some flee, and others depend on military allies like Egypt, Isaiah says, "we have waited for You." When "the time of trouble" comes to us, let us be willing to wait for God's provision. Much hurt has been caused when we rush out headlong to tackle problems in our own strength rather than wait for God's "gracious" provision. And once blessed by God's provision today, we must again depend on His provision tomorrow. He must be our strength "every morning," for today's victory does not grant us immunity from trouble tomorrow. We do not need to fear our enemies – even if they number 185,000 strong as in Isaiah's case. Isaiah is confident that "when You lift Yourself up" all enemies will melt away. Like swarms of locusts and caterpillars could strip away a green field down to the nubs, so God "shall run upon them" and crush their enemies' evil plans. Isaiah's example is instructive and inspiring. In desperate trial, he does not despair. He waits for God's gracious provision, trusting that God will be his strength every morning. When it is our turn to suffer at the hands of men with evil intent, let us agree to do the same. "Do not say, 'I will recompense evil'; wait for the LORD, and He will save you" (Proverbs 20:22).

33:5-6
The LORD is exalted, for He dwells on high; He has filled Zion with justice and righteousness. Wisdom and knowledge will be the stability of your times, and the strength of salvation; the fear of the LORD is His treasure.

The exact rendering of verse 6 varies among the major translators. Let me write it out combining 3 versions: "and He will be the stability of your times" (NASV), "a storehouse of salvation, wisdom, and knowledge" (HCS), "the fear of the LORD is the key to this treasure" (NLT). In unpredictable, unsettling times, God, Himself, provides "stability." Trusting in Him is compared to building a house on a rock (Luke 6:48), because He is stable, He is a "sure foundation" (Isaiah 28:16). Proverbs 29:4 says "A just king gives stability to his nation," and so God's people are provided unparalleled stability because our Lord has "filled Zion with justice and righteousness."

Our Lord is a "storehouse," He is a treasury of "salvation, wisdom, and knowledge." Do we need wisdom? Let us go to our Divine storehouse and find that He provides wisdom "generously to all" (James 1:5 ESV). Do we lack knowledge? We can come to this storehouse and find that the Lord gives this in generous supply as well! "For the LORD gives wisdom; from His mouth come knowledge and understanding" (Proverbs 2:6). And if we need salvation, we find that this, too, is found in our Lord's storehouse – and only in His storehouse, for "salvation belongs to the LORD" (Psalms 3:8).

Our Lord is a treasure! He offers wisdom to help us meet the complex challenges of life. He offers knowledge to answer life's hardest questions. And He grants salvation to rescue us from sin and death. But in order for us to be granted access to these treasures from the Lord, we must hold "the key," and verse 6 says that "the fear of the LORD is the key to this treasure." The fear of the Lord gives us wisdom. Psalms 111:10 says, "The fear of the LORD is the beginning of wisdom." The fear of the Lord gives us knowledge. Proverbs 1:7 says, "The fear of the LORD is the beginning of knowledge." And the fear of the Lord is the key to salvation. Psalms 33:18-19 says, "Behold, the eye of the LORD is on those who fear Him, on those who hope in His mercy, to deliver their soul from death." And Psalms 34:7 says "The angel of the Lord encamps all around those who fear Him, and delivers them." "The LORD is exalted"! He is worthy of our praise! He is a treasure, and those who fear Him – lovingly, wholeheartedly revere Him – are granted the key to the storehouse of treasures that He has laid up for those who are His.

ISAIAH 33

33:7-9
Surely their valiant ones shall cry outside, the ambassadors of peace shall weep bitterly. The highways lie waste, the traveling man ceases. He has broken the covenant, he has despised the cities, he regards no man. The earth mourns and languishes, Lebanon is shamed and shriveled; Sharon is like a wilderness, and Bashan and Carmel shake off their fruits.

In verse 2, Isaiah affirms that "we have waited for you." Our Lord provides His people with the "strength of salvation" (verse 6), but often we must wait through some very difficult times before we can see the joyous end of our salvation come to fruition. Such is the case in our verses here as a whole roll call of God's people are seen to suffer as they wait for God's promised deliverance to arrive. Israel's "valiant ones" cry, their "ambassadors" weep bitterly, travelers are forced to stay home, Lebanon, Sharon, and Carmel – all of Israel from east to west and to the top of their nation are "shamed and shriveled." No one is spared the effects of this trial – "the earth mourns and languishes." With such universal suffering depicted here, let us not think that we will be guaranteed an exemption from suffering in our day. Those who trust in the Lord are assured salvation. If we will wait for the Son who comes from heaven, He will deliver us from the wrath to come (I Thessalonians 1:10). But while we wait, we must often endure much hardship, as exemplified here as Israel endures Assyria's siege while waiting for God's deliverance that is to come.

33:10-13
"Now I will rise," says the LORD; "Now I will be exalted, now I will lift Myself up. You shall conceive chaff, you shall bring forth stubble; your breath, as fire, shall devour you. And the people shall be like the burnings of lime; like thorns cut up they shall be burned in the fire. Hear, you who are afar off, what I have done; and you who are near, acknowledge My might."

The Lord always has universal intentions even with His personal, localized rescues. He promises to deliver Israel, but He instructs even the nations that "are afar off" to pay attention to what He does to deliver His people and destroy His enemies. What God does to rescue His people in Israel provides hope for all who trust in Him the world over. And what God does to punish Assyria provides a warning to all who would reject Him the world over.

God has been patient with Assyria, but "Now...Now...now." Now He will act to punish their evil – and His punishments will be severe and complete.

His fire of judgment will "devour" them. They came with great designs to plunder God's people, but their plans to enrich themselves with their war machine will never come to fruition. They will "conceive chaff;" they will "bring forth stubble," meaning that their plans will yield no fruit.

God's purpose in the lives of man will not be denied. He has purposed that "I will be exalted." "I will be exalted among the nations, I will be exalted in the earth!" (Psalms 46:10). Man has no choice in the matter. We will exalt our Creator. We will exalt Him by obeying Him, praising Him, and having the world witness His blessings on His children – or we will reject Him, dishonor Him, and have the world exalt Him as they witness how He vanquishes evil.

33:14-16
The sinners in Zion are afraid; fearfulness has seized the hypocrites: "Who among us shall dwell with the devouring fire? Who among us shall dwell with everlasting burnings?" He who walks righteously and speaks uprightly, He who despises the gain of oppressions, who gestures with his hands, refusing bribes, who stops his ears from hearing of bloodshed, and shuts his eyes from seeing evil: he will dwell on high; his place of defense will be the fortress of rocks; bread will be given him, his water will be sure.

Seeing God destroy His enemies will inspire His children, filling them with joy in the Lord and hope for their future. But seeing God destroy rebellious people will cause "sinners" and "hypocrites" to fear for their lives, sensing within themselves that God sees their heart and is angered by their secret sins. God is a "devouring fire" (Psalms 18:8). And God does "not show personal favoritism" (Luke 20:21). The red-hot fire of His fury against hypocrites and sinners will consume all wicked people in wicked nations. His blazing intolerance for sin will also consume all sinners and hypocrites in good nations, as well as all sinners and hypocrites who go to church. Sinners who are thinking men and still have a working conscience will view God's punishments on others as a personal warning to themselves. "Who among us can hope to survive against such holy anger?" "What sinner can hope to avoid the 'everlasting burnings' that are ordained for the unholy?" God provides thinking men with a working conscience the answer to these questions: if sinners would protect themselves from the fires of God's judgment, they must stop sinning! They must walk "righteously" and speak "uprightly." They must "reject making a profit by fraud" (NLT), refuse bribes, and stop hanging out with evil people. If they will do so, God provides hope even for those who have sinned! Those who repent of sin and turn their life around "will dwell on high!" Sin makes us defenseless before the fires of God's judgment. But righteousness and forgiveness will be our "defense." Holy living and God's approval will build for us a "fortress of rocks" and become the bread and water sustaining our soul. We will be able to join David and say, "My defense is of God, Who saves the upright in heart" (Psalms 7:10). Hypocrites and sinners have nowhere to turn when the fires of God's judgment burn hot. But holiness will secure for us His constant provision, bread and water for our body and soul will be constantly supplied. David wrote, "I have been young, and now am old; yet I have not seen the righteous forsaken, nor his descendants begging bread" (Psalms 37:25). Our verses here remind us that a vision of God's judgment ignites fear in the heart of hypocrites and sinners. But repentance rekindles hope. God is a devouring fire that consumes sinners and hypocrites. But our God is also a fortress and a defense for the repentant. Let all thinking men and women take note.

33:17-19
Your eyes will see the King in His beauty; they will see the land that is very far off. Your heart will meditate on terror: "Where is the scribe? Where is he who weighs? Where is he who counts the towers?" You will not see a fierce people, a people of obscure speech, beyond perception, of a stammering tongue that you cannot understand.

Isaiah prophesies of the joy and feelings of relief in God's people when the Assyrians are overthrown by the angel of the Lord in II Kings 19. The "fierce people" of Assyria who speak a foreign tongue will be gone. The scribes, weighers (of spoils), and tower counters of the Assyrian army will all be gone as well. And in their place will stand "the King in His beauty." A king is never so grand as when he stands before his people after delivering them from a crisis. And here, after delivering His people from the Assyrian horde, His people are blessed to see Him "in His beauty." May the beauty of the Lord captivate us now, just as it does His people here. May the joy of seeing our King "in His beauty" always be our soul's highest aim. Let us join the psalmist in saying, "One thing I have desired of the LORD, that will I seek: that I may dwell in the house of the LORD all the days of my life, to behold the beauty of the LORD, and to inquire in His temple" (Psalms 27:4).

33:20
Look upon Zion, the city of our appointed feasts; your eyes will see Jerusalem, a quiet home, a tabernacle that will not be taken down; not one of its stakes will ever be removed, nor will any of its cords be broken.

Isaiah loves his hometown. Jerusalem, that he calls Zion, is "the city of our appointed feasts." He has a hundred happy memories of celebrating God's goodness by commemorating holy days with others who loved God too. Isaiah lived in turbulent times, but he promises his God-fearing readers that "your eyes will see Jerusalem, a quiet home." What a blessing it is to have "a quiet home." The Assyrian marauders will attack and pillage, but these "light and momentary troubles" (II Corinthians 4:17 NIV) will pass soon enough and God's people will be blessed to return to their "quiet home." May the Lord bless us with a "quiet home" for our children to return to each day. Let us train them up to leave the house each day to fight the good fight, to wrestle with the powers of this world, and to stand strong against the storms of life. But when they come home from school or work and time in the world, may they be blessed with the deeply spiritually nourishing environment of a "quiet home." The people of Isaiah's day faced tumultuous times. But he encourages them with this vision of the future, when their home will be peaceful, and their place of God-centered worship will be the center of their activities and a clear illustration of the stability that God has granted them. The tabernacle "will not be taken down; not one of its stakes will ever be removed." In the wilderness, the tabernacle was constantly being taken down and moved from one place to another for 40 years. In the exile, the people were removed from their homes and the cords that bound them to their place of worship were broken. But Isaiah invites his readers to lift their eyes and see this vision of the day that is approaching when all God's people will see (the new) Jerusalem. It will be a "quiet home," free of alarms and terrors. And the tabernacle of worship "will not be taken down." Jesus, our high priest will bring us to a "more perfect tabernacle that is not made with human hands" (Hebrews 9:11) that can never be removed from us. We will never be denied access to our blessed place of worship and never be disallowed entry into the presence of our Lord.

ISAIAH 33

33:21-22
But there the majestic LORD will be for us a place of broad rivers and streams, in which no galley with oars will sail, nor majestic ships pass by (for the LORD is our Judge, the LORD is our Lawgiver, the LORD is our King; He will save us);

    As broad rivers provide sustenance and prevent enemy armies from marching in, so the Lord will provide for and protect His people. No enemy ships can sail in, and no allied navy is needed, because the Lord Himself, protects His people. Isaiah 9:6 told us that the government would be upon the Lord's shoulder, and here, interestingly, we see that this includes all three branches of government. The judicial branch of government is provided by the Lord, for He is Judge. The legislative branch of government is provided by our Lord, for He is our Lawgiver. And the executive branch is provided as well, because He is our King. When our Lord reigns over nations and hearts He reigns completely – we need no one else to fill in the gaps in society that our Lord does not touch on – there are no gaps. He makes the laws, He interprets the laws and judges lawbreakers, and He enforces His laws as King. The government is on His shoulder, He bears the weight of governing His people as Judge, Lawgiver, and King. And where other governments may fail – their laws may fail to protect their people and their king may fail to protect them from enemies, God will not fail. "He will save us." As our Judge, He rises up to judge and to save us (Psalms 76:9 HCS). As our Lawgiver, He does the same -- "There is one Lawgiver, who is able to save and to destroy" (James 4:12). And as our King, He reigns with the same purpose in mind – to "save us." Psalms 74:12 says, "For God is my King from of old, working salvation in the midst of the earth." So then, seeing that it is the intention of our Lord's government to save those who are His, let us scorn all other pretend protectors and happily trust in our King to provide what He has promised to deliver. Let others trust in what they will, but may everyone in our family join David and say with confidence, "As for me, I will call upon God, and the LORD shall save me" (Psalms 55:16).

33:23-24
Your tackle is loosed, they could not strengthen their mast, they could not spread the sail. Then the prey of great plunder is divided; the lame take the prey. And the inhabitant will not say, "I am sick"; the people who dwell in it will be forgiven their iniquity.

    We are struck by this picture illustrating how spiritual victories and military triumphs go hand in hand. The armed forces of the enemy are seen defeated here. Their ships left lifeless; their broken war machine is plundered. Their defeat is so complete that even the lame among Israel can pick out their choice of the spoils. And God's people "will be forgiven their iniquity." We cannot miss the message that military victory is useless to us if unaccompanied by reconciliation with our Creator. We are quick to realize that this truth extends to every facet of life. Financial successes, career success, athletic prowess, academic accomplishments – none of these things are significantly beneficial if unaccompanied by God's forgiveness and a constant renewal of the joys of securing His approval. God will defeat their enemies, but even more significant is the fact that He will "heal their land" (II Chronicles 7:14), the people will no longer be "sick." May the Lord bless us with eyes like His that can correctly assess challenges and correctly discern the real need in crisis. God's people saw enemy armies threatening their security. God saw that sin was making them sick and ruining their walk with their loving Lord. The hearts of the people cried out for God to deliver them from their enemies, but their souls cried out for the Lord to deliver them from sin – and in mercy, God does both. God forgives. God defends us from enemies. What a blessed thought.

Isaiah 34

34:1-4
Come near, you nations, to hear; and heed, you people! Let the earth hear, and all that is in it, the world and all things that come forth from it. For the indignation of the LORD is against all nations, and His fury against all their armies; He has utterly destroyed them, He has given them over to the slaughter. Also their slain shall be thrown out; their stench shall rise from their corpses, and the mountains shall be melted with their blood. All the host of heaven shall be dissolved, and the heavens shall be rolled up like a scroll; all their host shall fall down as the leaf falls from the vine, and as fruit falling from a fig tree.

We must join Isaiah and do all we can to warn all the people of the world of God's impending judgment on us all. "Let the earth hear!" Everyone on earth needs to hear this warning of God's intention to judge all mankind. It may be up to us to choose what god we will worship and what god we will serve (Joshua 24:15), but it is not ours to choose which God decides our eternal fate. The Creator will judge all people in all nations whether they believe in Him or not. "The indignation of the LORD is against all nations."

All things were made by God and all things were designed to give Him glory (Colossians 1:16), and when we rebel against the very purpose of our existence, we infuriate our Creator, we incite "His fury" against us. God has given humanity a conscience that hears His call for us to be holy, and when we rebel against the demands of that conscience, we incite "His fury" against us.

Clearly, Isaiah's words here are not just directed against the Assyrian enemies attacking his people in his day. God's anger is said to be directed against "all nations." And the end of this judgment from God will result in "all the host of heaven shall be dissolved, and the heavens shall be rolled up like a scroll." Psalms 75:2-3 speaks to this day of judgment from the Lord just the same, "When I choose the proper time, I will judge uprightly. The earth and all its inhabitants are dissolved; I set up its pillars firmly. Selah."

II Peter 3:11 reminds us of how this ultimate dissolution of the world is personally applicable to all of us today: "Therefore, since all these things will be dissolved, what manner of persons ought you to be in holy conduct and godliness"? Our Creator will one day judge us, therefore, let us be holy and godly today. Then II Peter 3:12 adds to the godly man's response to the impending judgments of God: "looking for and hastening the coming of the day of God, because of which the heavens will be dissolved, being on fire, and the elements will melt with fervent heat". We are to be continually "looking for" God's judgments, and we are to continually be "hastening" the arrival of His day of judgment. In His discussion on the final Day of Judgment, Jesus says in Mark 13:37 - "And what I say to you, I say to all: Watch!" And as for hastening God's Day of Judgment, Jesus says in Matthew 24:14 – "And this gospel of the kingdom will be preached in all the world as a witness to all the nations, and then the end will come." The Day of Judgment will come when "this gospel of the kingdom will be preached in all the world." If we would hasten God's judgment, and we are instructed to do so, we must set our energies on seeing the gospel of God preached to all peoples everywhere. This is our ready means of hastening Christ's second coming, for He has promised that He will return after everyone, everywhere has heard the gospel.

34:5-7

"For My sword shall be bathed in heaven; indeed it shall come down on Edom, and on the people of My curse, for judgment. The sword of the LORD is filled with blood, it is made overflowing with fatness, with the blood of lambs and goats, with the fat of the kidneys of rams. For the LORD has a sacrifice in Bozrah, and a great slaughter in the land of

Edom. The wild oxen shall come down with them, and the young bulls with the mighty bulls; their land shall be soaked with blood, and their dust saturated with fatness."

With graphic language, the Lord is depicted by Isaiah here as coming down on the sinful nations of the earth (referred to as "Edom") to carry out "a great slaughter." God has prepared "a sacrifice" in Bozrah -- and in every land where evil dwells. Sin demands a sacrifice (Leviticus 4:22-26). Jesus offered His own body as "one sacrifice for sins forever" (Hebrews 10:12), but if we will not allow ourselves to be covered by the blood of Christ, our own blood is required as the cost of corrupting a God-given life with sin. And here we see the Lord exacting that terrible cost at the hands of the sinful nations of the earth. "Their land shall be soaked with blood." See the imperative for warning all people in all nations to turn from sin and turn to the Savior so that they might be rescued from the terrible punishment for sin! Sin demands a sacrifice! But if we will not obey our Lord and cling to His provision to make atonement for our wrongdoings, "there no longer remains a sacrifice for sins" (Hebrews 10:26), other than the sacrifice of our own life. On a personal level this is nothing less than tragic, and when seen on a national level, as depicted here, it is horrific. Sin demands a sacrifice. Reading this rightly moves us to deep gratitude for Jesus' redemptive sacrifice at Calvary, and moves us to warn others to "flee from this wrath to come" (Luke 3:7).

34:8-12
For it is the day of the LORD's vengeance, the year of recompense for the cause of Zion. Its streams shall be turned into pitch, and its dust into brimstone; its land shall become burning pitch. It shall not be quenched night or day; its smoke shall ascend forever. From generation to generation it shall lie waste; no one shall pass through it forever and ever. But the pelican and the porcupine shall possess it, also the owl and the raven shall dwell in it. And he shall stretch out over it the line of confusion and the stones of emptiness. They shall call its nobles to the kingdom, but none shall be there, and all its princes shall be nothing.

Once again, we see the timelessness of Isaiah's message. He is not only foretelling the downfall of Israel's enemies in his day, but the ultimate fall of all those who rebel against God. When the army of unbelievers is judged, "its smoke shall ascend forever." Revelation 14:11 says the same thing, "the smoke of their torment ascends forever and ever." And when Babylon falls in Revelation 19:3, the same prophecy is made, "Alleluia! Her smoke rises up forever and ever!" This vision of burning pitch and brimstone was seen by David as well. In Psalms 11:6 he writes, "Upon the wicked He will rain coals; fire and brimstone and a burning wind shall be the portion of their cup." God's hot anger will mete out burning coals of punishment on those who refuse to obey Him, and He will give His intended blessings to others who are less undeserving. Here, that means that the Lord turns the land over to "the pelican and the porcupine," to the "owl and the raven." And in Luke 14:21 the Master says, "Go out quickly into the streets and lanes of the city, and bring in here the poor and the maimed and the lame and the blind." It is God's heart to bless His people. If His people refuse His blessings, however, His intention to bless will not be undone. Just as He does here, He will take His blessings from the rebellious and give them to others (Matthew 25:28).

The result of incurring God's wrath is tragic. In addition to the coals and fire and brimstone, those who rebel against God are also destined to inherit "the line of confusion" and "the stones of emptiness." God promises that if we will not obey His voice that" "The LORD will strike you with madness and blindness and confusion of heart" (Deuteronomy 28:28). The Lord gives "skill to understand" (Daniel 9:22) to those who obey Him, but He gives "confusion" to those who refuse to obey. It is fascinating to see how the simplest spiritual truths are not understandable by those whose sin has moved God to pour out on them the "line of confusion." Unbelievers are also forced to carry the "stones of emptiness." They will find at the end of their days that they may have spent years acquiring riches and reputations, they may have filled their life with entertainment and adventure, but by failing to procure God's approval, even after all these acquisitions, "His soul is still empty" (Isaiah 29:8). What a tragedy (the ultimate tragedy!) to have one's life count as "nothing." A life and a soul filled with anything other than the Spirit of God is empty. It is nothing. And on judgment day it will be cast away from the presence and intended blessings of God, a tragic end for a horribly misdirected mind.

34:13-15

And thorns shall come up in its palaces, nettles and brambles in its fortresses; it shall be a habitation of jackals, a courtyard for ostriches. The wild beasts of the desert shall also meet with the jackals, and the wild goat shall bleat to its companion; also the night creature shall rest there, and find for herself a place of rest. There the arrow snake shall make her nest and lay eggs and hatch, and gather them under her shadow; there also shall the hawks be gathered, every one with her mate.

ISAIAH 34

When men and women desert the service and worship of their Creator, He will cause them to desert their monuments to themselves. Their palaces and fortresses – the hallmarks of their civilization and power, will be completely abandoned – so desolate that they will become the habitats of creatures that desire the loneliest of environments. Just as the Lord forced men and women to abandon their efforts at the tower of Babel in Genesis 11, so He does again here. Princes and generals, soldiers, sellers, and intellectuals – all forced to abandon their self-lauding pursuits. If we will surrender ourselves to the work of glorifying our Father and serving His children, *everything we do* matters forever and is remembered forever. The thought seems incredible, but how else can we take passages like Mark 9:41 "For whoever gives you a cup of water to drink in My name, because you belong to Christ, assuredly, I say to you, he will by no means lose his reward." And Mark 14:9 - "Assuredly, I say to you, wherever this gospel is preached in the whole world, what this woman has done will also be told as a memorial to her." In striking contrast, those who abandon their devotion to God for any other pursuit, will find that their monuments crumble, their palaces and fortresses are abandoned, and there is no remembrance of them in eternity. Proverbs 3:35 says, "The wise shall inherit glory, but shame shall be the legacy of fools." And such is the case here, as those who rebelled against God see their life's work come to nothing, replaced with shame as their only lasting legacy.

34:16-17
"Search from the book of the LORD, and read: not one of these shall fail; not one shall lack her mate. For My mouth has commanded it, and His Spirit has gathered them. He has cast the lot for them, and His hand has divided it among them with a measuring line. They shall possess it forever; from generation to generation they shall dwell in it."

The preceding verses showed how the great efforts of ungodly men were relegated to becoming nothing more than a home to brute beasts. All they had worked for in life was given over to others, and they had nothing left to show as a reward for their godless pursuits. In contrast, the godly shall never lose their reward, they will not lack a mate, their possessions will last forever, and they will be rewarded with an eternal home and dwell in it "from generation to generation." With this promise of eternal reward for the godly before us here, contrasted with the empty, hopeless outcome facing unbelievers given in verses 13-15, let us heed the warning of II John 1:8 – "Watch yourselves, so that you may not lose what we have worked for, but may win a full reward" (ESV).

Isaiah 35

35:1-2
The wilderness and the wasteland shall be glad for them, and the desert shall rejoice and blossom as the rose; it shall blossom abundantly and rejoice, even with joy and singing. The glory of Lebanon shall be given to it, the excellence of Carmel and Sharon. They shall see the glory of the Lord, the excellency of our God.

 The Assyrian invasion would devastate much of the country, leaving it a "wilderness" and a "wasteland." But God will deliver His people and cause that wasteland to "rejoice and blossom as the rose." Certainly, this prophecy looks far beyond the enemy invasion in Isaiah's day, however, and pictures for us the joyous transformation that takes place when men and women who were in the spiritual desert of ignorance, sin, and unbelief come to encounter the living God. "They shall see the glory of the Lord." They will experience "the excellency of our God." And their once desert-like soul "shall blossom abundantly and rejoice, even with joy and singing." In John 11:40, Jesus reaffirms for Martha what Isaiah promises here: "You will see God's glory if you believe" (NLT). How can we rightly respond to the enormity of this privilege of being able to experience "the glory of God?" What can we do other than praise Him for His greatness? Let us rise early each morning determined to praise Him for His greatness. Let us eagerly anticipate each Lord's Day that we might go into His house and praise Him for His "excellency." Let us "praise Him according to His excellent greatness!" (Psalms 150:2).

35:3-4
Strengthen the weak hands, and make firm the feeble knees. Say to those who are fearful-hearted, "Be strong, do not fear! Behold, your God will come with vengeance, with the recompense of God; He will come and save you."

Trials and dangers, like those that faced Isaiah's readers, can cripple us with anxiety. We are made "weak" and "feeble," not by the outside forces against us, but because we are "fearful-hearted." Isaiah calls on his anxious readers to "Be strong, do not fear!" In our day, when anxiety is nearly epidemic, even in the church, this word seems especially timely. Isaiah's reasons for dispelling his readers' anxiety are compelling: "Behold your God will come...and save you." When troubles and dangers come, let us steel our nerve and strengthen our resolve, confident that our God will come and save us. In Haggai 2:4, the promise of God's presence was the force behind the call to "be strong" just as it is here: "'Yet now be strong, Zerubbabel,' says the LORD; 'and be strong, Joshua, son of Jehozadak, the high priest; and be strong, all you people of the land,' says the LORD, 'and work; for I am with you,' says the LORD of hosts."

Hebrews 12 quotes verse three and provides us with a second reason to strengthen our resolve and firm up our physical and mental health, reminding us that "no chastening seems to be joyful for the present, but painful; nevertheless, afterward it yields the peaceable fruit of righteousness to those who have been trained by it. Therefore strengthen the hands which hang down, and the feeble knees" (Hebrews 12:11-12). Knowing that our present trial can instill in us "the peaceable fruit of righteousness" can also protect us from the anxieties and fears that weaken hands and make feeble knees. Godly men and women are by no means immune to the hardships and dangers of life. But we can be protected from the anxieties and fears that those dangers tend to stir. When danger comes, let us "be strong" and obey the command: "do not fear!" "God will come... and save you." His presence and promise of deliverance can embolden the "fearful-hearted." And the hope of being endowed with the "peaceable fruit of righteousness" can grant quiet assurance when enemies and dangers make the possibility of other pleasant outcomes less sure.

35:5-7
Then the eyes of the blind shall be opened. And the ears of the deaf shall be unstopped. Then the lame shall leap like a deer, and the tongue of the dumb sing. For waters shall burst forth in the wilderness, and streams in the desert. The parched ground shall become a pool, and the thirsty land springs of water; in the habitation of jackals, where each lay, there shall be grass with reeds and rushes.

When the Lord moves to deliver His people, His saving work is far-reaching. His rescue is rooted in His deep love for His creation, so it is not surprising that as He moves to rescue us from one trouble, His love moves Him to deliver us from other troubles as well. In James 5:15 we find, "And the prayer of faith will save the sick, and the Lord will raise him up. And if he has committed sins, he will be forgiven." When God moves to answer prayer and save from sickness – He will save from sin at the same time. Here, we see that when the Lord moves to save Israel from Assyria, He will save the people from their sicknesses at the same time. The nation's blind and deaf, their lame and mute will all be healed by the Lord's healing power just as He delivers them with His military power. Clearly, the verse also looks forward to the ministry of Jesus, who likewise healed His followers as the Great Physician, even while He overcame their sins as their Great High Priest. "Christ Jesus came into the world to save sinners" (I Timothy 1:15), but while He saved His people from their sins, He also opened the eyes of the blind (Mark 10:52); He healed the deaf and dumb (Mark 7:35); and He caused the lame to walk (John 5:9). Furthermore, as the Lord saved the nation from their enemies, He also healed the land's environmental difficulties too! Pools of water sprang up in desert places, grass and plant-life suddenly grew where the land had been barren, and the "thirsty land," became well-watered, a promise that carried both figurative and literal connotations, for when the Lord saves, He saves completely.

35:8-10
A highway shall be there, and a road, and it shall be called the Highway of Holiness. The unclean shall not pass over it, but it shall be for others. Whoever walks the road, although a fool, shall not go astray. No lion shall be there, nor shall any ravenous beast go up on it; it shall not be found there. But the redeemed shall walk there, and the ransomed of the LORD shall return, and come to Zion with singing, with everlasting joy on their

ISAIAH 35

heads. They shall obtain joy and gladness, and sorrow and sighing shall flee away.

After Assyria takes many from Israel captive, Babylon will invade and take many from Judah into captivity as well. But the Lord will call His people home. He will create a highway that will allow His people to escape bondage and find freedom. He will make a way for men and women to escape the penalty for their sin and find redemption. The way back to right standing with God is a "Highway of Holiness." God grants us means to return to Him, to enter His presence. But we cannot return to Him and drag our sin along with us. He will cleanse us of sin, and then we will delight in rejecting further sin. The way to God's blessings, the path to right standing with God is a holy way. It is inaugurated in God's cleansing forgiveness and continued with our constant fervor to remain pure.

God's way is clearly marked. His Spirit grants us road signs and His word is a road map clearly showing us the way to His blessings. With His clear guidance, even children can find the way, even fools will not go astray. To miss God's perfect plan, a man would have to intentionally exit the "Highway of Holiness" – he would have to "stumble off the ancient highways of good," and "walk the muddy paths of sin" (Jeremiah 18:15 NLT).

God's "Highway of Holiness" is a safe path. "No lion shall be there, nor shall any ravenous beast go up on it." Psalms 18:32 says, "God arms me with strength; he has made my way safe" (NLT). And Proverbs 3:23 promises that if we will trust in the Lord: "Then you will walk safely in your way, and your foot will not stumble."

And finally, God's "Highway of Holiness" is a path filled with joy. Those who come to the Lord on this path "come to Zion with singing." Those who walk in God's way will travel "with everlasting joy on their heads." Psalms 98:4 invites us to "Shout joyfully to the LORD, all the earth; break forth in song, rejoice, and sing praises." God does not require us to walk this highway alone, His presence is always with us, and in His presence is fulness of joy. The old King James version beautifully translates Psalms 16:11 this way: "Thou wilt shew me the path of life: in thy presence is fulness of joy; at thy right hand there are pleasures for evermore." As we walk with Him in the way, we can close our eyes in peace, we can lift our voice in praise, rejoicing that He has made us "exceedingly glad with Your presence" (Psalms 21:6). Some mistakenly believe that the way of sin is filled with more fun than God's path of holiness. We would strenuously disagree. God has "put gladness in my heart" (Psalms 4:7) and it is "joy unspeakable and full of glory" (I Peter 1:8 KJV).

Isaiah 36

36:1
Now it came to pass in the fourteenth year of King Hezekiah that Sennacherib king of Assyria came up against all the fortified cities of Judah and took them.

    Inserted now among Isaiah's many prophetical writings, we are granted a few chapters of narration that allow us a bird's eye view of the events in and around Assyria's invasion that Isaiah's prophecies speak so much about. King Hezekiah was a good king, one of Judah's best, in fact. But during his righteous reign, an evil army swarms on his nation and, except for Jerusalem, destroys every inch of it. Let us be neither shocked nor disheartened when we lose. Our Lord appears to be consistently willing to allow us to lose some battles as we fight to win His war against sin and unbelief. Job lost his children, his money, and his health, before he finally gained victory in the end. John lost his brother (Acts 12:2). Paul lost his freedom (Acts 16:23, Acts 21:33). The reasons behind our failures and defeats are many and varied. David lost his son because of his sin (II Samuel 12:15). But Israel lost their battle against Benjamin because they were obedient to God (Judges 20). Saul lost his kingdom because of his lack of devotion to God (I Samuel 15:28), and Job lost his family as proof of his devotion. Here, the nation of Judah loses every one of their fortified cities to the hands of their Assyrian invaders. Men died, families lost, cities were destroyed. Only Jerusalem remained – and through that lone standing city, God would win a great victory over His enemies and display His power and presence for all to see. God will win a great victory for His people at the end of chapter 37, but before that victory came, there were many horrible defeats here at the start of chapter 36. We must reject the notion that as children of God we are guaranteed to pass every test, win every fight, be immune from every disease, and that everyone in the world will like us. These things are not guaranteed. In fact, losing is one of our Lord's primary prescriptions to victory. Jesus teaches us in Matthew 16:25 – "...whoever loses his life for My sake will find it." God's people lost much before they gained their great victory in the end. Let us arm ourselves with this instruction from history so that we may face hardship and loss with godly resolve.

36:2-4
Then the king of Assyria sent the Rabshakeh with a great army from Lachish to King Hezekiah at Jerusalem. And he stood by the aqueduct from the upper pool, on the highway to the Fuller's Field. And Eliakim the son of Hilkiah, who was over the household, Shebna the scribe, and Joah the son of Asaph, the recorder, came out to him. Then the Rabshakeh said to them, "Say now to Hezekiah, 'Thus says the great king, the king of Assyria: "What confidence is this in which you trust?"'"

Hezekiah fights against an enemy far greater than he is, and with scorn and feigned disbelief, Rabshakeh curls his lip in scorn and asks, "What confidence is this in which you trust?" Yes, what is this confidence that is ours that makes us trust in our God so completely? Our confidence is founded in faith, that is true, but it is not blind faith nor unfounded confidence that inspires our trust in God. We are confident in our Lord's power because we see His unfathomable power manifested in His ability to create and maintain the universe. We are confident in His love for us because we read of His Son's willingness to suffer and die in order to win us to Himself. We are confident that He will come to rescue us today because of the massive volume of evidence supporting our trust in Him. Dozens of Bible stories and thousands of modern-day testimonies are more than adequate substantiation that we have good cause to place unwavering confidence in His provision.

Proverbs 14:26 says, "In the fear of the LORD there is strong confidence, and His children will have a place of refuge." God made the world. His power is limitless. Jesus died on the cross in a display of unparalleled love. And the testimonies of saints from Adam's day to ours assure us that "God shall bless us, and all the ends of the earth shall fear Him" (Psalms 67:7). "Therefore do not cast away your confidence, which has great reward" (Hebrews 10:35). Hezekiah's confidence in God's provision will grant him a front row seat allowing him to see God's miraculous rescue plan up close and personal. What confidence is this in which we entrust our life and our eternity? Our confidence is in the Lord our God, maker of heaven and earth (Psalms 146:5-6) and our confident hope "does not disappoint" (Romans 5:5).

36:5-7
I say you speak of having plans and power for war; but they are mere words. Now in whom do you trust, that you rebel against me? Look! You are trusting in the staff of this broken reed, Egypt, on which if a man leans, it will go into his hand and pierce it. So is Pharaoh king of Egypt to all who trust in him. But if you say to me, "We trust in the LORD our God," is it not He whose high places and whose altars Hezekiah has taken away, and said to Judah and Jerusalem, "You shall worship before this altar?"

Those who mock God's people tend to do so with a mixture of lies and misapplied truths just as Rabshakeh does with Hezekiah here and again in verse 10. The Rabshakeh insults Hezekiah's alliance with Egypt. Hezekiah needed to feel no intimidation or embarrassment from Rabshakeh's words, however – God had already instructed him not to depend on Egypt (Isaiah 31:1). Then Rabshakeh reveals his ignorance by ridiculing Hezekiah's dependence on God. Someone must have told him that Hezekiah had removed the "high places" and idol altars from the land. Apparently, Rabshakeh thought that this meant that Hezekiah had abandoned his religion, and so he mocks Hezekiah for depending on the God that he had reportedly so recently abandoned. But the Rabshakeh's assumptions were incorrect. Hezekiah had taken away those high places and altars as an act of devotion to God, not as a rejection of Him. When our detractors come to belittle us or intimidate us, let us be mindful of this ploy of the evil one. Sometimes there is the hint of logic to their criticism, a trace of truth to their arguments. But let us be moved by neither the weight of their words nor the threat of their violence. When faced with similar intimidators, Nehemiah says in Nehemiah 4:14 --"Do not be afraid of them. Remember the Lord, great and awesome and fight"!

36:8-10
Now therefore, I urge you, give a pledge to my master the king of Assyria, and I will give you two thousand horses – if you are able on your part to put riders on them! How then will you repel one captain of the least of my master's servants, and put your trust in Egypt for chariots and horsemen? Have I now come up without the LORD against this land to destroy it? The LORD said to me, "Go up against this land, and destroy it."

Rabshakeh continues his ridicule and threats toward Hezekiah just as he did in the previous three verses. First, he promises gifts to God's people if they will surrender. Evil people like to offer gifts. Satan offers Eve God-like powers of discernment if she will give in to him in Genesis 3:5. The temptress offers gifts to her would-be lovers in Proverbs 9:17 saying, "Stolen water is sweet, and bread eaten in secret is pleasant." Tempters and scoffers are likely to offer us something they think we will enjoy if we will join their side. But those who enjoy the gifts of sin and rebellion doom themselves to the "depths of hell" (Proverbs 9:18).

Then Rabshakeh points out the hopelessness of Hezekiah's situation. He points out the fact that Judah and Egypt combined could not "repel one captain of the least of my master's servants." This was the truth – but once again, it was misapplied truth – for it was not Judah and Egypt that Rabshakeh was fighting – it was God – who needed neither Egypt nor Judah to help Him.

Then, Rabshakeh spits out a savage, dangerous, yet brazen lie and says that God, Himself, was the one who directed him to "Go up against this land, and destroy it." The lie is savage, for if true, Hezekiah and his people truly have no hope. It is dangerously believable, however, because God has, indeed, allowed Assyria to destroy all of Israel and almost all of Judah. But it is a lie. In Isaiah 37:28 God says that Rabshakeh has not come at God's request to perform God's will, he has come to "rage against Me." Lies, threats, half-truths, and promises of gifts – these are the common weapons that Satan and his servants employ against God's people. These schemes of Satan can be effective, but we can overcome these tactics by knowing the truth. If we study and memorize and fix our minds on what God says, we will not be confused or disheartened when people try to browbeat us with bunk and nonsense. We must know God's truths in advance so that we are prepared to recognize Satan's lies in the future. Psalms 43:3 says,

"Oh, send out Your light and Your truth! Let them lead me; let them bring me to Your holy hill and to Your tabernacle." If we will follow God's "light" and His "truth," His truths will protect us from "deceitful and unjust man" (Psalms 43:1). We can expect unbelievers and sinners to attack us with lies, just as Satan attacked Eve in Eden and Rabshakeh attacked Hezekiah outside Jerusalem at the aqueduct from the upper pool. But our Lord offers us wonderful protection from the lies and half-truths of those who seek to subvert our faith: "He shall cover you with His feathers, and under His wings you shall take refuge; His truth shall be your shield and buckler" (Psalms 91:4).

36:11-12
Then Eliakim, Shebna, and Joah said to the Rabshakeh, "Please speak to your servants in Aramaic, for we understand it; and do not speak to us in Hebrew in the hearing of the people who are on the wall." But the Rabshakeh said, "Has my master sent me to your master and to you to speak these words, and not to the men who sit on the wall, who will eat and drink their own waste with you?"

Rabshakeh wants a public hearing. He demands to be heard. He has thrown his full devotion behind his god, his king, and his army and when the events play out, he wants everyone to know that he stands squarely, loudly in derision of God and all who believe in Him. Rabshakeh meets here with Hezekiah and these 3 leaders, not to make some sort of gentlemen's agreement, but to boast of his power, to ridicule God's people, and to scoff at God's ability to save. It will not go well for him. Job once lobbied to have his opinions known – "Oh that I had one to hear me!" (Job 31:35). But when God drew near and revealed His wisdom and might, Job regretted his words and said, "I abhor myself, and repent in dust and ashes" (Job 42:6). If this was the feeling of righteous Job after his public hearing, what hope does Rabshakeh have? The men on the wall will hear him, and they will tell others of his words. Everyone will know that he defies God and scorns His people. And then he will die along with 185,000 of his trusted troops. It is best for us to guard our words, and to guard who hears us even more. "Even a fool who keeps silent is considered wise; when he closes his lips, he is deemed intelligent" (Proverbs 17:28). If we are speaking the words of God, let us declare them boldly to everyone at every possible opportunity. But if we are merely expressing our own opinions, Ecclesiastes 5:2 gives us good advice: "Do not be rash with your mouth, and let not your heart utter anything hastily before God. For God is in heaven, and you on earth; therefore let your words be few."

ISAIAH 36

36:13-17
Then the Rabshakeh stood and called out with a loud voice in Hebrew, and said, "Hear the words of the great king, the king of Assyria! Thus says the king: 'Do not let Hezekiah deceive you, for he will not be able to deliver you; nor let Hezekiah make you trust in the LORD, saying, "The LORD will surely deliver us; this city will not be given into the hand of the king of Assyria."' "Do not listen to Hezekiah; for thus says the king of Assyria: 'Make peace with me by a present and come out to me; and every one of you eat from his own vine and every one from his own fig tree, and every one of you drink the waters of his own cistern; until I come and take you away to a land like your own land, a land of grain and new wine, a land of bread and vineyards.'"

Rabshakeh's speech is fascinating. He shamelessly and proudly attempts to make exile and slavery appear desirable. His reasoning for calling people to reject God and turn away from Hezekiah's holy example is that neither God nor Hezekiah can make them as happy as they will be enjoying the "grain and new wine" in Assyrian captivity. Who in their right mind would listen to such drivel? And yet the temptation to seek easy living that is self-pleasing rather than holy living that is God-pleasing continues to entice men and women in our day just as it did in Isaiah's day. Andrew Davis' "Christ-Centered Exposition" on Isaiah says, "For Christians, it is helpful to read Isaiah 36-37 with a similar eye to analogies, to see in the walled city of Jerusalem a type of our souls and to see in the Rabshakeh ("royal spokesman") a type of the devil, who uses an array of words to intimidate, allure, insult, and persuade the inhabitants of the town to open up and thereby be enslaved and killed by him." Here we see a good example of that, as Rabshakeh's words tempting his hearers to enjoy the pleasures of slavery appear ridiculous to those who prize their freedom over "bread and vineyards," just as modern day temptations to sin appear ridiculous to those who prize their purity over the pleasures promised by sin. And when we hear Jesus say, "Whoever commits sin is a slave of sin" (John 8:34), the allegory is clearer still. Let us not prize safety over obedience. Let us never prefer pleasure to purity. This was Rabshakeh's offer. May the choice be obvious to our spirit when similar temptations are presented to us today.

36:18-20
"Beware lest Hezekiah persuade you, saying, 'The LORD will deliver us.' Has any one of the gods of the nations delivered its land from the hand of the king of Assyria? Where are the gods of Hamath and Arpad? Where

are the gods of Sepharvaim? Indeed, have they delivered Samaria from my hand? Who among all the gods of these lands have delivered their countries from my hand, that the LORD should deliver Jerusalem from my hand?"

Those who lump all religions and all gods together are terribly mistaken and are destined to face crushing shame on their day of reckoning. Rabshakeh sees no difference between His Creator and the wooden idols of tiny Hamath. To him, the gods that the people of Arpad wore around their neck held the same rank as the Lord God who holds the universe in its place. It is deeply, hotly offensive to God to claim that devotion to other religions is comparable to obeying His laws and that other gods are comparable to His all-surpassing perfections. God is invisible, but it is His intention to reveal Himself to all humanity so that "you may know that there is none like Me in all the earth" (Exodus 9:14). It is His expectation that the people of the world will understand that "among the gods there is none like you, O Lord; nor are there any works like Your works" (Psalms 86:8). Soon, Isaiah will make it very plain that God demands for all people to understand that there is no other God. Isaiah 44:6 says, "I am the First and I am the Last; besides Me there is no God." He says again in Isaiah 45:5 – "I am the LORD, and there is no other; there is no God besides Me." God repeats the message in Isaiah 45:22,"Look to Me, and be saved, all you ends of the earth! For I am God, and there is no other." And 46:9 says it again, "I am God, and there is no other; I am God, and there is none like Me." Here, in blasphemous contradiction, Rabshakeh compares God to the idols and religions of pagan peoples. The comparison is blasphemous; it is profane; it is offensive to God. Rabshakeh's lie was that no god could save -- Hezekiah's God could save no better than any other god. His lie was no less offensive, no less profane, no less blasphemous, however, than the lie reported by people today that every god can save just like our God can. The lie that tells Buddhists and Hindus and kind-hearted unbelievers that their god is just as capable of saving their soul as the Lord God of heaven is repulsive to our Creator. God saves. God alone saves. Denying that God can save His children is blasphemous unbelief. And claiming that any other god can save us from death and hell is blasphemous misbelief. There is no one else under heaven known among men by whom we can be saved (Acts 4:12). Psalms 113:5 asks, "Who is like the LORD our God, Who dwells on high?" We must answer: "There is none like you" (II Samuel 7:22), or our sin is the same as that committed by the Rabshakeh in our verses before us.

ISAIAH 36

36:21-22
But they held their peace and answered him not a word; for the king's commandment was, "Do not answer him." Then Eliakim the son of Hilkiah, who was over the household, Shebna the scribe, and Joah the son of Asaph, the recorder, came to Hezekiah with their clothes torn, and told him the words of the Rabshakeh.

As Jesus stood silent before His accusers in Matthew 27:12-14, so the king's men stand silent before the insolence of Rabshakeh here. Often, words are not helpful and should be avoided. Proverbs 26:4 gives us the instruction: "Do not answer a fool according to his folly, lest you also be like him." Rabshakeh's loudmouthed blustering will earn him God's hot displeasure – so it was wise of Hezekiah and his servants to refuse to respond in kind. Psalms 62:1 says, "Truly my soul silently waits for God; from Him comes my salvation." As children of God, we need to feel no pressure to prove with words that our God will save us. Hezekiah exemplifies this verse nicely – confident that God would save him, indifferent to the rants and ravings of his attackers.

There are times, perhaps, when the best course of action is less clear. Proverbs 26:4 says, "Do not answer a fool according to his folly, lest you also be like him." But Proverbs 26:5 says, "Answer a fool according to his folly, lest he be wise in his own eyes." When do we answer fools and when do we give the Rabshakehs in our life the silent treatment? Let us seek discernment so that we will know when we should speak and when we should keep quiet (Ecclesiastes 3:7). Let us seek discernment so that if we speak, we will know how to speak, and not answer a fool "according to his folly." But above all, our verses here remind us that "The Lord will fight for you, and you have only to be silent" (Exodus 14:14 ESV). We have not been given the ministry of arguing with our enemies. Our work is to quietly wait for our Lord's salvation (Psalms 62:1), and then give testimony to the great things He has done after we have witnessed His works of rescue (Mark 5:19).

Isaiah 37

37:1-2
And so it was, when King Hezekiah heard it, that he tore his clothes, covered himself with sackcloth, and went into the house of the LORD. Then he sent Eliakim, who was over the household, Shebna the scribe, and the elders of the priests, covered with sackcloth, to Isaiah the prophet, the son of Amoz.

Where do we go when we're in trouble? Who do we turn to for counsel when hope is all but lost? If we will be like King Hezekiah, we will go to church. We will seek counsel from the godliest people we know. We will not seek the strongest people, the smartest people, nor the most influential people for our rescue and counsel. We will come again to God's house and sense again the peace of kneeling before His presence. When we are truly in trouble, we will know that only God can help us, so we will seek His face and seek the counsel of those who know Him best. That is what Hezekiah does here. He is at war. But he does not confer with generals, he does not hide out in his strongest fortress. He goes to God's house and seeks a word from Isaiah, the man of God. Let us follow this wonderful example. Some people stop going to church the moment trials or amusements provide the slightest distraction. But for those of us who have known the joy of kneeling in the presence of our loving Lord, we would not miss worship in the house of our God no matter what obstacles stand in our way. Hezekiah is soon to encounter one of the most powerful, miraculous Divine rescues of all time – and if we would have similar encounters, let us imitate his means of setting himself up to receive God's miraculous intervention. In the face of absolute desperation, Hezekiah went to the house of the Lord to worship and he sought the counsel of God's prophet. And by these two simple, God-pleasing efforts he gained both the Lord's approval and His rescue. When in need, may God grant us this holy craving for the fellowship of the saints and a longing for the presence of our Lord. Let us join Hezekiah and "Seek the LORD and His strength; seek His face evermore!" (I Chronicles 16:11).

37:3-4
And they said to him, "Thus says Hezekiah: 'This day is a day of trouble and rebuke and blasphemy; for the children have come to birth, but there is no strength to bring them forth. It may be that the LORD your God will hear the words of the Rabshakeh, whom his master the king of Assyria has sent to reproach the living God, and will rebuke the words which the LORD your God has heard. Therefore lift up your prayer for the remnant that is left.'"

Hezekiah has initiated a nation-wide revival. His heart is fixed on God. His desire is to obey God and to see Him glorified in his personal life, in the life of his nation, and in the nations surrounding. But now, just as he was in the midst of carrying out God's purposes and turning the hearts of his people to godly devotion, he is attacked by Assyria, and the nation's revival, yes, the nation's survival is in jeopardy. It is as if he was on the verge of seeing a national rebirth, of seeing the birth of unparalleled national revival, but just as these spiritual victories were taking place, Assyria comes with its army and destroys the strength of Hezekiah's people. They were on the verge of the birth of revival, but there is now no strength left in the nation to deliver on their desires to bring glory to their Maker. Hezekiah cannot stand the thought of this seemingly imminent miscarriage of justice. Like a woman in labor, Hezekiah cries out over the pangs of his labor to see God glorified, God's people rescued, God's name praised, and godly revival sweep across his land. He cries out his prayer to God and pleads with Isaiah to pray with him: "Lift up your prayer for the remnant that is left!" Rabshakeh has come to "reproach the living God." Hezekiah's prayer rings out to heaven -- Lord, please don't let him win! Save your people! Bring revival! Show your power on your enemies! Please, Lord! Have mercy on your people! Hezekiah longs to glorify God and deliver his people, but he has no strength to bring these things to pass. So, he prays. Like a woman who has no strength to push her baby from the womb, Hezekiah has no strength to deliver his people. But Matthew Henry says, "Prayer is the midwife of mercy." God's mercy will deliver what Hezekiah's weakness could not. Such is the power of prayer. Let us join Isaiah and answer Hezekiah's call to "lift up your prayer for the remnant that is left." People need us to pray for them. So many are dependent on the midwife of prayer to deliver them from the pains that have left them completely without strength. We are reminded here, however, that even when there is no strength left in our body, there is still great power remaining in our prayer. Let us pray. Let us pray for God's people. Let us pray that God's name will be revered and that the voice of those who "reproach the living God" will be silenced. Let us pray that days of "trouble and rebuke and blasphemy" will be replaced with days of triumph and blessing and reverence.

37:5-7

So the servants of King Hezekiah came to Isaiah. And Isaiah said to them, "Thus you shall say to your master, 'thus says the LORD: "Do not be afraid of the words which you have heard, with which the servants of the king of Assyria have blasphemed Me. Surely I will send a spirit upon him, and he shall hear a rumor and return to his own land; and I will cause him to fall by the sword in his own land."

Problems that are impossible for us to overcome, God can fix with ease. Here we see Hezekiah faced with an enemy he cannot hope to overcome – and then God steps in and announces His plan to overwhelm the Assyrian war machine. As easily as a mom checks off her list as she effortlessly places items in her grocery cart, so God tells Hezekiah His "grocery list" plans for the king of Assyria. God will 1) "send a spirit upon him." 2) He will cause Sennacherib to "hear a rumor and return to his own land." And 3) He will "cause him to fall by the sword in his own land." In Hezekiah's eyes, Sennacherib is unconquerable. But Proverbs 21:1 says, "The king's heart is in the hand of the LORD, like the rivers of water; He turns it wherever He wishes." And here, God "turns" away Sennacherib's plans to destroy Jerusalem. God sends "a spirit" on the king that prevents him from beginning the assault on the city. He sends a rumor that sends the king away on a fool's errand. And then the Lord executes the king by the hand of the king's own sons (verse 38). What Hezekiah could never have done, God carries out with ease. God tells Hezekiah not to be afraid, for His rescue is near, and this uplifting command to Hezekiah is extended to us as well: Proverbs 3:25-26 says, "Do not be afraid of sudden terror, nor of trouble from the wicked when it comes; for the LORD will be your confidence, and will keep your foot from being caught." In our day, if we are called upon to face dangers of any kind, may the Lord's rescue of Hezekiah provide us with the quiet assurance that He can do the same for us. Let us "Be strong and of good courage, do not fear nor be afraid of them; for the LORD your God, He is the One who goes with you. He will not leave you nor forsake you" (Deuteronomy 31:6).

37:8-13
Then the Rabshakeh returned, and found the king of Assyria warring against Libnah, for he heard that he had departed from Lachish. And the king heard concerning Tirhakah king of Ethiopia, "He has come out to make war with you." So when he heard it, he sent messengers to Hezekiah, saying, "thus you shall speak to Hezekiah king of Judah, saying: 'Do not let your God in whom you trust deceive you, saying, "Jerusalem shall not be given into the hand of the king of Assyria." 'Look! You have heard what the kings of Assyria have done to all lands by utterly destroying them; and shall you be delivered? Have the gods of the nations delivered those whom my fathers have destroyed, Gozan and Haran and Rezeph, and the people of Eden who were in Telassar? Where is the king of Hamath, the king of Arpad, and the king of the city of Sepharvaim, Hena, and Ivah?'"

The last days of Sennacherib are now at hand. He is moved to abandon his assault on Jerusalem and respond to a rumor – just as God foretold in verse 7. As God so often does, His judgment on Sennacherib does not fall in one swift stroke. God gives time, He gives such merciful, remarkable, repeated opportunities to repent. II Peter 3:15 says, "Remember, the Lord is waiting so that people have time to be saved" (NLT). It seems that Sennacherib is aware of the prophecy that says that he will leave Jerusalem to respond to a rumor, but rather than being convicted and repentant when he sees the prophecy unfold, he defies the prophecy, scorns God's authority, and adds to the blasphemy of his spokesman, Rabshakeh. As he turns away from Jerusalem (for a moment) he shouts back his final blasphemous contempt for God. Repeating Rabshakeh's sin, Sennacherib claims that God is no different than the wooden gods that his predecessors destroyed. He declares that God is no different than the idols that the people of Gozan wore around their neck or the clay statues that the people of Rezeph bowed down to. His army had destroyed many kings and many gods, and Hezekiah and his God would be no different. Sennacherib is fatally mistaken. What no king could do, what no army could do, Sennacherib accomplishes with tragic ease – he brings his reign to an end. His blasphemy incites God to anger, and before the chapter ends, Sennacherib's army will be destroyed and he will be murdered by his own sons – all because his words right here offended the One who "removes kings and raises up kings" (Daniel 2:21).

37:14-20
And Hezekiah received the letter from the hand of the messengers, and read it; and Hezekiah went up to the house of the LORD, and spread it before the LORD. Then Hezekiah prayed to the LORD, saying: "O LORD of hosts, God of Israel, the One who dwells between the cherubim, You are God, You alone, of all the kingdoms of the earth. You have made heaven and earth. Incline Your ear, O LORD, and hear; open Your eyes, O LORD, and see; and hear all the words of Sennacherib, which he has sent to reproach the living God. Truly, LORD, the kings of Assyria have laid waste all the nations and their lands, and have cast their gods into the fire; for they were not gods, but the work of men's hands – wood and stone. Therefore they destroyed them. Now therefore, O LORD our God, save us from his hand, that all the kingdoms of the earth may know that You are the LORD, You alone."

Sennacherib repeats the blasphemous sins of Rabshakeh in 36:18-20, and here Hezekiah repeats his godly response from 37:1. Hezekiah exemplifies for us once again that when crisis comes, we are to take the matter directly, immediately to God. "Spread it before the LORD." Kneel before the Lord and present Him with the details of our problem – not because He doesn't know them already, but to show that we are well aware of the matters before us that are offensive to God and beyond our ability to control. Hezekiah's godly response calls us to focus on these two matters. Too often we are over-agitated by things that bring us grief, but sadly under-concerned with the things that are offensive to God. Hezekiah is distressed because Sennacherib's words "reproach the living God." He is stirred to pray, not just for his own safety, but that the Lord would defend the glory of His name. Carnal men are concerned for their own well-being. Godly men are concerned that all men everywhere revere God's name.

Hezekiah also goes directly, immediately to the Lord because he knows that he cannot save himself. Too often, people think of God as their last resort. Only after every other means of fixing their problems has failed do they think to ask God for help. We are in a good place, however, when we recognize that we are hopeless to handle the crisis before us unless God intervenes. It is true that the kings of Assyria "have laid waste all the nations and their lands." Hezekiah recognizes that unless God intervenes, Judah will fall just as all the other nations in the past.

Hezekiah's godly response to crisis is grounded in two Spirit-given insights. First, Hezekiah shows that his highest priority in life is not self-preservation, but to honor God and see others honor Him as well. He has joined Isaiah in loving God so completely that in the face of Sennacherib's blasphemy, his first priority echoes Isaiah's: "the desire of our soul is for your name" (Isaiah 26:8). Hezekiah's prayer is not just to be rescued, his prayer is: "Now therefore, O LORD our God, save us from his hand, that all the kingdoms of the earth may know that You are the LORD, You alone."

Hezekiah's second Spirit-given insight is that apart from God, he is helpless to do anything that significantly helps people or that honors God in any meaningful way. In John 15:5 Jesus says, "...without Me you can do nothing." Hezekiah appears very cognizant of this truth. He does not trust in his army, his allies, or his own abilities. He throws himself at the feet of his Lord and prays for God to do what only He can do. Save His people. Glorify His name. Let us seek to emulate Hezekiah's wonderful example. May the desire of our soul be for the glory of our Savior's name. And may we be always, acutely aware that our own abilities are powerless to accomplish anything of eternal significance. We cannot save people. We cannot give Him all the glory He deserves.

But we can pray. We can spread our intercession before the Lord and cry out to Him to do what only He can do. And God's good pleasure to hear our prayers from heaven and uphold our cause (II Chronicles 6:35).

37:21-22
Then Isaiah the son of Amoz sent to Hezekiah, saying, "thus says the LORD God of Israel, 'Because you have prayed to Me against Sennacherib king of Assyria, this is the word which the LORD has spoken concerning him: "the virgin, the daughter of Zion, has despised you, laughed you to scorn; the daughter of Jerusalem has shaken her head behind your back!"'

"Because you have prayed to Me..." The weight of the words lies heavy on my chest. Our understanding of the sovereignty of God may sometimes interfere with our ability to grasp the importance of our prayers. Because Hezekiah prayed, his people will be saved and laugh their enemies to scorn. Because Hezekiah prayed, rescue will come from heaven and thousands upon thousands of people will see their families and loved ones delivered from certain death. So much good came about, so many people were so blessed because one man prayed. The alternative outcome that would have come to pass if Hezekiah had not prayed is almost too horrible to imagine. But, then again, we do not have to imagine, we see clearly what would have happened, because years later, in the face of a similar threat, God finds no one praying, and Ezekiel 22:30-31 tells us the terrible result. "'So I sought for a man among them who would make a wall, and stand in the gap before Me on behalf of the land, that I should not destroy it; but I found no one. Therefore I have poured out My indignation on them; I have consumed them with the fire of My wrath; and I have recompensed their deeds on their own heads,' says the Lord GOD." Hezekiah prayed and a nation was saved. When God heard no one praying, that same nation was later destroyed. The practical implications are impossible to miss. We must pray. "The intense prayer of the righteous is very powerful" (James 5:16 HCS). "The earnest prayer of a righteous person has great power and wonderful results" (James 5:16 NLT). God answers the prayers of His people. The absence of prayer is fatal to many. May Samuel's assertion be ours: "far be it from me that I should sin against the LORD in ceasing to pray for you" (I Samuel 12:23).

37:23-25

Whom have you reproached and blasphemed? Against whom have you raised your voice, and lifted up your eyes on high? Against the Holy One of Israel. By your servants you have reproached the Lord, and said, "By the multitude of my chariots I have come up to the height of the mountains, to the limits of Lebanon; I will cut down its tall cedars and its choice cypress tree; I will enter its farthest height, to its fruitful forest. I have dug and drunk water, and with the soles of my feet I have dried up all the brooks of defense."

Sennacherib and Assyria have conquered a vast array of gods and peoples. But here he makes a fatal mistake. He has "reproached and blasphemed" the Holy One of Israel. With his power he claims to possess the God-like ability to cut down forests and dry up rivers. It is interesting that even when men are endowed with remarkable power, we are still prone to exaggerate it. When Herod developed a similar pompous attitude, believing that his power rivalled God's, the Lord dealt him a worm-ridden death. Acts 12:23 says, "Then immediately an angel of the Lord struck him, because he did not give glory to God. And he was eaten by worms and died." Sennacherib's ego and blasphemy are similar to Herod's, and he will suffer a similar fate in just a few verses. Sennacherib claims that by his own power, he will overwhelm God and conquer His people. He might have saved his life if he had held the attitude insisted on by James 4:15, "Instead you ought to say, 'If the Lord wills, we shall live and do this or that.'" When Sennacherib boasted of his conquests over tiny pagan peoples, he was already on shaky ground, because "Pride goes before destruction, and a haughty spirit before a fall" (Proverbs 16:18). But when he boasted that he could conquer God's people and God, Himself, his shaky ground collapsed completely, for pride leads to a fall, but blasphemy leads to a headlong plummet into hell.

37:26-29
Did you not hear long ago how I made it, from ancient times that I formed it? Now I have brought it to pass, that you should be for crushing fortified cities into heaps of ruins. Therefore their inhabitants had little power; they were dismayed and confounded; they were as the grass of the field and the green herb, as the grass on the housetops and grain blighted before it is grown. But I know your dwelling place, your going out and your coming in, and your rage against Me. Because your rage against Me and your tumult have come up to My ears, therefore I will put My hook in your nose and My bridle in your lips, and I will turn you back by the way which you came.

Sennacherib was not condemned for conquering weaker countries. In fact, the Lord says that "I have brought it to pass, that you should be for crushing fortified cities into heaps of ruins." God had decreed "from ancient times" that Assyria would conquer the wicked nations around him. His actions were God-decreed. But his attitude was self-condemning. We are reminded of the importance of giving God glory for all our successes. We must acknowledge that apart from our Lord we can do nothing. The great works of great men may accomplish the great purposes of God, but in the eyes of our Lord, pride renders us unfit for the rewards He has stored up for those who carry out His bidding. His purposes are accomplished, but there is no reward awaiting those who do His will with a heart stained with pride. Such is the lesson before us here. God had decreed long before that Sennacherib would crush evil people. But when Sennacherib credits his own power with his victories, when he "rage(s) against" God rather than thank God for His blessings, he incurs God's wrath, even though he has carried out God's will. Prideful thoughts resonate very loudly in heaven. The HCS version says "your arrogance has reached My ears." Sennacherib's great works are before God's eyes, but his arrogance fills God's ears and so the reward for his feats of glory are negated. Instead of blessing Sennacherib, God says, "I will put My hook in your nose and My bridle in your lips, and I will turn you back by the way which you came." God will lead Sennacherib back home, and while in the act of worshiping his god, his own sons will murder him. Such is the unenviable reward awaiting the arrogant.

37:30-32
This shall be a sign to you: you shall eat this year such as grows of itself, and the second year what springs from the same; also in the third year sow and reap, plant vineyards and eat the fruit of them. And the remnant who have escaped of the house of Judah shall again take root downward, and bear fruit upward. For out of Jerusalem shall go a remnant, and those who escape from Mount Zion. The zeal of the LORD of hosts will do this.

People enjoy surprising their loved ones with good things. It may be surprising, however, to see how rarely God surprises people with blessings. Here, He tells His people 3 years in advance of the blessings that await them. In the third year, God's people will be able to once again plant and reap a God-blessed harvest. God loves to bless His people – and He wants us to know that all good things come from Him (James 1:17). God is so intentional about announcing in advance His intended blessings that the only example I can find of His people being "surprised" by His blessings in the Old Testament is in II Kings 7:5 when 4 lepers are surprised to find that the Syrian invaders have fled. But the only reason they were surprised is that they weren't nearby when Elisha clearly prophesied that this would happen the day before!

Sennacherib's siege has made life very difficult for God's people. But God promises that the future is bright. And a bright future can cast even a multitude of present hardships in a good light. God's people will "take root downward, and bear fruit upward." What a precious picture. God has called us to "bear fruit" (John 15:16), and when we are "rooted and built up in Him" (Colossians 2:7) He will nourish us so that we are able to bear fruit that honors Him. "The righteous shall flourish like a palm tree, he shall grow like a cedar in Lebanon. Those who are planted in the house of the

LORD shall flourish in the courts of our God. They shall still bear fruit in old age; they shall be fresh and flourishing, to declare that the LORD is upright; He is my rock, and there is no unrighteousness in Him" (Psalms 92:12-15).

37:33-35
Therefore thus says the LORD concerning the king of Assyria: "He shall not come into this city, nor shoot an arrow there, nor come before it with shield, nor build a siege mound against it. By the way that he came, by the same shall he return; and he shall not come into this city," says the LORD. For I will defend this city, to save it for My own sake and for My servant David's sake.

If we had to depend on our own self-worth to gain an audience with God and to gain anything from Him, we would be in trouble. Blessedly, the Lord is moved to protect and provide for His people for His name's sake, not because we have earned anything from Him. When we have sinned, we can cry out, "For Your name's sake, O LORD, pardon my iniquity, for it is great" (Psalms 25:11). When we are in danger, or don't know which way to turn, we can pray, "For You are my rock and my fortress; therefore, for Your name's sake, lead me and guide me" (Psalms 31:3). And when stress and fatigue have stolen the life from our service to Him, we can pray: "Revive me, O LORD, for Your name's sake! For Your righteousness' sake bring my soul out of trouble" (Psalms 143:11). God's motivation for protecting Jerusalem was bound up in His decree that His name must be honored among men. He says in Psalms 46:10 – "I will be exalted among the nations, I will be exalted in the earth!" If His people turn away from Him, He will punish them so that His name is not tarnished by their disobedience (Ezekiel 20:9). But if His people obey Him and openly and publicly depend on Him for their deliverance, He defends them with the exact same motivation – for His own name's sake. May our name and our well-being be so caught up in God's name and His purposes, that everything He does for His sake, turns out for our good as well.

Remarkably, God says that His second reason for defending Jerusalem is "for My servant David's sake." Amazing. David lived and died nearly 300 years before Isaiah and Hezekiah faced the Assyrian invasion. 300 years! And yet, God says that the reason He will deliver His people from Assyria is for the sake of His servant David. How long will our legacy last? How long will God continue to bless our children and their children for the sake of our service and devotion to Him? Not only is it reasonable to hope for this, it is proper for us to expect this! Deuteronomy 7:9 says, "Therefore know that the LORD your God, He is God, the faithful God who keeps covenant and mercy for a thousand generations with those who love Him and keep His commandments." What a precious thought. Through the mercies of my precious Savior, my devotion to His commands may bless my descendants for untold generations! Let us be faithful to God! Let us serve Him, honor Him, and obey Him! So much good can rise from one man's devotion to the Creator! David served the Lord in his generation (Acts 13:36), but the reward for his service was passed on to his descendants for generations on end. Let us be rightly inspired by these words to invest heavily in godly service today. The long-term dividends arising from our present godly devotion are incalculable.

37:36-38

Then the angel of the LORD went out, and killed in the camp of the Assyrians one hundred and eighty-five thousand; and when people arose early in the morning there were the corpses – all dead. So Sennacherib king of Assyria departed and went away, returned home, and remained at Nineveh. Now it came to pass, as he was worshiping in the house of Nisroch his god, that his sons Adrammelech and Sharezer struck him down with the sword; and they escaped into the land of Ararat. Then Esarhaddon his son reigned in his place.

In verse 29, God promised His people that He would put a hook in Sennacherib's nose and send him back to Nineveh and end the Assyrian invasion. How many days went by between verse 29 and verse 36? How did the people feel after God's promise in verse 29 and how did they feel after verse 36? True faith would allow their confidence to begin promptly in verse 29, and not have to wait until verse 36. But "when the Son of Man comes, will He really find faith on the earth?" (Luke 18:8). We cry out our desire for Him to find true faith in us, to see that we trust in His provision based on His promises in His word, and to see that we feel secure in His promises, even before we see His provision. When Thomas saw Jesus on the Cross he stopped believing, but when Jesus materialized before him in the house, Thomas believed in full (John 20:28). I suspect it was much the same for many of Hezekiah's people in the days of Isaiah 37. When they saw 185,000 enemy troops camped around them, they may have been tempted to disbelieve God's promise in verse 29. But when they awoke that fateful morning and saw "there were the corpses – all dead," it must have been giddily easy to believe. Trusting God in the presence of Jesus in the flesh and trusting God when your enemies lie dead at your feet is fine.

ISAIAH 37

(Though Jesus' response to Thomas in John 20:29 seems to indicate that our Lord finds this kind of faith unimpressive). May our faith in the promises of God, when our fate seems to hang in the balance, be just as strong as it is when the reward of victory is in our hand. May our faith in God's promises remain just as unflinching when our enemies stand armed before us as when our enemies are dead and gone.

Sennacherib defied the God of Hezekiah – and before Hezekiah's God his army died, and before his own god, he, himself lost his life. It is a fearful thing to fall into the hands of the living God" (Hebrews 10:31), and it is similarly suicidal to "pray to a god that cannot save" (Isaiah 45:20). Sennacherib is guilty of both of these self-endangerments, so we can hardly be surprised with how chapter 37 ends.

Sennacherib dies, and his son "reigned in his place." Such is the case when anyone refuses to honor God with his life. God will take what is his and give it to another. If He gives us talents and we refuse to use them for His glory, He gives them to another (Matthew 25:28). And if He gives us position and authority and we fail to give Him glory, that too He will remove from us and give to another (I Samuel 15:28). Saul's throne He gave to David, Sennacherib's throne was given to Esarhaddon, and the single talent of the unnamed servant in Matthew 25 was given to another all for the same reason – they failed to honor God with that which was given them. Present day application is not difficult to see. God has not given us thrones, but He has entrusted us with much. Let us gladly, tirelessly serve Him with all the talents, strengths, and opportunities He gives!

Isaiah 38

38:1-3
In those days Hezekiah was sick and near death. And Isaiah the prophet, the son of Amoz, went to him and said to him, "Thus says the LORD: 'Set your house in order, for you shall die and not live.'" Then Hezekiah turned his face toward the wall, and prayed to the LORD, and said, "Remember now, O LORD, I pray, how I have walked before You in truth and with a loyal heart, and have done what is good in Your sight." And Hezekiah wept bitterly.

James 5:13 says, "Is anyone among you suffering? Let him pray. Neither being king, nor being godly is protection from becoming sick. But although greatness does not protect us from sickness, neither does poverty nor our lack of prominence prevent us from being able to pray. Hezekiah had good reason to feel at peace as death approached. He had pleased the Lord with His godly devotion, and his eternity was secure in His Savior's hands. But for reasons of his own, Hezekiah "wept bitterly" at the news of his imminent demise. Even though God's people have good cause for uncommon peace in the midst of storms, it is fitting for godly people to weep in the face of devastating news and cry over things that trouble us. Jesus wept over the grief of Lazarus' sisters in John 11, Hannah wept over her humiliation in I Samuel 1, and David wept over the loss of his son in II Samuel 15. Sometimes, godly people cry. Blessedly, we are shown that God is moved to sympathy by the tears of His people. God was moved by the tears of Hagar and her son in Genesis 11, He will be moved by Hezekiah's tears here, and so we have good cause to believe that if we have cause to cry, that our Lord will deal with us tenderly in our distress.

38:4-6
And the word of the LORD came to Isaiah, saying, "Go and tell Hezekiah, 'Thus says the LORD, the God of David your father: "I have heard your prayer, I have seen your tears; surely I will add to your days fifteen years. I will deliver you and this city from the hand of the king of Assyria, and I will defend this city."'

In verse 1 God sent Isaiah the message that Hezekiah should set his affairs in order, "for you shall die and not live." Hezekiah is sick, and the Lord forewarns him that the natural outcome of his illness is that he will die. But here, the Lord promises to override the processes of nature and supernaturally heal Hezekiah, and miraculously protect His people in Jerusalem. We must not miss the reason for God's supernatural intervention: "I have heard your prayer, I have seen your tears." God is moved to sympathy by the tears of His people, and God is moved to act on behalf of His people who pray. In response to Moses' prayer, Exodus 32:14 says, "So the LORD relented from the harm which He said He would do to His people." God rescued Israel on behalf of Moses' prayer. In the New Testament, we again find the Lord moved to save by the prayers of His people. The night before Herod planned to execute Peter, Acts 12:5 says, "but constant prayer was offered to God for him by the church." God is moved by the prayers of His people. As He saved Israel from their punishment in Exodus 32, as He saved Peter from Herod in Acts 12, God now responds to prayer and heals Hezekiah in the verses before us. Let us pray. And let us pray specifically that God would heal the sick and rescue the perishing. In response to Hezekiah's prayer, God says, "I will deliver you and this city." Hezekiah is healed. His city is saved. And if God had not moved, neither of those things would have happened.

So then, seeing God's heart to answer prayer, let us pray! Let us plead with Him to heal the sick and save the lost. We are plainly shown that it is God's good pleasure to answer prayers such as these. May it be that if the sick are not healed they will have to be wrenched from our praying hands before they can pass away; and if the lost are not saved that they will have to walk over our backs as we kneel in impassioned prayer for their souls before they can enter the gates of hell. The Lord is moved by the prayers and tears of His people. Let us cry out our prayers to heaven on behalf of sick and sinful men. For the Lord hears our prayers and sees our tears.

38:7-8
And this is the sign to you from the LORD, that the LORD will do this thing which He has spoken: "Behold, I will bring the shadow on the sundial, which has gone down with the sun on the sundial of Ahaz, ten degrees backward." So the sun returned ten degrees on the dial by which it had gone down.

Once again we see the remarkable, miraculous extents to which the Lord will go so that His promises and provisions will not take us by surprise. Some people enjoy surprises, but it would seem that God is less interested in surprising us with His blessings. In order to inform Hezekiah in advance that God will heal his body and deliver his nation, God moves the sun! It is God's intention to intervene supernaturally, miraculously, and mercifully in Hezekiah's life. He will heal Hezekiah's terminal illness and He will deliver Hezekiah's people – and He insists that Hezekiah is shown beyond a shadow of a doubt that the blessings that come to him are provided by God. God moves the sun for the purpose of telling Hezekiah that the healing and rescue that comes to him does not arise from natural causes, nor from Hezekiah's personal prowess, but arises from the mercy and omnipotence of his Creator. We are, therefore, completely horrified to read in the very next chapter how Hezekiah proudly displays his health and wealth, without giving a single reference to the God who saved him and his nation. Still today, God speaks to us through the scriptures and through His Spirit to tell us His intentions in advance. May His communications have their desired effect in us. Let us trust Him in advance and praise Him and thank Him after His work is through. Let us not be like the 9 lepers who spoke no thanks to Jesus in Luke 17. When God blesses, we are to "give thanks to the LORD! Call upon His name; make known His deeds among the peoples!" (Psalms 105:1). And He tells us in advance of His blessings to come, so that we will not miss His provisions and be better prepared to praise Him publicly when His help arrives. Since God is intent on moving heaven and earth to tell us in advance that He intends to bless us, the least we can do is to be just as determined to praise Him after He blesses us.

38:9-11

This is the writing of Hezekiah king of Judah, when he had been sick and had recovered from his sickness: I said, "In the prime of my life I shall go to the gates of Sheol; I am deprived of the remainder of my years." I said, "I shall not see YAH, the LORD in the land of the living; I shall observe man no more among the inhabitants of the world."

From verse 10 onward to the end of the chapter we have recorded for us Hezekiah's prayer to the Lord at the time that "he had been sick and recovered from his sickness." As we read his prayer, it is helpful to remember that *God heard his prayer and answered it*. We may have cause to find flaws in some of his reasoning, and we can clearly see that after God answered his prayer, Hezekiah went on to do a number of things that dishonored the Lord and did himself much discredit, but even so, God answered Hezekiah's request here. It would stand to reason then, that if we would desire God to answer our prayers that we would do well to study Hezekiah's words here, so that we might benefit from a consideration of this prayer that moved the heart of God to send a powerful answer.

The news that his death is imminent fills Hezekiah with sorrow for two reasons: he will lose the precious gift of seeing "the LORD in the land of the living" and he will miss the opportunity to lead and serve and have fellowship with God's people. Certainly, of all the reasons to fear death, these two must rank as the most virtuous for doing so. In Philippians 1:23 Paul wrote that he looked forward to dying so that he could have a closer walk with the Lord, "having a desire to depart and be with Christ, which is far better." Paul, however, had the benefit of Jesus' words in John 14:2-3, "I go to prepare a place for you. And if I go and prepare a place for you, I will come again and receive you to Myself; that where I am, there you may be also." Paul had assurances that His fellowship with God would be sweeter and even more glorious than his fellowship with the Lord on earth. Hezekiah's imperfect understanding of the afterlife, however, likely did not allow him this strong assurance.

Hezekiah's second death-inspired sorrow was that he would no longer be able to enjoy the fellowship of "the inhabitants of the world." Hezekiah's thoughts here may not differ significantly from Paul's own reason for finding death less preferable to living. In Philippians 1:24, Paul wrote that it was better for him to remain among the living rather than join the ranks of the departed, because "to remain in the flesh is more needful for you."

Today, we can take great comfort in the prospect of our eventual death. We will depart and be in the presence of our Lord (Luke 23:43). We will depart and rest from our works on earth (Hebrews 4:9-10). And we will depart and join the company of untold millions of fellow believers who love God like we do (Revelation 21:24). Even so, as Hezekiah exhibits here, there are powerful reasons to appreciate the opportunity to remain among the living. It is altogether proper to crave the opportunity to worship and serve the Lord on earth; and it is altogether commendable to seek to live on earth, fueled by the Spirit-directed drive to encourage and serve God's people. Hezekiah was on the brink of departing this world and entering the presence of the Lord (which is far better). He begs to be excused from this opportunity however, and far from being angered, God appears pleased to grant his request. When we are called upon to pray for matters regarding a future that seems uncertain, may these great motivations guide our requests that we lift up to the Lord. If we are made to consider a move from a position, from our city, or from this earth, let us seek the option that best allows us what Hezekiah at least hints at here: that we would prefer to go where we might best worship and serve our Lord, and where we might best encourage and serve His people. We are granted good cause here to believe that if these things be our motivation, that our Lord is apt to grant our request.

38:12-14
My life span is gone, taken from me like a shepherd's tent; I have cut off my life like a weaver. He cuts me off from the loom; from day until night You make an end of me. I have considered until morning – like a lion, so He breaks all my bones; from day until night You make an end of me. Like a crane or a swallow, so I chattered; I mourned like a dove; my eyes fail from looking upward. O LORD, I am oppressed; undertake for me!

Hezekiah prays for God to intervene and save his life, and by chapter 39 verse 1, God will do just that. In the previous verses, we saw that Hezekiah's focus on worshiping God and blessing His people were components to his prayer that God found pleasing. Verses 12-14 here show us another healthy insight that Hezekiah exhibits that pleases God and moves Him to answer our requests. Hezekiah prays, "You make an end of me." He says that God "breaks all my bones." And then he repeats his line, "You make an end of me." Hezekiah does not blame his disease for his distress, he does not blame doctors for their inability to heal, and he does not blame circumstances that led to his infection. He looks for no other cause of his crisis, and so he looks for no other rescue from his crisis. His attention is riveted on God. "My eyes fail from looking upward." God is pleased with prayers of this sort. Those who blame people or problems for their sorrow are most likely to have their attentions misplaced when looking for their cure. Hezekiah's mind is fixed on His Lord. He does not seek a non-God cause for his trial and he does not seek a non-God answer to his urgent danger. Micah 7:7 says, "I will look to the LORD; I will wait for the God of my salvation; my God will hear me." Looking to the Lord in trial, and looking to Him only, places us in the best possible place to experience deliverance. Job held Hezekiah's same understanding. In Job 16:11 he says, "God has delivered me to the ungodly, and turned me over to the hands of the wicked." Job looked for no one else to blame for his troubles, and so, like Hezekiah, he looked for no one else to deliver him. And we find that the Lord was pleased to intervene and heal him, just as He does for Hezekiah here. Psalms 62:5 says, "My soul, wait silently for God alone, for my expectation is from Him." In trouble, let us fix our attention on our Creator. Let our "eyes fail from looking upward." When "God alone" is our hope, we will always find that our "hope does not disappoint" (Romans 5:5).

38:15-17
What shall I say? He has both spoken to me, and He Himself has done it. I shall walk carefully all my years in the bitterness of my soul. O LORD, by these things men live; and in all these things is the life of my spirit; so You will restore me and make me live. Indeed it was for my own peace that I had great bitterness; but You have lovingly delivered my soul from the pit of corruption, for You have cast all my sins behind Your back.

Hezekiah's prayer looks back over the bitterness of his soul that he felt as he faced death. His battle with his illness certainly brought him to a very low point spiritually and emotionally, but now he is able to say with remarkable insight, "It was for my own peace that I had great bitterness." The HCS renders his words as, "it was for [my own] welfare that I had such great bitterness." And the NLT says, "Yes, it was good for me to suffer this anguish." <u>Physical suffering can be very helpful to our spiritual well-being.</u>

Suffering helps us turn from sin. I Peter 4:1 says, "...he who has suffered in the flesh has ceased from sin."

Suffering helps us redirect our attentions to the purposes of God. I Peter 4:2 says that those who suffer desire to live "for the will of God."

Those who suffer are allowed to experience the joy of the Creator drawing near to comfort them in their trial. Psalms 94:19 says, "In the multitude of my anxieties within me, Your comforts delight my soul."

And here, we see that the bitterness of his illness brought Hezekiah the blessedness of God's peace. There are few things more spiritually rewarding, few things that bring our heart more peace than the opportunity to look back in time and retrace how God brought us through life-threatening ordeals and overwhelming hardships. Experiencing God's provision in the past provides the potential for limitless peace when facing the future.

Hezekiah's prayer here also grants us the invaluable reminder that our spiritual state is far more significant than our physical health. Hezekiah mourned over his illness. "I mourned like a dove" (verse 14). He cried over his life ending prematurely. "I am deprived of the remainder of my years" (verse 10). But when he recovers, he rejoices, not over his restored physical strength, but that "You have cast all my sins behind Your back." Psalms 32:2 says, "Blessed is the man to whom the LORD does not impute iniquity." It is not that God puts our sin behind His back and then can't remember them, as if He were like some forgetful old man. But our loving Lord "does not impute iniquity," He does not hold our sins against us. God cleanses us of sin and delights our soul with His grace – and the joy of possessing a cleansed soul filled with the joy of the Spirit's presence in us far surpasses all the joys of any creature comfort.

38:18-19
For Sheol cannot thank You, death cannot praise You; those who go down to the pit cannot hope for Your truth. The living, the living man, he shall praise You, as I do this day; the father shall make known Your truth to the children.

Revelation 19:5 reveals for us that the resurrected souls of God's people live to praise the Lord in heaven. Before that revelation in Revelation however, this was less well understood. Psalms 115:17-18 gives both Hezekiah's understanding as well as the hope for Revelation 19:5 – "The dead do not praise the LORD, nor any who go down into silence. But we will bless the LORD from this time forth and forevermore." Although all the resurrected saints will praise the Lord in heaven, it is true that it is the lot of the living to praise the Lord on earth. Hezekiah's joy is that his life has been extended, so now he is able to continue to praise his Lord. Man's highest endeavor is to bring praise to his Maker, "as I do this day," Hezekiah happily announces. Today, let us join Hezekiah's example and praise the Lord. If God will extend to us more time on earth, let us seek to spend the time allotted to us in the great enterprise of praising our Savior. Let us praise Him quietly, while alone with Him in our daily devotions, let us praise Him with our family beside us, and let us praise Him loudly and gladly in the company of His people in His house each Lord's day. May Psalms 104:33 echo our praise: "I will sing to the LORD as long as I live; I will sing praise to my God while I have my being."

If man's great work is to see God praised, His next great effort is to "make known Your truth to the children." Hezekiah will fail here. His son, Manasseh, will rebel against the Lord. Let us not fail. Let us pray for the next generation! We must make God's truths known to our children. Let us teach them God's ways, let us praise the Lord openly so our children can see the proper response to God's goodness. We must praise God and teach our children to praise God. The benefit for doing so can hardly be overstated! Jonadab made a vow to serve the Lord over 200 years before Jeremiah was born. He commanded his children to follow in his footsteps – to serve the Lord and abstain from alcohol (Jeremiah 35:6), and almost 300 years later, we find his descendants still committed to following his example! Generations upon generations committed to God and blessed by God (Jeremiah 35:19) because their father was faithful to God and made known God's truths to his children. Praise the Lord for His goodness; make His truths known to the next generation. This was Hezekiah's desire. May it be ours as well.

38:20-22
"The LORD was ready to save me; therefore we will sing my songs with stringed instruments all the days of our life, in the house of the LORD. Now Isaiah had said, "Let them take a lump of figs, and apply it as a poultice on the boil, and he shall recover." And Hezekiah had said, "What is the sign that I shall go up to the house of the LORD?"

Verse 22 repeats the historical record of this event found in II Kings 20:8. Isaiah informs Hezekiah that God will extend his life another 15 years and that he will be granted the joy of worshiping in the house of the Lord once again. Hezekiah asks for a sign that these wonderful things will take place, and God provides that sign (the sun went backwards 10 degrees) -- desiring that all might know that it is He that sustains life, and it is He that is blessing Hezekiah. King Hezekiah responds to God's kindness with praise, and by calling others to praise the Lord with him. Because God saved him, he calls on everyone around him to "sing my songs with stringed instruments all the days of our life, in the house of the LORD." Experiencing the grace and greatness of God rightly moves us to praise Him, and rightly moves us to move others to praise Him as well. God blesses us, and we praise Him in return. Since it is clearly in our best interest to continue this oldest of relationships, let us do our part and praise our Lord "all the days of our life." Let us teach our children to begin these songs of praise when they are yet very young, and may they see us continue these songs of praise even when we are very old. Let us praise the Lord "all the days of our life." On busy days, hard days, and vacation days, let us praise the Lord. When our days are filled with celebration and victory, and when they are filled with hardship and loss, let us praise the Lord "all the days of our life." Since God's goodness and mercy follow us all the days of our life (Psalms 23:6), let us respond rightly and sing Him our praises all the days of our life just the same.

Isaiah 39

39:1-2
At that time Merodach-Baladan the son of Baladan, king of Babylon, sent letters and a present to Hezekiah, for he heard that he had been sick and had recovered. And Hezekiah was pleased with them, and showed them the house of his treasures – the silver and gold, the spices and precious ointment, and all his armory – all that was found among his treasures. There was nothing in his house or in all his dominion that Hezekiah did not show them.

We might like to give Hezekiah the benefit of the doubt and say that his behavior here was simply his effort to be a gracious host. Sadly, the summary of this event in II Chronicles 32:31 will not allow us this hopeful view of Hezekiah's actions. "When the ambassadors of Babylon's rulers were sent to him to inquire about the miraculous sign that happened in the land, God left him to test him and discover what was in his heart" (HCS). When Babylon's ambassadors arrived to visit Hezekiah, "God left him." What a terrible thought. Hezekiah's actions here fail him. He does not honor God. He boasts of his own accumulations. He has the perfect opportunity to publicly praise God for healing him and for protecting him from his enemies, but his words fail him. But what hope does he have? "God left him." Let us be reminded that if God leaves us, we cannot succeed. We will always fail. We will look to our own well-being and take pride in our own accomplishments and neglect God's purposes and fail to bring Him honor. If God ever hints that He plans to leave us as He did with Moses, let us rush to follow Moses' example and stop in our tracks, kneel before the Lord, and refuse to go any farther unless God goes with us (Exodus 33:15). We must rise early and sit at our Father's feet and know for certain that He is with us. We must not allow ourselves to unwittingly walk out our door not realizing that God has left us. This is exactly what Hezekiah does here, and what Samson did before him. In Judges 16:20, Samson awoke from his sleep and rose to fight his enemies as he had done so often before, but then we read the bone-chilling line: "but he did not know that the Lord had departed from him." If we do not insist on kneeling in the presence of our Lord every morning, if we allow ourselves to walk in our own strength even for a single day, we may not recognize that God is not with us until it is too late – we have already said something, done something or shown something that causes irreparable damage. We may miss the opportunity to honor God and to make Him known – because we walked out our door without Him, and didn't recognize His absence until, like Hezekiah, we are forced to face the repercussions of our terrible mistake. Jesus said, "Without Me you can do nothing." So, let us make very sure we never do anything without Him. We must "Seek the Lord" (Deuteronomy 4:29) every morning, and make certain that He is "with us" before we start our day. Failure to do this one thing will inevitably lead to failures in everything that is most important.

39:3-4

Then Isaiah the prophet went to King Hezekiah, and said to him, "What did these men say, and from where did they come to you?" So Hezekiah said, "They came to me from a far country, from Babylon." And he said, "What have they seen in your house?" So Hezekiah answered, "They have seen all that is in my house; there is nothing among my treasures that I have not shown them."

Hezekiah felt at ease and among friends as he toured the Babylonian ambassadors around his palace. He felt no threat from them because "they came to me from a far country." Once again, we see that knowing God's word can protect us from a host of mistakes. Had Hezekiah remembered

Deuteronomy 28:49-50, he would likely have been better on his guard. "The LORD will bring a nation against you from afar, from the end of the earth, as swift as the eagle flies, a nation whose language you will not understand, a nation of fierce countenance, which does not respect the elderly nor show favor to the young." Perhaps we can't be expected to know in advance when troubles will hit home -- the Babylonian ambassadors may have put on a good show of flattery and respect for Hezekiah. But we can be well-versed in God's word, and His words are able to make us "wise for salvation" (II Timothy 3:15) – they can tell us how to keep our feet on a safe path. God's word would have taught Hezekiah that trusting strangers from distant lands is not safe, a lesson Joshua learned the hard way in Joshua chapter 9. And God's word teaches us that Hezekiah's boasting before Babylon was downright dangerous because we are shown in II Corinthians 12:1 that "It is doubtless not profitable for me to boast." James 4:16 may be even clearer, "But now you boast in your arrogance. All such boasting is evil." Instead of following Hezekiah's dangerous example, let us follow the pattern set out in Galatians 6:14 – "God forbid that I should boast except in the cross of our Lord Jesus Christ, by whom the world has been crucified to me, and I to the world."

39:5-6
Then Isaiah said to Hezekiah, "Hear the word of the LORD of hosts: 'Behold, the days are coming when all that is in your house, and what your fathers have accumulated until this day, shall be carried to Babylon; nothing shall be left,' says the LORD."

Daniel 1 details the sad fulfillment of this prophecy through Isaiah. The accumulated riches of Judah's kings were taken away to feed the pride and treasuries of pagan rulers in Babylon. Isaiah's words certainly caught Hezekiah off guard (as we can surmise from his terrible response in verse 8). He was fresh off a very enjoyable time entertaining foreign dignitaries who paid him a number of rich compliments. He had just finished surveying and boasting over the vast material wealth he had accumulated. And while his head was still in the clouds of conceit, Isaiah sent him a wake-up call. All his worldly riches will be carried away to Babylon. "Nothing shall be left." Let us shudder at this realization that everything that we work for will vanish away and become "vanity of vanities" unless it is safeguarded by our God. What can be salvaged when we forget God and live for our own personal pleasure? Nothing. "Nothing shall be left." If we set our heart on our accumulations and turn our backs on God's purposes, what monument will remain giving testimony to the meaningfulness of our life on earth? Again, nothing. "Nothing shall be left, says the LORD."

God promised that Hezekiah would live another 15 years. There was still time for Isaiah's words to do him much good. Perhaps he will cast off his confidence in his treasures and return his attentions to His Lord. Perhaps he will turn his boasting into humble mourning and pray for his children and their children, rather than add coins to a treasury that will soon enough enrich a pagan king. If we knew in advance that our house will burn in a fire in the coming days, we might have the good sense not to spend our resources adding to its worth. If we knew in advance that U.S. dollars would soon lose all their worth, we would likely have the sense to invest in other currency. And so, may the prophecy given Hezekiah have its good effect on us. Let us not spend ourselves on accumulations that will soon decay leaving nothing left. Proverbs 13:7 says, "There is one who makes himself rich, yet has nothing; and one who makes himself poor, yet has great riches." Hezekiah's riches gained him nothing but a few minutes of foolish pride. His riches and ours will be lost to us, "nothing shall be left." Let us intently seek to become "rich toward God" (Luke 12:21), for all other riches will fade away, "nothing shall be left, says the LORD."

39:7-8
And they shall take away some of your sons who will descend from you, whom you will beget; and they shall be eunuchs in the palace of the king of Babylon. So Hezekiah said to Isaiah, "The word of the LORD which you have spoken is good!" For he said, "At least there will be peace and truth in my days."

Hezekiah's lack of concern for his descendants is appalling. Jacob prayed that God would bless his sons and his son's sons (Genesis 48:9), but Hezekiah here demonstrates a revolting disinterest in the spiritual vitality and prosperity of his family line. It is God's heart to bless those who are His, and to bless the children of those who are His. The promise from Isaiah 59:21 was not just made to one man, but to all God's people! "As for Me," says the LORD, "this is My covenant with them: My Spirit who is upon you, and My words which I have put in your mouth, shall not depart from your mouth, nor from the mouth of your descendants, nor from the mouth of your descendants' descendants," says the LORD, "from this time and forevermore." Hezekiah missed God's heart for our future generations, and though he did much good for Judah during his lifetime, his self-centered lack of concern for the generations to follow contributed to the downward

ISAIAH 39

spiritual spiral that was to come. Manasseh, his son, would completely rebel against the Lord, and Amon, his grandson, was so evil that his own people murdered him in his own house (II Kings 21:23). Psalms 105:8 says that our Lord is concerned for the well-being of His people "for a thousand generations." Let us show similar concern for the spiritual welfare of all who follow us.

Isaiah 40

40:1-2
"Comfort, yes, comfort My people!" Says your God. "Speak comfort to Jerusalem, and cry out to her, that her warfare is ended, that her iniquity is pardoned; for she has received from the LORD's hand double for all her sins."

    Andrew Davis' Christ Centered Exposition on the book of Isaiah says, "Isaiah 40 is one of the greatest chapters in the Bible." Certainly, verse 31 is one of the most quoted verses in the Bible, and the entire chapter vibrates with the greatness of God. It draws sinners to be reconciled with their Creator, and encourages believers with reminders of the forgiveness, renewal, and strength that God gives to those who are His.
    God tells Isaiah to comfort His people. They have been at war with the armies of Assyria and God has been at war with the sins of their heart, but Jerusalem's "warfare is ended." Assyria has been defeated and Judah's "iniquity is pardoned." They have sinned and angered the Holy God, but He has dealt with their wrongdoings. They have received "double for all (their) sins" – that is they have received a fully adequate punishment for their

offenses. God is satisfied with His response to their sins. They are now "pardoned." He has cast their sins behind His back (38:17), and it is now time to comfort them with His tender forgiveness and renew their strength.

Matthew Henry says that the "commission and instructions" given us in these verses were not given to Isaiah only, but to all servants of the Lord "to proclaim comfort to God's people." The Christian life is like warfare, and there is much to grieve over in war. Isaiah's countrymen needed comfort. War had claimed the lives of many loved ones, and their sin had caused them much grief, but the "God of all comfort" (II Corinthians 1:3) is the God who "comforts the downcast (II Corinthians 7:6). Our Lord "heals the brokenhearted and binds up their wounds" (Psalms 147:3), and He calls for us to join Him in His work to comfort His people. When people sin, we must call on them to repent. But with the repentant we have the blessed task of bringing them the comforting news of God's forgiveness. Our God is the source of all comfort. Let us then, as His ambassadors, comfort those who mourn and ache and are trying to cope with heavy hearts.

40:3
The voice of one crying in the wilderness: "Prepare the way of the LORD; make straight in the desert a highway for our God.

All four gospel writers quote this verse and apply the words to John the Baptist. In John 1:23, John the Baptist says of himself, "I am the voice of one crying in the wilderness: 'Make straight the way of the LORD.'" When kings come, their way must be prepared. It is a dishonor to the king for his arrival to be greeted by unprepared people who have failed to un-busy themselves from less essential tasks. The Messiah is coming, and lest the people miss His arrival, John the Baptist will come first to "prepare the way of the LORD." And further still, lest people miss John the Baptist, Isaiah is granted this prophecy to direct the attention of his readers to watchfully anticipate the arrival of the one who would prepare for the arrival of the Messiah. God is calling Isaiah to comfort His people (verse 1). He has blessings and forgiveness and hope prepared for His people. He has a life of eternally significant, purpose-driven living intended for His children. But if left unprepared, if unawakened and unwarned, we may tragically miss all that God has intended for us. God has blessings prepared for us! But the world must be prepared in advance "lest anyone fall short of the grace of God" (Hebrews 12:15). God provides us with great hope! But the world must be prompted to pay attention to His offer, "lest any of you seem to have come short of it" (Hebrews 4:1). People live in the "wilderness" – they are lost and cannot find their way to God. So John the Baptist will go cry out to them there. People are in "the desert" – they have been living in a famine of words from the Lord. So John the Baptist will make a highway for God, a highway that leads them to God. Let us take up the gauntlet of John the Baptist and prepare people's hearts to hear from the Lord. He is speaking! He is coming! Let us join the great work of preparing hearts to receive Him.

40:4-5
Every valley shall be exalted and every mountain and hill brought low; the crooked places shall be made straight and the rough places smooth; the glory of the LORD shall be revealed, and all flesh shall see it together; for the mouth of the LORD has spoken.

Many commentators discuss how the exalted valleys and the hills brought low in verse 4 refer to the proud being humbled and the humble exalted. But verse 5 begins with "the glory of the LORD shall be revealed," which leads me to believe that verse 4 has a more global application. In Isaiah's day, God's revelation was given to Judah's prophets for Judah's people. But Isaiah prophecies of the day when God's revelation is granted to all mankind. The advantages of being Jewish will be "brought low" and the spiritually impoverished Gentiles will be "exalted." Just as Isaiah said in chapter 11 verse 9, "The earth shall be full of the knowledge of the LORD as the waters cover the sea," he now restates, "all flesh shall see (God's glory) together." Psalms 145:21 says that one day, "all flesh shall bless His holy name forever and ever." The glory of the Lord will be revealed in every nation, and men and women from every nation will rise up to "bless His holy name." And just as all nations will have access to the glory of God, all classes of peoples in all nations will have access to His revelation. No longer will God only speak to the class of prophets and priests. Joel 2:28 says, "And it shall come to pass afterward that I will pour out My Spirit on all flesh; your sons and your daughters shall prophesy, your old men shall dream dreams, your young men shall see visions." "The glory of the LORD shall be revealed." What a blessed thought. His glorious truths and glorious presence have been "hidden for ages and generations" (Colossians 1:26). The revelation of the glories of God had been "kept secret since the world began (Romans 16:25). But the Lord decrees for us through Isaiah that the glory of the knowledge of God, the knowledge of the glory of God (Habakkuk 2:14) will not be hidden forever. "The glory of the Lord will appear, and all humanity will see [it] together" (HCS). Seeing that the Lord has decreed that He will reveal His glory to all mankind, we take great delight in devoting ourselves to joining His work in making Him known. It is God's heart that all the earth will know Him, and it is our heart to make our contribution to seeing that this is so.

40:6-8
The voice said, "Cry out!" And he said, "What shall I cry?" "All flesh is grass, and all its loveliness is like the flower of the field. The grass withers, the flower fades, because the breath of the Lord blows upon it; surely the people are grass. The grass withers, the flower fades, but the word of our God stands forever."

    If we are to save ourselves from the vain pursuits of a misdirected life, if we would save our souls from the eternal consequences of sin, we must understand these words from Isaiah. "All flesh is grass." We are fleeting, temporary, short-lived creatures. We have no power to extend our lifespan. We may enjoy the flowering beauty of people around us, but we have no power to prolong their time in bloom. Our strength is temporary. Soon our bodies will weaken. Our wisdom is short-lived, soon our minds will fade. Our accomplishments, influence, insights, riches, beauty, and strength will all fade away. We should set our attentions on the eternal word of God which "stands forever," rather than focus on our own exploits and physical well-being which inevitably "fades." James 1:11 says, "For no sooner has the sun risen with a burning heat than it withers the grass; its flower fails, and its beautiful appearance perishes. So the rich man also will fade away in his pursuits."

    Furthermore, life on earth is short and full of troubles, but life in heaven is eternally satisfying. We should, therefore, make sure that our life on earth does not disqualify us from an eternity in heaven. Our sins and mortal nature, however, do just that – they disqualify us from heaven's eternal joys. And seeing that our accomplishments, influence, insights, riches, beauty, and strength all fade away, we can see that nothing we do can save us from the consequences of our sins. Our fading nature means that we cannot live forever on earth, and our fading glories mean that we cannot qualify to enter heaven. If we are to be saved forever and live in heaven forever, we must be resurrected by a power that is eternal. Blessedly, we have access to such power. In His mercy, God has spoken to us, and "the word of our God stands forever." I Peter 1:23 says that we have "been born again, not of corruptible seed but incorruptible, through the word of God which lives and abides forever."

We are frail, fading, fleeting creatures that cannot save themselves. This truth need not cause us sorrow, however. For the word of God is not like us. God's word "stands forever." And if we will trust in His word, we will be able to stand forever with Him, having been "born again" – revived and made new by His never-ending power.

40:9
O Zion, you who bring good tidings, get up into the high mountain; O Jerusalem, you who bring good tidings, lift up your voice with strength, lift it up, be not afraid; say to the cities of Judah, "Behold your God!"

God's people have been given "good tidings" to proclaim to the peoples of the world. Isaiah 40:9 calls on the people in Isaiah's day, just as Matthew 28:19 calls on us in our day to "bring good tidings" to the cities of Judah and beyond. The good tidings that we have been entrusted with to share to the world are summarized in a single phrase: "Behold your God!" This was the glad tiding spoken by John the Baptist in John 1:29 - "Behold! The Lamb of God who takes away the sin of the world!" And this was the same summarized glad tiding delivered by Pilate in John 19:14 when he said to the Jews: "Behold your King!" This is the simple, yet essential message which all people desperately need to hear: "Behold your Creator, your King, your Judge, your Savior!" At times, angels join us in proclaiming these glad tidings, "Then the angel said to them, 'Do not be afraid, for behold, I bring you good tidings of great joy which will be to all people'" (Luke 2:10). But primarily, it is God's people, not angels, who are responsible for delivering these good tidings the world over. Such a sacred, blessed task is ours! People have fallen under the weight of the guilt and penalty of sin, but we can say to them, "Behold, our Savior!" People are fighting their way through life's battles, with enemies and fears and hopelessness on every side, and we can say to them, "Behold your King!" People are squandering their life away on meaningless pursuits and unholy living, and we can warn them with "Behold your Judge!" Oh what a blessed task is ours to be called to deliver the good tidings of the greatness of God! No wonder Paul quotes Isaiah and says in Romans 10:15, "How beautiful are the feet of those who preach the gospel of peace, who bring glad tidings of good things!" We have such "good tidings" to deliver to the world! Let us take proper joy in the work and expend proper devotion to this sacred task.

40:10-11
Behold, the Lord GOD shall come with a strong hand, and His arm shall rule for Him; behold, His reward is with Him, and His work before Him. He will feed His flock like a shepherd; He will gather the lambs with His arm, and carry them in His bosom, and gently lead those who are with young.

The picture here is beautiful. God is coming. The world can be a lonely, frightening place...but God is coming. He comes "with a strong hand" and a mighty right arm. To sinners and unbelievers, God's arrival is not comforting. Isaiah 66:15 says, "For behold, the LORD will come with fire and with His chariots, like a whirlwind, to render His anger with fury, and His rebuke with flames of fire." But when our Lord comes to His children, His powerful arms do not bring a rod of punishment, no, they carry a prize. "His reward is with Him." Proverbs 11:18 promises that "he who sows righteousness will have a sure reward," and here we see that this reward is hand delivered by our Lord Himself.

"His work is before Him." It is the work of a shepherd. Our God is a Shepherd (Psalms 80:1), and like His Father, our Lord Jesus is "the good shepherd" (John 10:11). Our Lord feeds His flock with manna when His people are hungry, and feeds them with His word when they need that even more (Deuteronomy 8:3). He does not despise His children when they fail for lack of strength. He cherishes them, holding them close to His chest. He gives special attention to those with special needs, "gently" leading those with heavy burdens and stooping down to "carry" those who cannot carry on. And to those with God-given strength, He bids us to come and join Him in the work to feed and carry and care for His beloved lambs. Three times in John 21 Jesus invites Peter to tend to and feed His sheep. Responding to this same call, David "shepherded (God's people) according to the integrity of his heart, and guided them by the skillfulness of his hands" (Psalms 78:72). May Jesus' words to Peter in John 16, and our Lord's example set before us here, inspire us to join David and work untiringly to shepherd our Savior's sheep that He loves so much.

40:12-14
Who has measured the waters in the hollow of His hand, measured heaven with a span and calculated the dust of the earth in a measure? Weighed the mountains in scales and the hills in a balance? Who has directed the Spirit of the LORD, or as His counselor has taught Him? With whom did He take counsel, and who instructed Him, and taught Him in the path

of justice? Who taught Him knowledge, and showed Him the way of understanding?

The magnificence of God is briefly, but powerfully described. Look how great He is! The oceans cover almost three quarters of the world's surface, spreading out over nearly 140 million square miles. The oceans' deepest points are over 5 miles beneath the surface! It is estimated that there are some 352 quintillion gallons of water in the seas. And yet God can scoop the waters of the oceans in the cup of His hand. The incalculable expanse of space can only be imagined. In his commentary on these verses, Andrew Davis says that the visible universe is 46 billion light years across – travelling at the speed of light, it would take 46 billion years to go from one end of the universe to the other! And there are untold expanses of space beyond that! And yet God measures the heavens in a span – He can measure it all with His hand. Such is the limitless magnitude of our God. His vastness is incomparable, and His wisdom and knowledge are the same. He knows everything, and has never learned anything. His discernment is unsurpassable and infallible. Men may struggle to discern the proper "path of justice." When should we show mercy? When should we punish wrongdoing? How severely should we punish crimes? But God never struggles with these decisions. His understanding of every matter is perfect. Psalms 147:5 says "His understanding is infinite." His handling of every execution of justice is unflawed. He requires counsel from no one, for no one holds insights or perspectives that can match His own. His power and knowledge are endless, defying adequate descriptors. We call Him eternal, omnipotent, omniscient, and omnipresent. Who is like our God? We cannot match Him. We cannot adequately describe Him. But we can praise Him. We can submit to Him and serve Him. Let us be rightly awed by the greatness of our God, and may our awe inspire us to serve Him happily, thrilled with the matchless privilege of knowing and pleasing our peerless, perfect Savior.

40:15-17
Behold, the nations are as a drop in a bucket, and are counted as the small dust on the scales; look, He lifts up the isles as a very little thing. And Lebanon is not sufficient to burn, nor its beasts sufficient for a burnt offering. All nations before Him are as nothing, and they are counted by Him less than nothing and worthless.

Apart from God, mankind has no intrinsic value. Without the indwelling, purifying presence of our Creator, all the worth of all the nations combined is "less than nothing" and "worthless" in His eyes. David recognized this and wrote in Psalms 16:2 – "My goodness is nothing apart from You." Let us not fool ourselves. We have no significance apart from our relationship with God. Anyone who thinks otherwise is deluding himself. "For if anyone thinks himself to be something, when he is nothing, he deceives himself" (Galatians 6:3). So then, we see the horrifying consequences of sin. For sin separates us from God, and once separated from our Maker, we lose the relationship that is the sole means by which life retains meaning and value. The matter becomes even more horrifying when we see that, on our own, we are helpless to repair our relationship with God. Even if all the forests of Lebanon were used to fuel a sacred fire, and all the nations' creatures were offered as a burnt offering on our behalf, the sacrifice would be "not sufficient" to atone for our sins which have offended our Holy God. We are completely dependent on our Creator to be anything of significance, to do anything of significance (John 15:5), or to offer anything of significance that will permit us right standing with the only One who can change our worthless condition. When in right relationship with God, men and women are crowned with glory and honor (Psalms 8:5). Apart from God, we are "counted by Him less than nothing and worthless." With this fact before us, may all thinking men and women everywhere give the highest possible priority to gaining and maintaining a rightly united relationship with our Maker.

40:18-20
To whom then will you liken God? Or what likeness will you compare to Him? The workman molds an image, the goldsmith overspreads it with gold, and the silversmith casts silver chains. Whoever is too impoverished for such a contribution chooses a tree that will not rot; he seeks for himself a skillful workman to prepare a carved image that will not totter.

The majesty of God described in verses 12-17 is now thrown into striking contrast with the pathetic attributes of hand-made idols. Whether the gods are made of gold or silver or wood, none of them possess the ability to bless the lives of those who worship them. Psalms 115:4-8 says, "...idols are silver and gold, the work of men's hands. They have mouths, but they do not speak; eyes they have, but they do not see; they have ears, but they do not hear; noses they have, but they do not smell; they have hands, but they do not handle; feet they have, but they do not walk; nor do they mutter through their throat. Those who make them are like them; so is everyone who trusts in them." Those who trust in idols are so pitiful – just like the pitiful idols they worship! Look at the hope of the Christian compared to the hope of the idol worshipper: Those who hope in God, hope for the salvation of their souls! (Psalms 119:166). Those who hope in an idol, hope that it won't fall down. They seek out a "skillful workman" that can make them a god whose greatest achievement is that it "will not totter."

40:21-23
Have you not known? Have you not heard? Has it not been told you from the beginning? Have you not understood from the foundations of the earth? It is He who sits above the circle of the earth, and its inhabitants are like grasshoppers, who stretches out the heavens like a curtain, and spreads them out like a tent to dwell in. He brings the princes to nothing; He makes the judges of the earth useless.

"The heavens declare the glory of God" (Psalms 19:1), so Isaiah finds it difficult to believe that anyone has "not heard" or acts uninformed about His greatness. It may appear, from certain (poor) vantage points that poorly qualified men are in charge of the world. We are reminded here, however, that God "brings the princes to nothing." He is in charge, no one else. Psalms 107:40 says, "He pours contempt on princes, and causes them to wander in the wilderness where there is no way." When it looked as if Pilate had authority over Jesus, our Lord reminded him, "You could have no power at all against Me unless it had been given you from above" (John 19:11). Princes and judges cannot defy God for long, nor can they oppress His people in any eternally significant way. We need not "fear those who kill the body but cannot kill the soul" (Matthew 10:28). On the other hand, we cannot depend on the rulers and judges of the world to protect us in any significant way either. They are "useless" to defend us in any matters that are truly meaningful. Let us not be caught acting like we don't know who God is. Let us neither fear princes, nor depend on them. Let us take appropriate confidence in knowing that "My help comes from the LORD, who made heaven and earth" (Psalms 121:2).

40:24
Scarcely shall they be planted, scarcely shall they be sown, scarcely shall their stock take root in the earth, when He will also blow on them, and they will wither, and the whirlwind will take them away like stubble.

The world's greatest men are like "stubble" compared to God; they are "like grasshoppers" (verse 22) in His eyes. Those who oppose God and live for their own ambitions of glory will hardly be able to enjoy their time in the spotlight for more than a few moments before their self-absorbed aspirations "wither" and fade away. In light of the fleeting, temporary nature of ungodly success stories, David offers this counsel: "Do not fret because of evildoers, nor be envious of the workers of iniquity. For they shall soon be cut down like the grass, and <u>wither</u> as the green herb" (Psalms 37:1-2). Psalms 129:6 lifts up a prayer for God to cause the wicked to "be as the grass on the housetops, which <u>withers</u> before it grows up." And here, the Lord reveals His intention to do just that. The prospect of having all our life's work and hard-fought accomplishments wither and blow away should fill thinking men with a desire to avoid this possibility. We should desire to work for things that matter, accomplish things that will last, and succeed in efforts that will stand the test of time. How can we guarantee that our achievements will not "wither?" Two scriptures immediately leap to mind. Jesus says in John 15:6, "If anyone does not abide in Me, he is cast out as a branch and is <u>withered</u>; and they gather them and throw them into the fire, and they are burned." Separation from our Lord leads to a life that withers. Abiding in Christ, however, provides us with the assurance that our work will not wither, but we will instead, bear much fruit, "fruit that will last" (John 15:16). In addition, Psalm 1 reminds us that those who delight in the law of the Lord and meditate on God's words day and night will be "like a tree planted by the rivers of water, that brings forth its fruit in its season, whose leaf also <u>shall not wither</u>; and whatever he does shall prosper" (Psalms 1:3). We will not live on this earth forever. We do not need to. If we will delight in God's words and abide in the presence of our Lord day and night, our efforts here will never wither, they will not be blown away like stubble, and we will be blessed with the supreme satisfaction that we have devoted our life to bearing God-pleasing fruit – "fruit that will last."

40:25-26
To whom then will you liken Me, or to whom shall I be equal?" says the Holy One. Lift up your eyes on high, and see who has created these things, who brings out their host by number; He calls them all by name, by the greatness of His might and the strength of His power; not one is missing.

Psalms 147:4 says, "He counts the number of the stars; He calls them all by name." We are invited here to "lift up (our) eyes on high, and see who has created (the stars)." No one is like God. With His limitless power He has created the stars and put each one of them in their place. Though the stars in the universe are numberless, yet He knows all the details of each one. Observing the stars should move us to recognize that God – the One who created the sun and countless suns like it – is vastly, infinitely greater than anything else, anyone else in existence. "The greatness of His might and the strength of His power" is clearly revealed just by gazing at the stars. Some stars are so far away that we can't see them, all stars are so far away that we could never reach them, and even if we could, no star can be approached by man because of the overwhelming heat and power that radiate from their surface. Paul said that the Creator's "eternal power and Godhead" is so incontrovertibly revealed in the stars that men are "without excuse" (Romans 1:20) if they fail to recognize the reality and preeminence of God when we see His handiwork in the stars. "Lift up your eyes on high!" The grandeur of God is reflected in the grandeur of His creation. There is no one like Him. And we are held accountable for how fully we acknowledge that.

40:27-28
Why do you say, O Jacob, and speak, O Israel: "My way is hidden from the LORD, and my just claim is passed over by my God"? Have you not known? Have you not heard? The everlasting God, the LORD, the Creator of the ends of the earth, neither faints nor is weary. His understanding is unsearchable.

Job wondered this too. Like the people of Isaiah's focus here, Job wondered why God seemed to overlook his tears and troubles. In Job 19:7 he complained, "If I cry out concerning wrong, I am not heard. If I cry aloud, there is no justice." It seemed to Job that his plight was hidden from the mercies of God: "He has set darkness in my paths" (Job 19:8) – and that God had hidden His face from Job: "Why do You hide Your face, and regard me as Your enemy?" (Job 13:24). Though our tears may blind us to God's presence for a time, He is always near, and hears our groans and cries. Psalms 38:9 assures us that "my sighing is not hidden from You." Even as the people of Jacob and Israel cry out their question here, God rushes in with His answer. God's rescue has not been delayed because He lacks the strength to help, He "neither faints nor is weary." And God's provision has not been deferred because He could find no answer to their need – "His understanding is unsearchable." No, God knows exactly how to restore His people to vitality, and possesses unending strength with which to carry out His plans to make them new. He will answer their questions, He will uphold their cause, He will rescue their souls! In His arm is the strength to rescue, and in His "unsearchable" understanding is the plan to carry it out by His means and in His timing. When trouble besets us today , especially if the trouble lasts a long time, we may well be moved like Job and Israel to groan over our wounds and wonder why our Lord waits so long to deliver us. We may cry out as in Psalms 10:1 -- "Why do You stand afar off, O LORD? Why do You hide in times of trouble?" If we are called upon to suffer as Job did and as Israel did, may their encouragement be ours as well. After contemplating his sorrows, Job came to this exhilarating conclusion: "For I know that my Redeemer lives, and He shall stand at last on the earth" (Job 19:25). And when Israel groaned over their trials, the Lord encouraged them with a similar message that continues in the three verses to follow...

40:29-31
He gives power to the weak, and to those who have no might He increases strength. Even the youths shall faint and be weary, and the young men shall utterly fall, but those who wait on the LORD shall renew their strength; they shall mount up with wings like eagles, they shall run and not be weary, they shall walk and not faint.

The people of Israel were "weak." They had "no might" by which they could pick themselves up and move past their trouble. But even if they were strong, even if they had the energy of "youths" and even if they were as strong as "young men," their strength would eventually prove inadequate. The requirements of daily living overwhelm the strength of many, but the requirements of holy living overwhelm the strength of everyone. And all thinking men will acknowledge that the mandate in Galatians 6:2 to "Bear one another's burdens, and so fulfill the law of Christ," is also beyond the means of every mortal man. No one has the strength to carry the burdens of everyone else – and yet that is what we are called to do, and that is what we are enabled to do as described here. When troubles weigh heavy on us, we are promised the power to bear the burden and the pain if we will wait on the Lord. Those who trust Him, obey Him, and wait for His provision rather than rush out in self-dependence will find God faithful to "renew their strength." This constant renewal of the believer's strength enables us to carry on even when troubles last day after day and even if they last year after year! II Corinthians 4:16 says, "Therefore we do not lose heart. Even though our outward man is perishing, yet the inward man is being renewed day by day." And Psalms 103:5 reminds us that God "satisfies your mouth with good things, so that your youth is renewed like the eagle's." Troubles will eventually fade away. Blessedly, we are reminded here, that the strength that God gives our soul never diminishes. "The LORD shall renew (our) strength" day after day.

Psalms 69:2 says, "I sink in deep mire, where there is no standing; I have come into deep waters, where the floods overflow me." Sometimes troubles are murky, muddy affairs that bend our back, drag down our emotions, and darken our spiritual insights. They can blacken our outlook so badly that we forget the high purpose to which our Lord has called us, and divert our eyes from His lofty vantage point. Blessedly, when we seek His face and seek His strength (I Chronicles 16:11), He allows us to "mount up with wings like eagles" so that we can rise above the mud and mundane troubles that would try to drag our faces downward and focus only on our problems. Instead, God's renewing strength allows us to "mount up with wings like eagles" and see our troubles from His blessed viewpoint, rather than stare at them from ground level.

We are also able to "run with endurance the race that is set before us" (Hebrews 12:1), because "He increases our strength" so that we will not grow weary in our service to Him. II Thessalonians 3:13 compels us to "not grow weary in doing good." And here we have God's promise to empower what II Thessalonians 3:13 commands us to accomplish. In Psalms 81:13 God sounds out His command: "walk in My ways!" And as we strive to carry out His command to walk with Him, we are encouraged here, seeing that His ways are empowered by His strength, so that we can walk in His ways -- holy, helpful, and a blessing to others – without fear of fainting, for His strength will hold us up.

Isaiah 41

41:1
Keep silence before Me, O coastlands, and let the people renew their strength! Let them come near, then let them speak; let us come near together for judgment.

The unbelievers and disobedient of the world tend to trivialize their rejection of the sovereignty of God. They flippantly claim that one religion is as good as another. They make offhanded comments excusing their non-compliance with God's commands. They tritely dismiss the notion that God must be honored at all costs, and casually throw out complaints against Him whenever displeasing events occur. Here, God commands all unbelievers to "keep silence," stop thinking that they can flippantly scorn Him without consequence. He invites them, no, He demands them to draw near, not to carry on a casual conversation with their Creator, but to enter a formal tribunal with the One who will decide their eternal fate. The Lord would not have the peoples of the world face judgment unprepared. He calls them to gather their "strength," prepare their arguments and voice their reasons for rejecting His authority. Judgment is coming. Let all the world's peoples beware. Let them not take the matter casually, but rather expend all possible effort preparing their argument for why they do not submit to God. Perhaps a determined consideration of the matter will grant them insight to reconsider their position.

41:2-4
Who raised up one from the east? Who in righteousness called him to His feet? Who gave the nations before him, and made him rule over kings? Who gave them as the dust to his sword, as driven stubble to his bow? Who pursued them, and passed safely by the way that he had not gone with his feet? Who has performed and done it, calling the generations from the beginning? "I, the LORD, am the first; and with the last I am He."

    The Lord God, who is "the first," and "the last" has "raised up one from the east." He has "called him to His feet" in righteousness. There is not unanimous agreement on who is being referred to as the "one from the east" that God has called to His feet. Many say Cyrus of Persia, because he is discussed by name in chapters 44 and 45. Some say the passage speaks of Abraham, and others give different thoughts. We are encouraged by considering all the possibilities. If Isaiah is referring to Cyrus, as seems likely, we are cheered by the reminder that it is God who "removes kings and raises up kings" (Daniel 2:21). Even pagan kings are set in place by God, they reign only as long as He permits, and they are removed at His command. If Isaiah refers to Abraham, we are encouraged by God's elective grace that chose Abraham from among the world's peoples and granted him the highest privilege of sitting at His feet and gaining His blessings.

    We are further blessed by the picture for it reminds us that, with unending kindness, our Lord has also called us to His feet in righteousness. He has called "generations" of saints "from the beginning" of time, and He continues to call us to Himself even now. For He "has saved us and called us with a holy calling, not according to our works, but according to His own purpose and grace which was given to us in Christ Jesus before time began" (II Timothy 1:9).

41:5-7
The coastlands saw it and feared, the ends of the earth were afraid; they drew near and came. Everyone helped his neighbor, and said to his brother, "Be of good courage!" So the craftsman encouraged the goldsmith; he who smooths with the hammer inspired him who strikes the

anvil, saying, "It is ready for the soldering"; then he fastened it with pegs, that it might not totter.

"The coastlands saw it." They saw judgment coming, and "were afraid." The righteous requirements of their holy Creator were written on their conscience, and their heart warned them that their "evil heart of unbelief" (Hebrews 3:12) would condemn them for an eternity. But rather than rush to reconcile with their Creator, they encouraged one another to persist in rebelling against Him. They fashioned their own gods that had fewer expectations for righteous living. Their trust in these new gods was completely without foundation. Without help, their hand-made gods would "totter." The golden gods could not even stand up on their own, much less stand up against the Creator's verdict holding their worshipers culpable for their sin. As Dagon fell before the Lord in Ashdod (I Samuel 5), so all false and hand-fashioned gods will "totter" and fall when God draws near.

41:8-9
But you, Israel, are My servant, Jacob whom I have chosen, the descendants of Abraham My friend. You whom I have taken from the ends of the earth, and called from its farthest regions, and said to you, "You are My servant, I have chosen you and have not cast you away:"

The "coastlands" and "ends of the earth" (verse 5) have rejected their Creator and made their own gods. Blessedly, God's people need not share in the hopelessness and helplessness of dependence on gods who can't even stand up on their own. We take great comfort in our Lord's words, "I have chosen you and have not cast you away." When ignorance and depravity would have kept us apart from God, He chose us to be His own. "You did not choose Me, but I chose you and appointed you that you should go and bear fruit, and that your fruit should remain, that whatever you ask the Father in My name He may give you" (John 15:16). We are further blessed to see that our Lord finds us somehow fit to be His "servant." Though our past sins and present weaknesses make us hardly useful in our own eyes, our Lord has 'hired' us (Matthew 20) – He has given us purpose and value by calling us to be His servants and work for His eternal purposes in His vineyard. But even more remarkable is seeing that the eternal, holy God grants His chosen servants the priceless opportunity to be His "friend." James rightly finds it wholly remarkable that even a great man like Abraham could be considered for this honor – that "(Abraham) was called the friend of God" (James 2:23). But it is even more remarkable that *we* can have this treasured privilege extended to us! We might think that we are too lowly and sinful to be called the friend of God, but Jesus dispels this apprehension, for He is "a friend of tax collectors and sinners!" (Matthew 11:19). John 15 tells us the simple formula for becoming the friend of God, as well as what Jesus does when we become His friend. In John 15:14 Jesus says, "You are My friends if you do whatever I command you." The offer is simple. If we will obey our Lord, our God is willing to make us His friend. Certainly, this offer is too good for thinking people to pass up! Today, let us obey God! His friendship awaits those who obey Him! And then, for His friends, Jesus says in John 15:15 – "all things that I heard from My Father I have made known to you." If we obey our Lord, He will consider us His friend, and for His friends, the Lord reveals the mysteries of heaven made known by the Father, Himself. What a sacred privilege. What a priceless blessing. God has called us from the "farthest regions" of the earth. He has granted us purpose and value by allowing us to be His servant. And even more amazing still, He has granted us the unspeakable joy of allowing us to be His friend.

41:10
Fear not, for I am with you; be not dismayed, for I am your God. I will strengthen you, yes, I will help you, I will uphold you with My righteous right hand.

The world can be an unsettling place. Even for those of us living in the relative security of America, we may have cause to fear for our health, our children's well-being, our job security, or fear what the future holds. Here, however, our Lord gives us His simple comfort: "Fear not." And the reason that we can overcome fear is simpler still, "for I am with you." God is with us. Can there be a more comforting thought? We need not fear being alone, for God is always with us. We need not fear being overpowered by unfriendly forces, for He is God. When our strength is insufficient, He will "strengthen" us. When work is overwhelming, He will "help" us. And when we are burned out, used up, stressed out, and close to collapse, He will "uphold" us with His righteous right hand. Let us crave the presence of God. For when He draws near, He dispels all cause to fear. Psalms 73:23 says, "I am continually with You; You hold me by my right hand." And when His hand holds ours, we find no reason to fear anything. Fear is not always dispelled by the absence of danger. Plenty of people live in constant fear, even while living in perfect safety. Fear is dispelled when we enter the presence of the living God. It is the presence of God, not the absence of danger that grants us perfect peace and freedom from fear. Even if I walk through the valley of the shadow of death, I will not fear, for You are with me (Psalms 23:4). Psalms 34:4 says, "I sought the LORD, and He heard me, and delivered me from all my fears." Rather than seek safety, let us seek the Lord, for His presence provides what the absence of danger cannot. Psalms 46:1-2 says, "God is our refuge and strength, a very present help in trouble. Therefore we will not fear, even though the earth be removed, and though the mountains be carried into the midst of the sea." God is "very present." What a comforting thought. Today, may we take our eyes off our present troubles and set them on our Lord's "very present" help, constantly finding comfort in the assertion in Psalms 118:6 that "The LORD is on my side; I will not fear. What can man do to me?"

41:11-13
Behold, all those who were incensed against you shall be ashamed and disgraced; they shall be as nothing, and those who strive with you shall perish. You shall seek them and not find them – those who contended with you. Those who war against you shall be as nothing, as a nonexistent thing. For I, the LORD your God, will hold your right hand, saying to you, "Fear not, I will help you."

In Psalms 35:1 David prays, "Plead my cause, O LORD, with those who strive with me; fight against those who fight against me." And here, the Lord states His intention to answer David's request on behalf of all His people. Those who fight against the children of God are destined to be "ashamed and disgraced." "They shall be as nothing, as a nonexistent thing." "You shall seek them and not find them." Israel was conquered by Assyria – but today Assyria no longer exists. Jerusalem was conquered by Babylon, but today, Babylon is a nonexistent thing. God promises to hold His children by their right hand and help them when enemies "war against" them, when unkind people have "contended" with them. We have good cause to pity those who seek our hurt "since it is a righteous thing with God to repay with tribulation those who trouble you" (II Thessalonians 1:6). We need not seek to strengthen our hand to fight against those who fight against us. We simply need to tighten our grip on our Savior who holds our right hand in His. He will take care of those who war against us.

41:14-16
"Fear not, you worm Jacob, you men of Israel! I will help you," says the LORD and your Redeemer, the Holy One of Israel. "Behold, I will make you into a new threshing sledge with sharp teeth; you shall thresh the

mountains and beat them small, and make the hills like chaff. You shall winnow them, the wind shall carry them away, and the whirlwind shall scatter them; you shall rejoice in the LORD, and glory in the Holy One of Israel."

God sees clearly that His people possess no more power than a worm – and it is good for us not to think higher of ourselves than God does. With insight, David writes Psalms 22:6 -- "I am a worm, and no man; a reproach of men, and despised by the people." Our significance arises not from our inherent strength or beauty. Our significance rests entirely in the greatness of our Redeemer, the Holy One of Israel, who has decreed His intention to come to the aid of His people ("I will help you") and give them cause to "rejoice" when they see all that He has accomplished through them. Here He promises to turn His worm-like children into "a new threshing sledge with sharp teeth" – an unstoppable force that can clear away mountains. Though we are small and worm-like, the presence of the Lord in us beats mountains of troubles into small matters, and makes hills of trials like chaff that blow away in the wind. Let us not think that we are something, when we are nothing. Let us "glory in the Holy One of Israel," delighting in His great power, and rejoicing that He uses His power on our behalf. Psalms 105:1-3 echoes the call for us to "glory" in the joy of the presence and power of God, and to "rejoice" in the wondrous works that He carries out to "help" His people. "Oh give thanks to the LORD! Call upon His name; make known His deeds among the peoples! Sing to Him, sing psalms to Him; talk of all His wondrous works! Glory in His holy name; let the hearts of those rejoice who seek the LORD!"

41:17-20
The poor and needy seek water, but there is none, their tongues fail for thirst. I, the LORD, will hear them; I, the God of Israel, will not forsake them. I will open rivers in desolate heights, and fountains in the midst of the valleys; I will make the wilderness a pool of water, and the dry land springs of water. I will plant in the wilderness the cedar and the acacia tree, the myrtle and the oil tree; I will set in the desert the cypress tree and the pine and the box tree together, that they may see and know, and consider and understand together, that the hand of the LORD has done this, and the Holy One of Israel has created it.

God's words here likely held some literal fulfillment, seeing that God warned drought on the people if they disobeyed Him. "The LORD will change the rain of your land to powder and dust" (Deuteronomy 28:24).

But the heart of the words refers to the spiritual drought that had plagued the land and its people as a result of their sin and rejection of the lordship of their Creator. "'Behold, the days are coming,' says the Lord GOD, 'that I will send a famine on the land, not a famine of bread, nor a thirst for water, but of hearing the words of the LORD'" (Amos 8:11). When God's messages are rare and His presence seems far off, godly men are moved to pant for the water of His presence and thirst for a word from the Lord. Psalms 42:1 says, "As the deer pants for the water brooks, so pants my soul for You, O God." And Psalms 63:1 says, "O God, You are my God; early will I seek You; my soul thirsts for You; my flesh longs for You In a dry and thirsty land where there is no water." Sin leads to spiritual famine, which pains the souls of godly men and moves them to cry out to the Lord for His presence and His counsel. And here, we see the Lord answer: "I, the LORD, will hear them; I, the God of Israel, will not forsake them. I will open rivers in desolate heights, and fountains in the midst of the valleys; I will make the wilderness a pool of water, and the dry land springs of water." When "the poor and needy seek water," when the spiritually thirsty cry out for more of the Lord's presence – He "will hear them." He "will not forsake them." He will flow through their soul like "rivers of living water" (John 7:38). The presence of the Lord "will become in him a fountain of water springing up into everlasting life" (John 4:14). When service and harsh circumstance leave us dry, let us cry out to the Lord for the rivers of His refreshing presence. He hears the cries of a famished soul, and blessedly, it is His good pleasure to satisfy those who long for Him. "For He satisfies the longing soul, and fills the hungry soul with goodness" (Psalms 107:9), as He invites us to drink from the "river of His pleasures" (Psalms 36:8).

41:21-24

"Present your case," says the LORD. "Bring forth your strong reasons," says the King of Jacob. "Let them bring forth and show us what will happen; let them show the former things, what they were, that we may consider them, and know the latter end of them; or declare to us things to come. Show the things that are to come hereafter, that we may know that you are gods; yes, do good or do evil, that we may be dismayed and see it together. Indeed you are nothing, and your work is nothing; he who chooses you is an abomination."

God opens the courtroom and begins to examine the case for idol worship. He invites idolaters to "bring forth your strong reasons" for believing in their idols so that a proper judgment might be rendered determining whether or not it is reasonable for a man to center his religion on an idol. He invites idols to show us the future and so declare their powers. But they are pitifully incapable of that, so God sarcastically invites them to talk about the past – but even that, they cannot do. God invites them to do *anything*! Do a good deed – help someone. But they cannot do that, so God invites them to do "evil" – anything to show that the world can "see it together" – see that the idols have some power worthy of recognition. But the idols are inanimate. They are lifeless. They "are nothing" and their "work is nothing." The case is tried. Idols are found guilty of being a sham. Idols worn around the neck, idols set on shelves in the home, idols set on walls, car dashboards, or public squares, even beautifully adorned idols in elaborate temples are all deceptions. They cannot help anyone. In the courtroom of heaven it has been proven. Idols are deceptions, unworthy of the attentions, and certainly unworthy of the devotion and trust of mankind.

Verse 24 ends solemnly, "he who chooses you is an abomination." Men and women who worship idols are not well-meaning people with the right to choose their own religious preference. In God's eyes, those who worship idols are "an abomination," they are "detestable" (HCS). Idols are inanimate, and it is an affront to the intelligence of man to believe that a man-made statue can supernaturally help anyone. Idols are inanimate. It is an offence to the conscience of man to believe that idols have any spiritual value. To believe in an idol, men and women must refuse to listen to the rational instruction of their brains and turn their backs on the spiritual instructions of the God-given conscience in their soul. Idol worship is reprehensible, inexcusable, and condemnable. Paul was "provoked" by idol worship in Athens (Acts 17:16). May we be no less stirred by this sin of man that is an abomination to God, and unapologetically call all idol worshippers to throw away their lifeless gods, being lovingly compelled to do so, knowing that "Those who regard worthless idols forsake their own Mercy" (Jonah 2:8).

41:25-29

I have raised up one from the north, and he shall come; from the rising of the sun he shall call on My name; and he shall come against princes as though mortar, as the potter treads clay. Who has declared from the beginning, that we may know? And former times, that we may say, 'He is righteous'? Surely there is no one who shows, surely there is no one who declares, surely there is no one who hears your words. The first time I said to Zion, 'Look, there they are!' And I will give to Jerusalem one who

brings good tidings. For I looked, and there was no man; I looked among them, but there was no counselor, who, when I asked of them, could answer a word. Indeed they are all worthless; their works are nothing; their molded images are wind and confusion.

Some of the language here is shadowy, almost cryptic, at least to me. Multiple authors are confident that Isaiah speaks of Cyrus. I am less sure, though I see their reasoning. God declares that He will give to His people "one who brings good tidings." Giving good tidings to man is a frequent activity of God. An angel gives "good tidings" to the shepherds in Luke 2:10. Isaiah 61:1 predicts that Jesus will bring "good tidings" to the poor, and Jesus confirms Isaiah's words in Luke 4:18. Isaiah 52:7 is quoted by Romans 10:15, saying that all God's people who spread "good tidings" to the world are involved in a beautiful work. God's people have "good tidings" to bring to the world. In contrast, idolaters and their idols have nothing to say. There is "no counselor" with any helpful insights among the idol worshippers of the world. And there is no idol that can "answer a word" when God challenges them to refute the good tidings of great truths that He has communicated to mankind. Idols and idolaters are "worthless." No matter how impressive the labors of idol worshipers appear to be, Heaven's eye sees the temporary, futile nature of their efforts and says that "their works are nothing." It is a grief to the heart of old men to look back on their life and see that their life's work was all for nothing. Such is the inescapable destiny of everyone who trusts in and devotes his allegiance to hand-carved idols. Their life's work will all amount to "nothing." They will face judgment day before their Creator with nothing to show for the days on earth He allocated to them. The contrast is striking. God brings good tidings to His people. Idols offer nothing but "wind and confusion."

Isaiah 42

42:1
Behold! My Servant whom I uphold, My Elect One in whom My soul delights! I have put My Spirit upon Him; He will bring forth justice to the Gentiles.

"Behold!"

Though written, the word sounds loudly from the page. The Father is introducing His Son, and just as silence and attention is demanded when the king's entry is announced, so the Father calls for our attention as He introduces the arrival of His Son. The Father's introduction of His Son includes a powerful 5-fold accolade of "the only begotten Son" of God (John 1:18). Jesus is the Father's Servant. He was devoted to carrying out His Father's will (John 5:30), submitting to His Father's will even when it caused Him great suffering (Luke 22:42). Jesus is the "Elect One." Matthew 12:18 quotes Isaiah's words here, as Jesus Himself affirmed that the Father had "chosen" Him for His purposes. I Peter 2:4 says that Jesus was "chosen by God and precious." The soul of God the Father "delights" in His Son. In Matthew 3:17 the heart of God was so moved by this delight in His Son that

ISAIAH 42

He announced with a voice from heaven, saying, "This is My beloved Son, in whom I am well pleased." Fourthly, we see that the Spirit of the Father is in the heart of His Son. We are not surprised. How could it be any other way, seeing that Jesus affirms in John 17:21 that the Father was in His Son, and Jesus was in the Father? It is heartening to consider that Jesus came to save sinners, but we are reminded here by the Father's fifth descriptor of His Son that the mission of Jesus on earth was not just to bring salvation to God's children – He came to bring "justice to the nations" (ESV). He came to right wrongs and bring "justice to victory" (Matthew 12:20).

As we roll these thoughts around in our mind, contemplating the greatness of Jesus our Lord and examining what our Father said about His Son, we are struck by the fact that all five of these descriptors of the eternal Son of God, are also used to describe us, His adopted children. We, too, have been called to purpose and a life full of meaning as "servants of the Most High God" (Acts 16:17). Jesus called us His servants in John 12:26 saying, "If anyone serves Me, let him follow Me; and where I am, there My servant will be also. If anyone serves Me, him My Father will honor." David took proper joy in the privilege of being the servant of the living God, saying in Psalms 116:16, "O LORD, truly I am Your servant; I am Your servant, the son of Your maidservant; You have loosed my bonds." And just as the Father upheld His Servant-Son, so He will "uphold" all of us as we bear the weight of serving Him "For the LORD upholds (His people) with His hand" (Psalms 37:24).

Jesus is the "Elect One." And remarkably, so are we. Colossians 3:12 says that we are "the elect of God." I Thessalonians 1:4 encourages us to always remember "your election by God." We lift our hands and hearts in praise and gratitude, finding it difficult to find proper response when we consider that "The God of our fathers has chosen you that you should know His will, and see the Just One, and hear the voice of His mouth" (Acts 22:14).

And too, amazingly, just as God delights in His Son, we are told that He delights in us as well! "The steps of the godly are directed by the LORD. He delights in every detail of their lives" (Psalms 37:23 NLT). David took heart in knowing that the Lord "also brought me out into a broad place; He delivered me because He delighted in me" (Psalms 18:19). And Proverbs 11:20 reminds us that "Those who are of a perverse heart are an abomination to the LORD, but the blameless in their ways are His delight."

Jesus is God incarnate, so it is "natural" for Him to be filled with the Spirit of God. But this blessing of blessings has been extended to us as well. " I will pour out My Spirit on all flesh; your sons and your daughters shall prophesy, your old men shall dream dreams, your young men shall see visions" (Joel 2:28). We can understand the deep things of God and discern the teachings in His word because "the Helper, the Holy Spirit, whom the Father will send in My name, He will teach you all things, and bring to your remembrance all things that I said to you" (John 14:26).

And finally, just as the Father called His Son to administer justice to the nations, so He gives us this charge as well. "He has told you, O man, what is good; and what does the Lord require of you but to do justice, and to love kindness, and to walk humbly with your God?" (Micah 6:8). Psalms 82:3 calls on all of us to "Defend the poor and fatherless; do justice to the afflicted and needy." And Psalms 106:3 promises blessings for those who do so. "Blessed are they who observe justice, who do righteousness at all times!" (ESV).

I have now spent hours poring over this single verse. I must move on, but my soul finds so much joy in these words. This verse flows over me with a seemingly endless flood of visions of my Lord and inspiration for daily living. Over 500 years before Jesus is born in Bethlehem, the Father introduces the world to His Son. The Son of God is said to be God's Servant, the Elect One, the One in Whom God delights. The Spirit of God is upon Him, and He brings justice to the peoples of the earth. And all of these high privileges and pleasures, all of these honors and advantages have been freely offered to you and me as well. Remarkable. Amazing. I can hardly drink it in.

42:2-3
He will not cry out, nor raise His voice, nor cause His voice to be heard in the street. A bruised reed He will not break, and smoking flax He will not quench; He will bring forth justice for truth.

Jesus will "bring justice to the nations" (verse 1 ESV), but we are amazed by His method for bringing that justice. He will not "raise His voice." Some seek to win their disputes through intimidating anger and bully their points home with loud arguments rather than sound arguments. But Jesus is not like that. In Matthew 12, Jesus heals a man's hand on the Sabbath. In the most depraved response possible, the Pharisees seek to "destroy Him" for it. Then Matthew 12:15 says, "But when Jesus knew it He withdrew from there" so that people would know that He is a gentle Ruler as Isaiah predicted in these verses here. Jesus is the lion of Judah (Revelation 5:5), but He did not roar at His enemies. He "withdrew" from them, quietly teaching those who eagerly listened, and quietly enduring those who would not. Jesus demands justice and assures ultimate justice, but He did not carry out justice with a sword or with machines of war. His arrival was so gentle that even bruised reeds did not break when He passed through their midst. People are tender packages. Invisibly stamped on us all is the message: "fragile, handle with care." And Jesus handles us with care. The power He wields executes justice over even the world's most powerful people. But His tender concern keeps even "faintly burning" (ESV) hearts aglow, and sustains "the smallest hope" (NLT) of those who have suffered the bruising of their soul. Jesus does not force allegiance, nor does He lash His subjects to drive them to work for Him. Rather than roughly compelling us to work, He gently carries us to rest. Matthew 11:29 says, "Take My yoke upon you and learn from Me, for I am gentle and lowly in heart, and you will find rest for your souls."

42:4
He will not fail nor be discouraged, till He has established justice in the earth; and the coastlands shall wait for His law.

Jesus is gentle, but He will not be discouraged, He will not tire, and He will not stop working until He has "established justice in the earth." He could establish justice in the earth in an instant. He could execute all sinners and mete out fair justice on us all today. But He reigns with gentleness as well as justice, and that sort of reign must endure long seasons of prominent indecency before perfect justice is finally achieved. His gentle hands are cupped around the earth. He does not crush us with His displeasure, but gently molds us to His image and purposes. Though His works to make us righteous and establish justice may take millennia, we need not doubt His ultimate victory. "He will not fail." He is gentle with sinners, but He is certain to carry out His undeterrable intention to establish justice on the earth. Today, we wait with the coastlands for the law of the Lord to be established in the earth. But we can take heart. "He will not fail." God's law and His justice will certainly be established. May they be established in our hearts today, as the world awaits their establishment in that day to come.

42:5-7
Thus says God the LORD, who created the heavens and stretched them out, who spread forth the earth and that which comes from it, who gives breath to the people on it, and spirit to those who walk on it: "I, the LORD, have called You in righteousness, and will hold Your hand; I will keep You and give You as a covenant to the people, as a light to the

Gentiles, to open blind eyes, to bring out prisoners from the prison, those who sit in darkness from the prison house."

God is He "who created the heavens." He stretched out the earth like a scroll and formed everything "which comes from it." Life did not spontaneously erupt. It is God who "gives breath to the people." And apart from God, humanity has no soul, for it is He who infused "spirit to those who walk on (the earth)." The creative genius of God is beyond description. All things are made by Him. All life is sustained by Him. And the soul and spirit of human beings are instilled in us by Him. Sin and unbelief, however, have crippled humanity. Sin has made us "blind." Unbelief has made us "prisoners." The disruption of our unity with God has sentenced us to "sit in darkness." Blessedly, our Creator will not abandon us to life and death without Him. Our God has called His Servant, His Elect One (verse 1) to come and restore us! Jesus is the Father's "covenant to the people." In Luke 22:20 Jesus said, "This cup is the new covenant in My blood, which is shed for you." As the rainbow is God's covenant with man that He will not again destroy the world with a flood (Genesis 9:13-16), so Jesus is God's covenant with man that He will save man through His blood.

Jesus is also: "a light for the nations" (ESV). Psalms 107:10-11 says, "Those who sat in darkness and in the shadow of death, bound in affliction and irons" are in that darkness "because they rebelled against the words of God, and despised the counsel of the Most High." The nations of the world apart from God "do not know, nor do they understand; they walk about in darkness" (Psalms 82:5). Blessedly, Jesus has come to dispel the darkness that envelops all who are blinded by sin and unbelief. Matthew 4:16 says of Him, "the people who sat in darkness have seen a great light, and upon those who sat in the region and shadow of death light has dawned." Jesus is the light of the world. Unbelievers blinded by intentional ignorance and sin, as well as godly saints who face temporary dark times are blessed by the light that shines from our Savior and Lord, "For You will light my lamp; the LORD my God will enlighten my darkness" (Psalms 18:28). Jesus came to "give light to those who sit in darkness and the shadow of death, to guide our feet into the way of peace" (Luke 1:79). Because of Him, we are now "children of the light and of the day!" We no longer "belong to darkness and night" (I Thessalonians 5:5 NLT). II Corinthians 4:6 (NLT) says, "For God, who said, 'Let there be light in the darkness,' has made us understand that this light is the brightness of the glory of God that is seen in the face of Jesus Christ." The world can be a dark place. Blessedly, Jesus shines brightly, illuminating the truth, lighting the path to peace, and revealing hope.

ISAIAH 42

42:8
I am the LORD, that is My name; and My glory I will not give to another, nor My praise to carved images.

God is the Lord, He is Master, Owner, and Sovereign over all created things. It is an affront; it is a deep offence to Him to take the honor only He is due and give it to any other god. It is an offence to the sovereignty of God and to the intelligence of man to give praise to "carved images." God is amazingly patient. We could well expect Him to immediately destroy all idols and offenders that worship them the instant one begins to praise the other. But though He does not destroy them all straightway, as He did with Dagon in I Samuel 5, God is also relentlessly, unstoppably unswerving in His determination to see His name honored and His glory praised by all His creation. His defense of His own name, His holy intention to see all creation honor Him and worship Him is passed on to us, His children, and we cry out "Let the peoples praise You, O God; let all the peoples praise You" (Psalms 67:3). "Praise the LORD, all you Gentiles! Laud Him, all you peoples!" (Psalms 117:1). Our hearts join our Lord's and we long to see the day when "all the earth shall worship You and sing praises to You; they shall sing praises to Your name" (Psalms 66:4). And when others refuse to honor our Lord, we are determined to do it ourselves: "I will praise You, O Lord, among the peoples; I will sing to You among the nations" (Psalms 57:9). "I will praise You with my whole heart; before the gods I will sing praises to You" (Psalms 138:1). God is the Lord. There is no other. And He requires, yes, He demands, that all mankind honor and praise Him, and Him alone. Let us forever reject the notion that all religions are good and it is acceptable for men and women to choose the god that suits them. God condemns those who give His glory "to another." God alone is Lord. Let us praise Him with our whole heart, and call on everyone everywhere to do the same.

42:9
Behold, the former things have come to pass, and new things I declare; before they spring forth I tell you of them.

God foretold the descendants of Abraham becoming a great nation, God foretold that the kingdom of His people would be established under the reign of David and His sons, God foretold that captivity and tragedy would befall that nation if they abandoned their devotion to Him – and all of these things came to pass. And now, God declares the future once more. Verses 1-7 tell of the coming Savior, the Son of God who would be "a light to the Gentiles" (verse 6). God's past revelations and fulfillments of prophecy are well documented. All "the former things" which He declared would happen, did happen just as He said they would. And now, having proven His ability to foretell and fulfill, He announces that He will declare "new things." He will send His Savior-Son, the Messiah, who will "bring forth justice" (verse 1). Isaiah's listeners could be completely confident that the Messiah was coming, because all "the former things" that God revealed in advance had come to pass, so it stood to reason that since all former prophecies came true, all His new prophecies would come true just the same.

42:10-13
Sing to the LORD a new song, and His praise from the ends of the earth, you who go down to the sea, and all that is in it, you coastlands and you inhabitants of them! Let the wilderness and its cities lift up their voice, the villages that Kedar inhabits. Let the inhabitants of Sela sing, let them shout from the top of the mountains. Let them give glory to the LORD, and declare His praise in the coastlands. The LORD shall go forth like a mighty man; He shall stir up His zeal like a man of war. He shall cry out, yes, shout aloud; He shall prevail against His enemies.

In verse 8, God declares His intolerance of those who give His due praise to man-made gods, and Isaiah responds by calling on the peoples of the world to "sing," and "lift up their voice," and "shout," in order to declare God's praise and "give glory to the LORD." We praise God for His greatness, we praise Him for His love for us, and we are moved to praise Him because "He shall prevail over His enemies." God will defeat all His enemies, and it is within man's nature to praise winners and give honor to the victorious. Psalms 48:10 (CEV) says, "You are famous and praised everywhere on earth, as you win victories with your powerful arm." And in Exodus 14:4 (CEV), God foretells that He will overcome Pharaoh, and because of His triumph: "people everywhere will praise me for my victory." We praise God when we see Him triumph over His enemies, and we praise Him when He grants us victory over ours. Psalms 27:6 says, "And now my head shall be lifted up above my enemies all around me; therefore I will offer sacrifices of joy in His tabernacle; I will sing, yes, I will sing praises to the LORD." We praise God for His victories over His enemies. We praise God for giving us victory over our enemies, and, in a fascinating way, the act of praising God-Victorious gives us even more victories! Psalms 18:3 says, "I will call upon the LORD, who is worthy to be praised; *so shall I be saved from my enemies.*"

42:14-17

I have held My peace a long time, I have been still and restrained Myself. Now I will cry like a woman in labor, I will pant and gasp at once. I will lay waste the mountains and hills, and dry up all their vegetation; I will make the rivers coastlands, and I will dry up the pools. I will bring the blind by a way they did not know; I will lead them in paths they have not known. I will make darkness light before them, and crooked places straight. These things I will do for them, and not forsake them. They shall be turned back, they shall be greatly ashamed, who trust in carved images, who say to the molded images, "You are our gods."

God is slow to anger (Psalms 103:8). He "restrains" Himself from punishing evil for an incredibly long time. He is willing to "overlook" the offence of disobedience and unbelief (Acts 17:30) for a remarkably long time period. But here we see His patience come to an end. Like the sudden, startling cry of a woman in labor, He will cry out His intolerance for sin and sinners. And when He is at last stirred to act, two vastly different outcomes arise. He promises to "lay waste" and "dry up" the disobedient and unbelieving, and, in striking contrast, He will give "light" to His children and make their "crooked places straight." The great destruction on unbelievers, brought into such marked contrast with the great blessings poured out on the obedient, causes believers in false religion to "be greatly ashamed." Those who made gods out of self-carved images will be crushed by the weight of regret and repercussion. Their allegiance to gods with such pitiful inability to stand up to the Creator's power, will make them greatly ashamed. In Psalms 31:17 David prays, "Let the wicked be ashamed; let them be silent in the grave." And here, God promises to answer that request. David's prayer in Psalms 97:7 is "Let all be put to shame who serve carved images, who boast of idols." And God promises to answer that prayer as well. God is patient. He holds His peace "a long time." II Peter 3:15 tells us that the purpose of His patience is to give men time to be saved. But let all men and woman who scorn His salvation beware. God will not be patient forever. "The great day of the LORD is near; it is near and hastens quickly. The noise of the day of the LORD is bitter; there the mighty men shall cry out" (Zephaniah 1:14).

42: 18-20

Hear, you deaf; and look, you blind, that you may see. Who is blind but My servant, or deaf as My messenger whom I send? Who is blind as he who is perfect, and blind as the LORD's servant? Seeing many things, but you do not observe; opening the ears, but he does not hear.

Just as Jesus called on the man with the withered hand to stretch it out when his crippled arm could do no such thing (Mark 3:5), so God here calls on His deaf children to listen and His blind people to see. Faith, spiritual vigor, and zeal for the Lord will allow us to carry out His commands even though our crippled flesh can naturally do nothing our Lord requires. The Lord's rebuke is scathing. He has set so "many things" right in front of their eyes, He has displayed His will so many times. He has opened their ears to His voice, yet the disobedient man "does not hear." God has good cause to be infuriated. His very own servants, His own messengers, those with perfect opportunities to know Him have seen Him reveal His will but have not observed His efforts. He has spoken His word of truth, but they do "not hear" what He says. Jesus decried this same intentional blindness and deafness in the Pharisees, teaching us that it is a sin to be blind to God's revelation of Himself (John 9:41). Spiritual blindness is a terrible plague. "...blindness of the heart" causes us to be "alienated from the life of God" (Ephesians 4:18). Let us take all possible care to keep a sharp spiritual eye so that we can see what God is doing around us. Let us cup our hand around our spiritual ear so that we might intently listen to what our Lord may say. God is speaking! God is working in our midst! To miss His words and works is condemning.

42:21-22
The LORD is well pleased for His righteousness' sake; He will exalt the law and make it honorable. But this is a people robbed and plundered; all of them are snared in holes, and they are hidden in prison houses; they are for prey, and no one delivers; for plunder, and no one says, "Restore!"

God is holy, and He has called us to be holy (Leviticus 11:44). But when Israel insisted on sinning in Isaiah's day, and when men insist on sinning in our day, God does not wring His hands and wonder where He went wrong. God is pleased with the religious efforts and sacrifices made by righteous men and women (Psalms 51:19), but when men and women are irreligious and unrighteous, God is fully satisfied. He is still completely well pleased with His own perfect manifestation of righteousness. Sin among God's people is an absolute tragedy. It is shameful, that, in a manner of speaking, open sin committed by professing believers casts commitment to God in a bad light. II Peter 2:2 says that because of "evil teaching and shameful immorality," "Christ and his true way will be slandered" (NLT). But in a way, we can never cast God in a bad light. He is perfectly righteous, regardless of how well or poorly His servants represent Him, and He is perfectly content, pleased with His own perfect holiness, regardless of how well or poorly we are able to exemplify His holiness in the sight of others.

"He will exalt the law and make it honorable." Many in our day and Isaiah's scorned God's law. They scorned His laws regarding the exclusivity of worship, they scorned His laws regarding sexuality, they scorned His laws regarding honoring the Sabbath, and on and on it goes. But God exalts His law. He finds everything about His laws that govern the conscience of man to be good. "The law of the Lord is perfect" (Psalms 19:7). It is perfect whether or not we agree with it, whether or not we obey it, or whether or not we exchange it for another spiritual paradigm. God loves His law. He honors His law and makes it "honorable." All who disobey His law are 'dishonorable.' People who reject God's law do not make it archaic or out of touch with modern times, they simply disgrace themselves. Rejection of God's law causes people to be "robbed and plundered." They disqualify themselves from God's protective grace and make themselves vulnerable to all manner of attacks that rob them of wealth, health, spiritual vitality, and a future with hope. Those who scorn God's law are "snared in holes." Sin ensnares. On their own, sinners cannot see the way out or even fight their way out of their entrapment in sin. They are "hidden in prison houses." Good people, well-meaning, powerful people often cannot find them to help them. The godly in the church are often completely unaware of a sinner's struggle with sin, because sinners are "hidden." Their battle with sin is a secret battle. Both volitionally and not volitionally, the sins and the ailments caused by those sins are often hidden. Sin and rejection of God's law causes such terrible outcomes! Oh the tragedy of lives that are preyed upon and plundered because of their refusal to obey God! There is no way they can rescue themselves! Someone must pray for them! But tragically, no one does. God looks for someone to intercede on their behalf that He might "restore" them to spiritual health, but no one is praying. Seeing the certain doom facing those that had rejected His law, God says in Ezekiel 22:30, "I sought for a man among them who would make a wall, and stand in the gap before Me on behalf of the land, that I should not destroy it; but I found no one."

God is righteous, and He demands that we be holy too. God's law is good – very good – and He demands that we obey it. The result of rejecting His law is horrifying to contemplate. Let all thinking men adjust their lives accordingly.

42:23-2
Who among you will give ear to this? Who will listen and hear for the time to come? Who gave Jacob for plunder, and Israel to the robbers? Was it not the LORD, He against whom we have sinned? For they would not walk in His ways, nor were they obedient to His law. Therefore He has poured on him the fury of His anger and the strength of battle; it has set him on fire all around, yet he did not know; and it burned him, yet he did not take it to heart.

    Isaiah pleads with his people to please pay attention! God was not going to bless them! They were asking Him to deliver them from their enemies – and it was God who led their enemies and empowered them to defeat His own people! The people had "sinned," they "would not walk in His ways," and they were not "obedient to His law," and because of this trifold transgression "the fury of His anger" burned against them. But even as He torched them with His anger, the pain of their scalding wounds still did not alert their senses to the dangers of sinning. Even with God's painful warning system, His people "did not take it to heart," they did not repent of their rebellion, nor obey God's laws – yet absurdly, they continued to pray and ask Him to bless them! Isaiah ends his chapter with a plea for his people to "give ear" to the loud ringing of God's warning bells calling them to repent. He charges them to "listen and hear" the loud voice of God commanding them to repent and turn to Him in obedience. Failure to take God's chastisement to heart will certainly doom them to further catastrophe.

Isaiah 43

43:1
But now, thus says the LORD, who created you, O Jacob, and He who formed you, O Israel: "Fear not, for I have redeemed you; I have called you by your name; you are Mine."

Following His heavy words of warning and judgment in chapter 42, our Lord now gives great reason to hope. Though Israel has failed, and their sins and unbelief have caused them to endure God's discipline, yet the Lord will not disown them. "You are Mine." God does not relinquish the things that are His. He refines them, molds them, yes, corrects them and chastises them, but He does not abandon or give away the things that are His. His people have "sold themselves" (II Kings 17:17) to do evil in the sight of the Lord, but it is God's merciful intention to buy them back. "I have redeemed you." The cost of redemption is inestimably high. In Revelation 5:9 the elders and four living creatures fall before Jesus our Savior and praise Him because He has "redeemed us to God by Your blood." The sins of Israel have separated them from God, and their departure from Him has brought horrible consequences. But His gentle words of hope ring clear through Isaiah, "fear not, for I have redeemed you." The promise extends to us today. We have sinned, and the jaws of hell await sinners. We have sinned, and forfeited the right to ever again ask for God's blessings. But hope is here provided. "I have redeemed you." Sin separates us from God, "but now in Christ Jesus you who once were far off have been brought near by the blood of Christ" (Ephesians 2:13). Sin once made Satan our foster parent (John 8:44), but now we are the children of God through His redemptive act of mercy. "You are Mine." Nothing else can claim us anymore. We are no longer slaves to sin (Romans 6:6), slaves to circumstance, or slaves that are forced to conform to the ways of the world (I Corinthians 7:23). We belong to our loving Lord and no one else. What a blessed thought.

43:2-4

When you pass through the waters, I will be with you; and through the rivers, they shall not overflow you. When you walk through the fire, you shall not be burned, nor shall the flame scorch you. For I am the LORD your God, the Holy One of Israel, your Savior; I gave Egypt for your ransom, Ethiopia and Seba in your place. Since you were precious in My sight, you have been honored, and I have loved you; therefore I will give men for you, and people for your life.

"Through the waters" of trouble and "through the fire" of pain, God is with us. As with the Israelites when they crossed the Red Sea in Exodus 14, God is with us "through the waters." As with the next generation 40 years later at the crossing of the River Jordan in Joshua 3, God is with us "through the rivers." And as with Shadrach and his friends in Daniel 3, God is with us "through the fire." Even the threat of impending death fails to terrorize us as long as our Lord draws near. "Yea, though I walk through the valley of the shadow of death, I will fear no evil; for You are with me" (Psalms 23:4). What peace is ours being constantly reminded that "I am continually with You; You hold me by my right hand (Psalms 73:23). The soul of the saint will be forever safe as long as our Savior says, "I will be with you."

God's people are "precious" in His sight. He is willing to pay the highest possible price to redeem us to Himself (Matthew 13:46, I Corinthians 6:20), and He is willing to give other nations as "ransom" to provide rescue for His people. The firstborn of Egypt were destroyed as "ransom" for the rescue of Israel in Exodus 12, and the soldiers of Egypt were given as "ransom" to rescue God's people at the Red Sea in Exodus 14. God loves His people. We are precious to Him. Let us feel the weight of being clothed in our Savior's love. We "have been honored" to look in our Savior's face and see in His eyes the wonder of His love for us. The world does not love us. It despises us (John 15:19). The world gives no reward and no honor to those who love and are loved by God. Let us seek no such honor. Our God loves us, we are precious in His sight. This singular honor gives us good cause to seek no other reward and to despise any honors the world might think to bestow on us. Let us happily entrust our lives to Him, seeing that His love for us ensures that He will always seek the best for us. We are precious to Him, and His love for us is so, so precious to us. "How precious is Your lovingkindness, O God! Therefore the children of men put their trust under the shadow of Your wings" (Psalms 36:7).

43:5-7
"Fear not, for I am with you; I will bring your descendants from the east, and gather you from the west; I will say to the north, 'Give them up!' And to the south, 'Do not keep them back!' Bring My sons from afar, and My daughters from the ends of the earth – everyone who is called by My name, whom I have created for My glory; I have formed him, yes, I have made him."

Banishment and captivity are inevitable now. God has decreed that in punishment for their sins His people will be conquered and dispersed. But even as His punishment looms on the horizon, God repeats His astounding message of hope that He gave in verse 1: "Fear not, for I am with you." God had just given this same gentle reminder, this same word of hope in Isaiah 41:10 - "Fear not, for I am with you; be not dismayed, for I am your God. I will strengthen you, yes, I will help you, I will uphold you with My righteous right hand." When times are dark and sorrows unceasing, it is helpful for the cast-down soul to hear its dearest comforts frequently repeated. That is what the Lord does here, repeating for His people His gentle exhortation for them to rise above fear and to take comfort in His abiding presence. His people will be exiled into captivity, that is unavoidable now, but their trial will be bearable, because God will be with them.

And their troubles will be made even lighter still for the hope that the Lord gives that they will soon be gathered back home. God will call His people home, not because they are worthy, but because they are "called by My name." By faith we are adopted into God's family. And as His children, we are given His name. As a woman changes her last name by marriage, as a child changes his last name by adoption, so we change our last name when Christ redeems us. We are called Child-of-God, our name is changed to Christian. And we find life-changing purpose in our new family life. God here declares "I have created (you) for My glory." We were not born to live, eat, reproduce, and die as is the lot of lower creatures. We were not born to exact as much pleasure as possible out of living. We were born to give glory to God. "I have created (you) for My glory." Let the words sink deeply into our soul, and then let us rise each morning, enthused and inspired to live out our intended purpose. Joshua 7:19 calls Achan to give glory to God by confessing his sin. I Samuel 6:5 calls on the Philistines to give glory to God by honoring Him above all other gods. I Chronicles 16:29 calls on the people to give glory to God by bringing Him an offering. Psalms 29:2 says, "Give unto the LORD the glory due to His name; worship the LORD in the beauty of holiness." Psalms 96:8 urges us to give Him glory by coming to His court to worship. Luke 17:18 says that we give glory to God by thanking Him for His blessings. And Romans 4:20 says that Abraham gave glory to God by his faith. We have been designed by our Creator to give glory to God! And there are so many ways that we are able to carry out His glorious design for us! Let us rise early, work diligently, and focus our attention on the singular purpose of our existence! Give glory to God! Failure to do so is devastating! Malachi 2:2 warns us, "If you will not hear, and if you will not take it to heart, to give glory to My name," says the LORD of hosts, "I will send a curse upon you, and I will curse your blessings. Yes, I have cursed them already, because you do not take it to heart." Acts 12:23 provides a vivid example. When Herod failed to live out his purpose "an angel of the Lord struck him, *because he did not give glory to God*. And he was eaten by worms and died." God has made us, called us, and redeemed us to give Him glory. Today, let us strive to do exactly that.

43:8-10
Bring out the blind people who have eyes, and the deaf who have ears. Let all the nations be gathered together, and let the people be assembled. Who among them can declare this, and show us former things? Let them bring out their witnesses, that they may be justified; or let them hear and say, "It is truth." "You are My witnesses," says the LORD, "And My servant whom I have chosen, that you may know and believe Me, and understand that I am He. Before Me there was no God formed, nor shall there be after Me."

Once again, the peoples of the world are invited to gather together and present their reasons for choosing to worship gods of their own invention. What man-made gods can detail the future as our Creator can? Any who can are invited to present an example of a "former" experience where their god correctly described the future. The gods of this world can find no one to step forward on their behalf and bear witness to the powers that they supposedly wield. In contrast, God's people are His witnesses, confirming that He has foretold the future many times. He has many witnesses confirming that He alone is Creator and Sustainer, and He alone is able to foretell the future and bend all the world's events in order to fulfill what He has foretold. We are His witnesses. It is not necessary for us to be multitalented, endowed with unusual strength or intelligence, or wow our audience with good looks or personal charm. We simply need to be His "witnesses." God is great, and we bear witness to His greatness. God's love is inspiring, and we bear witness to His love. God saves, and we bear witness to His rescues. God speaks to mankind through the voice of His written word, and we bear witness to what His scriptures say. In Acts 1:8 Jesus gives the wonderful promise to give His disciples power. This supernatural power given by God to man is given to us for a single expressed purpose: "you will be my witnesses" (ESV). We are not required to perform great feats for God. We are not promised great power to make something of ourselves. We have been promised great power so that we can be witnesses to the greatness of God. With His power indwelling us, and His mighty acts and holy word before our very eyes, let us rise up to be His faithful witnesses, powerfully, comfortably, confidently detailing what we have seen Him say and do.

43:11
I, even I, am the LORD, and besides Me there is no savior.

No one else in the universe can save a human soul from the penalty of sin (Acts 4:12). Those who replace God with another god "forsake their own Mercy" (Jonah 2:8). We cannot stand quiet and idle while the world fills the heads of hell-bound souls with the condemning nonsense that all roads lead to heaven. "There is no savior" other than the One who is our Creator. There is no way to heaven other than via the One who is the Way (John 14:6). For the sake of others, we must rise up and boldly affirm that "we have seen and testify that the Father has sent the Son as Savior of the world" (1 John 4:14). And for our own sake we must "grow in the grace and knowledge of our Lord and Savior Jesus Christ" (II Peter 3:18). God is our savior. What a blessed thought. We join with Mary in rejoicing over this wonderful news: "my spirit has rejoiced in God my Savior" (Luke 1:47).

Our conscience confirms that we need a savior, and God confirms that He is the only savior available. The fact that He created the world confirms that He has the power to save us; the death of His Son on the cross confirms that He has a heart to save us; and the horrors of hell compared to His preparations for us in heaven, confirm that it is to our great benefit to reconcile with our Savior and not to "neglect so great a salvation" (Hebrews 2:3).

God is the Lord. Apart from Him there is no other opportunity for men and women to save their souls from the punishment of sins. The point could hardly be made more clearly.

43:12-13
"I have declared and saved, I have proclaimed, and there was no foreign god among you; therefore you are My witnesses," says the LORD, "that I am God. Indeed before the day was, I am He; and there is no one who can deliver out of My hand; I work, and who will reverse it?"

The NLT helps with verse 12's readability: "First I predicted your deliverance; I declared what I would do, and then I did it – I saved you. No foreign god has ever done this before. You are witnesses that I am the only God, says the LORD." The Lord, He is God. There is no other. The NLT's rendering of verse 13 is also easy to read, "From eternity to eternity I am God. No one can oppose what I do. No one can reverse my actions." He has always been God, long before anyone knew Him. Before creation He worked unopposed, and now, even with the devil, the demons, and evil men attempting to defy Him, He still cannot be opposed. No one can thwart His efforts. No one can reverse His judgments or successfully oppose His actions. Let us bear Him witness as Moses did in Psalms 90:1-2 – "LORD, You have been our dwelling place in all generations. Before the mountains were brought forth, or ever You had formed the earth and the world, even from everlasting to everlasting, You are God."

43:14-15
Thus says the LORD, your Redeemer, The Holy One of Israel: "For your sake I will send to Babylon, and bring them all down as fugitives – the Chaldeans, who rejoice in their ships. I am the LORD, your Holy One, the Creator of Israel, your King."

God declares that He will take vengeance on Babylon for their role in destroying His people in Jerusalem. Interestingly, God spends little time detailing His plans for Babylon's fall. Instead, He reminds His people who He is. It is more comforting to set our gaze on our God than it is to contemplate the destruction of our enemies. God is Lord. He is Master, He is Owner of the universe. All things belong to Him and all things exist to carry out His purposes (Colossians 1:16). He is our Redeemer. We had sold ourselves to sin, but our Redeemer bought us back – and the price of our redemption cost Him His life. Certainly, He is worthy of our indebted devotion. God is The Holy One. There is none like Him. He is perfectly pure without any trace of sin or shortcomings. All His plans are good. All His works are good. All His thoughts are good. We can trust Him, and we should make it our highest priority to be holy for He is holy (Leviticus 11:44). God is the Creator. He is the Creator of the world and He is the Creator of Israel – His own special people. "Without Him nothing was made that was made" (John 1:3), and without Him there is no body of believers, no family of faith, and no "chosen generation" (I Peter 2:9) that is chosen to be the recipients of His many mercies and His call to service. And God is our King. Psalms 10:16 says, "The LORD is King forever and ever." God is King, but He does not reign over a distant land, seen only by distant peoples. Psalms 24:9 invites the gates and doors before us to open up so that "the King of glory shall come in" and dwell among us. Our God is King – not a king who exacts taxes on us to add burden to our burdens, no He is our King who saves us. "For God is my King from of old, working salvation in the midst of the earth" (Psalms 74:12). Our God is King. He is not just one king among many, with rival kingdoms all around. He alone is King, His power and reign are infinitely greater than all other kings and gods. "For the LORD is the great God, and the great King above all gods" (Psalms 95:3). And how shall we respond in the face of such a great king who reigns over our hearts, and reigns over heaven? How shall we respond to the glory of the King of glories who reigns with majesty above all other gods and kings? Psalms 145:1 pictures our proper response: "I will extol You, my God, O King; and I will bless Your name forever and ever."

The enemies of God's people will be punished. Babylon will be cast down as fugitives. But this is not what gives the people of God their confidence. The destruction of their enemies is not the source of their joy. Our great joy is our great God displayed so gloriously before us. He is our Lord, He is our Redeemer, and He is the Holy One of Israel. He is the Lord, our Holy One, He is the Creator of Israel, and He is our King. Let us extol Him and bless His name forever.

43:16-18
Thus says the LORD, who makes a way in the sea and a path through the mighty waters, Who brings forth the chariot and horse, the army and the power (They shall lie down together, they shall not rise; they are extinguished, they are quenched like a wick): "Do not remember the former things, nor consider the things of old."

It is good for us to be continually inspired by the great things that God has done for us in the past. But in Isaiah's day, the people kept clinging to God's kindnesses to their forefathers in the past but sought no fresh visit from God in their own day. God highlights in verse 16 one of His many miraculous interventions in Israel's history – His rescue at the Red Sea, but He calls on His people to stop dwelling on the past. Great victories in the past are great victories – but they are in the past! We must dwell in the present with our eyes on eternity, and seek a fresh encounter with our Lord today. We must seek to obey Him today, honor Him today, and see Him glorify His own name today. We must not be content to continue giving testimonies only of God's great works for us in the distant past. And we certainly must not continue to wallow in failures or tragedies from our distant past. God calls His people to stop dwelling in the past. His presence today should demand our attention. We need His Divine intervention to see His will carried out around us today. Needs abound today that demand a new work from our Lord even now. We thank the Lord for His many kindnesses in the past, but we must cling to Him for new acts of mercy today. This is what our Lord calls His people to do in verse 18. This is not a call to forget the great promises and provisions of God in history. This is a call for God's people to stop dwelling in and dwelling on the past. Seek God's face, seek His strength, seek new shows of His glorious power, and seek these things today.

43:19-21
Behold, I will do a new thing, now it shall spring forth; shall you not know it? I will even make a road in the wilderness and rivers in the desert. The beast of the field will honor Me, the jackals and the ostriches, because I give waters in the wilderness and rivers in the desert, to give drink to My people, My chosen. This people I have formed for Myself; they shall declare My praise.

God declares His intention to do something new. As He revealed His heart to Abraham in Genesis 18:17, so He here once more reveals the intentions of His heart so His children will know in advance what He plans to do. "Shall you not know it?" His plans are great, and it will comfort His people to hear them. Look at this breathtaking plan of God! He will pour out His Spirit "in the wilderness" where He has never moved before. He will reveal His glory and call even the most remote peoples of the world to worship Him. Even "the jackals and ostriches" – those most improbable and inaccessible will come to know His greatness and declare His praises. The world's most barren spiritual wilderness areas will have access to the waters of His grace. The world's spiritual deserts that had never been refreshed by the rivers of life will now, for the first time ever, be watered by the breath and life of the Spirit of God. The Lord God will call pagan peoples to Himself. The Gentile world that had never known Him will now be spiritually awakened and their souls will be eternally refreshed. What a promise is given here! Here we have revealed God's intention to bring salvation and reconciliation to you and I, our forefathers, our children, and all the untold millions of Gentile saints who were once outside the promises of God, "being aliens from the commonwealth of Israel and strangers from the covenants of promise, having no hope and without God in the world" (Ephesians 2:12). Oh, how wonderful and merciful are the plans of the Lord who "turns a wilderness into pools of water, and dry land into watersprings" (Psalms 107:35). In John 7:38 Jesus said, "He who believes in Me, as the Scripture has said, out of his heart will flow rivers of living water." Long ago those rivers of living water were available only to the household of Israel. Now, however, the spiritually dry places on earth and the spiritually dry souls on earth will have ready access to the "fountain of life" (Psalms 36:9), the river of life (Revelation 22:1), and to the waters of life (Revelation 22:17). What a promise! What a plan. Still today, this epic plan of God continues to take center stage. You and I are beneficiaries of this world-changing plan of God to rescue and refresh the souls of men and women who waste away in spiritually barren places. What a promise! What a plan.

43:22-24
But you have not called upon Me, O Jacob; and you have been weary of Me, O Israel. You have not brought Me the sheep for your burnt offerings, nor have you honored Me with your sacrifices. I have not caused you to serve with grain offerings, nor wearied you with incense. You have bought Me no sweet cane with money, nor have you satisfied Me with the fat of your sacrifices; but you have burdened Me with your sins, you have wearied Me with your iniquities.

God has called His people to Himself that they might "declare My praise" (verse 21). Sadly, verse 22 tells Israel's terrible response, "you have not called upon Me, O Jacob; and you have been weary of Me, O Israel." How can such a thing be? God has opened up a "road in the wilderness" (verse 19) that will take people to a fulfilling, uplifting, joy-filled walk with their Creator, but the people have grown "weary" of walking down that road, and even worse, they have come to their Savior at the end of that road and grown "weary" of His company. How do people with such unending needs fail to call upon their omnipotent God? How do people look in the face of the perfectly holy and perfectly loving Creator and decide they no longer wish to be in His company? Even God seems to strain to find a logical explanation. He has not "burdened" (ESV) them with requirements that made compliance difficult. He has not "wearied" them with endless rituals that were a drudgery. "His commandments are not burdensome" (I John 5:3). He deserves all we have, and yet requires nothing of us that is not easy for His children to give. Yet, in spite of His infinite worthiness and minimal demands, His people were neither willing to sacrifice their possessions nor stop sinning to give Him His rightful honor. They were weary of God – and their sins and selfish living caused God to grow weary of them. "You have burdened Me with your sins, you have wearied Me with your iniquities." Our passage here fills our minds with probing questions. How can men so filled with needs turn their backs on such a holy, loving, powerful God? And our second question arises from this last line of verse 24. How does omnipotent, all-powerful God who formed the universe with His fingers – how does He grow tired? What could ever make God feel tired? The answer makes us hate our own sinful tendencies even more. "You have wearied Me with your iniquities." The sin of man is a weariness to the soul of God. He has given us a brain and a conscience and a heart to know His favor, and yet, flying in the face of all of that, we as a race insist on sinning. God's weariness with sinful, unbelieving hearts is pictured perfectly by Jesus' reaction to poor faith in Matthew 17:17 (HCS) -- "You unbelieving and rebellious generation! How long will I be with you? How long must I put up with you?" Sin and unbelief are so cosmically nauseating that they weary the heart of God whose strength is inexhaustible. How does He put up with us? We have good cause to join David's query in Psalm 8 and wonder why God would have any interest in us at all. We are even more amazed that He does not strike us all down in judgment and live happily with the angels. And then, when we consider that rather than destroy us, He sees fit to care for us and pour out His mercy on us – we are forced to realize that His patience and love are far beyond our comprehension. What will God do in the face of the transgressions of man that weary His eternal Spirit? The answer in verse 25 takes our breath away.

43:25-28
I, even I, am He who blots out your transgressions for My own sake; and I will not remember your sins. Put Me in remembrance; let us contend together; state your case, that you may be acquitted. Your first father sinned, and your mediators have transgressed against Me. Therefore I will profane the princes of the sanctuary; I will give Jacob to the curse, and Israel to reproaches.

God's people have grown weary of Him (verse 22), and their transgressions have wearied Him in return. What will He do in response? He "blots out your transgressions." Stunning. Remarkable. Of all the likely options: eternity in hell, banishment from His presence, or at least severe discipline – the least likely option of all is the course our Lord takes. He introduces Himself, as if His people have forgotten who He is: "I, even I, am He who blots out your transgressions." His people have not even a shred of decency. There is nothing in them God finds admirable. His mercy is completely generated from within, with no dependence at all on any virtue in the hearts of the objects of His kindness. The sole source of His decision to forgive is for His own name's sake. "For My own sake" "I will not remember your sins." Now, with His heart to forgive placed on the table before them, God invites them to reconsider their sin and unbelief. He is eternally holy and kind, worthy of all devotion. His commandments are not burdensome. And it is His good will to forgive and blot out their transgressions. So, with all these great attributes of God before them, the Lord invites them to "Put Me in remembrance." He invites them to "state your case," discuss this matter of highest import, talk back and forth with God and their fellow man to determine what God is worthy of receiving from them. Frightfully, it appears that even the Lord's heart to forgive is not enough to draw His people back to a right standing with Him. Adam, their first father sinned, and so have all their forefathers since Adam. God raised up "mediators" to mend their broken relationship with their God, but their priests and civic leaders turned their backs on God just as much as the general populace. So then, since they have profaned the name of God, God will "profane" the religious efforts of the priests and princes in their places of worship. Without holiness, without obedience, without devotion to God, all religious effort is "profane," it is "defiled" (HCS). Those who maintain that all religions are good must take notice. Those who refuse to come to God to forgive them of their sins will find that they have doomed themselves "to the curse." "Yes, all Israel has transgressed Your law, and has departed so as not to obey Your voice; therefore the curse and the oath written in the Law of Moses the servant of God have been poured out on us, because we have sinned against Him" (Daniel 9:11). Sin stands ready to curse. God stands ready to forgive. Let all thinking men choose their path accordingly.

Isaiah 44

44:1-5
"Yet hear now, O Jacob My servant, and Israel whom I have chosen. Thus says the LORD who made you and formed you from the womb, who will help you: 'Fear not, O Jacob My servant; and you, Jeshurun, whom I have chosen. For I will pour water on him who is thirsty, and floods on the dry ground; I will pour My Spirit on your descendants, and My blessing on your offspring; they will spring up among the grass like willows by the watercourses.' One will say, 'I am the LORD's'; another will call himself by the name of Jacob; another will write with his hand, 'The LORD's,' and name himself by the name of Israel."

    Could anyone rightly ask for a surer promise of greater blessings than what the Lord gives His people here? God reminds us that He has formed His children from the womb, and He has "chosen" them to be His own. We are twice His — both formed by and chosen by the Creator of all things. We might have good cause to fear His attention. He is holy; we are not. He is faithful; we are not. Yet He tells us to "Fear not." It is our Lord's loving intention to pour out on us His Spirit and heap out on us His blessings, even though rejection and punishment might seem more likely. He calls His people "Jacob" and "Jeshurun," "whom I have chosen." Psalms 135:4 says, "The LORD has chosen Jacob for Himself, Israel for His special treasure." We marvel over every facet of our Lord's willingness to choose Jacob (and choose us) to be His own. We marvel that God calls Jacob His "special treasure," when we see next to nothing that is "special" about him. We marvel that He chooses to pour out His blessings on His people, when (we) have done so little to deserve them. And we marvel that He calls His people "Jeshurun," meaning: "Upright One," being reminded of the joy of God's imputed righteousness when we had no righteousness of our own.

God's promise to His people extends not simply for the duration of their life, but to "your offspring" and to "your descendants." What a comfort to know that when we cannot be with our children, our Lord promises that His Spirit will never leave their side. Our ability to bless and nurture our children is limited. Our ability to provide for and instruct our grandchildren is even more limited. And our ability to inspire and protect distant generations is limited indeed. But we need not fear for them. Our wonderful Lord has promised that "I will pour My Spirit on your descendants, and My blessing on your offspring." God promises the presence of His Spirit and the provision of His blessings for the children and the children's children of those that He has called to be His own. What a precious hope.

The hope is so precious that God's people rightly rush to declare their allegiance to Him. One raises his hand above the crowd and shouts out "I am the LORD's"! Another proudly declares "I am a son of Jacob"! And another writes the simple declaration with pen on paper: "the LORD's," and seals his declaration of dependence with his signature, affirming for all to see that He has been adopted by God and has taken for himself "the name of Israel" as His family name.

What a pleasant picture. God calls His people to Himself. He makes them precious and upright in His sight. He pours out His Spirit and blessings upon them. And in response, His people happily, delightedly, exuberantly declare their allegiance to Him. May our family embody this picture forever.

44:6
Thus says the LORD, the King of Israel, and his Redeemer, the LORD of hosts: "I am the First and I am the Last; besides Me there is no God."

In Revelation 22:13 Jesus says the same thing: "I am the Alpha and the Omega, the Beginning and the End, the First and the Last." Being eternal, the first and the last, gives God unparalleled understanding. He sees the start and end of every life. He sees the rise and fall of every power. He sees the origins of all religions – and He sees that He has no rival. "Besides Me there is no God." This is the great theme flowing through chapters 43-46. In 43:11 He said, "I, even I, am the LORD, and besides Me there is no savior." And He will repeat this message in the next two chapters as well. There are not multiple paths to heaven. There are not multiple gods that can rescue men and women from hell. There is only one God who made the world and only one God who will judge the world. The world is full of gods made of plastic, wood, and precious metals. But only our Creator is "the First" and "the Last." He was there, He saw the day when every idol was made from scratch. He knows that although they are worshipped, they are not God. He was the One who set the sun in its place. He knows that although primitive peoples worship it, the sun is not God. He was there, He read the minds of the men who created gods and religions from the fluff in their own imaginations – He knows that made-up gods are not God. God is the ultimate authority on the matter. He is the First. He is the Last. He preceded the inception and manufacture of all other things that are called gods. His declaration is infallible. There is no other God besides Him. The first commandment He gave to Moses remains essential for everyone to submit to today: "You shall have no other gods before Me" (Exodus 20:3). We must not honor other gods, because there is no other God besides our Creator. The point is not open for debate. All men must either accept the truth or reject it – though rejecting it disregards the testimony of eternal God and dooms their own soul.

44:7-8
And who can proclaim as I do? Then let him declare it and set it in order for Me, since I appointed the ancient people. And the things that are coming and shall come, let them show these to them. Do not fear, nor be afraid; have I not told you from that time, and declared it? You are My witnesses. Is there a God besides Me? Indeed there is no other Rock; I know not one.

God declared in verse 6 that He alone is God, and here He gives evidence for His point. No other so-called god can "proclaim" the future as He can. No other god can set "in order" future events as God has done since He first "appointed the ancient people" – since He first created ancient Adam, forewarned and protected ancient Noah, chose ancient Abraham to be His own, and sheltered ancient Israel as His own special people. We need not "fear, nor be afraid" of the jeers of unbelievers nor fear the wrath of other gods. God took care of His people in "ancient" times, and He will take care of us as well. Time is like rain. It clears the air of false claims and melts the disguise of pretended greatness. Time proves idols to be fake gods and proves religions to be false hopes. But God is like a Rock. He stands immovable, unchangeable, and dependable when the storms of life and winds of doubting beat against Him. Psalms 18:31 asks, "For who is God, except the LORD? And who is a rock, except our God?" Psalms 62:2 says, "He only is my rock and my salvation; He is my defense; I shall not be greatly moved." And Psalms 62:7 adds, "In God is my salvation and my glory; the rock of my strength, and my refuge, is in God." God is our Rock. He is unfailingly dependable. We can stand on His promises. We can rely on His strength. We can base our career, our life's priorities, and our future on Him and know that we will never be disappointed. Our ability to completely depend on Him with absolute confidence moves us to join in the song of Psalms 18:46, "The LORD lives! Blessed be my Rock! Let the God of my salvation be exalted." God is a Rock. "Indeed there is no other Rock" but He. He, and He alone is worthy of our praise.

44:9-11
Those who make an image, all of them are useless, and their precious things shall not profit; they are their own witnesses; they neither see nor know, that they may be ashamed. Who would form a god or mold an image that profits him nothing? Surely all his companions would be ashamed; and the workmen, they are mere men. Let them all be gathered together, let them stand up; yet they shall fear, they shall be ashamed together.

The NLT's rendering of verse 10 is clear, "Who but a fool would make his own god – an idol that cannot help him one bit!" The point is plain. Idols are man-made images of self-imagined gods. "All of them are useless." "They shall not profit" the people who worship them. As he writes, Isaiah is surrounded by idol worshippers – and you can feel his shock and bewilderment at the absurdity of it all. "Who would do such a thing?" Who would mold a metal image that "profits him nothing?" Who would pray to a statue that cannot hear their prayers and cannot move a muscle to help them? What rational human being could think that this was an intelligent thing to do? If they would just consider their actions, surely all of them "would be ashamed." Indeed, the day is coming when "they shall all be ashamed together." The sight of God's people abasing themselves by worshipping inanimate statues and images was stunning and appalling to Isaiah, and the sight of the whole kingdom of Thailand continuing to do so today has a similar effect on me. We cry over the ridiculousness and vanity of it all. We groan over the shame of it all. And we fear, knowing that if they will not repent of this God-despising, conscience-scorning act of idol-worship, certain doom for their soul awaits. "They worshiped their idols, and this led to their downfall" (Psalms 106:36 NLT).

44:12-17

The blacksmith with the tongs works one in the coals, fashions it with hammers, and works it with the strength of his arms. Even so, he is hungry, and his strength fails; he drinks no water and is faint. The craftsman stretches out his rule, he marks one out with chalk; he fashions it with a plane, he marks it out with the compass, and makes it like the figure of a man, according to the beauty of a man, that it may remain in the house. He cuts down cedars for himself, and takes the cypress and the oak; he secures it for himself among the trees of the forest. He plants a pine, and the rain nourishes it. Then it shall be for a man to burn, for he will take some of it and warm himself; yes, he kindles it and bakes bread; indeed he makes a god and worships it; he makes it a carved image, and falls down to it. He burns half of it in the fire; with this half he eats meat; he roasts a roast, and is satisfied. He even warms himself and says, "Ah! I am warm. I have seen the fire." And the rest of it he makes into a god, his carved image. He falls down before it and worships it, prays to it and says, "Deliver me, for you are my god!"

With the hope of turning his early readers from the error of their ways, Isaiah walks through the process of god-making. A blacksmith hammers out an idol with the strength in his own (mortal) arms, after a craftsman designs it "according to the beauty of a (mortal) man." The makers and designers of the idols are not special. They are mortal men. The materials in the idol are nothing special. They are made from trees that a mortal man cut down "himself," after choosing it "himself" from among the many trees in the forest. Neither is the process for making an idol anything special. A man melts the metal and forms the image from simple fire that is also used to warm his skin and bake a roast. There is nothing supernatural about an idol. Idols are made by ordinary people, they are made by ordinary materials, and fashioned by an ordinary process. There is nothing extraordinary about them. Nothing! The only extraordinary thing about the matter is the spiritual insanity of the worshiper, who sees this inanimate image, made by ordinary men by ordinary means, and yet "falls down before it and worships it, prays to it and says, 'Deliver me, for you are my god!'" How can rational human beings still worship idols in our modern day? We are bewildered it. Can they not see that "Their idols are merely things of silver and gold, shaped by human hands"? (Psalms 135:15 NLT). David uses strong language in Psalms 31:6 to say, "I hate those who worship worthless idols. I trust in the LORD." His words are strong, but we can understand his emotional response. We are rightly moved to anger when we see a man leave his wife and children for the sake of an illicit lover – and so we would be right to be similarly angered by idol worship, seeing that "love of idols was adultery in the LORD's sight" (Psalms 106:39 NLT). We are further appropriately moved to an emotional response seeing people in this day and age insisting on attaching extraordinary powers to ordinary images that were created by ordinary people from ordinary materials in ordinary ways. May the Lord use us to inspire all idol worshipers to "trust in the LORD," rather than in "worthless idols," for idol worship is an affront to our Creator, an insult to our spiritual sensibilities, and an offense to the intelligence of man.

44:18-20
They do not know nor understand; for He has shut their eyes, so that they cannot see, and their hearts, so that they cannot understand. And no one considers in his heart, nor is there knowledge nor understanding to say, "I have burned half of it in the fire, yes, I have also baked bread on its coals; I have roasted meat and eaten it; and shall I make the rest of it an abomination? Shall I fall down before a block of wood?" He feeds on ashes; a deceived heart has turned him aside; and he cannot deliver his soul, nor say, "Is there not a lie in my right hand?"

People in Isaiah's day and in ours who worship idols fail to "understand." They have no "insight" (HCS), they never stop to "reflect" (NLT), ...they have no "discernment" (ESV). No matter how you translate Isaiah's words, the meaning is clear, idol worship is not an acceptable religious choice. People must abandon the instructions given them by both their conscience and their brain before they will kneel before a lifeless image in worship. The Lord grants no leniency for those who worship their household idol even if their family has been taught to do so for generations. Though the truth may be shrouded in those families who have worshiped idols for thousands of years, God still maintains that when they pick up an idol, everyone should recognize that there is "a lie in my right hand."

An idol worshipper "feeds on ashes." No one in their right mind would eat ashes. It would be a vain hope to try to nourish oneself with ashes.

So the idol worshipper indulges in a vain effort when he prays to a lifeless image. An idol cannot nourish his soul, nor can it answer his desperate prayers. Hosea 12:1 says "Ephraim feeds on the wind." They had placed their faith in men rather than God, and in so doing "he daily increases lies and desolation." We are engaged in a noble effort when we seek to turn people from the worship of idols and so protect them from the lies and desolation that inflicts those who do so. Bowing to an idol is like eating ashes. It is distasteful, unnourishing, and futile. As Paul does in Athens, let us first be "provoked" to action at the sight of idol worship (Acts 17:16), and then let us "reason" with them (Acts 17:17) that we might help them stop eating ashes and allow them to taste and see that the Lord is so much better in every way.

44:21-23
Remember these, O Jacob, and Israel, for you are My servant; I have formed you, you are My servant; O Israel, you will not be forgotten by Me! I have blotted out, like a thick cloud, your transgressions, and like a cloud, your sins. Return to Me, for I have redeemed you. Sing, O heavens, for the LORD has done it! Shout, you lower parts of the earth; break forth into singing, you mountains, O forest, and every tree in it! For the LORD has redeemed Jacob, and glorified Himself in Israel.

Jesus is "the light of the world." He shines brightly before our spiritual eyes to show us the way to heaven and show us the way to righteous living on earth. But sin is like a cloud, "like a thick cloud" that blinds our eyes to His glories and truths like black clouds block out the sun's rays. Sinners are not allowed into heaven; sinners are condemned to hell. It would stand to reason, then, that no one would dare to sin! But sinners stay sinners because sin is like a cloud, "like a thick cloud." Sin blinds our eyes to the light of the truth of the final outcome of our sin, and prevents us from feeling the warmth of the Son's love drawing us back to a right relationship with Him. Blessedly, we see the Lord's intention to dispel the clouds that darken men's souls. Though we have sinned, He will not forget His people. Through Jesus' death on the cross and resurrection from the tomb, He has redeemed us to God, and our redemption dissipates the clouds of sin that darken our way. When we could not save ourselves, indeed, even when we could not see that we needed a Savior, God redeemed us at great cost to Himself. The sight of such a great salvation – the sight of the clouds of sin being rolled away and the sight of the light of the Lord that brings salvation to man shining brightly upon His redeemed people moves heaven and earth to sing God's praise! The heavens sing! The caverns of the earth shout! The mountains and forests – even "every tree" in the forest are moved to sing and shout their praise to the Lord on high because He has "redeemed Jacob" and "glorified Himself in Israel." Romans 8:22-23 says that "the whole creation groans" in anticipation of and in longing for the redemption of mankind. And here, we see how "the whole creation" rejoices when the redemption of man is carried out. God's people are "redeemed" and God Himself is "glorified." These are the two great works that stir creation to cry out its praise – the salvation of men's souls and the Creator and Savior of man being glorified. "The whole creation" longs for, groans for, and erupts in praise for the Creator, when these great resolutions of God are fulfilled.

44:24-28
Thus says the LORD, your Redeemer, and He who formed you from the womb: "I am the LORD, who makes all things, Who stretches out the heavens all alone, Who spreads abroad the earth by Myself; Who frustrates the signs of the babblers, and drives diviners mad; Who turns wise men backward, and makes their knowledge foolishness; Who confirms the word of His servant, and performs the counsel of His messengers; Who says to Jerusalem, 'You shall be inhabited,' to the cities of Judah, 'You shall be built,' and I will raise up her waste places; Who says to the deep, 'Be dry! And I will dry up your rivers'; Who says of Cyrus, 'He is My shepherd, and he shall perform all My pleasure, saying to Jerusalem, "You shall be built," and to the temple, "Your foundation shall be laid."'"

God began the chapter presenting the weaknesses of idols. He now ends the chapter introducing himself. The disparity between the insufficiency of idols and the all-sufficiency of God is striking. Idols are helpless to generate anything. They depend on men to bring them into existence. In contrast, God is the One who formed us from the womb. He created the world; He created the order of its existence. He created the design for man to "be fruitful and multiply" (Genesis 1:28), and He created the ability of the womb to generate successive generations. Our God is our "Redeemer." He made us, we belonged to Him, but then we sold ourselves to sin and were estranged from Him because of it. Idols are powerless to convey their worshippers into their presence. But God is our Redeemer, He made us, then bought us with His own blood, and then brought us back to His good graces. Idols cannot even stretch their arms out from their sides without help, but God "stretches out the heavens all alone." The earth "spreads abroad" before Him, like a woman spreads out a tablecloth before her at the family meal. Before the omniscience of God, idol worshippers look like "babblers," unable to utter a single logical reason for the lunacy of their religious preference. "Diviners," those who look for Divine messages from ungodly sources, appear "mad" when they turn their backs on God's clear communication of His truths for the sake of allegiance to idols which cannot speak. God's truth "turns wise men backward" and makes the knowledge of educated doubters look "foolish."   Jeremiah 8:9 says, "The wise men are ashamed, they are dismayed and taken. Behold, they have rejected the word of the LORD; so what wisdom do they have?"

While idols sit silently behind their advocates, God speaks to the hearts of men and women, confirming the words of the testimony of His witnesses. And as a great example, God here foretells the destruction of the temple and the banishment of His people into "waste places." Then, with startling detail, God foretells the rebuilding of His temple and the reentry of His people into Jerusalem and the "cities of Judah." God's intention is to prove Himself infinitely superior to the abilities of idols, so He declares <u>by name</u> the "shepherd" who will perform all that God commands him and carry out God's plan to rebuild His nation. "Cyrus, He is My shepherd." Who could imagine that 150 years later the shepherd-servant of the Lord would prove to be a pagan king?

God is the Lord of all! He formed us, redeemed us, created the galaxies, speaks truth, and forms the future just as He formed the planets. In Isaiah 46:9 God says, "I am God, and there is no other; I am God, and there is none like Me." We read here God's 1 sentence, 5 verse introduction of Himself and find ourselves completely convinced.

Isaiah 45

45:1-3
Thus says the LORD to His anointed, to Cyrus, whose right hand I have held – to subdue nations before him and loose the armor of kings, to open before him the double doors, so that the gates will not be shut: "I will go before you and make the crooked places straight; I will break in pieces the gates of bronze and cut the bars of iron. I will give you the treasures of darkness and hidden riches of secret places, that you may know that I, the LORD, who call you by your name, am the God of Israel."

    One hundred fifty years before Cyrus comes to power in Persia, God calls him by his name and foretells His intention to bless him. When we read in Ezra all that Cyrus does to help God's people and beautify God's temple, we can easily see how these verses here would inspire him to do so. God will move his parents to give Cyrus his name, God will bring him to power and give him his reign, God will bless his military efforts so that he conquers his enemies with ease, and God will give him the treasures of the earth that were "hidden" from others, all so that Cyrus will know that God is the Lord, and that He is "the God of Israel." Why does God do what He does? It is a commonly, mistakenly believed notion that God's function in the universe is to make us happy. Making us happy is not God's prime directive. His desire is to see the peoples of the world come to know that He is God. God's purpose and motivation for naming, blessing, and predestining Cyrus' actions remain the same purpose and motivation which guide His actions in our lives today. Before his grandparents were even born, God gave Cyrus his name, God blessed Cyrus' efforts, and God moved Cyrus to bless His people, all so that "you may know that I, the LORD, who call you by your name, am the God of Israel." Though we cannot see Him with our eyes, it is God's desire for all of us to know who He is. God parted the waters of the Red Sea so that "the Egyptians may know that I am the LORD" (Exodus 14:4). God destroyed Ammon so that they "shall know that I am the LORD" (Ezekiel 25:7); He destroyed Moab so that "they shall know that I am the LORD" (Ezekiel 25:11); He destroyed Philistia so that "they shall know that I am the LORD" (Ezekiel 25:17). And in Ezekiel 39:7, God defeats the armies of Gog and Magog so that "the nations shall know that I am the LORD, the Holy One in Israel." It is God's desire for the world to know who He is and yield to Him His due honor. This is critical for our understanding because it helps cure us of the childlike foolishness that thinks that God exists to make us happy. It is not God's prime directive to make us happy. It is His desire that we know Him, relate rightly with Him, and honor Him. This understanding also helps fuel a proper motivation within us to make our life's great priority the same as His eternal priority – to see that the nations of the world know who He is. This understanding will help us abandon the comforts of home and follow our Lord's leading to the ends of the earth so that we can do everything in our power to see to it that everyone, everywhere may know that He is God.

45:4-7

For Jacob My servant's sake, and Israel My elect, I have even called you by your name; I have named you, though you have not known Me. I am the LORD, and there is no other; there is no God besides Me. I will gird you, though you have not known Me, that they may know from the rising of the sun to its setting that there is none besides Me. I am the LORD, and there is no other; I form the light and create darkness, I make peace and create calamity; I, the LORD, do all these things.

Three times in these 4 verses God declares that there is no other God besides Him. He will repeat the message again in the verses to come. We do not worship one god among many. We do not say that God is a good god to choose from. We bear testimony to the plain teaching of our Creator that He is the Lord and there is no other; He is God and there is no God besides Him. Peace and calamity await His orders before approaching anyone. Light and darkness are at His beck and call. No one can darken the eyes of those that God enlightens. No one can bring turmoil to the soul of those granted God's peace. God has no rivals that offer people a comparable spiritual enrichment package. He alone holds the keys to heaven and the keys to hell (Revelation 1:18). He alone is Creator. He alone is Redeemer. He alone is Judge. He decides what is right and what is wrong. He is God and there is no other god besides Him. "Among the gods there is none like You, O Lord; nor are there any works like Your works" (Psalms 86:8). We can boldly call people to repent of their former religious efforts and turn wholeheartedly to God, for we are not calling them to simply change religions – which is filled with frightening prospects. We are inviting them to embrace the truth and embrace their Creator – the only God there is.

45:8
Rain down, you heavens, from above, and let the skies pour down righteousness; let the earth open, let them bring forth salvation, and let righteousness spring up together. I, the LORD, have created it.

The beauty of God's provision for man is seen from heaven's eyes. The men and women of the earth are prone to sin. God did not create puppets, He created people – and those people are horribly prone to mar God's creation with rebellion and wickedness. But it is God's good pleasure to wash away our sin and to "pour down righteousness." What an uplifting picture. God's righteousness poured out on sin-prone men and women. In kindness, God blesses us. In kindness, He pours out His righteousness upon us so that each of His children "shall receive blessing from the LORD, and righteousness from the God of his salvation" (Psalms 24:5). Like rain washes pollution from the air, so God pours out His righteousness, washing sin from His people. And as trees and grass spring up from the earth in response to the rain, so salvation springs up from the earth in response to God's showers of righteousness. This picture in nature is pleasing to the eyes of men, and this picture in the spiritual realm is pleasing to the eyes of God who invites salvation and righteousness to "spring up together." God created the heavens that bring rain as well as the earth that receives that rain; and God created the means by which His righteousness rains down on man, and the salvation that we receive from His hand. What a beautiful picture. Righteousness and salvation springing up together across the earth. The picture is beautiful, and God has unveiled it for all to enjoy: "The LORD has made known His salvation; His righteousness He has revealed in the sight of the nations" (Psalms 98:2). And once enjoyed, it is our happy duty to direct the eyes of the world to this portrait of God's plan. "My mouth shall tell of Your righteousness and Your salvation all the day, for I do not know their limits" (Psalms 71:15).

45:9-10
Woe to him who strives with his Maker! Let the potsherd strive with the potsherds of the earth! Shall the clay say to him who forms it, "What are you making?" Or shall your handiwork say, "He has no hands"? Woe to him who says to his father, "What are you begetting?" Or to the woman, "What have you brought forth?"

Man is foolishly prone to argue with his Maker. Like Habakkuk questioned God in Habakkuk 1:14, and as Job questioned Him in Job 3:11, men are prone to misuse their opportunity to commune with God, by voicing their dissatisfaction with Him. The same opportunity provided us to know God and to praise God also allows us to quarrel with Him. But "woe to him who strives with his Maker." In Habakkuk and Job's cases, their humble and hurting inquiries were met with patiently loving responses from the Lord, but only bad outcomes can be imagined for those who hurl insulting arguments at their Creator. The very thought of arguing with God is ludicrous. Only a fool refuses to believe in God (Psalms 53:1), but only a fool destined for rebuke "strives with his Maker." Men who throw out complaints against God are like broken pieces of pottery that think they are more insightful than the potter. The disparity between the power and discernment of a broken pot and its creative potter is directly compared to the disparity between the power and discernment of people and their Creator. Those who question why God would make them sick, why God would allow them to fail, why God allows them to be disadvantaged – all these questions arise from cracked pots who should know better. Those who cast aspersions on God as they blame Him for wars, untimely deaths of loved ones, and all manner of painful life occurrences are simply voicing the complaints of so many cracked pots displeased with their Maker. Pain and sorrow can elicit pleas for understanding even from God's choicest saints, as Job and Habakkuk show, but even if pain moves us to ask God questions, we must choose the thoughts of our heart and words of our tongue very carefully, for men will never have ample reason to voice disrespect for God. If we are prone, like most all men, to say wrong things when we are injured, then let us take great care to say very little when we are in pain. "Do not be rash with your mouth, and let not your heart utter anything hastily before God. For God is in heaven, and you on earth; therefore let your words be few" (Ecclesiastes 5:2).

45:11-13
Thus says the LORD, the Holy One of Israel, and his Maker: "Ask Me of things to come concerning My sons; and concerning the work of My hands, you command Me. I have made the earth, and created man on it. I – My hands – stretched out the heavens, and all their host I have commanded. I have raised him up in righteousness, and I will direct all his ways; he shall build My city and let My exiles go free, not for price nor reward," says the LORD of hosts.

The thought of God calling Cyrus by name 150 years before he was born and ordaining that he would restore God's people to their homeland and work to reinstate God-directed worship in Jerusalem is all so fantastic that it would seem to defy imagination – except that we are reminded that God is the one who "made the earth." He is the one who "created man on it." By His own hands he "stretched out the heavens" and His voice commands the starry host. Given the omnipotence of God displayed in His creation of the universe, His ability to foretell, yes, His ability to control the future no longer appears so unusual. God created the world, and He tends to it and sustains it to this day. In like manner also, God formed Israel and called the nation to be His own "special possession" (Malachi 3:17, HCS), and it would stand to reason that He would tend to His people and sustain them just as He safeguards the earth. Cyrus will "build (God's) city," and he will "let (the Lord's) exiles go free," he will support God's people in rebuilding their homeland and worshipping their Lord – and he will do so without "price nor reward," without any financial incentive. In fact, he will give of his resources to support the effort to repatriate God's people and restore worship in Jerusalem (Ezra 1:1-4). God will raise up a pagan king and give him a heart to reign in "righteousness." God will "direct all his ways" so that Cyrus' reign is certain to accomplish His will. God will direct the hand of an unbelieving king to carry out His purposes for His people. And so that we will not miss the miracle, He foretells it in writing 150 years in advance. Remarkable.

What needs do we have today? We find a personal invitation in God's words, "Ask Me." What could we ever need that He cannot provide? He holds the hearts of kings in His hands. He holds the future and the expanse of the heavens in those hands as well. What need could we have that He cannot easily provide? We find God's reminder to us here of His creation of the cosmos and His control of an ancient king to be delightfully reassuring to us today.

45:14
Thus says the LORD: "The labor of Egypt and merchandise of Cush and of the Sabeans, men of stature, shall come over to you, and they shall be yours; they shall walk behind you, they shall come over in chains; and they shall bow down to you. They will make supplication to you, saying, 'Surely God is in you, and there is no other; there is no other God.'"

People cannot see God. Remarkably however, people can see God in His children. And His children's longing to draw near to their God will move onlookers to seek the fellowship and good graces of God's people. "Surely God is in you." They cannot see God, but they can clearly tell that God dwells in the midst of those who love Him. "And there is no other; there is no other God." Our devotion to our Savior and His devotion to us provides such palpable evidence of His Supremacy that even without seeing the Spirit of God, His presence is made obvious to all who would pay attention. Our verse here specifically discusses Egypt's response to God's hand on His people. David prophesied the same thing: "Envoys will come out of Egypt; Ethiopia will quickly stretch out her hands to God" (Psalms 68:31). But this truth extends far beyond Egypt to encompass every nation on earth. Zechariah 8:22-23 says, "'Yes, many peoples and strong nations shall come to seek the LORD of hosts in Jerusalem, and to pray before the LORD.' Thus says the LORD of hosts: 'In those days ten men from every language of the nations shall grasp the sleeve of a Jewish man, saying, "Let us go with you, for we have heard that God is with you."'" God lives with those who love Him, and this moves insightful people to seek the company of God's people. Oh, may our Lord be seen clearly in us! And when people seek our company, may they be blessed by their own encounter with our Savior and add their voices to ours in affirmation that "Surely God is in you, and there is no other; there is no other God!"

45:15
Truly You are God, who hide Yourself, O God of Israel, the Savior!

"Truly You are God, who hide Yourself." God hid Himself from the Gentile world for thousands of years, His "mystery" was "hidden from ages and from generations" until it was finally "revealed to His saints" (Colossians 1:26). Though we might wonder why God would hide His glories from us,

Jesus found cause to rejoice in this character of God, praising the Father in Luke 10:21 – "I thank You Father, Lord of heaven and earth, that You have hidden these things from the wise and prudent and revealed them to babes. Even so, Father, for so it seemed good in Your sight." It has seemed good in our Father's sight to "hide" Himself. One day, Jesus will appear in the clouds, the earth's end will come, and God's glory will be fully revealed. But that day has not yet come. Today, in many ways, our Lord remains hidden. Our Lord and His kingdom of heaven "is like treasure *hidden* in a field, which a man found and hid; and for joy over it he goes and sells all that he has and buys that field" (Matthew 13:44). God's greatest blessing for mankind is the opportunity to find Him, to know Him, to know His favor and see His smile of approval. These blessings are not given to the profane, the proud, or those who persist in unbelief, but those who seek Him will find Him when they seek Him with all their heart (Jeremiah 29:13). With this verse before us, let us rejoice that we have found God, our Savior. We have not found something obvious to all and so of little value to all. We have not found a wooden god like so much common driftwood on the shore. We did not stumble upon a clever religion as if tripping over a root in the forest. No, we have found God, our Savior, hidden to many, but precious, such a precious treasure to us. In Revelation 2:17, Jesus says that if His people will overcome, He will give then "some of the hidden manna to eat." "Truly, You are God who hide Yourself." But just as truly, in great mercy, He grants His people the joy of discovering His treasures and tasting His manna and finding our Savior-God, if we will overcome the distractions of the world and seek Him with all our heart.

45:16-17
They shall be ashamed and also disgraced, all of them; they shall go in confusion together, who are makers of idols. But Israel shall be saved by the LORD with an everlasting salvation; you shall not be ashamed or disgraced forever and ever.

Idol worshippers and idol makers will be in "confusion" in life and will be "ashamed" and "disgraced" when Judgment Day comes upon them. People are disgraced when secret shameful acts are finally brought to light, and that is the case for those who trust in idols. When the glory and power of God is revealed at Judgment, their shameful faith in inanimate idols will be their disgrace. They will be ashamed and humiliated. In contrast, those who trust in the Lord will be rewarded with an "everlasting salvation." Their dependence on God will save them from death and save them from hell and grant them a home in heaven "forever and ever." Victories are usually temporary. Winning today, in no way guarantees victory tomorrow. Rescues are usually temporary. Those cured of disease today, are prone to illness soon enough; and those rescued from danger today, are likely to face other dangers soon enough. But God's salvation for His people lasts forever. It is "an everlasting salvation." We will never be ashamed of our choice to follow Him. We will never be disgraced by His rescue of our soul.

45:18-19
For thus says the LORD, Who created the heavens, Who is God, Who formed the earth and made it, Who has established it, Who did not create it in vain, Who formed it to be inhabited: "I am the LORD, and there is no other. I have not spoken in secret, in a dark place of the earth; I did not say to the seed of Jacob, 'Seek Me in vain'; I, the LORD, speak righteousness, I declare things that are right."

The Lord is hidden from the eyes of unbelievers (verse 15), but His voice rings loud and clear for all to hear. Though He is a God who "hide(s) Himself" from the proud and profane, He will guide those who seek Him with clear directions, for He has "not spoken in secret." His voice calls us to Himself, directing our steps and comforting us in our service to Him, "for He will speak peace to His people and to His saints" (Psalms 85:8). When we are burdened by our weaknesses, our hearts find courage because "He has declared to His people the power of His works" (Psalms 111:6). Those in every nation who look for a Savior are blessed to know that God does not just speak where He is already well known: "You have declared Your strength among the peoples" (Psalms 77:14). Our Lord speaks to us! He declares to us His intentions and His commandments so that we will know how to please Him and how we can be best blessed. He did not create the world "in vain." He created all things for His glory – and all things will, indeed, eventually, give Him His due honor (verse 23). He has declared that no one will "seek Me in vain." He has promised that those who seek Him will find Him, and He guarantees that theirs will not be a vain pursuit. God has formed the earth "to be inhabited," and He declares the "things that are right" so that the inhabitants might live as He intends. Praise the Lord, when the voice of all our comforters falls silent, God still speaks peace. When we fear we have lost our way, His voice calls us home. And though the voices of false religion and deceitful counsel make an awful din in the world, they cannot drown Him out, for the voice of the LORD is powerful; the voice of the LORD is full of majesty" (Psalms 29:4).

ISAIAH 45

45:20-22
Assemble yourselves and come; draw near together, you who have escaped from the nations. They have no knowledge, who carry the wood of their carved image, and pray to a god that cannot save. Tell and bring forth your case; yes, let them take counsel together. Who has declared this from ancient time? Who has told it from that time? Have not I, the LORD? And there is no other God besides Me, a just God and a Savior; there is none besides Me. Look to Me, and be saved, all you ends of the earth! For I am God, and there is no other.

Three times! Three times in rapid succession God repeats His declaration: "I am God, *and there is no other!*" In verse 5 He said it, in verse 6 He says it twice! And here God says it for the 4th, 5th, and 6th time in this chapter alone. There is no other God in the universe. No one has the right to make up a new god, and anyone who puts his faith in another god is depending on a lie. God declares the matter very clearly and says it over and over for emphasis, so we can be confident when we pass His truth on to others – even though they may be distressed or offended by the news. No matter how many people deny this claim, and no matter how many eons they have being denying it, this is the truth that our Creator declares, "I am God, and there is no other." The missionary imperative can hardly be missed. We must expend all possible effort for the sake of the great multitudes who do not know the only God there is. Those who depend on any god other than the God who is speaking in these verses "forsake their own mercy" (Jonah 2:8). Let us lovingly, firmly, confidently relay this message to everyone who will listen.

45:23-25
I have sworn by Myself; the word has gone out of My mouth in righteousness, and shall not return, that to Me every knee shall bow, every tongue shall take an oath, he shall say, "Surely in the LORD I have righteousness and strength. To Him men shall come, and all shall be ashamed who are incensed against Him. In the LORD all the descendants of Israel shall be justified, and shall glory."

We find here the famous line twice quoted by Paul (Philippians 2:10-11 and Romans 14:11): "to Me every knee shall bow, every tongue shall swear allegiance" (ESV). On Judgment Day, all of us that love the Lord will bow before Him, worship Him, and rejoice that we belong to Him. And on that same day, all of those who reject Him will bow before Him just the same. We will rejoice at the sight of our Lord's exaltation, but "the wicked will see it and be grieved; he will gnash his teeth and melt away" (Psalms 112:10). The unbelievers will lament their life that gave God no honor and they will curse their self-deceit that turned a blind eye toward God. But they will defy Him no longer, they will deny Him no longer, and no longer will they defend their lack of faith. They will join us and bow before the Lord and at last "be ashamed" that they were once "incensed against Him." On that day, we who love our Lord will rejoice to see that all our devotion to Him was well placed. Our faith and sacrifice and service to our Creator will all be "justified" and we "shall glory" in the presence of our Savior-God. Those who gave God no glory in life, however, will join us in bowing before the Lord, but the honor they finally yield to God will bring them no personal joy. They will be "grieved." They will "gnash (their) teeth and melt away." But they will, indeed, bow before God and give Him His due honor. God has declared it, He has sworn it with an oath, "I will be exalted among the nations, I will be exalted in the earth!" (Psalms 46:10).

Isaiah 46

46:1-2
Bel bows down, Nebo stoops; their idols were on the beasts and on the cattle. Your carriages were heavily loaded, a burden to the weary beast. They stoop, they bow down together; they could not deliver the burden, but have themselves gone into captivity.

Before Babylon even rises as a power, God here declares their end, and the end of Bel and Nebo, their national gods. It appears that the people liked putting those names into the names of their children, because Daniel and Jeremiah mention a number of people named after these gods: Belteshazzar, Belshazzar, Nebuchadnezzar, and Nebuzaradan to name a few. These gods provided names for their people, but they provided little else. They were a burden on man and beast. They could not deliver their people from their enemies – they couldn't even deliver them from the burden of having to carry them. While others bow before their idols, Isaiah says that Bel bows and Nebo stoops. Their lack of power and lack of ability to deliver their people is a humiliation.

46:3-4
Listen to Me, O house of Jacob, and all the remnant of the house of Israel, who have been upheld by Me from birth, who have been carried from the womb: even to your old age, I am He, and even to gray hairs I will carry you! I have made, and I will bear; even I will carry, and will deliver you.

In contrast to the gods of Babylon that had to be carried, God carries His people. From the womb to the days when our hair turns gray, our Lord carries those He loves. "By You I have been upheld from birth; You are He who took me out of my mother's womb. My praise shall be continually of You" (Psalms 71:6). Our Lord will bear us up when days are heavy. Psalms 91:11-12 says, "For He shall give His angels charge over you, to keep you in all your ways. In their hands they shall bear you up, lest you dash your foot against a stone." False gods and Pharisees (Matthew 23:4) are a burden on their people, but our Lord bears us up, protecting us, bolstering our courage, and holding our heart in His hands when we are hurting. Our Lord bears us up in hardship to "deliver" us from trials, and He was once offered to bear our sins on Calvary to deliver us from death and Hell and grant us His salvation (Hebrews 9:28). God promises to deliver His people, and even Nebo's namesake Nebuchadnezzar was forced to profess that "there is no other God who can deliver like this" (Daniel 3:29).

46:5-7
To whom will you liken Me, and make Me equal and compare Me, that we should be alike? They lavish gold out of the bag, and weigh silver on the scales; they hire a goldsmith, and he makes it a god; they prostrate themselves, yes, they worship. They bear it on the shoulder, they carry it and set it in its place, and it stands; from its place it shall not move. Though one cries out to it, yet it cannot answer nor save him out of his trouble.

The omnipotence and omnipresence of God is compared to Bel and Nebo, Babylon's stationary gods. A craftsman takes gold out of a bag and makes a statue – and foolish people then bow before it or carry it on their shoulder to put it in a place of (supposed) honor. But from that place, it will never move. It cannot walk, cannot speak, "cannot answer nor save" those who pray to it. In what way can Babylon's gods, or any god compare to God our Creator? Once Bel and Nebo are set in place, they "shall not move." In contrast, God moves mountains and islands out of their places (Revelation 6:14). In contrast, our Lord moves the prophets of men to write of the great things of God (II Peter 1:21). And in stark contrast to the stone-faced demeanor of Babylon's idols, our Lord is moved with compassion to shepherd the "weary and scattered" (9:36). He is moved with compassion to heal the sick (Matthew 14:14). He is moved with compassion to forgive our debt (Matthew 18:27). In contrast, He is moved by compassion to cleanse us (Mark 1:41); and moved with compassion, our Lord is willing to teach us many things (Mark 6:34). Idols cannot move; but our God moves mountains, He moves prophets, and He is moved by compassion to care for us in so many ways. Who can compare to the Lord our God?

46:8
Remember this, and show yourselves men; recall to mind, O you transgressors.

"Remember this." Remember that no one compares to God. Remember that God moves among us with power and compassion to move mountains, move prophets, and take care of His people. When we remember all that God has done and all that He has done for us, and remember that there is no other God besides Him, our anticipated response to the greatness of God is to "show yourselves men." Interesting. The godly response to our Lord's glory is for us to be manly. Seeing the omnipotence of our Lord moves us to rise up and use all the strength in our arms, and all the strength in our back to take care of our family, take care of the needy, and protect those in danger. Remembering the greatness of God moves us to be courageous when facing the uncertainties that beset us, and inspire others to take courage as well. Remember God! Show yourselves men! This is the battle cry of our verse before us. David's last words to His son, Solomon, reflect the meaning here. On His deathbed, David charged his son saying, "I go the way of all the earth; be strong, therefore, and prove yourself a man" (I Kings 2:2). We are made in the image of God (Genesis 1:27), so in some respects, it should not surprise us that to be truly manly is to be truly godly. One gender is not capable of reflecting all the glories of God, so in I Thessalonians 2:7 Paul says that he and the godly men with him were like women, "we were gentle among you, just as a nursing mother cherishes her own children." Being truly feminine is godly. Being truly masculine is godly. Isaiah's words here remind us of the masculinity of godly men and women. We brush off challenges as minor hurdles, we carry the weak in our arms, we do not shirk from danger, we do not quit in the face of failures or criticism. We fight injustice and we take care of our own. We strive to be men, real men with nerves of steel and endurance that has no end – because we "remember this," we remember our Lord's words in verse 9 to follow,

"I am God, and there is no other; I am God, and there is none like Me." Remembering this makes us want to show ourselves men.

46:9
Remember the former things of old, for I am God, and there is no other; I am God, and there is none like Me,

Our Creator has made His point well. In Isaiah 42:8 God says, "I am the LORD, that is My name; and My glory I will not give to another. In 43:11 He says, "I, even I, am the LORD, and besides Me there is no savior." He repeats in 44:6 "I am the First and I am the Last; besides Me there is no God." In 45:5 He says it again, "I am the LORD, and there is no other; there is no God besides Me." In 45:22 the same message is stated with power again, "Look to Me, and be saved, all you ends of the earth! For I am God, and there is no other." And here, God makes His point once more – "I am God, and there is none like Me." The shame of believing in other gods, the shame of believing that all religions are good cannot be missed with these verses before us. There is only one savior from sin and hell. There is only one Creator. There is salvation in no other name (Acts 4:12), "there is one God and one Mediator between God and men, the Man Christ Jesus, who gave Himself a ransom for all" (I Timothy 2:5). The world desperately needs to know God. There is no other viable replacement. No one can take His place. No one else can take credit for creation, no one else has died for us to take away our sins, no one else is forming heaven for our eternal place to live, and no one else decides our eternal destiny. God alone does all these things, and so we call on all people everywhere to reconcile with Him – the only God there is.

46:10
Declaring the end from the beginning, and from ancient times things that are not yet done, saying, "My counsel shall stand, and I will do all My pleasure,"

Who is like our God who can declare "the end from the beginning"? The book of Revelation describes the end of the world. Peter declares "the end from the beginning as well, saying in II Peter 3:10 -- "the day of the Lord will come as a thief in the night, in which the heavens will pass away with a great noise, and the elements will melt with fervent heat; both the earth and the works that are in it will be burned up." God was there at the beginning of all things. He made the worlds Himself. He will be there at the end, dissolving the earth with the heat of His hands. And He will be with us every moment between these two great cosmic events. Since He started everything, and He will finish everything, He clearly knows how we can best respond to creation and prepare for Revelation. "My counsel shall stand." His counsel on how best to live and how best to be ready for judgment day will stand the test of time and stand the debate of doubters. Let us pay careful attention to His counsel in His scriptures, for in His word we find counsel that will stand throughout the millennia between creation and earth's final day. The world will melt away one day, but God's counsel "shall stand." Let us "bless the LORD" who has given us such (wonderful) counsel on how life should be lived (Psalms 16:7). Psalms 33:11 affirms "The counsel of the LORD stands forever, the plans of His heart to all generations." And Isaiah's words echo here the psalmist's words. God's omniscient perspective, seeing the "end from the beginning" means He clearly sees how men and women should live their lives. Blessedly, He does not keep that insight to Himself. He gives us His counsel. And that counsel will stand. The blameworthy sin of men and women is when they "rebelled against the words of God, and despised the counsel of the Most High" (Psalms 107:11). Without doubt, God "will do all My pleasure." He will bless those who please Him, and He will judge those who despise His counsel. His handwriting is on the wall before us just as it was for Belshazzar. His counsel is before our mind's eye. Let us obey Him, please Him, and bring Him honor, so that as He does all His pleasure, it will be His pleasure to bless us as we kneel before Him in adoration.

46:11-13
Calling a bird of prey from the east, the man who executes My counsel, from a far country. Indeed I have spoken it; I will also bring it to pass. I have purposed it; I will also do it. Listen to Me, you stubborn-hearted, who are far from righteousness: I bring My righteousness near, it shall not be far off; My salvation shall not linger. And I will place salvation in Zion, for Israel My glory.

Cyrus' banner was a golden eagle on a spear, and so it is not difficult to connect this description with God's plans to use Cyrus to 'execute His counsel.' Cyrus, God's "bird of prey," was "from a far country," but he was flying swiftly to rescue God's people. For the humble and obedient, God's promise of salvation and rescue was very dear. But for the "stubborn-hearted" and those who were "far from righteousness," God's promise was a warning. The Lord guarantees that salvation is coming. Though their benefactor, Cyrus, lives far away, God will certainly use Him to take care of

His people and "place salvation in Zion." "I have spoken it; I will also bring it to pass. I have purposed it; I will also do it." Salvation, God promises, is certainly coming. "My salvation shall not linger." At the same time, however, God's righteousness and judgment stand even nearer than their coming salvation! The people cannot live in unrighteousness and await God's salvation. If they think to live apart from Him in disobedience, His righteous judgment will fall upon them before His salvation arrives. The message is just as essential today as it was in the days of Isaiah's early readers. We cannot think that we can live unrighteous lives and expect God's salvation to come to us speedily. God saves. He will bring salvation to His people like a bird of prey swooping in from afar with rescue in his wings. It is comforting for the obedient to think of God's salvation flying to us on eagle's wings. It should, however, strike fear in the hearts of the stubborn-hearted and disobedient to see God's promise to also "bring My righteousness near" as well. Salvation is flying to the obedient. But God's righteous judgment is standing at the door of the disobedient. Let us forget neither picture.

Isaiah 47

47:1-3
Come down and sit in the dust, O virgin daughter of Babylon; sit on the ground without a throne, O daughter of the Chaldeans! For you shall no more be called tender and delicate. Take the millstones and grind meal. Remove your veil, take off the skirt, uncover the thigh, pass through the rivers. Your nakedness shall be uncovered, yes, your shame will be seen; I will take vengeance, and I will not arbitrate with a man.

Through Isaiah, God foretold the rise of Babylon and Judah's eventual captivity there (Isaiah 39:5-7); and through Isaiah here again, God foretells Babylon's fall. Babylon is called a "virgin daughter" because she had never been conquered and seemed impregnable. But her glory will be removed and her "tender and delicate" features will be lost. She will be removed from her throne and forced to "sit in the dust." Her servants will leave her, and she will be required to "grind meal" with a millstone like a common laborer. Her extravagant dresses will be stripped from her and she will expose her nakedness to the common eye as she wades across rivers in her attempt to flee. When God arises to "take vengeance" on her sinfulness, her "shame will be seen."

Though the prophecy is against Babylon, the wider application is easily seen. Peter refers to Rome as Babylon in I Peter 5:13, and Revelation 14:8 refers to Babylon as the "great city" that moves all the nations of the earth to rebel against God. So, although the prophecy certainly applies to Cyrus' conquest of Babylon in 539 BC, it also applies to the fall of other evil empires, and to the fall of evil man in general as well. Babylon's shame and nakedness will be revealed – and so will the shame and nakedness of all who rebel against God. "There is no creature hidden from His sight, but all things are naked and open to the eyes of Him to whom we must give account" (Hebrews 4:13). No sinner is too insignificant that his sin is hidden from God's eyes, and no evil empire is so powerful that it can overcome God's judgment. Sin against the commands of God's voice in our conscience is considered open rebellion by our Creator, and He will "take vengeance" on all who traitorously rebel against His call for holiness and faithfulness. God does not bargain. He calls us, yes He commands us to give Him honor (Psalms 46:10) and live in holiness (Leviticus 11:44), and He vows to "take vengeance" on all who fail to do so.

47:4
As for our Redeemer, the LORD of hosts is His name, the Holy One of Israel.

The gods of Babylon could not help them. The gods of all Creator-rejecters will fail to deliver them from the stain and shame of sin. In striking contrast, however, "our Redeemer" will save our soul. He will save us from the shame of trusting in false gods and false hopes. Blessedly, He is available to all! He is not just the God of a small Middle East nation – "the LORD of hosts" is His name. But neither does He answer to any and every reference to generic or personal deity preferences. Not all religions lead to God. He does not consider all requests and appeals made to personal gods to be directed toward Him. He is "the Holy One of Israel," and requests for salvation made to any other home-made god will fail to evoke the mercy of the only Redeemer available to save our souls from the eternal consequences of sin.

47:5-7
Sit in silence, and go into darkness, O daughter of the Chaldeans; for you shall no longer be called the Lady of Kingdoms. I was angry with

ISAIAH 47

My people; I have profaned My inheritance, and given them into your hand. You showed them no mercy; on the elderly you laid your yoke very heavily. And you said, "I shall be a lady forever," so that you did not take these things to heart, nor remember the latter end of them.

Babylon presumed that she would be "a lady forever." The foolish notion that we will be beautiful forever, desirable by all and forever, that we will be successful forever and bask in comfort forever is a foolhardy, evil belief. Of all people, Babylon should have known better. They were shown plainly that the result of Israel's rebellion against God led to their utter ruin. Daniel will even tell Babylon and her king how to avoid God's judgment. In Daniel 4:25-27, Daniel pleads with Babylon's King Nebuchadnezzar to not forget that "Heaven rules." "The Most High rules in the kingdom of men." All men are accountable to Him and will suffer eternal consequences if they do not live a life that pleases Him. Daniel counsels the king to "break off your sins by being righteous, and your iniquities by showing mercy to the poor." Babylon was gifted with Daniel's godly counsel, they were gifted with the opportunity to be eye-witnesses to what happens to people and nations when they reject God. But though they were granted such remarkable advantages, they "did not take these things to heart." They refused to "remember the latter end of them," that is they did not consider the outcome of a life separated from God – even though they saw the terrible consequences of sin right before their eyes. We must "remember" the lessons that our Lord teaches us. We must! As children are not permitted to forget their parents' instructions, so we are not allowed to forget what God commands and what God has allowed us to experience. Let us learn from Babylon's fall and remember God's commands, giving all possible devotion to carrying them out. God promises everlasting mercy "to those who remember His commandments to do them" (Psalms 103:18). We find great comfort in remembering the great words and great works of God. David wrote in Psalms 119:52 - "I remembered Your judgments of old, O LORD, and have comforted myself." Troubles are common, and our life on earth is most likely to give us heartaches. These trials and heartaches have been encountered by God's people since Adam and Eve lost their home in the garden and then lost their two sons in the aftermath. But the answer to life's trials and heartaches today is still the same as it was for God's people in ancient Israel when "they remembered that God was their rock, and the Most High God their Redeemer" (Psalms 78:35). Babylon fell when they failed to "remember" what God had taught them. Let us encourage people in our day not to make the same mistake.

47:8-9

Therefore hear this now, you who are given to pleasures, who dwell securely, who say in your heart, "I am, and there is no one else besides me; I shall not sit as a widow, nor shall I know the loss of children"; but these two things shall come to you in a moment, in one day: the loss of children, and widowhood. They shall come upon you in their fullness because of the multitude of your sorceries, for the great abundance of your enchantments.

Babylon's blasphemy that will doom their kingdom to destruction is in line 2, but we are struck by the prelude to their unforgiveable sacrilege that is found in line 1 – "Hear this now, you who are given to pleasures." Those who are a "lover of pleasures" (ESV) are called upon to take heed. May we take heed as well. When our attention is directed at pleasure seeking, we have become a people "given to pleasures." When the burdens of caring for Christ's church are a lesser priority than personal entertainment, we risk being viewed from heaven as a people "given to pleasures." Contemplating Isaiah's line here is sobering. We who are God's people are rightly repulsed by evil, but we are much less likely to be repulsed by the prospect of pleasure. Psalms 16:11 describes the godly man's greatest joy: "You will show me the path of life; in Your presence is fullness of joy; at Your right hand are pleasures forevermore." God's presence brings us unending pleasure. But when we are distracted from that pleasure for the sake of other pleasures, we place ourselves at great risk. The pursuit of pleasure can hardly be labelled an evil endeavor, and yet the danger of pleasure-basking and leisure-seeking is clearly seen, for the seemingly immediate attitude emanating from the pursuit of pleasure is articulated in the blasphemous, condemning statement that shortly follows, "I am, and there is no one else besides me." We review again that in Isaiah 43:11 God clearly states, "I, even I, am the LORD, and besides Me there is no savior." In 44:6 God says, "I am the First and I am the Last; besides Me there is no God." In 45:5 He says, "I am the LORD, and there is no other; there is no God besides Me." In 45:22 God says, "Look to Me, and be saved, all you ends of the earth! For I am God, and there is no other." And in 46:9 He says once more, "I am God, and there is no other; I am God, and there is none like Me." Yet after all of these declarations from God, after all His proofs from heaven, from His creation, and from our conscience – after all these statements of fact, facts of nature, and conscience-born affirmations of this truth, the people of Babylon denied that He alone is God, and declared, instead, that they themselves were the only thing that mattered – that they themselves were God! We are horrified by the deep, sinister, evil pride that would cause a thinking rational human being to say such nonsense – such blasphemous, condemning nonsense. What could deceive intelligent people into saying such wickedly stupid stuff? <u>Pleasure seeking</u>. When we revel in pleasure, we soon live for pleasure, and soon assume that our purpose is to seek pleasure, and that our personal pleasure is to be the foundation for all our life's investments. This self-centeredness sooner or later evolves to Self-centeredness and declares that no one has the right to interfere with our pursuit of pleasure, for there is no greater purpose for living that to enjoy physical pleasures, for there is no greater Being whose pleasures should take precedence over our own.

The height of man's greatest evil is displayed before us – creatures declaring their supremacy over their Creator. And the root of that foulest of evils is staggering. Those who are "given to pleasures" are soon given to blasphemy. At God's right hand are "pleasures forevermore." Let us hold all other pleasures very loosely.

47:10-11

For you have trusted in your wickedness; you have said, "No one sees me"; your wisdom and your knowledge have warped you; and you have said in your heart, "I am, and there is no one else besides me." Therefore evil shall come upon you; you shall not know from where it arises. And trouble shall fall upon you; you will not be able to put it off. And desolation shall come upon you suddenly, which you shall not know.

Intelligence is a gift from God. God "has put wisdom in the mind" of man (Job 38:36). Tragically, man often misuses His God-given intelligence and is "warped" by his intellect rather than blessed by it. Here, Babylon's collective wisdom is condemned because God saw that their warped understanding "led (them) astray" (ESV). The power of their mind and spiritual understanding allowed them to see that God exists. Tragically however, that understanding was warped and degraded into the mis-notion that they were that God and that "there is no one else (that matters) besides me." Without Holy God to whom we must give an account, people will naturally degrade themselves into the belief that if it feels good, it is good, and that it is their privilege to pursue whatever unholy passion their degraded mind now comes up with. The sinful, "warped" mind deceitfully claims that there is no Holy God that "sees me," "there is no one else besides me" whose opinion matters. The Lord here denounces Babylon for holding this belief, which has moved them to "have trusted in your wickedness." That is, they trusted that their wicked ways would offend no one of consequence and that wickedness that led to personal pleasure was actually something to be preferred. This trust in wickedness and this belief that we are God is a terrible perversion of knowledge – and the Lord holds those who hold these views accountable for how they have "warped" their God-given intellect into self-serving, self-aggrandizing pursuits of evil. He warns here that those who pursue evil and trust that evil has no consequence will suffer the frightening prospect that "evil shall come upon you." "Evil," and "trouble," and "desolation" are the lot of those who thought that they could sin without repercussion.

David writes Psalm 52 in response to the evil of Doeg the Edomite, who believed that evil betrayal of a godly man would somehow bring him personal benefit. David's words to Doeg echo Isaiah's words to Babylon: "Why do you boast in evil, O mighty man? The goodness of God endures continually. Your tongue devises destruction, like a sharp razor, working deceitfully. You love evil more than good, lying rather than speaking righteousness. You love all devouring words, you deceitful tongue. God shall likewise destroy you forever; He shall take you away, and pluck you out of your dwelling place, and uproot you from the land of the living. Selah. The righteous also shall see and fear, and shall laugh at him, saying, 'Here is the man who did not make God his strength, but trusted in the abundance of his riches, and strengthened himself in his wickedness.' But I am like a green olive tree in the house of God; I trust in the mercy of God forever and ever. I will praise You forever, because You have done it; and in the presence of Your saints I will wait on Your name, for it is good" (Psalms 52:1-9).

47:12-15
Stand now with your enchantments and the multitude of your sorceries, in which you have labored from your youth – perhaps you will be able to profit, perhaps you will prevail. You are wearied in the multitude of your counsels; let now the astrologers, the stargazers, and the monthly prognosticators stand up and save you from what shall come upon you. Behold, they shall be as stubble, the fire shall burn them; they shall not deliver themselves from the power of the flame; it shall not be a coal to be warmed by, nor a fire to sit before! Thus shall they be to you with whom you have labored, your merchants from your youth; they shall wander each one to his quarter. No one shall save you.

Having pronounced His judgment on the people of wicked Babylon, God here challenges them to defy His judgments as best they can. Sorcery and astrology have been the foundation of their counsels to this point. These things appeared to be satisfactory counsellors as long as circumstances were favorable. But now, God's judgment draws near and these ungodly counsellors will be like "stubble." "The fire shall burn them." God's judgment will burn away everything that men mistakenly trust in. These enchanters, stargazers, and unholy consultants will die out, and all who trust in them will suffer the same fate. "No one shall save you." If God does not save us from death and hell and pointless living, there is no replacement. No one else can save a soul. No one else can save us from the stain on our soul that sin creates. Babylon's own Nebuchadnezzar recognized this truth, saying in Daniel 3:29 – "There is no other God who can deliver like this." Those apart from God will one day all face the truth that "no one"—none of their chosen replacements for God -- can save us from sin and hell. In contrast, our abiding peace is carried with the confidence that our God saves. "As for me, I will call upon God, and the LORD shall save me" (Psalms 55:16). "Though I walk in the midst of trouble, You will revive me; You will stretch out Your hand against the wrath of my enemies, and Your right hand will save me" (Psalms 138:7). And Proverbs 20:22 provides the wonderful promise: "Wait for the LORD, and He will save you." God saves. Only God saves. All who join Babylon in rejecting God and trusting in anyone or anything else will find verse 15 to be devastatingly applicable to them: "no one shall save you."

Isaiah 48

48:1-2
Hear this, O house of Jacob, who are called by the name of Israel, and have come forth from the wellsprings of Judah; who swear by the name of the LORD, and make mention of the God of Israel, but not in truth or in righteousness; for they call themselves after the holy city, and lean on the God of Israel; the LORD of hosts is His name:

    What a blessing to be called by God's name, to bear the name "Christian," or as in this case, the "house of Jacob," "called by the name of Israel." What a remarkable blessing to be considered a part of the family of God! What a remarkable privilege it is to be able to "lean on the God of Israel" when trials come, and our way is unclear. Ah, we strain to adequately describe the honor and the opportunity that is ours to be allowed into God's family and gain access to His unbounding grace in time of need.

    This unrivaled privilege however, is accompanied by nonnegotiable requirements. If we claim to be children of God, but do not walk with Him "in truth or in righteousness," our relationship with Him is a pretended one, and our right to claim access to His blessings is null and void. We must walk with God "in truth." God is seeking those who will worship Him in truth (John 4:23). "God is Spirit, and those who worship Him must worship in spirit and truth" (John 4:24). God's people are condemned here for not worshipping in truth. They claimed to be His children, but also believed the lie that idols could help them too. We cannot be right with God and believe lies about Him. We cannot be right with God and promote the lie that other religions and other gods are viable alternatives.

Also, if we are to be right with God, we must worship Him "in righteousness." We cannot claim to be His children, we cannot claim access to His blessings and yet persist in sin. We must guard our personal holiness at all costs! Proper worship of our Creator is reliant on personal righteousness. But when the beauty of the Lord is worshipped in the beauty of holiness, men and women are allowed to encounter the very highest experience attainable by mortal man. David invites us to join in this epic privilege! "Give unto the LORD the glory due to His name; worship the LORD in the beauty of holiness" (Psalms 29:2). And Psalms 96:9 gives the same invitation: "Oh, worship the LORD in the beauty of holiness! Tremble before Him, all the earth." Let us rejoice that we are called children of the living God. And let us respond well to that privilege, worshipping our Lord in truth and in the beauty of righteousness.

48:3-5
I have declared the former things from the beginning; they went forth from My mouth, and I caused them to hear it. Suddenly I did them, and they came to pass. Because I knew that you were obstinate, and your neck was an iron sinew, and your brow bronze, even from the beginning I have declared it to you; before it came to pass I proclaimed it to you, lest you should say, "My idol has done them, and my carved image and my molded image have commanded them."

Knowing that His people are "obstinate," stiff necked, and hard-headed, the Lord makes His power plain through prophecy. People are very prone to missing the most essential truths that are imperative for us to understand. God is omnipotent, omniscient, omnipresent, holy and loving. We must understand that since God is omnipotent, He can take care of all our needs and He can lower punishment and judgment on all who defy Him. Since God is omniscient, His counsel from His word is infallible, applicable, and certain to bless us if we will obey Him and trust Him. Since He is omnipresent, we can pray to Him wherever we are, He can provide for us no matter where we are, and no sin of any dimension escapes His observation, no matter where we are. Since He is holy, we are commanded to be holy just the same. All unholiness on our part will separate us from God and open us up to His judgment, but since He is loving, He has provided a way -- one single opportunity – that will allow us to escape the punishment that sin demands and restore for us a right relationship with Him. All these things are essential for us to understand if we are to live rightly and eternally with fulfillment and joy. As essential as these truths are however, God's people (to say nothing of those who rebel against Him), are prone to missing it all! The world is prone to missing who God is, what power He wields, and the glorious holiness and love that make up His character. In order to help His people <u>not</u> miss these essential truths, God tells us the future in advance. He declares from "the beginning" what will happen "before it came to pass." He tells of the rise and fall of Babylon generations in advance here in Isaiah's book. He declares the rise of David as king years in advance in I Samuel 16. And He declares the end of the Syrian siege a day in advance in II Kings 7. God's advance warnings and advance promises pervade His messages throughout His communications to man – and He does this so that everyone will know that He is God. Events and dynasties, blessings and judgments come upon man by His design and for His purposes. No other god can mold the future to their design as God can, so no other god should be revered at any level – because God's ability to foretell and control the future plainly displays evidence that He alone is worthy of our total devotion.

This is the plainly stated purpose for God declaring the future and fulfilling His declarations before the eyes of men – so that no one will be tempted to give other gods the glory and honor and trust that only God is worthy to receive.

48:6-8
You have heard; see all this. And will you not declare it? I have made you hear new things from this time, even hidden things, and you did not know them. They are created now and not from the beginning; and before this day you have not heard them, lest you should say, "Of course I knew them." Surely you did not hear, surely you did not know; surely from long ago your ear was not opened. For I knew that you would deal very treacherously, and were called a transgressor from the womb.

God declares the future for the benefit of His people. Those who trust Him will use His prophecies to fill themselves with hope and guide their preparations for events to come. Apart from God's omniscience, however, the future is absolutely unpredictable. No one can predict what the world will be like in 100 years – and what the world will look like in 1000 years is laughably unknowable. The unpredictability of the future is an intentional invention of God designed to prevent wicked men from proudly saying "Of course I knew" that would happen! The inability to know the future apart from God's revelation is designed to spur men to seek the One who fashions the future with His hands. If the future was predictable, God knew that men would deal "very treacherously" with Him – they would take credit for matters that were ordained by and established by God alone. The tendency to take credit for the exploits of others, and feel pride in oneself over the merits of others, begins very early in life. Give a toy to a toddler and observe how quickly he claims ownership over that which he received from others due to no merit of his own. Such is the tendency of men and women to claim to know what tomorrow holds and claim to possess the power to decree how best to prepare for it. This tendency to claim to hold ownership over the future is the sin of the rich man in Luke 12:19, and this sin, along with all other sinful tendencies, begins in us very early. In fact, God says that each of us, by nature, is "a transgressor from the womb." Psalms 58:3 says, "The wicked are estranged from the womb; they go astray as soon as they are born, speaking lies." We are devastatingly prone to sin and unbelief right from our mother's womb. But we are reminded here again, of the kindness of God which communicates to both the spirit of man and the intelligence of man to help us overcome our sinful tendencies. The future appears unknowable – yet God knows it and declares it for the benefit of His people and to disclose His glorious power. Let all rational men and women refuse to give in to our inclination to transgress from the womb, and turn for inspiration, instruction, and revelation to the One who sees "the hidden things" of the future and declares them to all who would pay attention.

48:9-11
For My name's sake I will defer My anger, and for My praise I will restrain it from you, so that I do not cut you off. Behold, I have refined you, but not as silver; I have tested you in the furnace of affliction. For My own sake, for My own sake, I will do it; for how should My name be profaned? And I will not give My glory to another.

God will not allow His name to be profaned by being associated with evil people. Neither will God allow His name to be profaned by evil people claiming that He executes His own children. So then, in defense of His own name, He neither tolerates sin in His children, nor does He execute all His saints who are prone to sin. Instead, He has "refined" His people "in the furnace of affliction" so that sin might be removed, and their souls might not forever be separated from their Savior. We are not worthy of His refining efforts to redeem us. He does this for His name's sake. Knowing this,

Asaph prayed, "Oh, do not remember former iniquities against us! Let Your tender mercies come speedily to meet us, for we have been brought very low. Help us, O God of our salvation, <u>for the glory of Your name</u>; and deliver us, and provide atonement for our sins, <u>for Your name's sake</u>! Why should the nations say, 'Where is their God?'" (Psalms 79:8-10). As dross is removed from silver, God removes sin from His people. "For You, O God, have tested us; You have refined us as silver is refined" (Psalms 66:10). At the same time, however, although the processes have similarities, God's refining of men and the furnace's refinement of silver are not completely the same. God says, "I have refined you, but not as silver." The furnace removes dross from the silver, but it leaves the silver unchanged. In contrast, when God refines us and removes our impurities, He also completely remakes our spiritual chemistry.

We are reminded that the defining and refining of a saint is not a painless process. God refines His people with the "furnace of affliction." Furnaces are hot; afflictions hurt – so the process of making men holy and acceptable to God often involves painful times of affliction. But our comfort is not our Father's prime concern. His glory moves Him to refine us, even though we may be troubled and pained in the process. We must live to give glory to God. He will not allow His glory to be given to anyone else. He will move to assure that His name is honored and His glory upheld, and He will do so, not just by destroying sinners, but by refining saints as well.

48:12-15
Listen to Me, O Jacob, and Israel, My called: I am He, I am the First, I am also the Last. Indeed My hand has laid the foundation of the earth, and My right hand has stretched out the heavens; when I call to them, they stand up together. All of you, assemble yourselves, and hear! Who among them has declared these things? The LORD loves him; He shall do His pleasure on Babylon, and His arm shall be against the Chaldeans. I, even I, have spoken; yes, I have called him, I have brought him, and his way will prosper.

God gives a wonderful message of hope to the people that He has "called." He called His people out of Egypt, He promises through Isaiah that He will call them home from Babylon, and still today we are blessed by the knowledge that our Lord has called us to Himself. II Timothy 1:9 says that He "has saved us and called us with a holy calling, not according to our works, but according to His own purpose and grace which was given to us in Christ Jesus before time began." Remarkably, He has "called us by glory and virtue" (II Peter 1:3) to become "partakers of the divine nature"

(II Peter 1:4). What a precious thought. Our Lord has called us. He has not called us with evil intentions or selfish motives. He has called us by "glory and virtue." He has not called us to a life of leisure or ease or to any special physical pleasantries. He has called us to be "partakers of the divine nature," acting like God, loving like God, caring, teaching, and providing for others just as God does for us. Jacob and Israel were given the blessed privilege of being God's "called." So are we. He has called us to Himself and He will sustain us, providing all that we require. By His hand He "stretched out the heavens," and if He is capable of forming the galaxies, He can certainly provide for us.

Those God loves, He provides for, and here He promises to provide success to the unnamed Cyrus who will carry out His "pleasure" on Babylon and the Chaldeans. God promises when Cyrus comes against Babylon that "his way will prosper." Those God calls will certainly prosper. Psalms 35:27 rings out God's praise saying, "Let the LORD be magnified, who has pleasure in the prosperity of His servant."

48:16-17
Come near to Me, hear this: I have not spoken in secret from the beginning; from the time that it was, I was there. And now the Lord GOD and His Spirit have sent Me. Thus says the LORD, your Redeemer, the Holy One of Israel: "I am the LORD your God, Who teaches you to profit, Who leads you by the way you should go."

God calls us to live sacrificially, to give to those in need, to bear one another's burdens, and to seek the holiness of heaven, not the riches of the earth (Colossians 3:2). At the same time however, our Lord does not call us to a life of poverty, but to a life of "profit." His wisdom and His provisions "are better than the profits of silver, and (better) than fine gold" (Proverbs 3:14). Paul taught God's word, not so that godliness would lead his listeners to hardship and poverty, no, his intent was quite the opposite. In I Corinthians 7:35 he tells his readers: "And this I say for your own profit." The presence of our Savior in our life does not just bring profit to one or two lucky people, I Corinthians 12:7 tells us that "the manifestation of the Spirit is given to each one for the profit of all."

Furthermore, obedience to the Lord does not just help us thrive in a few arenas of life, but in all facets of living that truly matter: "For bodily exercise profits a little, but godliness is profitable for all things, having promise of the life that now is and of that which is to come (I Timothy 4:8). Psalm 1 gives the wholly remarkable assurance of the certain profit that awaits those who walk with God and delight in His words. "Blessed is the man who walks not in the counsel of the ungodly, nor stands in the path of sinners, nor sits in the seat of the scornful; but his delight is in the law of the LORD, and in His law he meditates day and night. He shall be like a tree planted by the rivers of water, that brings forth its fruit in its season, whose leaf also shall not wither; and <u>whatever he does shall prosper</u>." Amazing. Those who "suppose that godliness is a means of gain" are condemned as "men of corrupt minds and destitute of the truth" (I Timothy 6:5). Those who seek personal gain are not invited to find it in Christ, but those who seek to know God, obey God, and flood their minds with His words will find that "godliness with contentment is great gain" (I Timothy 6:6). The wonderful joy of walking with Christ is that we will never travel through life alone, nor will we be required to walk lost and confused through a maze of conflicting directives. God promises us here through the pen of Isaiah that He "leads you by the way you should go." And that way that He will lead us on will always lead "you to profit."

48:18-19
Oh, that you had heeded My commandments! Then your peace would have been like a river, and your righteousness like the waves of the sea. Your descendants also would have been like the sand, and the offspring of your body like the grains of sand; his name would not have been cut off nor destroyed from before Me.

Look at the wonderful results of obeying God's commandments! Those who obey God are granted peace like a river. As a great river's waters are replenished every day from an unending supply, so those who obey God are renewed with fresh peace every morning. Sin tears at our peace. Guilt nags at our nerves, the repercussions of our sin hound our steps and haunt our memory. The fear of punishment plagues the guilty. But those who obey God suffer none of these things. Their peace is unending for their obedience is unceasing.

Those who obey the Lord's commandments are also rewarded with righteousness that is like "the waves of the sea." Those who only listen to the voice of their flesh may be good one day, yet capable of horrible evil the next. They may be caring for a moment, but quickly their virtuous acts will change when personal pleasure takes center stage among their priorities once again. Those who delight in obeying God's commandments are not so. Their righteousness is as constant as the sea. Their good deeds are as endless as the waves on the ocean, for they do not obey God out of compulsion or fear, but because they agree with David in Psalms 119:47 "I will delight myself in Your commandments, which I love."

Following these two great blessings of obedience, the Lord mentions another – the descendants of those who obey God are "like the grains of sand" in number. As our righteous acts multiply, so, too do our descendants. And not only do they multiply, God says that they will be rescued from being "cut off," they will not be "destroyed," for they are under the eternal protection of the One that their righteous forefather obeyed.

God recites the numerous blessings assured those who obey Him, and mourns over His people who refused. "Oh that you had heeded My commandments!" Look at all that you might have had! God has such blessings in store for those who heed His commandments! The Lord's words here indicate that His promise to Jeroboam in I Kings 11:38 differs little from the promise given to all who obey Him: "if you heed all that I command you, walk in My ways, and do what is right in My sight, to keep My statutes and My commandments, as My servant David did, then I will be with you and build for you an enduring house." May our house – our family line – be enduring. May our obedience to the Lord's commandments be unending.

48:20-21

Go forth from Babylon! Flee from the Chaldeans! With a voice of singing, declare, proclaim this, utter it to the end of the earth; say, "The LORD has redeemed His servant Jacob!" And they did not thirst when He led them through the deserts; He caused the waters to flow from the rock for them; He also split the rock, and the waters gushed out.

Chapter 48 ends with the marvelous refrain, "The LORD has redeemed His servant Jacob!" He saved His people with water from the rock when they were dying of thirst in the desert. He saved them from Babylon when they were trapped in captivity there, and still today, we His people, join in rejoicing over the fact that the Lord our God redeems His people. These two examples are given here, but we can think of many more – God redeems our soul "from the power of the grave" (Psalms 49:15). He redeems our soul in peace from the battle that rages against us (Psalms 55:18). Psalms 72:14 says that "He will redeem (our) life from oppression and violence." And Psalms 103:4 says that God "redeems (our) life from destruction." Psalms 106:10 says that He saves us from the hand of those who hate us and redeems us from "the hand of the enemy." And perhaps most precious of all, we are reminded in Psalms 130:8 that "He shall redeem (His people) from all (our) iniquities." God redeems His people. When His people were desperate with thirst, when His people were languishing in captivity, and when they are ensnared in sin today, this is our hope – God redeems. "The LORD redeems the soul of His servants, and none of those who trust in Him shall be condemned" (Psalms 34:22). God redeems our soul from so many dangers, and we are given two great ways to respond to His soul-saving act of redemption. First, since God has redeemed us, brought us out of danger and brought us safe to His side, we must, in response, obey all His commandments. Psalms 119:134 says, "Redeem me from the oppression of man, that I may keep Your precepts." And secondly, in response to our Lord's life-saving acts of redemption, let us praise Him in return. The psalmist rightly responds to God's redeeming love when in Psalms 71:23 he says, "My lips shall greatly rejoice when I sing to You, and my soul, which You have redeemed." Let us obey our God in everything we do, giving our utmost devotion to obeying every edict He makes in His word. And as we obey, let us praise Him. Let us gather together as a church and praise Him, let us gather around our table as a family and praise Him, and let us rise early each morning with just our Savior and us in the room and sing His praise. He is worthy of our obedience. He is worthy of our praise. For He is our Redeemer.

48:22
"There is no peace," says the LORD, "for the wicked."

God gives His people peace. In John 14:27 Jesus says, "Peace I leave with you, My peace I give to you; not as the world gives do I give to you. Let not your heart be troubled, neither let it be afraid." God gives His people peace even when life is full of turmoil. This peace however, is only given to those who obey Him. Interestingly, Paul summarizes the vast intricacies of living on earth for the kingdom of God with three simple concepts. Romans 14:17 says, "...for the kingdom of God is not eating and drinking, but righteousness and peace and joy in the Holy Spirit." In the center of the summary of what it means to live on earth in the favor of God, we find these two matters inseparably intertwined: "righteousness and peace." As written above in the discussion of verse 18, there is no peace for those who disobey God: "Sin tears at our peace. Guilt nags at our nerves, the repercussions of our sin hound our steps and haunt our memory. The fear of punishment plagues the guilty." "There is no peace for the wicked." To the obedient, Christ says, "My peace I give to you." To the wicked, God solemnly warns, "There is no peace."

Isaiah 49

49:1
Listen, O coastlands, to Me, and take heed, you peoples from afar! The LORD has called Me from the womb; from the matrix of My mother He has made mention of My name.

Verse 6 says that this One that "the LORD has called...from the womb" is the One who will give "light to the Gentiles" and bring "salvation to the ends of the earth." We would suspect that this must be speaking of our Savior, and Acts 13:47 and Acts 26:23 confirm for us that these verses do indeed, refer to Jesus. From the womb, Jesus was called to carry out the Father's plan to redeem a lost world to Himself. He was called from the womb, not just Mary's womb, but from the womb of heaven, from the matrix of eternity Jesus was called to the task of redeeming mankind. Before He was born in Bethlehem, God the Father "made mention of (the Son's) name" -- an angel came to Joseph from heaven in Matthew 1:21 and said that his betrothed wife "will bring forth a Son, and you shall call His name JESUS, for He will save His people from their sins."

God needs no spur-of-the-moment plan to save His people. He needs no plan B when His intentions go awry. He has established His means for reconciling a world of lost sinners to Himself, and He desires that no one should be caught unaware and unprepared when His Son arrives to save the world. Here, the Lord calls on all the peoples of the world to pay careful attention to the advent of the Savior's birth. His coming is to fulfill the great plans of God to save the world from sin! His arrival must not be missed! The announcement here is at least partially successful, for in Luke 2 we find Simeon and Anna actively on the lookout for the arrival of the "Consolation of Israel" (Luke 2:25), hundreds of years after Isaiah's call for the nations of the earth to "take heed" and be watchful for the coming of the Lord.

As the people of Isaiah's day were called upon to look forward to the Lord's arrival with anticipation, so we are called upon to look back on the Lord's birth with celebration, and then maintain that same alert anticipation for the day when our Lord returns the second time. Revelation 22:12 spurs us to prepare for Jesus' return just as Isaiah 49:1 spurred His people to prepare for Jesus' birth. "And behold, I am coming quickly, and My reward is with Me, to give to every one according to his work." Jesus is coming! He is Savior to the world, and He carries an eternity of rewards with Him for those who anticipate His arrival. Let us "take heed" as the Lord compelled His hearers to do in Isaiah's day. He is coming soon. Let us work in His church and in His field just as Simeon and Anna did, so that His arrival will find us sharply alert at our posts, demonstrating all possible faithfulness to His purposes, and directing the attentions of everyone around us to prepare for His arrival as well.

49:2
And He has made My mouth like a sharp sword; in the shadow of His hand He has hidden Me, and made Me a polished shaft; in His quiver He has hidden Me.

Before He was born to Mary, Jesus saw Himself as He will be seen by all of us at the end of time. Revelation 1:16 describes the resurrected Jesus standing in glory in heaven, "He had in His right hand seven stars, <u>out of His mouth went a sharp two-edged sword</u>, and His countenance was like the sun shining in its strength." The words of our Lord are like a sword "piercing even to the division of soul and spirit, and of joints and marrow, and is a discerner of the thoughts and intents of the heart" (Hebrews 4:12). Jesus' words burn bright and pure in the hearts of His hearers still today. On the road to Emmaus, two men talked with Jesus as they travelled and were mesmerized by all that He said. They described their time with Jesus this way, "Did not our heart burn within us while He talked with us on the road, and while He opened the Scriptures to us?" (Luke 24:32). The words of our Lord are like a sharp two-edged sword. They cut through our arguments and excuses. They pierce our conscience and cut away all the nonsense we once believed. The words of our Lord are a weapon of war. They bring death to groundless lies and conniving deceits. They protect the weak from doubts and defend the innocent from false teaching. Such are the war-like effects of our Savior's words.

The words of our Lord are like a "sharp sword" and He, Himself, is like a polished arrow, hidden in the Father's quiver. At precisely the right time, the Father will take Him out of Heaven's quiver, and shoot Him straight and true to Bethlehem. Our Lord is sharp; He is piercing; and He is polished. Ezekiel 21:28 says, "A sword, a sword is drawn for the slaughter. It is polished to consume and to flash like lightning" (ESV). Our Lord is a sharpened sword and a polished arrow and these traits of His are ominous. He is "polished to consume." Moses feared the Lord with a holy fear, for he saw what happened to his people when they turned their backs on God: "We have been consumed by Your anger, and by Your wrath we are terrified" (Psalms 90:7). Hebrews 12:29 gives the stern and simple warning: "our God is a consuming fire." The coming of Jesus, the Savior of the world is here foretold! And He is said to be like a weapon when He comes. In Isaiah 53, Jesus' coming will again be foretold. He will be described there as a gentle, praying, healing, wounded lamb. But here, He is described as a sharp sword and a polished arrow. Men in Isaiah's day, in Jesus' day, and in ours, have unceasingly proven themselves prone to rejecting the sovereignty of God and despising His Son who came to remove our sin. Our Father is divinely patient with people on this matter. His Son is a lamb, gentle and wounded for the sake of giving men time to repent and hope for forgiveness. But let there be no mistake, those who fight against the Lamb will find that "God shall shoot at them with an arrow; suddenly they shall be wounded" (Psalms 64:7). Our Lord is a lamb; but He carries weapons of war. Let all thinking men make their peace with the Son of God. For if we war with Him, we cannot win.

49:3-4
And He said to me, "You are My servant, O Israel, in whom I will be glorified." Then I said, "I have labored in vain, I have spent my strength for nothing and in vain; yet surely my just reward is with the LORD, and my work with my God."

Jesus, here called Israel, will glorify the Father. This was His desire from the beginning, and He will not be disappointed. In Jesus, the Father "will be glorified." As Jesus felt His death on the cross was imminent, and His work was soon to be finished, He prayed out loud in John 12:28 -- "Father, glorify Your name." "Then a voice came from heaven, saying, 'I have both glorified it and will glorify it again.'" A few verses later, in that same chapter, Jesus said, "Now the Son of Man is glorified, and God is glorified in Him. If God is glorified in Him, God will also glorify Him in Himself, and glorify Him immediately" (John 13:31-32). The work of the Son would successfully glorify the Father. Tragically, however, it would not bring salvation to all men. The sorrow of seeing men and women reject His provision of salvation moves Jesus to say, "I have labored in vain, I have spent my strength for nothing and in vain." Jesus came to save sinners, but so many sinners refused His salvation. "He came unto his own, and his own received him not" (John 1:11 KJV). Jesus came into the world so "that the world through Him might be saved" (John 3:17) – but even after all of the sacrifice and efforts of our Savior, not everyone in the world will be saved. Even so, Jesus' reward is undiminished. His "reward is with the LORD" and His work is neither overlooked nor unrewarded by the Father.

May our Lord's work inspire us today. Let us devote ourselves fully to the extraordinary effort to see God glorified. So much of what Jesus came to do was thwarted because of unbelief. So many people rejected His lordship and so denied themselves His salvation. But the response of the crowd in no way diminished Christ's effort to glorify the Father. Let us tolerate much that hinders our work, just as Jesus tolerated so much that hindered His. But let us tolerate nothing that hinders this great work of God – to see His name glorified. Our final reward is not based on the success of our various efforts, but on the unquenchable desire of our soul to see God glorified in us. Circumstances, troublesome people, and a host of other matters can hinder every effort of our work on earth -- except the only work that really matters. Let us rise up to praise and serve our Lord and see Him glorified. Our final reward and His pleasure with us now ride solely on this singular concern.

49:5-6
And now the LORD says, Who formed Me from the womb to be His Servant, to bring Jacob back to Him, so that Israel is gathered to Him (For I shall be glorious in the eyes of the LORD, and My God shall be My strength), indeed He says, "It is too small a thing that You should be My Servant to raise up the tribes of Jacob, and to restore the preserved ones of

Israel; I will also give You as a light to the Gentiles, that You should be My salvation to the ends of the earth."

    Jesus was formed from the womb "to bring Jacob back" to the Father. Jesus came to earth so that the nation of Israel might be "gathered" together in right standing with their Creator. From the grand account of God's covenant with Abraham in Genesis we have followed God's supreme efforts to bring salvation to the nation of Israel. We see Him rescue Israel from slavery in Egypt and from difficulties in the desert in the book of Exodus. We watch the Lord rescue His people from one enemy after another in Joshua and Judges. And in Samuel and in the chronicles of the kings we read with great interest of God's good will to establish the kingdom of Israel and the kingdom of Judah, and to bless and defend His people and glorify His own name. God's work to save Israel has seemed to us to be such a grand work! The world degraded itself into idol worship and wicked living, but God saved one nation – He preserved and reserved Israel so that the world might know at least one people that were rescued from sin and maintained a right relationship with their Creator. The rescue and salvation and blessing of Israel! What a great work! And yet now, the magnificent heart of our Father is set on brilliant display for us here. The great work of rescuing Israel – even this marvelous work – is "too small a thing" for our Savior-Son to condescend to carry out. God declares His intention to send His Son to save the world! The world! Jesus will not just come to save a small nation in the Middle East. God says that He will come "to be My salvation to the ends of the earth"!

    The missionary imperative floods forward from our Father's words. Jesus has come to bring "salvation to the ends of the earth!" Let us join Him! It is too small a thing for us to be concerned with our own family's well-being. Let us lift up our eyes and adopt our Father's viewpoint as our own. It is the will of our God to save the world from their sins. May it be our driving desire to carry out His stated will to rescue the peoples of the earth. Paul was driven to his marvelous missionary efforts on the wings of these very words – In Acts 13:47 he quotes Isaiah's words here, "For so the Lord has commanded us: 'I have set you as a light to the Gentiles, that you should be for salvation to the ends of the earth.'" The Father sent the Son into the world so that "the world through Him might be saved" (John 3:17). Saving the nation of Israel, as marvelous as that is, is "too small a thing" for such a magnificent Savior. In John 12:32 Jesus said, "And I, if I be lifted up from the earth, will draw all men unto me." God's desire, the Son's desire is to "draw all men" to know and embrace and be blessed by their Creator. Let us join our God in this work of the ages to draw all men in all nations to the saving knowledge of Christ the Lord.

49:7
Thus says the LORD, the Redeemer of Israel, their Holy One, to Him whom man despises, to Him whom the nation abhors, to the Servant of rulers: "Kings shall see and arise, princes also shall worship, because of the LORD who is faithful, the Holy One of Israel; and He has chosen You."

As a dog bites the hand of the one who feeds it, so mankind "despises," he "abhors" the Holy One, the Redeemer, the only one who can feed and save his soul. Who would tolerate such base treatment from such inferior creatures? When Shimei despises King David in II Samuel 16, Abishai is understandably incensed beyond measure. II Samuel 16:9 says "Then said Abishai the son of Zeruiah unto the king, 'why should this dead dog curse my lord the king? Let me go over, I pray thee, and take off his head.'" When vile men show disrespect for good men, onlookers are moved by natural instinct to find beheading a just response. We are moved to awe however, when we see that this is not our Savior's response to the contempt that men pour out toward Him. Though He is the Savior of man, He is called "the Servant of rulers." Though those He came to save are unworthy of His saving grace, yet He is "faithful" to the task of saving them. Our Savior is faithful, He is Holy, and He has chosen us – and for all these reasons and so many more, ultimately "kings shall see and arise, princes also shall worship" because of these marvelous attributes of our Lord. We worship our Lord and seek to be like Him because He is our "Holy One." We revere Him with uncontainable gratitude, because He is our "Redeemer," bringing us back into right standing with God after our sins had taken us far away. But our love for Him is multiplied a hundred times over when we remember the insults and offences He endured while carrying out His saving acts. God works to save the men and women who despise and abhor the One who came to save them. How can we possibly thank Him adequately?

49:8-10
Thus says the LORD: "In an acceptable time I have heard You, and in the day of salvation I have helped You; I will preserve You and give You as a covenant to the people, to restore the earth, to cause them to inherit the desolate heritages; that You may say to the prisoners, 'Go forth,' to those who are in darkness, 'Show yourselves.' They shall feed along the roads, and their pastures shall be on all desolate heights. They shall neither

hunger nor thirst, neither heat nor sun shall strike them; for he who has mercy on them will lead them, even by the springs of water He will guide them."

Christ the Son came to earth to save the souls of men. His time on earth was filled with sorrow and discomfort. Let us not forget that Jesus' work to redeem us was a painful ordeal. He was not left to face His trials alone, however. When the Son prayed, the Father softly whispered: "I have heard You." When the Son shook beneath the weight of His burden, the Father lifted the weight of His cross and said, "I have helped you." And when Jesus shuddered in the garden as His death drew near, the Father promised, "I will preserve You." All these wonderful pictures of the Father's love for the Son are illustrated here hundreds of years before the Son was even born. The word pictures do not end here, however. The Father's love for His Son will enable the Son to carry out works that will change the world. Filled with the Father's strength, the Son will save countless millions. He will rescue "prisoners" and allow them to "go forth" in the freedom of a soul unbound by sin. He will be the light "to those who are in darkness." Luke 1:79 says that He will "give light to them that sit in darkness and in the shadow of death, to guide our feet into the way of peace" (KJV). John 1:4 says, "In Him was life; and the life was the light of men." In John 8:12 Jesus said, "I am the light of the world. He who follows Me shall not walk in darkness, but have the light of life." And II Corinthians 4:6 says, "For God, who commanded the light to shine out of darkness, hath shined in our hearts, to give the light of the knowledge of the glory of God in the face of Jesus Christ" (KJV). In addition to freeing prisoners and shining in the darkness, Jesus also fed the hungry "along the roads" and "on all the desolate heights." By His Father's uplifting hand, He was able to take His focus off of His own pain and show "mercy" on the needy and "lead them" when they did not know which way to go. When the people become thirsty for fulfillment in life and parched for a word from their Creator, Jesus "will guide them" to "springs of water" that will grant them life and peace that will both last forever. And as our Lord provides all these things, He will shine because the Father sustains Him.

Jesus will be "oppressed" and "afflicted" (Isaiah 53:7), yet with the Father's loving watch care which "heard" our Lord's prayers, "helped" our Lord's efforts, and "preserved" our Lord's well-being, Jesus was able to feed the hungry, have mercy on the needy, free prisoners, shine in the darkness, and "restore the earth" to a right standing with the Creator. Goodness! What remarkable things come to pass when the Father hears prayers, helps

His servants, and preserves the faithful. As we contemplate the great things that the Son was able to do as a result of the great favor shown to Him by the Father, let us humbly be filled with awe, knowing that the Father has promised to do these great things for us as well. He hears our prayers just as He heard His Son's. Psalms 65:2 says, "O You who hear prayer, to You all flesh will come." He helps His servants just as He helped His Son. Luke 1:54 affirms, "He has helped His servant Israel, in remembrance of His mercy." And He preserves the faithful just as He did for Jesus. Psalms 31:23 says, "Oh, love the LORD, all you His saints! For the LORD preserves the faithful." Since, then, our Father has promised to do for us just as He promised to do for Jesus, let us set our sights on carrying out the same works that Jesus did as well. Let us shine in the darkness, show mercy on the needy, feed the hungry, and preach the gospel so that repentance and faith might "restore the earth" to our loving Lord. May this remarkable picture of God's sustaining love for His Son inspire us to imitate the Son's remarkable response to His Father's love, so that we may work to bear fruit as Jesus did -- "Fruit that will last" (John 15:16 NLT).

49:11-12
I will make each of My mountains a road, and My highways shall be elevated. Surely these shall come from afar; Look! Those from the north and the west, and these from the land of Sinim.

Chapter 49 is a prophecy looking forward to the coming of Jesus, the Son of God. He will be "a light to the Gentiles" and bring "salvation to the ends of the earth" (verse 6). Through Jesus, the obstacles that once rose like "mountains" and prohibited people from coming to a saving knowledge of their Creator will be transformed into "a road" that will now carry people to God.

There are many obstacles that stand in the way of men and women coming to God. Poor examples, hard living, distracting dangers, false teachers, deceptive allurements, disappointments, and our constant tendency to sin all loom before us as mountains obscuring the path to God. But Jesus is a road, He is "the way" (John 14:6) through those mountains. The Lord's highways that take people to unity with the Father are "elevated." As an elevated road is safe to travel on even in the midst of severe flooding, so the way of Jesus rises above the floodwaters of life's distracting and painful challenges to grant us a straight, unimpeded pathway to God. Jesus opens the road to salvation! And this superhighway of eternal life is not a one lane country road from Israel alone, it has arteries that bring people in "from the north and the west" and from the obscure far-off land of Sinim. Jesus will usher the peoples of the world to a saving knowledge of the Father. He delights in "bringing many sons to glory" (Hebrews 2:10), and He will bring them on well-lit, well-marked, elevated highways that He has built to provide sure passage for all who crave the presence of God.

49:13
Sing, O heavens! Be joyful, O earth! And break out in singing, O mountains! For the LORD has comforted His people, and will have mercy on His afflicted.

Some people are not very good comforters. Job chided his friends for this, saying, "Miserable comforters are you all!" (Job 16:2). Life is often harsh, people unfair, and loved ones often do not know how to comfort us in our hour of need. Sometimes it is hard to know what to say to someone that is hurting, sometimes our depraved nature moves us to blame victims rather than comfort victims, and sometimes our insensitive nature makes us completely overlook the fact that people near us are hurting. Seeing so many hurting people, and seeing so many poor comforters causes both the heavens and the earth to sing out with a burst of joy when they see that "the LORD has comforted His people, and will have mercy on His afflicted." Pain is a common side effect of living – but Jesus "has comforted His people." The psalmist rejoiced that "You shall increase my greatness, and comfort me on every side" (Psalms 71:21). And Psalms 94:19 says, "In the multitude of my anxieties within me, Your comforts delight my soul." Jesus did not promise a life of leisure, in fact, He promised quite the opposite (John 16:33). But our Lord does promise comfort, even as He promises "tribulation."

Jesus comforts His people, and He "will have mercy on His afflicted." David drew deep comfort in this knowledge praying in Psalms 25:16 - "Turn Yourself to me, and have mercy on me, for I am desolate and afflicted." The world may ignore or even blame the afflicted, but God does not. "For He has not despised nor abhorred the affliction of the afflicted; nor has He hidden His face from Him; but when He cried to Him, He heard" (Psalms 22:24).

Afflictions come. Hardships come. Tragedy strikes. But God comforts His people and shows mercy on His afflicted. Heaven and earth watch God's merciful comforts and they "break out in singing" a "joyful" song of praise. When God's grace fills our day with happiness, let us join the heavens, the earth, and the mountains in singing praises to the Lord for His kindness.

And when troubles rend our heart, let us kneel before Him, expectantly looking to Him for His comfort and His mercy. And as His presence uplifts our soul, let us once again join heaven and earth and the mountains and praise Him for His comfort.

49:14-15
But Zion said, "The LORD has forsaken me, and my Lord has forgotten me." Can a woman forget her nursing child, and not have compassion on the son of her womb? Surely they may forget, yet I will not forget you."

God's love for us is compared to the love of a nursing mother for her newborn baby. A nursing mother cannot possibly forget her child. Even if the child never cried, the physiology of her body will remind her of her child's needs regularly day and night. In similar fashion, our Lord's divine love for us makes it impossible for Him to forget our needs. In the midst of the darkness of unpredictable dilemmas, and while in the throes of seemingly unanswered prayer, God's people may sometimes feel that God has "forgotten" them, that He has "forsaken" them. Even righteous David once prayed, "How long, O LORD? Will You forget me forever? How long will You hide Your face from me? (Psalms 13:1). But this can never be true. Our Lord cannot possibly forget us, He cannot possibly forsake us. "For He Himself has said, 'I will never leave you nor forsake you'" (Hebrews 13:5). Our Lord "does not forget the cry of the humble" (Psalms 9:12). When our eyesight and insight grow dim, when circumstance is so overwhelmingly tragic that we cannot feel the Lord's presence beside us for a moment, let us take heart by what our Lord teaches us here. He is here when we cannot sense Him, He remembers our pain when we cry out our needs to Him. His promise is true even when our feelings are not, "I will not forget you."

49:16-18
See, I have inscribed you on the palms of My hands; your walls are continually before Me. Your sons shall make haste; your destroyers and those who laid you waste shall go away from you. Lift up your eyes, look around and see; all these gather together and come to you. "As I live," says the LORD, "You shall surely clothe yourselves with them all as an ornament, and bind them on you as a bride does."

God's people feared that He had forgotten them (verse 14). Their enemies had defeated them, they lived in fear and danger and disgrace. But God gives His reassurance here that His people are not forgotten. God cannot forget His people (verse 15). He has inscribed our names on the palms of His hands. His hands bear the scars of the nails that hammered home the proof that His love for us is unfailing. The "walls," the protections of His people, are "continually" the focus of our Lord's concern. He is constantly working behind the scenes to take care of His people, even when danger and disgrace appear to take center stage.

Our Lord gives His endangered people His guarantee: Israel's enemies "shall go away from you," but "I will never leave you" (Hebrews 13:5). Israel's enemies will "gather together" adorned and armed with both wealth and weapons, but God promises that just as the four lepers enriched themselves with the silver and gold and clothing of their enemies in II Kings 7, so will all God's people be enriched with the abandoned possessions of their enemies. Let us not be embarrassed when enemies criticize us or even lay us low for a time. We would like to think that obeying God will move everyone to love us, we tend to think that criticism indicates that we are doing something wrong. This is simply not the case. Let us be content to suffer the abuses of enemies who do not love our Lord. In the end, having ungodly enemies will turn out to our honor. Their riches and glory will be given to us as a reward.

49:19-21
For your waste and desolate places, and the land of your destruction, will even now be too small for the inhabitants; and those who swallowed you up will be far away. The children you will have, after you have lost the others, will say again in your ears, "The place is too small for me; give me a place where I may dwell." Then you will say in your heart, "Who has begotten these for me, since I have lost my children and am desolate, a captive, and wandering to and fro? And who has brought these up? There I was, left alone; but these, where were they?"

God restores. The once crowded streets of Jerusalem will become "desolate." The land of "milk and honey" (Numbers 14:8) will become "the land of your destruction." Enemies will be many, children will be few. But God restores. As He restored Job's family and riches in Job 42, so He promises to restore Israel to glory here. God's people will be so blessed that they will wonder out loud, "Where did all these children come from? How did all these blessings come to be mine? They will muse on their past troubles and say to themselves, 'there I was, left all alone...' and then all of a sudden, blessings started springing up from everywhere. Blessings from burdens, beauty from ashes. Goodness! How great are the kindnesses of God who restores that which "you have lost." God restores joy (Psalms 51:12). God restores health (Jeremiah 30:17). God restores lost years (Joel 2:25), and God restores wounded souls (Psalms 23:3). The pain of losing battles, losing health, and losing dignity can drive us to our knees. But God restores. God wonderfully restores. Isaiah's words from long ago still provide great hope for those who suffer loss today.

49:22-23
Thus says the Lord GOD: "Behold, I will lift My hand in an oath to the nations, and set up My standard for the peoples; they shall bring your sons in their arms, and your daughters shall be carried on their shoulders; kings shall be your foster fathers, and their queens your nursing mothers; they shall bow down to you with their faces to the earth, and lick up the dust of your feet. Then you will know that I am the LORD, for they shall not be ashamed who wait for Me."

God moved the Egyptians to give of their possessions to provide for His people on their journey to the Promised Land in Exodus 12:36. God moved Cyrus to carry His sons and daughters to Jerusalem in Ezra chapter 1. And throughout history's past and throughout the future to come, He will continue to call the world's people to care for His children. God will set His banner in the camp of His people and declare that His church is where His presence dwells. His banner will inspire His people to fight for His causes, and will also serve as a rally cry to the world at large to come to the aid of those who are His – so that the blessings that He pours out on His own people may spill over on them as well. God plants His standard – He unfurls His banner in the midst of His people and declares "I will bless those who bless you!" (Genesis 12:3), and all the world's people with good sense for self-advancement will see the Lord's banner and rush to uphold His people. Many will do this with the good intentions of blessing God's people and joining them in honoring the Lord just as the Centurion Cornelius does in Acts chapter 10. Others will do so outside of their own volition, ushered along in their support of God's people by the unseen hands of God's Spirit as does the city clerk of Ephesus in Acts 19. But whether volitionally or not, the Lord will move kings and queens to "foster" good will with His people, to "carry" God's people on their shoulders, to "nurse" them to health, and to "bow" before them in acknowledgement of the presence of God in their midst. God will move the world to aid and honor His people so that everyone everywhere "will know that I am the LORD." Aid for God's people however, is not the end point that God desires. His purpose is that His blessed people will serve as catalysts that will speed the world's willingness to glorify their Creator. His banner is unfurled for the world to see. God reigns! And He reigns in the midst of His people. All who trust in Him, all "who wait for Me" will not be ashamed of their allegiance. God's people will be cared for, the world will know who God is, and at last He will be honored by all the world's peoples when every knee shall bow, and every tongue confesses that Jesus Christ is Lord (Philippians 2:10).

49:24-26
Shall the prey be taken from the mighty, or the captives of the righteous be delivered? But thus says the LORD: "Even the captives of the mighty shall be taken away, and the prey of the terrible be delivered; for I will contend with him who contends with you, and I will save your children. I will feed those who oppress you with their own flesh, and they shall be drunk with their own blood as with sweet wine. All flesh shall know that I, the LORD, am your Savior, and your Redeemer, the Mighty One of Jacob."

A lion will not be deprived of his prey. A prize fighter will not be denied his prize. "To the victor go the spoils" so the old adage says. But here, God promises to reverse that trend. Though Israel has fallen "prey" to their captors, though God's people have become captives of a "mighty" and "terrible" people, God "will contend with him who contends with you" and will deliver His people even from the jaws of a lion-like conqueror. The evil empires of the world which oppress millions, and appear undefeatable, will be overcome by the power of the Lord who seeks to protect His own. God will defeat these enemies by turning them on themselves – feeding, as it were, "on their own flesh" and becoming drunk "with their own blood as with sweet wine." It is interesting and instructive to walk through history and see how often this plan of God for overthrowing evil empires is illustrated. Gideon saw God deliver him from the insurmountable forces of Midian, not by giving him a great army of his own, but because the Midianite army turned on itself: "the Lord set every man's sword against his companion throughout the whole camp (Judges 7:22). King Jehoshaphat saw the Lord deliver him from the combined armies of Ammon, Moab, and Mount Seir, again, not by giving him a powerful army, but by causing Judah's enemies to devour themselves. II Chronicles 20:23 says, "For the people of Ammon and Moab stood up against the inhabitants of Mount Seir to utterly kill and destroy them. And when they had made an end of the inhabitants of Seir, they helped to destroy one another." This means of destroying nations from within did not end in Biblical times. The great empire of the Soviet Union, which appeared indestructible, completely collapsed before the eyes of a shocked world in 1991 without a shot being fired. And most recently, we have seen the nation of Syria completely devastated by civil war. When seemingly all-powerful armies and empires collapse, the weaknesses of man are fully exposed. And when God rescues His people from the conquests of all-powerful armies and empires, His power and protective love are likewise fully exposed, so that "all flesh shall know that I, the LORD, am your Savior, and your Redeemer, the Mighty One of Jacob."

Verse 26 reminds us that God is our "Savior." The great danger of man is failure to recognize that he must be saved and that there is only a single opportunity to gain that salvation. "And we have seen and testify that the Father has sent the Son as Savior of the world" (1 John 4:14). Sin condemns us to hell – but Jesus came to save us from that horrible destiny! The price of saving us is inestimably high, however. It requires a life to save a life. "Without the shedding of blood there is no forgiveness of sins" (Hebrews 9:22). In addition to a Savior, therefore, we need a "Redeemer" as well, One who will buy us back when we sell ourselves to sin (Romans 7:14). Blessedly, our Lord is both our Savior and our Redeemer, for "The LORD redeems the soul of His servants" (Psalms 34:22). But to save us from sin and redeem us from death and hell requires power unimaginable. Our Savior must have power over the grave. He must be able to resurrect us from the dead. Once again, we find our Lord sufficient, for He is Savior, He is Redeemer, and He is "the Mighty One of Jacob." Some would love us enough to try to save us, some are generous enough to willingly try to redeem us, but there is only One who holds the power to redeem lost souls. Praise the Lord, our "Redeemer is mighty" (Proverbs 23:11). Blessedly, our "Redeemer is strong; the LORD of hosts is His name" (Jeremiah 50:34).

Isaiah 50

50:1-3
Thus says the LORD: "Where is the certificate of your mother's divorce, whom I have put away? Or which of My creditors is it to whom I have sold you? For your iniquities you have sold yourselves, and for your transgressions your mother has been put away. Why, when I came, was there no man? Why, when I called, was there none to answer? Is My hand shortened at all that it cannot redeem? Or have I no power to deliver? Indeed with My rebuke I dry up the sea, I make the rivers a wilderness; their fish stink because there is no water, and die of thirst. I clothe the heavens with blackness, and I make sackcloth their covering."

When troubles come, the tendency of men and women is to ask "why." Why did this happen to me? More than 100 years after Isaiah's prophecy, Judah will fall, and the people will be taken captive and exiled to Babylon. The Lord knows that when the suffering of their captivity comes upon them that His people will wonder why He let this happen to them. And here, a century in advance, God answers their future questions by describing 2 factors that were the cause of their troubles, and 2 matters that were not the problem.

The problem was not that God had abandoned His people. He did not divorce them. He did not sell them to a creditor to pay off a debt or sell them as slaves because He was displeased with them. Though Judah had been unfaithful to the Lord, Malachi 3:7 openly voices His invitation: "Return to Me and I will return to you."

Neither did Judah's woes stem from any inability on God's part to save those who belong to Him. God dried up the Red Sea so His people could cross, He covers the skies with clouds. All the natural order of the world – all the natural order of the universe is under His control. God is omnipotent, there is no end to the power He wields over the earth. Judah was not exiled to Babylon because God had disowned them, nor were they suffering because He lacked the power to rescue them. These 2 factors were not the cause of their troubles.

Judah's trouble was caused by 2 serious matters of concern. First, Judah was punished "for your iniquities." They had "sold" themselves to sin and they had been "put away" because of their "transgressions." Let us not blame God for the repercussions of sin. This refrain will soon be repeated in Isaiah 59:1-2, "Behold, the LORD's hand is not shortened, that it cannot save; nor His ear heavy, that it cannot hear. But your iniquities have separated you from your God; and your sins have hidden His face from you, so that He will not hear."

And secondly, Judah's trouble was heightened because when God called to them, they did not answer. He taught them and they did not listen. He commanded them and they did not obey. He offered His protection and they fled from His sheltering wings. It is the height of God's kindnesses that He condescends to speak to men and women, and it is the depth of man's depravity when he refuses to listen. In Matthew 23:34, Jesus promises to "send you prophets, wise men, and scribes" who will communicate His will and expectations. Judah's response to God's communicators however, is reprehensible: "some of them you will kill and crucify, and some of them you will scourge in your synagogues and persecute from city to city." It is God's heart to communicate His love, to protect His people, and to provide for their needs in love. Failure to listen when he speaks however, moves Jesus to say with sorrow "O Jerusalem, Jerusalem, the one who kills the prophets and stones those who are sent to her! How often I wanted to gather your children together, as a hen gathers her chicks under her wings, but you were not willing!" (Matthew 23:37). God speaks to the conscience of man, and men and women are held accountable for how they respond.

ISAIAH 50

"And it shall be that every soul who will not hear that Prophet shall be utterly destroyed from among the people." (Acts 3:23). The people of Judah will be sent off into captivity in Babylon, not because God's power was insufficient to protect them, but because when He spoke, they refused to listen.

50:4
The Lord GOD has given Me the tongue of the learned, that I should know how to speak a word in season to him who is weary. He awakens Me morning by morning, He awakens My ear to hear as the learned.

Isaiah pens the words of Jesus, foretelling the heart of our Lord hundreds of years before He was born in Bethlehem. Jesus credits the Father with giving Him "a word in season to him who is weary." The Gospels will later confirm that the Lord will have a heart to uplift the weary around Him. Matthew 9:36 says that when Jesus "saw the multitudes, He was moved with compassion for them, because they were weary and scattered, like sheep having no shepherd." And in Matthew 11:28 (NLT) Jesus said, "Come to me, all of you who are weary and carry heavy burdens, and I will give you rest." Having the right things to say to people who are weary and struggling with the weight of crisis can be a gift of inestimable worth. Proverbs 25:11 says, "A word fitly spoken is like apples of gold in settings of silver." May the Father grant us "the tongue of the learned" that knows how to encourage the weary with gentle words of comfort when they need them most. In times of crisis, we are prone to turn inward and think only of our own pain and our own needs. Inspired by our Lord's example however, let us seek to be a giver of good words to those around us, even when we feel low ourselves. Proverbs 15:23 (NLT) says, "Everyone enjoys a fitting reply; it is wonderful to say the right thing at the right time!" Let us seek then, to always "say the right thing" as Jesus did, and say it the right way at the right time. For most of us, all of these things are very challenging. Our tongue is not very insightful, we tend to be not very sensitive, and we tend to be consumed with our own troubles not the troubles of others. So then, just as Jesus awakened "morning by morning" to hear from the Father. Let us awaken each day and rush into His presence so that we might be blessed with His words of instruction and comfort -- and then let us go into the world and comfort others as our Lord has comforted us. II Corinthians 1:4 says that God "comforts us in all our tribulation, that we may be able to comfort those who are in any trouble, with the comfort with which we ourselves are comforted by God." Let us listen carefully to all that our Lord says, let us rise early to seek His presence and hear His voice, as our Lord is seen doing in Mark 1:35, so that it might be for us as it was for Christ who rejoiced that the Father "awakens Me morning by morning, He awakens My ear to hear as the learned." What a precious gift – to hear our Savior's voice morning by morning and day by day. If we are to serve Him, if we are to comfort the hurting, and care for the weak, if we are to have wisdom in dark times and answers for those who seek the truth, we must hear from our Lord every day. We must hear Him speak and then rush to tell others what we have heard Him say. This was our Savior's example, and it is our happy privilege to imitate His actions and hear our Father speak in our spiritual ear morning by morning as He awakens us to sit with Him once more.

50:5-6
The Lord GOD has opened My ear; and I was not rebellious, nor did I turn away. I gave My back to those who struck Me, and My cheeks to those who plucked out the beard; I did not hide My face from shame and spitting.

The task that the Father called upon His Son to carry out was incomparably difficult. He must leave His home in heaven, suffer the disgrace of taking on human form, further suffer physical and verbal abuse, and finally, succumb to a torment-filled death – all to rescue the very people that were abusing Him. Despite all this, He did not "turn away." He did not shirk the role of suffering Savior. He was not "rebellious" and run from His calling as Jonah did. He was not "rebellious" and give in to Satan's temptations in the wilderness. He was not "rebellious" and turn back from the Father's purposes in Gethsemane. Jesus was "subject" to His earthly parents (Luke 2:51), and He was subject to His heavenly Father: "He humbled Himself and became obedient to the point of death, even the death of the cross" (Philippians 2:8). Jesus obeyed the Father and carried out His purposes even though the purposes of God meant much physical and emotional suffering. May His example inspire us. Let us never be "rebellious." Let us never "turn away" from the responsibilities designated for us. "The Lord GOD has opened (our) ear"! He has allowed us to hear His words of encouragement and instruction so that we will not lose hope or vision in our quest to serve Him. Our Lord has opened our ears so that we can hear Him speak! What a precious thought. Let us not "turn away" from His words, but rush to hear them, obey them, and pass them on to others.

50:7
For the Lord GOD will help Me; therefore I will not be disgraced; therefore I have set My face like a flint, and I know that I will not be ashamed.

Verses 5 and 6 highlighted some of the humiliating, painful abuses that Jesus endured in order to carry out His Father's will. Jesus' responsibility was of the highest magnitude imaginable – the salvation of mankind. The burdens placed on Him were also of the highest magnitude imaginable – hunger (Luke 4:2), thirst (John 19:28), fatigue (John 4:6), sorrow (John 11:35), and torture (Matthew 27:26-30). But Jesus was not left to endure these things alone, or to carry the weight of service on His own. "The Lord GOD will help Me." The service of our Lord and His church can cause us pain, sleepless nights, sore backs, and heavy hearts. Let us not be surprised. The same was true for our Lord. But just as serving God may cause us similar trials, our godly service will also grant us access to the same strength that empowered our Savior. Psalms 146:5 says, "Happy is he who has the God of Jacob for his help, whose hope is in the LORD his God." When we encounter troubles and trials, failure and fatigue, let us "set (our) face like a flint" as Jesus did, turn our faces into the wind and endure the trial without shirking or shaking. Let us call out with confidence for the Father to help us just as He helped His Son: "O God, do not be far from me; O my God, make haste to help me!" (Psalms 71:12). When we need help, let us ask for it. Psalms 109:26 says, "Help me, O LORD my God! Oh, save me according to Your mercy." Jesus faced terrible humiliation on the cross. In Matthew 27:42 the scornful crowd hurled their insults, "He saved others; Himself He cannot save." And in Matthew 27:49 the scorners cried, "Let Him alone; let us see if Elijah will come to save Him." We may face similar scorn, but like Jesus, we can be confident that "I will not be ashamed." David spoke of the humiliation he felt as he ran away from Absalom: "Many are they who say of me, 'There is no help for him in God'" (Psalms 3:2). But just as Jesus and David were comforted by the Father's help in time of humiliating troubles, so can we take comfort in His sure help for us. Psalms 40:17 says, "I am poor and needy; yet the LORD thinks upon me. You are my help and my deliverer; do not delay, O my God."

The picture is dear to me, and one I want to emulate. "I have set My face like a flint." In the face of the winds of challenge, Jesus did not flinch. His confidence in His Father's help assured Him that He would be victorious and "not be ashamed" in the end. Bolstered by my Savior's example and the promise of my Father's help, I want to demonstrate this same confidence.

50:8-9
He is near who justifies Me; who will contend with Me? Let us stand together. Who is My adversary? Let him come near Me. Surely the Lord GOD will help Me; who is he who will condemn Me? Indeed they will all grow old like a garment; the moth will eat them up.

Paul applied these verses to himself, and thus to all believers. Romans 8:31 says, "If God is for us, who can be against us?" There are those who will "contend" that believers have trusted in a false hope, there are those who will contend that believers are just as evil, or more evil than everyone else. But Paul extends Christ's hope described here, and applies it to all His children, saying in Romans 8:33-34, "Who shall bring a charge against God's elect? It is God who justifies. Who is he who condemns? It is Christ who died, and furthermore is also risen, who is even at the right hand of God, who also makes intercession for us." As the world did with Jesus on His cross and before the cross, so it is liable to do with us, arguing with our message and accusing us of misrepresenting the truth. But Matthew 11:19 says that "wisdom is justified by her children" and verse 8 here says that those followers of Wisdom are justified by their Father as well. "He is near who justifies me." When enemies and scoffers draw near, we will find that our Father is nearer still. When we are required to stand toe to toe with our enemies, we will find that no matter how powerful they are, or how weak we are, "surely the Lord GOD will help Me" and thus relieve our anxieties, knowing that He can outwrestle any contenders who challenge us in the ring. The fight against enemies of the cross is long-lasting. "But those who wait on the LORD shall renew their strength" (Isaiah 40:31), whereas those who fight against us will "grow old like a garment" and weaken over time even while our strength is continually renewed.

50:10-11
Who among you fears the LORD? Who obeys the voice of His Servant? Who walks in darkness and has no light? Let him trust in the name of the LORD and rely upon his God. Look, all you who kindle a fire, who encircle yourselves with sparks: walk in the light of your fire and in the sparks you have kindled – this you shall have from My hand: you shall lie down in torment.

Our chapter ends with two fascinating pictures. One of the godly man, and one of the unbeliever. The picture begins the same. Both are walking in the dark. "Who walks in darkness and has no light?" Even godly men who fear the Lord and have the assurance that those who walk with the Lord "shall not walk in darkness, but have the light of life" (John 8:12), will have moments, not long perhaps, but moments when the way is dim and our sight is darkened. "For now we see through a glass, darkly" (I Corinthians 13:12 KJV). In Psalms 143:3 David writes, "For the enemy has persecuted my soul; he has crushed my life to the ground; he has made me dwell in darkness, like those who have long been dead." Sometimes, for our Lord's own purposes, He may choose to allow us to walk a path that seems very dark. Psalms 88:6 says, "You have laid me in the lowest pit, in darkness, in the depths." Blessedly however, these dark times for the believer are temporary. Psalms 18:28 says, "For You will light my lamp; the LORD my God will enlighten my darkness." In dark times, our Lord extends to us the blessed invitation of verse 10: "Let him trust in the name of the LORD and rely upon His God." He who trusts in the Lord, "fears the LORD" and "obeys" the Lord in the dark times will be soon warmed and illuminated by His guiding light. The way may be dark and dim for a moment, but the godly man trusts in and relies on the Lord God to be the light that guides his way. Psalms 118:27 says, "God is the LORD, and He has given us light." We find His light to be all the light we need; we look for no other.

In striking contrast, when the unbeliever finds himself in similar dark surroundings, he makes up his own light. He tries to see by "the sparks (he) has kindled." He chooses to "walk in the light" of his own fire, made by his own imagination. The hope extended to those who wait for the Lord's guiding light is not extended to those who chart their course by their own light source, however. "The light of the righteous rejoices, but the lamp of the wicked will be put out" (Proverbs 13:9). Those who make their own light and trust in their own insights are given the frightening warning here that they "shall lie down in torment."

The world can be a dark place. The future is unforeseeable, solutions often un-seeable. But when dark days come, let us follow the admonition here: "Let him trust in the name of the LORD and rely upon his God." Light is promised to all who trust in and walk with the Lord (John 8:12). Only eventual "torment" is promised those who invent their own lamp fueled with the oil of their own imagination.

Hosea 10:13 warns: "You have plowed wickedness; you have reaped iniquity. You have eaten the fruit of lies, because you trusted in your own way." Let us rise up to warn the people around us not to trust in their own way, but to trust in the One who is "the true Light which gives light to every man coming into the world" (John 1:9). The world can be a dark place, discouraging, depressing, and deceiving. Blessedly, we have a great message for those who are in the dark: "the darkness is passing away, and the true light is already shining" (1 John 2:8).

Isaiah 51

51:1-2
Listen to Me, you who follow after righteousness, you who seek the LORD: look to the rock from which you were hewn, and to the hole of the pit from which you were dug. Look to Abraham your father, and to Sarah who bore you; for I called him alone, and blessed him and increased him.

For those who "follow after righteousness" and "who seek the LORD," uplifting words are offered here. God does not change (Malachi 3:6), so He reminds us here that the promises that He extended to Abraham when he walked in righteousness and when he sought the Lord are similarly extended to us when we walk as he did. "Look to Abraham your father," remember what the Lord did for Him when he obeyed at Mount Moriah. Remember the promises given to him when he obeyed the Lord in Genesis 12:1-3 and in Genesis 15:1. Look to how the Lord listened to his prayers of intercession in Genesis 18:32. Remember how the Lord blessed Sarah with a son when she was long past the age for bearing children. The Lord extends an invitation: "Listen to Me." All who are driven with a passion for "righteousness," all who zealously "seek the LORD," "look" and "listen" to what God has done for Abraham when he followed after righteousness and sought the Lord in the past. God "called him alone" to do His bidding, and when Abraham obeyed Him, God "blessed him" and God "increased him." We who seek righteousness and seek God's favor are "hewn" out of the same rock of faith that birthed Abraham. We are formed from the same clay that was dug from the same pit that made Abraham such a blessed vessel in the Lord's service. In Acts 10:35, Peter encourages Cornelius' household by saying, "in every nation whoever fears Him and works righteousness is accepted by Him." And our verses here grant us a similar encouragement. Great blessings, great tasks, and great promises were granted Abraham, and similar blessings, tasks, and promises are granted those even today who are hewn from the same rock of faith and fashioned from the same clay that made Abraham such a chosen vessel.

51:3

For the LORD will comfort Zion, He will comfort all her waste places; He will make her wilderness like Eden, and her desert like the garden of the LORD; joy and gladness will be found in it, thanksgiving and the voice of melody.

"The LORD will comfort Zion." What a precious thought. His people had disobeyed Him, and as a result they were condemned to tragic consequences. But, praise the Lord, discipline and punishment are not God's final words to His people. "Comfort," "joy and gladness," "thanksgiving and the voice of melody" is the final chorus that God's people sing. The people's disobedience had brought them great sadness. Blessedly, however, our Lord is the "God of all comfort" (II Corinthians 1:3) and comforts even those who have been banished to "waste places" and forced to live in the "wilderness." Sometimes, our troubles are the result of our own sin as is the case for Zion here. Sometimes, however, our sorrow and stress do not arise from sin, but are the result of our service to the Lord. In II Corinthians 7:5 Paul writes, "For indeed, when we came to Macedonia, our bodies had no rest, but we were troubled on every side. Outside were conflicts, inside were fears." Paul's troubles however, were soothed by the God of all comfort, just as Zion is comforted here. In the very next verse, Paul wrote, "Nevertheless God, who comforts the downcast, comforted us by the coming of Titus." God is a God of comfort. Psalms 94:19 says, "In the multitude of my anxieties within me, Your comforts delight my soul." Even when trials and troubles hit us from every direction, God's comforts uplift us on every side as well. "You shall increase my greatness, and comfort me on every side" (Psalms 71:21). Isaiah writes for the benefit of hurting people.

God promises comfort to His people who will face extreme hardship in exile, and this "joy and gladness" is offered to all His people in turmoil from Isaiah's day to ours, for in every age, God's people are provided with the opportunity to experience that the word of God "is my comfort in my affliction" (Psalms 119:50).

51:4
Listen to Me, My people; and give ear to Me, O My nation: for law will proceed from Me, and I will make My justice rest as a light of the peoples.

God's law and His justice are given "as a light of the peoples." Without God's guiding light, the social conscience of mankind quickly decays. Powerful people will decide that "might makes right" and choose to believe that if they have the power to do anything, then it is proper for them to do anything. Others may not think to inflict pain on other members of society, but their social conscience erodes just the same, feeling that they are free to do any actions that do not overtly cause pain for someone else. Still others might espouse altruistic causes, but never give a thought to honoring their Creator in the things they do. Without God's guiding light, the world becomes a dark place. People do evil things, do good things with evil motives, and squander the opportunity to secure heavenly rewards through earthly godliness. Blessedly, the Lord grants us His "law," He displays His "justice" as a light for all the peoples of the world. God's law teaches that purity, not power is of utmost importance. His law teaches that even private sins such as immorality and pride carry dangerous, eternal repercussions even though they may not threaten the well-being of others. God's law is a light for the peoples of the world. "The commandment is a lamp, and the law a light; reproofs of instruction are the way of life" (Proverbs 6:23). His commandments show us the right way to live so that we will not miss it.

Similarly, God's justice joins God's law and "rests" on the world as a light to the nations. Zephaniah 3:5 says that "Every morning He brings His justice to light." His justice destroyed Sodom and Gomorrah so that the world would see the light that sin leads to a terrible outcome. The Lord meted out justice on David after his sin with Bathsheba and murder of Uriah to shed light on the fact that justice awaits even powerful men, even moral men who sin against God's commands. Matthew 12:18 says that the Father sent Jesus into the world in order to "declare justice to the Gentiles," to enlighten the world that justice awaits wrongdoers. All men are born spiritually blind, and in the darkness of their understanding they become self-seeking, short-sighted, and sometimes, downright evil. But the Lord does not leave them to a dark fate. He grants us His law, He shows the peoples of the world His justice so that we will know the truth and then fear the failure to follow it.

51:5
My righteousness is near, My salvation has gone forth, and My arms will judge the peoples; the coastlands will wait upon Me, and on My arm they will trust.

God is holy, and when His righteousness draws near, His holy presence leads to different outcomes for different people. Unbelievers cringe when the Lord arrives, because His arms "will judge the peoples." The believer, however, rejoices when God's "righteousness is near" because it means that His "salvation appears" (HCS). The grace of God brings salvation (Titus 2:11), and so His children throughout the world, from the "coastlands" of the nations across the seas, "will wait upon" the Lord because He brings salvation when He comes. Psalms 62:1 says, "Truly my soul silently waits for God; from Him comes my salvation." Knowing this, Proverbs 20:22 compels all God's people to "Wait for the LORD, and He will save you."

God's people "will wait" with confidence for God to save them, "they will trust" in His arms that bring them their rescue. While unbelievers fear the coming of the righteous Lord, His children eagerly await His coming, for they know that their trust in Him will be rewarded with a sure salvation. Psalms 18:2 says, "The LORD is my rock and my fortress and my deliverer; my God, my strength, in whom I will trust; my shield and the horn of my salvation, my stronghold." Before Judah's captivity in Babylon, and before our trials that will dawn upon us tomorrow, our Lord sends this promise in advance, "My salvation has gone forth."

God's "salvation has gone forth." What a blessed hope. May our family always "wait upon (Him)" and "trust" in His redeeming arm (Psalms 77:15) so that we will have no cause to fear when His righteousness draws near to "judge the peoples."

51:6
Lift up your eyes to the heavens, and look on the earth beneath. For the heavens will vanish away like smoke, the earth will grow old like a garment, and those who dwell in it will die in like manner; but My salvation will be forever, and My righteousness will not be abolished.

The sun and stars in the heavens seem ageless, untouched by time. The earth appears hardly less securely established. Yet these things "will vanish away like smoke." At the time appointed by our Creator "the earth will grow old like a garment" and disintegrate like a threadbare cloth exposed to the elements over time. Perhaps even more ominously, mankind – the people who dwell in the earth and depend on the sun "will die in like manner." The sun is not eternal. It will vanish away. The earth will not last forever. It, too, will grow old and melt away. How much more, then, should we be aware of our own mortality and impending judgment? Blessedly, the amazing assurance is given here that God's children will outlast the sun. "My salvation will be forever." If a benefactor saves us from debt, we will soon enough need money once again. If a doctor heals our wounds, his treatments will not protect us from future illness. If a rescuer saves us from danger, our lives will, inevitably, face death once more. But God's rescue is far superior to all of those. His salvation "will be forever." God is "the author of <u>eternal salvation</u> to all who obey Him" (Hebrews 5:9). The world is passing away, but we need not fear the end of the world. In Matthew 24:35 Jesus said, "Heaven and earth will pass away, but My words will by no means pass away." God's word which teaches the way of salvation lasts forever. God's home in heaven which is prepared for His children lasts forever. And God's salvation which extends to His children the opportunity to reach that heaven endures forever. Everything about God is eternal. Everything about man is temporary. Our trials, failures, pains, and pitfalls are all real, but they are temporary. Everything about the world we live in is temporary. The sun and stars of the heavens will vanish away, and the earth will tatter and fray into disarray. But those who trust in the grace of God and the righteousness that He imputes to His children will be saved forever. Mankind will not live on earth forever, but God's people are assured that we will "dwell in the house of the Lord forever" (Psalms 23:6). And unlike the sun and moon, whose last days are drawing near, God's people "are preserved forever" (Psalms 37:28). Isaiah's words remind us that "The world is passing away along with its desires, but whoever does the will of God abides forever" (I John 2:17). With this reminder before us, let us be careful to heed the call of Colossians 3:2 and "Set your mind on things above, not on things on the earth."

51:7-8
Listen to Me, you who know righteousness, you people in whose heart is My law: do not fear the reproach of men, nor be afraid of their insults. For the moth will eat them up like a garment, and the worm will eat them like wool; but My righteousness will be forever, and My salvation from generation to generation.

Continuing the theme of verse 6, God encourages His people to not lose heart when they face "the reproach of men" and show courage in the face of "insults." Just as the heavens and the earth are temporary (verse 6), the threats and insults of enemies and persecutors are temporary as well. Like moths eat shirts in the closet and caterpillars eat woolen coats, so the test of time will eat away the threats and insults hurled on God's people. It is good for us to remember that evil is temporary, but God's righteousness is eternal. Judah would temporarily be defeated by Babylon, but the salvation that God provides for the souls of His people will last forever. God calls on Isaiah's readers (including us) to "Listen to Me!" Do not be discouraged by the insults of unbelievers! Their painful barbs are temporary, whereas God's righteous right hand will uphold His people forever. Godly people have good cause to be patient people. We can endure the insults of unbelievers because we know that God will protect our heavenly reputation and safeguard our eternal home. Proverbs 19:11 says, "Smart people are patient; they will be honored if they ignore insults" (NCV).

51:9-11

Awake, awake, put on strength, O arm of the LORD! Awake as in the ancient days, in the generations of old. Are You not the arm that cut Rahab apart, and wounded the serpent? Are You not the One who dried up the sea, the waters of the great deep; that made the depths of the sea a road for the redeemed to cross over? So the ransomed of the LORD shall return, and come to Zion with singing, with everlasting joy on their heads. They shall obtain joy and gladness; sorrow and sighing shall flee away.

The confident cry of the souls of embattled saints is exemplified here. "Awake, awake, put on strength, O arm of the LORD!" The believer cries out for the Lord to rise up and help Him. He has read of all the Lord's great deeds on behalf of His people "in the ancient days." "The generations of old" have passed on all the stories of how God did such great and powerful things for His people, leaving the next generation with an expectancy, a confident hope that God will save them just as He saved their forefathers. In ancient days, the Lord "cut Rahab apart." Some say Rahab refers to a mythological sea serpent (Psalms 89:10). Some say this refers to God's delivering His people from Egypt (Isaiah 30:7). And still others point to the future when the Lord defeats that "serpent of old" in Revelation 20:2. In any event, the Lord has proven over and over throughout history that His compassion moves Him to defend His people, His power enables Him to overpower His enemies with ease, and His immutability means that Isaiah's hearers and today's readers can "come boldly to the throne of grace" (Hebrews 4:16) and expectantly, confidently, call out for the Lord to rescue His children once again.

Judah will be exiled into Babylon, but "the ransomed of the LORD shall return." The sorrow of their captivity will be replaced with "joy and gladness." "Everlasting joy" will be on their heads. They will be brought low by temporary circumstance, but their "sorrow and sighing shall flee away." Because of their sin and rebellion, discipline and punishment, troubles and trials are in store for the people of Jerusalem. But once again we see that chastisement is not God's final word for His people. "Ransom" and "return," "joy and gladness" comprise the happy future of all those who come to Him in repentance and expectancy in their time of need.

51:12
I, even I, am He who comforts you. Who are you that you should be afraid of a man who will die, and of the son of a man who will be made like grass?

The world is full of injustice, pain, ridicule, insults, grieving, failure, and an endless list of concerns and heartaches. God does not remove from us the pangs of living on earth, but He does promise to comfort us in these times. "I, even I, am He who comforts you." Our Lord does not leave us to fend for ourselves when our hearts are heavy. He comes to comfort us Himself. For all God's infinite power, it is remarkable to see how gentle and comforting He is. Paul calls our Lord the "God of all comfort" (II Corinthians 1:3). God gives us His scriptures to comfort us (Romans 15:4). He gives us fellow believers to comfort us (II Corinthians 7:6, Colossians 4:11). And, then, above all that, He gives us Himself as the comfort of comforts, the Comforter of comforters. "I will pray the Father, and he shall give you another Comforter, that he may abide with you for ever" (John 14:16 KJV).

Our God comforts us in times of pain and uncertainty, and it is our responsibility, in return, to bask in His presence, take proper consolation in His comfort, and cast off all fear. Psalms 118:6 exemplifies the proper response to the Lord's comforting presence, saying: "The LORD is on my side; I will not fear. What can man do to me?" Fear in the heart of the believer is an offense to God. "Who are you that you should be afraid of a man who will die" when the Lord God Almighty is your Guardian and Comforter? Courage and contentment are the expected responses in the hearts of God's people when He draws near to comfort us in our distress. We must not persist in fearing men who are "made like grass" when God's comforting presence draws near.

ISAIAH 51

51:13-15
And you forget the LORD your Maker, Who stretched out the heavens and laid the foundations of the earth; you have feared continually every day because of the fury of the oppressor, when he has prepared to destroy. And where is the fury of the oppressor? The captive exile hastens, that he may be loosed, that he should not die in the pit, and that his bread should not fail. But I am the LORD your God, Who divided the sea whose waves roared – the LORD of hosts is His name.

Isaiah's readers are called on to lift their eyes above their troubles. They have "feared continually." They have lived in constant dread of "the fury of the oppressor." They are terrified that their enemies will "destroy" them. But the Lord God Almighty has decreed that the "captive exile" will be freed, that His children will not "die in the pit" of despair, and that His children will not go hungry. With these assurances before them, why would God's people ever despair? God is great! He "stretched out the heavens and laid the foundations of the earth!" He controls the roaring waves of the sea! He is able to do all things, and His loving concern for His people means that He is both capable and desirous of moving heaven and earth to protect and provide for His people. With this reminder of the greatness of God and the goodness of God, why would the people of Judah live in fear? Why would any Christian ever suffer from anxiety? The first phrase tells us the formula for worry: "you forget the LORD your Maker." When troubles loom on the horizon, it is sometimes difficult to wrest our attention from those worrisome matters. But as long as our attention remains fixed on troubles, anxiety and fear will remain. We must not "forget the LORD your Maker." We must keep our eyes fixed on His greatness and His love for us. Staring at problems is a prescription for fear. Remembering God is the cure. Nehemiah demonstrates this nicely. In the face of powerful enemies, he tells God's people: "Do not be afraid of them. <u>Remember the Lord</u>, great and awesome, and fight..." (Nehemiah 4:14). May the words of Psalm 42 be our refrain when we are tempted to fixate on our trouble rather than on our Savior. "Why am I discouraged? Why is my heart so sad? I will put my hope in God! I will praise him again – my Savior and my God! Now I am deeply discouraged, <u>but I will remember you</u>" (Psalms 42:5-6 NLT).

51:16
And I have put My words in your mouth; I have covered you with the shadow of My hand, that I may plant the heavens, lay the foundations of the earth, and say to Zion, "You are My people."

Ah, what a rich verse stands before us here! It is tempting to spend days here, rolling over the truths and possibilities presented by Isaiah's words. God declares, "I have put My words in your mouth." He promises Moses that He will "raise up for them a Prophet like you from among their brethren, and will put My words in His mouth." Do these two passages speak only of Jesus, of whom John 3:34 says, "He whom God has sent speaks the words of God?" Or do they speak of all God's prophets of whom II Peter 1:21 tells us, "holy men of God spoke as they were moved by the Holy Spirit," and Jeremiah 1:9 says, "Then the LORD put forth His hand and touched my mouth, and the LORD said to me: 'Behold, I have put My words in your mouth?'" Or is the Lord referring to His willingness to place His words in the mouth of each one of His children? Luke 12:12 provides all of God's children – every one of us that are called upon to represent Him – with the assurance that "the Holy Spirit will teach you in that very hour what you ought to say." God places His word in our mouths so that we might speak the same message of holiness, love, and reconciliation that He speaks. Our Lord speaks to us the words of life (John 6:63). He speaks to us the words that teach us how to live a fulfilling life, a holy life, and how to gain eternal life. God tells us the purpose for living, the standard for living, and His provision for redemption. God speaks His remarkable words to His people, and then He places His word in our mouth so that we might tell others what we have heard Him say. God's word is not so distant that man cannot hear it – His words are echoed in the voices of His people so that His message is never far from the people of the world who are in desperate need of it. Deuteronomy 30:14 promises, "The word is very near you, in your mouth and in your heart, that you may do it." Psalms 138:4 says, "All the kings of the earth shall praise You, O LORD, when they hear the words of Your mouth." Hearing the words of God moves the peoples of the world to praise Him. May the world be moved to praise God often because they hear the words of God often, and may they hear those words from us. Balaam said, "The word that God puts in my mouth, that I must speak" (Numbers 22:38). Let us obey this edict better than Balaam did. Let us look expectantly to hear God's word spoken to our spiritual ear each morning (Isaiah 50:4). Let us listen carefully for His words of instruction telling us to turn right or turn left (Isaiah 30:21). And let us faithfully tell others what we have heard Him say. "I have put My words in your mouth." What a sacred privilege. We have heard God speak. We have read His Word. He has placed His words inside us. Let us now tell others, so that they too, might know what He says.

The wonder of God speaking to the world through us is thrilling to contemplate. But the depth and riches of this verse continue as the Lord tells us that He is speaking to us and putting His words in our mouth so that He can "plant the heavens" and "lay the foundations of the earth, and "say to Zion, 'You are My people.'" In the beginning of time, God created the heavens and the earth through the words of His voice. "God said, 'Let there be light'; and there was light" (Genesis 1:3). He "planted the heavens" with His words. And now, it is His continuing work to plant His Kingdom of Heaven by this same means. God is planting the heavens, His Kingdom of Heaven, on earth even now, and He does so be speaking His word to His people and inspiring His people to speak His words to others. The kingdom of heaven is in the hearts of God's people (Luke 17:21). And it is established there the same way the heavens and the earth were established long ago – by the spoken, implanted word of God.

And once the Lord establishes His kingdom in His people, as a mother softly calls the name of her newborn son as she holds him to her chest, so our Father calls to us with His word to gently remind us that we are His and He is ours. With both maternal care and a father's protective love, our Lord whispers His word to His children: "You are My people." In Isaiah 43:1 the Father says, "I have called you by your name; You are Mine." God calls us to Himself, and then places His words in our mouth so that our words might be His words, demonstrating to the world that we belong to Him – and that they can belong to Him just the same.

51:17-20

Awake, awake! Stand up, O Jerusalem, you who have drunk at the hand of the LORD the cup of His fury; you have drunk the dregs of the cup of trembling, and drained it out. There is no one to guide her among all the sons she has brought forth; nor is there any who takes her by the hand among all the sons she has brought up. These two things have come to you; who will be sorry for you? – Desolation and destruction, famine and sword – by whom will I comfort you? Your sons have fainted, they lie at the head of all the streets, like an antelope in a net; they are full of the fury of the LORD, the rebuke of your God.

God calls on His people to wake up. He commands them to stand up. They have fallen under the full measure of His wrath. The have drunk from the "cup of His fury" and "drained it out." Their sin has caused them "desolation and destruction, famine and sword." How could they sleep through that? Why are they lying around as if drunk or half asleep when their nation and families and lives are falling apart? It is important for us to remember that sin is sedating. Sin anesthetizes the conscience and numbs us from the helpful pangs of guilt. Even while suffering the horrible consequences of sin, we find people insisting on persisting in sin. Their sin has ruined their family, ruined their career, and ruined their health – and yet they refuse to stop rebelling against God and continue to sin. Why? Because sin is sedating. It makes people lie down and close their eyes to the fall-out of their sin. As if in a drunken stupor, sinners cannot feel the sting of remorse, they ignore the pain of guilt, and refuse to repent of the error of their ways. So, as if addressing a sleeping drunkard, God commands Jerusalem to get up. Wake up! Stand up! They are like an antelope in a net. They are trapped in the repercussions of sin. They are facing the full fury of the Lord and there is no escape except standing up in repentance. They must not sleep through judgment. They cannot dream away God's rebuke. They must wake up and repent! They must stand up and set their minds on holy action. Revelation 6:17 says, "For the great day of His wrath has come, and who is able to stand?" All who refuse to stand in repentance now, will one day fall and kneel before our Righteous Judge.

51:21-23
Therefore please hear this, you afflicted, and drunk but not with wine. Thus says your Lord, the LORD and your God, Who pleads the cause of His people: "See, I have taken out of your hand the cup of trembling, the dregs of the cup of My fury; you shall no longer drink it. But I will put it into the hand of those who afflict you, who have said to you, 'Lie down, that we may walk over you.' And you have laid your body like the ground, and as the street, for those who walk over."

God's people have sinned, they are "drunk" with sin, and as a result, the Lord has made them drink "the dregs of the cup of My fury." But now, in great kindness toward His people, and in defense of His own name, the Lord promises Isaiah's hearers that He will take the cup of suffering from their hands and give it, instead, to "those who afflict you." Judah's enemies have walked all over them. In their captivity in Babylon, Judah will be brought very low. They will lie, as it were, on the ground, lie down in the middle of the street for their enemies to tramp on their backs in cruelty and derision. But God "pleads the cause of His people." The HCS says that God "defends His people." He takes up our cause and defends us from enemies and dangers – even when those dangers and enemies are at our doorstep through faults of our own! God's defense of His people moves David to write the comforting blessing of Psalms 5:11 – "Let all those rejoice who put their trust in You; let them ever shout for joy, because You defend them; let those also who love Your name be joyful in You." God defends those that are His. It is His good will to draw near and rescue His people from disaster so that He might be glorified. After witnessing God's miraculous rescue of Daniel from the lion's den, King Darius was moved to praise Daniel's God in Daniel 6:27, exalting God's care for Daniel by saying: "He (God) delivers and rescues, and He works signs and wonders In heaven and on earth, Who has delivered Daniel from the power of the lions." If we find ourselves in crisis, let us trust in our Lord and pray. And when He delivers us, may those who see us, praise our Lord just as Darius did for His rescue of Daniel from the lion's den.

Isaiah 52

52:1-2
Awake, awake! Put on your strength, O Zion; put on your beautiful garments, O Jerusalem, the holy city! For the uncircumcised and the unclean shall no longer come to you. Shake yourself from the dust, arise; sit down, O Jerusalem! Loose yourself from the bonds of your neck, O captive daughter of Zion!

Again, just as in 51:17, the Lord calls on His people in Jerusalem to "Awake, awake!" Too often people seem to sleep through the exploding reverberations of sin. God's message of repentance rings loudly in their ears, the bombardment of painful repercussions for sin thunders all around them – and yet they sleep – happy to keep on sinning, content to continue to displease their loving Creator. Here, the Lord invites His people to wake up! The background for these words is their eventual captivity in Babylon, where the Lord invites them to wake up and "put on your beautiful garments." As one might wake up in the morning and put on their best clothes in preparation for a special occasion, the Lord calls them to set aside their tattered pajamas and put on a tux and gown. They have been lying in the dust, dirtied by sin and degraded by defeat and captivity, but the Lord will cleanse them of sin and put away the embarrassment of their enslavement. He will loose them from the bonds around their neck and restore their freedom in Jerusalem. Sin has terrible repercussions, but sleepers are not aware of them. God has wonderful blessings in store for those who obey Him, but sleepers do not care. So God repeats His command from chapter 51: "Awake!"

52:3
For thus says the LORD: "You have sold yourselves for nothing, and you shall be redeemed without money."

It is amazing how fiscally uninsightful sinners are. "You have sold yourselves for nothing." People get so little out of sin! They ruin their careers, their reputation, and their families – selling themselves to the grip of sin – and gain only ruin and embarrassment in exchange! Godly men shake their heads in wonder over why anyone would be willing to sell themselves so cheaply just to "enjoy the passing pleasures of sin" for a season (Hebrews 11:25). In great contrast, we are also awed in wonder over the terrible cost that is required to redeem sinners out of their sin. "You shall be redeemed without money." I Peter 1:18-19 says, "You were not redeemed with corruptible things, like silver or gold, from your aimless conduct received by tradition from your fathers, but with the precious blood of Christ, as of a lamb without blemish and without spot." Money cannot redeem a sin-stained soul. Something of far greater worth is required. "The wages of sin is death" (Romans 6:23). Nothing less than a life can redeem a life, and so Jesus our Lord gave His life to redeem ours. Sin brings us "nothing" of value and the cost of sin is so terrible – Jesus suffered and died as a result of our sin. Sin is a terrible investment. It profits us nothing, and the cost is beyond reckoning. May we be reminded again, to make all possible effort to keep ourselves from sin.

52:4-6
For thus says the Lord GOD: "My people went down at first into Egypt to dwell there; then the Assyrian oppressed them without cause. Now therefore, what have I here," says the LORD, "That My people are taken away for nothing? Those who rule over them make them wail," says the LORD, "And My name is blasphemed continually every day. Therefore My people shall know My name; therefore they shall know in that day that I am He who speaks: 'Behold, it is I.'"

God's people "went down at first into Egypt," and when they were enslaved there they cried out to the Lord and He delivered them through the hand of Moses. Later, "the Assyrian oppressed them without cause" and the Lord delivered them by destroying an army of 185,000 Assyrians overnight (II Kings 19:35). "Now therefore," says the Lord – look what we have here – God's people "wail" because of their humiliation and suffering in Babylon, and God's "name is blasphemed continually every day" as Babylon despises both the people and the God of defeated Israel. As a result, the cry of His people and the discredit to His own name will move the Lord to act once more. He will deliver His children, He will defend His name, and His people will know that it is He that calls them to Himself. It is He that upholds the honor of His name. God will make sure that His people will not be "taken away for nothing." His purposes will be upheld and His name will be glorified. None of God's actions are "for nothing." If He speaks His message to the world, His word will call people to Himself just as He intends (Isaiah 55:11). If He rescues His people, He will do so in order to carry out His purpose of bringing glory to His own name (Exodus 14:18, etc.). And if He punishes His people, as He does when He allows them to be sent off as captives to Babylon, His punishment will not be "for nothing." The discipline and eventual rescue of His people will once again accomplish His purposes. When Job came face to face with the greatness of God, He acknowledged "I know that You can do everything, and that no purpose of Yours can be withheld from You" (Job 42:2). God will send His people as captives into Babylon. But His ultimate intention to redeem a remnant and glorify His name will not be "withheld" from Him. His people will not be "taken away for nothing." We can take hold of that same reassurance. All things that befall us can be turned to carry out the Lord's purposes. Nothing that happens to us is "for nothing."

52:7
How beautiful upon the mountains are the feet of him who brings good news, who proclaims peace, who brings glad tidings of good things, who proclaims salvation, who says to Zion, "Your God reigns!"

Paul quotes Isaiah's words here in Romans 10:15 and applies them to God's servants who take the gospel to the world. The feet of God's messengers are described specifically, emphasizing that God's messengers must travel to distant places in order to make known the "good news" that "God reigns!" The message that we carry to the distant mountains and far off peoples is a message of "salvation." Mankind is in desperate need of salvation. It is a lie that proposes that all men are inherently good or that all roads lead to heaven. People are born into darkness (Ephesians 5:8) and ignorance (Ephesians 4:18). They are born into sin. Psalms 58:3 says, "The wicked are estranged from the womb; they go astray as soon as they are born, speaking lies." This darkness and ignorance and sin moves us to be at war with God, we fight against His commands and His purposes. "For the sinful nature is always hostile to God. It never did obey God's laws, and it never will" (Romans 8:7). The nature of self-centeredness and sin-centeredness causes everyone to be "hostile," to be at war with our Maker. But the "good news" that is brought by God's messengers is a message of "peace." The good news tells us that we can have "peace with God through our Lord Jesus Christ" (Romans 5:1). The "good news" that we bring to people is also a message of "glad tidings of good things." The world brings a train load of troubles. But like news of reinforcements to a city under siege, like the voice of a doctor telling their patient she is cured, like the joy of hearing that a loved one is finally returning home, so God's message brings glad tidings of good things to heavy hearted people who are in need of good news. God's messengers proclaim "salvation!" We do not simply tell people how they can be healthier, live a little longer, or make a little more money – we tell them that they can be rescued from the guilt of sin, the specter of death, and the horror of hell. We can inspire them that we should not and need not "let sin reign in your mortal body" (Romans 6:12), because "God reigns" -- not temptation and sin. We can inspire them with the knowledge that they need not live under the weight of anxiety and fear because "God reigns" -- not random circumstance. And we can call the world's peoples to repent of sin and seek reconciliation with God hurriedly because on judgment day "God reigns," and it is He who will judge the living and the dead (Acts 10:42).

52:8
Your watchmen shall lift up their voices, with their voices they shall sing together; for they shall see eye to eye when the LORD brings back Zion.

See here this role of the watchmen that is perhaps sometimes overlooked. Ezekiel 3:17 describes the familiar responsibility of watchmen in the Kingdom of God: "Son of man, I have made you a watchman for the house of Israel; therefore hear a word from My mouth, and give them warning from Me." Here however, Isaiah describes for us a different role of the watchman. We are to lift up our voices and "sing together" when we see the Lord provide for His people. God saves, and we praise Him in return.

This is the relationship that the Lord has offered us since He placed Adam in Eden. And since the arrangement is so clearly in our favor it is to our great benefit to successfully carry out our blessed responsibility to sing God's praises in response to His saving work. Some people can be so inwardly focused that they fail to appreciate God's saving work in others. They are prone to giving inadequate praise to the Lord who expends so much grace, extends so much mercy, and even offers His own blood in the effort to bring salvation to men and women. So, since self-centeredness, lack of empathy, and inadequate adoration of the Savior can all cause the church to be overly quiet regarding God's saving works, the Lord calls on watchmen to inspire their fellow believers to "sing together" the praises of the Lord. When God's people, when His watchmen see with their own eyes, when they see God save people right "before their very eyes" (NLT), they lift up their voices and sing God's praises; and their eye witness testimony and the sound of their praises will inspire others to join in the song of singing praise to the God who saves.

Come, let us join the watchman who penned Psalms 95:1. When we see the saving works of the Lord, let us sing out His praises, and call on all His people to join us, saying, "Oh come, let us sing to the LORD! Let us shout joyfully to the Rock of our salvation." Seeing people at worship beckons others to join in singing the Savior's due praise. It is the great work of the watchmen, the sons and servants of the Lord, to carefully look for the Lord's works and carefully listen to the Lord's words – and then sound the bell in our watchtower – a bell that calls on sinners to repent and calls on saints to sing His praise.

52:9
Break forth into joy, sing together, you waste places of Jerusalem! For the LORD has comforted His people, He has redeemed Jerusalem.

We are reminded here that it is the greatness of God that summons us to praise Him, not our own well-being. Sickness, poverty, failure, and troubles should be no hindrance to giving God praise, for He is great even when we are not. Though we live in "waste places," though God's people that had returned to Jerusalem faced many challenges, yet it was right for them to lift up their voice and "sing together." It was right for them to "break forth into joy" because "the LORD has comforted His people, He has redeemed Jerusalem." The comforts of our Lord and the joy of being "redeemed" by Him outweigh all outward discomforts. Troubles may abound, but God is great and worthy to be praised. Hardships may surround us, but

God's comfort in hard times lift our hearts to praise Him. In II Corinthians 7:5 Paul writes, "When we came to Macedonia, our bodies had no rest, but we were troubled on every side. Outside were conflicts, inside were fears. Nevertheless God, who comforts the down cast, comforted us by the coming of Titus." As the comforts of God and the coming of Titus allowed Paul to "break forth into joy," so the comforts of the Lord and the arrival of His people in Jerusalem moved them to "sing together" a song of praise to the One "who comforts the downcast" and redeems lost people to Himself.

52:10
The LORD has made bare His holy arm in the eyes of all the nations; and all the ends of the earth shall see the salvation of our God.

    God is sovereign. The earth and all living things are at His beck and call. And yet, though He reigns over all, with angels and mankind subservient to Him, God is a God who works. The salvation of mankind requires superhuman effort to accomplish, and blessedly, "(our) Father never stops working" to see men saved (John 5:17 NLT). He "has made bare His holy arm," He rolls up His sleeves and goes to work to save us. Our works cannot save us (Titus 3:5), but God's work does save us, and He invites "all the ends of the earth" to watch Him work and bring "the salvation of our God" to the lives of men. It is normal for sons to love to watch their father work, and it is our Heavenly Father's good will to grant opportunity for His children to watch with fascination as He works to rescue His people. In Exodus 14:13 the Lord speaks through Moses to invite His people to "Stand still, and see the salvation of the LORD, which He will accomplish for you today." And in II Chronicles 20:17 God speaks through Jahaziel to give His people the same invitation: "stand still and see the salvation of the LORD." God works to save us, and He invites us to watch Him work. John the Baptist quotes Isaiah's words here in Luke 3:6 when he foretold the coming of Jesus who would come to save the world and allow all His children the joy of watching Him save. God works. We watch. And then we tell the world of God's saving works so that "all the ends of the earth (can) see the salvation of our God."

52:11-12
Depart! Depart! Go out from there, touch no unclean thing; go out from the midst of her, be clean, you who bear the vessels of the LORD. For you shall not go out with haste, nor go by flight; for the LORD will go before you, and the God of Israel will be your rear guard.

THE DERBYSHIRE FAMILY COMMENTARY

Long before God's people are taken captive into Babylon, Isaiah pens these words from the Lord foretelling their rescue and return home. The happy command will ring out: "Depart! Depart!" Return to your homeland! Return and bring glory to God once more! Their return to Jerusalem would not be like the frantic flight of a criminal who fears recapture by the law. They will not "go out with haste," running away as if their captors were pursuing them. They will not "go by flight," hiding, running, secretly concealing their position to avoid detection. Ezra 1 tells of the fulfillment of Isaiah's words here, and how Cyrus, king of Persia, will sanction and sponsor Israel's return home. They will return home openly, even triumphantly, led by the Lord their Savior. The people will be vulnerable to attack, but they will need no army to protect them. Ezra 8:23 tells how the Lord fulfilled Isaiah's prophecy that "the LORD will go before you, and the God of Israel will be your rear guard."

They will not be returning home empty handed. They will "bear the vessels of the LORD." They will return home with an offering to give to the Lord in thanks and with instruments of reverence to use in worship of their Savior. Ezra 1:5-11 gives the remarkable inventory of the "vessels of the Lord" that were given to God's people to take back to the Promised Land.

God's people will return in safety, they will return enriched by their former captors, carrying vessels of worship, and they are instructed to return "clean." "Be clean." "Touch no unclean thing," are the instructions given by the Lord generations in advance. God's provision, His protection, His salvation is promised to those who are His -- and holiness on the part of His people is required in return. It is not acceptable to receive God's blessings and remain attached to "unclean thing(s)." Our Lord is Immanuel! God with us! He walks with us through life, He blesses us beyond measure, providing and protecting our eternal security. We must, in return, walk holy and pure in every facet of our lives. Deuteronomy 23:14 says, "For the LORD your God walks in the midst of your camp, to deliver you and give your enemies over to you; therefore your camp shall be holy, that He may see no unclean thing among you, and turn away from you."

Just as it was in Deuteronomy and in Isaiah and in Ezra, so it is today. God blesses His children, and we walk with Him in holiness in return. Proper gratitude for God's provision requires holiness. God's directive to "be clean" remains imperative for us today!

ISAIAH 52

52:13-15
Behold, My Servant shall deal prudently; He shall be exalted and extolled and be very high. Just as many were astonished at you, so His visage was marred more than any man, and His form more than the sons of men; so shall He sprinkle many nations. Kings shall shut their mouths at Him; for what had not been told them they shall see, and what they had not heard they shall consider.

Verse 13 reminds us of the greatness of our Savior. Verse 14 reminds us of the great sacrifice that He made for us. And verse 15 hints at the great outcome that will arise as a result of the great sacrifice made by our great Savior.

Verse 13 says that the "Servant," the Father's chosen Servant – His Son and our Savior will "deal prudently." The ESV says that He will "act wisely." Luke 2:40 says that from the time He was a youth Jesus was "filled with wisdom." And Matthew 13:54 says that those who heard Him teach were astonished by His teachings and asked among themselves: "Where did this Man get this wisdom and these mighty works?" As a result of His great wisdom and mighty works (especially His work on the cross), Jesus will be "exalted and extolled and be very high." Jesus will be exalted by both heaven and earth, extolled by both mortal man and the eternal Father. Philippians 2:9 says, "God also has highly exalted Him and given Him the name which is above every name." And in Acts 19:17 both Jews and Greeks are amazed by, of all things, the testimony of evil spirits so that "fear fell upon them all, and the name of the Lord Jesus was extolled" (ESV).

Verse 15 then hints at the great result of our Savior's wisdom and works – He will "sprinkle many nations." "I will sprinkle clean water on you, and you shall be clean; I will cleanse you from all your filthiness and from all your idols" (Ezekiel 36:25). When we look at the sin and rebellion and depravity of mankind, the claiming and cleansing of the nation of Israel seems to us to be such a magnificent endeavor! Man deserves death and punishment! But look! Our Creator has called a nation to Himself so that not everyone would be annihilated because their sin. Saving Israel is such a magnificent work! But here we are reminded that God's work surpasses even this great endeavor. He will "sprinkle many nations." He will rain down His cleansing mercy on all peoples. He will flood the whole earth with the purifying power of His grace. Kings will be silent before Him. Those who had been ignorant of God's plan to sprinkle all nations with His grace will be told the good news and they "shall see" and "they shall consider" the great work of God which overcomes the fallen nature of man. What a great hope is extended to man – the purifying works of God will "sprinkle many nations," allowing some from every tribe, nation, and tongue to be cleansed of the guilt and penalty of sin.

Between the uplifting look at the greatness of the Savior in verse 13 and the blessed sprinkling of many nations with purity in verse 15, however, lies the somber, heart-wrenching reminder in verse 14, which pictures the great cost, the incomparable sacrifice that Jesus endured in order to gain His exultation in verse 13 and sprinkle the world with salvation in verse 15. People were "astonished" at the level of degradation that Jerusalem endured when God's people were taken captive to Babylon, but that degradation could not compare with that which our Savior endured. "His visage was marred more than any man." His face was bloodied by a twisted crown of thorns (Mark 15:17). He was disfigured from the beatings of those He came to save. Matthew 26:67 says, "...they spat in His face and beat Him; and others struck Him with the palms of their hands." Christ's "visage was marred." He was beaten, bruised, bloodied, and murdered – all so that we might be saved.

As we read the verses before us, let us remember that our Lord's wisdom and great works make Him worthy to be exalted and extolled "very high." Let us remember that His wisdom and great works allowed "many nations" to be sprinkled with His cleansing grace so that men from every tribe and tongue might be saved. And let us not forget the great cost that was paid by our Lord to carry out His great work to purify the nations – that it is His blood that sprinkles the nations that they may be made holy. The wisdom of our Lord is unsurpassable, the sufferings of our Lord are unimaginable, and the results of His sacrificial efforts are epic in proportion. They brought salvation, not just to Israel, but sprinkled the nations of the world with His cleansing blood so that "the world through Him might be saved" (John 3:17).

Isaiah 53

53:1
Who has believed our report? And to whom has the arm of the LORD been revealed?

John 12:38 quotes these words from Isaiah and says that they refer to the poor response of man to the great revelations of God. John 12:37 says, "Although He had done so many signs before them, they did not believe in Him." They heard the "report" of Jesus' power and wisdom. They saw with their own eyes that the power of the Lord had been "revealed." But rather than respond with repentance and devotion to the "revealed" power of "the arm of the LORD" the people insisted instead, on remaining "willingly ignorant" (II Peter 3:5 KJV), refusing to believe the report of the Savior's power and plans for His people. Isaiah's words here, as well as John's reference to them in his gospel are a lament. They grieve over the fact that the Lord would reveal His plans and power to man, and yet men would refuse to believe the wonderful report. Man's failure to believe what God has reported to be true is condemning. John 3:19 says, "And this is the condemnation, that the light has come into the world, and men loved darkness rather than light, because their deeds were evil." It is not ignorance that keeps men from God. It is not well-intentioned devotion to other religions. God has "revealed" His greatness; His "report" has sounded forth around the world. But men and women the world over continue to refuse to believe the report because "their deeds were evil."

53:2
For He shall grow up before Him as a tender plant, and as a root out of dry ground. He has no form or comeliness; and when we see Him, there is no beauty that we should desire Him.

Jesus will be born in a stable without pomp or pageantry to welcome Him. His arrival will be less like a king, and more like "a tender plant." His arrival will resemble an inconspicuous bush in an inconspicuous field. Those looking for beauty will find little cause to follow Him. He will be filled with power, glory, wisdom, love, mercy, and truth, but none of these things will be visible from the outside, and the invisibility of His glory will be a stumbling block to many. Nathaniel will be unimpressed with Jesus' birthplace (John 1:46). The crowd by the sea was unimpressed with Him because of the ordinariness of His father and family (Matthew 13:55). In John 7:27 the crowd is unimpressed with Jesus because they knew where He was from, and in John 9:29 the crowd is unimpressed with Jesus because they didn't know where He was from! Jesus arrived on earth "as a root out of dry ground." Nothing about His arrival or His appearance impressed His onlookers. Those who were looking for God in man found Him in Jesus – as exemplified by Simeon (Luke 2:25-35), Anna (Luke 2:36-38), and John the Baptist (John 1:29-34). But those who were only impressed by beautiful and powerful people found no reason to be impressed with Jesus. I Samuel 16:7 says that God does not see people as men see people. "For man looks at the outward appearance, but the LORD looks at the heart." God is unimpressed with outward appearances, and so He was uninterested in embellishing Jesus' arrival on earth with showy displays aimed at impressing shallow people. Those who seek the Lord will find Him: "And you will seek Me and find Me, when you search for Me with all your heart" (Jeremiah 29:13). But those who are looking only for beauty (that fades) and power (that wanes) will likely miss Jesus altogether.

53:3
He is despised and rejected by men, a Man of sorrows and acquainted with grief. And we hid, as it were, our faces from Him; He was despised, and we did not esteem Him.

Jesus had no outer "comeliness," no "beauty" (verse 2) and so the world (which adores these things) "despised and rejected" Him. Andrew Davis' "Christ-Centered Exposition" on Isaiah says that the word "despised" here means "grossly underestimated." And so He was. Unbelievers underestimated His ability to forgive sin in Mark 2. They underestimated His relation to King David and His right to the praise of men in Luke 19, and they underestimated His ability to save Himself in Matthew 27:42. Unbelievers despised Jesus, they "grossly underestimated" Him, and they rejected His authority. And "we," those who believed in Him, who were devoted to Him, who recognized that He was the Messiah, sent from God to save us from sins – "we" treated Him not much better. We hid our faces from Him. When Jesus was arrested in the garden, His disciples ran away (Matthew 26:56), and when pressured, Peter denied knowing Him (Luke 22:54-62). "We," His own children "did not esteem Him." The NLT says, "He was despised, and we did not care." John 1:11 says, "His own did not receive Him." This double rejection by both the sinful world and His own uninsightful children caused our Lord to be "a Man of sorrows and acquainted with grief." Our Lord is often seen weeping, and never once do the scriptures say He laughed. It is a painful reminder to us that our sin filled Jesus' life with sorrow. Jesus wept over the sorrow of Martha in John 11:35, He wept over the imminent destruction of Jerusalem in Luke 19:41. Jesus mourns when Jerusalem rejects Him in Luke 13:34. And He was overcome with sorrow and "deeply distressed" over the terrors of His impending crucifixion in Matthew 26:37. The rejection by His people, the pain of seeing His people punished for sin, and the torment of crucifixion and death all caused our Lord to be "a Man of sorrows and acquainted with grief." Let us forever overflow with humble thanks to the One who loved us so much that He was willing to bear so much sorrow for our sake. And too, let us take proper solace from knowing that our Lord's experience with suffering allows Him a perfect understanding and empathy for ours. Hebrews 2:17-18 says, "In all things He had to be made like His brethren, that He might be a merciful and faithful High Priest in things pertaining to God, to make propitiation for the sins of the people. For in that He Himself has suffered, being tempted, He is able to aid those who are tempted."

53:4
Surely He has borne our griefs and carried our sorrows; yet we esteemed Him stricken, smitten by God, and afflicted.

Matthew 8:17 says that this verse was fulfilled in Jesus' constant care for the sick, and Holman's translation makes that even easier to see: "He

Himself bore our sicknesses, and He carried our pains..." Jesus does not only commiserate with our troubles, He does not simply sympathize with us in our griefs – "He has borne our griefs and carried our sorrows." "He Himself bore our sicknesses, and He carried our pains." He does not simply feel empathy for the sick. He heals the sick! He does not simply care for sinners, He forgives sinners! Jesus was constantly curing. In Mark 1 He heals Peter's mother-in-law and all her neighbors. In Mark 2 He heals a paralytic. In Mark 3 He heals a man with a withered hand. In Mark 5 He heals a demon-possessed man, a woman with a flow of blood, and raises a girl back to life. In Mark 6 He heals a few sick people in Nazareth and many more in Gennesaret. In Mark 7 He heals the Syro-Phoenician's daughter. In Mark 8 He heals a blind man at Bethsaida. In Mark 9 He heals a boy with a mute spirit. In Mark 10 He heals blind Bartimaeus. And even the night before He is crucified we find Jesus healing the ear of Malchus in John 18:10. Surely, "Jesus Himself bore our sicknesses and carried our pains."

Yet after all Jesus did to relieve the pains of sickness and sorrow, no one came to relieve His. Instead, many blamed Jesus for His own demise. The NLT renders the verse's final phrase: "And we thought his troubles were a punishment from God, a punishment for his own sins!" It appears that Jesus spent more time healing than He did teaching. He took our pains on Himself and bore our troubles as His own. Yet as soon as He was "afflicted," His people left Him to suffer alone. Today, we are moved with deep gratitude for how our Lord has willingly "borne our griefs and carried our sorrows" even as He groaned under the weight of His own suffering. We know from our own experience how difficult it is to ease the burdens of others while reeling under challenges of our own. We are, therefore, all the more moved to love our Savior Jesus, who bore our sicknesses and carried our sorrows even as He carried the immeasurable weight of His own suffering alone.

53:5
But He was wounded for our transgressions, he was bruised for our iniquities; the chastisement for our peace was upon Him, and by His stripes we are healed.

In the NLT, verse 4 ends with: "And we thought his troubles were a punishment from God, a punishment for his own sins!" Verse 5 however, puts to rest that condemnable accusation. Jesus did not die for any wrongdoing on His part. He was not punished for mistakes of His own. He was wounded for "our transgressions." "Our iniquities" were the cause of His bruises. "Peace" with God required that our sins must be cleansed. We cannot enter the presence of God and drag our sins in with us. We cannot enjoy the favor of God and persist in sin. So then, if we are to enjoy "peace" with our Holy God, sinners must endure a purifying "chastisement." A "punishment" (HCS) that would provide necessary recompense for our sins in order to make us right with God was required. Jesus took that "punishment," He took that "chastisement" upon Himself. "His stripes," the beatings He endured, healed the wounds created by our sins. The punitive actions required to grant us peace with God were meted out at His expense.

Good men groan in remorse when their mistakes cause problems for someone else. Our verse here reminds us of the terrible pain that our sins caused our loving Lord. As Judas hurled away the coins that were given Him to betray Jesus (Matthew 27:5), let us hate and hurl away all vestiges of sin and all benefits of sin. Looking on the innocent yet injured face of Jesus made Judas regret all his sin and cast all gains from that sin far from Him. Since even Judas had this insight, let us not fail to remember how our sin caused such great pain to our innocent, loving Lord. And with the picture placed before us illustrating how our sin inflicted such great pain on Jesus, let us dread and flee sin with all possible intensity.

53:6
All we like sheep have gone astray; we have turned, every one, to his own way; and the LORD has laid on Him the iniquity of us all.

I Peter 2:24-25 quotes verses 5-6 of Isaiah given here. Peter's take on these verses is that we should be encouraged to embrace suffering in our lives seeing all the suffering that our Lord endured, and that we have cause to be deeply grateful, seeing that we were once like "sheep going astray," but now we have "returned to the Shepherd and Overseer of (our) souls."

No one is right with God on His own merits or his own insights. "All" of us, every one of us, without exception, have "turned" from God. God makes His will and ways known through our conscience, but like sheep, we go "astray." Isaiah somewhat defines what going astray means by adding "we all have turned to our own way" (HCS). The NLT puts it: "We have left God's paths to follow our own." This is the specific sin which Judges 21:25 concludes is the root cause of Israel's many, constant problems – "everyone did what was right in his own eyes." Sin is not relegated to the confines of cruelty and dishonesty. Isaiah's words remind us that the fabric of sin is woven with the threads of self-centeredness. Self-centered living, rather than God-centered living is the core of sinful living. It sends us "astray" from God's intended lifestyle and God's intended blessings. Like sheep who leave the good pasture of their shepherd and wander off to a place with less food and less safety, so we wander from God's commandments, following our own path, which allows us the appearance of autonomy, but condemns us to a life void of the fulfillment and blessings that only the Good Shepherd can provide.

Like sheep who cannot find their way back to the shepherd without help, so we are incapable of returning to a holy relationship with God on our own. The cost of overturning the effects of sin is immeasurably high. As sheep are unable to carry heavy burdens, neither can we bear the cost required to cover sins and return us to the Shepherd. So, then, because we cannot bear the punishment and guilt of our sin, "The LORD has laid on Him (Jesus) the iniquity of us all." As if all our various personal sins were bound together in a single package, the sins of mankind were bundled together and placed on the shoulders of our Lord. He carried our sins to the cross, and there the burden of our sin was fully, eternally relieved. We have all gone astray. We have all chosen to reject God's way and live "(our) own way." Blessedly, we have been offered the opportunity to repent of that decision. Our Lord has chosen to take the burden and punishment of our sins on Himself so that we can return to the blessings and provisions of the Good Shepherd once more.

53:7
He was oppressed and He was afflicted, yet He opened not His mouth; He was led as a lamb to the slaughter, and as a sheep before its shearers is silent, so He opened not His mouth.

Twice in this verse and three times in Matthew (Matthew 26:63, 27:12, 27:14) our Lord is seen to keep silent before His (false) accusers. It is very difficult to hold our tongue when people who seek our hurt falsely accuse us. Our righteous indignation mixes with our personal pride to provoke our tongue to burst out in rapid fire self-defense. Knowing this about ourselves heightens our reverent awe over Jesus' ability to remain silent when His base, villainous accusers railed against Him with false testimony. A heart devoted to seeing God honored and seeing men saved will be compelled to speak of the greatness of God and the spiritual needs of men. But that same heart will feel no pressure at all to speak up in self-defense. Jesus demonstrates for us that it is virtuous to remain silent in the face of verbal insults. "Fools quickly show that they are upset, but the wise ignore insults" (Proverbs 12:16 NCV). Proverbs 19:11 says the same thing: "Smart people are patient; they will be honored if they ignore insults" (NCV). Jesus exemplified this perfectly. Let us be loudly vocal in defending our Lord's honor and proclaiming His message to the lost world. But when the insults are hurled at us, not at our Savior, let us take them patiently and quietly, submitting them to the Lord. Our quiet response may win the respect of fellow believers, and our Defender will take care of the others soon enough.

53:8
He was taken from prison and from judgment, and who will declare His generation? For He was cut off from the land of the living; for the transgressions of My people He was stricken.

    The gospel writers tell how Jesus was arrested and taken for "judgment" before Annas (John 18:13), Caiaphas (John 18:24), Pilate (John 18:28-29), Herod (Luke 23:7), and then back to Pilate again (Luke 23:11). The outcome of this sham judgment was that "He was cut off from the land of the living." Jesus would give His life away "for the transgressions of My people." The unavoidable result of sin is death. Romans 6:23 says, "The wages of sin is death." Ezekiel 18:4 affirms: "The soul that sinneth, it shall die" (KJV). Blessedly, although there is no substitute for the consequence of sin – that will always be death -- there *is* a substitute for *who* must die. We, the people of God, have all sinned, but our destiny is no longer death and hell. Our destiny has changed to eternal life and heaven, because Jesus "was stricken" "for the transgressions of (His) people." The death of Jesus brought eternal life to me. How can I rightly respond? Paul's words in Galatians 2:20 provide me direction: "I have been crucified with Christ; it is no longer I who live, but Christ lives in me; and the life which I now live in the flesh I live by faith in the Son of God, who loved me and gave Himself for me."

53:9
And they made His grave with the wicked – but with the rich at His death, because He had done no violence, nor was any deceit in His mouth.

    Jesus died beside the wicked, but he was entombed beside the rich. Matthew 27:38 shows how the former prophecy was fulfilled, and Matthew 27:57 tells how the latter prophecy came to be. I Peter 2:22 then quotes the next half of the verse: "Who committed no sin, nor was deceit found in His mouth." Many modern translations transition to the 2nd half of the verse with the word "although" rather than "because," which the NKJV inserts here, in keeping with the tone and sense of the passage. Jesus was crucified even though He had done nothing wrong. Jesus spoke only the truth and always the truth, without any trace of "deceit." Jesus does not trick people to come to Him, He calls men and women to walk with Him with the truth. Neither does He force people to walk with Him. He needs no coercion to convince His followers to seek His presence. He refused to resort to "violence" even in self-defense, even though at least 12 legions of angels stood ready to fly to His assistance (Matthew 26:53). Truth and love are the great means by which the Lord calls people to Himself. While tyrants and charlatans use force and deceit to gather followers, Jesus calls the world to Himself by the power of the truth and the appeal of His great love.

53:10
Yet it pleased the LORD to bruise Him; He has put Him to grief. When You make His soul an offering for sin, He shall see His seed, He shall prolong His days, and the pleasure of the LORD shall prosper in His hand.

Evil men did not overpower Jesus and force Him to the cross. It was the Father's will, He was "pleased," as it were, to "bruise," to sacrifice His Son, to allow Him to suffer "grief" for the sake of saving mankind. Look at the terrible cost necessary to save sinners! Our Father, our God, must take His Son and "make His soul an offering for sin." The body and soul of Jesus were put to death on Calvary, and though He was God's own son, His deity provided no pain relief. Jesus' death was a "grief" to Him. We see Him praying in desperation before His crucifixion and we are overwhelmed with the intensity of the grief that our Lord felt in the hours before His soul was made an offering for our sin. The Father bruised His Son, put His Son to grief, and led Him to die as an offering for sin.

How could a loving Father bear to watch His Son suffer like that? First, "He shall see His seed." He will see the blessed salvation that Jesus' death will bring to all "His seed" on the earth. He saw the great multitudes around the world who would become the seed of His Son through faith, and He saw how the death of His Son would so wonderfully bless all the souls of all the men and women of all the earth who would trust in His name. Acts 3:25 confirmed that because of Jesus' death on the cross, "in your seed all the families of the earth shall be blessed." God was able to bear the pain of seeing His Son suffer on the cross, He was "pleased" to "bruise" Him, and willing to "put Him to grief," because He was able to "see His seed." He could see all the saved souls that would honor the Son as a result of His sacrifice, and He could see all the blessings that His "seed" would enjoy because of the Son's willingness to die.

And, too, the Father was able to bear watching the "grief" of His Son, for He knew that His Son's death and grief were temporary. After Jesus' sacrifice was complete, the Father would "prolong His days," He would restore the Son's eternal power and Godhead (Romans 1:20) and replace His grief with "the pleasure of the Lord." Hebrews 10:12 says, "But this Man, after

He had offered one sacrifice for sins forever, sat down at the right hand of God." And I Peter 3:22 adds that Jesus "has gone into heaven and is at the right hand of God, angels and authorities and powers having been made subject to Him." Our Lord's suffering, and grief, and death were temporary. Once His sacrifice was complete, the Father knew that the full measure of His Son's good pleasures would be restored forevermore.

53:11
He shall see the labor of His soul, and be satisfied. By His knowledge My righteous Servant shall justify many, for He shall bear their iniquities.

Jesus will "bear (our) iniquities." The One who "knew no sin" rescued us from ours. "For He made Him who knew no sin to be sin for us, that we might become the righteousness of God in Him" (II Corinthians 5:21). The One who had never sinned bore our sin so that we could die to sin and "live for righteousness." "(Jesus) bore our sins in His own body on the tree, that we, having died to sins, might live for righteousness--by whose stripes you were healed" (I Peter 2:24). The pain inflicted on Jesus as He bore our iniquities can hardly be imagined. The beatings, the thorns, and the nails, as well as the mockery, cruelty, and treachery that Jesus endured in order to "bear (our) iniquities" is impossible to imagine. The result of His efforts however, are overwhelmingly joyous. He shall "justify many." All humanity was destined for death and hell – billions of human souls doomed to hell! But through the efforts of the Father's "righteous Servant" many will be "justified" -- they will be cleansed of their sin, made right with the Author of life, and saved from the eternal consequences of sin. "Having now been justified by His blood, we shall be saved from wrath through Him" (Romans 5:9). "Having been justified by His grace, we should become heirs according to the hope of eternal life" (Titus 3:7).

Bearing our sin brought Jesus much agony. But the result of His efforts brought justification and salvation to many, and Jesus our Lord takes divine satisfaction in the blessed, eternal, remarkable fruit of His labor. Men and women – "many" men and women are justified, reconciled with God, and saved from sin because of what Jesus did for us on the cross. Our Lord felt the pain, the agony of bearing our sins, but when He saw what would come of it, He was "satisfied." "He shall see the labor of His soul, and be satisfied." On the cross, the sting of our sin would bring Him death, but the "labor of His soul" would overpower both sin and death and allow many human souls to be eternally saved. On the cross, His labor now ended, Jesus will say, "It is finished" (John 19:30). The price of our redemption will be paid, and Jesus will be satisfied with the fruits of His labor.

53:12
Therefore I will divide Him a portion with the great, and He shall divide the spoil with the strong, because He poured out His soul unto death, and He was numbered with the transgressors, and He bore the sin of many, and made intercession for the transgressors.

The Father lists 4 great works of His Son, the "righteous Servant" (verse 11), which make Him worthy of great reward. First, the Father applauds His Son for how He "poured out His soul unto death." "The wages of sin is death" (Romans 6:23). Without death, there is no means by which men can be saved from sin. "Without the shedding of blood there is no forgiveness of sins" (Hebrews 9:22 ESV). All humanity would be doomed to death in hell unless the Son of God willingly came to lay down His life for us. Today, we rightly give thanks to those who donate a pint of their blood for the sake of others. Of how much more honor is Jesus worthy, when He offered, not a unit of blood, but all His blood for the sake of others. Good men are willing to sacrifice for others. Some are even willing to sacrifice much for the sake of those they hold dear. But who would sacrifice so much for people so ungrateful and undeserving? The Father rewards His Son, not just because "He poured out His soul unto death," but because He did so for the sake of so many people who were so undeserving.

Secondly, the Father commends His Son because He was willing to be "numbered with the transgressors." Rescuing mankind from the penalty of sin required the death of a perfect sacrificial atonement. Only God is perfect. But God cannot die. He is Spirit. He is eternal. In order to die to save humanity, He must first 'take on flesh' (Hebrews 2:14) and be "numbered with the transgressors" that He came to save. The Father finds great virtue in His Son's willingness to lower Himself and become one with flawed, selfish people. The self-righteous Pharisees criticized Jesus for associating with low-life mortal men (Mark 2:16), but the Father commends His Son for this humble trait which allowed Him to rescue untold millions of souls from sin.

Thirdly, the Son is honored by the Father because He "bore the sin of many." Carrying the weight of the guilt and the repercussions of our own sins and failures is certainly heavy enough. Many are crushed and never recover from the weight of their past sins. Momentary lapses in judgment lead to career losses, moral failures lead to unrecoverable breaks in families. Guilt over past sins haunts many to the day they die. The burden of the weight of a single sin can crush a man for a lifetime – and our Lord "bore the sin of many." He carried the weight of the sins of all humanity. The pain and weight and darkness of our sin was so terrible that for a moment, our

Lord could not see His Father, crying out in Matthew 27:46 -- "My God, My God, why have You forsaken Me?" The weight of our sin was crushing – it broke His heart (John 19:34). And for His willingness to suffer the weight of bearing the sins of the world, the Father will see to it that the Son is glorified.

And fourthly, the Father commends the Son because Jesus "made intercession for the transgressors." We see Jesus praying for His people in John 17 and the Father still sees Jesus praying for us even now. Romans 8:34 says, "It is Christ who died, and furthermore is also risen, who is even at the right hand of God, <u>who also makes intercession for us</u>." And Hebrews 7:25 tells us that our Savior will never stop praying for us! "Therefore He is also able to save to the uttermost those who come to God through Him, since <u>He always lives to make intercession for them</u>." "We have an Advocate with the Father, Jesus Christ the righteous" (I John 2:1). He died for us long ago, and He continues to be our Advocate even now, praying for us to this very hour, knowing that without His prayers of intercession, we would "go our own way" and forfeit the blessings of the great work that He carried out for us on the cross.

Look at the greatness of our Savior. He "poured out His soul unto death" for us. He was willing to number Himself among us, even though we are sin-filled unworthy people. He bore our sins on the cross – suffering the terrible weight of feeling the guilt and shame of every sin of every person the world over. And still today, our Lord is still our Advocate, praying on our behalf that we will be able to flee temptation, endure hardship, and "take hold of that for which Christ Jesus took hold of me" (Philippians 3:12 NIV). For all these things, (and we can list many more), the Father finds His Son worthy of glory. Let us join the Father and give praise to our Lord Jesus; He is worthy of praise.

Isaiah 54

54:1
"Sing, O barren, you who have not borne! Break forth into singing, and cry aloud, you who have not labored with child! For more are the children of the desolate than the children of the married woman," says the LORD.

Isaiah's people, God's people, are compared to a "desolate" woman, a "barren" woman. They have been taken captive and forced to live in desolate exile. They are like a barren woman, unable to carry on the family line, powerless to pass on anything of value to the next generation. But then the Lord calls on them to "sing." He invites His people to "break forth into singing." He promises that His barren children will be fruitful, they will be blessed with children without number and joy without limit at the sight of their enlarging family.

The prophecy will begin its fulfillment when the exiles return from Babylon in the book of Ezra. But Isaiah's words portend much greater events than the return of a few thousand Jews to Jerusalem. Paul quotes Isaiah's words in Galatians 4:27 and teaches us that they apply to the expansion of Christ's church, the birth of believers in Jesus all over the world. The nations had been barren! No one trusted in their Creator, no one obeyed Him or sought to give Him glory. The world at large had been a spiritually desolate place for centuries, for millennia! But the promise is given that this will change, and Paul's letter to the Galatians declares that the time had come at last for the barren nations of the earth to rejoice, for they would (at last) bring forth children of faith – far, far more children than Israel ever had.

Oh, it is such a great cause for rejoicing to see barren nations at last bear children of faith! It is right to "break forth into singing" when cities that had never had a single Christian, cities that had never offered God-directed worship finally see churches born and bodies of believers lift up praise to their Savior. "Sing, O barren, you who have not borne!" It has been my joy to sing this song. It has been my joy to see our Lord call people to Himself in Thailand, in places where He had never been praised before. Those "who have not borne" songs of praise to their Creator now sing! Those "who have not borne" children into the family of faith now crowd around the throne in grateful praise and service! Oh, it is such a deep, abiding joy to see children of God born in places that had never known Him before. Long ago, Isaiah was granted this glimpse of the expansion of Christ's kingdom on earth, and his vision continues to fill us with hope and joy today.

54:2-3
Enlarge the place of your tent, and let them stretch out the curtains of your dwellings; do not spare; lengthen your cords, and strengthen your stakes. For you shall expand to the right and to the left, and your descendants will inherit the nations, and make the desolate cities inhabited.

What a great picture of the expanding borders of Christ's influence! God's people will "expand to the right and to the left"! This is not just a picture of the exiles returning from Babylon, this is a picture of the ever-expanding family of faith. It is an invitation, yes, it is a command to "strengthen your stakes," to *stake a claim* in Jesus' name over all the nations of the earth. As the marines planted their nation's flag on Iwo Jima after the terrible island battle in 1945, as settlers staked out their holdings in the old west, so God's people are called upon to plant their flag and stake out the borders of God's kingdom for the Savior's ever-expanding domain. Isaiah 9:7 says that "of the increase of His government and peace there will be no end," and here, that promise is affirmed, saying that the kingdom of God will forever "enlarge," "stretch," "lengthen," "strengthen," and "expand." Isaiah's words are a call to missions, yes, even more than that, they state the certainty of missions. On the shoulders of missionaries and by the beautiful feet of those who bring good news, Christ's kingdom will expand to every nation on earth, making "desolate cities" that had never given God His due praise finally "inhabited" with God-fearing, Christ-honoring, Savior-praising people of faith. William Carey, the one called the founder of the modern missionary movement, preached from this very text as he inspired God's people to rise up and set their sights on expanding the kingdom of God. Let us join him in taking proper delight in enlarging, stretching, lengthening, strengthening, and expanding the kingdom of God.

54:4-5
Do not fear, for you will not be ashamed; neither be disgraced, for you will not be put to shame; for you will forget the shame of your youth, and will not remember the reproach of your widowhood anymore. For your Maker is your husband, the LORD of hosts is His name; and your Redeemer is the Holy One of Israel; He is called the God of the whole earth.

God's people are assured here that they "will not be ashamed," or rather, we will "forget the shame of (our) youth." Israel could well feel ashamed. Their country was defeated in battle and they were exiled as servants of foreigners. As Ruth arrived in her new home in Israel, so the people of Judah arrived in their new home in Babylon – penniless, protector-less, strangers in a strange land. But just as Ruth's disgrace and desperation ended when Boaz became her husband, so Judah's disgrace and desperation ended when God came down to take His people as His bride. "Your Maker is your husband." What a precious thought. As a bride feels secure and filled with joy in the arms of her husband, so do God's people delight in the protective love of their Savior. "They looked to Him and were radiant, and their faces were not ashamed" (Psalms 34:5).

Israel had good cause to be "ashamed" by the sins of its "youth." They had ample reason to feel the "reproach" of the failures of their "widowhood" and old age. But the Lord's wedding vows change their disgrace to pure joy. "I will betroth you to Me forever; yes, I will betroth you to Me In righteousness and justice, In lovingkindness and mercy" (Hosea 2:19). As a husband gives His name to His bride, so our Lord gives us His name -- and His name is wonderful. "The LORD of hosts is His name." He is our Redeemer, the Holy One of Israel. "He is called the God of the whole earth." With our God, the God of the whole earth, as our redeemer, protector, and companion, the shame of our past sins and past failures and present weaknesses melt away. Our Lord loves us, forgives us, and has called us to be His own. We "will not (now) be ashamed."

54:6-8
"For the LORD has called you like a woman forsaken and grieved in spirit, like a youthful wife when you were refused," says your God. "For a mere moment I have forsaken you, but with great mercies I will gather you. With a little wrath I hid My face from you for a moment; but with everlasting kindness I will have mercy on you," says the LORD, your Redeemer.

The sins of God's people had brought them very low. They were like a "woman forsaken," a woman whose husband had left her. But the Lord had left them "for a mere moment." Of necessity, God must deal with sin in His people, but He deals with sin only with "a little wrath" — much less wrath than our sins deserve. Having dealt with sin with temporary anger, His "everlasting kindness" will take center stage once more. "For the LORD is good; His mercy is everlasting, and His truth endures to all generations" (Psalms 100:5). God displays anger with His children to purify us from sin and warn others to fear disobedience. God's anger, however, is blessedly short-lived. In wonderful contrast to the quick passing of His anger, "the mercy of the LORD is from everlasting to everlasting" (Psalms 103:17).

54:9-10
"For this is like the waters of Noah to Me; for as I have sworn that the waters of Noah would no longer cover the earth, so have I sworn that I would not be angry with you, nor rebuke you. For the mountains shall depart and the hills be removed, but My kindness shall not depart from you, nor shall My covenant of peace be removed," says the LORD, who has mercy on you.

In Genesis 9:11 God promises that He will never again destroy the earth with a flood. Here, however, the Lord tells us that His promise in Genesis extends further still. Though we sin against Him, yet the Lord makes this covenant that His kindness will never depart from His people. He has signed a "covenant of peace" with His children of faith, and His covenant will never be nullified. Though mountains melt and hills be removed, yet His love for us will never be removed. Flood waters will never again cover the earth, and God's anger will never cover the earth either. Psalms 46:1-2 shows the great comfort that God's promise here provides. "Though the earth be removed, and though the mountains be carried into the midst of the sea," yet the sons of Korah who penned the psalm "will not fear," because "God is our refuge and strength, a very present help in trouble." The Lord now extends to all of His children the promise that He made to David and His sons long before. "If (David's) sons forsake My law and do not walk in My judgments, if they break My statutes and do not keep My commandments, then I will punish their transgression with the rod, and their iniquity with stripes. Nevertheless My lovingkindness I will not utterly take from him, nor allow My faithfulness to fail. My covenant I will not break, nor alter the word that has gone out of My lips" (Psalms 89:30-34). God insists on showing mercy on the undeserving. He swears that He will show us mercy. Sin He will punish, but sons He will never send away. Mountains may melt, but God's mercy is "great above the heavens" (Psalms 108:4).

54:11-13
O you afflicted one, tossed with tempest, and not comforted, behold, I will lay your stones with colorful gems, and lay your foundations with sapphires. I will make your pinnacles of rubies, your gates of crystal, and all your walls of precious stones. All your children shall be taught by the LORD, and great shall be the peace of your children.

Isaiah writes of a future day when the house of Israel had collapsed. Their homes, homeland, hopes, and family lines lay in ruins. But here, our Lord promises to make them beautiful once again. He would beautify their homes, houses of worship, and future with the precious stones of His favor. As Solomon decorated the temple with "precious stones" to reflect the beauty of the Lord (II Chronicles 3:6), the Lord promises here to adorn His people with precious stones of beauty once more. Verse 13 describes the motherlode of precious stones, the vein of precious metals which is the source of the spiritual sapphires which beautify God's people. "All your children shall be taught by the LORD." Oh, the joy of seeing the eternal God teach your children! Nothing glorifies, beautifies, enriches a family as when the Spirit of God is seated at the family dining table and teaches your children as you eat. Nothing compares to the precious work of the Savior as He calls your children to sit with Him in daily devotions while He teaches His great truths to their spiritual ear. Oh, how beautiful is the family that sees the Savior teach their children how to follow Him, serve Him, and devote themselves to His will and ways. Solomon set precious stones in the wall of the temple "for beauty," and our Lord teaches our children the great things of God so that our families might be filled with the beauty of the Father. From my seat on the hill of fatherhood, I have seen nothing more beautiful than this sight of my Father teaching my children. The encouragement is more excellent still because He is careful to say: "All your children" shall be taught by the Lord. One black sheep, one wayward son, a single daughter who does not care for the Lord can bring great grief to godly parents. But the Lord has granted me this blessing that He speaks of here. My Lord has granted me the unsurpassed blessing of teaching <u>all</u> my children. Gary, Jonathan, Becky, and Sandi have all been called to my Savior's table of instruction and have heard and have obeyed His voice instructing them on the way that they should go. I am deeply, deeply grateful. When the Lord is the great Teacher of our children, He makes them to prosper and He fills them with peace. "And great shall be the peace of your children." The law of the Lord brings beauty to families, and His instructions fill children with peace. "Those who love your teachings will find true peace, and nothing will defeat them" (Psalms 119:165 NCV)." Prosperity and peace. Beauty and abundance. These are the blessings that our Lord brings when He comes to teach our children. Let us crave nothing but God and let us dread nothing but sin – not only for ourselves, but also for our children. Let us leave off praying for shallow blessings for our children. Let us plead with the Lord that He will sit with them each day and teach them His ways. For true prosperity and true peace will belong to our children and to their children when they listen to and obey the magnificent tutoring of our Lord.

54:14-15
In righteousness you shall be established; you shall be far from oppression, for you shall not fear; and from terror, for it shall not come near you. Indeed they shall surely assemble, but not because of Me. Whoever assembles against you shall fall for your sake.

The promise is offered to the captives in Babylon that they will be established in their homeland once more. But clearly the prophecy extends beyond assurances to Israel's returnees from Babylon and is meant to comfort God's people in all nations and in all eras. God's people will be established "in righteousness." For ages on end the Lord has established His people in mercy, even though they constantly struggled with rebellion and sin. At last, however, the people of God will "be established," they will be built up together, unified by the common bonds of inner love for God and outward acts of righteousness. For generations on end, Israel had risen and fallen, risen and fallen again because of their continual rebellion and return to unrighteous living. At last, however, the Lord will remove rebellion and their penchant for wickedness, and they will finally be permanently established in the security of holiness. Proverbs 12:3 says, "A man is not established by wickedness, but the root of the righteous cannot be moved."

In the past, the Lord raised up Assyria and raised up Babylon to punish Israel for their rebellion. But the time is coming when those who rise up against God's people will not do so at His behest, nor with His blessings. "If any nation comes to fight you, it will not be because I sent them to punish you. Your enemies will always be defeated because I am on your side" (NLT). Unrighteousness will fall out of our thinking and enemies will fall before reaching our gates. What a great picture of the blessed state of the holy, healthy church. Temptations may lure us, but our longing will always be to remain righteous in our Father's eyes. And enemies may seek our hurt, but our Lord's longing will always be to remain watchful and protective of those whose eyes are on Him.

54:16-17

"Behold, I have created the blacksmith who blows the coals in the fire, who brings forth an instrument for his work; and I have created the spoiler to destroy. No weapon formed against you shall prosper, and every tongue which rises against you in judgment you shall condemn. This is the heritage of the servants of the LORD, and their righteousness is from Me," says the LORD.

This is the "heritage" that belongs to all God's children: righteousness and safety. "Their righteousness is from Me." Without this inheritance from our Lord, we would all be without hope, for apart from the Lord's kindness: "As it is written: 'There is none righteous, no, not one'" (Romans 3:10). There can be no more important matter in life, for only the pure are allowed to see God (Matthew 5:8), and only those who are perfectly righteous are allowed to enter heaven (Matthew 5:20). So then, we are deeply grateful for our imputed righteousness (Romans 4:6), knowing that if we were not granted our righteousness by our Father, we would have no other source to obtain such a gift.

And too, we are grateful for our heritage of safety granted us by our Lord. God knows how to create weapons. God knows how to raise up warriors and spoilers who wreak havoc on the lives of others. He also knows, however, how to combat these weapons and how to silence these enemies, and He assures us here that it is His intent to do so. "No weapon formed against you shall prosper." Weapons of war, weapons of prejudice, jealousy, cruelty, and deceit will all fail when they are aimed at God's people. Even the judging, cursing tongues of our enemies will be condemned when

ISAIAH 54

they lash out at us – not because we are greater than our enemies, but because our Father grants these two great gifts as our inheritance of faith: righteousness and safety. On our own, we are perpetual sinners – stained by past sins and prone to present ones. But our inheritance from our Father makes us a people "made righteous" (Romans 5:19) and the benefits of being made righteous are unending. "For You, O LORD, will bless the righteous; with favor You will surround him as with a shield" (Psalms 5:12).

Isaiah 55

55:1
Ho! Everyone who thirsts, come to the waters; and you who have no money, come, buy and eat. Yes, come, buy wine and milk without money and without price.

Our God, our Creator invites us to come. He invites us to drink in abundant living. He invites us to come and to taste life "in all its fullness" (John 10:10 NLT). All too many people the world over live their whole lives and never see the point of it all! They never once experience the deepest joys God intends for us to feel. They never experience the fulfillment of carrying out God's purpose for us. Some find life filled only with pain. Others find life filled only with guilt. Some find nothing in life worth living for at all. For all these, our Lord says, "Come." Set your heart on living a life that overflows with satisfaction in carrying out the great eternal purpose that our Creator-God has set before us. The offer is remarkable – "waters" – "living water" Jesus called it in John 4:10 – water that will allow all our souls to feel abundantly, richly satisfied with an overwhelming sense of fulfillment, contentment, and joy. The offer is an unparalleled bargain. It will cost us nothing yet gains for us an eternity of fulfilment. The only requirement placed on us is to "thirst." Those who are happy with life, feel no remorse over sin, find no reason to concern themselves with eternity, and who are content to feed their flesh with temporary pleasures are not extended the invitation. Only those who thirst for a life on a higher spiritual plane are invited. Those who are content with temporary pleasures are not offered eternal joys. They "have their (lesser) reward" (Matthew 6:2), and they are promised nothing more.

55:2
Why do you spend money for what is not bread, and your wages for what does not satisfy? Listen carefully to Me, and eat what is good, and let your soul delight itself in abundance.

Psalms 53:2 says, "God looks down from heaven upon the children of men, to see if there are any who understand…" And here, as if God is looking down from heaven and wondering how so many people can fail to understand, He shakes His head and asks humanity 'why are you spending all your attention on things that don't matter? Why do you eat what is not filling and spend money on things which do not satisfy your soul?' It is our loving Lord's intention to fill our lives with "good" things, things that will cause our soul to "delight itself in abundance." Even when facing hardships, our Lord is ready to grant our soul unquenchable, abundant delight. Psalms 94:19 says, "In the multitude of my anxieties within me, Your comforts delight my soul."

Isaiah's words compel us to examine how we use our time and how we invest our energies. The soul delights in setting God as the great focus of our lives. When we serve our Lord sacrificially, worship Him wholeheartedly, and set His commands and His purposes constantly in the forefront of our lives, our soul will love it! We will never regret anything we give in pursuit of carrying out our Savior's purposes. In contrast, there will be great regret felt over money spent which procured nothing in heaven, time spent on matters which distracted from godly endeavors, and passions followed which left the soul feeling empty in the end. If we will delight ourselves in the Lord (Psalms 37:4), our soul will "delight itself in abundance." If anything else becomes the object of our desire, we will find that it "does not satisfy."

55:3-5
Incline your ear, and come to Me. Hear, and your soul shall live; and I will make an everlasting covenant with you – the sure mercies of David.

Indeed I have given him as a witness to the people, a leader and commander for the people. Surely you shall call a nation you do not know, and nations who do not know you shall run to you, because of the LORD your God, and the Holy One of Israel; for He has glorified you."

    If we will set our Lord as the object of our affections as David did, our Lord will do for us as He did for him. He will make an "everlasting covenant" to bless us as He did with David. He will show us His constant "sure mercies" as He did for David. And He will use us to call the nations to Himself as He did with David. God does not change. We can, therefore, be assured that if we will demonstrate the passionate devotion to God that David did, God will bless us as He did David: "Your soul shall live." These remarkable 5 verses from Isaiah 55 inspire us to scorn creature comforts and desire instead "soul delight." David is used as both the example for how to thirst for God and how God blesses those who do. Psalms 63:1-6 picture David's thirst: "O GOD, You are my God; early will I seek You; my soul thirsts for You; my flesh longs for You in a dry and thirsty land where there is no water. So I have looked for You in the sanctuary, to see Your power and Your glory. Because Your lovingkindness is better than life, my lips shall praise You. Thus I will bless You while I live; I will lift up my hands in Your name. My soul shall be satisfied as with marrow and fatness, and my mouth shall praise You with joyful lips. When I remember You on my bed, I meditate on You in the night watches." This was David's thirst to "come to the waters" (verse 1) and set his affection on his Father. And when David did so, not only did God bless Him, but He blessed David's descendants for generations on end (Psalms 132:11-12). And even greater still, the Lord's blessings on David for His devotion extended to a blessing for all the world's people! "Nations who do not know you shall run to you." They run because they see how God blesses those who love Him. The floodwaters of God's blessings are so deep and so wonderfully wide that they extend far beyond the shores of those who first know Him -- bringing delight to the souls of all the world's people. The remarkable promise is given in Psalms 67:7 -- "God shall bless us, and all the ends of the earth shall fear Him."

    Let us thirst for God. Let us expend all possible effort and display all possible devotion to His purposes. Doing so will delight our soul and bring blessings to our children's children for endless generations and will add grease to the wheels that turn the hearts of the nations to find their soul's delight in the Lord as well.

55:6
Seek the LORD while He may be found, call upon Him while He is near.

ISAIAH 55

    The world's greatest invitation is coupled with a warning of critical importance. We are invited to "seek the Lord." We are granted the great privilege of calling upon Him when we are in need. Psalms 105:4 invites us to "Seek the LORD and His strength; seek His face evermore!" The search for God is not a fool's errand, it is not a blind search for the mystical. We are assured by Deuteronomy 4:29 that if we will seek the Lord, we will not be disappointed. "You will seek the LORD your God, and you will find Him if you seek Him with all your heart and with all your soul." The benefits of seeking are without measure. Psalms 34:10 says, "But those who seek the LORD shall not lack any good thing." The danger of not seeking the Lord is frightful. II Chronicles 12:14 says of Rehoboam: "He did evil, because he did not prepare his heart to seek the LORD." And to top it off, Acts 17:27 tells us that the very reason we were created is so that we might "seek the Lord" -- so failure to seek Him is a crime against our own existence. For all these reasons, let us seek the Lord! Let the needy seek the Lord's help. Let sinners seek the Lord's forgiveness. Let the lonely seek the Lord's presence. And may all men and women seek the Lord's blessings and approval. The Lord has invited us to seek Him! What a remarkable invitation – an offer to seek audience with the Maker of the universe. Let us rush to respond as the psalmist does in Psalms 27:8 - "When You said, 'Seek My face,' my heart said to You, 'Your face, LORD, I will seek.'"

    The incredible offer to seek and to find the Creator God is coupled with an implied warning of utmost importance. "Seek the LORD <u>while He may be found</u>." "Call upon Him <u>while He is near</u>." The implication is that although God's invitation is astounding, it is time sensitive. God offers salvation to sinners. He offers cleansing and renewal for those wracked by a guilty conscience. He offers meaning and fulfillment to those who recognize that the state of our eternal soul is vastly more important than the comforts of the physical and temporary. Everyone – every single man and woman on earth – should fully recognize that God's offer to their conscience is the opportunity of a lifetime. Failure to immediately rush to take advantage of God's offer is offensive to our Creator and seriously endangers our soul. II Corinthians 6:2 says, "Behold, now is the accepted time; behold, now is the day of salvation." We must not put God on hold when He offers us forgiveness, heaven, and His eternal blessings in exchange for nothing but our trust. The parable of the foolish virgins in Matthew 25:1-13 re-affirms for us that we must be ready at all times to seek and to receive the presence of the Lord. God's offer of forgiveness and blessings is too good to pass up. In fact, it is inexcusable to pass up. Failure to seek the Lord when His voice calls us to Himself places us at grave risk of so offending our Father that He never calls us again. Oh, how terribly often I have watched men and women cry over their need for God. I have watched so many rock back and forth, often in tears, as they hear the Father call, and weigh in the balance the cost of heeding His voice. I have seen them, after an extended session in a spiritual battle – their conscience crying out their need for God and their flesh crying out their preference to sin – but finally, they choose sin instead of the Savior. And then, so often, I see them steadily fall away – never again hearing the Father call, never again sensing their need for forgiveness, never again seeking the face of God. "Now is the accepted time." Tomorrow may prove too late. Our Lord invites us to seek Him! Let us seek His face! Let us seek His glory and His grace, His forgiveness and His help in time of need. And let us seek Him today "while He is near." God calls us to Himself! But the offence of giving Him a cold shoulder denies us any guarantee that He will call again.

55:7
Let the wicked forsake his way, and the unrighteous man his thoughts; let him return to the LORD, and He will have mercy on him; and to our God, for He will abundantly pardon.

In verse 3 our loving Lord calls us to Himself. He promises in that verse that if we come to Him in faith that our "soul shall live." This is not an offer for good men to become better. It is an offer which allows wicked men and women to be forgiven of their sins and gain eternal life. It is an offer for unrighteous men and women to be cleansed of the nagging guilt that plagues their conscience and gain, instead, a pure soul that lives abundantly forever. In response to this great offer from God that our "soul shall live," we are called upon to "forsake" our wicked ways and evil thoughts. The best of men must kneel and confess to actions that they are ashamed of and thoughts that are even worse. We are invited to come to God (verse 1), but we are not allowed to come to Him and drag our sins in with us. We must "forsake" all things that are unholy if our fellowship with the Lord is to endure. Blessedly, no matter how far we have walked from God, no matter how horrible our actions have been, our Lord promises to "abundantly pardon." He promises to "have mercy." Though our actions have been shameful and our thoughts have been even worse, mercy and pardon are promised to all who "return to the LORD." "'Return to Me, and I will return to you,' says the LORD of hosts" (Malachi 3:7). Unlike our tendency to not forgive, or begrudgingly forgive those who wrong us, our Lord "abundantly" forgives when we return to Him. He multiplies His pardons; He lavishes His forgiveness on us. What a precious thought – our God "abundantly" pardons. We are moved to join the 8 Levites in Nehemiah 9 and humbly acknowledge and gratefully praise our Lord, saying: "You are God, ready to pardon, gracious and merciful, slow to anger, abundant in kindness" (Nehemiah 9:17).

55:8-9

"For My thoughts are not your thoughts, nor are your ways My ways," says the LORD. "For as the heavens are higher than the earth, so are My ways higher than your ways, and My thoughts than your thoughts."

We read of God's offer to "abundantly pardon" and show mercy on evil doers and we are happy with God's mercy – as long as it applies to His forgiveness of our "small" (in our own minds) miscues and minor misdeeds. Major sins however, especially those carried out by people we don't know or don't like, we may prefer for God to deal with more stringently. God sees our hesitance to forgive; He sees our desire to mete out swift punishment for sins carried out by complete strangers, and He says to us here: "My thoughts are not your thoughts." Men forgive loved ones and punish strangers. Men want great sins of cruelty punished, but moral indiscretions with no apparent victims they find acceptable. God however, finds our inability to forgive to be a character flaw. He finds our double standards regarding punishing strangers versus punishing loved ones to be far lower, far baser than His ways. "As the heavens are higher than the earth, so are My ways higher than your ways." God finds all sin – all sin – to be abhorrent, detestable, a perversion of the human holiness He created us to exemplify, and punishable by death and hell. At the same time, God finds pardon for the guilty and mercy for the repentant to be a higher response to sin than universal judgment. In the eyes of God, "Mercy triumphs over judgment" (James 2:13). Man grades sin on a curve. God does not, for His thoughts are higher than ours. Man wants to punish bad strangers immediately. God desires to show mercy, because His ways are higher than ours. Man has trouble discerning when mercy should be shown and when judgment should be meted out. God has no such trouble. His ways are higher than ours and can discern these matters perfectly.

55:10-11

For as the rain comes down, and the snow from heaven, and do not return there, but water the earth, and make it bring forth and bud, that it may give seed to the sower and bread to the eater, so shall My word be that goes forth from My mouth; it shall not return to Me void, but it shall accomplish what I please, and it shall prosper in the thing for which I sent it.

The word of God from the mouth of God will always, forever accomplish the will of God. As rain always makes the plants grow, God's word will always successfully lead to budding faith in unbelievers. His words will always nourish the souls of His children. At times in history we see His word bring about great revivals when whole cities, whole people groups turn to Him. At times His words seem to fall on deaf ears, but even then, His words will call a remnant to Himself and His chosen few will find His words to be food for their souls. God's word will never return void. It will always produce fruit. "It will accomplish all I want it to, and it will prosper everywhere I send it" (NLT). Seeing then, that God's word will always prosper and bear spiritual fruit when it is presented, let us present it constantly in every venue and under every circumstance. Let us present God's word to the lost so that faith might be birthed inside them. Let us teach God's word to young believers that they may grow thereby. Let us encourage the downcast with words from heaven so that their spirits might be lifted. Let us have God's word on the tip of our tongue all day, every day, for God's word will always be the right thing to say, His words will always carry the day, and they will always "accomplish" His purposes and benefit our hearers.

55:12
For you shall go out with joy, and be led out with peace; the mountains and the hills shall break forth into singing before you, and all the trees of the field shall clap their hands.

The initial fulfillment of Isaiah's prophecy occurred when God's people returned from Babylon. The Lord led them home with joy and with peace. These words continue to be fulfilled even in our day however, as God's people "go out" to work for Him each day, as missionaries go out to the nations with the good news year by year, and as servants of the Lord are "led out" by the Savior to carry out the works of the Lord filled with His joy and peace. Those who serve the Lord are filled with the "joy" of the Lord. Psalms 28:7 says, "The LORD is my strength, my shield from every danger. I trust in him with all my heart. He helps me, and my heart is filled with joy. I burst out in songs of thanksgiving" (NLT). And those who serve the Lord are filled with peace. Psalms 29:11 says, "The LORD gives his people strength. The LORD blesses them with peace" (NLT). Joy and peace are the wonderful travel companions of all those who "go out" to serve the Lord. The joy of the Lord is so pervading that it bursts from the lives of God's people and brings joy to all around them as well. Even "the mountains and the hills shall break forth into singing" at the sight of God's people. The joy of the presence of the Lord is so overwhelming that if mankind did not sing God's praises, the vacuum of praise would pull the songs of praise from the stones! (Luke 19:40). Psalms 98:8 says, "Let the rivers clap their hands; let the hills be joyful together before the LORD," because the greatness of God is so transcending, that the sound of His praise from the lips of His children summons all nature to sing His praise as well.

55:13
Instead of the thorn shall come up the cypress tree, and instead of the brier shall come up the myrtle tree; and it shall be to the LORD for a name, for an everlasting sign that shall not be cut off.

Multiple views are offered by authors as to Isaiah's meaning here, and each view is very pleasant to contemplate. Some say this is a picture of the reversal of the curse given on humanity after Adam's fall in the garden. Genesis 3:18 says, "thorns and thistles" will grow up and impede man's efforts. Here, the Lord promises the day when those thorns will be replaced by the cypress tree and briers will be replaced by the myrtle tree – the shade and beauty of God's protective grace will replace the choking, stinging effects of man's sin.

Some find Isaiah's words to relate to God's heart to bless the efforts of His children. Instead of fruitless briers, God will prosper His people so that they flourish in all they do. His people will return to Israel from Babylon and harvest fields and see forests grow where the land hand been desolate during the time that Israel was in exile. The words picture how God's blessings grant His children fruitfulness and successfulness when, by natural means, our efforts would fail to provide for our needs and fail to give Him glory. As Jacob became "exceedingly prosperous" when God blessed his curious strategy in Genesis 30, as Jesus blessed the disciples' fishing efforts in John 21, so the Lord promises here to bless the efforts of His people as "an everlasting sign" that will reveal to the world that God reigns over all and He blesses the efforts of His people.

Isaiah 56

56:1
Thus says the LORD: "Keep justice, and do righteousness, for My salvation is about to come, and My righteousness to be revealed."

God saves. What a blessed thought. He saves us from enemies (Psalms 18:3). He saves from sin (Matthew 1:21). He saves from death (James 5:20). He does not just save a few people, from a few places, from a few minor mishaps. Jesus is "able to save to the uttermost those who come to God through Him" (Hebrews 7:25). God saves! He saves souls! (Psalms 72:13, Hebrews 10:39). He saves lives (Genesis 19:19). He saves peoples (Deuteronomy 33:29) and saves nations (Revelation 21:24).

"His salvation is near to those who fear Him" (Psalms 85:9), but "Salvation is far from the wicked" (Psalms 119:155). So then, seeing that God saves, but seeing that this salvation is near the righteous (Psalms 37:39), but is far from the wicked, how should we respond? Our verse here tells us plainly: "Keep justice, and do righteousness, for My salvation is about to come." God saves. And as His saving heart draws near to us, we are compelled to "keep justice" and "do righteousness" as our proper welcome to His approaching salvation. Failure to repent of sin and live "righteously and godly" in this present world (Titus 2:12) is a failure to properly respond to the salvation that our Savior-God presents. John the Baptist's opening sermon centered on this theme: "Repent, for the kingdom of heaven is at hand!" (Matthew 3:2). Jesus taught the same (Matthew 4:17). And when Paul wrote with joy that the salvation of the Lord had drawn near, he gave his readers the same charge as Isaiah, John and Jesus. Seeing that "now our salvation is nearer than when we first believed," Paul called on his readers to "cast off the works of darkness, and let us put on the armor of light" (Romans 13:11-14). God saves! And we must "keep justice," we must live righteous lives in response. No one is saved because they are righteous. But everyone who is saved by God will devote himself to righteousness. The salvation of God brings righteousness to men. Persistent sin even in religious people is a frightful indication that their salvation is a long way off.

56:2
Blessed is the man who does this, and the son of man who lays hold on it; who keeps from defiling the Sabbath, and keeps his hand from doing any evil.

We are to "keep justice" and "do righteousness" because God is coming to save (verse 1). In response to God's provision to save us, we must keep ourselves from "any evil" – any form of evil, any degree of evil. Every kind of wrongdoing is included, but only one virtuous endeavor is mentioned by name: keeping oneself from "defiling the Sabbath." Honoring the Sabbath Day honors the God who created the world in six days and is a far cry from just a head nod to Old Testament ritual. In Ezekiel 20:12 God says that He gave His people the Sabbath Day instructions "as a sign between them and Me, that they might know that I am the LORD who sanctifies them." He repeats the call to "hallow My Sabbaths" in Ezekiel 20:20 so that all might know "that I am the LORD your God." God is made known, God is revealed more clearly to everyone when His people honor Him on the Sabbath Day. "Blessed is the man who does this." The Lord blesses those who honor the Sabbath. "Those who are planted in the house of the LORD shall flourish in the courts of our God" (Psalms 92:13). David wrote "I was glad when they said to me, 'Let us go into the house of the LORD'" (Psalms 122:1). I hope that our family will always delight in honoring our Lord in His house on His day. Yes, let us honor Him every day, but honoring our Creator on the Sabbath is a sign to the world that our God is the God who sanctifies us. "Blessed is the man who does this."

56:3-5
Do not let the son of the foreigner who has joined himself to the LORD speak, saying, "The LORD has utterly separated me from His people"; or let the eunuch say, "Here I am, a dry tree." For thus says the LORD: "To the eunuchs who keep My Sabbaths, and choose what pleases Me, even to them I will give in My house and within My walls a place and a name better than that of sons and daughters; I will give them an everlasting name that shall not be cut off.

A precious promise is given to all who follow the example of Abraham and Ruth and leave their homeland for the sake of pleasing and serving the Lord God. More will be said of this group in the next 3 verses, but here, Isaiah first focuses on the blessed hope of the "eunuch," those who can have no children of their own. For singles and couples that cannot have children, God's promise is very sweet. The legacy of those who love the Lord is secure. The desire to have children and leave a lasting legacy will be more than fulfilled by the Lord's promise to give His children "a place and a name better than that of sons and daughters." No one need to fear that they have no son to carry on the family name, the Lord pledges to us that "I will give them an everlasting name that shall not be cut off." Dying alone in the world as a "dry tree," without any fruit that will last or descendants that will continue the works that we have begun can be a frightful prospect for some. But the Lord removes this fear from His people. All that we do for Him will be remembered forever. All our spiritual gains and spiritual children that have been won to the Lord through our prayers and efforts will be credited to our account and remain cause for rejoicing for all eternity. Our family name will never die out. Our Father gives us His name, "an everlasting name" that will be remembered forever. The Lord "grants the barren woman a home, like a joyful mother of children. Praise the LORD!" (Psalms 113:9).

56:6-8
Also the sons of the foreigner who join themselves to the LORD, to serve Him, and to love the name of the LORD, to be His servants – everyone who keeps from defiling the Sabbath, and holds fast My covenant – even them I will bring to My holy mountain, and make them joyful in My house of prayer. Their burnt offerings and their sacrifices will be accepted

on My altar; for My house shall be called a house of prayer for all nations." The Lord GOD, who gathers the outcasts of Israel, says, "Yet I will gather to him others besides those who are gathered to him."**

Not everyone who moves to a different country is included in this promise, but all those who "join themselves to the LORD," all who leave their home and heartland because they desire to "serve Him" and "to love the name of the LORD" are here encouraged with the promise of God's intention to bring them to His holy mountain and "make them joyful in My house of prayer." In Matthew 19:29, Jesus addresses this promise again, saying, "everyone who has left houses or brothers or sisters or father or mother or wife or children or lands, for My name's sake, shall receive a hundredfold, and inherit eternal life." Abraham left his home in Haran to become a foreigner in Canaan in Genesis 12. Ruth did so as well in Ruth 1:16. Each received great reward for their willingness to become foreigners in a foreign land for the sake of faithfulness to God, and we see here that it is the Lord's heart to similarly bless all who similarly forsake the comforts of home for the cause of Christ.

The Lord's grace toward the foreigner is extended to "the outcast" as well. He "gathers" outcasts from society's fringe and places them in the midst of His loving family of faith. He sends out His servants to gather in "the poor and the maimed and the lame and the blind" (Luke 14:21). He declares in Micah 4:7 that "I will make the lame a remnant, and the outcast a strong nation." We tend to seek the sociable, the talented, and the influential. Our Lord seeks the outcasts. "The LORD builds up Jerusalem; He gathers together the outcasts of Israel" (Psalms 147:2). Let the rich take care of the rich. Let society's favorites find comfort in their crowd of friends. But let us make special effort to care for foreigners and outcasts, for this is the pattern that our Father demonstrates for us here.

Interestingly, Jesus quotes verse 7 in Matthew 21:13, but He does so to emphasize a different point. Jesus refers to Isaiah's words here and reminds His hearers that "My house shall be called a house of prayer." God's house, our times of worship in His house are to center on prayer, not profit. Let us repeat David's vow to "give myself to prayer" (Psalms 109:4), for "the prayer of the upright is His delight" (Proverbs 15:8). And let us remember that our time in the Lord's house is to center on our prayerful communion with Him, and not on those things which feed us, enrich us, or entertain us.

56:9-12
All you beasts of the field, come to devour, all you beasts in the forest. His watchmen are blind, they are all ignorant; they are all dumb dogs, they

cannot bark; sleeping, lying down, loving to slumber. Yes, they are greedy dogs which never have enough. And they are shepherds who cannot understand; they all look to their own way, every one for his own gain, from his own territory. "Come," one says, "I will bring wine, and we will fill ourselves with intoxicating drink; tomorrow will be as today, and much more abundant."

Isaiah gives a scalding rebuke for the "watchmen" and "shepherds" of his people. Isaiah rebukes the leaders of his day and in every day that are "blind" and "ignorant" and "who cannot understand." It is inexcusable to be ignorant of the heart and commands of God. The attributes of God are "plainly seen" (Romans 1:20). The commandments of God are written on our hearts and inscribed in our conscience (Romans 2:15). I John 2:20 says, "But you have an anointing from the Holy One, and you know all things." Since then, the Lord gives us His Spirit, His word, and our conscience so that we can know spiritual truths, it is a great failure for the leaders of Israel to be "ignorant." It is shameful not to know God's word. It is criminal not to follow our God-given conscience. And for all men in general, but for leaders especially, it is condemning to live as if unaware of the commandments of God and the unavoidable penalty for disobeying those commands. Jesus rebuked Nicodemus for this sin of ignorance that is made even more serious when present in those who rise to positions of leadership. In John 3:10 Jesus asks him, "How can you be a teacher of Israel and not know these things?" (CEV). It is man's highest privilege to know God (Philippians 3:8), and it is man's highest condemnation when he acts like he is unaware of God's truths. Israel's leaders are supposed to teach God's word – but they don't know it themselves. They are supposed to warn their people that the kingdom of God is at hand! The imminent arrival of God's blessings for those who obey and His punishment for those who rebel is at hand, but they act as if they are blind to this matter of utmost, urgent importance. Isaiah condemns the leaders for their ignorance. Ignorance of God's commands is inexcusable.

Isaiah also condemns the leaders of Israel who are "dumb dogs" that "cannot bark." They have been assigned to be "watchmen" for the people and warn them of actions and attitudes that set them at odds with their Creator. But though they see the people rebel, they provide neither caution nor counsel that would turn the people from their wicked ways and save their souls from death (James 5:20). It is inexcusable for watchmen to remain silent when they are at their posts and see the enemy approaching. Lives are at stake! When they see danger, watchmen must speak! They must sound the alarm! On the battlefield they must warn their fellow soldiers, and in life leaders must warn the people around them that God punishes evil and sin disqualifies us from His most precious blessings. In Ezekiel 3:17, the Lord tells Ezekiel, "Son of man, I have made you a watchman for the house of Israel; therefore hear a word from My mouth, and give them warning from Me." Later, God cites the culpability of those who refuse to do their duty as watchmen – who fail to warn people of the dangers of disobeying God. Ezekiel 33:6 says, "But if the watchman sees the sword coming and does not blow the trumpet, and the people are not warned, and the sword comes and takes any person from among them, he is taken away in his iniquity; but his blood I will require at the watchman's hand." Isaiah condemns the leaders for their silence. Silence regarding God's commands is inexcusable.

    Isaiah continues his condemnation of Israel's leaders, saying that they are "sleeping, lying down, loving to slumber." Laziness, contentedly sitting idle, and twiddling away life's precious time is shameful. Love for God will drive a man to work. He will see life as precious. He will see infinite joy and unending pleasure in all that he does to serve his Creator. He will see needs among God's people, and a rushing urge will well up in his chest to rise up and rush out to help. He will see the lostness of those who are not right with the Lord and he will be compelled to work to see them reconciled to God and praise Him as He deserves. He will see the need to accomplish great things for God and He will see vast importance in the most trivial of chores, for all work is God-honoring. God-directed work when carried out as Ephesians 6:7 dictates: "Work with enthusiasm, as though you were working for the Lord rather than for people" (NLT). There is no place for leisure-seeking laziness in the house of God. Laziness among God's leaders is a spiritual irritant. Leaders who lounge when they should be working irritate the Lord like smoke irritates the eyes (Proverbs 10:26). Isaiah condemns the leaders for their silence. Laziness and leisure-centered living is inexcusable.

    Isaiah further condemns Israel's leaders for being "greedy dogs which never have enough." They are only looking out for themselves, each man seeks only "his own gain" in striking disobedience to the Lord's command for us to "Let each of us please his neighbor for his good, leading to edification" (Romans 15:2). As leaders, we must think of others as better than ourselves (Philippians 2:3) and consider helping others to be a higher priority to taking care of our own desires. As leaders we are to focus on the needs of others, and as followers we are to focus on our satisfaction in Christ. Isaiah condemns the leaders here for their greed which illuminates their dissatisfaction with what God has provided them. Hebrews 13:5 plainly tells us: "Your life should be free from the love of money. Be satisfied with what you have, for He Himself has said, 'I will never leave you or forsake you'" (HCS). May we, as leaders, demonstrate David's heart of the godly leader: "Turn my heart to Your decrees and not to material gain" (Psalms 119:36 HCS). Isaiah condemns the leaders for their greed and self-centeredness. When blessed with the presence of God and the wonder of His unending provisions, greed and focus on personal wealth is inexcusable.

And finally, Isaiah condemns the leaders for their focus on temporal pleasures and their inattention to eternal security. They indulge in wine and intoxicating excitements while giving no thought to the fact that judgment on their soul was just over the horizon. Jesus leveled the same condemnation for all those who would mistakenly think to live life only to "eat, drink, and be merry" (Luke 12:19). The warning that Jesus levels on those who live for present pleasures rather than eternal rewards is perhaps even severer than Isaiah's: "Fool! This night your soul will be required of you; then whose will those things be which you have provided?" (Luke 12:20). We have been gifted with a spiritual soul that is capable of communing with the holy, eternal Creator of all things. We have the opportunity to be reconciled with Him, please Him, be blessed by Him, and enjoy His favor forever. Exchanging that for "the passing pleasures of sin" (Hebrews 11:25) is inexcusable.

The "watchmen," Israel's leaders that God had called to take care of His people are ignorant of His teachings, they are silent instead of sounding the alarm of impending danger. They are lazy and greedy, and focused on pleasure today rather than God's reward in heaven. Because of their multiple failures, their nation is at great risk. The "beasts of the field" and the "beasts in the forest" are invited to come and "devour" the defenseless people. Their leaders have abandoned their God-given work to protect and provide for their people and so the beasts come to gnash and tear at those who could have been safe behind the shield of godly leaders. Oh family! Let us rise up and take this rebuke to heart. Let us lead as God intended! Let us protect His people from the beasts of tempters, distracters, and falsifiers of the truth. Beasts abound! But much can be gained by the fruits of godly leaders – those who will study God's word, faithfully teach it to God's people, who diligently work for God's purposes, who seek no earthly riches, and set their hearts on God's eternal kingdom and not on earthly pleasures. In a single paragraph, Isaiah provides us a remarkably helpful treatise on spiritual leadership. May his words yield their intended purpose in us.

Isaiah 57

57:1-2
The righteous perishes, and no man takes it to heart; merciful men are taken away, while no one considers that the righteous is taken away from evil. He shall enter into peace; they shall rest in their beds, each one walking in his uprightness.

The vast disparity between how the world views the death of good men and how God views the death of good men is placed on display here. Let us first take note as Isaiah does that "the righteous perishes." Righteousness is no protector from death. If anything, righteous living makes men more vulnerable to dangers. The first person to die on earth died *because* he was righteous. David cried out for God to intervene in Psalms 12:1 saying, "Help, O Lord, for the godly are fast disappearing! The faithful have vanished from the earth!" (NLT). Death comes to the righteous as well as the unrighteous, but God views the death of His children far differently than the world does. The carnal world looks only to their own well-being, no one cares when good men die. "No man takes it to heart." "No one considers" that the loss of a righteous man leaves the world worse off than it was before.

"No one considers" that the death of righteous men is a warning that they should likewise prepare their souls for death. Righteous men die, and the self-absorbed world couldn't care less. Our Lord in heaven however, gives the death of His servants His utmost attention. "Precious in the sight of the LORD Is the death of His saints." (Psalms 116:15). The Lord carries His people "into peace" when they pass away. He gives "rest" to those who walked "in his uprightness" while living on earth. Revelation 14:13 says, "Blessed are the dead who die in the Lord from now on. 'Yes,' says the Spirit, 'that they may rest their labors, and their works follow them.'"

The uncaring world offers no reward to the righteous in their dying days. Fortunately, we seek no reward from them anyway. Our prize is from the Lord of heaven who rewards uprightness with peace and repays works of righteousness with heaven's rest.

57:3-6

But come here, you sons of the sorceress, you offspring of the adulterer and the harlot! Whom do you ridicule? Against whom do you make a wide mouth and stick out the tongue? Are you not children of transgression, offspring of falsehood, inflaming yourselves with gods under every green tree, slaying the children in the valleys, under the clefts of the rocks? Among the smooth stones of the stream is your portion; they, they, are your lot! Even to them you have poured a drink offering, you have offered a grain offering. Should I receive comfort in these?

The wicked and unbelievers of Isaiah's day are severely chastised. They are called children of witches and the illegitimate children of prostitutes. They are accused of the most horrible sin imaginable: murdering their children and giving them as sacrifices to their gods. As is often the case, the more wicked men and women become, the more they scoff at and ridicule those that are more righteous than they. The Lord, however, puts the question to them, "Whom do you ridicule?" Who are you sticking your tongue at? Who are you scoffing at with your "wide mouth?" Scoffing at preaching, at sound doctrine, ridiculing God's messengers and God's message is a serious matter. God considers abuse of His messengers to be an offense aimed at Him, and those who ridicule God's servants offend the God who sent them. Those who set their heart on evil and who scoff at the messengers that God has sent to call them to repent will have only rocks as their "portion." Their eternal reward will amount to nothing more than pebbles in a stream. Although they have "poured a drink offering" and "offered a grain offering" their religious efforts grant them no good standing with God. He asks with holy sarcasm: "Should I receive comfort in these?" Isaiah's words are powerful reminders that not all religions are good. Not all spiritual activity leads to God. These were very religious people. They were so dedicated and earnest in their belief that they sacrificed their own children to their gods. But the end result of replacing God with other gods, the final outcome of trading holy living for a life of sin is that pebbles become their "portion," rocks become their "lot" in life. Some say that the reference to river stones being the lot of idol worshippers refers to the law's command to stone to death those who worship idols, indicating that death is the lot and final punishment that is meted out on those who spurn God for the sake of idol worship.

57:7-10
On a lofty and high mountain you have set your bed; even there you went up to offer sacrifice. Also behind the doors and their posts you have set up your remembrance; for you have uncovered yourself to those other than Me, and have gone up to them; you have enlarged your bed and made a covenant with them; you have loved their bed, where you saw their nudity. You went to the king with ointment, and increased your perfumes; you sent your messengers far off, and even descended to Sheol. You are wearied in the length of your way; yet you did not say, "There is no hope." You have found the life of your hand; therefore you were not grieved.

As He does so often, the Lord, again compares idol worship and other religions to adultery and sexual sin. Those who are unfaithful to God are like those who are unfaithful to their husband. They are so savagely intent on being impure and finding sexual pleasure in impure places that they have willingly "even descended to Sheol" to give their impure affection to impure lovers. They are so intent on spurning God's love that they are willing to descend to Hell to find another lover. May the Spirit of God empower our words and fill us with humble boldness so that we can communicate with misguided souls that their devotion to other religions is viewed as nothing less than adultery in God's eyes. In our day, it is felt to be progressive to accept all religions as acceptable. This is clearly not God's view. Those who worship other gods and follow other religions are compared to those who climb mountains – who go to "a lofty and high mountain" just to sleep with someone not their husband. They "enlarged" their bed, they "loved their bed" – they slept around with all sorts of people – so are those who leave God to worship gods and religions of their own making. Hosea 1:2 says, "...the land has committed great harlotry by departing from the LORD."

Maintaining that all religions are good is equivalent to saying that sleeping with every man you can find is good. God's word says that worship of other gods is like adultery. We must maintain God's view and not be lured by the deceptively happy proposition that all religions are created equal. It is not cruel or narrow-minded to call people to worship God and Him alone – just as it is not narrow-minded to call people to live pure lives and abandon illicit relationships. Those who follow empty religions, like those who sleep around and cheat on their husbands "are wearied in the length of your way." They come to the end of their rope and find "there is no hope," they find emptiness, guilt, and futility. Tragically, like their immoral counterparts, followers of false religion refuse to turn from their futile ways, even when the pangs of guilt and vanity weigh heavily on their heart. When they should seek to amend their ways, they, instead, "were not grieved," they do not admit that "there is no hope." They insist on persisting in their impurity until they are crushed by reality when both lovers and religions abandon them on the day of recompense.

57:11
And of whom have you been afraid, or feared, that you have lied and not remembered Me, nor taken it to your heart? Is it not because I have held My peace from of old that you do not fear Me?

The people have rebelled against God, and God says that the reason they do not fear His judgment on them is because "I have held My peace from of old." God's decision to not level immediate punishment on sinners leads some people to brazenly continue to disregard God's authority and keep on sinning. God is patient with us. He is slow to anger (Psalms 145:8). II Peter 3:15 says, "And remember, the Lord is waiting" (holding back His judgment and punishment) "so that people have time to be saved" (NLT). Some however, mistake God's patient mercy for acceptance, they mistake His seeming silence regarding their sin for tolerance of their sin. In response to the persistent rebellion of His people, the Lord says in Psalms 50:21 - "While you did all this, I remained silent, and you thought I didn't care. But now I will rebuke you, listing all my charges against you" (NLT). Let there be no mistake. God punishes sin and unbelief. There is no such thing as sinning without consequence. We cannot ignore God without eternal repercussions. God asks the people, "of whom have you been afraid, or feared?" The people had foolishly feared the immediate displeasure of man rather than the eternal, but delayed displeasure of God. Fearing people rather than revering God leads to terrible outcomes.

57:12-13
I will declare your righteousness and your works, for they will not profit you. When you cry out, let your collection of idols deliver you. But the wind will carry them all away, a breath will take them. But he who puts his trust in Me shall possess the land, and shall inherit My holy mountain.

The NLT translates verse 12 as: "Now I will expose your so-called good deeds that you consider so righteous. None of them will benefit or save you." Most people want to go to heaven. Most would prefer to think that God is happy with them. Sadly, many if not most, think they can write up their own list of good deeds that will get them to heaven, and they think it reasonable to decide for themselves what actions will precipitate blessings from God and secure eternal reward and spiritual well-being. God's words here put an end to such self-deluding nonsense. Good deeds and religious activity that do not come from God and are not directed toward pleasing God "will not profit you." If anyone thinks that this sounds unfair, God invites them to take it up with their idols. He invites them to take their case to their personal gods and have these idols "deliver" them from God's judgment. Those who trust in God's grace and live to serve Him with holy devotion will "possess the land" and "inherit" a holy dwelling place here and holy heaven in the hereafter. Those who trust in good deeds apart from God-directed faith however, will find that "the wind will carry them all away," "a breath" will blow away all their self-endorsed good deeds. The teaching is of utmost importance. Good deeds and religious effort that do not come from God nor are aimed at honoring God "will not profit you."

57:14-15
And one shall say, "Heap it up! Heap it up! Prepare the way, take the stumbling block out of the way of My people." For thus says the High and Lofty One who inhabits eternity, whose name is Holy: "I dwell in the high and holy place, with him who has a contrite and humble spirit, to revive the spirit of the humble, and to revive the heart of the contrite ones."

Verse 15 exalts the glory of God. He is "the High and Lofty One." "The LORD is high above all nations, His glory above the heavens" (Psalms 113:4). His power is beyond reckoning, His glory is beyond compare. His realm includes everything in existence. He is infinitely superior to everything!

He "inhabits eternity." We are bound by time. Our work on earth is limited by the years of our lives. Our productivity is limited by the number of hours in the day. We had no effect on the world before we were born and will have extremely limited effect on the world after our time on earth is done. But God transcends all our time-suppressed capabilities because He "inhabits eternity." His works began before time began, and His works and His glory will know no end when time on earth is done. "Bless the LORD, the God of Israel, who lives forever from eternal ages past. Amen and amen!" (Psalms 41:13 NLT).

And thirdly, God's name "is Holy." He is holy. Everything He does is virtuous. His motives are perfect. His actions are holy in intent and He is righteous as He carries His intentions out.   "Sing praise to the Lord, you saints of His, and give thanks at the remembrance of His holy name" (Psalms 30:4).

Remarkably, amazingly, despite all our limitations and all the ways we are pitifully inferior to Him, yet the Lord is pleased to allow us access to His presence. He will let us live with Him, to "dwell in the high and holy place" with Him, if we will put on "a contrite and humble spirit." When we are cast down by failures and worry, the Lord is pleased to come "to revive the spirit of the humble." When we are crushed by the pain of loss or hopeless despair, the Lord is pleased to come "to revive the heart of the contrite ones."

Oh let us come to Him! James 4:8 rejoins the invitation: "Draw near to God and He will draw near to you." He is so great, so lofty! He is holy – He never does anything selfish or wrong. He is eternal, there is never a time when He will not be omnipotent and loving – we can entrust our lives here to Him, as well as entrust our eternities to Him! Let us draw near to Him, allowing nothing to inhibit us as we come. And let us inspire others to draw near to Him as well. Let us join the cry of verse 14 to see that nothing inhibits men and women from drawing near to their loving Lord. "Prepare the way!" "Take the stumbling block out of the way of My people." Let us do all we can do to make the path to Jesus easy to travel for those who need Him. Let us pray that the "stumbling blocks" of false teachings, sin among believers, worldly deceptions, the pressure of unbelieving peers, and a host of other stumbling blocks will be removed so that people in need can plainly see and easily follow the way to right standing with our wonderful, lofty, eternal, holy God who loves us and allows us to live in close communion with Him.

57:16-18

For I will not contend forever, nor will I always be angry; for the spirit would fail before Me, and the souls which I have made. For the iniquity of his covetousness I was angry and struck him; I hid and was angry, and he went on backsliding in the way of his heart. I have seen his ways, and

will heal him; I will also lead him, and restore comforts to him and to his mourners.

    Psalms 85:5 cries out, "Will You be angry with us forever? Will You prolong Your anger to all generations?" And here, our loving Lord answers, No, "I will not contend forever, nor will I always be angry." David took great comfort in this, writing in Psalms 103:8-9, "The LORD is merciful and gracious, slow to anger, and abounding in mercy. He will not always strive with us, nor will He keep His anger forever." The NLT translates it in clear English, "For I will not fight against you forever; I will not always show my anger. If I did, all people would pass away – all the souls I have made." God's mercy and patience are incredible. Because of the "iniquity" of man's "covetousness" God was angry. He "struck" His people so that the sting of discipline would turn them back to their loving Father. Sadly, they did not return. He "hid" from them and left their prayers unanswered so that their desperation would turn their hearts back to their loving Father. But once again, His people "went on backsliding in the way of his heart." After repeated efforts to discipline and turn His people from their evil ways, God's people persisted in unbelief and insisted on continuing to sin. When we would likely have given up and turned our back on such constant rebellion, God's mercy shines brilliantly yet again. "I have seen his ways…" they are evil ways, rebellious ways, but if I leave them alone, their ways will doom them to death and hell. So, instead of abandoning mankind to their deserved outcome, God says that He will "heal him." "I will also lead him, and restore comforts to him and to his mourners." Remarkable. When God looks down from heaven and sees His people rebel and ignore Him on every side, His response is to "heal him" of his rebellious heart, and "lead him" in the path that will "restore comforts" to those who mourn over their sin and their desperate need for God's mercies. Sin and unbelief call for God's judgment. But once again we see that "mercy triumphs over judgment" (James 2:13).

57:19
"I create the fruit of the lips: peace, peace to him who is far off and to him who is near," says the LORD, "And I will heal him."

    God's mercy on our sin and His provision granting our soul reconciliation with our Creator yields three great outcomes. First, He brings praise to our lips. The "fruit of the lips" is the "sacrifice of praise" (Hebrews 13:15). When God shows us mercy, we sing His praise. That is the intended outcome of God's merciful efforts, and since the arrangement is wholly in our favor, let us do our part and sing His praises continually in both public worship and private devotions. Let us join David in Psalms 59:17 and sing, "To You, O my Strength, I will sing praises; for God is my defense, my God of mercy."

Secondly, God's mercy ushers in our peace. As Ephesians 2:17 says, "He came and preached peace to you who were afar off and to those who were near." Isaiah's words presaged the gracious determination of God to draw not just Israel to a peaceful walk with Him, but the whole world as well. When God draws near, He brings His people peace. "We have peace with God through our Lord Jesus Christ" (Romans 5:1), and when we have peace with God, all other spheres of life are filled with peace as well. Our conscience is at peace, for our guilt has been cleansed. Our mind is at peace for our eternal future is secure. Let all who are in turmoil come and bow in submission to the Lord, for "The LORD will bless His people with peace" (Psalms 29:11).

And thirdly, in mercy, the Lord looks on His people who are sickened by the effects of sin and godlessness and says, "I will heal him." "He heals the brokenhearted and binds up their wounds" (Psalms 147:3). He "heals all your diseases" (Psalms 103:3), both the diseases that infect the body as well as those that afflict the soul. Knowing this, David cries out in Psalms 41:4, "Heal my soul, for I have sinned against You."

In mercy, our Lord calls us to Himself, even when we are so unworthy. He heals us of heartache, diseases, and the pangs of a guilty conscience. He brings us peace. He brings us peace with God and peace of mind, a peace "which surpasses all understanding," and "will guard (our) hearts and minds through Christ Jesus" (Philippians 4:7). In response to this unsurpassable peace and His tender healing power, we are called upon to respond to Him with "the fruit of the lips," the sacrifice of our praise. Let us, however, take note that it is our Lord Himself who "creates" the praise that rises from our lips. He is both the inspiration of our praise and the One who forms the words of praise in our inner being. We would say that peace and healing come from God and praise comes from us, but we are reminded by Isaiah's wording that our words of praise come from God well, for He is careful to remind us that "I create the fruit of the lips." We are completely dependent on our Lord for all the good things that He does – and all the right responses on our part as well.

57:20-21
But the wicked are like the troubled sea, when it cannot rest, whose waters cast up mire and dirt. "There is no peace," says my God, "for the wicked."

ISAIAH 57

In verse 19 the Lord promises peace for His people – both for those in Israel as well as those across the world that will be drawn to Him by His grace. God gives some gifts to everyone. Matthew 5:45 says, "He makes His sun rise on the evil and on the good, and sends rain on the just and on the unjust." Some of His most precious gifts however, He reserves only for His children. This peace that surpasses all understanding is one such gift. It is denied those who rebel against Him. The wicked have no peace. They may have happy moments. They may live in luxury. But God is forever at war with them. Let the wicked and unbeliever be warned. "There is no peace," says the Lord, "for the wicked." Leisure, health, power, and wealth can be dangerous deceptions to wicked men who reject the Lord. Looks can be deceiving, and easy living on earth can be very deceiving. It can make the wicked and unbelievers forget that God is at war with them. If they are not careful, they will not see the banners of God's army of judgment until it is too late, when the picture of Revelation 19:11 is revealed and they see at last what John has already seen: "Now I saw heaven opened, and behold, a white horse. And He who sat on him was called Faithful and True, and in righteousness He judges and makes war." Our Lord wages holy war with those who reject Him. Let all thinking men take proper warning.

Isaiah 58

58:1-5
Cry aloud, spare not; lift up your voice like a trumpet; tell My people their transgression, and the house of Jacob their sins. Yet they seek Me daily, and delight to know My ways, as a nation that did righteousness, and did not forsake the ordinance of their God. They ask of Me the ordinances of justice; they take delight in approaching God. "Why have we fasted," they say, "and You have not seen? Why have we afflicted our souls, and You take no notice?" In fact, in the day of your fast you find pleasure, and exploit all your laborers. Indeed you fast for strife and debate, and to strike with the fist of wickedness. You will not fast as you do this day, to make your voice heard on high. Is it a fast that I have chosen, a day for a man to afflict his soul? Is it to bow down his head like a bulrush, and to spread out sackcloth and ashes? Would you call this a fast, and an acceptable day to the LORD?

Isaiah's words deliver a powerful reminder that proper motives and personal holiness are necessary if religious efforts are to have any spiritual value. Isaiah's listeners were religious people. They prayed often (they sought God daily), they read the Bible often and listened to religious speakers (they "delight to know My ways"). They fasted often. Despite these religious activities however, God was firm in His rebuke. The Lord rebukes the motives behind their religious acts: "You fast for strife and debate." The ESV translates verse 4 as: "you fast only to quarrel and to fight and to hit with a wicked fist." They did not fast to be more holy, they fasted in order to leverage their religious diligence as a club in their disputes with others. They did not fast to better hear God speak His message to them. They fasted with the expectation that their voice would be "heard on high" and God would give them what they wanted. Impure motives ruin religious effort. Those who are religious because it betters their station do not please God with their spiritual efforts. Those who are religious, but believe they can tell God what to do, rather than listen to and obey God's commands will find that their efforts "will not make your voice to be heard on high" (NLT).

In addition, the people's religious efforts were tainted by their failure to live holy lives. "In the day of your fast you find pleasure, and exploit all your laborers." By mistreating and "oppressing" (ESV) their employees, they polluted their prayers and made filthy their religious fasts. We must be holy and we must care for the needy or our religion looks gross in the eyes of the Lord. James 1:27 says it clearly, "Pure and undefiled religion before God and the Father is this: to visit orphans and widows in their trouble, and to keep oneself unspotted from the world."

58:6-7
Is this not the fast that I have chosen: to loose the bonds of wickedness, to undo the heavy burdens, to let the oppressed go free, and that you break every yoke? Is it not to share your bread with the hungry, and that you bring to your house the poor who are cast out; when you see the naked, that you cover him, and not hide yourself from your own flesh?

The spiritual instinct to deny physical pleasure for the sake of spiritual good is a God-given one. It is interesting to see how sacrifice, fasting, and self-denial are a part of most all major religions. This spiritual insight can easily be twisted and mis-applied, however. Verse 3 called to attention the fact that outwardly fasting while secretly indulging in "pleasure" is unacceptable to God. In Matthew 6:16-18 Jesus repeats this warning that God does not reward those who fast while seeking personal gain. Not all fasts, not all religious efforts please God. Here, the Lord tells us the type of "fast" that pleases Him – the acts of sacrifice and self-denial that He is looking for: to defend the safety of those who are oppressed by wickedness, to help carry the burdens of those who are struggling, to free those who are chained by those who are taking advantage of them, and to share what we have with those in need. Plainly our Lord sees service to man and taking care of the needy as a large part of our service to Him. We cannot rightly approach the presence of the Lord and ignore the needs of people beside us. In Psalms 82, we see the Lord standing in the congregation of the mighty and calling on His people to "Defend the poor and fatherless; do justice to the afflicted and needy. Deliver the poor and needy; free them from the hand of the wicked" (Psalms 82:3-4). Psalms 41:1 says that there are blessings in store for those who take care of those in need: "Blessed is he who considers the poor; the LORD will deliver him in time of trouble." It is in the heart and character of God to: "bring justice to the poor of the people; He will save the children of the needy, and will break in pieces the oppressor" (Psalms 72:4). If we are to imitate our Lord, we must seek to do the same.

58:8-9a
Then your light shall break forth like the morning, your healing shall spring forth speedily, and your righteousness shall go before you; the glory of the LORD shall be your rear guard. Then you shall call, and the LORD will answer; you shall cry, and He will say, "Here I am."

The wonderful rewards for taking care of the oppressed, and the poor and needy are described here. "Your light shall break forth like the morning!" Goodness! Such a remarkable outcome of helping out our fellow man! Caring for the needy allows us to "shine forth as the sun in the kingdom of their Father" (Matthew 13:43). When we provide for the poor, we "shine as lights in the world" (Philippians 2:15). The "true light" of Jesus our Savior is "already shining" (1 John 2:8), but some are sadly afflicted with a poor vantage point – the injustices forced upon them, their poverty, and their needs may darken their vision so markedly that the light of the Savior becomes very dim to them. When we provide care for the needy however, the glorious light of the Savior's truth and love once again breaks forth "like the morning" and blesses those that we bless with a bright glimpse of the Father's radiant love.

Secondly, when we care for others, our own healing "shall spring forth speedily." We need not wait until we are healthy, wealthy, and care-free before we take care of others. Even when we are weak and sick and oppressed, let us take care of those around us, for often, <u>our personal healing lies in our own acts of kindness toward others</u>. "Healing" springs "speedily" to those who treat the wounds of others. Proverbs 11:25 gives the promise similarly: "A generous person will prosper; whoever refreshes others will be refreshed" (NIV).

In addition, those who care for the needs of others will be protected on every side. Their righteousness will be their vanguard, protecting them like a shield from the dangers of temptation and the accusations of critics; and the "glory of the LORD" will be their rear guard, protecting them from enemies and events that scheme to attack us when and where we are most vulnerable.

And, too, when we seek to meet the needs of others, the Lord promises to answer our prayers and walk closely with us in our own difficult times. When we cry out for His help, "the LORD will answer," and when we cry out that we are lonely, "He will say, 'Here I am.'" I Peter 3:7 reminds us that a husband's prayers are "hindered" when he does not adequately care for his wife, and Isaiah's words here expand that concept, illustrating that when we take care of the needs of anyone around us, our prayers are facilitated, and when we come alongside a burdened soul, our Lord comes to walk alongside us.

58:9b-12

If you take away the yoke from your midst, the pointing of the finger, and speaking wickedness, if you extend your soul to the hungry and satisfy the afflicted soul, then your light shall dawn in the darkness, and your darkness shall be as the noonday. The LORD will guide you continually, and satisfy your soul in drought, and strengthen your bones; you shall be like a watered garden, and like a spring of water, whose waters do not fail. Those from among you shall build the old waste places; you shall raise up the foundations of many generations; and you shall be called the Repairer of the Breach, the Restorer of Streets to Dwell In.

How sacrificial should we be willing to be for the sake of others? Where do we draw the line? Verse 10 gives a thought-provoking guideline: "extend your soul to the hungry." The HCS translates the phrase as, "offer yourself" for the sake of the hungry. The ESV renders it "pour yourself out" for the hungry. Let us not be over-concerned with self-preservation. The Lord has assured us that if we will pour ourselves out in care of others, He will refill us with His unending supply of energy and strength. He will "satisfy your soul in drought." He will "strengthen your bones." If we will abandon thoughts of self-care and pour ourselves out in caring for others, we are promised here that the Lord will make us "like a watered garden, and like a spring of water, whose waters do not fail." We can afford to be generous; we can provide for the needs of others, because we are assured that our Lord will stoop down and take care of us. The legacy of those who care for others is beautiful. They are remembered by the generations following as "Repairers" of ruined lives, they will be seen as "Restorers" of vitality to those that had lost vision and lost their grip on their Savior's hand. Let us freely abandon ourselves for the sake of caring for the needs of the people that God has placed before us. The promises from heaven given to those who care for the needy are remarkable. When we are unsure how to best meet overwhelming needs, "The LORD will guide you continually." When we fear that our own strength may fail us, we are reassured that the waters of God's sustaining love "do not fail." When the fear arises that we may dry out if we continually give of ourselves to others, the Lord softly reassures us that He will "satisfy your soul in drought." The disciples recommended to Jesus in Mark 6:36 that He send the crowd away because their needs were great. But just as He commanded them in Mark 6:37 – "You give them something to eat" – so He directs us to continue feeding the hungry and providing for the needy in our day. Blessedly, just as He empowered the disciples as they fed the 5,000, so Isaiah's words remind us of His heart to empower us even now. "Give, and you will receive. Your gift will return to you in full —pressed down, shaken together to make room for more, running over, and poured into your lap. The amount you give will determine the amount you get back" (Luke 6:38 NLT).

58:13-14
If you turn away your foot from the Sabbath, from doing your pleasure on My holy day, and call the Sabbath a delight, the holy day of the LORD honorable, and shall honor Him, not doing your own ways, nor finding your own pleasure, nor speaking your own words, then you shall delight yourself in the LORD; and I will cause you to ride on the high hills of the earth, and feed you with the heritage of Jacob your father. The mouth of the LORD has spoken.

Verse 6 described the kind of religious fasts that please the Lord, and here we are told what it looks like to observe the Sabbath in a manner that pleases Him. These verses do not give us a list of rituals to carry out on the Sabbath or a list of activities that are prohibited on the Sabbath. God calls us, He invites us to "call the Sabbath a delight." Those of us who do, indeed, find God's Sabbath a delight will likely smile and feel warmly affirmed by Isaiah's words. Our soul finds delight in the presence and favor of the One who is our Lord, Savior, and Creator. Our Lord and Savior calls us to Himself! He invites us to receive His forgiveness and delight in His presence! We are granted access to His throne room, we are invited to approach Him with our prayers, our eyes are allowed to gaze on His glory, and every week we are encouraged to gather together as a family and enjoy all these highest of enjoyments together in corporate worship. Oh, how the soul delights in the presence of God! And oh, how those delights are doubled when His presence is enjoyed in the company of the saints that have been saved and transformed just like us! This is what our Father calls us to do each week! Not to endure a dry weekly religious ritual, but to "delight" in His presence, delight in His favor, delight in His forgiveness, delight in His blessings, delight in the promise of heaven, and delight in all these things in the company of others who delight in them as well. Sunday, the Sabbath Day, is a day to "delight yourself in the LORD." It is a day to delight in His Word and not "your own words." It is a day to delight in His ways and not "your own ways." It is a day to focus on God's unequalled power, God's glorious purposes, God's unfailing love, God's deep truths, God's unending promises, and God's merciful kindness. The Sabbath is a day that we can set aside doing as we please and focus on that which pleases our Savior. Far from being an inconvenience, those who love God find His Sabbath Day a delight. Psalms 26:8 says, "LORD, I have loved the habitation of Your house, and the place where Your glory dwells." In Psalms 27:4 the writer says that his favorite thing in the world is to go to the Father's house to worship: "One thing I have desired of the LORD, that will I seek: that I may dwell in the house of the LORD all the days of my life, to behold the beauty of the LORD, and to inquire in His temple." David's testimony is permanently recorded in Psalms 122:1 - "I was glad when they said to me, 'Let us go into the house of the LORD.'" May our family experience and demonstrate this same delight in honoring our Lord on the Sabbath Day. Let us delight in His nearness, delight in His Word, delight in the fellowship of the saints, delight in singing His praises, and delight in the opportunity to do all these things in His house on His day.

If we will honor God on the Sabbath and delight in Him on this special day, He will cause us to "ride on the high hills of the earth" and taste "the heritage of Jacob." The trials of the world can sink even the most stalwart believer into pits that are very low. When at our lowest, let us go to church. Honoring the Father in His house on the Sabbath is the key to rising from the pit of despair to the "high hills" of God's blessed encouragements. When we feel spiritually starved and hungry to do something meaningful, let us go to church. Our Lord feeds those who come to His house with the heritage of Jacob. Our soul is fed and our spirits are lifted when we come to God's house on God's Sabbath. Asaph says that life had become "too painful for me" (Psalms 73:16), he could hardly bear the turmoil caused him by evil men, and he found no relief from his pain, "until I went into the sanctuary of God" (Psalms 73:17). If we will honor God on the Sabbath and delight in Him in His house on His day, we will find Him worthy of all we give, and we will find that He richly blesses those who "call the Sabbath a delight." Let us "Lift up (our) hands in the sanctuary, and bless the LORD" (Psalms 134:2). God blesses all who do.

Isaiah 59

59:1-2
Behold, the LORD's hand is not shortened, that it cannot save; nor His ear heavy, that it cannot hear. But your iniquities have separated you from your God; and your sins have hidden His face from you, so that He will not hear.

Sin "separates" us from God. Sin rises up like a black cloud, its stench causing our Lord to turn His face away from our repulsive actions. The prayer of repentance is always heard, but when we pray for anything else, our requests for His blessings are hidden in the smog of sin "so that He will not hear." Psalms 66:18 says, "If I regard iniquity in my heart, the Lord will not hear." Jeremiah 5:25 says, "Your wickedness has deprived you of these wonderful blessings. Your sin has robbed you of all these good things" (NLT). We have been granted the extraordinary invitation to "draw near to God" (James 4:8). How can we possibly measure the preciousness of such an offer? But we are not invited to come to God and drag our sin in with us. Habakkuk 1:13 says "[Your] eyes are too pure to look on evil, and You cannot tolerate wrongdoing" (HCS). Sin must be repented of and turned from, we cannot persist in sin and hope to continue to enjoy blessings from

God. The Lord is omnipotent, and He is all-loving, He is all-attentive to His people's needs. It is not that He was too weak to save, or too aloof to save Israel from their enemies in Isaiah's day. God was fully aware of His people's needs; His power was fully capable of meeting those needs. But Israel's sin obstructed the receipt of God's blessings and rescue. The application for us today is easy to see. Israel is struck with the horrifying reality that sin "separated you from your God." May the Lord please help us recognize sin, groan over our sin, and repent of our sin immediately. We have many needs that we are completely dependent on the Lord to provide. The world has many needs and they depend on us to pray for them. Let us not allow anything to inhibit our prayers!

59:3-5
For your hands are defiled with blood, and your fingers with iniquity; your lips have spoken lies, your tongue has muttered perversity. No one calls for justice, nor does any plead for truth. They trust in empty words and speak lies; they conceive evil and bring forth iniquity. They hatch vipers' eggs and weave the spider's web; he who eats of their eggs dies, and from that which is crushed a viper breaks out.

It was not for slips of the tongue or isolated lapses in judgment that Israel is condemned. God's judgment on His people is handed down because of their systemic immersion in sin. Blood is on their hands. Murderers are not brought to justice – no one even "calls for justice." Their nation has eroded into a state of complete apathy toward the delivery of justice for the oppressed. Their hands are dirty with guilt, and so is their mouth. They speak lies without regret, and their conversations are laced with perverse subjects that good men would be disgusted by. Lies and deceit pervade the culture, but no one cares. There is no one with the sense to "plead for truth." They have found sin acceptable, and their acceptance of sin is like hatching viper's eggs. Those who eat the eggs – those who commit the sins -- will die of the poison within them, and those who come along later are bitten by the venomous fangs of the vipers hatched by that sin. The devastating results of sin continually perpetuate. Sin is like a "spider's web" trapping both sinners and bystanders in the guilt and consequences and judgment on that sin. Personal sin is damaging. National sin, systemic sin, when whole groups of people band together in support of sin is overwhelmingly destructive. Personal sin will always, eventually lead to a fall, and national sin will lead to total collapse – as it will do for the people of Israel here. "Behold, the wicked brings forth iniquity; yes, he conceives trouble and brings forth falsehood. He made a pit and dug it out, and has fallen into the ditch which he made. His trouble shall return upon his own head, and his violent dealing shall come down on his own crown" (Psalms 7:14-16).

59:6-8
Their webs will not become garments, nor will they cover themselves with their works; their works are works of iniquity, and the act of violence is in their hands. Their feet run to evil, and they make haste to shed innocent blood; their thoughts are thoughts of iniquity; wasting and destruction are in their paths. The way of peace they have not known, and there is no justice in their ways; they have made themselves crooked paths; whoever takes that way shall not know peace.

Isaiah ended chapter 57 with the warning, "'There is no peace,'" says my God, "'for the wicked.'" And here, Isaiah repeats that warning: "whoever takes that way (of unrighteous living) shall not know peace." People desire peace for themselves. They may delight in oppressing others; they may rush to carry out "acts of violence." They may "make haste to shed innocent blood." But for themselves, everyone wants to lie down at night and enjoy peace of mind. The fact is, however, peace comes to the righteous. There is no peace for those who persist in sin. Psalms 85:10 says, "Righteousness and peace will embrace" (HCS). Peace is denied the wicked. The men and women of Isaiah's day sought the path to peace, but "they made themselves crooked paths" – paths that could never bring them to peace of mind. Those who are searching for peace but indulging in evil are walking the paths of life with their shame fully exposed. "Their webs (of sin and deceit) will not become garments, nor will they cover themselves with their (wicked) works." Their sins are like spider webs – sticky and difficult to escape – and incapable of covering one's naked shame. Being right with Jesus brings us "peace with God" (Romans 5:1). Walking with the Lord in righteous obedience grants us peace that surpasses all understanding (Philippians 4:7). But abandoning the ways of God for the "crooked paths" of sin-filled living will deny us that peace. "Whoever takes that path shall not know peace."

59:9-12
Therefore justice is far from us, nor does righteousness overtake us; we look for light, but there is darkness! For brightness, but we walk in blackness! We grope for the wall like the blind, and we grope as if we had no eyes; we stumble at noonday as at twilight; we are as dead men in desolate places. We all growl like bears, and moan sadly like doves; we look for justice, but there is none; for salvation, but it is far from us. For

our transgressions are multiplied before You, and our sins testify against us; for our transgressions are with us, and as for our iniquities, we know them:

As if he were the voice of sinful Israel, Isaiah laments the sad state of his people and confesses that the cause of their troubles is that "our transgressions are multiplied before You." See the sorry state of men and women when they refuse to turn from their sin. They "look for light," but "walk in blackness." Problems in life are common to most everyone. Many times, however, these problems are not overly grievous because we can see the light at the end of the tunnel – we recognize that the problem is a temporary one or we can see solutions that will eventually lift us out of our difficulty. This encouragement is denied those who persist in sin, however. For them there is no light at the end of the tunnel. There is only constant "darkness." They "grope" for the way out of their sin-induced troubles, but find no escape. They try to pull themselves up by their own bootstraps, relying on their own smarts and skills and strengths, but all their powers are reduced to those of "dead men." They run to their friends for help but find no one to lend them a hand in the "desolate places" to which their sin has taken them. They groan and growl in anger and resentment; they moan and groan in lonely desperation. Sin has brought them very low and they see no hope for rescue. They seek salvation, but God reminds them in Isaiah 43:11 that "I, even I, am the LORD, and besides Me there is no savior." Their sin has taken their hearts far from God and so their only hope for salvation now seems far from their sight. Psalms 119:155 affirms what the Isaiah's sinful listeners were fearing: "Salvation is far from the wicked, for they do not seek Your statutes." Sin is devastating. We must confess it and turn from it. We must call on others to confess it and turn from it. Isaiah's words remind us that those who insist on persisting in sin face dreadfully dark days ahead.

59:13-15
In transgressing and lying against the LORD, and departing from our God, speaking oppression and revolt, conceiving and uttering from the heart words of falsehood. Justice is turned back, and righteousness stands afar off; for truth is fallen in the street, and equity cannot enter. So truth fails, and he who departs from evil makes himself a prey. Then the LORD saw it, and it displeased Him that there was no justice.

Speaking for all of Israel, Isaiah continues the list of his people's sins. Once they began "departing from our God," they fell into a host of other sins. They became "unfair" and "oppressive" (NLT). They lied about everything. No one could trust anything anyone said. "For truth is fallen in the street." Oppression by the powerful was prevalent and "justice" was denied the injured. Individuals, families, and societies can be inspired to repent of sinful living and devote themselves to godly purposes when they are blessed to see examples of godly living and can be inspired by the words of godly teachers. But Israel was doomed when they refused to give godly men and women a voice. Rather than listen to and be inspired by godly people, they "attacked" them (NLT). When good men and women are afraid to speak up because society "preys" on them and attacks them, the fall of that society is close at hand.

The condemnation levelled here on Israel is dreadful: "truth fails." Knowing the truth of who God is and what He desires us to do will set people free from a life without purpose and a death without hope (John 8:32). But when that truth "fails," when the truth fails to turn people to God, fails to turn people from sin, or even fails to gain an audience, the fall of that people is imminent. The picture painted of Israel here is heart-breaking. God is "displeased" because the land does not uphold justice and the truth has failed to call people to righteous living. Goodness, what a picture of spiritual ruin.

59:16
He saw that there was no man, and wondered that there was no intercessor; therefore His own arm brought salvation for Him; and His own righteousness, it sustained Him.

The great work of God is to see man saved. It is a glorious work. Billions of souls of men and women over thousands of years and endless generations are condemned by their sin and doomed to face an eternity in the torment of hell unless someone intervenes. And God, blessedly, wonderfully, and fantastically intervenes. God saves! He saves people from the guilt of sin and the punishment for sin! He saves people from Hell and offers the means for bringing them to Heaven instead! God's work is such a wonderful work! The salvation of the souls of men and the reconciliation of men and women to their Creator is such a tremendous work! It is such a lofty, noble enterprise that everyone should be swept away with inspiration to join Him in this great work and strive with all possible diligence to see souls saved. It is nothing less than shocking when people are not swept away with exuberance to save souls. Everyone should be so inspired by the great work of God that they rush to join Him in His saving work. Here, we see that <u>no one</u> in Israel, "no man" in Israel was devoted to bringing people to God. There was not a single "intercessor" in the nation, no one was praying that God would forgive the sins of his fellow man, no one was praying that his loved ones would turn to God in repentance. No one was pleading with men to reach out to God and no one was pleading with God to forgive men. No one. This lack of concern for the souls of men and women "astonished" (NASB) God. God was "amazed" (HCS) that no one joined Him to save people. God, who created mankind and gave men and women a soul, a conscience, a heart capable of compassion, and the instinct to imitate their Creator – God looked down on the people that He had made and "wondered" how on earth they could be so callous, so uninsightful, so depraved that no one sought to save the souls of those around them. We are rightly taken aback to see God "astonished." And we are rightly astonished and brought to our knees in awe to see God's response. When God looks down from heaven and sees no one trying to see souls saved, He says, 'I will save them Myself." "His own arm brought salvation for Him." God was astonished, but He did not despair – though He found no righteous souls with a heart like His, God's "own righteousness, it sustained Him."

In Ezekiel 34, the Lord gives this same response to this same problem. Since Israel's leaders failed to call people to God, He makes His own powerful pledge to His people. "*I Myself* will search for My sheep and seek them out… *I* will seek out My sheep and deliver them from all the places where they were scattered on a cloudy and dark day… *I* will bring them out from the peoples… *I* will gather them from the countries, and will bring them to their own land… *I* will feed them on the mountains of Israel… *I* will feed them in good pasture…" and "*I* will feed My flock, and *I* will make them lie down, says the Lord GOD" (Ezekiel 34:11-15). God saves. When men fail, God does not. When mankind continually shows himself spiritually uninsightful, God continues to save. His righteous, compassionate heart will draw men to Himself, even when no one else joins Him in this highest of noble tasks.

59:17
For He put on righteousness as a breastplate, and a helmet of salvation on His head; He put on the garments of vengeance for clothing, and was clad with zeal as a cloak.

The garments of God are here described. God wears righteousness as a soldier would wear a breastplate. Young people are prone to being slaves to fashion. They wear what everyone else wears. They follow the trends of fashion carefully, and every morning they dress themselves in accordance with the current fad. God is not like that. Even when no one else is wearing it, God wears righteousness. Even when "there is none righteous, no, not one" (Romans 3:10), even when no one else is willing to place the breastplate of righteousness on their chest, God never takes it off. He remains righteous, He remains pure and holy, even when He can find no one else dressed as He is.

God wears salvation like a soldier wears a helmet. The distinctives of a helmet reveal the army the soldier fights for. In World War II, you could look at a soldier's helmet and easily recognize if he was fighting for America or fighting for Germany. God fights for salvation. He wears it as a helmet. Deuteronomy 20:4 says, "for the LORD your God is He who goes with you, to fight for you against your enemies, to save you." The Lord gave a similar promise in Jeremiah 15:20 - "'I am with you to save you and deliver you,' says the LORD." God saves. He wears salvation as a helmet.

God puts on "vengeance" as His clothing. In Ephesians 6 and again in I Thessalonians 5:8 Paul refers to Isaiah's words here and tells us that we should dress like our Father dresses. We should wear the same breastplate and the same helmet that our Father wears. There are limits to this, however. As all soldiers wear the same uniform, but only the general wears stars on his epaulets, so the "garments of vengeance" are only suitable for God to wear. Romans 12:19 says, "Beloved, do not avenge yourselves, but rather give place to wrath; for it is written, 'Vengeance is Mine, I will repay,' says the Lord." Vengeance is a garment that only God is to wear – and we can be sure that He will put vengeance on. II Thessalonians 1:8 promises that "in flaming fire" the Lord will take "vengeance on those who do not know God, and on those who do not obey the gospel of our Lord Jesus Christ." The world is constantly afflicted with the wounds inflicted by evil men. The righteous saints in heaven continually cry out for vengeance to be taken on those who persecute the holy and murder the innocent. Revelation 6:10 says "And they cried with a loud voice, saying, 'How long, O Lord, holy and true, until You judge and avenge our blood on those who dwell on the earth?'" Vengeance on evil acts of violence is a righteous longing, and our righteous Judge promises to carry vengeance out with His own hand. He brings salvation to the faithful, but He brings vengeance on "those who do not know God, and on those who do not obey the gospel of our Lord Jesus Christ."

And, too, the Lord is "clad with zeal as a cloak." Everything God does is important – terribly important! He does nothing listlessly, casually, or indifferently. He is zealous, exuberant, enthusiastic, and passionate about everything He does. God cares for and protects His people with great zeal. Zechariah 8:2 says, "Thus says the LORD of hosts: 'I am zealous for Zion with great zeal; with great fervor I am zealous for her.'" God is passionate about protecting the holy honor of His house. After Jesus whipped the merchants out of the Father's temple, John 2:17 records, "Then His disciples remembered that it was written, 'Zeal for Your house has eaten Me up.'" God is zealous for the things that He does. He wears zeal like a cloak. May we be similarly dressed, as it is written: "it is good to be zealous in a good thing always" (Galatians 4:18).

59:18-20
According to their deeds, accordingly He will repay, fury to His adversaries, recompense to His enemies; the coastlands He will fully repay. So shall they fear the name of the LORD from the west, and His glory from the rising of the sun; when the enemy comes in like a flood, the Spirit of the LORD will lift up a standard against him. "The Redeemer will come to Zion, and to those who turn from transgression in Jacob," says the LORD.

Isaiah reiterates that the Lord "puts on the garments of vengeance" (verse 17). The Lord is not arbitrary or unfair in His demonstration of "fury" on His enemies. "According to their deeds, accordingly he will repay." God punishes in accordance with the level of sin committed. He does not punish more than people deserve, He gives "recompense" – He gives fair and equal compensation for the evils committed. Obadiah 1:15 says the same thing. In that verse the Lord describes the punishment He plans to level on His enemies: "as you have done, it shall be done to you; your reprisal shall return upon your own head." Let there be no mistake, God punishes evil and unbelief. But He does so fairly, never meting out punishment that is not in keeping with the evil that is committed. God's "fury" that punishes His enemies is designed to ignite a holy fear of the Lord in His enemies and to inspire His saints to ride out and confront wickedness in the world without fear. The Lord will "lift up a standard" against those who rebel against Him and persecute His people. His standard, God's banner will be unfurled and inspire His people to join Him as elite troops form ranks around their nation's flag. "But you have raised a banner for those who honor you – a rallying point in the face of attack" (Psalms 60:4 NLT). We do not fight alone against the evils of the world. "The Redeemer will come," winning back the lands and peoples that were lost in previous battles with the enemy and reinforce the battle strength of all those "who turn from transgression."

Let us walk closely with the Lord. Let us not seek friendship with those who are against God (James 4:4). For if we will make God's enemies our enemies, He will hold that our enemies are His, and we can pray with assurance as David did in Psalms 54:4-7 – "Behold, God is my helper; the Lord is with those who uphold my life. He will repay my enemies for their evil. Cut them off in Your truth. I will freely sacrifice to You; I will praise Your name, O LORD, for it is good. For He has delivered me out of all trouble; and my eye has seen its desire upon my enemies."

59:21

"As for Me," says the LORD, "this is My covenant with them: My Spirit who is upon you, and My words which I have put in your mouth, shall not depart from your mouth, nor from the mouth of your descendants, nor from the mouth of your descendants' descendants," says the LORD, "from this time and forevermore."

It may be that in all of scripture there is no word that is more precious to me personally than these words here. One pre-dawn morning as I knelt in the little prayer corner that I had knelt in so many times before, I cried out my intercession for my children. I wept my prayer. My body shook as I prayed. My fists were clenched and through tears I poured out a desperate prayer for my Lord to call my children to Himself. I felt so fearful. I was terrified that my children would grow up and turn their back on the Lord. I was terrified at the prospect of my children not honoring my Father, and was acutely and painfully made aware that there was nothing that I could do to place the Spirit of the Lord in my children. I was completely incapable of filling my children's voices with the words of my Savior. The thought nearly tore me apart. My body and soul shook. I pleaded with the Lord, I begged Him to please call my children to Himself. I felt my heart breaking over just the possibility of the prospect that my children could grow up and demonstrate no devotion to the Lord. And then, at last, as I shook in desperate prayer, I heard these words inside me: "This is My covenant with you, My Spirit who is upon you, and My words which I have put in your mouth, shall not depart from your mouth, nor from the mouth of your children, nor from the mouth of your children's children from this time forth and forevermore." Instantly, I knew my prayer was answered. I thanked my Lord, rose from my knees and went to work. And the relief and flood of gratitude that swept over me in those moments has been matched and more by the past 25 years of watching my Lord call my children to Himself. I am so eternally grateful. John wrote, "I have no greater joy than to hear that my children walk in the truth" (III John 1:4). I am so grateful that my Lord has condescended to grant me this highest of joys. We find here that it is His good will and His delight to grant this request for His children. This heart of the Lord to call the children of His servants to Himself is a joy of the highest possible magnitude. Neither John nor I can find its equal.

Isaiah 60

60:1-3
Arise, shine; for your light has come! And the glory of the LORD is risen upon you. For behold, the darkness shall cover the earth, and deep darkness the people; but the LORD will arise over you, and His glory will be seen upon you. The Gentiles shall come to your light, and kings to the brightness of your rising.

    Heaven's great summons rings out over the Lord's sleeping children and calls them to "arise" and "shine." The light has come! Though the darkness of sin and spiritual ignorance has covered the earth for so long, now the light of Christ's truth has been revealed! The peoples of the earth are privileged to know the truth! They are blessed with the opportunity to see the light! The nations of the world in Isaiah's day and ours are covered with great swaths of land that are in darkness. There are great groups of people that are groping in the dark without even the semblance of understanding of who they are, who God is, and the purpose of living. Sin brings darkness on people; spiritual ignorance is like "deep darkness" which blinds people from the fundamental truths of life. Isaiah however, brings good news for his readers: "your light has come!" Ephesians 5:14 says, "Awake, you who sleep, arise from the dead, and Christ will give you light." This message of hope is not just for Israel, but for the Gentiles – for all the world's people as well. Luke 2:32 says that Jesus came as "a light to bring revelation to the Gentiles." So many nations in Isaiah's day were in darkness, not knowing God's truths, and still in our day, there remain places and peoples that do not know their Creator. It is God's will to fix that. It is God's heart to "give light to those who sit in darkness and the shadow of death, to guide our feet into the way of peace" (Luke 1:79). Matthew noted that Jesus came in fulfillment of Isaiah's words. Speaking of Jesus, he wrote: "The people who sat in darkness have seen a great light, and upon those who sat in the region and shadow of death Light has dawned" (Matthew 4:16). Jesus came to begin fulfilling Isaiah's prophecy, but the continued fulfillment of these words occurs in our day when we take the light of His word to nations and people that do not know Him. The prophecy has global significance, revealing the heart of God to enlighten all the nations of the world. But even with the global significance of Isaiah's words, his message is also intensely personal. David wrote in Psalms 18:28 – "You will light my lamp; the LORD my God will enlighten my darkness." We read Isaiah's words and rejoice because "God is the LORD, and He has given us light" (Psalms 118:27). God gives light to the world, and when I am in the dark, my Lord gives His light to me. Blessed, then, by the light of God's truths and the glory of God's presence, let us seek to reflect His light to others as purely as possible, so that we "may become blameless and harmless, children of God without fault in the midst of a crooked and perverse generation, among whom you shine as lights in the world" (Philippians 2:15).

60:4
Lift up your eyes all around, and see: they all gather together, they come to you; your sons shall come from afar, and your daughters shall be nursed at your side.

Verse 3 before and verse 5 to come both talk about the Gentiles, so we are hard put not to attribute Isaiah's words in verse 4 to the Gentiles as well. Look at the great prospect presented to and through Isaiah! God's children, those adopted as the sons and daughters of Israel by faith, flock to worship Him and bless His people in "The City of the Lord" (verse 14). What a great future is about to dawn! Throughout history, Israel rejected the Lord time and again, and the nations of the world despised Him completely or were completely ignorant of His greatness. But now, the days are foretold when that will change. Israel will worship the Lord and the peoples of the world will "come to you," they will "gather together" from afar with the intent of worshiping the Lord as children of God and co-heirs of His promises to the people of Israel. Though the peoples of the world had lived in spiritual darkness for so long, without hope and without God in this world, yet now, Isaiah foretells the day when the nations of the earth will turn to their Creator in droves. Psalms 22:27 says, "All the ends of the world shall remember and turn to the Lord, and all the families of the nations shall worship before You." Psalms 86:9 repeats the wonderful chorus: "All nations whom You have made shall come and worship before You, O Lord, and shall glorify Your name." And Revelation 15:4 echoes the final refrain: "Who shall not fear You, O Lord, and glorify Your name? For You alone are holy. For all nations shall come and worship before You, for Your judgments have been manifested."

60:5-7
Then you shall see and become radiant, and your heart shall swell with joy; because the abundance of the sea shall be turned to you, the wealth of the Gentiles shall come to you. The multitude of camels shall cover your land, the dromedaries of Midian and Ephah; all those from Sheba shall come; they shall bring gold and incense, and they shall proclaim the praises of the LORD. All the flocks of Kedar shall be gathered together to you, the rams of Nebaioth shall minister to you; they shall ascend with acceptance on My altar, and I will glorify the house of My glory.

Isaiah encourages his readers and listeners with the wonderful hope that God sets here before His people. They will "become radiant." They "shall see" what God has done in their lives, they "shall see" that God has called others with the same calling (verse 4). They will bask in the glow of the magnificent glory of God, they will become radiant as they reflect the holy, loving ways of God, and they will beam as they delight in the company of all the like-minded, like-chosen peoples of the world who have been "gathered together" from all corners of the planet so that they might bring offerings to God and gifts to His people. Just as Revelation 5:9 affirms that Jesus will "(redeem) us to God by Your blood out of every tribe and tongue and people and nation" – so Isaiah sees the day when many from every nation, every people "shall swell with joy" because they have been chosen and have chosen to follow Jesus. Even the people of Kedar and Nebaioth are included – those who were the descendants of Ishmael (Genesis 25:13) and initially denied the blessings given to Abraham's son Isaac, are now welcomed into the Holy City as they offer their gifts of praise and "minister" to God's people who may have come to faith before them. Even the descendants of Midian and Ephah were there. Those who were the sons of Abraham by Keturah, who were also (initially) denied the blessings promised the descendants of Isaac, are now welcomed into the great body of believers bringing gold and incense and praises to the Lord as well. Even the descendants of Sheba are there. Solomon prophesied of this day, saying in Psalms 72:10 "The kings of Tarshish and of the isles will bring presents; the kings of Sheba and Seba will offer gifts. Yes, all kings shall fall down before Him; all nations shall serve Him." Are these the descendants of Sheba, whose uncle Nimrod built the tower of Babel? If so, we see that God's redemptive love for mankind will overcome all previous curses to grant salvation and fellowship to all the world's people – even those who were once far off. Or does it speak of the land of Sheba, whose queen exemplified this picture so beautifully, when in I Kings 10:10 "She gave the king one hundred and twenty talents of gold, spices in great quantity, and precious stones. There never again came such abundance of spices as the queen of Sheba gave to King Solomon." Regardless, we are blessed by this picture of the peoples of the world who had once been denied blessings, who had once been cursed, who had once been "without Christ, being aliens from the commonwealth of Israel and strangers from the covenants of promise, having no hope and without God in the world" (Ephesians 2:12), yet now, in the day Isaiah speaks of, all these people will be joined to the family of faith, honoring God and blessing His people as "heirs of God and joint heirs with Christ" (Romans 8:17). What a blessed day is here described when all the elect from all the nations "swell with joy" and become "radiant" as they give gifts of praise and "minister" to God's people in wonderful, holy, exuberant, joyous union.

60:8-9
Who are these who fly like a cloud, and like doves to their roosts? Surely the coastlands shall wait for Me; and the ships of Tarshish will come first, to bring your sons from afar, their silver and their gold with them, to the name of the LORD your God, and to the Holy One of Israel, because He has glorified you.

What a blessed sight is described here! New believers flocking to Christ, flying "like a cloud," rushing to Him in great numbers, hastened by the winds of the Spirit. Matthew Henry says of this verse, "What a pleasant sight is it to see poor souls hastening to Christ, with a full resolution to abide with him!" Those once far from God will ever be drawn to Him. They will come bearing gifts of praise to the Savior and gifts of gold and silver for all His people. Their love for God will well up inside them and spur them to bless His people. They seek to draw near to God, and their longing to be near Him will call them to gather together to be near to His people. The glory of God beckons them and His blessings on His people "has glorified" those that draw near to Him, which beckons even more people to join the ever expanding, glorious, happy, unified, rescued people of God.

60:10-12
The sons of foreigners shall build up your walls, and their kings shall minister to you; for in My wrath I struck you, but in My favor I have had mercy on you. Therefore your gates shall be open continually; they shall not be shut day or night, that men may bring to you the wealth of the Gentiles, and their kings in procession. For the nation and kingdom which will not serve you shall perish, and those nations shall be utterly ruined.

The people and nations that oppose God's people in Israel and God's people in His church "shall perish." God's people will bask in safety. They will need no gates on the city walls – their enemies will all be "utterly ruined." Enemies will flee, but friends and well-wishers will join God's people in great "procession." Isaiah's words likely speak of the gold and gifts that Cyrus and Darius gave to see God's people restored in Jerusalem, but we cannot help but see his allusion to the end of time and the dawn of the New Jerusalem when "The city had no need of the sun or of the moon to shine in it, for the glory of God illuminated it. The Lamb is its light. And the nations of those who are saved shall walk in its light, and the kings of the earth bring their glory and honor into it. Its gates shall not be shut at all by day (there shall be no night there). And they shall bring the glory and the honor of the nations into it" (Revelation 21:23-27). And even now, we see his words applicable to our day, bolstering the courage of the Lord's missionaries and gospel-sharers as we see that those who presently oppose the proclamation of God's message and persecute God's people will ultimately, completely fail and fall.

60:13-16
The glory of Lebanon shall come to you, the cypress, the pine, and the box tree together, to beautify the place of My sanctuary; and I will make the place of My feet glorious. Also the sons of those who afflicted you shall come bowing to you, and all those who despised you shall fall prostrate at the soles of your feet; and they shall call you the City of the LORD, Zion of the Holy One of Israel. Whereas you have been forsaken and hated, so that no one went through you, I will make you an eternal excellence, a joy of many generations. You shall drink the milk of the Gentiles, and milk the breast of kings; you shall know that I, the LORD, am your Savior and your Redeemer, the Mighty One of Jacob.

ISAIAH 60

Isaiah looks forward to the day (our day) when the people of God no longer add to the strength of their ranks from the nation of Israel alone. "The City of the LORD," the body of believers, will be nourished by and flourish by the reinforcements arriving from all the Gentile nations and by the aid provided by great kings. Lebanon is given specific mention. Just as they provided fine wood for the temple of the Lord in II Chronicles 2, so Lebanon will join with the nations of the world and once again "beautify the place of My sanctuary." They will come to worship at the feet of the Lord, and they will find that "the place of My feet (is) glorious." It is glorious to sit at the Lord's feet and worship Him in unhindered praise! The people of the world will join God's people in worship, they will be a blessing to God's children, and in turn, God's people will be a blessing to the world. God will make us "an eternal excellence, a joy of many generations." Oh the joy of seeing God elevate His people to a place of "excellence." The ESV says that God will make us "majestic forever." Oh! The list of those that I have seen God make "majestic" seems endless. Let us take delight in these words from Isaiah! God calls people to Himself from among all the world's peoples! Their arrival "beautifies" the place of godly worship and godly service! Even those who once oppressed God's people are transformed by grace to become God's people! And once enjoined to the people of God, they are infused by His excellent greatness so that they radiate their own "eternal excellence" and the presence of God among them brings joy to "many generations." And all of this takes place so that "you shall know that I, the LORD, am your Savior and your Redeemer, the Mighty One of Jacob." God calls; God saves; God transforms; God fills us with joy; and then, God receives His due honor as we acknowledge that He alone is our Savior, Redeemer, and the Mighty One over Jacob and over all mankind.

60:17-18
Instead of bronze I will bring gold, instead of iron I will bring silver, instead of wood, bronze, and instead of stones, iron. I will also make your officers peace, and your magistrates righteousness. Violence shall no longer be heard in your land, neither wasting nor destruction within your borders; but you shall call your walls Salvation, and your gates Praise.

When God reigns in our lives everything gets better! Our investments that gave us bronze will be replaced by those that yield gold. Our efforts that provided iron will be changed to those that have a silver lining. Our outlook will be brighter, our motives will be purer, our causes will be nobler, and our hearts will be richer when Christ reigns in our mortal body. When individuals walk with God, they are singularly blessed, and when nations walk with God they are blessed en masse. Officers and magistrates, "overseers" and "taskmasters" (ESV), rulers (NLT), and "guard(s)" (HCS) will no longer need to protect those in danger, enforce laws, or arbitrate disputes, because violence, ill-will, in-fighting, and dishonesty will be replaced with "peace" and "righteousness." Our security will rest in God's Salvation rather than our own less certain self-preservation. And all who visit us at our gates will hear us praising our God rather than exalting our own achievements. Such is the happy description delivered here of the state of the people and nation whose God is the Lord. "Happy are the people who are in such a state; happy are the people whose God is the LORD!" (Psalms 144:15).

60:19-20
The sun shall no longer go down, nor shall your moon withdraw itself; for the LORD will be your everlasting light, and the days of your mourning shall be ended.

Today, some matters are hard to understand. Today, sorrows and anxieties often darken the doors of even the godliest of men and women. But it will not be like this for us forever. Isaiah tells us of this coming day when we will no longer be in the dark. The Lord will be our light – our "everlasting" light. Our mourning will end because the glow of His light will warm and cheer us. Our disorientation will be cured because His light will guide us. Isaiah's readers once suffered the gloom of defeat by their enemies and captivity in Babylon. His words here allowed them to lift their eyes off their dark circumstances and see the light of hope. May his words do the same today.

Hundreds of years after Isaiah wrote, John would be granted this same vision to remind us of this hope before us. Our home in heaven has no need of sun or moon. It is "illuminated" by the "glory of God" because "the Lamb is its light" (Revelation 21:23). When sorrows strike us here, let us mourn as is fitting for those who care about the things that God cares about. But let us not "sorrow as others who have no hope" (I Thessalonians 4:13). The light of the Lamb of life awaits us in heaven and even now we can bask in the glow! Psalms 89:15 reminds us: "Blessed are the people who know the joyful sound! They walk, O LORD, in the light of Your countenance." Today, even now we are blessed with the unsurpassable privilege of walking in the light of the countenance of God. Let us walk with our Lord! May our souls be illumined, and our spirits brightened by the everlasting glow of the Lord. Let us rejoice that "God is the LORD, and He has given us light" (Psalms 118:27).

60:21-22
Also your people shall all be righteous; they shall inherit the land forever, the branch of My planting, the work of My hands, that I may be glorified. A little one shall become a thousand, and a small one a strong nation. I, the LORD, will hasten it in its time.

Let us walk with the Lord in a spirit of prayer, inviting and hastening this day pictured before us here. One day to come, God's people "shall all be righteous." Goodness, what a pleasant prospect. Today, we love the Lord so much. We long to serve Him. Our worship both in church and our worship at home alone in His presence is so sweet. Our worship in the glory of His nearness and our service in His presence is so near to heaven on earth – and it would be nearer still were it not for the weight and guilt and grip of sin. The consequences of our past sins, our battle with present temptations, and our undeniable, aggravating inclination to sin again remain thorns in our side that temper all life's joys. The day is coming however, when our love for God, our service to Him, and our worship of Him will no longer be tainted by our maddening predisposition to sin. We shall "all be righteous." What a precious day awaits us. Proverbs 20:9 asks, "Who can say, 'I have made my heart clean, I am pure from my sin'?" On our own, none of us can say this. But here, our Father promises to do for us that which we crave but cannot do ourselves. He will make us righteous. At last, we will be able to worship and serve our Lord in purity. We will at last be able to "go and sin no more" (John 8:11) as our Lord commands and our soul aspires.

Our coming righteousness will come to us by an act of God. He says that it is "the work of My hands." His grace cleanses us from our past sins, the work of His Spirit keeps us from further sins, and His death on the cross cleanses us from all our guilty stains. Our devotion to purity arises within us because He is "planting" within us the seed of righteousness. I John 3:9 says, "Whoever has been born of God does not sin, for His seed remains in him; and he cannot sin, because he has been born of God." God's Spirit plants within us a heart for holiness, and that implanted seed will germinate, "branch," and yield "much fruit" (John 15:8) so that the Father "may be glorified."

God's work in us prospers us beyond measure: one little child of God "shall become a thousand," and a single "small" saint will become "a strong nation." But our advancement is not merely for our personal enjoyment. We are purified, we are blessed so that God "may be glorified." And this great motivation of our Creator to see His great name glorified will move Him to "hasten" our purification and hasten our spiritual prosperity so that He, our Lord, will receive His due praise.

Isaiah 61

61:1-3
The Spirit of the Lord GOD is upon Me, because the LORD has anointed Me to preach good tidings to the poor; He has sent Me to heal the brokenhearted, to proclaim liberty to the captives, and the opening of the prison to those who are bound; to proclaim the acceptable year of the LORD, and the day of vengeance of our God; to comfort all who mourn, to console those who mourn in Zion, to give them beauty for ashes, the oil of joy for mourning, the garment of praise for the spirit of heaviness; that they may be called trees of righteousness, the planting of the LORD, that He may be glorified.

Isaiah wrote these words some 700 years before Jesus was born in Bethlehem, but in Luke 4, Jesus reads this passage in the synagogue on the Sabbath day and tells a captivated, but flammable crowd of listeners that these words were written of Him. This prophetic description of Jesus centuries before His birth provided the evidence that John the Baptist desperately sought after to confirm for him that Jesus was, indeed, the Christ (Luke 7:22). Many in the world from Isaiah's day to ours are not seeking the Son of God, and even if they were seeking, they would be prone to miss Him, because their self-made expectations of a Savior differ greatly from those we see in these descriptors. Some assume that a kind-hearted God would prevent all ills and all brokenness. But our world is broken, and life in a broken world will lead to broken hearts. God does not prevent these things, instead, He heals them. The Father sent His Son to "heal the brokenhearted." Like His Father, Jesus "heals the brokenhearted and binds up their wounds" (Psalms 147:3). Those who ignore God in their brokenness will miss it, those who blame God for their troubles will miss it too, but those who carry their pains to Jesus will find that He comes with gentleness and kindness "to heal the brokenhearted" and "to comfort" and to "console" all who mourn.

It is interesting to note the significance that Jesus came to "preach good tidings to the poor." Preaching as a means to get one's point across is regarded as foolishness by many (I Corinthians 1:21), yet it is by preaching "good tidings" that our Creator has chosen to communicate His truths to us. We might think that displays of power or pre-death tours of heaven could be methods better suited to convince man to obey His Creator, but no, it is by "the foolishness of the message preached" that our Lord has chosen to "save those who believe." We might also choose a different target audience than the Messiah chooses. We might guess that God would send His message and Messenger to speak deep truths to the wisest of men, the most gifted of men, or to the most powerful of the world's people. But instead, He preaches His simple truths to simple people. He preaches the riches of His wisdom to the poorest of His hearers. James 2:5 tells us that rather than targeting the rich and powerful, God has intentionally "chosen the poor of this world to be rich in faith and heirs of the kingdom which He promised to those who love Him." Psalms 112:9 says that God "has given to the poor," and prominent among His many gifts to them, we see included this great privilege of hearing the gospel truths peached from the lips of the Son of God.

Jesus came to "free those who are bound" and to grant "liberty to the captives." He would free the apostles from prison in Acts 5:19, set Peter free in Acts 12, and release Paul from His imprisonment in Acts 16. The Messiah's rescue of those in bondage is by no means limited to freeing those in jail, however. His truth sets us free (John 8:32) from the bonds of ignorance, guilt, and hopelessness; and through Jesus, His children are "set free from sin" (Romans 6:18). Jesus frees us from the nagging, soul-wrenching guilt of sin. He sets us free from the addiction to sin. And, blessedly, He sets us free from the eternal punishment of sin.

Jesus came to heal and to comfort and to set free, but He also came to warn men and women of the imminence of the coming of the "day of vengeance of our God." He came to "preach good tidings." He came to proclaim the festive, Jubilee-like arrival of "the acceptable year of the LORD." But He also came to warn the men and women of our world of the imminence of the "day of vengeance of our God." God has given great gifts to men (Ephesians 4:8). God gives us all a conscience to tell right from wrong (Romans 2:15). He gives us "eternity in (our) hearts" (Ecclesiastes 3:11) so that we will use all His gifts to seek Him (Acts 17:27). He promises to bless those who obey Him (Deuteronomy 28:2) and bless those who bless His people (Numbers 24:9). Sadly, those who desecrate God's gifts to man, those who rebel against their conscience, refuse to seek to know and honor their Creator, despise His promises, and treat His children cruelly are all too easy to find. Jesus may treat these rebels with patience for a while, maybe even a long while, but there is coming a day when Jesus the Messiah will take "vengeance" on all who rebel against Him. In Micah 5:15 our Lord warns "In anger and wrath I will execute vengeance on the nations that did not obey." Isaiah prophesies of the coming of the Son of God, not only giving hope for holy men living in dark times, but also to warn the world not to make the mistake of thinking that the Messiah comes as a Santa Clause giving goodies to all. He comes with gifts and glad tidings to men; but He comes with vengeance on those who despise His gifts.

Jesus comes to give "beauty for ashes." He gives "pheer" (beauty) for "epher" (ashes). When life falls apart and there seems to be no way to redeem the terrible tragedy that is before us, Isaiah would have us remember that our Lord has come to restore joy and hope and beauty. And when rescue appears impossible from our vantage point, we are reminded that our Lord can change tragedy and ashes into rescue and beauty as easily as a child can erase and replace a single letter on a page.

The world is full of cause for sorrow, but our Lord comes to salve our sorrows with the "oil of joy." David's life was scarred by betrayals, violence against him, and the curses of lesser men. But in Psalms 23:5-6 he wrote the oft-quoted words: "You anoint my head with oil; my cup runs over. Surely goodness and mercy shall follow me all the days of my life; and I will dwell in the house of the LORD forever." The sting of worldly sorrows is real, but the Lord anoints His hurting people with the "oil of joy" which is able to cure even the deepest of wounds.

When God's people experience the glory of His goodness, when we hear His "glad tidings," when we feel our shackles fall away by His freeing power, when His comforts and consolations re-invigorate our soul, the tattered rags of self-centeredness are put away, and we delight to put on the "garments of praise" instead. Preoccupation with our personal problems, fixation on the pressures placed on us, will weigh on our hearts like a "spirit of heaviness." Those who fix their eyes on the Lord, however, will find that their hearts are filled with peace (Isaiah 26:3) and their lips are filled with praise. The crushing weight of the spirit of heaviness is replaced with the soul-restoring garments of praise.

These great gifts brought to us by the Messiah are not provided so that we can sin and yet be saved. God implants His gifts in man so that we might grow to be "trees of righteousness." Jesus does all that He does for us so that we might: "live for righteousness" (I Peter 2:24) -- not that we might be exalted as anything great, but that "He may be glorified" in His remarkable work in men and women that teaches us, cleanses us, consoles and comforts us, frees us, and fills our lives with "beauty" and our tongues with "praise."

61:4-7

And they shall rebuild the old ruins, they shall raise up the former desolations, and they shall repair the ruined cities, the desolations of many generations. Strangers shall stand and feed your flocks, and the sons of the foreigner shall be your plowmen and your vinedressers. But you shall be named the priests of the LORD, they shall call you the servants of our God. You shall eat the riches of the Gentiles, and in their glory you shall boast. Instead of your shame you shall have double honor, and instead of confusion they shall rejoice in their portion. Therefore in their land they shall possess double; everlasting joy shall be theirs.

Isaiah foretells the coming of the Messiah in verses 1-3, and now he foretells the restoration and elevation of God's people here. Isaiah's words will begin to be fulfilled when God's people return from Babylon to "rebuild the old ruins" and "repair the ruined cities" that had been deserted and desolate for "many generations." Translators offer varying renderings of verse 7, but we see that God's people will see their "shame" replaced with "double honor." And in this "double honor" we see that Isaiah's words transcend far beyond a simple promise that Israel's captives will one day return home. All of us who trust in God and become His children by faith "shall be named the priests of the LORD," all who see us will acknowledge that we are "the servants of our God." Revelation 1:6 says that Jesus "has made us kings and priests to His God and Father." Jesus will call us His priests, and onlookers will confirm that it is so when they see that we live for His purposes and sing His praises. We will live to work for God and we will love our work – "everlasting joy" will be ours. We will live for God and when He becomes the center of all things, we will love our life – "everlasting joy" will be ours. God's people will delight to serve Him as servants, they will find great pleasure in praising Him as priests. All that they get out of life will come from Jesus, for He is their "portion." They look to Jesus for all their rewards in life and all their purpose in life, and they are not disappointed in the end. They "rejoice in their portion," for they find God's rewards and His purposes to be completely satisfying. The Lord can rightly claim ownership of all creation, yet He finds satisfaction in the service and praise of those who are His by faith: "For the LORD's portion is His people" (Deuteronomy 32:9). If God is satisfied with having us as His portion, how much more then, ought we delight to join the refrain of Psalms 142:5 and say, "I cried out to You, O LORD: I said, 'You are my refuge, my portion in the land of the living." "The LORD is my portion," says my soul, "Therefore I hope in Him!" (Lamentations 3:24). When the everlasting Lord is our portion "everlasting joy" will be our reward. The fulfillment of Isaiah's words here may have begun with the return of God's people from Babylon, but the greater, fuller fulfillment of Isaiah's words will never end. Jesus continues to call people to Himself as His servants and His priests, and as we serve Him in this most pleasant of roles, "everlasting joy" shall be ours.

61:8-9
For I, the LORD, love justice; I hate robbery for burnt offering; I will direct their work in truth, and will make with them an everlasting covenant. Their descendants shall be known among the Gentiles, and their offspring among the people. All who see them shall acknowledge them, that they are the posterity whom the LORD has blessed.

God loves justice. It may seem like some people get away with murder, but they never do. God loves justice and He metes it out perfectly in His perfect timing. He hates "robbery and wrongdoing" (NLT) and promises to "reserve the unjust under punishment for the day of judgment" (2 Peter 2:9). For His children who walk in the truth and uphold justice, however, He grants a different covenant: "Their descendants will be known and honored among the nations. Everyone will realize that they are a people the LORD has blessed" (Isaiah 61:9 NLT). What a deep, abiding joy is ours to see how God has blessed us. We acknowledge that we are completely undeserving. We acknowledge that all of our Lord's blessings on us flow from His well of kindness and mercy and His Divine intention to bless His children: "For you bless the godly, O LORD, surrounding them with your shield of love" (Psalms 5:12 NLT). It is God's desire to bless His children in order to awaken the conscience of the lost and to inspire all to reverently obey Him. "God shall bless us, and all the ends of the earth shall fear Him" (Psalms 67:7). When others declare that God has blessed us, let us bow our heads and humbly acknowledge that we see it too, and publicly, frequently, gratefully voice our highest praises to our God from whom all blessings flow.

61:10-11
I will greatly rejoice in the LORD, my soul shall be joyful in my God; for He has clothed me with the garments of salvation, He has covered me with the robe of righteousness, as a bridegroom decks himself with ornaments, and as a bride adorns herself with her jewels. For as the earth brings forth its bud, as the garden causes the things that are sown in it to spring forth, so the Lord GOD will cause righteousness and praise to spring forth before all the nations.

Speaking on behalf of all God's people, Isaiah writes that he "will greatly rejoice in the LORD." His "soul shall be joyful" in God. Isaiah is filled with joy and rejoices in the Lord because of two great gifts: salvation and righteousness. No one can make us righteous but God alone. We have already committed sins without number that taint our past and stain our soul so indelibly that on our own there is no hope for recovery. Our spirit hates being a sinful creature. Our conscience stings from the guilt, our soul is shamed by the awareness that we have failed to live up to our Creator's standards, and our heart is haunted by the fear of sin's repercussions. Everyone has sinned (Romans 3:23), everyone is doomed by sin (Romans 6:23), and no one is able to fix their sin (Romans 7:24), and these 3 truths cause all thinking men to suffer intelligent desperation. We rightly groan over our sin until that day when our Lord takes it all away. Oh, the joy of Christ's imputed righteousness – when He administers His righteousness to us! Well does Isaiah say that His soul is joyful in God, for "He has covered me with the robe of righteousness." Good deeds can never erase sinful actions, but blessedly, Christ's blood can! On Christ's behalf the Father declares us righteous, not because we have never sinned, but because the stain of our sins has been erased by the blood of Christ, and when Christ then comes to live in us, the Father sees only His righteousness in us, not our sinful flesh that remains visible to the naked eye. Oh, the joy of sinful men made righteous! "Blessed is the man to whom the Lord shall not impute sin" (Romans 4:8). The exhilarating transformation from sinful man to righteous child of God causes joy and praise to impulsively spring from inside us. Let us not hold it back. "Rejoice in the LORD, O you righteous! For praise from the upright is beautiful" (Psalms 33:1).

Isaiah also finds cause to rejoice, because God has clothed Him with "the garments of salvation." The Psalms are filled with praises of gratitude for God's salvation. "I will rejoice in Your salvation" (Psalms 9:14). "My heart shall rejoice in Your salvation" (Psalms 13:5). "We will rejoice in your salvation, and in the name of our God we will set up our banners!" (Psalms 20:5). And Psalms 35:9 says, "My soul shall be joyful in the LORD; it shall rejoice in His salvation." Christ has saved us! What else do we need to rejoice? Sin no longer dictates our destiny. Death and hell no longer loom over our future! We are saved! We will one day leave this world of suffering and enter perfect heaven – saved from the death that nature offers, saved from the hell that sin secures. Praise the Lord!

Verse 11 then grants us a very pleasant picture of the garden of God. God plants righteousness and salvation in His children, and He is certain that His efforts will yield "righteousness and praise" in return. God imputes righteousness to us, and we dedicate our lives to living righteously for Him in proper response. God saves us from sin and death, and we praise Him in proper response – the seeds of righteousness and salvation will "spring forth" into righteousness and praise before the watchful eyes of "all the nations" beckoning them to rush forward to meet the Gardener (John 15:1) that He might implant His righteousness and salvation into them as well.

Isaiah 62

62:1
For Zion's sake I will not hold my peace, and for Jerusalem's sake I will not rest, until her righteousness goes forth as brightness, and her salvation as a lamp that burns.

If this is the Lord speaking, we are greatly encouraged by His unceasing Divine efforts to save His people and dress them in righteousness. What a precious thought that He "will not rest" until His children shine in righteousness and His people are rescued from the penalty of their sin. In Ezekiel 34:12 the Lord declares, "I will be like a shepherd looking for his scattered flock. I will find my sheep and rescue them from all the places to which they were scattered on that dark and cloudy day" (NLT). Jesus plainly stated that His mission on earth was to "seek and to save the lost" (Luke 19:10). He will not rest until all His lambs are accounted for.

If however, these words are from Isaiah himself, we find them hardly less inspiring. It would be easier for Isaiah to hold his peace; he would be far less vulnerable to opposition if he would not be so vocal about God's call for men and women to repent. Jeremiah voiced this temptation: "Then I said,

'I will not make mention of Him, nor speak anymore in His name'" (Jeremiah 20:9a). It is apparent however, that Jeremiah was compelled by the Spirit of God to seek the salvation of his people, just as Isaiah was, because he finishes Jeremiah 20:9 by saying: "But His word was in my heart like a burning fire shut up in my bones; I was weary of holding it back, and I could not." Paul expressed the same godly burden to see his people saved. "My heart's desire and prayer to God for Israel is that they may be saved." In Romans 9:2 Paul says, "I have great sorrow and continual grief in my heart" because his countrymen were not reconciled with the Lord. Here, Isaiah expresses this same theme which inspires us to rise up as he did to do all we can to see the people around us walk in righteousness and see our nation saved. Let us fervently pray as David did, "Oh, save your people and bless your heritage! Be their shepherd and carry them forever" (Psalms 28:9 ESV).

62:2
The Gentiles shall see your righteousness, and all kings your glory. You shall be called by a new name, which the mouth of the LORD will name.

God will see to it that His people are saved from sin and shine in righteousness, and the unbelievers around them cannot help but take notice. They "shall see your righteousness." Their flesh may lure them to sinful living, but when they see a righteous life lived out before them, their conscience recognizes that righteous living is the right way to live. Even kings and enjoyers of success will acknowledge that the glory of righteous living exceeds their own. The lost see the glory of the saints – and so does the Savior. He looks on His people that He has cleansed and redeemed and His heart wells up with such love that He gives them a new name. When His grace-filled covenant was handed to Abram, God renamed him Abraham (Genesis 17:5). When Jacob prevailed with God in prayer, the Lord changed his name to Israel (Genesis 32:28). And so shall it be for all God's people when we overcome the temptations of the world and are transformed from a hell-bound sinner to a heaven-bound saint. Revelation 2:17 says, "He who has an ear, let him hear what the Spirit says to the churches. To him who overcomes I will give some of the hidden manna to eat. And I will give him a white stone, and on the stone a new name written which no one knows except him who receives it." Being reconciled with God is likened to being "born again" (John 3:3), and just as babies are named after birth, so our Lord looks down from heaven and is likewise moved to give a new name to His cherished baby-saints.

62:3
You shall also be a crown of glory in the hand of the LORD, and a royal diadem in the hand of your God.

Those who belong to God are like "a crown of glory" in His hand. God's cleansing, saving works in us make us glorious – like a "royal diadem." Our faith in God and praise for His name make us precious to Him – we become His treasure, His crown – not that He wears on His head, but that He holds in His hand – suggesting that we are not ornamental crowns, but useful ones, designed to be about His work as He holds us as instruments of glory in His hands. Paul called his fellow believers his "crown of rejoicing" (Philippians 4:1, I Thessalonians 2:19), and here we see Isaiah describe God's children the same way. Sin bankrupts us, tarnishes us, degrades, demeans, and disgraces us. But once reconciled to the Lord, our spiritual luster returns! Without Christ we are "broken pottery" (Isaiah 45:9 NCV), with Him we are crowns. Listening to other gods and false teachers "make you worthless" (Jeremiah 23:16), but obeying the words of the Lord causes our value to soar like royal diadems. See how God's work in the souls of man instills such remarkable value in us!

62:4
You shall no longer be termed Forsaken, nor shall your land any more be termed Desolate; but you shall be called Hephzibah, and your land Beulah; for the LORD delights in you, and your land shall be married.

Such an overwhelmingly precious promise is given to God's people here. Their sin had separated them from the Lord (Isaiah 59:2). He had named them "Lo-Ammi" – "not My people" (Hosea 1:9). They had become "Forsaken." But due to no beauty or effort of their own, the Lord here promises to court them once again. In verse 2 God promised His people a new name, and here He gives them 2 – Hephzibah and Beulah. Hephzibah means "My delight is in her!" Such a remarkable thing for God to say about such an unattractive people. Beulah means "married." The Lord will look down from His heavenly home and find delight in His people. And adding grace upon grace, blessing upon blessing, He will not just admire them from afar, He will take them to Himself as His bride, granting them all the privileges and joys of married union with the King of Kings.

62:5
For as a young man marries a virgin, so shall your sons marry you; and as the bridegroom rejoices over the bride, so shall your God rejoice over you.

God says His love for us is like the love that a young husband has for his bride. And because we are moved to imitate our Father, He says that in the same way, men and women in God's kingdom will love one another, will love the church in the same way. Isaiah's words certainly include the Jew's love for their nation and their return from captivity in Babylon, but they reach far further than that, describing God's great love for His people and His people's great love for the church. The final descriptor we have of the body of Christ is this same picture – a bride for her Husband. Revelation 21:9 says, "Then one of the seven angels who had the seven bowls filled with the seven last plagues came to me and talked with me, saying, 'Come, I will show you the bride, the Lamb's wife.'" Our Father loves us. He loves us like a young man loves his bride. What a precious thought.

62:6-7
I have set watchmen on your walls, O Jerusalem; they shall never hold their peace day or night. You who make mention of the LORD, do not keep silent, and give Him no rest till He establishes and till He makes Jerusalem a praise in the earth.

God sets His watchmen over His people to call them from sin, call them to dedicate themselves to His purposes, call them to listen to His word, and warn them of approaching dangers to their faith and service. We are so greatly stirred by the Lord's promise: "they shall never hold their peace day or night." No matter how far God's chosen ones stray, He will always call them back to Himself. His watchmen will always be His voice, calling men from sin and inspiring then to live for the honor and glory and purposes of God. God's servants will never "hold their peace." They will continually grant the world the great opportunity to hear and know His will. As great as that work is, the blessed role of the watchman is not limited to speaking God's words to God's people, however. God's servants, His watchmen will never hold their peace, they will always, ever speak God's truths to man. But they will also "not keep silent" before God on behalf of men. Their constant prayers of intercession on man's behalf will give God "no rest." They will pray without ceasing until the Lord "establishes" His people as a banner of praise throughout the earth.

Let us raise our hand and volunteer to carry out this great task of the watchman! May our family never fail to have successive generations that stand on the rampart of godly service and call men to God and call down God's blessings on man. Our Lord ever lives to make intercession for the sake of men and women who are ever at risk of physical and spiritual ruin (Hebrews 7:25). Let us join Him in this great work that He forever lives to do. Let us never hold our peace. Never. Let us warn our fellow man of the great error and terrible outcome of sin. Let us inspire our fellow man with the very words of God that have been passed on to us through the scriptures. And let us pray for all around us. Let us "not keep silent" before the Lord. Let us "pray without ceasing" (I Thessalonians 5:17). The role of God's watchmen is not limited to watching. We must vocalize His words to men and verbalize the needs of men in intercession before God. Let us follow Samuel's example when he said, "Moreover, as for me, far be it from me that I should sin against the LORD in ceasing to pray for you; but I will teach you the good and the right way" (I Samuel 12:23). Teach men God's ways. Pray for men in the presence of God. This is the great work of the watchman. May our family be forever filled with the sound of watchmen at their holy work.

62:8-9
The LORD has sworn by His right hand and by the arm of His strength: "Surely I will no longer give your grain as food for your enemies; and the sons of the foreigner shall not drink your new wine, for which you have labored. But those who have gathered it shall eat it, and praise the LORD; those who have brought it together shall drink it in My holy courts."

As captives in Babylon, Israel's labors led to the comforts of others. Later, while under Roman rule, once again they could not enjoy the fruits of their labor – others benefited from what should have been theirs to enjoy. But here, the Lord promises the coming day when godly men will find satisfaction in the fruit of their own honest efforts. They will find fulfilment and contentment in their labors, and thus enriched by the enjoyment of the fruits of their efforts, they will come to God's "holy courts" and "praise the LORD" for the simple pleasures inherent in gaining an honest wage for an honest day at work. The picture is pleasant and simple. God's people work for a living, they are paid for it, and they praise God in His house for the simple joy of working hard and getting paid for it. No one takes what is mine, I take nothing from others, and my focus through it all is on giving praise to my Lord for whom I work, and through whom I have strength to work.

62:10-12
Go through, go through the gates! Prepare the way for the people; build up, build up the highway! Take out the stones, lift up a banner for the peoples! Indeed the LORD has proclaimed to the end of the world: "Say to the daughter of Zion, 'Surely your salvation is coming; behold, His reward is with Him, and His work before Him.'" And they shall call them the Holy People, the Redeemed of the LORD; and you shall be called Sought Out, a City Not Forsaken.

    The cry goes out! "Go through the gates" and enter the kingdom of God!" The initial fulfillment may have been witnessed when captives from Israel returned to Jerusalem from Babylon, but God's call through Isaiah rings out to include all peoples from every age. "Lift up a banner!" Swell the ranks of the army of God by summoning the world's people to join His advancing throng that marches under His direction with flag unfurled! Clearly the message is not only directed toward returnees from Babylon, for the message is to be "proclaimed to the end of the world." God's work is to save men's souls (Luke 19:10), and with "His work" and "His reward" before Him He calls His "Holy People," those that He has "Redeemed" to Himself. Though His people have rebelled against Him for so long, yet He reassures them that they are "a City Not Forsaken;" He has "Sought Out" all His people from the ends of the earth and signaled for them to return to Him with banners of blessings waving and His truth "proclaimed to the end of the world." Such a picture of victory is presented here! Though so many men and women insist on rebelling against the Lord, yet His army will forever call people to His ranks. He will forever call, forever save, forever reward His followers. As for our part, let us join the roadbuilders that will "prepare the way for the people." Let us "build up, build up the highway!" Let us join the holy construction crew that builds the roads that convey men and women to the Savior! Our Lord's banner is unfurled! It waves high above the temporal, mundane matters of distraction and calls the world to follow Him. People in the cities and in the jungles and in all the Father's fields the world over can see it wave. May all who see our Father's banner find ready-made roads that we have built that will aid their travel to Him.

Isaiah 63

63:1-6
Who is this who comes from Edom, with dyed garments from Bozrah, this One who is glorious in His apparel, traveling in the greatness of His strength? – "I who speak in righteousness, mighty to save." Why is Your apparel red, and Your garments like one who treads in the winepress? "I have trodden the winepress alone, and from the peoples no one was with Me. For I have trodden them in My anger, and trampled them in My fury; their blood is sprinkled upon My garments, and I have stained all My robes. For the day of vengeance is in My heart, and the year of My redeemed has come. I looked, but there was no one to help, and I wondered that there was no one to uphold; therefore My own arm brought salvation for Me; and My own fury, it sustained Me. I have trodden down the peoples in My anger, made them drunk in My fury, and brought down their strength to the earth."

Isaiah describes the Lord coming in "glorious apparel" that is "stained" with the blood of those that He has "trodden down" in the "fury" and "anger" of His judgment. The picture is very similar to the portrait of

Christ given us in Revelation 19:11-16. In Revelation 19:11 the Lord is called "Faithful and True" and "in righteousness He judges and makes war." Revelation 19:13 says "he was clothed with a robe dipped in blood, and His name is called the Word of God." And verse 19:15 says "He Himself treads the winepress of the fierceness and wrath of Almighty God."

Several matters of interest catch my attention. First, we are reminded that God is furious with those who do not obey Him and do not worship Him. Unrighteousness and devotion to false religion incite red-hot anger in the heart of holy God. "For the wrath of God is revealed from heaven against all ungodliness and unrighteousness of men, who suppress the truth in unrighteousness" (Romans 1:18). Psalms 2:12 reminds us to "Pay homage to the Son, or He will be angry, and you will perish in your rebellion, for His anger may ignite at any moment. All those who take refuge in Him are happy" (HCS). For all God's mercy, He is not soft on sin. We must remember this. "The LORD is longsuffering and abundant in mercy, forgiving iniquity and transgression; but He by no means clears the guilty, visiting the iniquity of the fathers on the children to the third and fourth generations" (Numbers 14:18).

Secondly, there appears to be little difference in the heart of God between His saving work and His work of judgment. His fury toward the ungodly "sustained" His efforts to bring salvation for His children (verse 5). His "Day of vengeance" comes in the "year of My redeemed" (verse 4). What I tend to separate into 2 distinct works of God – rescue for His people and destruction on the rebellious, He appears to view as a single act. He is "mighty to save" in verse 1 and He tramples the ungodly to death in verse 3. Interestingly, it appears to be His "fury" that is the driving force behind both His salvation of His saints (verse 5) and His destruction of the ungodly (verse 6). It is interesting to ponder why God's anger would move Him to save people, and we are moved to remember again that God is the center of all things, not man. His priority to exalt His name takes precedence over and is the driving force behind both His heart to save the elect and to bring judgment on unbelievers. Psalms 106:8 says that the Lord "saved them (his people) for His name's sake, that He might make His mighty power known." And Exodus 14:18 says that God punished the Egyptians for much the same reason: "Then the Egyptians shall know that I am the LORD, when I have gained honor for Myself over Pharaoh...." Isaiah 5:16 says "the LORD of hosts shall be exalted in judgment" and Psalms 18:46 says that He is exalted when He saves. God saves and God judges, and it is His fierce defense of His name that drives both actions.

ISAIAH 63

And thirdly, we see both that God alone is judge: "I have trodden the winepress alone" (verse 3). And God alone saves: "there was no one to help," "therefore My own arm brought salvation" (verse 5). We do not get to choose who judges us. We do not get to pick the god that most closely aligns with our personal preferences. Our Creator made us, taught us what He expects from us, and then judges us for how we respond to His commands. There is no other judge to overrule Him or to set up a separate system of spiritual arbitration. God judges all of us, and He judges alone. And too, God alone possesses power to save us from spiritual and eternal ruin. God alone judges. God alone saves. Isaiah 43:11 says, "I, even I, am the LORD, and besides Me there is no savior." With God alone as the Savior and Judge of all the universe, we have no hope but to reconcile with Him. There is no means of securing our soul's salvation and escaping the consequences of sin other than by reconciling with the One who stands as Savior and Judge of the whole earth.

63:7-10
I will mention the lovingkindnesses of the LORD and the praises of the LORD, according to all that the LORD has bestowed on us, and the great goodness toward the house of Israel, which He has bestowed on them according to His mercies, according to the multitude of His lovingkindnesses. For He said, "Surely they are My people, children who will not lie." So He became their Savior. In all their affliction He was afflicted, and the Angel of His Presence saved them; in His love and in His pity He redeemed them; and He bore them and carried them all the days of old. But they rebelled and grieved His Holy Spirit; so He turned Himself against them as an enemy, and He fought against them.

Isaiah sets his pen to write of the great list of "lovingkindnesses" that the Lord has "bestowed on us." The list is long and wonderful to revisit over and over again. It is full of a "multitude" of loving blessings that are so amazing that they defy adequate descriptors. Our loving Lord has poured out on us a vast, remarkable array of "lovingkindnesses" – blessings so dear and so wonderful that a specially-invented word must be used to describe the unique preciousness of the Father's matchless gifts to us. Isaiah begins the list by considering our Lord's elective grace. "For He said, 'Surely they are My people.'" Our Lord has called us to be His own. When we were sinful and ignorant and did not seek forgiveness or knowledge of the truth, yet our Lord declared that He had chosen us to be His people. What a kindness it is, what a blessed encouragement to our soul -- to rest in the knowledge that our God has chosen us to belong to Him. Jeremiah 30:22 declares, "You shall be My people, and I will be your God." What a precious lovingkindness.

Next on Isaiah's list, our Lord "became" our Savior. The Angel of the Divine presence, "The Angel of His Presence" certainly refers to Jesus, who saw Israel's need and saved them from their enemies and saw our need and saved us from our sin. Our rescue did not come easily. It brought Him "affliction." We see Jesus tormented in the garden as He cried out agonized prayers over His impending crucifixion. We see Him tormented again as His body endured the torture of the scourging, the cruel mockery, and the cross. And we see our Lord afflicted time and time again as both the sins and the sufferings of His people brought Him grief. Our Lord was "grieved in His heart" over the sins of man in Genesis 6:6; and Psalms 78:40 says that the sins of His people "grieved Him in the desert." And such are the tender sympathies of our Lord, that our pain causes Him the affliction of Godly empathy as well. Jesus wept at the sight of the tears of Lazarus' sisters (John 11:35), and verse 9 here says that when His people suffered affliction that "He was afflicted" in His heart as well.

Our Lord has given us so many precious lovingkindnesses. His gifts to us did not come without pain to Himself. He groans and grieves over our sins and sorrows and the extreme measures that He endured to overcome them. And His gifts to us did not come without expectations. Our Lord expected that His goodness to us would generate love and loyalty in us. He said, "Surely they are My people, children who will not lie." "Children who will not be disloyal" (HCS). Sadly, almost unimaginably, His people did rebel against Him "and grieved His Holy Spirit" (verse 10). Our rebellion, completely without cause and completely to our discredit brings righteous, understandable anger to our Lord. Our Lord is willing to call us His friend (John 15:15). Disobedience and disloyalty however, make us His enemy. Our Lord's heart is to fight for us (Deuteronomy 20:4 etc.). Disobedience and disloyalty however, cause God to fight against us instead (verse 10). Certainly, all thinking men and women will clearly see that it is in our best interest to loyally love and obey our Lord in response to His unending lovingkindnesses to us. Failure to respond in kind to God's love will move the omnipotent, omniscient, omnipresent God of creation to come against us as our enemy. Who in their right mind would trade God's unending blessings for God's unbridled anger?

63:11-14

Then he remembered the days of old, Moses and his people, saying: "Where is He who brought them up out of the sea with the shepherd of His flock? Where is He who put His Holy Spirit within them, who led them by the right hand of Moses, with His glorious arm, dividing the water before them to make for Himself an everlasting name, who led them through the deep, as a horse in the wilderness, that they might not stumble?" As a beast goes down into the valley, and the Spirit of the LORD causes him to rest, so You lead Your people, to make Yourself a glorious name.

We see with our mind's eye a man standing over wreckage. Perhaps he is a captive from Israel looking over his oppressed people in Babylon. Perhaps he is a man in our day, broken by tragedy. The pain and problems before him appear unsalvable, innumerable, inescapable. Today is nearly unbearable, and there is no hope that tomorrow will be any better. But then, "he remembered the days of old." In the midst of his present hardship, he called to mind the great deeds of God from the past. He remembered what God did through Moses, how He saved the people at the Red Sea, and how He sustained Moses with His Holy Spirit. He remembered God's great works in the past, and thus refreshed his soul in the present. The psalmist in Psalms 77:10-12 does the same thing. When his soul is in "anguish" he writes: "I will remember the years of the right hand of the Most High. I will remember the works of the LORD; surely I will remember Your wonders of old. I will also meditate on all Your work, and talk of Your deeds." *Considering God's past provisions is a good cure for present anxieties.* God does not change (Malachi 3:6), if He provided for His people in Moses' time, we have proper cause to believe that He will do so in our day as well. He filled Moses with His Holy Spirit, and He promises to do the same for us if we will ask (Luke 11:13). He gives rest to beasts in the valley (verse 14). He promised rest to His people in Exodus 33:14 -- "My Presence will go with you, and I will give you rest." Jesus again promised rest in Matthew 11:28 – and if we will contemplate and meditate on these promises and provisions of our Lord in the past, we will find rest for our souls in the here and now. It is God's intention to make for Himself "a glorious name." And He intends to do so by providing for His people and demonstrating His power before us. So then, armed with the memory of His great works in the past, and inspired by the vision of His glorious name flying like a banner before us, let us not lose hope in our present trial. God has done so many great things. And for His own great name's sake He will do many more.

63:15-16
Look down from heaven, and see from Your habitation, holy and glorious. Where are Your zeal and Your strength, the yearning of Your heart and Your mercies toward me? Are they restrained? Doubtless You are our Father, though Abraham was ignorant of us, and Israel does not acknowledge us. You, O LORD, are our Father; our Redeemer from Everlasting is Your name.

The prophet speaks as the voice of those who will face days of tragedy when it seems that God is gone. He asks, "Where are you Lord?" Where is your zeal for protecting your people? Where is your powerful hand providing for us? Where is your merciful heart that cares for those in need? What is holding you back? The prophet communicates the common question that comes to the minds of those in desperation. "Where are you Lord?" But though he is distressed by not knowing where God's mercy is, he is strengthened by his assurance of who God is. "You are our Father." Even if it were possible for Abraham and Israel to forget us, You would never leave us alone. You are "our Redeemer." With Your own flesh and blood, You redeemed us to become Your own flesh and blood, so we are certain that You will never abandon us. God is our Father. No matter how dark times become, He always sees us. He cannot forget us. "Can a woman forget her nursing child, and not have compassion on the son of her womb? Surely they may forget, yet I will not forget you" (Isaiah 49:15). Our Lord's name is "Everlasting." In our darkest days let us remember that His love for us will never end.

63:17-19
O LORD, why have You made us stray from Your ways, and hardened our heart from Your fear? Return for Your servants' sake, the tribes of Your inheritance. Your holy people have possessed it but a little while; our adversaries have trodden down Your sanctuary. We have become like those of old, over whom You never ruled, those who were never called by Your name.

"O LORD," "Return for Your servants' sake"! The only thing that separates us from everyone else in the world is the presence of God. The prophet groans because he knows that if God does not draw near, he and his people are no different from those "who were never called by Your name." Moses realized this same essential matter: "If Your Presence does not go with us, do not bring us up from here. For how then will it be known that Your people and I have found grace in Your sight, except You go with us? So we shall be separate, Your people and I, from all the people who are upon the face of the earth" (Exodus 33:15-16). God's people have strayed from His ways. They have hardened their heart. They have not honored Him at home nor worshipped Him in His sanctuary, so the Lord removed His protection on their nation and their adversaries were granted license to trample down the sanctuary. The people strayed from His ways, so the Lord left them to their own devices, and His absence finally stirred the people to their senses. Please, Lord! "Return for Your servants' sake!" It is not God's blessings that separate us from the pagan peoples of the earth. God blesses both the just and the unjust (Matthew 5:45). It is not ritual, riches, or even righteousness that separate us from the pagan peoples of the earth. It is the presence of God. And this is what the prophet here pleads for above all else. Please, Lord, "return for Your servants' sake." Without Your presence, "we have become like those of old, over whom You never ruled." It is good to seek God's blessings. It is good to seek God's wisdom and strength. But let us be faithful to rise each morning, desperately hungry for the presence of God once more. The only thing that makes us different from lost people on their way to hell is the presence of God in us. May the fullness of His blessed presence never leave us.

Isaiah 64

64:1-2
Oh, that You would rend the heavens! That You would come down! That the mountains might shake at Your presence – as fire burns brushwood, as fire causes water to boil – to make Your name known to Your adversaries, that the nations may tremble at Your presence!

Our Lord has made it clear that although He hates sin, He is slow to anger (Psalms 103:8) and does not rush to lower judgment on sinful man because He does not want anyone to die apart from Him (II Peter 3:9). It is God's desire to overcome unbelief and defeat rebellion with mercy rather than with judgment. At the same time however, may no one ever delude himself into thinking that it is safe to sin. Judgment and punishment for sin and unbelief are at the door of all those who fail to heed God's commands. God warns us in Malachi 3:5 -- "'I will come near you for judgment; I will be a swift witness against sorcerers, against adulterers, against perjurers, against those who exploit wage earners and widows and orphans, and against those who turn away an alien-- because they do not fear Me,' says the LORD of hosts." Added to that warning, Revelation 14:7 gives us the vision of the angel in heaven saying with a loud voice, "Fear God and give glory to Him, for the hour of His judgment has come; and worship Him who made heaven and earth, the sea and springs of water."

It is good for us to patiently wait for God's judgment on the ungodly. He is patient. We can be too. But the writer here joins the writers of Malachi and Revelation to remind us that the passionate soul with a longing to see God rightly honored will sometimes be moved to plead with the Lord to come in judgment and power today. He will clench his fists and cry out to God to come today and silence the scornful derision of unbelievers. Watching evil men oppress the innocent, watching hypocrites bring shame on the name of Christ, and watching God's people suffer at the hands of God-scoffers can rightly move godly men to pray as Isaiah does here: Oh Lord please tear the heavens in two and consume with Your holy fire all Your enemies so that "the nations may tremble at Your presence!" David prayed like this in Psalms 144:5-6 – "Bow down Your heavens, O LORD, and come down; touch the mountains, and they shall smoke. Flash forth lightning and scatter them; shoot out Your arrows and destroy them." Godly men and women "tremble" in the presence of the Lord, and they are moved with great zeal to call on everyone else to "tremble" before the Lord as well. When rebellious souls scorn God, ignore God, and persecute God's people, godly souls find just cause to plead with the Lord to act. For the sake of God's holy name, Isaiah prays that He will shake the mountain and pour out the hot fire of judgment on evil men so that His name might be revered. Let us be less inclined to pray for God to make our name great, and completely consumed with a vehement longing for our Lord to defend His name before the eyes of our sinful world.

64:3-4
When You did awesome things for which we did not look, You came down, the mountains shook at Your presence. For since the beginning of the world men have not heard nor perceived by the ear, nor has the eye seen any God besides You, who acts for the one who waits for Him.

God does "awesome things" for His people. Even those with weakened faith that "did not look" for God's provision have seen Him move mountains on their behalf. The world has many gods. The peoples of the world have created several major religions and have bowed down to worship nearly an uncountable number of gods. But the imaginations of men have never created a god that rivals our God. No one has ever heard or seen a God that is capable of doing what God can do or is as compassionate as God is toward His people. When God draws near, the mountains shake. No other god possesses anything even remotely resembling this level of power. Exodus 19:18 describes the trembling of the mountains when God drew near. "Now Mount Sinai was completely in smoke, because the LORD descended upon it in fire. Its smoke ascended like the smoke of a furnace, and the whole mountain quaked greatly." God's power shakes mountains. Perhaps even more earth shattering, however, is the fact that God moves mountains in His effort to care for His people. In a moving reflection, Mary notes that not only has God done great things like create the universe and sustain life on earth – He has used His great power to take care of her! "He who is mighty has done great things for me" (Luke 1:49). David marveled over God's care for His people: "Oh, how great is Your goodness, which You have laid up for those who fear You, which You have prepared for those who trust in You in the presence of the sons of men! Blessed be the LORD, for He has shown me His marvelous kindness in a strong city!" (Psalms 31:19, 21). God's power is beyond reckoning. Just His presence causes mountains to shake. And God's "marvelous kindness" toward us is no less awe inspiring. "He acts for the one who waits for Him." Since, then, God is all-powerful and all-loving, let us happily and trustingly "wait for Him." Let us trust in His provision, trust in His timing, and trust in His holy ways, even when He seems far off and His ways seem unlikely to succeed. Waiting on God and trusting in His provision places us in the hands of the One who has inexhaustible, irresistible power and unending care for our condition – quite an enviable position. Let others trust in themselves or wait for help from another source. As for our family, let us agree with Micah's testimony in Micah 7:7 – "I will look to the LORD; I will wait for the God of my salvation; my God will hear me."

64:5
You meet him who rejoices and does righteousness, who remembers You in Your ways. You are indeed angry, for we have sinned – in these ways we continue; and we need to be saved.

"You meet him…" What a precious thought. God meets with those who are His. He draws near to those who draw near to Him (James 4:8). He enters the home and sits at the table with those who invite Him in (Revelation 3:20). He grants access to His throne of mercy to all who come to Him with their concerns (Hebrews 4:16). We are overwhelmed with this precious contemplation: "My God of mercy shall come to meet me" (Psalms 59:10). He meets with all those who are His, especially with those who delight in doing "righteousness" and remember His will and His "ways." Ah, let us take proper delight in meeting with God, and let us not forget these 2 matters that usher in and enhance those meetings. Let us guard our righteousness at all costs, for it is the righteous that are granted access to the Creator. Psalms 15:1-2 teaches: "LORD, who may abide in Your tabernacle? Who may dwell in Your holy hill? He who walks uprightly, and works righteousness, and speaks the truth in his heart." And secondly, the one who "remembers You in Your ways" is granted these precious personal meetings with the Father. Remembering His ways, contemplating His laws, meditating on His words – these efforts draw us into the very presence of the Holy God who smiles on and rewards those who set their thoughts on Him and prioritize His purposes above all other pursuits. The correlation between remembering God and drawing near to His presence is beautifully pictured in Psalms 63:6-8 -- "I remember you upon my bed, and meditate on you in the watches of the night; for you have been my help, and in the shadow of your wings I will sing for joy. My soul clings to you; your right hand upholds me" (ESV).

Then promptly after considering the joy of entering the presence of God, Isaiah recalls quickly the great enemy that denies us intimacy with our Creator: sin. We imagine that his pen reflects his audible groans – "we have sinned!" Oh, our Father drew us to His arms! We embraced Him! He heard and answered our requests! We looked on His face and His smile brought such joy to our soul! And then we ruined it all with sin! We sin and then never stop sinning! "In these ways we continue!" Oh, the horror of it all! When walking righteously with our Lord we enjoyed incomparable joy as He poured out His constant lovingkindnesses on us. We loved being righteous! We loved the presence of God! But then our sin that we could not seem to stop ruined it all! Oh, how we need rescue from this sin that rises up in us so readily! Oh "how we need to be saved" from this body of sin and death. Isaiah's cry over the ravages of sin is carried to the pen of Paul, who joins Isaiah's cry against sin and then rejoices over the coming of the Savior that Isaiah longed to see. In Romans 7:24-25 Paul writes, "O wretched man that I am! Who will deliver me from this body of death? I thank God – through Jesus Christ our Lord!"

There is so much here in this single verse! We have access to the presence of God! Sin denies us that privilege of privileges! We cannot overcome the horrible consequences of sin ourselves – we need a Savior! But thanks be to God, Romans 7:25 reminds us that we have a Savior! And through our Savior Jesus we have access to the presence of God once more.

"Now in Christ Jesus you who once were far off have been brought near by the blood of Christ" (Ephesians 2:13).

64:6
But we are all like an unclean thing, and all our righteousnesses are like filthy rags; we all fade as a leaf, and our iniquities, like the wind, have taken us away.

I have quoted this verse perhaps 100 times. It is essential for those who are not right with God to understand this truth. This is God's view of the human race apart from Christ's saving work on the cross. "We are all like an unclean thing." No one is good. No one can get to heaven because they are a good person, for apart from Christ's imputed righteousness there are no good people. All our good deeds drape across our filthy body like even filthier rags. Apart from God we have no goodness; and we have no permanence. We "fade" like leaves and blow away in the winds of time. Until Christ cleanses us with His blood, our finest merits are unpleasing to God, our purest thoughts are filthy, and our religious efforts are unclean. "There is none righteous, no, not one" (Romans 3:10). These words blaze brightly like a beacon of truth summoning man to his senses. Religious rites and good deeds cannot save a man from the penalty of his sins. Religious rites and good deeds do not cleanse away the stain and vulgar stench of sin. No good deed of man can clear away even the smallest indiscretion. Sin makes our souls filthy in God's eyes. And nothing – nothing – short of the life-blood of Jesus Christ His Son contains the virtue required to detach sin from our souls. Without Jesus, we are "unclean," and "filthy" in God's sight no matter what good deeds we have done. Sin has "taken us away" from God and there is no means to transport us back to God other than the forgiveness and cleansing that is found in faith in Christ.

64:7
And there is no one who calls on Your name, who stirs himself up to take hold of You; for You have hidden Your face from us, and have consumed us because of our iniquities.

Verse 6 described mankind as "an unclean thing." We debase and dirty ourselves with sin and find that our Creator is the only One who can cure us of our both our penchant for sin and the penalty of sin. Tragically, after sinning, few seek the only One who can forgive them of their sin. "There is no one who calls on Your name." No one "stirs himself up to take hold of You." See how prayer is here described – prayer is *taking hold of God*.

ISAIAH 64

We do not recite prayers, we wrestle prayers. We grapple with our needs before the Lord, we cling to His promises. As Jacob wrestled with the Lord and refused to let Him go until He blessed him (Genesis 32:24-28), so prayer is likened to a wrestling match here. Sadly, Isaiah finds no one wrestling with the Lord in prayer. God has left the wrestling ring of prayer "because of our iniquities." The people are not seeking the Lord, and He is not showing His face to the uninsightful crowd. All who call on the name of the Lord will be saved (Romans 10:13), but there is no hope for persons or peoples who turn their back on their Creator and refuse to take hold of Him and call on His name for help. In Psalms 14:2-4, David too, lamented the fact that no one sought to be righteous, and no one prayed that God would take away their sin. "The LORD looks down from heaven upon the children of men, to see if there are any who understand, who seek God. They have all turned aside, they have together become corrupt; there is none who does good, no, not one." Just as Isaiah noted in verse 6, David found no one devoted to righteous living, and just as verse 7 here, David found no one praying that God would remove their sin – no one was insightful enough to "call on the LORD" (Psalms 14:4). Sin and prayerlessness go hand in hand. Absence of prayer, or cold, unengaged prayers do not protect us from sin, and sin anesthetizes our soul into cold and unengaged prayers that soon stop completely.

64:8-9
But now, O LORD, You are our Father; we are the clay, and You our potter; and all we are the work of Your hand. Do not be furious, O LORD, nor remember iniquity forever; indeed, please look – we all are Your people!

Isaiah intercedes on behalf of his people, pleading with the Lord to exercise divine selective memory loss. He asks the Lord to remember that the people belong to Him – but not to "remember iniquity forever." He uses a potter as his illustration. As a potter would tend to try not to break the clay creation he formed with his own hands, so Isaiah asks the Lord to handle with care His pottery-like people. The Lord will use this same illustration in Jeremiah 18:6 when He warns His people: "O house of Israel, can I not do with you as this potter? Look, as the clay is in the potter's hand, so are you in My hand, O house of Israel." Here however, rather than destroy the pottery as is the potter's right, Isaiah asks the Lord to care for His people in keeping with a potter's natural favor toward His creation. This same reasoning framed David's prayer for God's help in Psalms 138:8 – "The LORD will perfect that which concerns me; Your mercy, O LORD, endures forever;

do not forsake the works of Your hands." And in Psalms 119:94 David said it even more simply: "I am Yours, save me!"

64:10-12
Your holy and beautiful temple, where our fathers praised You, is burned up with fire; and all our pleasant things are laid waste. Will You restrain Yourself because of these things, O LORD? Will You hold Your peace, and afflict us very severely?

Israel's only quality used to attract God's kindness is their need. Israel's only attribute qualifying them for God's blessings is their severe hardship. They have no noteworthy merits that might invite God to help them. All their troubles flow from their own faults and flaws and poor decisions. They deserve nothing from God. So they do not pray asking God to respond to their virtue, they pray to God asking Him to respond to their need. And they do so because He has wonderfully, graciously, repeatedly shown that He extends His mercy to His children when we cry out to Him for help. Jonah, perhaps, is a perfect example. After rebelling against God and refusing service to God, He found himself drowning in the sea and then smothering in a fish's belly. His danger and discomfort were all well deserved. And then, from the fish's belly he prays: "I cried out to the LORD because of my affliction, and He answered me. Out of the belly of Sheol I cried, and You heard my voice" (Jonah 2:2). A near-death experience and "affliction" were Jonah's only qualifications for his prayer. And though catastrophe was his only quality, God "answered" his request. Even though Jonah's prayer was offered up from a desperate heart rather than a devoted heart, Jonah gratefully acknowledged that "You heard my voice."

By all means, let us "add to (our) faith virtue" (II Peter 1:5). But let us take great solace and confidence in the graciousness of God which moves Him to care for our needs based on His virtues not ours. If answers to prayer were contingent on our merits, we would pray and then boast of God's answers. But because God's provision in our need and God's answers to our requests flow from His lovingkindness, we pray and then thankfully praise Him for His wonderful grace. Psalm 116 demonstrates the heart behind prayers such as these that are cried out in these three verses in Isaiah 64. "I love the Lord, because He has heard my voice and my supplications. Because He has inclined His ear to me, therefore I will call *upon Him* as long as I live. The pains of death surrounded me, and the pangs of Sheol laid hold of me; I found trouble and sorrow. Then I called upon the name of the Lord: "O Lord, I implore You, deliver my soul!"

ISAIAH 64

Gracious *is* the Lord, and righteous; yes, our God *is* merciful. The Lord preserves the simple; I was brought low, and He saved me. Return to your rest, O my soul, for the Lord has dealt bountifully with you. For You have delivered my soul from death, my eyes from tears, and my feet from falling. I will walk before the Lord In the land of the living. I believed, therefore I spoke, "I am greatly afflicted." I said in my haste, "All men are liars." What shall I render to the Lord for all His benefits toward me? I will take up the cup of salvation, and call upon the name of the Lord. I will pay my vows to the Lord now in the presence of all His people. Precious in the sight of the Lord is the death of His saints. O Lord, truly I *am* Your servant; I *am* Your servant, the son of Your maidservant; You have loosed my bonds. I will offer to You the sacrifice of thanksgiving, and will call upon the name of the Lord. I will pay my vows to the Lord now in the presence of all His people, in the courts of the Lord's house, in the midst of you, O Jerusalem. Praise the Lord!"

Isaiah 65

65:1
I was sought by those who did not ask for Me; I was found by those who did not seek Me. I said, "Here I am, here I am," to a nation that was not called by My name."

Paul quotes Isaiah's words here and speaks of their fulfillment in Romans 10:20, and decades of living in Thailand has granted me an eyewitness account of the Lord continuing to fulfill these words today. I have seen men and women find God who were not seeking Him. I have seen the Lord announce His presence and present His power before those who did not ask for an audience with Him. Though many do not seek the Lord, yet He seeks them (Luke 19:10) and is pleased to pour out His truths and His kindness even on those who do not know enough to ask for His blessings. Isaiah speaks of the day when nations who had never been associated with God – they had never been called by His name, nor had they called on His name for help – even these nations will come to know God and worship Him as Lord. Paul was overjoyed as he saw this promise come to fruition when nations and cities and families came to know Christ as Lord that for "ages and generations" (Colossians 1:26) had been apart from Him. God calls to Himself even those who are not seeking Him. Let us then follow Jesus' example in Luke 19:10 and go out to seek the lost, for they do not know enough to seek the Lord, but we know that our Lord is seeking them.

65:2-5
I have stretched out My hands all day long to a rebellious people, who walk in a way that is not good, according to their own thoughts; a people who provoke Me to anger continually to My face; who sacrifice in gardens, and burn incense on altars of brick; who sit among the graves, and spend the night in the tombs; who eat swine's flesh, and the broth of abominable things is in their vessels; who say, "Keep to yourself, do not come near me, for I am holier than you!" These are smoke in My nostrils, a fire that burns all the day.

Paul repeated these words as a stern caution to his people in Romans 10:21, and the message remains a strong warning to all in our day as well. Those who refuse to obey God's commands are called "rebellious people." Rather than walk with God according to His will and ways, they have chosen, instead, to "walk in a way that is not good." Living against God's ways is not good for us, it brings no good to us. Nothing good comes of rejecting God's ways. The ways of the unbeliever are not good. There is nothing virtuous or upright about the ways of those who reject God. Their rebellion against God causes them to do all manner of things that God finds repulsive. God draws near to His people, looks on them with love, and guides them with the look in His eyes (Psalms 32:8). But His people brazenly, openly scorn His love and commands, provoking Him to anger to His face.

God's thoughts "are very deep" (Psalms 92:5), His people love to think about them, meditate on them, delight in them, and obey them. Psalms 139:17 says, "How precious also are Your thoughts to me, O God! How great is the sum of them!" In contrast, those who rebel against God, prefer their own thoughts to the thoughts of God. They "walk in a way that is not good, according *to their own thoughts*." They have the audacity to believe not only that their ways are wiser than God's ways, they believe their ways are holier than God's ways as well! They push away God's spokesmen saying, "Keep to yourself, do not come near me, for I am holier than you!" We shake our heads in amazement as we see people demonstrate this in our day today. How often we hear community leaders and famous people scorn God's word because it conflicts with their "values" concerning abortion, homosexuality, and tolerance for what the Bible calls sin. Those that rebel against God and feel holy in their rebellion are a stench in the nose of God. "They are smoke in My nostrils," a repugnant smell that "never goes away" (NLT).

65:6-7

"Behold, it is written before Me: I will not keep silence, but will repay – even repay into their bosom – your iniquities and the iniquities of your fathers together," says the LORD, "Who have burned incense on the mountains and blasphemed Me on the hills; therefore I will measure their former work into their bosom."

God is an excellent manager of His accounts. If we will take care of His needy ones, He is careful to repay us. Proverbs 19:17 says, "If you help the poor, you are lending to the LORD – and he will repay you!" (NLT). Isaiah's words here are ominous to consider however, for he teaches that the Lord will also repay "your iniquities and the iniquities of your fathers together." Though it may look like it for a moment, no one gets away with murder – or any other sin. God will repay everyone for the spiritual debt they incur when they sin. God "will not keep silence" in the face of sin for long. He will certainly repay those who rebel against Him what they deserve. "Our God shall come, and shall not keep silent; a fire shall devour before Him, and it shall be very tempestuous all around Him. The Lord "repays to their face those who hate him, by destroying them. He will not be slack with one who hates him. He will repay him to his face" (Deuteronomy 7:10). Since God will always repay sin, and the payment required for sin is death (Romans 6:23), let us sense the urgency to call people everywhere to come to Jesus by faith that He might take the debt of our sin on Himself, so that we will enjoy a reward in heaven based on His work on the cross, rather than suffering the repayment of sin based on our "former work" of unbelief.

65:8-10

Thus says the LORD: "As the new wine is found in the cluster, and one says, 'Do not destroy it, for a blessing is in it,' so will I do for My servants' sake, that I may not destroy them all. I will bring forth descendants from Jacob, and from Judah an heir of My mountains; My elect shall inherit it, and My servants shall dwell there. Sharon shall be a fold of flocks, and the Valley of Achor a place for herds to lie down, for My people who have sought Me."

As one would save a cluster of grapes even if there were few good grapes left, or as one would save a grapevine even when it produced very little fruit, so the Lord will do for His people. Though Israel had become so spiritually barren that it resembled a dried-out grapevine or a grape cluster with only a couple good grapes remaining, yet for the sake of the few that remained loyal to Him, the Lord would not destroy them all. God promised to defend wicked Jerusalem for the sake of David, His righteous servant. In Isaiah 37:35 the Lord declared: "For I will defend this city, to save it for My own sake and for My servant David's sake." See the remarkable, far-reaching protection for society and blessings for a family that a single godly life can impart. God promised to save a wicked city for the sake of 10 righteous men (Genesis 18:32), and He delivered a family for the sake of a single righteous man (Genesis 19:15). Let us walk with the Lord! So many people might find rescue and mercy from the Lord by means of a single righteous man or woman living in their midst. Such cause for rejoicing is found here for the missionary when his work at last sees the first soul saved in a village long held captive by sin and unbelief. That single righteous soul, like a single good grape, may summon the protective mercies of the Lord for their entire cluster, just as illustrated here.

Let us examine these "servants" of the Lord that gain rescue for their people. God calls them "My elect," but He also calls them "My people who have sought Me." Men perhaps, find it difficult to balance God's sovereignty and man's responsibility. It may be difficult for some to couple our understanding of predestination with our understanding of man's responsibility to choose his path and choose his actions rightly. But God finds no such difficulty. He presents both these matters simultaneously so that we can see that they are not mutually exclusive. We, His children are His "elect." He has chosen us; He has called us to Himself before we had any spiritual sensitivities at all. "You did not choose Me, but I chose you" (John 15:16). And we in response, have "sought" Him, we have "followed hard" after Him (Psalms 63:8 KJV). We rise up early and ardently, urgently seek to serve Him and please Him with our whole being, for we have both been chosen by God and we have chosen to belong to Him. The Kingdom of God is comprised of those that He has chosen as His "elect," and it is comprised of those who have chosen to obey Him as His "servants." The picture presented here is sweet. God will call people to be His own, and from Sharon (in the west) to the Valley of Achor (in the east) His people will respond wonderfully. They will serve Him and honor Him, and so confirm that though their tribe had failed so many times, yet "a blessing is in it," good things would yet arise from God's redemptive work in their land.

65:11-12
But you are those who forsake the LORD, who forget My holy mountain, who prepare a table for Gad, and who furnish a drink offering for Meni. Therefore I will number you for the sword, and you shall all bow down to the slaughter; because, when I called, you did not answer; when I spoke, you did not hear, but did evil before My eyes, and chose that in which I do not delight.

Israel's many spiritual crimes are listed here along with the one punishment that is meted out on those guilty of these God-dishonoring corruptions. They are condemned because they "forsake the LORD." Joshua 24:20 warned that there were grave circumstances ahead for those who turn their back on God: "If you forsake the LORD and serve other gods, he will turn against you and destroy you, even though he has been so good to you" (NLT). Sympathy is appropriately extended to those who have never heard of God's truths (Jonah 4:11), but no sympathy can be expected for those who hear God's truths, see Him move, understand His heart – and then forsake Him, discarding Him for another god that seems to suit better. The punishment for forsaking God is death. "I will number you for the sword."

Israel's second spiritual crime is that they "forget My holy mountain." They have heard Him call them to come and worship. They have seen His greatness and recognize that He is worthy of worship in His holy place, but when the time arrives to worship Him, they "forget." They are distracted with other pursuits, they attend to business matters, pleasurable pursuits, and restful activities, but they "forget" to worship the Holy God in His holy place on His holy day. Failure to worship the Lord in His holy place on His holy day is a serious spiritual crime. It is punishable by death. "You shall all bow down to the slaughter."

God further chastises His people because "when I called, you did not answer; when I spoke, you did not hear." In Mark 3, Jesus asks the leaders a question and they refuse to answer. Mark 3:5 says that when they refused to respond, Jesus "looked around at them with anger." Failure to respond when the Lord commands, failure to listen when the Lord speaks is a serious matter. It angers the Lord and is punishable by death. When Jonah refused to listen to God's call, his life was immediately put on the line. When Esther hesitated to obey God's call, Mordecai warned her that if she failed to answer God's call, "you and your fathers' house will perish" (Esther 4:14).

The Lord also rebukes the people because they "did evil before My eyes." How important it is that we recognize that God sees all things! Nothing is hidden from Him. Jeremiah 16:17 says, "For My eyes are on all their ways;

they are not hidden from My face, nor is their iniquity hidden from My eyes." Psalms 69:5 acknowledges that "O God, You know my foolishness; and my sins are not hidden from You." We must be aware that "there is no creature hidden from His sight, but all things are naked and open to the eyes of Him to whom we must give account" (Hebrews 4:13). Perhaps some people will do some imperfect things if they think no one is looking, but very few will show so little regard to personal safety that they will disobey those in authority right before their very eyes. This however, is exactly what God is accusing the people of – "doing evil before My eyes." Brazenly defying God and disobeying His commands right in front of Him is punishable by death.

And finally, the Lord accuses the people of choosing "that in which I do not delight." We might not be surprised to see that abandoning God's laws to do evil things is punishable by death. God is so holy, He demands that we respond to His holiness with holiness of our own. But God's love for us is also so remarkable, His love for us so transcends any other love shown by any other creature, that to scorn His love is likewise a terrible evil. God's love for us demands that our hearts return a great love for Him. We must love Him so completely that it is our delight to do all things that delight Him. We love what He loves, and we hate what He hates. All God's delights are our delights, and we take no interest in things that He takes no delight in. Here the people are condemned for this slight. They delight in things that God does not delight in. Those who love the Lord will delight in pleasing Him, failure to delight in those things which delight the Creator is a terrible evil and is punishable by death.

Any one of these evils would be enough to condemn Isaiah's hearers to the death penalty – and they were guilty of them all. They were busy placating the gods of Gad and Meni, and took no effort to please the Most High God. Though God is slow to anger and rich in mercy, these offences are so odious that they incite the Lord to mete out justice on the perpetrators. Let all thinking men take note.

65:13-14
Therefore thus says the Lord GOD: "Behold, My servants shall eat, but you shall be hungry; behold, My servants shall drink, but you shall be thirsty; behold, My servants shall rejoice, but you shall be ashamed; Behold, My servants shall sing for joy of heart, but you shall cry for sorrow of heart, and wail for grief of spirit."

There is no guarantee from our Lord that the life of godly men and women on earth will be easy or pain-free. It is quite possible that some who despise God and live wicked lives will eat better, drink more, and live merrier lives than their Christian counterpart. We have no cause to envy them, however. In the end, we win. In heaven, it is the godly believer that will be "glad and rejoice" (Revelation 19:7). In heaven, it is the child of God who will feast at the "marriage supper of the Lamb (Revelation 19:9). And in the end, all unbelievers "shall cry for sorrow of heart, and wail for grief of spirit." Regret, remorse, shame, and grief will be the only fare made available to those who fed their body but starved their soul on earth. In the parable of the rich man and Lazarus we see the unbelieving rich man "in torment," unable to experience the comforts of God in heaven. In the parable, Lazarus was given this explanation in Luke 16:25 - "Remember that in your lifetime you received your good things, and likewise Lazarus evil things; but now he is comforted and you are tormented." Forfeiting bliss in heaven for the sake of the "passing pleasures of sin" (Hebrews 11:25) is an extremely poor long-term investment strategy. Perhaps poor insight will make it seem that unholy people are happy people, but that will certainly not be the case for long. When judgment comes, Psalms 112:10 says, "The wicked will see it and be grieved; he will gnash his teeth and melt away; the desire of the wicked shall perish."

65:15-16
You shall leave your name as a curse to My chosen; for the Lord GOD will slay you, and call His servants by another name; so that he who blesses himself in the earth shall bless himself in the God of truth; and he who swears in the earth shall swear by the God of truth; because the former troubles are forgotten, and because they are hidden from My eyes.

Israel – God's chosen people – had rebelled against Him and incited Him to anger over and over again. Reading the Bible's account of Israel's constant disloyalty through the wilderness in Exodus, throughout the book of Judges and then into the books of the kings, we are amazed at God's constant faithfulness to His people, even when they are so unfaithful to Him. This will never change. God will always remain faithful to His people. God has called a people to Himself and declared with an oath "You shall be My people, and I will be your God" (Jeremiah 30:22). Here however, we come upon a turning point in history. God will always be faithful to His people -- II Timothy 2:13 says, "If we are faithless He remains faithful; He cannot deny Himself." But here, in response to Israel's wholesale, continual rebellion, the Lord declares that He will "call His servants by another name." God will remain faithful to His people, but His people will no longer be confined to a single nation, and Israel will not be permitted to deceive themselves into thinking that bloodline alone will make them "a holy nation" or qualify them to be God's "own special people" (I Peter 2:9). Romans 9 will follow through with Isaiah's epic announcement and declare that God's children are not defined by heredity, but by faith (Romans 9:30). God will be faithful to His people, but His people will be called "by another name." The children of God will no longer be called the children of Israel, "For they are not all Israel who are of Israel" (Romans 9:6). Instead, since Acts 11:26, as foretold here, God's people are called Christians. Our new name is wonderful. We do not depend on our nation or our family for our access to God. We depend on Christ. And through Christ, not just Israel, but "the earth shall bless himself in the God of truth."

65:17-19
For behold, I create new heavens and a new earth; and the former shall not be remembered or come to mind. But be glad and rejoice forever in what I create; for behold, I create Jerusalem as a rejoicing, and her people a joy. I will rejoice in Jerusalem, and joy in My people; the voice of weeping shall no longer be heard in her, nor the voice of crying.

It is difficult not to see these verses as describing the same thing John described in Revelation. "Now I saw a new heaven and a new earth, for the first heaven and the first earth had passed away" (Revelation 21:1). Life on this "new earth" is filled with joy. Sorrow and weeping "shall no longer be heard in her," just as Revelation 21:4 affirms: "And God will wipe away every tear from their eyes; there shall be no more death, nor sorrow, nor crying. There shall be no more pain, for the former things have passed away." When the Lord, at last, will draw His people to Himself in His New Jerusalem, everyone will love it! The Lord invites us to "be glad and rejoice forever" out of anticipation for the coming of the new heavens and the new earth that He promises to create. God "will rejoice in Jerusalem" and His people will rejoice in what He has created. Such is the happy picture of our certain future. Our present world is full of sorrow and worry over impending sorrows. But in this great paradise to come, our Lord will take delight in us, His children; and we, His children, will take delight in Him.

65:20-23
No more shall an infant from there live but a few days, nor an old man who has not fulfilled his days; for the child shall die one hundred years old, but the sinner being one hundred years old shall be accursed. They shall build houses and inhabit them; they shall plant vineyards and eat their fruit. They shall not build and another inhabit; they shall not plant and another eat; for as the days of a tree, so shall be the days of My people, and My elect shall long enjoy the work of their hands. They shall not labor in vain, nor bring forth children for trouble; for they shall be the descendants of the blessed of the LORD, and their offspring with them.

Here now the picture remains glorious, though the setting perhaps, becomes less sure. If this is looking forward to heaven, what is the meaning of infants living to old age and the offspring of the saints being blessed of the Lord? Do Isaiah's words here refer to the new earth in heaven, or to the glorious prospect of living so closely united with Christ that life is like heaven on earth? Isaiah writes of the day when the plans and efforts of the saints succeed just as Joshua 1:8 promises and Psalms 92:12-15 pictures – "The righteous shall flourish like a palm tree, he shall grow like a cedar in Lebanon. Those who are planted in the house of the LORD shall flourish in the courts of our God. They shall still bear fruit in old age; they shall be fresh and flourishing, to declare that the LORD is upright; He is my rock, and there is no unrighteousness in Him."

Does Isaiah write of the new earth in heaven or to heaven on earth? We are filled with a sudden joy in contemplating how little the two differ. Whether in heaven or on earth, God's children "shall not labor in vain." May this wonderful hope before us here yield rightful inspiration within us. Seeing that nothing we do for our Lord is in vain, let us stand firm in our devotion to His purposes, just as Paul calls us to do in I Corinthians 15:58 -- "Therefore, my beloved brethren, be steadfast, immovable, always abounding in the work of the Lord, knowing that your labor is not in vain in the Lord."

65:24
It shall come to pass that before they call, I will answer; and while they are still speaking, I will hear.

A dearer incentive to pray, a clearer promise of God's heart to answer our requests can hardly be found. Daniel could not see God's answer immediately, but the angel assured him in Daniel 9:23 that God was moved to answer his request even will he was "still speaking." "The moment you began praying, a command was given. I am here to tell you what it was, for God loves you very much." In Acts 12 the people gathered together to pray for Peter's release from prison, and while they were "still speaking," Peter knocked at their door. The examples of God's remarkably timely answers to prayer go on and on in Bible times, in our times, and in our own family as well. Let us run to our Lord in prayer. He is famous for His heart to answer the requests of His children and He knows what we need even before we do. Matthew 6:8 says "your Father knows the things you have need of before you ask Him." The Pulpit Commentary says, "God is always more ready to hear than we are to pray." Oh let us pray! So often needs come upon us unexpectedly and answering those needs in time would require great preparation that we could not anticipate. But our Lord has already anticipated all our future needs and has already set His provisions in motion. All that remains is for us to approach His throne of grace so that we might there obtain mercy – and obtain that mercy even while we are "still speaking" (Hebrews 4:16).

65:25
"The wolf and the lamb shall feed together, the lion shall eat straw like the ox, and dust shall be the serpent's food. They shall not hurt nor destroy in all My holy mountain," says the LORD.

When God draws near, sworn enemies suddenly reconcile, and certain dangers become somehow safe. Isaiah foretells the coming day in Heaven when we are free from dangers of all sorts, and also pictures for us how it is at times when God draws close and makes life here like heaven on earth. Isaiah says now in summary as he said in more detail in 11:6-9. In that passage, this peace on earth was not just referring to heaven, but to the expansion of the kingdom of heaven on earth. "They shall not hurt nor destroy in all My holy mountain, for the earth shall be full of the knowledge of the LORD as the waters cover the sea" (Isaiah 11:9). When men are at peace with God, not only are they also drawn to peace with one another, but all nature is able to rest in peace as well. Carnivores stop killing, snakes stop biting, and everyone comes to God's "holy mountain," not to satisfy their appetites, but to worship the Holy God.

Isaiah 66

66:1-2
Thus says the LORD: "Heaven is My throne, and earth is My footstool. Where is the house that you will build Me? And where is the place of My rest? For all those things My hand has made, and all those things exist," says the LORD. "But on this one will I look: on him who is poor and of a contrite spirit, and who trembles at My word."

The enormity of the magnificence of God is beyond reckoning. The magnitude of the glory of God cannot be measured. When He sits in heaven, His feet rest on the earth. The vastness of His power is unlimited. All things were created by Him, and all life in heaven and on earth is sustained by Him. "He sustains the universe by the mighty power of his command" (Hebrews 1:3 NLT). We can build Him no monument that will impress Him, we can accomplish no mighty deed that will win His admiration. How then can we gain the approval of the One who owns all things, knows all things, and can do all things? Happily, the means for winning God's approval is not a secret, He tells us plainly right here. "On this one I will look: on him who is poor and of a contrite spirit, and who trembles at My word." It is not man's might that impresses God, it is our demonstration of our understanding that we have no might, that we are poor and ignorant and completely dependent on His provision for our survival – this understanding is pleasing in God's sight. Psalms 34:18 says: "The LORD is near to those who have a broken heart, and saves such as have a contrite spirit." Psalms 51:17 repeats the same message: "The sacrifices of God are a broken spirit, a broken and a contrite heart – these, O God, You will not despise."

God is well pleased with those who bow low before Him, and He is pleased with those who lift His word high before their mind's eye. He looks approvingly on all who reverently *tremble at His word.* His word is life-giving (Luke 4:4), His words give eternal life (John 6:68). Hebrews 11:3 says that "the worlds were framed by the word of God," and Luke 21:33 says that His words will never "pass away." The words of God which formed the created order of the universe and which impart life and meaning to mankind have been revealed to us that we might drink them in, meditate on them, study then, obey them, and teach them to others. It would be man's greatest folly to ignore the words of his Creator, but we please our Father when we reverently lift up His words to us and tremble beneath the weight of the truths that He reveals through His written word.

What thinking man or woman would demonstrate no concern for the opinions of his Creator? And here we are told exactly what our Creator is pleased to find in His people – not great deeds or great capabilities – but a humble soul that finds no greatness in himself, but finds no end to the greatness of God and the preciousness of His word. The men and women who seek to please God will use every possible moment to hold His word in two trembling hands, drink them in, and strain to respond in the best way possible. Since God approves of those who rightly handle His word, let us follow the instruction in II Timothy 2:15 and "be diligent" (HCS) to prove that we are approved by God, by "rightly handling the word of truth" (ESV).

66:3-4
"He who kills a bull is as if he slays a man; he who sacrifices a lamb, as if he breaks a dog's neck; he who offers a grain offering, as if he offers swine's blood; he who burns incense, as if he blesses an idol. Just as they have chosen their own ways, and their soul delights in their abominations, so will I choose their delusions, and bring their fears on them; because, when I called, no one answered, when I spoke they did not hear; but they did evil before My eyes, and chose that in which I do not delight."

The Lord now repeats the accusations made against His people in 65:12. They rejected God's ways and followed "their own ways" instead. Their "soul delights" in doing spiritually abhorrent "abominations." He called them to change their ways, but their suppressed conscience could not hear His call. They brazenly "did evil" right "before My eyes." It is instructive to us to see the result of their rejection of the Lord. When they refused to "delight" in the things He delights in, and when they chose "their own ways" to be religious rather than His ways, they made their religion gross in the sight of God. It is a bald-faced lie to say that all religions lead to God. The Lord clearly spells out how much the religious efforts of Isaiah's readers disgusted Him. In God's eyes, their religious acts were just as evil as murder! They were just "as if he slays a man." Their religious acts were no better than bowing to a wooden idol or pouring out swine's blood on the temple floor. We must delight in walking rightly with our Lord if our religious efforts are to be holy acts of proper worship. Sin ruins religion. Delighting in activities or beliefs that God does not delight in ruins religion. All religions which overlook what God defines as evil and which fail to delight in pleasing God our Creator are "delusions." They offer no spiritual gain, contain no spiritual merit, and, instead, incite anger in the God who made us.

66:5
Hear the word of the LORD, you who tremble at His word: "Your brethren who hated you, who cast you out for My name's sake, said, 'Let the LORD be glorified, that we may see your joy.' But they shall be ashamed."

Isaiah has many words of rebuke for those among his people that had turned their backs on God. But he does not lash out at all his readers equally, as if everyone listening was equally guilty. No, he has words of rebuke for his ungodly hearers (in verse 4 and in verse 6), but here we see him interject words of hope for those "who tremble at (God's) word." Godly men and women who, like Isaiah's hearers, live among ungodly people in ungodly times are often the brunt of much harassment and ridicule. Isaiah noted the sarcastic attacks made by those who mockingly wished for God to bless His followers and sarcastically cheered for God to give His people joy – "Let the LORD be glorified" they taunted, and mockingly asked that God's followers be happy. But the Lord will turn the tables soon enough, and it will not be His people who will be ashamed by the harassing criticism of the unbelieving world, it will be those who reject God and persecute His people that "shall be ashamed." Psalms 37:12-20 grants us an illustration of Isaiah's point, "The wicked plots against the just, and gnashes at him with his teeth. The Lord laughs at him, for He sees that his day is coming. The wicked have drawn the sword and have bent their bow, to cast down the poor and needy, to slay those who are of upright conduct. Their sword shall enter their own heart, and their bows shall be broken. A little that a righteous man has is better than the riches of many wicked. For the arms of the wicked shall be broken, but the LORD upholds the righteous. The LORD knows the days of the upright, and their inheritance shall be forever. They shall not be ashamed in the evil time, and in the days of famine they shall be satisfied. But the wicked shall perish; and the enemies of the LORD, like the splendor of the meadows, shall vanish. Into smoke they shall vanish away."

66:6
The sound of noise from the city! A voice from the temple! The voice of the LORD, who fully repays His enemies!

Constant verbal attacks from the sneering crowd can be a sore trial for even solid believers. But here, as if the voice of the Lord suddenly drowned out the sound of the crowd's scorn, God's children hear Him speak. His words fill His children with confidence and fill the ungodly with dread. The Lord "fully repays His enemies!" Let us live for the Lord! May our lives be so firmly entrenched in God's ways and our heart so sweetly tuned to God's heart, that all God's enemies see us as their enemy as well, and God sees that all our enemies are His enemies also. When that is our blessed state, our spirits will be wonderfully lifted when God loudly drowns out all the unpleasant sounds of ungodly people to echo once again His intention to bless His children and "fully repay His enemies" for how they have brought hurt to those He loves.

66:7-11
"Before she was in labor, she gave birth; before her pain came, she delivered a male child. Who has heard such a thing? Who has seen such things? Shall the earth be made to give birth in one day? Or shall a nation be born at once? For as soon as Zion was in labor, she gave birth to her children. Shall I bring to the time of birth, and not cause delivery?" says the LORD. "Shall I who cause delivery shut up the womb?" says your God. "Rejoice with Jerusalem, and be glad with her, all you who love her; rejoice for joy with her, all you who mourn for her; that you may feed and be satisfied with the consolation of her bosom, that you may drink deeply and be delighted with the abundance of her glory."

Isaiah addressed a nation that was hurting. Their sins had brought them to a painful time. But here, the Lord promises that their pains preceded something wonderful. As a woman suffers pain before she delivers a wonderful son or daughter, so Israel's suffering would compare to childbirth – a nation of the children of God would be birthed out of her pains. It takes 9 months for a child in the womb to be ready for birth, it takes even longer for a nation to be born, but the Lord promises that this great nation of saints that will be birthed from Israel's womb will be delivered "in one day." It will "be born at once." Isaiah's words immediately take our mind's eye to Acts 2, when suddenly, the blood-bought, Spirit-filled nation of saints was born in a day when the Spirit fell, Peter preached, and 3,000 souls were saved.

Israel's pain was real, but the Lord calls on all who love her to "be glad with her," and to "rejoice for joy with her," for the children that will be born from her labor pains will be a wonderful "consolation." As a mother could hardly imagine holding a newborn son or daughter in her arms and then lament that she was no longer pregnant, so those who love Israel need not mourn Israel's labor pains, for the holy nation of saints that will be birthed from her womb will be cause for everyone to be "delighted with the abundance of her glory."

66:12-13
For thus says the LORD: "Behold, I will extend peace to her like a river, and the glory of the Gentiles like a flowing stream. Then you shall feed; on her sides shall you be carried, and be dandled on her knees. As one whom his mother comforts, so I will comfort you; and you shall be comforted in Jerusalem."

The Lord continues to liken Israel's trials to labor pains and encourages Isaiah's readers to take heart, for a wonderful child (the Gentile saints) will be born from the midst of her pain. Israel's pains did not signify her coming death, but the coming life of her children of faith. The Lord would fill her with peace like a river when the Gentile saints were added to her like a "flowing stream." As a mother carries her baby on "her sides" – balancing her child on her hip, and as she "dandles" her child on her knees, so will the babes in Christ from all the nations be held by the Lord, gaining both the protection and comfort that He extends to all His children, both Jew and Gentile.

66:14-17

"When you see this, your heart shall rejoice, and your bones shall flourish like grass; the hand of the LORD shall be known to His servants, and His indignation to His enemies. For behold, the LORD will come with fire and with His chariots, like a whirlwind, to render His anger with fury, and His rebuke with flames of fire. For by fire and by His sword the LORD will judge all flesh; and the slain of the LORD shall be many. Those who sanctify themselves and purify themselves, to go to the gardens after an idol in the midst, eating swine's flesh and the abomination and the mouse, shall be consumed together," says the LORD.

When the Lord moves to judge the world, His children will "rejoice." The "hand of the LORD" will protect us from the fires of His judgment. We will be safe; our bones and our souls will "flourish;" and we will be filled with joy, knowing that the Judge of the world has both made us pure and declared us not guilty. Those who are "enemies" of God however, those who do not trust in His Son and do not obey His word, they will not know this joy, they will only see God's "indignation." We see again how much God hates disobedience and unbelief. Even people with seemingly good intentions – they go to "sanctify themselves," they go to "purify themselves" – even if they have a heart to be pure, even if they religiously seek to sanctify themselves – if they ignore God in their efforts, if they trust in idols and engage in religious acts that God finds offensive, these observers of false religions "shall be consumed together." God considers idol worship to be the most serious of crimes. God holds that false religion is highly offensive. These things fill Him with "anger" and with "fury" that He will finally let loose to judge those who have scorned His ambassadors and have refused to heed the voice of their conscience pleading with them to obey their Creator's call. Ezekiel 7:1-4 tells us the desired endpoint of the unleashing of the wrath of God on the disobedient. "Moreover the word of the Lord came to me, saying, 'And you, son of man, thus says the Lord God to the land of Israel: 'An end! The end has come upon the four corners of the land. Now the end *has come* upon you, and I will send My anger against you; I will judge you according to your ways, and I will repay you for all your abominations. My eye will not spare you, nor will I have pity; but I will repay your ways, and your abominations will be in your midst; then you shall know that I *am* the Lord!'" If we will not declare by faith that God is the Lord, He will declare by His fury that He is the Lord. One way or the other, His glory will be declared. Let all rational men and women take note.

66:18-21
For I know their works and their thoughts. It shall be that I will gather all nations and tongues; and they shall come and see My glory. I will set a sign among them; and those among them who escape I will send to the nations: to Tarshish and Pul and Lud, who draw the bow, and Tubal and Javan, to the coastlands afar off who have not heard My fame nor seen My glory. And they shall declare My glory among the Gentiles. Then they shall bring all your brethren for an offering to the LORD out of all nations, on horses and in chariots and in litters, on mules and on camels, to My holy mountain Jerusalem," says the LORD, "as the children of Israel bring an offering in a clean vessel into the house of the LORD. And I will also take some of them for priests and Levites," says the LORD.

For ages and generations, the Lord had allowed Israel the incomparable privilege of *seeing His glory* (verse 18). Israel saw His glory as the Red Sea walled up on 2 sides and allowed them to escape their enemies. They saw His glory when He led them with a pillar of fire by night and a pillar of cloud by day in the wilderness. They saw His glory when He gave them the 10 Commandments at Mount Sinai. They saw His glory when He made the sun stand still in Joshua 10. And on and on the examples flow. What a joy, what confidence it gave them that they were believing rightly and acting rightly when they focused all their attentions on pleasing this God of such unending glory. And now the Lord declares His intention to allow the entire world to witness His glory, not just the nation of Israel. Psalms 97:6 spoke of this purpose of God as well: "The heavens declare His righteousness, and all the peoples see His glory." Oh, the thought of this breathtaking privilege of seeing the glory of God! How can we rightly respond to this privilege of privileges? Let us lift up our praise to our God daily for the gift of seeing His glory. Praise is the response that our Lord looks for from His children as exemplified by His people at the dedication of the temple during Solomon's reign. "When Solomon had finished praying, fire came down from heaven and consumed the burnt offering and the sacrifices; and the glory of the LORD filled the temple. And the priests could not enter the house of the LORD, because the glory of the LORD had filled the LORD's house. When all the children of Israel saw how the fire came down, and the glory of the LORD on the temple, they bowed their faces to the ground on the pavement, and worshiped and praised the LORD, saying: "For He is good, for His mercy endures forever." God is great, and He has allowed us to see His greatness. In response, let us do our best to praise Him as He deserves. Psalms 148:13 repeats the call to praise our God of glory: "Let them praise the name of the LORD, for His name alone is exalted; His glory is above the earth and heaven."

When God reveals His glory, His people first respond in praise. And then we rise to serve Him. Verse 21 says that after revealing His glory to the world, He will "take some of them (the Gentiles) for priests and Levites." The Lord has declared to us His glory! He has called us to be His priests, His "royal priesthood" (I Peter 2:9), and as His priests it is our happy duty to continue to declare His glory to the world. "And they shall declare My glory among the Gentiles." This is our great privilege and responsibility, to see the glory of God, and then declare His glory to the world. Psalms 96:3 rings out the call to all God's people: "Declare His glory among the nations, His wonders among all peoples." And though some may not lift their eyes to gaze on the beauty of the Lord, many will. They will hear us present His gospel, their soul will be stirred by the beckoning of His Holy Spirit, they will experience His glory, and they will flock to Him. Soldiers will drive to Him in their chariots, the sick will be dragged to Him on their litters, from the deserts they will come on camels, from the mountains they will come on mules, from the plains they will come on horses, but they will come! Nations and millions across the globe will come to God for the joy of seeing His glory! And as we come to His holy mountain to worship Him as He deserves, we will proclaim His glory to still others, and they will join us too. God will be praised, men and women will be made children of the God of glory, and they will be made priests and Levites who will declare His glory to the nations so that all the world may enjoy the highest attainment of man – to see the glory of God and to praise Him in His glorious presence.

66:22-24

For as the new heavens and the new earth which I will make shall remain before Me," says the LORD, "So shall your descendants and your name remain. And it shall come to pass that from one New Moon to another, and from one Sabbath to another, all flesh shall come to worship before Me," says the LORD. "And they shall go forth and look upon the corpses of the men who have transgressed against Me. For their worm does not die, and their fire is not quenched. They shall be an abhorrence to all flesh."

Men and women had lived and died on the earth from Adam's day to Isaiah's. When they died, they went to Sheol, the place of the dead. What happened there, and what people did there was shrouded in mystery to the Old Testament writers. But, now, at the close of Isaiah's wonderful scroll, the Father promises just as the Son promised in John 14:2 to create "the new heavens and the new earth" which will be home for all who trust in Him. John saw this new creation of the Lord in Revelation 21:1 – "Now I saw a new heaven and a new earth, for the first heaven and the first earth had passed away." Though many of God's children live in anonymity and obscurity on earth, in heaven, all the names of all God's children will be known and remembered forever – "your descendants and your name remain." Psalms 112:6 confirms that "The righteous will be remembered forever" (HCS). And as God prepares the new earth and the new heavens as the eternal dwelling place of His people, HIs people now sing His praises in His temple, His dwelling place on earth. In the past, God's people would come to worship the Lord in His temple only a few times a year at the appointed feast gatherings. But now, as Isaiah foretold, we His people, gather to meet with Him every week – "from one Sabbath to another." Once it was only Jewish men that arrived at the appointed feast times to worship, but now "All humanity will come to worship me from week to week and from month to month" (verse 23 NLT). Women and children will come, and people from every nation and people group will come to worship the Lord every Sabbath. They will know the Lord, love the Lord, and enjoy Him forever. The worship that they sing out on earth will be continued on into heaven for an eternity.

In striking contrast, the unbelieving and disobedient will be executed by the Lord, and their memory will become "an abhorrence to all flesh." The praise on the lips of the saints and the joy in the soul of the saints will last forever. Sadly, the pain and remorse of the ungodly is long lived as well. "For their worm does not die, and their fire is not quenched."

Isaiah's great book comes to a close with a striking picture of the disparity between the destiny of the believer and the destiny of those who reject God's authority and offer of forgiveness. The believers are blessed with the joy of standing in the presence of their Creator and adoring Him forever. But "the corpses of the men who have transgressed" against the Lord will become "an abhorrence to all flesh," with no end to the pain and tragedy of their rebellion. Let all thinking men and women take note.

Author's Note

Tell The Kids was created with a heart to bring the coming generations to saving faith in Jesus. Although this commentary on Isaiah may not be considered a children's book by some, it, too, was born out of family times together studying God's word, as a mom and dad hungered to see saving faith nurtured in their children. If families read this together, or if moms and dads read this book and then pass on to their children what they learned in these pages, it is our desire that children might sense their need to place their faith in Jesus.

All of us must place our trust in Jesus because Isaiah 53:6 tells us that we have all "gone astray." We have all "gone astray," we have all sinned, and the consequences of sin are horrifying. Sin ruins our relationship with God, bans us from heaven, and condemns us to death and hell. The action required to take away our sin was so painfully difficult! Isaiah 53 describes for us the pain and grief that Jesus endured to take away our sins. Jesus suffered and died for our sake, but the very happy news is that He came back to life! And if we will turn from our sin and ask Jesus to forgive us, He will forgive us and make us clean – as if we had never sinned.

If you want Jesus to cleanse you of your sins, you can pray right now:

Pray and admit to God that you believe that He made the world and that everything exists to give Him honor.

Tell God that you believe He is holy and perfect and confess to Him that you are not.

Thank God for His love and thank Him that His Son Jesus came to take away our sins by dying for us on the cross.

Ask Him to cleanse you of all your sins, and tell Him your commitment to live to honor Him from this day on.

-Dr. Doug Derbyshire MD

www.ingramcontent.com/pod-product-compliance
Lightning Source LLC
Chambersburg PA
CBHW030115240426
43673CB00002B/82